A Ricoeur Reader:
Reflection and Imagination

A Ricoeur Reader:
Reflection and Imagination

Edited by Mario J. Valdés

UNIVERSITY OF TORONTO PRESS

Toronto and Buffalo

© University of Toronto Press 1991
Toronto and Buffalo

Printed in Canada

ISBN 0-8020-5880-9 (cloth)
ISBN 0-8020-6814-6 (paper)

Theory/Culture 2

∞
Printed on acid-free paper

Canadian Cataloguing in Publication Data

Ricoeur, Paul
   A Ricoeur reader : reflection and imagination

   (Theory/culture ; 2)
   Includes bibliographical references.
   ISBN 0-8020-5880-9 (bound)   ISBN 0-8020-6814-6 (pbk.)

   1. Hermeneutics.   2. Criticism.   3. Ricoeur, Paul
   I. Valdés, Mario J., 1934-   . II. Title.
   III. Series.

   B2430.R551 1991   121'.68   C91-093222-0

6-1-92

To Simone Ricoeur and María Elena de Valdés

and in memory of Northrop Frye

Contents

IV / The Dialogical Disclosure: Interviews with Paul Ricoeur

Acknowledgments

An editor of a volume of collected papers has a long list of acknowledgments to include, and I am no exception. My major debt is to Paul Ricoeur, who made his work available for my scrutiny and whose generosity is matched only by his intellectual honesty and professional rigour. His concern throughout his work has been with the quality of writing presented to the reader.

I also wish to acknowledge María Elena de Valdés's assistance with this project, beginning with her suggestion that I collect Ricoeur's papers on literary criticism and theory. I would also like to thank David Pellauer of De Paul University and *Philosophy Today* for his generous assistance in locating some of the more obscure publications, and my colleague L.M. Findlay, at the University of Saskatchewan, who took time to advise me on the selection of the papers included in this collection. I have profited from his counsel, as he will recognize from this volume's contents. I wish to acknowledge the dedication and hard work on this project of my research assistant, Mr Luis Torres.

Finally, I wish to thank all the editors and publishers listed in the following brief publication history of the papers included here for their kind permission to reprint.

'What is a Text? Explanation and Understanding' (1970). From *Hermeneutics and the Human Sciences*, translated and edited by John B. Thompson (Cambridge: Cambridge University Press; Paris: Editions de la Maison des Sciences de l'Homme, 1981), pp. 145–64. Reprinted with permission.

This article was originally published in French as 'Qu'est-ce qu'un texte? Expliquer et Comprendre,' in *Hermeneutik und Dialectic*, vol.

2, edited by Rudiger Bubner (Tübingen: J.C.B. Mohr, 1970), pp. 181 –200. An abridged version appeared in English in David Rasmussen's *Mythic-Symbolic Language and Philosophical Anthropology* (The Hague: Martinus Nijhoff, 1971), pp. 135–50.

'Word, Polysemy, Metaphor: Creativity in Language.' Translated by David Pellauer and reprinted, with permission, from *Philosophy Today* 17, no. 2 – 4 (Summer 1973): 97–128.
    Under the title 'Creativity in Language: Word, Polysemy, Metaphor,' this article was first presented as a lecture at the Fifth Lexington Conference on Pure and Applied Phenomenology, 13–15 April 1972, at the Veterans Administration Hospital in Lexington, Kentucky. It was published in the proceedings of the conference: *Language and Language Disturbances: The Fifth Lexington Conference on Pure and Applied Phenomenology 1972,* edited by Edwin R. Straus (Pittsburgh: Duquesne University Press, 1974), pp. 49–71. It has also been reprinted in *The Philosophy of Paul Ricoeur: An Anthology of His Work,* edited by Charles Reagan and David Stewart (Boston: Beacon Press, 1978), pp. 120–33.

'Appropriation' (1972). From *Hermeneutics and the Human Scences*, translated and edited by John B. Thompson (Cambridge: Cambridge University Press; Paris: Editions de la Maison des Sciences de l'Homme, 1981), pp. 182–93. Reprinted with permission.
    The article was originally given as a lecture in Toronto in October 1972.

'The Human Experience of Time and Narrative' (1979). Translated by David Pellauer and reprinted, with permission, from *Research in Phenomenology* 9: 17–34.
    This article was presented as a paper at the International Colloquium on Phenomenology and the Human Sciences at Duquesne University in 1978.

'The Function of Fiction in Shaping Reality' (1979). Translated by David Pellauer. Reprinted, with permission, from *Man and His World* 12, no. 2 (1979): 123–41.

'Mimesis and Representation' (1980). Translated by David Pellauer. Reprinted, with permission, from *Annals of Scholarship: Metastudies of the Humanities and Social Sciences* 2, no. 3 (1981): 15–32.

Acknowledgments xi

This article was the kernel for the vast project that became *Time and Narrative*. It was read at the XVIIIth Congrès des Sociétés de Philosophie de la langue française, in 1980, in Strasbourg. The French title is 'Mimesis et représentation'; it was published in *Actes du XVIIIᵉ Congrès des Sociétés de Philosophie de la langue française* (Strasbourg: Université des Sciences Humaines de Strasbourg, 1982), pp. 51–63.

'Habermas' (1975) and 'Geertz' (1975). Reprinted, with permission, from *Lectures on Ideology and Utopia*, edited and introduced by George H. Taylor (New York: Columbia University Press, 1986), pp. 232–53 and 254–66.
These articles were given as part of a lecture series at the University of Chicago in 1975.

'Construing and Constructing: A Review of *The Aims of Interpretation* by E.D. Hirsch, Jr' (1977). Reprinted, with permission, from *The Times Literary Supplement* 197, no. 3911 (25 February 1977): 216.

'Review of *Ways of Worldmaking* by Nelson Goodman' (1980). Reprinted, with permission, from *Philosophy and Literature* 4, no. 1 (Spring 1980): 107–20.

The Conflict of Interpretations: Debate with Hans-Georg Gadamer' (1982). Reprinted, with permission, from *Phenomenology: Dialogues and Bridges,* edited by R. Bruzina and B. Wilshire (Albany: State University of New York, 1982), pp. 299–320.
The symposium remarks and discussion were tape-recorded by Professor Sal Winer and transcribed for publication by Ronald Bruzina and Bruce Wilshire.

'Northrop Frye's *Anatomy of Criticism*, or the Order of Paradigms' (1983). Translated by David Pellauer. Reprinted, with permission, from *Centre and Labyrinth: Essays in Honour of Northrop Frye,* edited by E. Cook, C. Hošek, J. Macpherson, P. Parker, and J. Patrick (Toronto, Buffalo, London: University of Toronto Press, 1983), pp.1–13.

'Greimas's *Narrative Grammar*' (1980). Translated by Frank Collins and Paul Perron. Reprinted, with permission, from *New Literary History: A Journal of Theory and Interpretation* 20 (1980): 581–608.
This essay first appeared as 'La *Grammaire narrative* de Greimas,' in

Documents de recherche du Groupe de Recherche semio-linguistiques (Paris: Centre National de Recherche Scientifique) 2, no. 15 (1980).

'On Narrativity: Debate with A.J. Greimas' (1984). Translated and adapted by Frank Collins and Paul Perron. Reprinted, with permission, from *New Literary History: A Journal of Theory and Interpretation* 20 (1980): 551–62.

This debate was held on 17 June 1984, at the University of Toronto Colloquium on Universals of Narrativity, Fifth International Summer Institute for Semiotic and Structural Studies.

'Metaphor and the Main Problem of Hermeneutics' (1974). Translated by David Pellauer. Reprinted, with permission, from *New Literary History* (On Metaphor) 6, no. 1 (1974–5): 95–110.

This essay was originally published as 'La Métaphore et le problème central de l'herméneutique (Résumé et summary), in *Revue philosophique de Louvain* 70 (février 1972): 93–112, 115. The first English translation, with notes and comments, appeared in *Graduate Philosophical Journal* 3, no. 1 (1973–4): 42–58. It was reprinted without notes and comments in *New Literary History* (see above) and subsequently published as 'Metaphor and the Main Problem of Hermeneutics,' in *The Philosophy of Paul Ricoeur: An Anthology of His Work,* edited by Charles Reagan and David Stewart (Boston: Beacon Press, 1978), pp. 134–48. Another translation was included in *Hermeneutics and the Human Sciences,* translated and edited by John B. Thompson (Cambridge: Cambridge University Press; Paris: Editions de la Maison des Sciences de l'Homme, 1981), pp. 165–81.

'Writing as a Problem for Literary Criticism and Philosophical Hermeneutics' (1977). Reprinted, with permission, from *Philosophic Exchange* 2, no. 3 (Summer 1977): 3–15.

This article was originally given as a lecture at the Center for Philosophic Exchange, State University of New York at Brockport.

'Narrated Time' (1984). Translated by Robert Sweeney. Reprinted, with permission, from *Philosophy Today* 29, no. 4/4 (Winter 1985): 259–72.

The article first appeared as 'Le Temps raconté,' in *Revue Métaphysique et de morale,* octobre – décembre 1984: 436–52.

'Time Traversed: Remembrance of Things Past' (1984). Translated by K. McLaughlin and David Pellauer. Reprinted, with permission, from *Time and Narrative*, Vol. II, translated by K. McLaughlin and D. Pellauer (Chicago, London: University of Chicago Press, 1985), pp. 130–52.

The article, in part, was given as a lecture at the University of Toronto in 1982 and was expanded into chapter 4, 'L'Expérience temporelle fictive,' of *Temps et récit*, Tome II: *La Configuration du temps dans le récit de fiction* (Paris: Seuil, 1984), pp. 194–255.

'Between the Text and Its Readers' (1985). Translated by K. McLaughlin and David Pellauer. Reprinted, with permission, from *Time and Narrative*, Vol. III, translated by K. McLaughlin and D. Pellauer (Chicago, London: University of Chicago Press, 1985), pp. 159–79.

This essay was first given as a lecture in Toronto in 1982 and was subsequently incorporated into chapter 4, 'Monde du texte et monde du lecteur,' of *Temps et récit*, Tome III: *Le temps raconté* (Paris: Seuil, 1985), pp. 238–61.

'Life: A Story in Search of a Narrator' (1987). Translated by J.N. Kraay and A.J. Scholten. Reprinted, with permission, from *Facts and Values: Philosophical Reflections from Western and Non-Western Perspectives,* edited by M.C. Doeser and J.N. Kraay, translated by J.N. Kraay and A.J. Scholten (Dordrecht: Martinus Nijhoff, 1987), pp. 121–32.

'Phenomenology and Theory of Literature: An Interview with Paul Ricoeur' (1981). Interview by Erik Nakjavani. Reprinted, with permission, from *Modern Language Notes*, 96, no. 5 (December 1981): 1084–90.

'Poetry and Possibility: An Interview with Paul Ricoeur' (1982). Interview by Philip Fried. Reprinted, with permission, from *The Manhattan Review* 2 (1982): 6–21.

The interview took place at the University of Chicago in 1982.

'The Creativity of Language' (1984). Interview by Richard Kearney. Reprinted, with permission, from *Dialogues with Contemporary* xiv Acknowledgments

Continental Thinkers (Manchester: Manchester University Press, 1984), pp. 17–36.
   The interview took place in Paris in 1981.

'Myth as the Bearer of Possible Worlds' (1984). Interview by Richard Kearney. Reprinted, with permission, from *Dialogues with Contemporary Continental Thinkers* (Manchester: Manchester University Press, 1984), pp. 36–45.
   A shortened version of this interview was first published in *The Crane Bag Journal of Irish Studies* 2, no. 1–2 (1978): 260–6.

'World of the Text, World of the Reader: An Interview with Paul Ricoeur' (1986). Interview by Joël Roman; translated by Kara Vissler. Reprinted, with permission, from *Préfaces*.
   The interview originally appeared as 'Monde du texte, monde du lecteur,' in *Préfaces*, no. 1 (mars-avril 1987): 98–101.

A Ricoeur Reader:
Reflection and Imagination

Introduction:
Paul Ricoeur's Post-
Structuralist Hermeneutics

Ricoeur's Theory of Interpretation

It is almost unprecedented for a major philosopher to turn his attention to the theoretical problems of literary criticism. Yet, beginning with *Interpretation Theory: Discourse and the Surplus of Meaning* in 1976 and culminating with *Time and Narrative*, Vol. III, in [1985],* Paul Ricoeur has addressed every major theoretical issue of the undisciplined discipline we call literary criticism. During this decade he has written five books and numerous articles, eleven of which have been collected and edited by John B. Thompson in a volume titled *Hermeneutics and the Human Sciences* (which I will treat here as a sixth book).

In the introduction to *Interpretation Theory*, Ricoeur defines his goal as 'step-by-step approximations of a solution to a single problem, that of understanding language at the level of such productions as poems, narratives, and essays, whether literary or philosophical' (*IT*, p. xi). The central problem can be restated in terms of literary criticism as a systematic examination of the concept of textual unity as a construct of language. The philosophical means used in the pursuit of this goal is phenomenological dialectic and hermeneutic exegesis.

Ricoeur's argument has four parts: first, the examination of language as discourse; second, the adjustment needed in order to focus on written discourse as distinct from spoken; third, a theory of text –

---

* Years cited are for first publication. All titles have been cited in English; however, where first publication was in French, the year appears in brackets.

this part takes up the contributing factors of the polysemy of words and the ambiguity of sentences in order to confront the problem of plurivocity in full works such as poems and essays – and fourth, the culmination of textual theory of interpretation, which is a dialectic of explanation and understanding.

Ricoeur begins by acknowledging the importance of modern linguistics for the study of discourse, but he also insists on the need to return to the roots of the Western philosophical tradition – Plato's *Cratylus*, *Theaetetus*, and *Sophist*, and Aristotle's *On Interpretation*.

After a critique of de Saussure's *Course in General Linguistics*, Ricoeur addresses the crucial shortcoming of structural linguistics and its parent discipline, semiotics, namely, the inability to pass from the consideration of the word as a lexical sign to the sentence as the basic unit of meaning. He writes: 'The sentence is not a larger or more complex word, it is a new entity. It may be decomposed into words, but the words are something other than short sentences. A sentence is a whole irreducible to the sum of its parts. It is made up of words, but it is not a derivative function of its words. A sentence is made up of signs, but is not itself a sign' (*IT*, p. 7). The salient point is that there is no linear progression to move from words to sentences to texts: each stage of the language spectrum requires new structures and a new description.

But the key distinction that will be the fundamental premise for the entire argument is that which Ricoeur makes between semantics and semiotics. Semantics, as the science of the sentence, is concerned with making sense, or with the communication of meaning, and thus responds to the integrative capacity of language. Semiotics, as the science of signs, relies on the capacity of separation of language into constitutive parts. Once the distinction has been made, there follows the need to establish adequate criteria to differentiate between the two. At this point, Ricoeur introduces the concept of discourse as a dialectic of event and meaning. The event is experience as expression, but it is also the intersubjective exchange itself and communication with the recipient. Ricoeur's point is crucial and will be essential in confronting deconstruction. What is communicated in the event of the speech act is not the experience of the speaker as experienced, but its meaning. The lived experience remains private, but its sense, its meaning, becomes public through discourse. Thus the poet's private feelings must remain part of his or her psychological world, but the poem as expression relates some sense of the lived experience.

Related to the dialectic of event and meaning, which encompasses the expressive act itself, is the inner dialectic of sense and reference.

> To refer is what the sentence does in a certain situation and according to a certain use. It is also what the speaker does when he applies his words to reality. That someone refers to something at a certain time is an event, a speech event. But this event receives its structure from the meaning as sense. The speaker refers to something on the basis of, or through, the ideal structure of the sense. The sense, so to speak, is traversed by the referring intention of the speaker. In this way the dialectic of event and meaning receives a new development from the dialectic of sense and reference. (*IT*, p. 20)

The argument that follows is so fundamental, so basic to the entire operation of literary criticism and to the five books that follow, that we must take time to gloss it: 'Only this dialectic [sense and reference] says something about the relation between language and the ontological condition of being in the world. Language is not a world of its own. It is not even a world. But because we are in the world, because we are affected by situations, and because we orient ourselves comprehensively in those situations, we have something to say, we have experience to bring to language' (*IT*, pp. 20–1). One could not ask for a bolder, more direct rejection of the trivialization of the issues raised by contemporary deconstructionist criticism. The argument continues:

> This notion of bringing experience to language is the ontological condition of reference, an ontological condition reflected within language as a postulate which has not immanent justification; the postulate according to which we presuppose the existence of singular things which we identify. We presuppose that something must be in order that something may be identified. This postulation of existence as the ground of identification is what Frege ultimately meant when he said that we are not satisfied by the sense alone, but we presuppose a reference. And this postulation is so necessary that we must add a specific prescription if we want to refer to fictional entities such as characters in a novel or a play. (*IT*, p. 21)

Ricoeur insists on the priority of the experience of being in the world and that, proceeding from this ontological condition of belonging, we can move towards its expression in language. 'It is because there is first something to say, because we have an experience to bring to language, that conversely language is not only directed towards ideal meanings but also refers to what is' (*IT*, p. 21).

In summing up this first part of *Interpretation Theory*, Ricoeur makes a statement that will later lead into the centre of the concept of split reference, the basic thesis of *The Rule of Metaphor*:

> This universal signification of the problem of reference is so broad that even the utterer's meaning has to be expressed in the language of reference as the self-reference of discourse, i.e., as the designation of its speaker by the structure of discourse. *Discourse refers back to its speaker at the same time that it refers to the world.* This correlation is not fortuitous since it is ultimately the speaker who refers to the world in speaking. Discourse in action and in use refers backwards and forwards, to a speaker and a world. Such is the ultimate criterion of language as discourse. (*IT*, p. 22; my emphasis)

This dialectic concept is not only essential to the development of Ricoeur's philosophy of language, it also has far-reaching implications for literary criticism, for within it is the basis of a theory that will provide a post-structural alternative to deconstruction.

The second chapter of *Interpretation Theory* addresses the necessary adjustments that must be made in the treatment of writing as distinct from speaking. Ricoeur's argument now narrows the scope of the inquiry to written language as distinct from spoken language. He begins by pointing out that through writing the meaning of language is separated from the speech-act event: 'But this detachment is not such as to cancel the fundamental structure of discourse ... The semantic autonomy of the text which now appears is still governed by the dialectic of event and meaning ... writing is the full manifestation of discourse' (*IT*, pp. 25–6). The chapter is organized on the basis of five topics: fixation of the message, message and encoder, message and decoder, message and code, and message and reference.

Fixation: 'What writing actually does is fix not the event of speaking but the "said" of speaking, i.e., the intentional exteriorization constitutive of the couple "event–meaning." What we write, what we inscribe is the noema of the act of speaking, the meaning of the speech event, not the event as event' (*IT*, p. 27). Not only does written language mean that the message is free from the presence of a speaker, it also means that the message must do without the speaker's authority and replace it through the material medium.

Message and encoder: 'With written discourse ... the author's intention and the meaning of the text cease to coincide ... Inscription becomes synonymous with the semantic autonomy of the text which results from the disconnection of the mental intention of the author from the verbal meaning of the text, of what the author meant and what the text means. The text's career escapes the finite horizon lived by its author. What the text means now matters more than what the author meant when he wrote it' (*IT*, pp. 29–30). This autonomy does not mean that the author's intention has been completely lost. It means only that the author's intention cannot stand outside the text as the criterion for interpreting the text. A text remains discourse, a human construct written by someone for someone about something. The author's intentions thus have become a part of the text.

Message and decoder: Because the text is addressed to an unknown reader and to potential readers beyond the anticipation of the author, it stands on its own. The same reader also has the possibility of returning to the text time and time again and, perhaps most important of all, the reader has the possibility of discussing his or her reading and thus enlarging the scope of the reading experience from the private confines of the individual to a community of other readers. The convergence of the author's configuration of the text and the reader's refiguration is the dynamic merger that makes possible the net gain of new meaning in metaphorical writing. It should be understood that, although Ricoeur has suggested this direction of inquiry in *Interpretation Theory*, not until *The Rule of Metaphor* will the dynamics of metaphor be treated fully, and not until Volume I of *Time and Narrative* will Ricoeur take up the relationship of configuration and refiguration.

Message and code: The author is not only the encoder, but also the craftsman, the maker of the work. The conventions of writing are the rules of the craft: writing plays a decisive role precisely in the application of the categories of practice, technique, and work to discourse. There is production when a form is applied to some matter in order to shape it.

Message and reference: Once again Ricoeur sketches out what will be the corner-stone of *The Rule of Metaphor*: 'My contention is that discourse cannot fail to be about something. In saying this, I am denying the ideology of absolute texts ... In one manner or another, poetic texts speak about the world. But not in a descriptive way. As Jakobson himself suggests, the reference here is not abolished, but divided or split' (*IT*, pp. 36–7). The consequence of this position for literary criticism is far-reaching, for within it lies the concept of literature itself, i.e., literature is *written discourse with the capacity to redescribe the world for its readers.*

The direct consequence of Ricoeur's theory of the text÷reader dialectic for literary criticism is the transformation of interpretation into a dynamic dialectic between the distanciation of the text and the appropriation of the reader. By 'distanciation' Ricoeur means the semantic autonomy of the text, which stands removed from its unknown multiple readers. By 'appropriation' he means the process of making one's own what was not. In all of our experiences in the world of action, there is a general need for making our own what is alien to us in order to understand it. This is 'the principle of a struggle between the otherness that transforms all spatial and temporal distance into cultural estrangement and the ownness by which all understanding aims at the extension of self-understanding ... Reading is the *pharmakon*, the remedy, by which the meaning of the text is rescued from the estrangement of distanciation and put in a new proximity, a proximity which suppresses and preserves the cultural distance and includes the otherness within the ownness' (*IT*, p. 43). Literary criticism thus is re-formed from a search for absolutes into a dynamic encounter of continuous refiguration within a tradition of commentary: 'The dialectic of distanciation and appropriation is the last word in the absence of absolute knowledge' (*IT*, p. 44).

The third chapter of *Interpretation Theory*, 'Metaphor and Symbol,' turns to the capacity of the message to carry more than one meaning. The seven pages devoted to metaphor in this chapter are a précis of the major undertaking that is *The Rule of Metaphor*. The first task taken up is an inquiry into how two meanings are possible for the same expression. Ricoeur recognizes that literary criticism under the influence of the positivists of the nineteenth century has responded to this problem methodologically by making a distinction between denotation and connotation. In this way, only the denotation is cognitive and therefore the object of semantic inquiry. Connotation is considered to be extrasemantic because it includes emotive evocations, which do not have cognitive standing. In essence the nineteenth-century practice of literary criticism will be challenged by Ricoeur's philosophy of language: 'Live metaphors are metaphors of invention within which the response to the discordance in the sentence is a new extension of meaning, although it is certainly true that such inventive metaphors tend to become dead metaphors through repetition. In such cases, the extended meaning becomes part of our lexicon and contributes to the polysemy of the words in question whose everyday meanings are thereby augmented. There are no live metaphors in a dictionary' (*IT*, p. 52).

Ricoeur is arguing that live metaphors have more than emotive value because they create new meaning. 'A metaphor, in short, tells us something new about reality' (*IT*, p. 53). A host of issues that affect literary criticism arises from these comments. For example, how can semantic theory account for the creating of new meaning in literature? How is the literary text's figurative language related to the world of action? What is meant by the information level of figurative language? And, how can critical analysis be done on an expression that is caught up in a dynamic tensional relationship?

Ricoeur's tensional theory of metaphor is extended to the consideration of the symbol: 'The metaphorical twist, which our words must undergo in response to the semantic impertinence at the level of the entire sentence, can be taken as the model for the extension of meaning operative in every symbol' (*IT*, p. 55). The fundamental control in the interpretive process is the return to the world of action as the basis for all meaning; this is the corner-stone of Ricoeur's theory of interpretation, which has given literary criticism a contemporary philosophical argument in the tradition of Giambattista Vico, Wilhelm von Humboldt, and Benedetto Croce. Ricoeur continues: 'As in metaphor theory, this excess of signification in a symbol can be opposed to the literal signification, but only on the condition that we also oppose two interpretations at the same time' (ibid.). There are two levels of signification since it is the recognition of the literal meaning that allows us to see that a symbol still contains more meaning. 'This surplus of meaning is the residue of literal interpretation. Yet for the one who participates in the symbolic signification there are really not two significations, one literal and the other symbolic, but rather a single movement which transfers him from one level to the other and which assimilates him to the second signification by means of, or through, the literal one' (ibid.) The argument thus concludes that symbolic signification is so constituted that *we can attain the secondary signification only by way of the primary signification.*

Ricoeur cites with approval the oft-quoted passage from Northrop Frye's *Anatomy of Criticism* that characterizes poetic language as centripetal, as opposed to centrifugal, as is didactic discourse, and goes on to make a strong case for the cultural world-making role of literature: 'this redescription is guided by the interplay between differences and resemblances that gives rise to the tension at the level of the utterance. It is precisely from this tensive apprehension that a new vision of reality springs forth, which ordinary vision resists because it is attached to the ordinary use of words. The eclipse of the objective, manipulable world thus makes way for the revelation of a new dimension of reality and truth' (*IT*, p. 68). Literature therefore is about reality and truth, and literary criticism's function is to comment on the shared meaning, the intersubjective truth of the redescription of the world that is the reading experience.

The fourth, and final, chapter of *Interpretation Theory* outlines the philosophical basis for the act of interpretation itself. Working within the hermeneutic tradition, Ricoeur is nevertheless careful to distance his theory from romanticist hermeneutics, which sought to reconstruct the genius of the author through his works. Ricoeur postulates an interpretation theory that is fully linked to the reading of the literary work itself. In other words, the process of interpretation is, in part, determined by phenomena that are to be interpreted and, in part, by phenomena of the reading experience. Ricoeur takes care to establish the strength of the two concepts of explanation and understanding before entering into their relationship:

> understanding, which is more directed towards the intentional unity of discourse, and explanation, which is more directed towards the analytic structure of the text, tend to become the distinct poles of a developed dichotomy. But this dichotomy does not go so far as to destroy the initial dialectic of the utterer's and the utterance meaning ... In the same way the polarity between explanation and understanding in reading must not be treated in dualistic terms, but as a complex and highly mediated dialectic. Then the term interpretation may be applied, not to a particular case of understanding, that of the written expressions of life, but to the whole process that encompasses explanation and understanding. Interpretation as the dialectic of explanation and understanding or

comprehension may then be traced back to the initial stages of interpretive behavior already at work in conversation. And while it is true that only writing and literary composition provide a full development of this dialectic, interpretation must not be referred to as a province of understanding. It is not defined by a kind of object – 'inscribed' signs in the most general sense of the term – but by a kind of process: the dynamic of interpretative reading. (*IT*, p. 74)

Rather than a transposition of meaning from author to reader's reader, to reader, literary criticism becomes a process, a movement back and forth between text and critic for the benefit of the critic and all those who share in the textual commentary. There can be no completion of the interpretive process, but only a temporary pause necessary to allow another player to enter the court. This does not mean that there is no sense of truth or of knowledge in the interpretive process, for the very goal of interpretation must be to share one's insights with others. But what this theory does mean is that there can be no valid claim to definitive meaning of the text, for this claim would kill the text, would remove it from the process and render it consumed and empty. Nor can a critic substitute the reconstituted historicity of the text for the text itself. The historical context of the text must be inserted into the dialectic process of interpretation as part of the thrust of explanation. Similarly, the formal considerations of a text are not the text itself, but only one factor among many that are needed to move the analytic structure of the text into an engagement with the intentional unity of the text as the essential feature of understanding.

The driving force behind the desire to know is the need to make the world over in terms that are meaningful. This is the polar force of the reader's appropriation. On the other side, the thought of another when separated from that other by writing, and thus forced to stand alone, comes to the reader as otherness, as a different and disturbing view of the world. If one chooses to engage the otherness as constituted by a text one has entered into the struggle between appropriation and distanciation. The theory of phenomenological hermeneutics is the theory of the productive engagement between text and reader as a process of redescribing the world, my world first, and others' worlds subsequently. This interpretive process begins with the analytic power of explanation and is then challenged by the unitary force of understanding. The engagement of explanation and understanding will thus produce the interpretation that, in return, responds to the initial need to engage distanciation and appropriation. Literature is consequently the corpus of texts that have the capacity to promote the redescription of the world in their readers.

Ricoeur concludes *Interpretation Theory* with these words: 'Interpretation is the process by which disclosure of new modes of being – or, if you prefer Wittgenstein to Heidegger, of new forms of life – gives to the subject a new capacity for knowing himself. If the reference of the text is the project of a world, then it is not the reader who primarily projects himself. The reader rather is enlarged in his capacity of self-projection by receiving a new mode of being from the text itself' (*IT*, p. 94). I have gone through an extended description of this slim book of 1976 because it is still the best introduction to Ricoeur's theory of interpretation and it clearly anticipates the direction the major books of the next decade will take.

The Rule of Metaphor (begun in 1971 and published in 1975), and *Interpretation Theory* (begun in 1972 and published in 1976) are part of the same intensive examination Ricoeur devoted to metaphorical meaning. In *The Rule of Metaphor*, Ricoeur gave the central issues dealt with in an introductory manner in *Interpretation Theory* full philosophical treatment.

The Rule of Metaphor aims not only to deal with metaphor and the history of metaphor study, but to use metaphor as a paradigm for all creativity through language. The book contains eight studies, each of which can be taken as a single study on an aspect of the subject, but which collectively take the reader through five stages of inquiry: 1 / the foundations of the substitution theory of metaphor that limit it to a figure of speech (ch. 1 and 2), 2 / the challenge to the substitution theory (Max Black), as well as 3 / to the interaction theory (Monroe Beardsley), 4 / the full exposition of Ricoeur's theory, and 5 / its extension into the role of a paradigm for creativity (ch. 6, 7, and 8).

The significance of Ricoeur's philosophy of language for a major rethinking of literary criticism becomes clear in chapter 7, 'Metaphor and Reference.' Here Ricoeur introduces his commentary with clear awareness of the consequences for literary criticism: 'The postulate of reference requires a separate discussion when it touches on those particular entities of discourse called texts, that is, more complex compositions than the sentence. The question henceforth arises in the context of hermeneutics rather than semantics. For which the sentence is at once the first and the last entity' (*RM*, p. 219). In other words, the disciplines have been matched to the corresponding problematic, semiotics to the word, semantics to the sentence, and hermeneutics to the text. Ricoeur continues: 'The question of reference is posed here in terms that are singularly more complex; for certain texts, called literary, seem to constitute an exception to the reference requirement expressed by the preceding postulate' (*RM*, p. 219). The challenge of highly structured, figurative language texts is taken up.

The essential first point is Ricoeur's concept of the text. By text he means written discourse that has been produced as a work, as a totality irreducible to a simple sum of sentences. Furthermore, a work is organized not as language but as discourse with clearly codified perimeters, and finally it has an identifiable character that makes it an individual among other individuals with which it cannot be merged or confused.

The complex nature of the literary text demands a more elaborate concept of reference. Although the literary text suspends the descriptive reference that is common to didactic texts, there can be no doubt that, if all reference to the world of action had been eliminated, literary discourse would have been locked into a closed circle with no possibility of communication. Ricoeur puts it this way: 'The literary work through the structure proper to it displays a world only under the condition that the reference of descriptive discourse is suspended. Or to put it another way, discourse in the literary work sets out its denotation as a second-level denotation, by means of the suspension of the first-level denotation of discourse' (*RM*, p. 221). This essential postulate is demonstrated by and, indeed, derived from the study of metaphor as a paradigm of creativity. 'Just as the metaphorical statement captures its sense as metaphorical midst the ruins of the literal sense, it also achieves its reference upon the ruins of what might be called … its literal reference' *(RM*, p. 221). It should now be clear that the emergence of this double reference, or split reference, of literary texts is not to be located at the semantic level of the sentence, but rather at the hermeneutic level of the work. The primacy of the poetic function over the referential function does not eliminate reference but only makes it ambiguous. Thus literature has a double-sensed message that is in dynamic tension and, as Ricoeur shall point out, is the basis of creativity. A theory of literary criticism is now in view, for it is within the very analysis of metaphor as paradigm that the referential nature of poetic language is revealed. This referential concept must take into account the eclipse of a first level of reference and the emergence of a second level of reference, that is, the concept of split reference. It therefore follows that the task of interpretation demands an understanding of poetic meaning grounded in the eclipsed literal meaning. To sum up this argument: Ricoeur is saying that the referential power of poetic discourse is linked to the eclipse of ordinary meaning, to the creation of a heuristic fiction, and finally to the redescribed reality brought to the reader.

The concluding chapter of *The Rule of Metaphor* brings the argument to fruition, and indicates the future course of Ricoeur's development of his philosophy of language. The gain in meaning in poetic discourse is inseparable from the tension not just between the terms of a metaphorical statement, but also between two levels of interpretation: the literal level, which is restricted to the established value of words in the lexicon, and a metaphorical level resulting from innovation thrust upon these words in order to make sense of them in terms of the whole work. The resulting gain in meaning is not yet the conceptual gain of interpretation; it is a kind of semantic shock that produces the need for interpretation. Because the gain in meaning is caught in the conflict of 'same' and 'different,' it is unstable and volatile. This tensional situation of the split reference is lodged within the copula of the utterance. The ontological implications are clear: 'Being as ... means being and not being. In this way, the dynamism of meaning allowed access to the dynamic vision of reality which is the implicit ontology of the metaphorical utterance' (*RM*, p. 297). Ricoeur's theory of language has five essential postulates that we will be able to translate to a theory of literary criticism:

1 / Language's power to signify lies in the intersection of two movements. 'One movement aims at determining more rigorously the conceptual traits of reality, while the other aims at making reference appear' (*RM*, p. 298).
2 / 'On this groundwork the tension ... of metaphorical utterance can then be located: the tension between the terms of the statement, the tension between literal interpretation and metaphorical interpretation and the tension in the reference between is and is not' (*RM*, pp. 298–9).
3 / 'The metaphorical utterance functions in two referential fields at once. This duality explains how two levels of meaning are linked

together in the symbol. The first meaning relates to a known field of reference, that is, to the sphere of entities to which the predicates considered in their established meaning can be attached. The second meaning, the one that is to be made apparent, relates to a referential field for which there is no direct characterization, for which we consequently are unable to make identifying descriptions by means of appropriate predicates' (*RM*, p. 299).

4 / 'Two energies converge here: the gravitational pull exerted by the second referential field on meaning, giving it the force to leave its place of origin; and the dynamism of meaning itself as the inductive principle of sense ... On the one hand, as regards its sense, the metaphorical utterance reproduces the form of a movement in a portion of the trajectory of meaning that goes beyond the familiar referential field where the meaning is already constituted. On the other hand, it brings an unknown referential field towards language, and within the ambit of this field the semantic aim functions and unfolds' (*RM*, p. 299).

5 / 'An experience seeks to be expressed which is more than something undergone. Its anticipated sense finds in the dynamism of simple meaning, relayed by the dynamism of split meaning a sketch that now must be reconciled with the requirements of the concept' (*RM*, p. 300).

These postulates, translated to a theory of literary criticism, give us what I have previously called a phenomenological hermeneutics.

1 / The task of hermeneutic interpretation must be focused at the intersection of the two directions of language, that is, neither exclusively with the writer's text nor with the reader, but in the encounter between the two.

2 / Any attempt to reduce or remove the tensional aspect of poetic discourse will impose an arbitrary closure on it. Interpretation must maintain the tensional character of the text.

3 / The interpretation must bring forward both the historicity of the writer's text, and the historicity of the reader so that the interpretive encounter can engage the two spheres of discourse.

4 / The interpretation itself must be dialectical and produce on a higher level of conceptual meaning the meaning of the reader.

5 / The task of interpretation is never completed, for the aim cannot

be to deplete the text of its dynamism. The aim must be to arrive at a temporary statement that participates in a tradition of commentary of texts.

The eleven essays published in *Hermeneutics and the Human Sciences*, edited by John B. Thompson, were written during the 1970s. All but one, 'Appropriation,' were published previously in books and journals in French, German, and English. The extraordinary value of this collection is that it presents both the continuity and the evolution of Ricoeur's philosophy during this decade, almost entirely during this period, his philosophy of language. The collection is divided into three parts: 'Studies in the History of Hermeneutics,' 'Studies in the Theory of Interpretation,' and 'Studies in the Philosophy of Social Science.' More than half of the essays are crucial to our concern with literary criticism. I limit my discussion to the essays most relevant to the problems of literary theory.

In 'Phenomenology and Hermeneutics,' Ricoeur's aim is not to contribute to the history of phenomenology, or to that of hermeneutics, but rather to alter both and map out a future direction – one that leads directly into the major issues of literary theory and culminates in the elaboration of a philosophy of interpretation a decade later.

We can extrapolate the following considerations for literary criticism:

1 / The question of meaning is the fundamental and most general presupposition of the critical commentary.
2 / The historical lived experience mediated by texts becomes the present of the historical past.
3 / The linguistic sign is engaged within a game of redescription between the reader and the text, but it must ultimately return to the lived experience of the individual and of the community; thus it is that the hermeneutic commentary addresses this intersubjective shared meaning.
4 / The role of literary criticism in this philosophy is to withdraw from the objectifications and explanations of historical science and sociology and concentrate on the artistic and historical experience of encountering the life-world that precedes and, indeed, supports the objectifications and explanations. But life-world should not be confused with some ineffable immediacy of experience or with the emotional environment of human experience. Life-world designates only the reservoir of shared meaning, the surplus of sense in living

experience, which renders the objectifying and explanatory attitude possible.

The most powerful implication of Ricoeur's philosophy with regard to literary criticism answers the fundamental question as to the role of this discipline. He writes: 'The dominant problematic is that of the text, which reintroduces a positive and, if I may say so, productive notion of distanciation. In my view, the text is much more than a particular case of intersubjective communication: it is the paradigm of distanciation in communication. As such, it displays a fundamental characteristic of the very historicity of human experience, namely, that it is communication in and through distance' (*Hermeneutics and the Human Sciences* [*HHS*], p. 131). If we add Ricoeur's concept of literature as texts whose capacity to redescribe reality is taken up by the reader in the dialectic process of appropriation, we have a clearcut sense of purpose and well-defined objectives for the tradition of commentary of these texts. These views of Ricoeur have been repeated in a number of essays and books during the 1970s, and are today the most effective hermeneutic counterpoint to deconstruction within post-structural criticism. What then, we may ask, is the program for literary criticism that Ricoeur is advocating? Once again his views are clear and to the point:

> To interpret ... is to appropriate *here and now* the intention of the text ... the intended meaning of the text is not essentially the presumed intention of the author, the lived experience of the writer, but rather what the text means for whoever complies with its injunction. The text seeks to place us in its meaning, that is – according to another acceptation of the word *sens* – in the same direction. So if the intention is that of the text and if this intention is the direction which it opens up for thought, then depth semantics must be understood in a fundamentally dynamic way. I shall therefore say: to explain is to bring out the structure, that is, the internal relations of dependence which constitute the statics of the text; to interpret is to follow the path of thought opened up by the text, to place oneself *en route* towards the *orient* of the text. (*HHS*, pp. 161–2; emphasis mine)

Literary criticism therefore not only has a goal, but also has a general methodological road to follow. The initial dialectical situation between text and reader is the one of the conflict between the distance and difference proper to another's text and the appropriation – the need to make sense – belonging to the reader. Out of this conflict the creative gain in metaphorical meaning is produced. Literary criticism is not accidental; it is neither a subjective intuition of the poem nor a search for the historical clue to the true meaning of the text.

Although Ricoeur's essays and books were continually building up a philosophical overview of the claims and methods of literary criticism, especially the work of such notable writers as Jacques Derrida, A.J. Greimas, and Northrop Frye, there was a profound change with the three-volume project *Time and Narrative*.

Time and Narrative evolved from a seminar taught by Paul Ricoeur at the University of Toronto in 1981 and culminated in a four-part study published in 1983–5, in three volumes. Volume I, *Time and Narrative*, takes up the argument of *The Rule of Metaphor* of split reference in poetic language and enlarges it considerably in order to address the full spectrum of man's creative invention through language.

The essays published between 1975 and 1981 attest to Ricoeur's dissatisfaction with the conclusion to *The Rule of Metaphor* and with the possible misunderstanding of the dynamics of split reference. It was with the incentive of making these issues clear that once again he returned to two of the masters, Aristotle and St Augustine. There is, therefore, more than the affinity of succession between *The Rule of Metaphor* and *Time and Narrative*. They are both concerned with the philosophical problem of giving an account of semantic innovation. While the semantic innovation of metaphor is accepted without difficulty, it is another matter with narrative prose and its long tradition of representation in both history and fiction. In the narrative mode, Ricoeur argues, the semantic innovation lies in the invention of synthesis: 'By means of the plot, goals, causes, and chance are brought together within the temporal unity of a whole and complete action. It is the synthesis of the heterogeneous that brings narrative close to metaphor' (*TN*, I: ix).

The heart of the philosophical argument addresses the role of understanding in response to semantic innovation. Understanding of semantic innovation is the process of grasping the text; this operation unifies into a whole the multiplicity of circumstances, human aims and plans, initiatives, intentions and interaction, as well as the rise and fall of personal and collective fortunes attended by all the unforeseen and unintended consequences of human life in the world of action. The epistemological problem lies in the creation of a unique synthesis from an acquired familiarity and use of language, which is both collective and common to all. Ricoeur's answer is that time as human time exists only through narrative expression, and that narrative achieves its full objective only by creating time. Ricoeur states it succinctly at the beginning of Volume I, chapter 3: 'Time becomes human to the extent that it is articulated through a narrative mode, and narrative attains its full meaning when it becomes a condition of temporal existence' (*TN*, I: 52).

Volume I of *Time and Narrative* is divided into two parts: 'The Circle of Narrative and Temporality' and 'History and Narrative.' The first part acts as a general introduction to all three volumes of the work. Each part is divided into three chapters; the organization of the book, far from being fortuitous, is demanded by the logic of the entire argument. In Part I, chapter 1 presents fundamental concepts of the experience of time that are in a dialectical relationship with the concepts of emplotment in chapter 2; chapter 3 presents the relationship itself. Thus, we have Augustine in dialectic encounter with Aristotle, and this inquiry yields the threefold mimesis outlined in chapter 3.

Similarly, in Part II, chapter 4, 'The Eclipse of Narrative,' is countered by chapter 5, 'Defenses of Narrative," and this dialectic exchange brings about chapter 6, 'Historical Intentionality.' This logical method applies to the entire three-volume project. Thus, Part I of *Time and Narrative* is the introduction to the entire argument, whereas Part II, on historical narrative, is directly countered by Volume II on fictional narrative, with Volume III serving as the synthesis to the initial problem of human time created through narrativity.

Ricoeur takes care to point out the issues of literary theory treated in this book. In introducing his concept of threefold mimesis, Ricoeur makes it quite clear that he is concerned with a hermeneutics of texts:

> It is the task of hermeneutics, in return, to reconstruct the set of operations by which a work lifts itself above the opaque depths of living, acting, and suffering, to be given by an author to readers who receive it and thereby change their acting. For a semiotic theory, the only operative concept is that of the literary text. Hermeneutics, however, is concerned with reconstructing the entire arc of operations by which practical experience provides itself with works, authors, and readers. It does not confine itself to setting mimesis$_2$ [the configuration of the text, i.e., the organization of written language into a work] between mimesis$_1$ [the

prefigured basis for narrative itself] and mimesis$_3$ [the refiguration of the text by the reader]. It [hermeneutics] wants to characterize mimesis$_2$ by its mediating function. What is at stake, therefore, is the concrete process by which the textual configuration [mimesis$_2$] mediates between the prefiguration of the practical field and its refiguration through the reception of the work. It will appear as a corollary, at the end of this analysis, that the reader is that operator *par excellence* who takes up through doing something – the act of reading – the unity of the traversal from mimesis$_1$ to mimesis$_3$ by way of mimesis$_2$. (*TN*, I: 53)

The conjunction of Augustine's concept of temporality and Aristotle's views on plot brings forth a creative mimesis in place of the static concept of imitation that has restricted all inquiry into representational discourse. The creative mimesis is enlarged by Ricoeur into a tripartite theory of the human capacity of figuration. The dialectic between the prefiguration of human understanding of the world of action and the work of composition or configuration is played out by the reader, the operator, whose act of reading is a refiguration of the configured work. This refiguration is possible because both the writer of the text and its reader have shared in the prefiguration of language in the world of action. The dynamics of *The Rule of Metaphor* are clearly in evidence in this work, but the clarity and force of the argument attain a mastery of the 'arc' of operations not fully presented in the former work.

Ricoeur sums up the theoretical direction: 'We are following therefore the destiny of a prefigured time that becomes a refigured time through the mediation of a configured time' (*TN*, I: 54). Within that statement is contained an entire theory of literary criticism.

Time and Narrative, Volume II (*Configuration of Narrative Fiction*) is the most directly pertinent of Ricoeur's books to the practice of literary criticism. Indeed, this book constitutes the central argument for the criticism of phenomenological hermeneutics. Although it is the second of three volumes in the logical order of the project, it is part three of the four parts.

The concentration here is on configuration, that is, mimesis$_2$ of the threefold mimesis discussed in the previous book. Configuration is the realm of the world of the work itself. It is an inquiry into the mode of organization, of composition, of that world that looms as the necessary task. In other words, it is the analysis of the very principle of internal *order* that gives the work its unity and identity and that is, of course, the object of all formal inquiry. The only notable difference between this mode of inquiry and the many valuable formalist approaches of narratology is that, in this case, configuration is one phase in the process of interpretation that will not attain its final goal until the refiguration of the reader is considered in mimesis$_3$. The examination of textual configuration proceeds through a dialectic of inquiry. The two levels of inquiry are the organizational structure of the work and the world-view that emerges from the work. This is not a mere recasting of the form–content bifurcation of traditional criticism, for Ricoeur is arguing for interaction, not for separation. With structure, the critic moves from the parts towards a total organization, and, with world-view, from a unitary understanding towards an illumination of the parts. Ricoeur does not shy away from applying the theoretical outline; in chapter 4 he takes up *Mrs. Dalloway* by Virginia Woolf, *The Magic Mountain* by Thomas Mann, and *Remembrance of Things Past* by Marcel Proust.

Volume III of *Time and Narrative* contains the fourth and last part of the project: narrated time, which 'is aimed at as complete an explication as possible of the hypothesis that governs our inquiry, namely, that the effort of thinking which is at work in every narrative configuration is completed in a refiguration of temporal experience' (*TN*, III: 3).

In chapter 7, 'The World of the Text and the World of the Reader,' Ricoeur acknowledges the general outline for a literary theory he has been approaching. 'A literary hermeneutics worthy of the name must assume the threefold task ... of understanding ... explanation ... and application. In contrast to a superficial view, reading must not be confined to the field of application even if this field does reveal the end of the hermeneutical process; instead reading must pass through all three stages' (*TN*, III: 174). The main argument of this chapter is addressed in the first paper of this collection.

The Two Faces of Post-Structuralism

Post-structuralism, or the idea that the signified of each signifier is another signifier in turn, has been developed from the first by the union and the conflict of two very different sets of concepts, the one urging us towards analysis, the other groping beneath surface meaning in search of an elusive deeper meaning. From the research of Ferdinand de Saussure to the structuralism of the 1960s, there have been important achievements through only one of these sets as in the work of A.J. Greimas and Gerard Genette; others, such as H.-G. Gadamer, resist the call for a scientific method as a response to the search for the meaning gained when the injunctions of the text come together with the reader's historicity. But the most influential theoreticians of the last quarter of this century have been philosophers who have brought together both analysis and interpretation. The attempt to relate the two has made this an era of speculation, debate, and in general, enormous enrichment of the study of literature.

Before attempting an explicit characterization of the analytical and reflective tendencies, I will illustrate them by examples from Ricoeur and Derrida, the two philosophers whose work has given post-structuralism its two faces of hermeneutics and deconstruction.

Derrida, as is well known, has developed a philosophical deconstruction of Western metaphysics. He writes, in *Positions*, the following succinct formulation: 'To "deconstruct" philosophy is thus to work through the structured genealogy of its concepts in the most scrupulous and immanent fashion, but at the same time to determine, from a certain external perspective that it cannot name or describe, what this history may have concealed or excluded, constituting itself as history through this repression in which it has a stake' (p. 6).

In general, the aim of deconstruction is to show how the very discourse under scrutiny subverts the ideological position it maintains. The means to this disclosure is to show up the rhetorical devices and operations that have been used to produce the 'irrefutable' foundation for the text. Derrida has argued, from *Of Grammatology* to his most recent essays, that philosophers attempt to characterize writing as a translucent means of expression for thought, when in fact the writing itself is thoroughly grounded in ideological positions and is never either neutral or an indifferent means.

Derrida's most revolutionary concept, which has had far-reaching consequences for criticism, is to reverse the normal order of absence and presence: 'to posit presence ... no longer as the absolutely matrical form of being but as a "determination" and an "effect." Presence is a determination and effect within a system that is no longer that of presence but that of difference' (*Speech and Phenomena,* p. 147). Thus rather than think that absence is that void left by the removal of presence, Derrida postulates that the general condition is that of absence and that this state obliges the philosopher to fill the void, to insert presence, which is always a metaphysical imposition of one's own.

At this point we come up against the fundamental post-structuralist issue: the meaning of meaning. To Derrida, the meaning, that is, what the speaker intends to say, is already inscribed in the structure of language. There is no origin, in the absolute sense of the word; there are only endless circles of differentiation.

The consequences of even these basic Derridean concepts are at the same time powerful and self-defeating. Paul De Man sums up the overview: 'The innumerable writings that dominate our lives are made intelligible by a preordained agreement as to their referential authority; this agreement however is merely contractual, never constitutive. It can be broken at all times and every piece of writing can be questioned as to its rhetorical mode' (*Allegories of Reading*, p. 204).

This state of affairs, of course, produces a critical process of constant reiteration. Each critic will detect the failings of prior critics, but will, in turn, produce new errors of his or her own. The critic is thus caught on a treadmill of describing and disclosing the logocentric impositions of others as they produce, unavoidably, impositions of their own.

I do not propose to enter upon a full examination of Derrida's philosophy. I wish only to point out that the motives and interests that move it in essay after essay are so exclusively analytical, and the problems with which it deals so metaphysical, that it can hardly be regarded as subversive or negative. The predominant interest in this introduction is to outline the common ground of post-structuralism and the important differences that, within post-structuralism, separate Derrida from Ricoeur.

Earlier in this introduction, I have described how Ricoeur argues in each of the six major books that to maintain a dichotomy between explanation and understanding is tantamount to rejecting the relationship of reason and reflection. Explanatory analyses, while they clarify the objective internal operations of texts, leave unanswered the questions of unintended ideological bias as well as intended promotion of ideas, the questions of reception in differing contexts by future readers unknown and entirely unpredicted by the author.

On the other hand, reflective approaches assume a subjective communion of author and reader similar to a face-to-face dialogue. While they can uncover important elements of signification, they ignore the factual distinction between dialogue and reading. Ricoeur argues, as I have sketched above, that there must be a dialectic of explanation and understanding if we are to share meanings. In dialogue, understanding and explanation almost coincide; if I do not understand what my dialogical partner has said, I ask for an explanation, which, when given, helps me to understand. But written texts, while they may be founded on this discursive basis of spoken language, are clearly and markedly distinguished from it. Written texts stand apart temporally and intentionally from the immediacy of dialogue. The written text is, above all, a composition, a strategy of communication that is subjected to a process of exteriorization, using a collective multifaceted, polysemic, and highly valorized system of cultural signs. In so far as the written text is a composition, explanation and semiotic analysis are not only appropriate, but necessary, and in so far as the reading of the text is the concretization of meaning, understanding is called for.

Although there are significant disagreements between Ricoeur and Derrida, let us first review the basic agreement. Both would agree that, in the making of meaning, there is always a pattern of reiteration. As early as *Of Grammatology*, Derrida stated that iterative questioning of the text is not a capricious exercise in self-indulgence, but a rigorous exposition of the text's *inherent* indeterminacies. Therefore, Derrida argued, what is deconstructed is the logocentric assumption of fixed meaning.

Equally forcefully, Ricoeur has insisted that the polysemic nature of language rules out all interpretive absolutisms, and that the trap of an anti-rational psychologism or subjectivism, into which reflective understanding is prone to fall, can be overcome through a relation of mutual implication between analytical reason and reflective understanding. The reiteration of cultural ideological constructs can be revealed through analysis, and the ensuing understanding will, in its own turn, be the subject of still another round of interpretation in the unending chain of belonging to the community.

Both Derrida and Ricoeur attribute indeterminacy to the inherent polysemic nature of language, not to any skill or the lack of it in performance. And since there is no absolute origin, culture is a continuing chain of iterations and reiterations. These are the general points of agreement.

A major area of disagreement is on the point of how extensive indeterminacy is. For Derrida, textual indeterminacy is always, and without exception, already there in the text. Ricoeur, in contrast, works with ordered, predictable conceptual systems, such as the dialogical nature of creative meaning, although these systems are seen as the determinate framework within which indeterminacy operates. Derrida characterizes his philosophy as a radical break with the logocentric metaphysics of Western thought. Ricoeur considers his work to be a continuation of a tradition of inquiry from Aristotle and Augustine to Heidegger and Wittgenstein. For deconstruction, the emergence of indeterminacy invalidates all claims to a sense of order that is not one of presence; for Ricoeur, disorder leads to the revelation of creative order or tensional order on a different scale.

To sum up, post-structuralist thought comes from Heidegger's conception of human existence that rules out the possibility of an errorless reliable origin. Derrida and Ricoeur share in this concept. And the fundamental separation between the two philosophers is the possibility of shared meaning. Hermeneutics is an alternative to deconstruction because its dialectic orientation keeps it open ended as a dynamic process, but does not sacrifice transmission. In post-structuralist hermeneutics, a metaphor posits a connection rather than a congruence. It makes possible a similarity that rises out of the ruins of semantic impertinence. The level of indeterminacy is regulated by the degree of impertinence in the segments. The more radical and dissimilar the elements, the more will the ensuing gain in meaning be unpredictable.

Perhaps the most significant consequence of Ricoeur's philosophy for literary criticism is that it establishes the basis for meaningful shared commentary. In other words, it offers critics an alternative of post-structuralist scholarship that overcomes the contemporary either/or trap of historicist absolutism and the deferral of deconstruction. The goal of criticism thus returns to being the elucidation of the critic and of those readers who share the same texts, as it was with Juan Luis Vives during the Renaissance. Elucidation is accomplished by critics and their readers when they put into play the knowing appropriation of the literary work. 'Putting into play' is a key concept that Ricoeur has taken from Gadamer and that we should take care to define since it is the activity that will take us from the level of configuration of the text to that of refiguration by readers. Ricoeur defines the boundary that 'putting into play' will cross in these words: 'The boundary between configuration and refiguration has not yet been crossed, as long as the world of the work remains a transcendence immanent in the text' (*TN*, II: 160).

The activity of putting a text into play is not determined exclusively by the consciousness that plays, that is, by the reader. The players are participants, for the activity itself has its own way of being. Putting a text into play is an experience that transforms those who participate in it – critics and their readers. The subject of the aesthetic experience is not the critic, but rather what takes place in the activity. Ricoeur puts it this way: 'The threshold separating these problematics [configuration and refiguration] is, in fact, crossed only when the world of the text is confronted with the world of the reader. *Only then does the literary work acquire a meaning in the full sense of the term, at the intersection of the world projected by the text and the life-world of the reader'* (*TN*, II: 160; my emphasis). But how accurate is the term 'putting into play'? What does it entail? We often say that we play with an idea; what we mean by this common expression is that we take up an idea and engage it; there is an essential give and take, a to-and-fro movement in this activity. We also say that an idea is played out, or that a part is played, or that something is in play between one place and another. All of these expressions from ordinary language reveal that there is a linguistic category for this common activity of mental engagement, but there is something other than the exclusive mental activity of a subject. The *in-itself* of putting into play is such that, even in a solitary situation, there must be something with which one plays. And more important, we must recognize that whoever is engaged in putting into play is also played himself or herself, for the rules of the game impose themselves upon the player, prescribing the to-and-fro and delimiting the field where the activity takes place. The essential point that Ricoeur makes is that there is a strict relation between putting into play and the presentation of a world, and this relation is fully reciprocal. Since the idea of literature Ricoeur holds is that of a tradition of texts with a maximum capacity to induce the redescription of the world in the reader, it follows that the game we play as readers of and commentators on literature is that of world-making. As a corollary of this proposition, we can surmise that the literary dimension of texts, their literariness, is precisely their propensity for putting into play the heuristic fiction of the world. The literary critic of the past well understood that art abolished only the non-metamorphosed aspects of reality. In this sense, the task of the critic has always been one of recognition rather than of cognition. The problem with traditional criticism was that it was caught in a trap between the reflective Kantian tradition and the speculative Hegelian tradition of philosophy. However, the place of criticism, as elaborated by Ricoeur, is not in either camp, but rather at equal distance from both, accepting as much from one as from the other but opposing both with equal vigour.

A careful study of *The Rule of Metaphor* and the essays in *Hermeneutics and the Human Sciences* reveals that Ricoeur's examination of the literary text posits four dimensions: the formal, the historical, the phenomenological (reading experience), and the hermeneutic (self-understanding). These dimensions can now be recast as stages of operation for literary criticism. Let us examine them as a sketch of an approach to practical criticism.

The formal dimension of the text is the system of signs, their rules of operation and their interrelationships. This level of inquiry is one of semiotic analysis of the linguistic and structural features, which every text has as composition. At this level, we respond to the general question: How does the text function?

The second dimension of the text is the historical. This level of inquiry stems from the basic presupposition that all texts and all readers are historical and that the historical dimension is always a factor of some consequence. The historicity of the text has an implicit tension with the historicity of the reader. As discourse, it is written language addressed to someone about something. Thus, in its split reference between internal and external references, there is the undeniable dialectic of the historical ground of the text and the distinct ground of the reader. At this level, we operate on semantic inquiry as we seek to bring the dialectic of past significance and present meaning into focus. The general question we respond to is: What does the text speak about?

The third dimension of the text is the phenomenological level of the reading experience. At this level, we turn to the consideration of experiential aspects of the text–reader relationship as we examine the textual strategies and the reader's modes of reception. Obviously this stage of Ricoeur-based criticism coincides with the reader-reception theory of our colleagues from Constance, as is acknowledged in *Time and Narrative*, Vol. III (p. 171). This third dimension of the text therefore yields the critical reading experience that we can identify as the essence of the critical commentary. It should be stated once again that neither Ricoeur nor Jauss and Iser are concerned with the subjective experience of reading, but only with the intersubjective dimension of such an experience. The general question we pursue at this level is: What does the text say to me that is common to the reading experience of others?

The fourth and final dimension of the text is the hermeneutic level of self-knowledge. At this level, we encounter the undercurrent of tension between the text's autonomy and the assimilating force of the reader's appropriation. At this level, there is a reflective assessment of what Gadamer has called the fusion of horizons; it is this act of dialogic unity with the text that is the hermeneutical experience. The question here is: How has my world changed because of reading the text?

If four dimensions of the literary text can be discerned in Ricoeur's philosophy, we must also note the three areas of engagement of the critic who responds to the text. The critic's areas of engagement are, of course, the tripartite exposition of mimesis that Ricoeur has developed in *Time and Narrative*: prefiguration (mimesis$_1$), configuration (mimesis$_2$), and refiguration (mimesis$_3$). The three are the areas of critical study that are the necessary counterparts to the four dimensions of the literary text. Let us bring the text and the critic together and thus establish the Ricoeur-based mode of literary criticism. Prefiguration is the area of cultural participation through language and, as such, is the pre-condition for textuality. There can be no text if there is not the common ground of language and culture. Configuration is the area of analysis of the composition and, as such, corresponds to the formal and historical dimensions of the text, which has been discussed above. Refiguration is the area of actualization of the text by the critical reader and therefore corresponds to the phenomenological and hermeneutic dimensions of the text. In both configuration and refiguration, we have a dialectic examination of corresponding dimensions of the text.

The critical commentary on a literary text moves progressively through the four dimensions of literary text after establishing the necessary conditions of prefiguration. The crossing between configuration and refiguration, that is, from the consideration of the formal and historical dimensions of the text to that of the phenomenological and hermeneutic, is a major passage from virtual structure to actual meaning. But let us not make the mistake of treating this approach as if it were a method for determining the meaning of the text. Every reader achieves meaning and does not need the critic to expand or enhance it. The essential aim of this mode of literary criticism is not to establish objective truth about any aspect of the text but, rather, to elucidate the shared experience of reading the text with the essential claim of refiguration – the redescription of the world – that the only form of truth we have is self-truth on an intersubjective level.

One of the strongest objections made to a literary theory that holds the literary text to be indeterminate and the work of art inexhaustible is the charge of inconsequential commentary, since absolute truth is held to be an illusion, and one interpretation is purportedly as good as any other. The response to this objection will be the last issue I address here. To put it strongly, there is no possible distinction of merit between one reading experience and another. But it is quite another matter where there is an implicit or explicit claim of authority and knowledge by the writer of a commentary that is based on the reading experience and is disseminated for the use of other readers. We are here involved with the general issue of the validity of critical statements. It is clear that, in critical discourse as in any other human pursuit, there will be a wide range of varied talent and ability used in its execution. The means that Ricoeur suggests as a basis for evaluation of psychoanalysis can be transferred to literary criticism. In summary form, they are the following: the critical commentary must have coherence in keeping with its own stated principles; it must also be able to meet its stated aims; further, criticism must be of consequence to its readers, that is, perform a useful function for them; and, finally, criticism must be written as an intelligible narrative. There is no doubt that we must make numerous value judgments when dealing with literary criticism; what Ricoeur has proposed is, in fact, a general guide to judge all interpreters' performances. Consequently, a critic has as much claim as anyone else to the truth she or he purports to have discovered in reading a literary text, but her or his performance in sharing this truth is another matter. It can be coherent, accomplished, consequential, and well written, or it can be wanting in one or all of these aspects. Literary criticism based on Ricoeur's philosophy rejects the romantic pretension of recovering the genius of the author. Equally set aside is the historicist attempt to reconstruct the author's meaning or the purported meaning perceived by the original audience. Ricoeur's approach posits a mode of literary criticism that is concerned with the relationship between the text and its readers. The literary text remains the mediator in the process of the fusion of present meaning and past significance. Finally, Ricoeur offers an alternative to deconstruction within post-structuralism and its continuous iteration of values. The reader–critic's appropriation of the text does not warrant the disregard of the formal features of the text or the whimsical unravelling of the discourse. The dialectical process of appropriation is primarily the projection of a world, a proposal of a mode of being-in-the-world that the text discloses.

In post-structuralist hermeneutics, the critic does not project the *a priori* of his or her own understanding, nor does he or she interpolate this *a priori* into the text. Quite the contrary: appropriation is the process by which the revelation of new modes of being in the experience of reading the text gives the critic a new capacity for self-knowledge. If the power of a text is to be found in its capacity to project a redescription of the world, then the critic does not project herself or himself onto the text; rather, the text projects the discovery of refiguration upon the critic. Appropriation is not a remaking of the text in our own perspective, but rather a response to the text that can become a commentary rooted in self-understanding. Because absolute knowledge is an illusion, the conflict of interpretations is inescapable. Ricoeur's philosophy, however, gives us the means to transcend the finite character of being-in-the-world and to celebrate the participation of text and readers in the community of commentary.

The Scope and Aim of This Collection

This book is, of course, by Ricoeur, but it is also about Ricoeur, since the plan that I have put in place seeks to exemplify Ricoeur's own theory of interpretation. Attentive readers of *The Rule of Metaphor* (1977) were struck by the richness and depth of his 'tensional conception of metaphor' as a paradigm for the interpretation of overdetermined literary texts. When Ricoeur writes in chapter 7, 'Metaphor raises this reciprocity from confusion and vagueness to bipolar tension' (p. 246), he has in fact begun laying the groundwork for a post-structuralist hermeneutics.

The four-part approach or method that I have drawn from his book has been used as the organizing principle in this volume. Part I aims at giving the reader the philosophical context for a post-structuralist hermeneutics; Part II seeks to put in evidence Ricoeur's dialectic thinking through his reviews and debates; Part III presents his theory of the interpretation process; and Part IV discloses the redescriptive power of hermeneutics through a series of glimpses into the redescriptive reader: Paul Ricoeur in dialogue about literature.

Part I consists of six papers written between 1970 and 1980 that explore the tensional elements of discourse as the foundations for a radical hermeneutics: 'What Is a Text? Explanation and Understanding' (1970), 'Word, Polysemy, Metaphor: Creativity in Language' (1973), 'Appropriation' (1973), 'The Human Experience of Time and Narrative' (1978), 'The Function of Fiction in Shaping Reality' (1979), and 'Mimesis and Representation' (1980).

I have selected 'What Is a Text?' to begin this collection because it offers the reader the most succinct review of what the hermeneutic tradition consists of and, at the same time, gives Ricoeur's starting-point for a post-structuralist theory of interpretation:

> We shall take another step in the direction of this reconciliation between explanation and interpretation if we now turn towards the second term of the initial contradiction. So far we have worked with a concept of interpretation which remains very subjective. To interpret, we said, is to appropriate here and now the intention of the text. In saying that, we remain enclosed within Dilthey's concept of understanding. Now what we have just said about the depth semantics unveiled by the structural analysis of the text invites us to say that the intended meaning of the text is not essentially the presumed intention of the author, the lived experience of the writer, but rather what the text means for whoever complies with its injunction. The text seeks to place us in its meaning, that is – according to another acceptation of the word *sens* – in the same direction. So if the intention is that of the text, and if this intention is the direction which it opens up for thought, then depth semantics must be understood in a fundamentally dynamic way. (p. 60)

The essential points expressed in this paragraph are four: 1 / interpretation is a dialectic process that engages both the reader's sense-making appropriation and the text's formal directions and injunctions; 2 / the author's intentions have become irrelevant as norms for the interpretation of the text; 3 / the analysis of depth semantics becomes a dynamic process when the reader's participation in the making of sense is considered; and 4 / meaning is neither stable nor fixed, but is, rather, an engagement that is in process.

The second paper, 'Word, Polysemy, Metaphor' was one of

Ricoeur's first writings in which he turned to the examination of metaphor as a way into the implications of creativity in language. Ricoeur begins by recalling Wilhelm von Humboldt's aphorism that describes language as 'an infinite use of finite means.' Ricoeur remarks: 'Looking for a striking illustration of this contrast, I found it in some recent interpretations of metaphor which depart from the traditional interpretation of rhetoric and show it to be not an ornament of language nor a stylistic decoration, but a semantic innovation, an emergence of meaning' (p. 65). With these lines, Ricoeur embarks on one of the most radically innovative and revolutionary inquiries into the polysemic nature of language and its function in social reality. This trajectory will culminate in *The Rule of Metaphor.* Ricoeur's conclusion constitutes a philosophical premise for a theory of literature. He holds that the strategy of metaphorical discourse is aimed not at facilitating communication or at improving the efficacy of argumentation, but, rather, at challenging and even shattering our sense of reality through reflective redescription.

'Appropriation' also dates from 1972. It is the third paper in this collection. In it, the basic issue taken up by Ricoeur is how to free the concept of the subject from the subject–object dichotomy in which it has been trapped for more than half a century of interpretation theory. Ricoeur follows the direction laid out by Heidegger in *Being and Time* that *Dasein* 'belongs' before the subject can assert presence, and by Gadamer in *Truth and Method*, which exemplifies the text–reader relation as one of playing a game. To be in play is not the activity of the subject but, rather, an activity in which subjects participate in the playing of the game or the making of the text.

'The Human Experience of Time and Narrative' (1978) was written after publication of *The Rule of Metaphor* and marks the new direction Ricoeur takes that will result in the three volumes of *Time and Narrative*. This lecture was the first attempt to link up the concept of narrative function, which he had developed in his work with Greimas, and the phenomenology of time experience. He writes: 'The main thesis of this paper will be that narrativity and temporality are as closely linked as a "language-game," in Wittgenstein's terms, is to a "form of life"' (p. 99).

'The Function of Fiction in Shaping Reality' (1979) is Ricoeur's first philosophical essay directly linking the reading of literature to the process of world-making that every reflective person engages in. He draws support from Nelson Goodman's *Languages of Art* and the general thesis that symbolic systems 'make' and 'remake' the world. The argument presented in this paper is the basis for Ricoeur's imperative on the function of literature as a primary impetus to the reader's redescription of his or her sense of reality and its values.

Ricoeur works with two symbolic systems, the verbal and the pictorial, which come together in reality, shaping it instead of merely referring to it. The final outcome of this line of thought will be mimesis$_3$ of *Time and Narrative* as the basic referential concept of refiguration.

The last article in this section, 'Mimesis and Representation' (1980), is, in fact, the nucleus that developed into the major theoretical work we know as the three volumes of *Time and Narrative*. In this article, Ricoeur presents his argument for an expansion of the concept of mimesis into a threefold paradigm of representation.

The second part of this collection highlights Ricoeur's exceptional way of engaging in debate with philosophies relevant to his project. The reader of his books is struck by the extent to which he carries out the dialogic encounter. He engages his dialogic partners by giving them the first word through a careful presentation of their position. Ricoeur then counters with his own position, disputing specific issues. He concludes with the insight gained by the dialectic encounter, demonstrating how the relationship between the two positions is different from either one and, because of its dynamic relationship, is always unfolding.

In *The Rule of Metaphor*, he debates with major commentators on theory of metaphor, including Max Black, Nelson Goodman, Jacques Derrida, and Mary Hesse, and in *Hermeneutics and the Human Sciences* he mediates the debate between Gadamer and Habermas. In this section I have included his lectures on Habermas and Geertz, the reviews of E.D. Hirsch's *Aims of Interpretation* and Nelson Goodman's *Ways of Worldmaking*, as well as his review articles on Northrop Frye's *Anatomy of Criticism* and A.J. Greimas's *Narrative Grammar*, and, finally, two debates: the highly significant exchange with A.J. Greimas held in 1984 at the University of Toronto and an earlier debate with H.-G. Gadamer.

The first two papers in this section were part of a much longer series of lectures delivered at the University of Chicago in autumn 1975. We are all indebted to George H. Taylor's excellent edition of the entire lecture series, *Lectures on Ideology and Utopia*. I have selected only the second of the two lectures on Habermas and the one on Geertz for inclusion in this volume because they offer a clear introduction to Ricoeur's concept of ideology as the social fabric within which communication operates.

Although Ricoeur enthusiastically supports Habermas's development of a social critique as the metascience of the social sciences, he objects to Habermas's implicit claim that the critique stands outside the social process. Ricoeur draws Habermas's argument for analysis of social distortion into a hermeneutic position wherein the critical theorist starts knowingly in the encounter with the text from his or her own historicity, which comes from varying cultural and temporal distances.

Ricoeur's discussion of Clifford Geertz's hermeneutics is the culmination of a long process of analogical thinking that was first sketched out in his essay 'The Model of the Text: Meaningful Action Considered as Text.' Ricoeur argues that, since social action is already symbolically mediated, it is ideology that plays the primary mediating role, and that, in turn, we must see ideology as constructed socially on the basis of countless layers of narrativity. Thus, he argues, ideology can be compared to the rhetorical devices of discourse: symbolic mediation is essential to both social action and language. Consequently, the interpretation of literary texts will always offer this primary link to the world of social action.

The reviews of *Aims of Interpretation* by E.D. Hirsch, Jr, and *Ways of Worldmaking* by Nelson Goodman are significant, but for very different reasons. Hirsch represents a hold-over from an earlier hermeneutics and a vehement rejection of Gadamer's philosophical hermeneutics. Clearly, this encounter is essential for a clarification of the direction Ricoeur's hermeneutics has taken. Nelson Goodman's book, on the other hand, offers Ricoeur the opportunity to respond to the distinguished North American nominalist in a manner that establishes strong links between the two philosophers and the two traditions they represent. As a rule, Ricoeur never writes a negative or merely positive review. He engages in a dialectic encounter, with the aim of generating a net gain in understanding of the issues debated.

The debates with Greimas and Gadamer represent the nexus between the configuration of the text (the reader's response to the injunctions of the text) and the refiguration (the reader's redescription of his or her own sense of world). The debate with Greimas both sharpens Greimas's own project and makes possible Ricoeur's appropriation of the semiotic power of explanation for his hermeneutics. The debate with Gadamer is less focused but more far-reaching since it brings out the central concern of hermeneutics with social values and the redescription of value paradigms as the achievement of literature. The understanding of being-in-the-world must, however, be seen in the light of the explanatory process of semiotics.

The third part of this collection aims to give some idea of the scope and direction of Ricoeur's post-structuralist hermeneutics. It consists of six papers: 'Metaphor and the Main Problem of Hermeneutics' (1974), 'Writing as a Problem for Literary Criticism and Philosophical Hermeneutics' (1977), 'Narrated Time' (1984), 'Time Traversed: Remembrance of Things Past' (1984), 'Between the Text and Its Readers' (1985), and 'Life: A Story in Search of a Narrator' (1987).

The first paper, 'Metaphor and the Main Problem of Hermeneutics,' reviews the context presented in Part I of this collection, but also focuses the issues and problems of literary interpretation, which aims to be a dialogue on the reading experience. A post-structuralist hermeneutics approaches the literary text as a facilitating basis for performances by the reader that are variations on a theme. A fundamental corollary of this principle is that intentionality of the text itself is variational. This idea takes into account an implicit inventiveness in the text that must be put into play if it is to be actualized. Thus considered, the essential activity of the writer and of the reader is playing the game of realization.

Ricoeur's theory of dialectic tension is best depicted as the intersection between two spheres of discourse. This intersection of the separate spheres can be understood if we recognize that their difference is based on separate modalities of each discourse. Consequently the intersection is the encounter that is possible because of the oppository relationship implicit in the semantic aims of each discourse.

The essential characteristic of the poetic text, to Ricoeur, is a creative gain in meaning. The metaphorical utterance in the poem stands before us as a statement expressed in specific formal patterns. Ricoeur holds that the utterance is about something, and the inquiry into what this is, the task of interpretation. The metaphorical utterance functions in two referential fields at once. This duality explains how two levels of meaning are linked up in the same symbol. The dynamism of metaphorical meaning is seen as an unstable convergence of the referential field of experience as it moves towards expression and encounters the referential field of language that has been forced out of the familiar, where it began.

The second paper of this section, 'Writing as a Problem for Literary Criticism and Philosophical Hermeneutics,' is still closely attached to the line of argument presented in *The Rule of Metaphor*, but there is an important distinction; in this essay, Ricoeur considers the metacritical question that will become the post-structuralist issue: What is the ultimate justification for the externalization of critical discourse? He writes: 'the problem of writing becomes a hermeneutical problem when it is referred to its complementary pole which is reading' (p. 336). Ricoeur's response at this point is a re-elaboration of Gadamer's *Truth and Method*.

The remarkable philosophical *tour de force* of *Time and Narrative* has a number of extraordinary papers incorporated into the finely woven tapestry of temporality in history and fiction. In one of these papers, Ricoeur's study of Proust: 'Time Traversed: Remembrance of Things Past,' Ricoeur examines the Gadamerian concept of distance that joins together rather than separates; the idea of meaning in and through distance is central to Ricoeur's dialectic between the historicity of the text and that of the reader. He writes: 'The itinerary of *Remembrance* moves from the idea of a distance that separates to that of a distance that joins together. This is confirmed by the final figure of time proposed in *Remembrance*, that of an accumulated duration that is, in a sense, beneath us' (p. 380).

'Narrated Time' essentially comprises a schematic synthesis of the theoretical issues developed in the long trajectory of the three-volume *Time and Narrative* (1984–6). The central question for that project, and for post-structural hermeneutics, is: 'In what way is the ordinary experience of time, borne by daily acting and suffering, refashioned by its passage through the grid of narrative?" (p. 338).

This is the response to the earlier query on the justification of externalizing critical commentary. In the seven years that have passed between 'Writing as a Problem ...' and the present essay, Ricoeur has written the three volumes of *Time and Narrative*, and can now give the short answer that refiguration as the redescription of the world has its own tradition and function to perform, which moves the idea of re-enactment to the actual making of our everyday reality through the numberless fragments of narrativity in which we are immersed from birth.

The fifth paper in this section, 'Between the Text and Its Readers,' is something of an anomaly. It was first written in French for presentation in English at a seminar, 'Time and Narrative,' given in 1982 in Toronto. Subsequently it was expanded, altered, and, for a time, shelved as Ricoeur struggled to compress the ever-expanding manuscript of *Time and Narrative* into what had been planned as a single volume. Finally, Ricoeur decided to turn the project into the three volumes we know as *Time and Narrative*. One of the most remarkable aspects of this trajectory is that the final version of 'The World of the Text and the World of the Reader,' now part of chapter 7 of Volume III, is essentially the same as the original manuscript 'Between the Text and Its Readers.' I have kept the original version for this collection.

This paper is Ricoeur's most extensive study of reader-reception theory and, of course, the work of Wolfgang Iser and Hans Robert Jauss. In many respects this paper presents the very core of Ricoeur's post-structuralist hermeneutics: 'The act of reading is thereby included within a reading community which, under certain favourable conditions, develops the sort of normativity and canonical status that we acknowledge in great works, those that never cease decontextualizing and recontextualizing themselves in the most diverse cultural circumstances' (p. 413).

In the last article of this part Ricoeur inverts the traditional discussion of the movement from life to art and treats the countermovement from art to life, and by doing so culminates the process that began to develop in theory some thirty years ago. The artist's movement from life to art has been a corner-stone of criticism because of the critical concentration on the author's perspective and creative process. Post-structuralist criticism, however, has shelved the commentary on the author's viewpoint as irrelevant to aesthetic creation, as a marginal curiosity or, at best, part of the historicity of creative writing. The emphasis now is on the reader's configuration of the text and the aesthetic experience of the act of reading. Consequently, the counter-questions are related to how art comes together in our own personal identity. In a phrase, Ricoeur gives the primary aim of post-structuralist hermeneutics: to recover the narrative identity that constitutes us. The subject that we are is never given at the beginning of this story, but only as an achievement constituting a self taught by cultural symbols, first among which are the stories received in the literary tradition.

Literary criticism derived from Ricoeur's hermeneutics starts with the recognition that the text is analytically accessible as distinct from the psychological recesses of the author's intentions. The data brought forth by the analysis of the text do not comprise the hidden meaning; rather, they are the injunction for response addressed to the reader. The interpretation that follows analysis accordingly is a kind of obedience to this injunction that comes from the text.

The concept of hermeneutical circle is not ruled out by Ricoeur's shift in hermeneutics. Indeed, the hermeneutical circle is formulated, but in new terms. It no longer proceeds from an intersubjective relation linking the subjectivity of the author and that of the reader. The hermeneutical program is a connection between two discourses, the discourse of the text and the discourse of interpretation. This connection means that what has to be interpreted in a text is what it says and what it speaks about – the kind of world it opens up, discloses. The final act of appropriation is less the projection of the reader's prejudices into the text than the fusion of horizons that occurs when the world of the text and the world of the reader merge into each other.

The fourth and last part of this collection attempts to give some insight into Ricoeur responding and thinking as he speaks, always intent on the question being asked and, through dialogue, creating a remarkable insight into the dialogic process of self-discovery.

Paul Ricoeur has given a number of interviews over the last twenty years; in this collection, I have selected five published over the last decade that reflect on the issues of literary theory. The major value of these interviews is that the paradigm of inquiry is not the carefully designed dialectic method of Ricoeur's philosophy. The implicit paradigm in the interviews is, without exception, the existing tradition of inquiry in philosophy and literary theory. Ricoeur's responses constitute a gradual process of appropriation of the issues until he manages to construct a working model of his dialectic wherein he can demonstrate his views and not merely state his position as an abstract formulation. Ricoeur himself does not put much value on interviews because they lack the carefully constructed model of his essays. Nevertheless, in their own genre they constitute a glimpse of a philosopher at work.

Ricoeur's theory of interpretation is a post-structuralist hermeneutics, in both the historical and the theoretical attributions of the term. This theory has developed over the last two decades and not only has taken structuralism and semiotics into full consideration and responded to them but, most significantly, has built on this debate. The two Greimas articles attest to the extent of the encounter.

Ricoeur's theory is a hermeneutics in so far as it remains a reflective theory of interpretation, but it is a phenomenological hermeneutics since it turns the focus of inquiry on the textual experience rather than on the writing, and it is post-structural not only because he appropriates the functional analysis of form, but because he radically redirects the aims of interpretation from fixing truth in the work to discovering truth in the reader's response to the tensional interaction of a dynamic system. Ricoeur's work is post-structuralist in its dismissal of the logocentric illusions of the absolute object or definitive interpretation.

Bibliographical Note

Ricoeur's works examined in this introduction are:

Interpretation Theory: Discourse and the Surplus of Meaning. Forth Worth, Tex.: Texas Christian University Press, 1976. Cited here as *IT.*

'The Model of the Text: Meaningful Action Considered as Text.' *Social Research* 38 (1971): 529–62.

The Rule of Metaphor. Trans. by Robert Czerny. Toronto: University of Toronto Press, 1977. Cited here as *RM.*

Hermeneutics and the Human Sciences. Trans. and ed. by J.B. Thompson. Cambridge: Cambridge University Press, 1981. Cited here as *HHS.*

Time and Narrative. Trans. by Kathleen McLaughlin and David Pellauer. Chicago: University of Chicago Press, 1984–6. Cited here as *TN* I, II, and III.

Other works referred to in this introduction are:

Beardsley, Monroe C. *Aesthetics: Problems in the Philosophy of Criticism.* New York: Harcourt, Brace and World, 1958.

– 'Textual Meaning and Authorial Meaning.' *Genre* 1, no. 3 (1968): 169–81.

Black, Max. 'Metaphor.' *Proceedings of the Aristotelian Society* 55 (1954–5): 273–94.

– 'More about Metaphor.' *Dialectica* 31, no. 3–4 (1977): 431–57.

De Man, Paul. *Allegories of Reading.* New Haven: Yale University Press, 1979

Derrida, Jacques. 'Difference.' *Speech and Phenomena*, pp. 126–60. Trans. by David B. Allison. Evanston: Northwestern University Press, 1973.

– *Of Grammatology.* Trans. by Gayatri Chakravorty Spivak. Baltimore: Johns Hopkins University Press, 1974

– *Positions.* Trans. by Alan Bass. Chicago: University of Chicago Press, 1981

Iser, Wolfgang. *The Implied Reader: Patterns of Communicating in Prose Fiction from Bunyan to Beckett.* Baltimore: Johns Hopkins University Press, 1974

– *The Act of Reading: A Theory of Aesthetic Response.* Baltimore: Johns
Hopkins University Press, 1978
Jauss, Hans Robert. 'Theses on the Transition from the Aesthetics of Literary
Works to a Theory of Aesthetic Experience.' In *Interpretation of Narrative*, ed.
Mario J. Valdés and Owen J. Miller, pp. 137–47. Toronto: University of
Toronto Press, 1978

I

Philosophical Context
for a Post-Structuralist
Hermeneutics

What Is a Text?
Explanation and
Understanding

This essay will be devoted primarily to the debate between two
fundamental attitudes which may be adopted in regard to a text.
These two attitudes were summed up, in the period of Wilhelm
Dilthey at the end of the last century, by the two words 'explanation'
and 'interpretation.' For Dilthey, 'explanation' referred to the model
of intelligibility borrowed from the natural sciences and applied to
the historical disciplines by positivist schools; 'interpretation,' on the
other hand, was a derivative form of understanding, which Dilthey
regarded as the fundamental attitude of the human sciences and as
that which could alone preserve the fundamental difference between
these sciences and the sciences of nature. Here I propose to examine
the fate of this opposition in the light of conflicts between contemporary schools. For the notion of explanation has since been displaced,
so that it derives no longer from the natural sciences but from
properly linguistic models. As regards the concept of interpretation,
it has undergone profound transformations which distance it from
the psychological notion of understanding, in Dilthey's sense of the
word. It is this new position of the problem, perhaps less contradictory and more fecund, which I should like to explore. But before
unfolding the new concepts of explanation and understanding, I
should like to pause at a preliminary question which in fact domi-
nates the whole of our investigation. The question is this: what is a
text?

I. What Is a Text?

Let us say that a text is any discourse fixed by writing. According to
this definition, fixation by writing is constitutive of the text itself. But

what is fixed by writing? We have said: any discourse. Is this to say that discourse had to be pronounced initially in a physical or mental form? that all writing was initially, at least in a potential way, speaking? In short, what is the relation of the text to speech?

To begin with, we are tempted to say that all writing is added to some anterior speech. For if by speech [*parole*] we understand, with Ferdinand de Saussure, the realization of language [*langue*] in an event of discourse, the production of an individual utterance by an individual speaker, then each text is in the same position as speech with respect to language. Moreover, writing as an institution is subsequent to speech, and seems merely to fix in linear script all the articulations which have already appeared orally. The attention given almost exclusively to phonetic writings seems to confirm that writing adds nothing to the phenomenon of speech other than the fixation which enables it to be conserved. Whence the conviction that writing is fixed speech, that inscription, whether it be graphics or recording, is inscription of speech – an inscription which, thanks to the subsisting character of the engraving, guarantees the persistence of speech.

The psychological and sociological priority of speech over writing is not in question. It may be asked, however, whether the late appearance of writing has not provoked a radical change in our relation to the very statements of our discourse. For let us return to our definition: the text is a discourse fixed by writing. What is fixed by writing is thus a discourse which could be said, of course, but which is written precisely because it is not said. Fixation by writing takes the very place of speech, occurring at the site where speech could have emerged. This suggests that a text is really a text only when it is not restricted to transcribing an anterior speech, when instead it inscribes directly in written letters what the discourse means.

This idea of a direct relation between the meaning of the statement and writing can be supported by reflecting on the function of reading in relation to writing. Writing calls for reading in a way which will enable us shortly to introduce the concept of interpretation. For the moment, let us say that the reader takes the place of the interlocutor, just as writing takes the place of speaking and the speaker. The writing–reading relation is thus not a particular case of the speaking–answering relation. It is not a relation of interlocution, not an instance of dialogue. It does not suffice to say that reading is a dialogue with the author through his work, for the relation of the reader to the book is of a completely different nature. Dialogue is an exchange of questions and answers; there is no exchange of this sort between the writer and the reader. The writer does not respond to the reader. Rather, the book divides the act of writing and the act of reading into two sides, between which there is no communication. The reader is absent from the act of writing; the writer is absent from the act of reading. The text thus produces a double eclipse of the reader and the writer. It thereby replaces the relation of dialogue, which directly connects the voice of one to the hearing of the other.

The substitution of reading for a dialogue which has not occurred is so manifest that when we happen to encounter an author and to speak to him (about his book, for example), we experience a profound disruption of the peculiar relation that we have with the author in and through his work. Sometimes I like to say that to read a book is to consider its author as already dead and the book as posthumous. For it is when the author is dead that the relation to the book becomes complete and, as it were, intact. The author can no longer respond; it only remains to read his work.

The difference between the act of reading and the act of dialogue confirms our hypothesis that writing is a realization comparable and parallel to speech, a realization which takes the place of it and, as it were, intercepts it. Hence we could say that what comes to writing is discourse as intention-to-say and that writing is a direct inscription of this intention, even if, historically and psychologically, writing began with the graphic transcription of the signs of speech. This emancipation of writing, which places the latter at the site of speech, is the birth of the text.

Now, what happens to the statement itself when it is directly inscribed instead of being pronounced? The most striking characteristic has always been emphasized: writing preserves discourse and makes it an archive available for individual and collective memory. It may be added that the linearization of symbols permits an analytic and distinctive translation of all the successive and discrete features of language and thereby increases its efficacy. Is that all? Preservation and increased efficacy still characterize only the transcription of oral language in graphic signs. The emancipation of the text from the oral situation entails a veritable upheaval in the relations between language and the world, as well as in the relation between language and the various subjectivities concerned (that of the author and that of the reader). We glimpsed something of this second upheaval in distinguishing reading from dialogue; we shall have to go still farther, but this time beginning from the upheaval which the referential relation of language to the world undergoes when the text takes the place of speech.

What do we understand by the referential relation or referential function? In addressing himself to another speaker, the subject of discourse says something about something; that about which he speaks is the referent of his discourse. As is well known, this referential function is supported by the sentence, which is the first and the simplest unit of discourse. It is the sentence which intends to say something true or something real, at least in declarative discourse. The referential function is so important that it compensates, as it were, for another characteristic of language, namely, the separation of signs from things. By means of the referential function, language 'pours back into the universe' (according to an expression of Gustave Guillaume)[1] those signs which the symbolic function, at its birth, divorced from things. All discourse is, to some extent, thereby reconnected to the world. For if we did not speak of the world, of what should we speak?

When the text takes the place of speech, something important occurs. In speech, the interlocutors are present not only to one another, but also to the situation, the surroundings, and the circumstantial milieu of discourse. It is in relation to this circumstantial milieu that discourse is fully meaningful; the return to reality is ultimately a return to this reality, which can be indicated 'around' the speakers, 'around,' if we may say so, the instance of discourse itself. Language is, moreover, well equipped to secure this anchorage. Demonstratives, adverbs of time and place, personal pronouns, verbal tenses, and in general all the 'deictic' and 'ostensive' indicators serve to anchor discourse in the circumstantial reality which surrounds the instance of discourse. Thus, in living speech, the *ideal* sense of what is said turns towards the *real* reference, towards that 'about which' we speak. At the limit, this real reference tends to merge with an ostensive designation where speech rejoins the gesture of pointing. Sense fades into reference and the latter into the act of showing.

This is no longer the case when the text takes the place of speech. The movement of reference towards the act of showing is intercepted, at the same time as dialogue is interrupted by the text. I say intercepted and not suppressed; it is in this respect that I shall distance myself from what may be called henceforth the ideology of the absolute text. On the basis of the sound remarks which we have just made, this ideology proceeds, by an unwarranted hypostasis, through a course that is ultimately surreptitious. As we shall see, the text is not without reference; the task of reading, *qua* interpretation, will be precisely to fulfil the reference. The suspense which defers the reference merely leaves the text, as it were, 'in the air,' outside or without a world. In virtue of this obliteration of the relation to the world, each text is free to enter into relation with all the other texts which come to take the place of the circumstantial reality referred to by living speech. This relation of text to text, within the effacement of the world about which we speak, engenders the quasi world of texts or *literature*.

Such is the upheaval which affects discourse itself, when the movement of reference towards the act of showing is intercepted by the text. Words cease to efface themselves in front of things; written words become words for themselves.

The eclipse of the circumstantial world by the quasi world of texts can be so complete that, in a civilization of writing, the world itself is no longer what can be shown in speaking but is reduced to a kind of 'aura' which written works unfold. Thus we speak of the Greek world or the Byzantine world. This world can be called 'imaginary,' in the sense that it is *represented* by writing in lieu of the world *presented* by speech; but this imaginary world is itself a creation of literature.

The upheaval in the relation between the text and its world is the key to the other upheaval of which we have already spoken, that which affects the relation of the text to the subjectivities of the author and the reader. We think that we know what the author of a text is because we derive the notion of the author from that of the speaker. The subject of speech, according to Emile Benveniste, is what designates itself in saying 'I.' When the text takes the place of speech, there is no longer a speaker, at least in the sense of an immediate and direct self-designation of the one who speaks in the instance of discourse. This proximity of the speaking subject to his own speech is replaced by a complex relation of the author to the text, a relation which enables us to say that the author is instituted by the text, that he stands in the space of meaning traced and inscribed by writing. The text is the very place where the author appears. But does the author appear otherwise than as first reader? The distancing of the text from its author is already a phenomenon of the first reading, which, in one move, poses the whole series of problems that we are now going to confront concerning the relations between explanation and interpretation. These relations arise at the time of reading.

II. Explanation or Understanding?

As we shall see, the two attitudes which we have initially placed under the double title of explanation and interpretation will confront each other in the act of reading. This duality is first encountered in the work of Dilthey. For him, these distinctions constituted an alternative wherein one term necessarily excluded the other: either you 'explain' in the manner of the natural scientist, or you 'interpret' in the manner of the historian. This exclusive alternative will provide the point of departure for the discussion which follows. I propose to show that the concept of the text, such as we have formulated it in the first part of this essay, demands a renewal of the two notions of explanation and interpretation and in virtue of this renewal, a less contradictory conception of their interrelation. Let us say straight away that the discussion will be deliberately oriented towards the search for a strict complementarity and reciprocity between explanation and interpretation.

The initial opposition in Dilthey's work is not exactly between explanation and interpretation, but between explanation and understanding, interpretation being a particular province of understanding. We must therefore begin from the opposition between explanation and understanding. Now if this opposition is exclusive, it is because, in Dilthey's work, the two terms designate two spheres of reality which they serve to separate. These two spheres are those of the natural sciences and the human sciences. Nature is the region of objects offered to scientific observation, a region subsumed since Galileo to the enterprise of mathematization and since John Stuart Mill to the canons of inductive logic. Mind is the region of psychological individualities, into which each mental life is capable of transposing itself. Understanding is such a transference into another mental life. To ask whether the human sciences can exist is thus to ask whether a scientific knowledge of individuals is possible, whether this understanding of the singular can be objective in its own way, whether it is susceptible of universal validity. Dilthey answered affirmatively, because inner life is given in external signs which can be perceived and understood as signs of another mental life: 'Understanding,' he says in the famous article 'The Development of Hermeneutics,' is the process by which we come to know something of mental life through the perceptible signs which manifest it.'[2] This is the understanding of which interpretation is a particular province. Among the signs of another mental life, we have the 'manifestations fixed in a durable way,' the 'human testimonies preserved by writing,' the 'written monuments.' Interpretation is the art of understanding applied to such manifestations, to such testimonies, to such monuments, of which writing is the distinctive characteristic. Understanding, as the knowledge through signs of another mental life, thus provides the basis in the pair understanding–interpretation; the latter element supplies the degree of objectification, in virtue of the fixation and preservation which writing confers upon signs.

Although this distinction between explanation and understanding seems clear at first, it becomes increasingly obscure as soon as we ask ourselves about the conditions of scientificity of interpretation. Explanation has been expelled from the field of the human sciences; but the conflict reappears at the very heart of the concept of interpretation between, on the one hand, the intuitive and unverifiable character of the psychologizing concept of understanding to which interpretation is subordinated and, on the other hand, the demand for objectivity which belongs to the very notion of human science. The splitting of hermeneutics between its psychologizing tendency and its search for a logic of interpretation ultimately calls into question the relation between understanding and interpretation. Is not interpretation a species of understanding which explodes the genre? Is not the specific difference, namely, fixation by writing, more important here than the feature common to all signs, that of presenting inner life in an external form? What is more important: the inclusion of hermeneutics in the sphere of understanding or its difference therefrom? Friedrich D.E. Schleiermacher, before Dilthey, had witnessed this internal splitting of the hermeneutical project and had overcome it through a happy marriage of *romantic genius* and *philological virtuosity*. With Dilthey, the epistemological demands are more pressing. Several generations separate him from the scholar of

Romanticism, several generations well versed in epistemological reflection; the contradiction now explodes in full daylight. Listen to Dilthey commenting upon Schleiermacher: 'The ultimate aim of hermeneutics is to understand the author better than he understands himself.' So much for the psychology of understanding. Now for the logic of interpretation: 'The function of hermeneutics is to establish theoretically, against the constant intrusion of romantic whim and sceptical subjectivism into the domain of history, the universal validity of interpretation, upon which all certitude in history rests.'[3] Thus hermeneutics fulfils the aim of understanding only by extricating itself from the immediacy of understanding others – from, let us say, dialogical values. Understanding seeks to coincide with the inner life of the author, to liken itself to him (*sich gleichsetzen*), to reproduce (*nachbilden*) the creative processes which engendered the work. But the signs of this intention, of this creation, are to be found nowhere else than in what Schleiermacher called the 'exterior' and 'interior form' of the work, or again, the 'interconnection' (*Zusammenhang*) which makes it an organized whole. The last writings of Dilthey ('The Construction of the Historical World in the Human Sciences') further aggravated the tension. On the one hand, the objective side of the work was accentuated under the influence of Edmund Husserl's *Logical Investigations* (for Husserl, as we know, the 'meaning' of a statement constitutes an 'ideality' which exists neither in mundane reality nor in psychic reality: it is a pure unity of meaning without a real localization). Hermeneutics similarly proceeds from the objectification of the creative energies of life in works which come in between the author and us; it is mental life itself, its creative dynamism, which calls for the mediation by 'meanings,' 'values,' or 'goals.' The scientific demand thus presses towards an ever greater depsychologization of interpretation, of understanding itself, and perhaps even of introspection, if it is true that memory itself follows the thread of meanings which are not themselves mental phenomena. The exteriorization of life implies a more indirect and mediate characterization of the interpretation of self and others. But it is a self and another, posed in psychological terms, that interpretation pursues; interpretation always aims at a reproduction, a *Nachbildung*, of lived experiences.

This intolerable tension, which the later Dilthey bears witness to, leads us to raise two questions which guide the following discussion: Must we not abandon once and for all the reference of interpretation to understanding and cease to make the interpretation of written monuments a particular case of understanding the external signs of an inner mental life? But if interpretation no longer seeks its norm of intelligibility in understanding others, then does not its relation to explanation, which we have set aside hitherto, now demand to be reconsidered?

III. The Text and Structural Explanation

Let us begin again from our analysis of the text and from the autonomous status which we have granted it with respect to speech. What we have called the eclipse of the surrounding world by the quasi world of texts engenders two possibilities. We can, as readers, remain in the suspense of the text, treating it as a worldless and authorless object; in this case, we explain the text in terms of its internal relations, its structure. On the other hand, we can lift the suspense and fulfil the text in speech, restoring it to living communication; in this case, we interpret the text. These two possibilities both belong to reading, and reading is the dialectic of these two attitudes.

Let us consider them separately, before exploring their articulation. We can undertake a first type of reading which formally records, as it were, the text's interception of all the relations to a world that can be pointed out and to subjectivities that can converse. This transference into the 'place' – a place which is a non-place – constitutes a special project with respect to the text, that of prolonging the suspense concerning the referential relation to the world and to the speaking subject. By means of this special project, the reader decides to situate himself in the 'place of the text' and in the 'closure' of this place. On the basis of this choice, the text has no outside but only an inside; it has no transcendent aim, unlike speech which is addressed to someone about something.

This project is not only possible but legitimate. For the constitution of the text as text and of the body of texts as literature justifies the interception of the double transcendence of discourse, towards the world and towards someone. Thus arises the possibility of an explanatory attitude in regard to the text.

In contrast to what Dilthey thought, this explanatory attitude is not borrowed from a field of knowledge and an epistemological model other than that of language itself. It is not a naturalistic model subsequently extended to the human sciences. The nature–mind opposition plays no role here at all. If there is some form of borrowing, it occurs within the same field, that of signs. For it is possible to treat the text according to the explanatory rules that linguistics successfully applies to the simple system of signs which constitute language [*langue*] as opposed to speech [*parole*]. As is well known, the language–speech distinction is the fundamental distinction which gives linguistics a homogenous object; speech belongs to physiology, psychology, and sociology, whereas language, as rules of the game of which speech is the execution, belongs only to linguistics. As is equally well known, linguistics considers only systems of units devoid of proper meaning, each of which is defined only in terms of its difference from all of the others. These units, whether they be purely distinctive like those of phonological articulation or significant like those of lexical articulation, are oppositive units. The interplay of oppositions and their combinations within an inventory of discrete units is what defines the notion of structure in linguistics. This structural model furnishes the type of explanatory attitude which we are now going to see applied to the text.

Even before embarking upon this enterprise, it may be objected that the laws which are valid only for language as distinct from speech could not be applied to the text. Although the text is not speech, is it not, as it were, on the same side as speech in relation to language? Must not discourse, as a series of statements and, ultimately, of sentences, be opposed in an overall way to language? In comparison to the language–discourse distinction, is not the speaking–writing distinction secondary, such that speaking and writing occur together on the side of discourse? These remarks are perfectly legitimate and justify us in thinking that the structural model of explanation does not exhaust the field of possible attitudes which may be adopted in regard to a text. But before specifying the limits of this explanatory model, it is necessary to grasp its fruitfulness. The working hypothesis of any structural analysis of texts is this: in spite of the fact that writing is on the same side as speech in relation to language – namely, on the side of discourse – the specificity of writing in relation to speech is based on structural features which can be treated as analogues of language in discourse. This working hypothesis is perfectly legitimate; it amounts to saying that under certain conditions the larger units of language [*langage*], that is, the units of a higher order than the sentence, display organizations comparable to those of the smaller units of language, that is, the units which are of a lower order than the sentence and which belong to the domain of linguistics.

In *Structural Anthropology*, Claude Lévi-Strauss formulates this working hypothesis for one category of texts, the category of myths:

> Like every linguistic entity, myth is made up of constitutive units. These units imply the presence of those which normally enter into the structure of language, namely the phonemes, the morphemes and the semantemes. The constituent units of myth are in the same relation to semantemes as the latter are to morphemes, and as the latter in turn are to phonemes. Each form differs from that which precedes it by a higher degree of complexity. For this reason, we shall call the elements which properly pertain to myth (and which are the most complex of all): large constitutive units.[4]

By means of this working hypothesis, the large units which are minimally the size of the sentence, and which placed together constitute the narrative proper to the myth, can be treated according to the same rules that are applied to the smaller units familiar to linguistics. To indicate this analogy, Lévi-Strauss speaks of 'mythemes' in the same way that one speaks of phonemes, morphemes, and semantemes. But in order to remain within the limits of the analogy between mythemes and the linguistic units of a lower level, the analysis of texts will have to proceed to the same sort of abstraction as that practised by the phonologist. For the latter, the phoneme is not a concrete sound, to be taken absolutely in its sonorous substance; it is a function defined by the commutative method and its oppositive value is determined by the relation to all other phonemes. In this sense it is not, as de Saussure would say, a 'substance' but a 'form,' an interplay of relations. Similarly, a mytheme is not one of the sentences of the myth but an oppositive value which is shared by several particular sentences, constituting, in the language of Lévi-Strauss, a 'bundle of relations.' 'Only in the form of combinations of such bundles do the constituent units acquire a signifying function.'[5] What is called here the 'signifying function' is not at all what the myth means, its philosophical or existential import, but rather the arrangement or disposition of mythemes, in short, the structure of the myth.

I should like to recall briefly the analysis which, according to this method, Lévi-Strauss offers of the Oedipus myth. He divides the sentences of the myth into four columns. In the first column he places all the sentences which speak of overrated blood relations (for example, Oedipus marries Jocasta, his mother; Antigone buries Polynices, her brother, in spite of the order forbidding it). In the second column, we find the same relation, but modified by the inverse sign: underrated or devalued blood relations (Oedipus kills his father, Laios; Eteocles kills his brother, Polynices). The third column concerns monsters and their destruction; the fourth groups together all those proper names whose meaning suggests a difficulty in walking straight (lame, clumsy, swollen foot). The comparison of the four columns reveals a correlation. Between the first and second columns we have blood relations overrated or underrated in turn; between the third and fourth we have an affirmation and then a negation of the autochthony of man. 'It follows that the fourth column is related to the third column as the first is to the second ...; the overrating of blood relations is to their underrating as the attempt to escape from autochthony is to the impossibility of succeeding in it.' The myth thus appears as a kind of logical instrument which brings together contradictions in order to overcome them: 'the impossibility of connecting the groups of relations is overcome (or, more exactly, replaced) by the assertion that two contradictory relations are identical, insofar as each is, like the other, self-contradictory.'[6] We shall return shortly to this conclusion; let us restrict ourselves here to stating it.

We can indeed say that we have thereby explained the myth, but not that we have interpreted it. We have brought out, by means of structural analysis, the logic of the operations which interconnect the packets of relations; this logic constitutes 'the structural law of the myth concerned.'[7] We shall not fail to notice that this law is, *par excellence*, the object of reading and not at all of speech, in the sense of a recitation whereby the power of the myth would be reactivated in a particular situation. Here the text is only a text and the reading inhabits it only as such, while its meaning for us remains in suspense, together with any realization in present speech.

I have just taken an example from the domain of myths; I could take another from a nearby domain, that of folklore. This domain has been explored by the Russian formalists of the school of Vladimir Propp and by the French specialists in the structural analysis of narratives, Roland Barthes and A.J. Greimas. In the work of these authors, we find the same postulates as those employed by Lévi-Strauss: the units above the sentence have the same composition as the units below the sentence; the sense of the narrative consists in the very arrangement of the elements, in the power of the whole to integrate the subunits; and conversely, the sense of an element is its capacity to enter in relation with other elements and with the whole of the work. These postulates together define the closure of the narrative. The task of structural analysis will be to carry out the segmentation of the work (horizontal aspect), then to establish the various levels of integration of the parts in the whole (hierarchical aspect). Thus the units of action isolated by the analyst will not be psychological units capable of being experienced, nor will they be units of behaviour which could be subsumed to a behaviourist psychology. The extremities of these sequences are only the switching points of the narrative, such that if one element is changed, all the rest is different. Here we recognize the transposition of the method of commutation from the phonological level to the level of narrative units. The logic of action thus consists in an interconnected series of action kernels which together constitute the structural continuity of the narrative. The application of this technique ends up by 'dechronologizing' the narrative, in a way that brings out the logic underlying narrative time. Ultimately the narrative would be reduced to a combination [*combinatoire*] of a few dramatic units (promising, betraying, hindering, aiding, etc.) which would be the paradigms of action. A sequence is thus a succession of modes of action, each closing off an alternative opened up by the preceding one. Just as the elementary units are linked together, so too they fit into larger units; for example, an encounter is comprised of elementary actions such as approaching, calling out, greeting. To explain a narrative is to grasp this entanglement, this fleeting structure of interlaced actions.

Corresponding to the nexus of actions are relations of a similar nature between the 'actants' of the narrative. By that we understand, not at all the characters as psychological subjects endowed with their own existence, but rather the roles correlated with formalized actions. Actants are defined entirely by the predicates of action, by the semantic axes of the sentence and the narrative: the actant is the one by whom, to whom, with whom ... the action is done; it is the one who promises, who receives the promise, the giver, the receiver, etc. Structural analysis thus brings out a hierarchy of *actants* correlative to the hierarchy of *actions*.

The narrative remains to be assembled as a whole and put back into narrative communication. It is then a discourse which a narrator addresses to an audience. For structural analysis, however, the two interlocutors must be sought only in the text. The narrator is designated by the signs of narrativity, which belong to the very constitution of the narrative. Beyond the three levels of actions, actants, and narration, there is nothing else that falls within the scope of the science of semiology. There is only the world of narrative users, which can eventually be dealt with by other semiological disciplines (those analysing social, economic, and ideological systems); but these disciplines are no longer linguistic in nature. This transposition of a linguistic model to the theory of the narrative fully confirms our initial remark: today, explanation is no longer a concept borrowed from the natural sciences and transferred to the alien domain of written artefacts; rather, it stems from the very sphere of language, by analogical transference from the small units of language (phonemes and lexemes) to the units larger than the sentence, such as narratives, folklore, and myth. Henceforth, interpretation – if it is still possible to give a sense to this notion – will no longer be confronted by a model external to the human sciences. It will, instead, be confronted by a model of intelligibility which belongs, from birth so to speak, to the domain of the human sciences, and indeed to a leading science in this domain: linguistics. Thus it will be upon the same terrain, within the same sphere of language [*langage*], that explanation and interpretation will enter into debate.

IV. Towards a New Concept of Interpretation

Let us consider now the other attitude that can be adopted in regard to the text, the attitude which we have called interpretation. We can introduce this attitude by initially opposing it to the preceding one, in a manner still close to that of Dilthey. But, as we shall see, it will be necessary to proceed gradually to a more complementary and reciprocal relation between explanation and interpretation.

Let us begin once again from reading. Two ways of reading, we said, are offered to us. By reading we can prolong and reinforce the suspense which affects the text's reference to a surrounding world and to the audience of speaking subjects: that is the explanatory attitude. But we can also lift the suspense and complete the text in present speech. It is this second attitude which is the real aim of reading. For this attitude reveals the true nature of the suspense which intercepts the movement of the text towards meaning. The other attitude would not even be possible if it were not first apparent that the text as writing, awaits and calls for a reading. If reading is possible, it is indeed because the text is not closed in on itself but opens out onto other things. To read is, on any hypothesis, to conjoin a new discourse to the discourse of the text. This conjunction of discourses reveals, in the very constitution of the text, an original capacity for renewal which is its open character. Interpretation is the concrete outcome of conjunction and renewal.

In the first instance, we shall be led to formulate the concept of interpretation in opposition to that of explanation. This will not distance us appreciably from Dilthey's position, except that the opposing concept of explanation has already gained strength by being derived from linguistics and semiology rather than being borrowed from the natural sciences.

According to this first sense, interpretation retains the feature of appropriation which was recognized by Schleiermacher, Dilthey, and Rudolf Bultmann. In fact, this sense will not be abandoned; it will only be mediated by explanation, instead of being opposed to it in an immediate and even naïve way. By 'appropriation,' I understand this: that the interpretation of a text culminates in the self-interpretation of a subject who thenceforth understands himself better, understands himself differently, or simply begins to understand himself. This culmination of the understanding of a text in self-understanding is characteristic of the kind of reflective philosophy which, on various occasions, I have called 'concrete reflection.' Here hermeneutics and reflective philosophy are correlative and reciprocal. On the one hand, self-understanding passes through the detour of understanding the cultural signs in which the self documents and forms itself. On the other hand, understanding the text is not an end in itself; it mediates the relation to himself of a subject who, in the short circuit of immediate reflection, does not find the meaning of his own life. Thus it must be said, with equal force, that reflection is nothing without the mediation of signs and works, and that explanation is nothing if it is not incorporated as an intermediary stage in the process of self-understanding. In short, in hermeneutical reflection – or in reflective hermeneutics – the constitution of the *self* is contemporaneous with the constitution of *meaning*.

The term 'appropriation' underlines two additional features. One of the aims of all hermeneutics is to struggle against cultural distance.

This struggle can be understood in purely temporal terms as a struggle against secular estrangement, or in more genuinely hermeneutical terms as a struggle against the estrangement from meaning itself, that is, from the system of values upon which the text is based. In this sense, interpretation 'brings together,' 'equalizes,' renders 'contemporary and similar,' thus genuinely making one's *own* what was initially *alien*.

Above all, the characterization of interpretation as appropriation is meant to underline the 'present' character of interpretation. Reading is like the execution of a musical score; it marks the realization, the enactment, of the semantic possibilities of the text. This final feature is the most important because it is the condition of the other two (that is, of overcoming cultural distance and of fusing textual interpretation with self-interpretation). Indeed, the feature of realization discloses a decisive aspect of reading, namely, that it fulfils the discourse of the text in a dimension similar to that of speech. What is retained here from the notion of speech is not the fact that it is uttered but that it is an event, an instance of discourse, as Benveniste says. The sentences of a text signify *here and now*. The 'actualized' text finds a surrounding and an audience; it resumes the referential movement – intercepted and suspended – towards a world and towards subjects. This world is that of the reader, this subject is the reader himself. In interpretation, we shall say, reading becomes like speech. I do not say 'becomes speech,' for reading is never equivalent to a spoken exchange, a dialogue. But reading culminates in a concrete act which is related to the text as speech is related to discourse, namely, as event and instance of discourse. Initially the text had only a sense, that is, internal relations or a structure; now it has a meaning, that is, a realization in the discourse of the reading subject. By virtue of its sense, the text had only a semiological dimension; now it has, by virtue of its meaning, a semantic dimension.

Let us pause here. Our discussion has reached a critical point where interpretation, understood as appropriation, still remains external to explanation in the sense of structural analysis. We continue to oppose them as if they were two attitudes between which it is necessary to choose. I should like now to go beyond this antithetical opposition and to bring out the articulation which would render structural analysis and hermeneutics complementary. For this it is important to show how each of the two attitudes which we have juxtaposed refers back, by means of its own peculiar features, to the other.

Consider again the examples of structural analysis which we have borrowed from the theory of myth and narrative. We tried to adhere to a notion of sense which would be strictly equivalent to the arrangement of the elements of a text, to the integration of the segments of action and the actants within the narrative treated as a whole closed in upon itself. In fact, no one stops at so formal a conception of sense. For example, what Lévi-Strauss calls a 'mytheme' – in his eyes, the constitutive unit of myth – is expressed in a sentence which has a specific meaning. Oedipus kills his father, Oedipus marries his mother, etc. Can it be said that structural explanation neutralizes the specific meaning of sentences, retaining only their position in the myth? But the bundle of relations to which Lévi-Strauss reduces the mytheme is still of the order of the sentence; and the interplay of oppositions which is instituted at this very abstract level is equally of the order of the sentence and of meaning. If one speaks of 'overrated' or 'underrated blood relations,' of the 'autochthony' or 'non-autochthony' of man, these relations can still be written in the form of a sentence: the blood relation is the highest of all, or the blood relation is not as high as the social relation, for example, in the prohibition of incest. Finally, the contradiction which the myth attempts to resolve, according to Lévi-Strauss, is itself stated in terms of meaningful relations. Lévi-Strauss admits this, in spite of himself, when he writes: 'The reason for these choices becomes clear if we recognize that mythical thought proceeds from the consciousness of certain oppositions and tends towards their progressive mediation,'[8] and again, 'the myth is a kind of logical tool intended to effect a mediation between life and death.'[9] In the background of the myth there is a question which is highly significant, a question about life and death: 'Are we born from one or from two?' Even in its formalized version, 'Is the same born from the same or from the other?,' this question expresses the anguish of origins: whence comes man? Is he born from the earth or from his parents? There would be no contradiction, nor any attempt to resolve contradiction, if there were not significant questions, meaningful propositions about the origin and the end of man. It is this function of myth as a narrative of origins that structural analysis seeks to place in parentheses. But such analysis does not succeed in eluding this function: it merely postpones it. Myth is not a logical operator between any propositions whatsoever, but involves propositions which point towards limit situations; towards the origin and the end; towards death, suffering, and sexuality.

Far from dissolving this radical questioning, structural analysis reinstates it at a more radical level. Would not the function of structural analysis then be to impugn the surface semantics of the recounted myth in order to unveil a depth semantics which is, if I may say so, the living semantics of the myth? If that were not the function of structural analysis, then it would, in my opinion, be reduced to a sterile game, to a derisory combination [*combinatoire*] of elements, and myth would be deprived of the function which Lévi-Strauss himself recognizes when he asserts that mythical thought arises from the awareness of certain oppositions and tends towards their progressive mediation. This awareness is a recognition of the *aporias* of human existence around which mythical thought gravitates. To eliminate this meaningful intention would be to reduce the theory of myth to a necrology of the meaningless discourses of mankind. If, on the contrary, we regard structural analysis as a stage – and a necessary one – between a naïve and a critical interpretation, between a surface and a depth interpretation, then it seems possible to situate explanation and interpretation along a unique *hermeneutical arc* and to integrate the opposed attitudes of explanation and understanding within an overall conception of reading as the recovery of meaning.

We shall take another step in the direction of this reconciliation between explanation and interpretation if we now turn towards the second term of the initial contradiction. So far we have worked with a concept of interpretation which remains very subjective. To interpret, we said, is to appropriate *here and now* the intention of the text. In saying that, we remain enclosed within Dilthey's concept of understanding. Now what we have just said about the depth semantics unveiled by the structural analysis of the text invites us to say that the intended meaning of the text is not essentially the presumed intention of the author, the lived experience of the writer, but rather what the text means for whoever complies with its injunction. The text seeks to place us in its meaning, that is – according to another acceptation of the word *sens* – in the same direction. So if the intention is that of the text, and if this intention is the direction which it opens up for thought, then depth semantics must be understood in a fundamentally dynamic way. I shall therefore say: to explain is to bring out the structure, that is, the internal relations of dependence which constitute the statics of the text; to interpret is to follow the path of thought opened up by the text, to place oneself *en route* towards the *orient* of the text. We are invited by this remark to correct our initial concept of interpretation and to search – beyond a subjective process of interpretation as an act *on* the text – for an objective process of interpretation which would be the act *of* the text.

I shall borrow an example from a recent study which I made of the exegesis of the sacerdotal story of creation in Genesis 1–2, 4a.[10] This exegesis reveals, in the interior of the text, the interplay of two narratives: a *Tatbericht* in which creation is expressed as a narrative of action ('God made ...'), and a *Wortbericht*, that is a narrative of speech ('God said, and there was ...'). The first narrative could be said to play the role of tradition, and the second of interpretation. What is interesting here is that interpretation, before being the act of the exegete, is the act of the text. The relation between tradition and interpretation is a relation internal to the text; for the exegete, to interpret is to place himself in the meaning indicated by the relation of interpretation which the text itself supports.

This objective and, as it were, intratextual concept of interpretation is by no means unusual. Indeed, it has a long history rivalling that of the concept of subjective interpretation, which is linked, it will be recalled, to the problem of understanding others through the signs that others give of their conscious life. I would willingly connect this new concept of interpretation to that referred to in the title of Aristotle's treatise *On Interpretation*. Aristotle's *hermenetia*, in contrast to the hermeneutical techniques of seers and oracles, is the very action of language on things. Interpretation, for Aristotle, is not what one does in a second language with regard to a first; rather, it is what the first language already does, by mediating through signs our relation to things. Hence interpretation is, according to the commentary of Boethius, the work of the *vox significativa per se ipsam aliquid significans, sive complexa, sive incomplexa*. Thus it is the noun, the verb, discourse in general, which interprets in the very process of signifying.

It is true that interpretation in Aristotle's sense does not exactly prepare the way for understanding the dynamic relation between several layers of meaning in the same text. For it presupposes a theory of speech and not a theory of the text: 'Words spoken are symbols or signs of affections or impressions of the soul; written words are the signs of words spoken.'[11] Hence interpretation is confused with the semantic dimension of speech: interpretation is discourse itself, it is any discourse. Nevertheless, I retain from Aristotle the idea that interpretation is interpretation *by* language before being interpretation *of* language.

I would look in the work of Charles Sanders Peirce for a concept of interpretation which is closer to that required by an exegesis relating interpretation to tradition in the very interior of a text. According to Peirce, the relation of a 'sign' to an 'object' is such that another relation, that between 'interpretant' and 'sign,' can be grafted onto the first. What is important for us is that this relation between interpretant and sign is an open relation, in the sense that there is always another interpretant capable of mediating the first relation. G.-G. Granger explains this very well in his *Essai d'une philosophie du style*:

> The interpretant which the sign evokes in the mind could not be the result of a pure and simple deduction which would extract from the sign something already contained therein ... The interpretant is a commentary, a definition, a gloss on the sign in its relation to the object. The interpretant is itself symbolic expression. The sign–interpretant association, realised by whatever psychological processes, is rendered possible only by the community, more or less imperfect, of an experience between speaker and hearer ... It is always an experience which can never be perfectly reduced to the idea or object of the sign of which, as we said, it is the structure. Whence the indefinite character of Peirce's series of interpretants.[12]

We must, of course, exercise a great deal of care in applying Peirce's concept of interpretant to the interpretation of texts. His interpretant is an interpretant of signs, whereas our interpretant is an interpretant of statements. But our use of the interpretant, transposed from small to large units, is neither more nor less analogical than the structuralist transfer of the laws of organization from units of levels below the sentence to units of an order above or equal to the sentence. In the case of structuralism, it is the phonological structure of language which serves as the coding model of structures of higher articulation. In our case, it is a feature of lexical units which is transposed onto the plane of statements and texts. So, if we are perfectly aware of the analogical character of the transposition, then we can say that the open series of interpretants, which is grafted onto the relation of a sign to an object, brings to light a triangular relation of object–sign–interpretant; and that the latter relation can serve as a model for another triangle which is constituted at the level of the text. In the new triangle, the object is the text itself; the sign is the depth semantics disclosed by structural analysis; and the series of interpretants is the chain of interpretations produced by the interpreting community and incorporated into the dynamics of the text, as the work of meaning upon itself. Within this chain, the first interpretants serve as tradition for the final interpretants, which are the interpretation in the true sense of the term.

Thus informed by the Aristotelian concept of interpretation and above all by Peirce's concept, we are in a position to 'depsychologize' as far as possible our notion of interpretation, and to connect it with the process which is at work in the text. Henceforth, for the exegete, to interpret is to place himself within the sense indicated by the relation of interpretation supported by the text.

The idea of interpretation as appropriation is not, for all that, eliminated; it is simply postponed until the termination of the process. It lies at the extremity of what we called above the *hermeneutical arc*: it is the final brace of the bridge, the anchorage of the arch in the ground of lived experience. But the entire theory of hermeneutics consists in mediating this interpretation-appropriation by the series of interpretants which belong to the work of the text upon itself. Appropriation loses its arbitrariness insofar as it is the recovery of that which is at work, in labour, within the text. What the interpreter says is a resaying which reactivates what is said by the text.

At the end of our investigation, it seems that reading is the concrete act in which the destiny of the text is fulfilled. It is at the very heart of reading that explanation and interpretation are indefinitely opposed and reconciled.

Notes

1 Gustave Guillaume, *Le Temps et l'eternité chez Plotin et Saint Augustin* (Paris: Vrin, 1933, 1971)

2 W. Dilthey, 'Origine et développement de l'herméneutique,' in *Le Monde de l'esprit*, Vol. I (Paris: Aubier, 1947), p. 320 [English translation: 'The Development of Hermeneutics,' in *Selected Writings*, ed. and trans. by H.P. Rickman (Cambridge: Cambridge University Press, 1976), p. 248]

3 Ibid, p. 333 [259–60]

4 Claude Lévi-Strauss, *Anthropologie structurale* (Paris: Plon, 1958), p. 233 [English translation: *Structural Anthropology*, trans. by Claire Jacobson and Brooke Grundfest Schoepf (Harmondsworth: Penguin Books, 1968), pp. 210–11]

5 Ibid, p. 234 [211]

6 Ibid, p. 239 [216]

7 Ibid, p. 241 [217]

8 Ibid, p. 248 [224]

9 Ibid, p. 243 [220]

10 See Paul Ricoeur, 'Sur l'exégèse de Genèse 1, 1–2, 4a,' in Roland Barthes et al., *Exégèse et herméneutique* (Paris: Seuil, 1971), pp. 67–84.

11 Aristotle, *The Art of Poetry*, trans. by Philip Wheelwright (New York: Odyssey Press, 1951), p. 115

12 G.-G. Granger, *Essai d'une philosophie du style* (Paris: A. Colin, 1968), p. 115 [Ricoeur's translation]

Word, Polysemy, Metaphor: Creativity in Language

This paper is about the creative aspects of language. However we must avoid platitudes about this formidable topic. A helpful suggestion and guide may be found, I think, in the famous aphorism of Wilhelm von Humboldt which describes language as an infinite use of finite means. Looking for a striking illustration of this contrast, I found it in some recent interpretations of metaphor which depart from the traditional interpretation of rhetoric and show it to be not an ornament of language or a stylistic decoration, but a semantic innovation, an emergence of meaning. In order to introduce this theme I thought that it might be fruitful to present it as an alternative strategy of discourse, distinct from and opposed to other strategies, particularly those of ordinary language and scientific language.

These diverse strategies seem to me to be different answers which may be given to the specific perplexity and challenge proposed by the crucial phenomenon of natural languages which we call polysemy. By polysemy I shall mean that remarkable feature of words in natural languages which is their ability to mean more than one thing. I was thus led to inquire into the creative potentialities already contained in this nuclear phenomenon and to connect it to the focus of all creativity in language, the sentence.

Hence the strategy of this essay about the strategy of language. First, we shall speak of the sentence as the actual bearer of all creativity in language. Then we shall consider polysemy as the potential creativity contained in the word. Third, we shall consider the range of alternate strategies opened by polysemy, and finally, and this will be the aim of this paper, we shall describe metaphor as the main procedure of the third kind of strategy of discourse considered in this paper, that of poetic discourse. My goal will be to show that this strategy preserves best the potential creativity of the words of our language.

The Sentence as Infinite Use of Finite Means

My first task is to relate the fundamental structures of language to the Humboldtian opposition between finite means and infinite use. As I already suggested in my introductory remarks, it is not first the word, but the sentence which has to be considered as the focus of creativity. It is not that I identify infinite use with the sentence and finite means with the words. The relation is more complex, since, as we shall see, the word as related to the sentence is itself the depository of the creativity of language. Therefore the first opposition is not between the sentence and the words, but between the sentence and some other entities which are more fundamental than words, signs.

I am using here the terminology of the great French Sanskritist Emile Benveniste from his *Essays on General Linguistics*. According to him, language relies not on one, but on two kinds of entities: the semiotic entities, that is to say the signs, and the semantic entities, the bearers of meaning. I want to explain this distinction and to relate it to the Humboldtian distinction between finite means and infinite use.

Semiotic entities or signs are merely distinctive and oppositive units within specific systems: phonemes within phonological codes, morphemes or sememes within lexical codes, syntactic forms of rules within syntactic systems. In saying that they are merely distinctive and oppositive units we mean that they are defined by their difference with regard to other units of the same system. It follows from this main trait that these entities are not related to extralinguistic realities such as things, events, properties, relations, actions, passions, or states of affairs. They are purely intralinguistic phenomena. This feature is true even of the most primitive difference which we may find within the linguistic signs themselves and which distinguishes them from other semiotic systems. I mean the difference which Ferdinand de Saussure introduced between the signifier and the signified, which Louis Hjelmslev reformulated as the difference between the expression and its content. This difference borrowed from the Stoic tradition is a difference within the sign itself and not an external relation between sign and thing. Signifier and signified – or in psychological terms, acoustic images and concepts – represent the two sides of the same sign like the two sides of one and the same coin. Like the coin the sign is the unity of both.

Now how does this description of semiotic entities satisfy Wilhelm von Humboldt's aphorism? In what sense can semiotic entities be said to be finite? It follows from the immanent nature of all the relations between signs and within signs that semiotic systems are closed systems and for that reason they constitute finite sets of entities. Furthermore, among all semiotic systems, linguistic systems have the peculiarity of being twice closed or twice finite. On the one hand, the analysis of the signifier, or of the expression, yields a finite number of distinctive elements: the phonemes, a few dozen in each language. On the other hand, the signified, or the content, may be submitted to a similar analysis which at least in principle should lead to those symbols which would constitute the elementary constituents of all lexical systems. In conjunction with specific combinatory rules, these elementary constituents should provide a basis for a complete analysis of all lexical codes. If this hypothesis holds, we should have to assume that lexical systems too are finite systems. As concerns the syntactic systems, it is obvious that the paradigms of tenses constitute finite lists of forms and imply a finite enumeration of rules. Now, in what sense may we speak of an infinite use of these finite sets? The first entity which has to be considered is not the word, but the sentence. Our task will be to describe the features of the sentence which contribute to the creative process of language that we call discourse. The first trait to be noticed is the temporal character of these new entities. Language as sentence and as discourse appears and disappears. It happens. Whereas systems of signs are merely virtual, language as discourse is actual.

As a second trait we can consider the remarkable capacity of an instance of discourse to refer back to its own speaker, thanks to specific linguistic functions such as the personal pronouns, the tenses of the verbs, the demonstratives, and so on. Whereas systems of signs are properly anonymous, discourse requires a speaker who may express himself in it.

In the same manner, the instance of discourse refers to a hearer to whom it is addressed as the second person. This I–thou structure of discourse belongs to the semantic order and has no place in semiotic systems.

Finally the sentence as a whole is the bearer of the meaning. Here we mean to designate something other than and more than the signified of the individual signs. It is a distinctive feature which may be identified as the predicative function. (The sentence, of course, may be reduced to its predicate. Then we have a one-word sentence as in the imperative, but it is a sentence nevertheless inasmuch as it is a predicate.) The predicative constitution of the sentence provides it with a meaning. This meaning should be called the intended rather than the signified of the sentence, if we want to preserve the distinction between the semiotic and the semantic order. This intended is what we seek to translate when we transpose a discourse from one language into another. The signified is untranslatable in principle. It cannot be transposed from one system to another since it characterizes one system in opposition to the other. The intended, on the contrary, is fundamentally translatable since it is the same intended unit of thought transposed from one semiotic system into another. Let us therefore say that the intended is the semantic element in discourse. As we shall see later, the intended of discourse is the focus of all creative process in language. But before considering the aspect of creativity and infinity which belongs to the semantic element as such, let us consider a last semantic feature of the sentence.

The intended can be considered from two different points of view. It is something immanent within the sentence, merely resulting from the connection between the terms in the predicative operation of a sentence, and at the same time a claim to express reality. To this claim is linked the possibility of truth and error in discourse. Let us call the immanent character of the meaning 'sense' and its truth claim 'reference.' Then we may say that where there is meaning there is also a question of reference, that is, a claim which can be fulfilled or which can remain null or void. As you may see, I am using the expression coined by Gottlob Frege in a very free way. This thinker called *Sinn* (sense) the ideal content, the objective side of the meaning, the intended as such. And he called *Bedeutung* (reference or denotation) the directedness of discourse towards reality which it may reach or miss. With this consideration of reference the opposition between semiotic and semantic is complete. Whereas semiotic units are systems of inner dependencies, and for that reason constitute closed and finite sets, the sentence, as the first semantic unit, is related to extralinguistic reality. It is open to the world.

Now in what sense are semantic entities infinite? Discourse is infinite because sentences are events, because they have a speaker and a hearer, because they have meaning, and because they have reference. Each of these traits has an infinite character. With the event comes the openness of temporality, with the speaker and hearer the depth of individual fields of experience, with meaning the limitlessness of the thinkable, and with reference the inexhaustibility of the world itself. On all these counts language as discourse appears as an open process of mediation between mind and world. To return to Humboldt, discourse is the creative process of giving form to both the human mind and the world, of forming (*Bildung*) man and reality at the same time. This process is infinite in the sense that the boundary between the expressed and the unexpressed endlessly keeps receding. Discourse is this power of indefinitely extending the battle-front of the expressed at the expense of the unexpressed.

Word and Polysemy

We may now relate the function of the word to that of discourse and introduce polysemy.

The main implication of the preceding analysis is that words have meaning only inasmuch as sentences have meaning. Once again I am taking meaning in its semantic sense as an intended content and as a claim to refer to something outside language. In this sense, words do not mean outside the sentence. Their intended content is a part of the whole intended content of the sentence, and they designate something inasmuch as sentences themselves refer to states of affairs. In brief, words function as meaningful entities only within the framework of the sentence. That they have partial meaning only in connection with the whole meaning of the sentence could be very easily demonstrated by showing that words have no meaning before they are used either as logical subjects of a proposition or as predicates, that is, before they serve either to identify individuals or to assert universal characteristics of these individuals. In this sense, words belong to the linguistics of the sentence, not to the linguistics of the sign. They are semantic entities, not semiotic entities.

Of course, words are based on lexical entities which are undoubtedly semiotic things. But a lexical entity is not yet a word. It is only the possibility of a word. This is why a lexical entity is defined merely by its opposition to other lexical entities within the same system. It has nothing to do with reality. This is not the case with the word in the sentence. It bears a part of the sentence meaning and shares the referential function of the whole discourse. It is about things, it points to things, it represents things. When *Sprache spricht*, then words themselves co-operate in the shaping of reality.

We are now prepared to consider our second theme, the polysemy of words. As I said in my introduction, I relate this specific topic to the general topic of my paper in the following way. If metaphor is one of the strategies of discourse which exploits the creativity of language, then we may ask about the kind of challenge which this strategy claims to come to grips with. It is this question which leads me to focus on polysemy as the crucial phenomenon of natural languages and to ask about the place of the word itself in the fabric of language. Having done the required analysis of the word, we can now consider polysemy.

Polysemy is readily defined as the property of words in natural language of having more than one meaning. As Stephan Ullmann puts it in his *Principles of Semantics*, polysemy means one name with several senses. This feature is a universal feature of words in natural languages. Before considering the challenge which results from this constitutive trait, let us describe its functional character. Before all other possible advantages, a polysemic language satisfies the most elementary requirement of a natural language, I mean economy. A lexicon which would be based on the opposite principle of total univocity of all its elements, that is to say, on the principle of only one sense for one name, would be infinite if it were destined to convey from one person to another the richness of concrete and qualitative experience. It would even be doubly infinite because of the limitless variety of each individual sphere of experience and because of the innumerable plurality of individual perspectives on the world.

This first functional trait has for its counterpart a second feature which we shall call the sensibility to context. Thanks to the contextual use, language based on polysemy may draw practically innumerable meanings from the finite set of lexical entities codified by the dictionary. We shall see in a moment how ordinary language proceeds to make this procedure appropriate to its ends. Let us say in general terms that polysemic language is characterized by its sensibility to the context.

By context we mean not only the linguistic environment of the actual words, but the speaker's and the hearer's behaviour, the situation common to both, and finally the horizon of reality surrounding the speech situation. Furthermore, the context is already implied in the very definition of the words. Each of the partial values enumerated by the dictionary represents a potential use in a typical context which has been identified and classified by lexicology. The sum of these potential uses in potential contexts is what we call in an improper sense the meaning of the word. This is an improper sense because the lexical entities are not yet words in the strong sense. But this way of speaking is not wholly improper since the partial meanings of a word summarize previous uses which have been classified according to corresponding contexts. In this sense, a polysemic language is contextually determined not only in its use, but in its very constitution.

Such are the two functional traits of a polysemic language, economy at the level of the code, contextual dependence at the level of the message. This dialectics of economy and novelty foreshadows the dialectics of finite means and infinite use which will be unfolded when we consider the various strategies by which we make use of these polysemic traits. This dialectic takes place in the concrete process by which we decode a given message and which we may call interpretation in the most general sense of the word. The simplest message conveyed by the means of natural language has to be interpreted because all the words are polysemic and take their actual meaning from the connection with a given context and a given audience against the background of a given situation. Interpretation in this broad sense is a process by which we use all the available contextual determinants to grasp the actual meaning of a given message in a given situation.

It was already in this broad sense, or maybe an even broader sense, that Aristotle used the word *hermeneia*, that is to say interpretation, in the second treatise of the *Organon* which its editors have called by the same name. His sense may have been still broader than ours because it seems that language has to be interpreted not only because words are the symbols of states of mind, and written signs of oral signs, but because discourse is fundamentally the interpretation of reality. We shall return to this still broader sense of interpretation at the end of this paper. Let us therefore call interpretation the decoding of messages based on polysemic words. It is interpretation which calls for the various strategies which we shall now consider.

Why this diversity of strategies? Because of a challenge, a threat which is implied in all processes of interpretation. This challenge is the threat of ambiguity or of equivocity which appears to be the permanent counterpart of polysemy or, so to speak, the price to pay for a polysemic language. But let us be accurate. Ambiguity or equivocity is not the same thing as polysemy. Polysemy is a feature of words, several senses for one name. Ambiguity is a feature of discourse, that is to say, of the stretch of speech longer than or equal to the sentence. Ambiguity or equivocity means that for one string of words we have more than one way of interpreting it. Whereas polysemy is a normal phenomenon, ambiguity may be a pathological phenomenon. I say 'may be' because, as we shall see, we must preserve the possibility of highly significant ambiguities, the possibility of a functional ambiguity. That will be the case with poetic language. But ambiguity remains a case of dysfunction each time that the situation of discourse requires only one interpretation for reasons which will be proper to each type of strategy. Each time that the present stretch of discourse gives no sufficient clue to eliminate equivocity in interpretation, then misunderstanding becomes unavoidable, and as Friedrich D.E. Schleiermacher said, there is a hermeneutical task where there is misunderstanding and when understanding proceeds from the rectification of misunderstanding.

In the preceding remarks I used equivocity, ambiguity, and misunderstanding as synonymous terms. In order to distinguish these terms, we could perhaps call ambiguity the character of the discourse itself as opened to several interpretations; and call equivocity the process of interpretation hesitating between these interpretations. Misunderstanding would be the effect of both ambiguity and equivocity on the intersubjective process of communication.

Such is the balance of advantages and disadvantages of a polysemic language. On the one hand, it satisfies the principle of economy, which is the basic principle for all kinds of languages, at the same time that it allows the contextual game to draw an infinite variety of meaningful effects from this economic structure. But, on the other hand, it delivers language to the precarious and haphazard work of interpretation and therefore to the risks of ambiguity, equivocity, and misunderstanding.

Polysemy and the Strategies of Language

Let us now introduce the various strategies capable of meeting the challenge of misunderstanding. I shall consider three of them: ordinary language, scientific language, and poetic language, without pretending that these are the only possible solutions.

By ordinary language I mean that use of natural languages (English, French, German, and so on) whose aim is communication and whose means are a tactic of polysemy reduction. By communication I mean the attempt to convey information from speaker to hearer concerning the concrete situations of everyday life which are differently experienced by the individual members of the speech community. A certain amount of univocity is reached by specific means requiring a minimal technicity in the use of words which I call the reduction of polysemy. This tactic relies mainly on the clever use of the context's effect on the individual terms of discourse. This reductive action of contexts is easy to understand. The use of language is governed not only by syntactic rules of grammaticality, but also by semantic rules of sense compossibility. In order to make sense together, words must have a mutual appropriateness, a semantic pertinence. This rule of semantic pertinence requires that when we speak, only a part of the semantic field of a word is used. The remainder is excluded, or, rather, repressed, by the process of mutual selection exerted by the sentence as a whole and by the context of discourse on its parts. If the sentence is not enough to screen the convenient contextual values, the topic will help to eliminate the unwanted meaning under the control of the whole speech situation. Finally it is the function of the exchange of questions and answers within the dialogue or conversation to allow the hearer to check the semantic choice of the speaker and to allow the speaker to verify that the message has been correctly decoded by the hearer. The speaker's utterances must provide the hearer's interpretation with some specific clues or guidelines for this screening of polysemy.

Such is the way in which ordinary language succeeds to a certain extent in reducing the initial polysemy of the words and in making relatively univocal statements with polysemic words. But if this strategy is enough in everyday life, it does not radically exclude polysemy. It cannot claim more than to reduce it. The threat of misunderstanding, as we too well know, is not fundamentally dispelled. Very often a long speech, if not a whole book, is not enough to insure understanding and agreement. Misunderstanding finally prevails.

This ultimate failure of ordinary language to meet the challenge of misunderstanding explains why a quite different strategy had to be introduced, a strategy which would no longer aim at reducing polysemy, but at eradicating it. This strategy is that of scientific language.

In the following analysis I shall not speak of scientific language in general but only from the point of view of the therapy of misunderstanding, and therefore in connection with the treatment of ambiguity. From this limited point of view, scientific language may be defined by the defensive measures it takes against ambiguity. I will mention only the most striking of them.

As a first step, scientific language only pushes farther a procedure rooted in ordinary language, that of definition. As is well known, language is constructed in such a way that it is always possible to designate an element of our lexical code by means of other elements belonging to the same code. It is possible in principle to say that a bachelor is an unmarried man. Thanks to this reflective action of language, we expand our vocabulary and control the meaning of our words. Scientific language pushes this definatory procedure farther by refining it with the help of classificatory and taxonomic measures.

The second step is to introduce technical terms into our vocabulary which satisfy a specific rule, that of denoting only quantitative entities, to the exclusion of the qualitative aspect of our experience. Some previous words borrowed from ordinary language such as 'stream,' 'mass,' 'speed,' may be retained, but they are reformulated and redefined according to the requirements of a *mathesis universalis*.

At a further stage of abstraction, words similar to those of our dictionaries are replaced by mathematical symbols, that is to say, by signs which can be read but not vocally uttered. The link with natural language is broken. Scientific language henceforth is beyond the boundary line which divides artificial language from natural language.

Finally, at a stage corresponding to an advanced degree of formalization, the meaning of all the formulas and all the laws of a formal system is governed by a set of axioms which assign each elementary meaning its place in the theory and prescribe the rules for reading the whole symbolism. Of course there is still room for interpretation in the sense that a formal system has still to be applied to a diversity of empirical domains of experience, but this interpretation is itself governed by new rules of translation which exclude all ambiguity. These rules of translation and the prescription which they imply take the place of contextual interpretation in ordinary discourse. Therefore the constitution of formal systems and the rules for interpreting them in relation to empirical fields constitute the ultimate procedure directed by scientific language against ambiguity.

At this point we might be tempted to reformulate the whole fabric of our language according to the procedures which we just defined. Does it not seem reasonable to construct a *langue bien faite* ruled by the principle of a one-to-one relation between signs and entities, of one meaning for each word, and to extend this artificial language to ethical and political problems, and why not even to conversation? This dream of a radical and complete reformulation of the whole of our language haunted philosophers like Leibniz, conceiving his *characteristica universalis*, Russell, writing the *Principia Mathematica*, and Wittgenstein, in his *Tractatus*, stating the rules of a language which would be the exact picture of the structure of facts.

But there are fundamental reasons for thinking that this project must fail. Ordinary language and artificial language not only belong to two irreducible strategies, but have different aims. The theme of ordinary language is communication, and its field of application is reality as it is differently experienced by the individual members of the speech community. Strictly speaking, however, communication is not the aim of a scientific language. When we read a scientific paper, we are not in the position of an individual member of the speech community just invoked. All readers are, in a sense, one and the same mind, and the purpose of discourse is not to build a bridge between two spheres of experience, but to insure the identity of meaning from the beginning to the end of an argument. This is why there are no contextual variations of meaning in a *langue bien faite*. The meaning is contextually neutral, or, if you prefer, insensible to the context, because the main purpose of this language is that the meaning remain the same all through the arguments. This continual sameness of the meaning is secured by the one-to-one relation between name and sense and by the indifference to the context. Thus I should say that the aim of a scientific language is not communication, but argumentation. It follows that there is something irreducible in ordinary language. The variability of meanings, their displaceability, and their sensibility to the context are the condition for creativity and confer possibilities of indefinite invention in both poetic and scientific activity. Here indeterminateness and creativity appear to be completely solidary. This is why *langues biens faites* are, at best, insular languages. The conclusion could be, as Roman Jakobson says, that both mathematical and ordinary languages are required, and that each of them has to be considered as the metalanguage required for the structural analysis of the other.

Metaphor and Polysemy

In this last part of my paper, I want to consider metaphor within the limits of my present concern, that is with respect to creativity in language, and in continuity with my previous remarks about polysemy. In other words, I shall treat metaphor as a creative use of polysemy and in that way as a specific strategy of language. Instead of reducing or suppressing polysemy, metaphor uses polysemy as a means to preserve polysemy and to make it work in a most effective way. For what purpose? We shall reserve the answer for the end of this essay.

The decisive step in the direction we are now taking has been indicated by writers such as I.A. Richards, Max Black, Colin Turbayne, Monroe Beardsley, Douglas Berggren, and others who departed from the tradition of rhetoric for which metaphor conveyed no information and appeared merely as a stylistic ornament, whose function it was to please. They could break with this tradition because they approached the problem of metaphor from a quite new perspective. For traditional rhetoric, metaphor was one of the figures of speech called tropes because they proceeded from a deviating use of the meaning of words. Tropes therefore affected just the names and the giving of names. Instead of giving their proper names to certain things, or facts, or experiences, the writer chooses to use the name of something else by extending the meaning of this foreign name. The task of rhetoric thus is to classify the different figures according to the kind of deviation which generated them. Metaphor was traditionally classified as a trope by resemblance or by analogy. This treatment of metaphor by rhetoric has been characterized by Richards and his followers as a substitution theory. The decisive factor is that the borrowed word taken with its deviating use is substituted for a potential proper name which is absent in the context, but which could be used in the same place. The writer chooses not to use the convenient word in its proper sense and to replace it with another word which seems to be more pleasant.

To understand the metaphor, then, is to restitute the term which has been substituted. It is easy to understand that these two operations – substitution and restitution – are equivalent. Therefore it is possible to give an exhaustive paraphrase of a given metaphor. From these presuppositions, it follows that metaphor offers no new information. It teaches nothing. For the same reason, metaphor is a mere decorative device. It has no informative value; it merely adorns language in order to please. It gives colour to speech, it provides a garment to cover the nudity of common usage.

Such is the train of presuppositions implied in a rhetorical treatment of metaphor. Between the starting-point, that metaphor is an accident in the process of naming, and the conclusion, that metaphor is merely decorative and intended to please, the road is continuous and the turning-point is constituted by the action of substitution. The weakness of this model is obvious. It is impossible on its basis to give an account of the difference between a bad metaphor, like the leg of a chair, and a novel metaphor, like the poetic verse, 'La terre est bleue comme une orange,' or 'time is a beggar.' The aspect of semantic novelty which, I believe, is the fundamental problem of metaphor remains unexplained in a substitution theory which covers both cases. Furthermore, the theory is unable to explain the process itself by which the meaning of a word is extended beyond its common use. What Beardsley called the 'metaphorical twist' remains an enigma. This is why rhetoric contented itself with classifying the figures of speech, being unable to generate them.

The reason why rhetoric could not give an account of the process which generates metaphor is that it limited its description to the words, and more precisely, to the name. As we shall see, the metaphorical process occurs at another level, at the level of the sentence and of discourse as a whole. This is why rhetoric could only identify the effects of the process on the word, the lexical impact, so to speak, and classify the metaphor among other figures such as metonymy, synecdoche, irony, and so on.

The new approach initiated by I.A. Richards in his *Philosophy of Rhetoric* starts from his remark that words alone cannot be metaphoric. They are metaphoric only in the context of a sentence. More precisely, only a statement, an entire proposition, can be metaphorical. In Richards's terms, metaphor has to pose a tenor and a vehicle. It is a unity of both. It proceeds from the tension between these two poles. In this sense, we may oppose a tension theory of metaphor to a substitution theory.

Within this new framework, some new features appear which had been previously overlooked and which allow us to recognize the informative character of metaphor as opposed to its mere decorative character for rhetoric. For me, the recognition of this informative character is the nucleus of the whole discussion since it implies and reveals the creative dimension of metaphoric statements.

This recognition proceeds from an analysis which underlines two complementary features of the metaphorical statement, a negative and a positive trait.

On the one hand, the strategy of discourse put into action in metaphor relies on the purposive creation of a semantic discrepancy in the sentence. For a literal interpretation the metaphorical statement breaks down. Monroe Beardsley goes so far as to say that the privileged procedure of metaphor is self-contradiction. The function of metaphor is to make sense with nonsense, to transform a self-contradictory statement into a significant self-contradiction. In more general terms, we could say that a metaphorical statement proceeds from the violation of semantic rules which determine appropriateness in the application of predicates. In the terms of a French critic, Jean Cohen, in *Structure du langage poétique*, metaphor relies on the violation of semantic pertinence. It consists in the reduction of semantic impertinence generated by the violation of semantic rules through the imposition of a deviation of another kind at the level of the word. Metaphor in this way appears as the solution of an enigma. What appears as the deviation in the meaning of the word, as the metaphorical twist, is the positive counterpart of the initial deviation from semantic pertinence. It is a deviating use of words responding to the deviating way of predicating attributes to things.

This analysis of the negative side of the metaphorical process already allows us to acknowledge its creative dimension. But what about the positive character of metaphor? Or, to put it in another way, how do we make sense with nonsense? We spoke of the intuitive grasp of resemblances. Was it not Aristotle who said that 'to have command of metaphor is to have an eye for similarities'? There is something true in this thesis. The creative moment of metaphor is concentrated on this grasping of resemblance, in the perception of analogies. But a metaphysics of imagination, which we might be tempted to draw from the tradition of Romanticism, could destroy the benefits of the previous analysis if applied inaccurately. The problem is a semantic one, not a psychological one. How do we make sense with self-contradictory statements? In invoking imagination, we lose sight of the decisive factor that, in novel metaphors, the similarity is itself the fruit of metaphor. We now see a similarity that nobody had ever noticed before. The difficulty therefore is to understand that we see similarity by construing it, that the visionary grasping of resemblance is, at the same time, a verbal invention. The iconic element has therefore to be included in the predicative process itself.

This is why the most effective analysis of metaphor concerns the construction which accompanies the vision. Even if it is true that there is something irreducible in the grasping of similarities as a kind of sudden insight, the only progress that can be achieved by an epistemology of metaphor concerns the discursive and not the intuitive process involved in the creation of meaning.

The case of trivial metaphor is the easiest to treat. Metaphors like 'man is a wolf' proceed from a kind of predication in which some of the connotative values attached to our words are applied in a new way to the principal subject. By connotative values we mean, with Max Black, the 'system of associated commonplaces' which enlarge the meaning of our words, adding cultural and emotional dimensions to the literal values codified by our dictionaries. Of course there are no metaphors in a lexicon, but beyond the lexicon there is what Aristotle called the *topoi*, the cultural treasure of meanings. The art of metaphor is to apply a part of this treasure to new subjects, to use it as a screen which not only selects, but which brings forth new aspects in the principal subject. In this way, even trivial metaphors have an informative value.

The case of novel metaphor is more difficult to treat. The new fact is that the solution of the enigma raised by the tension or the semantic clash on which the metaphor is built no longer relies on the existence of a previous system of associated commonplaces, on a range of connotative values which would be already at our disposal. The novel metaphor creates a new semantic situation. We can no longer speak of connotative meanings waiting for our use. We may only speak of properties which have not yet been brought to language. Here lies precisely the difference between novel and trivial metaphor. We do not merely apply already existing connotations, we create a new framework of connotation which exists only in the actual act of predication. In other words, a novel metaphor does not merely actualize a potential connotation, it creates it. It is a semantic innovation, an emergent meaning. From these metaphors we may see that no paraphrase can exhaust them. They are untranslatable. They say what they say, and what they say cannot be said in another way.

We are now as far as possible from the ornamental interpretation from which we started.

From these remarks derives the role of likeness in the construction of good metaphors. There is indeed something paradoxical and circular in the way in which a good metaphor is produced. Likeness is the guideline of the process which constructs it as likeness. Metaphor is a unitive process which produces a kind of assimilation between remote ideas. As such, it is the object of the kind of insight to which Aristotle pointed when he said that 'while the proper use of all those various poetic devices is important, by far the greatest thing for a poet is to be master of metaphor. Such mastery is the one thing that cannot be learned from others. It is the mark of genius (*euphuia*), for to be good at metaphor is to be intuitively aware of hidden resemblances.'[1] But at the same time this assimilation between remote ideas is a discursive process which we express by new metaphors like that of a screen or a filter, by which we designate the way in which the predicate selects and organizes some features of the principal subject.

This paradox is not only a psychological paradox, like that which Gestalt psychology describes under the title of insight when it shows that each change in a structure, each transition from one structure to another, occurs as a sudden intuition in which the new structure emerges from the collapse of the previous one. This paradox is a semantic paradox, a paradox linked to the reallocation of predicates. Nelson Goodman describes the metaphor as 'the reassignment of a label,' and he says that this reassignment takes the form of an affair between a predicate which has a past and an object which yields while protesting. This paradox of protesting and yielding is another metaphor about metaphor. It speaks of the paradox between insight and construction, between genius and calculus.

Moreover, this paradox is a logical paradox. By this I mean that the paradox is not only between insight and construction, but about the essence of likeness as a relation. Likeness is itself a compound relation which correlates sameness and difference. To see sameness in the difference is the genius of metaphor. It was not by accident that Aristotle spoke of the 'similar' as the 'same' perceived in things which are 'remote.' Likeness is the key word of metaphor because, in metaphor, sameness and difference are not merely mixed, but remain opposed. The tension is not only between tenor and vehicle, between focus and frame, but in the relation itself, in the copula. In metaphor, sameness works in spite of difference. This specific feature explains the kinship between metaphor and riddle.

This conspicuous trait has been seen in one way or another by several authors. Ruth Herschberger speaks of 'a likeness of unlike things able to reconcile opposites and containing tension.' Douglas Berggren sees 'the indispensable principle for integrating diverse phenomena without sacrificing diversity' in the metaphor. And in *The Myth of Metaphor*, Turbayne correctly compares what happens in metaphor to what Gilbert Ryle called a category mistake, that is, a mislocation of names and of predicates. Instead of giving the name of the species to the genus, of the genus to the species, or of the species to another species, metaphor merely blurs the conceptual boundaries of the terms considered.

Could we not say therefore that the dynamics of metaphor consists in confusing the established logical boundaries for the sake of detecting new similarities which previous categorization prevented our noticing? In other words, the power of metaphor would be to break through previous categorization and to establish new logical boundaries on the ruins of the preceding ones. If we take this last remark seriously, we may wish to draw the ultimate consequence and say that the dynamics of thought which breaks through previous categorization is the same as the one which generated all classifications. In other words, the figure of speech which we classify as metaphor would be at the origin of all semantic fields, since to contemplate the similar or the same – and we know now that the similar is also the same – is to grasp the genus, but not yet as genus; to grasp the same in the difference, and not yet as above or beside the difference. To grasp the kinship in any semantic field is the work of the metaphoric process at large. We are now allowed to speak of metaphoric process in so general a way because the so-called metaphor, the metaphor as trope or as a figure, as it is defined by rhetoric, presents the same process, but under the paradoxical structure of sameness in spite of difference. This is why we may say from the likeness at work in metaphor what we say about the genus as it is grasped in logical thought. We may say that we learn from it, that it teaches us something. Aristotle once more observes that it is from metaphor that we can best get hold of something fresh, for 'when Homer calls old age stubble, he teaches and informs us through the genus, for both have lost their bloom.'

These remarks may allow us to do justice to the iconic element of the metaphor. This factor has been carefully left aside because it introduces psychological considerations alien to a mere linguistic or semantic explanation. But is the pictorial, the figurative, so obviously alien to semantic consideration? Once more let us follow the preceding analysis of the paradoxical structure of likeness, that is, the inner conflict between sameness and difference in the process of metaphor. Does not imagination have something to do with this conflict? An old prejudice stemming from Hume, according to which an image is the residue of an impression, stops us from giving a purely semantic description of imagery and imagination. Misled by this prejudice, we look at imagery in connection with the sensory fields – sight, hearing, touch, and so on. But if we follow Kant rather than Hume, I mean the theory of schematism and that of productive imagination, we have to look at imagination as the place of nascent meanings and categories, rather than as the place of fading impressions.

In a similar way, we should have to say that the iconic in metaphor is nothing else than grasping of similarities in a preconceptual way. In popular terms, figurative thinking is the presentation of abstract ideas and their concrete appearance. But what is a concrete presentation of an abstract idea, if not the learning and the teaching of a genus thanks to the interplay between sameness and difference? To my mind a philosophy of imagination is badly needed. Could we not say by anticipation that imagination is the emergence of conceptual meaning through the interplay between sameness and difference? Metaphor would be the place in discourse where this emergence may be detected because sameness and difference are in conflict. If metaphor can be treated as a figure of speech, it is because it overtly presents in the form of a conflict between sameness and difference the process which is covertly at work in the construction of all semantic fields, that is, the kinship which brings individuals under the rule of a logical class. Metaphor helps us to detect this process because it works against previous categorization at the level of rhetoric. It cleverly bypasses given categories in order to reveal unnoticed similarities in the field of our experience.

We will now relate this analysis of metaphor to our previous analysis of polysemy. It is essential to the structure of metaphor that the old and the new are present together in the metaphorical twist. The kind of tension which we described at the level of the sentence, and even within the copula itself, now dwells in the words themselves. When we receive a metaphorical statement as meaningful, we perceive both the literal meaning which is bound by the semantic incongruity and the new meaning which makes sense in the present context. Metaphor is a clear case where polysemy is preserved instead of being screened. Two lines of interpretation are opened at the same time and several readings are allowed together and put into tension. This effect has been compared to stereoscopic vision. Several layers of meaning are noticed and recognized in the thickness of the text.

This first relation between metaphor and polysemy is not the only one. We have treated it as a synchronistic phenomenon, but it is also a diachronic one. If we consider the long history of a metaphor, we may say that it passes from the state of novelty to that of faded or dead metaphor. At the first stage metaphor does not belong to the lexicon. It exists only in discourse, in the present and actual instance of discourse. But as soon as it is received by a speech community, it tends to be used in the same way as the literal meanings already classified by our dictionaries. At the last stage, when the tension between literal and metaphorical sense is no longer perceived, we may say that the metaphorical sense has become a part of the literal sense. Then it is merely added to the previous polysemy of the word. In this way we may say that metaphor is the procedure by which we extend polysemy.

In this way we come to the following hypothesis. If metaphor extends polysemy, is not polysemy the results of previous metaphor? But now metaphor is no longer a rhetorical device, no longer a trope; it designates the general process by which we grasp kinship, break the distance between remote ideas, build similarities on dissimilarities.

We are now prepared to answer the decisive question: what is the function of metaphor? By this question we are sent back to the strategy underlying the use of metaphor. If ordinary language aims at communication by cleverly reducing ambiguity, and if scientific language aims at univocity in argumentation by suppressing equivocity, what is the finality of metaphorical language? Our concept of likeness as the tension between sameness and difference implies that a discourse which makes use of metaphor has the extraordinary power of redescribing reality. This is, I believe, the referential function of a metaphorical statement.

This heuristic function of the metaphor appears clearly when we bring metaphor and models together, as Max Black does in *Models and Metaphors*, and as Mary Hesse does in *Models and Analogies in Science*. The function of a model is to describe an unknown thing or a lesser-known thing in terms of a better-known thing thanks to a similarity of structure. Two things have therefore to be considered in a model. On the one hand, it is a fiction, that is, it is a way of making an object easier to handle. On the other hand, this fiction is a heuristic fiction inasmuch as we may transfer the description of this better-known object to the field to be described on the basis of a partial isomorphism.

This concept of heuristic fiction may be extended from the theory of models in science to the theory of poetry. In his *Poetics*, Aristotle paved the way for a generalization of metaphor conceived as heuristic fiction by linking metaphor as a rhetorical trait to the main operation of poetry which is the building of a *mythos*, of a fable. The invention of the fable in tragedy is the creative act of poetry *par excellence*. This creative act gives its title to the work, *Poetics*, that is to say, creative fiction. Therefore if we say that the function of poetry is to imitate nature, we must not forget that this *mimesis* is not a copying of reality, but a redescription in light of a heuristic fiction. Thanks to tragedy, we are prepared to look at human beings in a new way because human action is redescribed as greater, nobler, than actual life is. Thanks to this disclosure of the depth structure of human life by poetry, we may say once more with Aristotle that poetry is closer to philosophy than to history. History remains caught in anecdotes, poetry reaches the essence of things.

What we just said about tragedy, what must be said about poetic narrative, can be said also of lyrics, although at first sight lyrical poetry has no reference. Language constitutes a world of its own. In the terms of Jakobson, the poetic dimension of language emphasizes the message as such at the expense of the reference to the context. Sound and sense tend to make a solid object, a closed totality. But if it is true that lyrical poetry suspends all didactic references and even abolishes the world, can we not say that this *epoché* of reference in the terms of the descriptions already given by ordinary language is the negative condition for the disclosure of new aspects of reality which could not have been said in a more direct way? If this is true, we can say that poetic language has a mimetic function inasmuch as it is a heuristic fiction preparing a redescription of reality. If it is true that poetry gives no information in terms of empirical knowledge, it may change our way of looking at things, a change which is no less real than empirical knowledge. What is changed by poetic language is our way of dwelling in the world. From poetry we receive a new way of being in the world, of orientating ourselves in this world. Even if we say with Northrop Frye that poetic discourse gives articulation only to our moods, it is also true that moods as well as feelings have an ontological bearing. Through feeling we find ourselves already located in the world. In this way, by articulating a mood, each poem projects a new way of dwelling. It opens up a new way of being for us.

If this analysis is sound, we should have to say that metaphor shatters not only the previous structures of our language, but also the previous structures of what we call reality. When we ask whether metaphorical language reaches reality, we presuppose that we already know what reality is. But if we assume that metaphor redescribes reality, we must then assume that this reality, as redescribed, is itself novel reality. My conclusion is that the strategy of discourse implied in metaphorical language is neither to improve communication nor to insure univocity in argumentation, but to shatter and to increase our sense of reality by shattering and increasing our language. The strategy of metaphor is heuristic fiction for the sake of redescribing reality. With metaphor we experience the metamorphosis of both language and reality.

Note

1 Aristotle, *The Art of Poetry*, trans. by Philip Wheelwright (New York: Odyssey Press, 1951), p. 317

Appropriation

This essay will attempt to explicate a key idea which governs the methodology of interpretation. It concerns the way in which a text is *addressed to* someone. Elsewhere[1] we have noted that the writing–reading relation is distinguished from the speaking–hearing relation not only in terms of the relation to the speaker, but also in terms of the relation to the audience. We have asked: for whom does one write? and we have answered: for anyone who can read. We have also spoken of the 'potentialization' of the audience, which is no longer the partner in dialogue but the unknown reader that the text procures. The culmination of reading in a concrete reader who appropriates the meaning will thus constitute the theme of this essay.

It is obvious that we shall rediscover the old problem of the role of subjectivity in understanding and, therefore, the problem of the hermeneutical circle. But this problem is presented in new terms, as a result of the fact that it has been postponed for so long. Instead of considering it as the first problem, we have pushed it back to the end of our investigation. What we have said in other essays about the notion of interpretation is, in this respect, decisive. If it is true that interpretation concerns essentially the power of the work to disclose a world, then the relation of the reader to the text is essentially his relation to the kind of world which the text presents. The theory of appropriation which will now be sketched follows from the displacement undergone by the whole problematic of interpretation: it will be less an intersubjective relation of mutual understanding than a relation of apprehension applied to the world conveyed by the work. A new theory of subjectivity follows from this relation. In general we may say that appropriation is no longer to be understood in the tradition of philosophies of the subject, as a constitution of which the subject would possess the key. To understand is not to project oneself into the text; it is to receive an enlarged self from the apprehension of proposed worlds which are the genuine object of interpretation. Such is the general line of this essay, which will be pursued in detail as follows.

1 / To begin with, the necessity of the concept of appropriation will be shown. It will be introduced as the counterpart of a concept of distanciation which is linked to any objective and objectifying study of a text. Hence the first section: 'distanciation and appropriation.'

2 / Then we shall take up the relation between the concept of appropriation and that of the revelation of a world. Following Hans-Georg Gadamer's analysis in *Truth and Method*, we shall introduce the theme of 'play.' This theme will serve to characterize the metamorphosis which, in the work of art, is undergone not only by reality but also by the author (writer and artist), and above all (since this is the point of our analysis) by the reader or the subject of appropriation. Appropriation will thus appear as the 'playful' transposition of the text, and play itself will appear as the modality appropriate to the reader *potentialis*, that is, to anyone who can read.

3 / Next we shall identify the illusions and errors which the concept of appropriation must overcome. Here the critique of the illusions of the subject will be the necessary path to the sound appreciation of the concept of appropriation. Appropriation will be the complement not only of the distanciation of the text, but also of the relinquishment of the self.

The conclusion will sketch the place of hermeneutic philosophy in relation to the reflective Kantian tradition on the one hand, and the speculative Hegelian tradition on the other. It will be shown why a hermeneutic philosophy must situate itself at an equal distance from both.

I. Distanciation and Appropriation

The dialectic of distanciation and appropriation is the final figure which the dialectic of explanation and understanding must assume. It concerns the way in which the text is addressed to someone.

The potentialization of the audience implies two ways of reconnecting the discourse of the reader to that of the writer. These possibilities pertain to the status of *history* in the whole process of interpretation. The general tendency of literary and biblical criticism since the mid-nineteenth century has been to link the contents of literary works, and in general of cultural documents, to the social conditions of the community in which these works were produced or to which they were directed. To explain a text was essentially to consider it as the expression of certain socio-cultural needs and as a response to certain perplexities localized in space and time. In contrast to this trend, which was subsequently called 'historicism,' an alternative tendency arose, stemming from Frege and from the Husserl of the *Logical Investigations*. According to these thinkers, meaning (they were interested in the meaning of a proposition rather than that of a text) is not an idea which someone has in mind; it is not a mental content but an ideal object which can be identified and reidentified, by different individuals in different periods, as being one and the same object. By 'ideality,' they understood that the meaning of a proposition is neither a physical nor a mental reality. In Frege's terms, *Sinn* is not *Vorstellung*, if *Vorstellung* (idea, representation) is the mental event linked to the actualization of meaning by a given speaker in a given situation. The identify of 'sense' in the infinite series of its mental actualization constitutes the ideal dimension of the proposition. In a similar way, Husserl described the contents of all intentional acts as the 'noematic' object, irreducible to the mental aspect of the acts themselves. The notion of ideal 'sense,' borrowed from Frege, was thus extended by Husserl to all mental operations – not just logical acts but also perceptual acts, volitional acts, affective acts, etc. For a phenomenology 'turned towards the object,' all intentional acts without exception must be described in terms of their noematic side, understood as the 'correlate' of the corresponding noetic acts.

The inversion in the theory of propositional acts has an important implication for hermeneutics, insofar as this discipline is conceived as the theory of the fixation of life expressions by writing. After 1900, Dilthey himself made a great effort to incorporate into his theory of meaning the kind of ideality which he found in Husserl's *Logical Investigations*. In Dilthey's later works, the interconnection (*Zusammenhang*) which gives a text, a work of art, or a document its power to be understood by another and to be fixed by writing is somewhat similar to the ideality that Frege and Husserl discerned at the basis of all propositions. If this comparison holds, then the act of 'understanding' is less 'historical' and more 'logical' than the famous article of 1900 declares.[2] The whole theory of the 'human sciences' is affected by this important shift.

A comparable change in the domain of literary criticism, in America and on the Continent, can be related to the turn from history to logicity in the explanation of cultural expressions. A wave of 'anti-historicism' followed the earlier excesses of psychologism and sociologism. For this new attitude, a text is not primarily a message addressed to a specific range of readers; in this sense, it is not a segment of a historical chain. Insofar as it is a text, it is a kind of atemporal object which has, as it were, broken from its moorings to all historical development. The rise to writing implies the 'suspension' of the historical process, the transference of discourse to a sphere of ideality which permits an indefinite expansion of the sphere of communication.

I must say that I take this 'anti-historicist' trend into account and that I accept its principal presupposition concerning the objectivity of meanings in general. It is because I concur with the project and the method of this sort of literary criticism that I am ready to define, in new terms, the dialectic between explanation and understanding which results from the recognition of the specificity of the literary object.

Let us develop this new dialectic: the objectification of meaning is a necessary mediation between the writer and the reader. But as mediation, it calls for a complementary act of a more existential character which I shall call the appropriation of meaning. 'Appropriation' is my translation of the German term *Aneignung. Aneignen* means to make one's own what was initially 'alien.' According to the intention of the word, the aim of all hermeneutics is to struggle against cultural distance and historical alienation. Interpretation brings together, equalizes, renders contemporary and similar. This goal is attained only insofar as interpretation actualizes the meaning of the text for the present reader. Appropriation is the concept which is suitable for the actualization of meaning as addressed to someone. It takes the place of the answer in the dialogical situation, in the same way that 'revelation' or 'disclosure' takes the place of ostensive reference in the dialogical situation. The interpretation is complete when the reading releases something like an event, an event of discourse, an event in the present time. As appropriation, the interpretation becomes an event. Appropriation is thus a dialectical concept: the counterpart of the timeless distanciation implied by any literary or textual criticism of an anti-historicist character.

II. 'Play' as the Mode of Being of Appropriation

The following theme was suggested by reading Gadamer;[3] but it is also called for by the theory of the *heuristic fiction*. I should like to show that it is not only reality which is metamorphosed by the heuristic fiction, but also the author and the reader. Thus the metamorphosis of the reading subject results initially from the metamorphosis of the world, and then from the metamorphosis of the author.

1. The Heuristic Fiction as Play

Gadamer develops his conception of play in the course of a meditation on the work of art. This meditation is wholly directed against the subjectivism of the aesthetic consciousness which stems from the Kantian theory of the 'judgment of taste,' itself linked to the theory of 'reflecting judgment.' Play is not determined by the consciousness which plays; play has its own way of being. Play is an experience which transforms those who participate in it. It seems that the subject of aesthetic experience is not the player himself, but rather what 'takes place' in play. In a similar way we speak of the play of waves, of light, of parts of a machine and even of words. We play with a project, with an idea; we can equally 'be played.' What is essential is the 'to and fro' (*Hin und Her*) of play. Play is thereby close to dance, which is a movement that carries away the dancer. Thus we say that the part 'is played,' or again that something 'is in play' between ... All of these expressions betray that play is something other than the activity of a subject. The to-and-fro of play occurs as if by itself, that is, without effort or applied intention. This 'in-itself' of play is such that, even in solitary play, there must be something with which or against which one plays (with luck as one's partner in times of success!). In this risk of an unknown partner lies the 'charm' of play. Whoever plays is also played: the rules of the game impose themselves upon the player, prescribing the to-and-fro and delimiting the field where everything 'is played.' Hence play shatters the seriousness of a utilitarian preoccupation where the self-presence of the subject is too secure. In play, subjectivity forgets itself; in seriousness, subjectivity is regained.

In what respects does this analysis, which we have briefly recalled, clarify our problem of hermeneutic understanding? In the first place, the presentation of a world in a work of art, and in general in a work of discourse, is a playful presentation. Worlds are proposed in the mode of play. The analysis of play thus enables us to recover in a new way the dialectic between the suspension of didactic reference and the manifestation of another sort of reference, beyond the *epoché* of the former. Play displays the same dialectic, developing a serious side of its own – what Gadamer calls 'presentation' (*Darstellung*). In play, nothing is serious, but something is presented, produced, given in representation. There is thus an interesting relation between play and the presentation of a world. This relation is, moreover, absolutely reciprocal: on the one hand, the presentation of the world in a poem is a heuristic fiction and in this sense 'playful'; but, on the other hand, all play reveals something true, precisely because it is play. To play, says Gadamer, is to play at something. In entering a game we hand ourselves over, we abandon ourselves to the space of meaning which holds sway over the reader.

In play there occurs what Gadamer calls a 'metamorphosis' (*Verwandlung*), that is, both an imaginary transposition marked by the reign of 'figures' (*Gebilde*) *and* the transformation of everything into its true being. Everyday reality is abolished and yet everyone becomes himself. Thus the child who disguises himself as another expressed his profoundest truth. The player is metamorphosed 'in the true'; in playful representation, 'what is emerges.' But 'what is' is no longer what we call everyday reality; or rather, reality truly becomes reality, that is, something which comprises a future horizon of undecided possibilities, something to fear or to hope for, something unsettled. Art only abolishes non-metamorphosed reality. Whence the true *mimesis*: a metamorphosis according to the truth. In this sense, we shall speak of recognition rather than cognition. In a theatrical representation, we recognize characters and roles. Therein lies the paradox: the most imaginary creation elicits recognition. 'As recognised, the presented being is what is retained in its essence, what is detached from its haphazard aspects,'[4] stripped of all that is fortuitous and accidental. This is the sense in which Aristotle could dare to say that poetry (he was thinking of tragedy) is more philosophical than history. For poetry proceeds to the essential, whereas history remains content with the anecdotal. Such is the significant link between fiction, figuration, and recognition of the essential.

2. The Author as Playful Figure

A second implication emerges which is no less interesting than the first. It is not only the presentation of the world which is 'playful,' but also the position of the author who 'puts himself on stage' and hence gives himself in representation. Is this not the key to what we have called the potentialization of the reader? Is he not also 'metamorphosed' by the play upon the world which unfolds in the work of art? The hypothesis of a playful relation between the author and his work is supported by diverse analyses which come from quite a different perspective, in particular from German and Anglo-Saxon literary criticism.[5] The discussion in this critical literature was polarized, above all, by the problem of the relation between the novelist and his characters. The term 'point of view' was used to describe the various possible solutions contributed by novelists of the past to this difficult problem: a total view of the characters by an omniscient author, the identification with one of the characters through whose eyes the author sees everything that is shown, the annihilation of the author in a story which tells itself all alone, and so on.

How can this debate be clarified by our earlier reflections on play? The very fact that there have been numerous solutions to this technical problem results, in my opinion, from the playful character of the relation itself. The author is rendered fictitious; and the different modalities of the relation of author to narration are like so many rules of this playful relation. The solutions classified by Norman Friedman and F.K. Stanzel may be reconsidered from this point of view.[6] That these solutions constitute so many fictions of the author seems to me confirmed by the remark of one of the critics: 'The author can, to a certain extent, choose to disguise himself, but he can never choose to disappear.'[7] To disguise oneself, to assume different 'voices,' is this not to play?

For their part, the French, more affected by the structuralist concern to cut the links between the text and the author, emphasize the non-coincidence of the 'psychological' author and the 'narrator,' where the latter is 'marked' by the signs of the narrator in the text. But this non-coincidence cannot imply the elimination of the author;

just as Benveniste spoke of split reference with respect to poetic language, so too we must introduce the idea of a 'split speaker.' This splitting marks the irruption of the playful relation into the very subjectivity of the author. We are no longer very far from Dilthey when he speaks of 'the position of the poet's imagination before the world of experiences.'[8] In the same sense, Wolfgang Kayser speaks of the 'mythical creator' in order to designate the situation of the narrator. The narrator is the one who abstracts from his personality so that a voice other than his is heard. Thus the very disappearance of the subject is still an imaginative variation of the writer's *ego*. The imaginative variation then consists in being part of the narrative, in disguising oneself according to the narrative. In any case, it is still a matter of a role assumed by the narrator. For the omniscient narrator is just as much a fiction of the subject as is the narrator identified with a character or as is the narrator dispersed among the characters who appear to speak and to act all alone. The omniscient narrator is also an 'autonomous figure created by the author in the same way as the characters'[9] even more so if the narrator is identified with a character or hidden behind all. The objective and Olympian narrator may well disappear: play is displaced towards the partial and restricted viewpoints of the characters; or, as in *The Sorrows of Young Werther*, it is hidden in an imaginary character inserted between the character and ourselves, such that this third person is sensed to have put together the words of the poor Werther, addressing us in the preface and engaging us in a pseudo-dialogue.

It makes little difference, therefore, whether a text is written in third or in first person. In every case, the distanciation is the same and the variety of solutions proves that we have not gone beyond rule-governed play. Thus the novelist may change his perspective and become suddenly omniscient when he reads the thoughts of his characters. So while it is true to say that the narrator is never the author, nevertheless the narrator is always the one who is metamorphosed in a fictional character which is the author. Even the death of the author is a game that the author plays. In all cases he remains, according to Kayser's expression, a 'creator of the universe.'[10]

3. The Reader as Playful Figure

It is now possible to transfer the remarks on the author to the reader, and to treat the reader in turn as a fictive or playful figure. For the author's subjectivity, submitted to imaginative variations, becomes a model offered by the narrator to the subjectivity of his reader. The reader as well is invited to undergo an imaginative variation of his *ego*. When the fictive author of the preface of *Werther* addresses us, 'and you, good soul ...,' this 'you' is not the prosaic man who knows that Werther did not exist, but is the 'me' who believes in fiction. As Kayser says, 'the reader is a fictive creation, a role which we can assume in order to look at ourselves.'[11] In this sense, we may speak of metamorphosis, as Gadamer speaks of the metamorphosis of reality in play. The reader is this imaginary 'me,' created by the poem and participating in the poetic universe.

We may still speak of a relation of congeniality, but it is exercised from the playful author to the playful reader. For the work itself has constructed the reader in his role. So the congeniality does not signify anything other than the double metamorphosis of the author and the reader: 'Assuming the role of reader corresponds to the mysterious metamorphosis which the audience undergoes in the theatre when the lights go out and the curtains are drawn.'[12]

It is easy, therefore, to generalize beyond the novel or the story: even when we read a philosophical work, it is always a question of entering into an alien work, of divesting oneself of the earlier 'me' in order to receive, as in play, the self conferred by the work itself.

III. The Illusions of the Subject

The concept of appropriation has hardly been introduced when it becomes the victim of errors linked to the primacy of the subject in modern philosophy, in so far as the latter originates in the writings of Descartes, Kant, and Husserl. The role of the subject seems to imply that appropriation is a form of the constitution of objectivity in and by the subject. This inference results in a series of errors about the very meaning of appropriation. The first of these errors is a surreptitious return to the Romantic pretension of recovering, by congenial coincidence, the genius of the author: from genius to genius! Another error is to conceive of appropriation in terms of the primacy of the original audience with which one seeks to coincide: to discover to whom a text was addressed and to identify oneself with that original audience, such would be the task of hermeneutics. Or, more bluntly, appropriation would consist in subsuming interpretation to the finite capacities of understanding of the present reader.

This way of conceiving of appropriation, ensnared in these various errors, is responsible for the distrust which scientific minds display towards hermeneutics, understood as a form of subjectivism or of subjectivist existentialism. Even Heidegger has been read this way: his 'pre-understanding' (*Vorverständnis*) is taken as indistinguishable from a simple projection of the prejudices of the reader into his reading. The same could be said of Bultmann's hermeneutical circle: 'to believe in order to understand,' is this not to project the reading self into the text read?

Here I shall say that the notion of subject must be submitted to a critique parallel to that which the theory of metaphor exercises on the notion of object. In fact, it is the same philosophical error which must be taken by its two extremities: objectivity as confronting the subject, the subject as reigning over objectivity.

At this stage, everything gained from the critique of the illusions of the subject must be integrated into hermeneutics. This critique, which I see conducted in either a Freudian or a Marxist tradition, constitutes the modern form of the critique of 'prejudice.'

According to the Marxist tradition, the critique of the subject is one aspect of the general theory of ideology. Our understanding is based on prejudices which are linked to our position in the relations of force of society, a position which is partially unknown to us. Moreover, we are propelled to act by hidden interests. Whence the falsification of reality. Thus the critique of 'false consciousness' becomes an integral part of hermeneutics. Here I see the place for a necessary dialogue between hermeneutics and the theory of ideology as developed, for instance, by Habermas.[13]

According to the Freudian tradition, the critique of the subject is one part of the critique of 'illusions.' Here I am interested in psychoanalysis, not as a grid for reading a text, but as the self-criticism of the reader, as the purification of the act of appropriation. In *Freud and Philosophy*, I spoke of an effect of self-analysis which I called the relinquishment of the subject. As Freud said, the subject is not master in his own house. This critique is addressed to what could be called the 'narcissism of the reader': to find only oneself in a text, to impose and rediscover oneself.

Relinquishment is a fundamental moment of appropriation and distinguishes it from any form of 'taking possession.' Appropriation is also and primarily a 'letting-go.' Reading is an appropriation-divestiture. How can this letting-go, this relinquishment, be incorporated into appropriation? Essentially by linking appropriation to the revelatory power of the text which we have described as its referential dimensions. It is in allowing itself to be carried off towards the reference of the text that the *ego* divests itself of itself ...

The link between appropriation and revelation is, in my view, the corner-stone of a hermeneutics which seeks both to overcome the failures of historicism and to remain faithful to the original intention of Schleiermacher's hermeneutics. To understand an author better than he understood himself is to unfold the revelatory power implicit in his discourse, beyond the limited horizon of his own existential situation.

On this basis, it is possible to refute fallacious views about the concept of interpretation. In the first place, appropriation does not imply any direct congeniality of one soul with another. Nothing is less intersubjective or dialogical than the encounter with a text; what Gadamer calls the 'fusion of horizons' expresses the convergence of the *world* horizons of the writer and the reader. The ideality of the text remains the mediator in this process of the fusion of horizons.

According to another fallacious view, the hermeneutical task would be governed by the original audience's understanding of the text. As Gadamer has firmly demonstrated, this is a complete mistake: the Letters of Saint Paul are no less addressed to me than to the Romans, the Galatians, the Corinthians, etc. Only dialogue has a 'you,' whose identification proceeds from the dialogue itself. If the meaning of a text is open to anyone who can read, then it is the omnitemporality of meaning which opens it to unknown readers; and the historicity of reading is the counterpart of this specific omnitemporality. From the moment that the text escapes from its author and from his situation, it also escapes from its original audience. Hence it can procure new readers for itself.

According to a third fallacious view, the appropriation of the meaning of a text would subsume interpretation to the finite capacities of understanding of a present reader. The English and French translation of *Aneignung* as 'appropriation' reinforces this suspicion. Do we not place the meaning of the text under the domination of the subject who interprets? This objection can be dismissed by observing that what is 'made our own' is not something mental, not the intention of another subject, nor some design supposedly hidden behind the text; rather, it is the projection of a world, the proposal of a mode of being-in-the-world, which the text discloses in front of itself by means of its non-ostensive references. Far from saying that a subject, who already masters his own being-in-the-world, projects the *a priori* of his own understanding and interpolates this *a priori* in the text, I shall say that appropriation is the process by which the revelation of new modes of being – or, if you prefer Wittgenstein to Heidegger, new 'forms of life' – *gives* the subject new capacities for knowing himself. If the reference of a text is the projection of a world, then it is not, in the first instance, the reader who projects himself. The reader is rather broadened in his capacity to project himself by receiving a new mode of being from the text itself.

Thus appropriation ceases to appear as a kind of possession, as a way of taking hold of ... It implies, instead, a moment of dispossession of the narcissistic *ego*. This process of dispossession is the work of the sort of universality and atemporality implied by the explanatory procedures. Only the interpretation which satisfies the injunction of the text, which follows the 'arrow' of meaning and endeavours to 'think in accordance with' it, engenders a new *self*-understanding. By the expression '*self*-understanding,' I should like to contrast the *self* which emerges from the understanding of the text to the *ego* which claims to precede this understanding. It is the text, with its universal power of unveiling, which gives a *self* to the *ego*.

It would require, at the end of this excursion, a long explanation in order to situate hermeneutic philosophy in relation to the reflective Kantian tradition, on the one hand, and the speculative Hegelian tradition, on the other. We shall restrict ourselves here to offering a few remarks in support of the thesis that hermeneutic philosophy must place itself at equal distance from both traditions, accepting as much from one tradition as from the other but opposing each with equal force.

By its concern to secure the link between understanding meaning and self-understanding, hermeneutic philosophy is a continuation of reflective philosophy. But the critique of the illusions of the subject and the permanent recourse to the great detour of signs distances it decisively from the primacy of the *cogito*. Above all, the subordination of the theme of appropriation to that of manifestation turns more towards a hermeneutics of the *I am* than a hermeneutics of the *I think*.[14]

It may be thought that what distances hermeneutic philosophy from reflective philosophy brings it nearer to speculative philosophy. That is largely true. Thus, Gadamer can say that his hermeneutics revives Hegel in so far as it breaks with Schleiermacher. Fundamentally, the concept of manifestation of a world, around which all other hermeneutical concepts are organized, is closer to the idea of the 'self-presentation' (*Selbstdarstellung*) of the true, following the preface to *The Phenomenology of Mind*, than to the Husserlian idea of constitution. But the permanent return of this self-presentation to the event of speech in which, *ultimately*, interpretation is accomplished signifies that philosophy mourns the loss of absolute knowledge. It is because absolute knowledge is impossible that the conflict of interpretations is insurmountable and inescapable.

Between absolute knowledge and hermeneutics, it is necessary to choose.

Notes

1 See 'The Hermeneutical Function of Distanciation,' in *Hermeneutics and the Human Sciences*, ed. by J.B. Thompson (Cambridge: Cambridge University Press, 1981), pp. 131–44

2 W. Dilthey, 'Origine et développement de l'herméneutique' (1900) in *Le Monde de l'esprit*, Vol. I (Paris: Aubier, 1947) [English translation: 'The Development of Hermeneutics,' in *Selected Writings*, ed. and trans. by H.P. Rickman (Cambridge: Cambridge University Press, 1976)

3 Hans-Georg Gadamer, *Wahrheit und Methode* (Tübingen: J.C.B. Mohr, 1960) [English translation: *Truth and Method*, trans. by Garret Barden and John Cumming (London: Sheed and Ward, 1975)]

4 Ibid, p. 109 [102]

5 See F. van Rossum-Guyon, 'Point de vue ou perspective narrative'; Wolfgang Kayser, 'Qui raconte le roman?'; and Wayne C. Booth, 'Distance et point de vue'; all in *Poétique*, Vol. IV (1970). In France a related problem was posed by J. Pouillon in his work *Temps et roman* (Paris: Gallimard, 1946)

6 Cf. F. van Rossum-Guyon, 'Point de vue ou perspective narrative,' pp. 481–2 and 485–90.

7 W.C. Booth, quoted in van Rossum-Guyon, ibid, p. 482

8 W. Dilthey, quoted in van Rossum-Guyon, ibid, p. 486

9 F.K. Stanzel, quoted in van Rossum-Guyon, ibid, p. 490

10 Wolfgang Kayser, 'Qui raconte le roman?' p. 510

11 Ibid, p. 502

12 Ibid, p. 510

13 See 'Hermeneutics and the Critique of Ideology,' in *Hermeneutics and the Human Sciences*, pp. 63–100.

14 See Paul Ricoeur, 'The Question of the Subject: The Challenge of Semiology,' trans. by Kathleen McLaughlin, in *The Conflict of Interpretations: Essays in Hermeneutics*, ed. by Don Ihde (Evanston: Northwestern University Press, 1974), pp. 236–66.

The Human Experience of
Time and Narrative

My aim in this paper is to bring together two problematics that are not usually connected: the epistemology of the narrative function and the phenomenology of time experience.

On the one hand, the epistemology of narrative, whether it considers narrative in the sense of history-writing or of story-telling, scarcely questions the concept of time which is implicit in narrative activity. It takes it for granted that narratives occur *in* time, i.e., within a given temporal framework, and it uncritically identifies this given temporal framework with the ordinary representation of time as a linear succession of abstract 'nows.'

On the other hand, the phenomenology of time-experience usually overlooks the fact that narrative activity, in history and in fiction, provides a privileged access to the way we articulate our experience of time.

The main thesis of this paper will be that narrativity and temporality are as closely linked as a 'language-game' in Wittgenstein's terms is to a 'form of life.' Or, to put it in different terms, narrativity is the mode of discourse through which the mode of being which we call temporality, or temporal being, is brought to language.

I shall first give a rough outline of the temporal problematics from the point of view of the ambiguities and paradoxes which may receive a specific clarification from our narrative activity. Then I shall turn to the narrative activity itself from the point of view of its temporal structures and inquire to what extent these temporal structures constitute an answer to the ambiguities and paradoxes of our ordinary experience of time.

I. The Problematics of Time

I have taken as evidence of the specific opaqueness of the human experience of time the eleventh book of Augustine's *Confessions* and Heidegger's *Sein und Zeit*, section II. In the context of this paper, the convergence of their analyses will be held as more relevant than their obvious differences. I have selected three problems which seemed to me appropriate to further inquiry.

The first concerns the specificity of the human experience of time compared to the ordinary representation of time as a line linking together mathematical points. According to this representation, time is constituted merely by relations of simultaneity and of succession between abstract 'nows,' and by the distinction between extreme end-points and the intervals between them. These two sets of relationships are sufficient for defining the *time when* something happens, for deciding what came *earlier* or *later* and *how long* a certain state of affairs might last. But the deficiency of this representation of time is that it takes into account neither the centrality of the present as an *actual* now nor the primacy of the future as the main orientation of human desire, nor the fundamental capacity of recollecting the past in the present.

The drastic move made by Augustine and by Heidegger was to say that there is no past, no present, and no future in any substantive sense, but rather a dialectic of intentionalities, which Augustine referred to as memory, attention, and expectation. For that purpose, he assumed the paradox of a threefold present: a present about the future, a present about the past, and a present about the present.

Heidegger takes the same position when he substitutes for the substantive terms of 'future,' 'past,' and 'present' three modalities of what he calls 'Care,' which connect cognitive, practical, and emotional components within one and the same ontological structure. I shall not consider at this stage the shift of emphasis thanks to which the present is deprived by Heidegger of its priority for the sake of the future. I shall focus instead on the phenomenology common to both Augustine and Heidegger in order to emphasize the conflict between an experience of time rooted in the dialectic of Care and its representation in the terms of a linear succession of abstract 'nows.' This problem constitutes an enigma to the extent that the recovery of the genuine constitution of time does not seem to be able to abolish the representation of time as a linear succession of nows in spite of the radical misunderstanding of the transcendental constitution of time that it generates. This resistance of the ill-famed reference of time must have some right of its own.

The second problem arises from the very paradox that both Augustine and Heidegger – albeit in very different ways – were compelled to introduce the above-mentioned opposition into our experience of time. For Augustine, the present of man is not the eternal present of God; for that reason, it is not a harmonious interplay of intentions – between memory, expectation, and attention – but a discordant experience which Augustine called, in a very appropriate way, *distentio*, which means both extension and distraction. Let us reserve for the third paradox the quantitative aspects of *distentio* as extension and focus on the dialectic of intention and distraction. Intention is what prevails when, for example, in reciting a poem, we hold together the whole of the poem, in spite of the fact that a part of it is still ahead of us and another part has already sunk into the past and thus only a phase of the work is present.

Distraction is what prevails when we are torn between the fascination with the past in regret, remorse, or nostalgia; the passionate expectation of the future in fear, desire, despair, or hope; and the frailty of the fleeting present. *Human* time is the dialectic of intention and distraction, and we have no speculative means of overcoming it. Heidegger meets a similar enigma when he distinguishes between *authenticity* and *inauthenticity* in our relating to time. But inauthenticity, which reminds us of distraction, is not extrinsic to the purpose of an analytic of *Dasein*. On the contrary, inauthenticity has its own existential claim, which is that of *everyday life*. And since the description of everyday life belongs in an organic way to the analytic, we must introduce into our account of temporality the dialectic of authenticity and inauthenticity. To this drastic move we owe the most remarkable attempt to organize the phenomenology of time in terms of several *levels of radicality*. Accordingly, three such levels are distinguished. The most radical one is temporality, properly so-called. It is characterized by the primacy of the future in the dialectic between the three temporal intentionalities and, above all, by the finite structure of time arising from the recognition of the centrality of death, or, more exactly, of *being-towards-death*. (The resoluteness with which we face our own being-towards-death, in the most intimate structure of Care, provides the criterion of authenticity for all of our temporal experience.) We move in the direction of the inauthentic pole when we proceed from *temporality* to *historicity*. Historicity, in its technical sense, refers first to our way of 'becoming' between birth and death. The *stretching-along* of life is thus more emphasized than the *wholeness* provided to life by its mortal termination. In this *stretching-along* we may recognize Augustine's *distentio*. But this *distentio* is preserved from sheer dispersion thanks to *Dasein's* capacity to recapitulate – to *repeat*, to *retrieve* – our inherited potentialities within the projective dimension of Care. This *Wiederholung* is the counterpart of the stretching-along of life. It bears witness to the continuity in the process of deriving historicity from temporality. We shall show at the end of this paper the tremendous relevance of *Wiederholung*, which surfaces in any attempt to ground historical *and* fictional narratives in a common temporal structure. We may now reach the pole of inauthenticity, in the sense of the prevailing of everyday-life structures over and against those of temporality ruled by being towards death and of historicity ruled by repetition. The temporal structure corresponding to this stage is called *within-timeness*, because, at that level, time is held as that 'in' which events occur. We get closer to the linear representation of time, but the important claim of Heidegger is that before any *levelling* of *within-timeness* for the sake of the linear representation of time, its structure may still be referred to an analytic of *Dasein*. *Within-timeness* is still a feature of Care, but of Care as falling prey to its own objects, the subsisting and manipulable things of one's concern. It is in this state of *thrownness* that the present becomes the predominant category. (But, even then the 'now' is not the abstract 'now' of the linear representation; it is the 'now that' of human initiatives. It is also for within-timeness that we make use of calculations and measurement. But we measure time because we *reckon with* time, and *reckoning with* time is part of the character of Care as mundane *concern*. Within-timeness implies also public time, but this time is public not because it is *neutral*, indifferent to the distinction between things and men, but because human action is common action and because *Mitsein* – being together – may always and has always been reduced to anonymity. Even then, the anonymity of common time is not the abstractness of linear time according to the popular representation.)

Such is the Heideggerian reading of Augustine's dialectic of *intention* and *distention*. But there is no speculative way to overcome this dialectic, which remains unsolved and open.

A third and ultimate paradox arises from this very dialectic. It appears that *extension* is not the result of some fall, the sin of abstraction, but is a constitutive trait of the most radical temporality. We can trace it back from the mere extension of within-timeness to the *stretching-along* of historicity and finally the *ausser sich* of the three ecstasies of time. *Distentio*, then, is not merely a kind of disease of time-consciousness, but the *extension* which is dialectically connected to the intentionality of consciousness. It can ultimately be ascribed to the radical passivity pertaining to our human experience of time.

Such are the main paradoxes which plague our experience of time. They are so intractable that they keep eliciting from each of us the outcry which opens Augustine's meditation on Time: 'If nobody asks me, I know; but if I were desirous to explain it to one that should ask me, plainly I know not' (Augustine, *Confessions* XI, XIV).

II. The Narrative Kernel

We now turn to narrative discourse and ask how it deals with these paradoxes, whether it provides a solution of its own, and how this solution relates to the lack of speculative resolution which we recognized.

As an immediate rejoinder to our last complaint – we know time when nobody asks us about it, we don't know it when we are asked to explain it – we are first of all overwhelmed by the incredible abundance and variety of narrative expressions (oral, written, graphic, gestural), and of classes of narratives (myth, folk-tale, fable, epic, tragedy, drama, novel, movies, comics, as well as history, auto-biography, analytical case-histories, testimony of witnesses before the court, and, of course, ordinary conversation). If time-experience is *mute*, narrating is *eloquent*. We find the scattered diversity of story-telling uniquely puzzling. To handle this overwhelming proliferation of narrative forms, the first natural move has been to reduce the number of its classes. A second, more artificial move has been to submit them to constructed models. As concerns classification, we may say that the development of our Western culture has produced a major dichotomy, that drawn between history and story; i.e., between narratives which claim to be *true*, empirically verifiable or falsifiable, and fictional stories which ignore the burden of corroboration by evidence, and so this dichotomy constitutes an important obstacle for our inquiry, for it makes questionable the claim that these two large classes share some common narrative structures whose temporal features in turn could be easily acknowledged. As concerns the second, more artificial device – the recourse to constructed narrative models and codes – it offers a still more dangerous threat to our enterprise, to the extent that the interest in narrative models and codes often results in a trend, both in the theory of history and in literary criticism, to deny the narrative component, whatever it may be. Some historians speak, after Braudel, of *histoire non-événementielle* – eventless history – and many epistemologists in the field of historical knowledge contend that inquiry – in the strong sense of argumentative inquiry – has excluded history writing from traditional narrative forms (folklore, myths, epics, and legendary chronicles). On the side of literary criticism, we have a similar and even more radical trend to submit the intractable variety of narrative forms to constructed models which should be radically atemporal (e.g., Roland Barthes's 'Introduction to the structural analysis of narratives'). Thus, a more manageable deductive approach can be substituted for an impossible inductive approach. The result is that the narrative component as such is identified only with the surface grammar of the message, with the level of manifestation, whereas only achronological codes would rule the level of constitution, to use the vocabulary of A.J. Greimas, the main French exponent of this structuralist treatment.

My suspicion is that both anti-narrativist epistemologists in the field of the theory of history and structuralist literary critics' theory of story have overlooked the temporal complexity of the narrative matrix in both narrative classes. Because most historians have a poor concept of event – and even of narrative – they consider history as an explanatory endeavour which has severed its ties with story-telling. The underscoring of the surface grammar in literary narration leads critics to what seems to me to be a false posing of radical choices: either to remain caught in the labyrinthine chronology of the told story, or to radically move to an achronological model. The dismissal of narrative as such implies a similar lack of concern in both camps for the properly *temporal* aspects of narrative and therefore for the contribution that the theory of narrative could offer to a phenomenology of time experience. To put it bluntly, this contribution has been almost null because *time* has disappeared from the horizon of the theories of history and narrative. Theoreticians of these two broad fields seem even to be moved by a strange mistrust of time, the kind of mistrust that Nietzsche expressed in his *Zarathustra*.

I suggest that we take as the leading thread of our discussion the decisive concept of *plot*. If plot is not the only structure of narrative and if its role in modern narratives has become controversial, at least it may be held that, for an inquiry into the temporal aspect of narrative, plot functions as the narrative *matrix*. This emphasis on narrative as plot has several advantages: first, it provides us with a structure which could be common to both historical and fictional narratives. Of course, in order that this advantage remain un-challenged, it must be proved, that history-writing itself continually arises from this narrative matrix, and therefore that inquiry and explanatory procedures are constantly grafted upon the kind of intelligibility displayed by narratives as plots. In the same way, it must be proved that in fictional narratives, the plot is a basic struc-ture which no achronological model is able to generate.

This paper will not give the arguments which support my conten-tion that history writing and fictional narratives not only proceed historically from some common matrix in which plot is an important component, but also continue, in fact, to share in this common narrative structure.

The second advantage which I see in an analysis starting from *plot* is one which would be less dependent on further arguments not developed in this paper: an examination of *plot* may allow us mo-mentarily to bracket one of the main differences between historical and fictional narratives, the difference resulting from the *truth-claim* of history vs. that of fiction. In other words, plot may be seen as pertaining to the *sense* of narrative as distinct from its *reference*. This distinction must not be emphasized too strongly, since the complete meaning of the most fictional narrative cannot be assessed without taking into account its relation to the real world, whether it be a relation of imitation in the narrow sense of copying, or an imitation which incorporates such complexities as irony, decision, conscious distortion and negation, and so on. Ultimately it is our very inquiry into the function of narrative as *shaping* our temporal experience which will compel us to go beyond the obvious but provisory opposi-tion between the *direct truth-claim* of history concerning past events, and the *indirect truth-claims* of fictional narrative which are implied in the various forms of the mimetic function.

Such are the two advantages of an inquiry into the narrative structures common to history and fiction starting from plot as the most significant of those structures. I will say nothing of the third and last advantage, that plot displays some remarkable temporal structures which help us to bridge the gap between an inquiry into narrativity and an inquiry into temporality. The description of these temporal structures is, in fact, the main purpose of this paper, and I freely acknowledge that the desire to disentangle these temporal implications was the main motive which led me to pick out 'plot' as my main topic. This implication is already suggested by the fact that the notions of historical *event*, as a temporal concept, and *plot*, as a narrative concept, are mutually definable. To be historical, an event must be more than a singular occurrence, a unique happening. It receives its definition from its contribution to the development of a plot. Reciprocally, a plot is a way of connecting event and story. A story is *made out of* events, to the extent that plot makes events *into* a story.

This notion of events made *into* story through the plot immediately suggests that a story is not bound to a merely chronological order of events. All narratives combine in various proportions, two dimensions – one chronological and the other non-chronological. The first may be called the episodic dimension. This dimension characterizes the story as made out of events. The second is the configurational dimension, according to which the plot construes significant wholes out of scattered events. Here I borrow from Louis O. Mink the notion of the configurational act, which he interprets as a 'grasping together.' I understand this act to be the act of the plot, as eliciting a pattern from a succession. I am ready to ascribe to this act the character of *the* judgment, and more precisely of reflective judgment in the Kantian sense of this term.[1] To tell and to follow a story is already to reflect upon events in order to encompass them in successive wholes. Such is the dimension which is completely overlooked in the theory of history by the anti-narrativist writers. They tend to deprive narrative activity of its complexity and, above all, of its twofold characteristic of confronting and combining in various ways both sequence and pattern. But this antithetical dynamic is no less overlooked in the theory of fictional narratives proposed by structuralists. They take it for granted that the surface grammar of what they call the 'plane of manifestation' is merely episodic, and therefore purely chronological. They conclude that the principle of order has to be found at the higher level of achronological models or codes. Anti-narrativist writers in the theory of history and structuralist writers in literary criticism share the same prejudice. They do not see that the humblest narrative is always more than a chronological series of events and that, in turn, the configurational dimension cannot overcome the episodic dimension without suppressing the narrative structure itself.

III. Temporal Structures of the Plot

We may now try to assess the contribution of the theory of narrative to the 'solution' of the paradoxes of time experience.

I shall not attempt to do that in a direct and straightforward way. Rather, I shall use as an intermediate step towards this solution the kind of *parallelism* which can be established between the levels of temporalization that we described in the first section, following Augustine and Heidegger, and some corresponding levels which have yet to be acknowledged in the temporal structures of the plot. This parallelism between levels of temporality and levels of narrativity will pave the way for understanding the ways in which narratives, on the one hand, are the modes of discourse appropriate to our experience of time; and time experience, on the other hand, is the ultimate referent of the narrative mode. Instead of claiming to grasp directly the connection between narrative as a language-game and temporality as a form of life, this more analytical and piecemeal approach will help us to construe in a meaningful way the unity of time as narrated and narrative as temporal.

The present paper will remain within the boundaries of an analysis of plot as the structure common to both historical and fictional narrative. We shall not attempt to lift the brackets put on the differences between the truth-claims of these two broad classes of narratives. In other words, we shall speak of plot as the *sense* of narrative isolated from its reference.

In spite of its abstract character – or, maybe, thanks to it – the analysis of the plot is already very rich in temporal implications. We have already anticipated some of them in making the distinction between the chronological and the non-chronological dimensions of plot. But the temporal features of the plot will appear in a more articulate manner if we apply to them the grid of the threefold structure of time experience as temporality, historicity, and within-timeness.

a / The first function of narratives – whether 'true' or fictional – is to establish man at that level of temporalization that Heidegger calls 'within-timeness' – the time of everyday life. But in spite of its way of locating events 'in time,' narrative activity already marks the threshold between the existential traits of within-timeness and the abstract representation of time in a linear way. The art of telling makes meaningful use of most adverbial expressions which characterize this lower level of temporality: 'then,' 'earlier,' 'later,' 'until that ...' 'now that ...' When story-tellers start telling, everything is already *extended* in time.

It could be said, then, that narrative activity, taken unreflectively, contributes to the dissimulation of the more authentic levels of temporality. It is more appropriate, however, to say that narrative activity *tells the truth* of within-timeness as a genuine dimension of human Care. All the categories which, according to Heidegger, differentiate within-timeness from the other levels of temporality make sense at the ordinary level of story-telling. The heroes of the narrative 'reckon with' time. They 'have' or 'don't have' time 'to' (do this or that). Their time may be 'lost' or 'won.' Furthermore, narratives show men thrown into circumstances which, in turn, deliver them over to the change of light and night. It is, accordingly, a time in which 'datation' obtains, but according to natural measures, like days and seasons, which have not yet been replaced by the artificial measures of astronomy and physics. Of this time it can be rightly said that 'we measure time because we reckon with it' and not the contrary. In the same manner, narrative time is public time, not because it is indifferent to man as acting and suffering. The art of telling keeps the public character from falling back into anonymity. It is the time proper to the 'being-together' of heroes, antagonists, and helpers, the time of action as interaction – 'inter-time,' if we dare say, not abstract time. Thus narrative time shares with within-timeness the same public character, in so far as neither has yet been levelled to the abstract representation of time.

Finally, the 'now' characteristic of within-timeness, which Heidegger defines as the present which 'makes present,' is not yet the now of linear time. It is the 'from now on ...' of human decision, and the 'now that...' of human intervention. This present, as Heidegger says, 'temporalizes in union with expectation and retention.' It is concern understood as 'expectation-that-retains.'

To summarize this first point, it belongs to a hermeneutics of story-telling to initiate the return from the *abstract representation* of time as linear to the *existential interpretation* of temporality. Story-telling achieves that in a fundamental way by revealing the existential traits of within-timeness over and against the abstraction of linear time.

b / But narratives do more than establish man – his actions and passions – 'in' time. Story-telling brings us back from within-timeness to historicity – from 'reckoning with' time to recollecting time. As such, the narrative function provides the *transition* from within-timeness to historicity.

What we said earlier concerning the dialectic between the episodic and configurational dimensions of plot may help us to take this new step; we only have to make the temporal implications of this dialectic explicit. Here we hit upon a temporal constitution which is completely overlooked in the theory of action by anti-narrativist arguments and in literary criticism by structuralist claims. Both take it for granted that narrative, as such, is merely chronological and that chronology means abstract succession. This is why no other device seems to remain open except a subordination of sequential history to explanatory history, on the one hand, or the reduction of the chronology of the narrative message to the atemporality of narrative codes. What is overlooked in both camps is the tremendous complexity of narrative time. We could display in the following way the temporal dialectic implied in the basic operation of eliciting a configuration from a succession. Thanks to its episodic dimension, narrative time tends towards the linear representation of time in many ways: first, the 'then' and 'and then,' which provide an answer to the question 'what next?' suggest a relation of exteriority between the phases of the action. Besides this, the episodes constitute an open-ended series of events which allow one to add to the 'then' an 'and then,' and an 'and so on ...' Finally, the episodes follow one another in accordance with the irreversible order of time common to human and physical events.

The configurational dimension, in turn, displays temporal features which may be opposed one by one to those 'features' of episodic time. First, the configurational arrangement makes the succession of events into significant wholes which are the correlate of the act of grouping together. Thanks to this reflective act – in the sense of Kant's *Critique of Judgment* – the whole plot may be translated into one 'thought.' 'Thought,' in that narrative context, may assume various meanings. It may characterize, according to Aristotle's *Poetics*, the 'theme' – in Greek, the *dianoia* – which accompanies the 'fable' – in

Greek, the *mythos* – of the tragedy. (It may be noticed that this correlation between 'theme' and 'plot' is the basis of Northrop Frye's 'Archetypical' criticism.) 'Thought' may also designate the 'point' of the Hebraic maschal or of the biblical parable (hereto, Jeremias observes that the 'point' of the parable is what allows us to translate it into a proverb or an aphorism). The term 'thought' may also apply to the 'colligatory terms' used in history writing; such terms as the Renaissance, the Industrial Revolution, and so on, which, according to Walsh[2] and Dray,[3] allow us to apprehend a set of historical events under a common denominator (here 'colligatory terms' correspond to the kind of explanation that Dray puts under the heading of 'explaining what'). In a word, the correlation between thought and plot supersedes the 'then' and 'and then' of mere succession. But it would be a complete mistake to consider such a 'thought' as achronological. 'Fable' and 'theme' are as closely *tied* as are episode and configuration. The time of fable-and-theme, if we may put that in a one-word expression, is more deeply temporal than the time of merely episodic narratives.

Secondly, the plot's configuration superimposes 'the sense of an ending' – to use Kermode's expression – on the open-endedness of mere succession. As soon as a story is well known – and such is the case with most traditional and popular narratives, as well as with the national chronicles of the founding events of a given community – retelling takes the place of telling. Then following the story is less important than apprehending the well-known end as implied in the beginning and the well-known episodes as leading to the end. Time, once more, is not abolished by the teleological structure of the judgment which 'grasps together' the events under the heading of the end. This strategy of judgments is one of the means through which time experience is brought back from within-timeness to repetition.

Finally, the recollection of the story ruled as a whole by its way of ending constitutes an alternative to the representation of time as flowing from the past forward into the future, according to the well-known metaphor of the 'arrow of time.' It is as though recollection inverted the so-called natural order of time. By reading the end in the beginning and the beginning in the end, we learn also to read time itself backwards, as the recapitulation of the initial conditions of a course of action in its terminal consequences. In that way, a plot establishes human action not only within time, as we said at the beginning of this section, but within memory. Memory, accordingly, *repeats* the course of events according to an order which is the counterpart of time as stretching-along between a beginning and an end.

This third temporal character of plot has brought us as close as possible to Heidegger's notion of *repetition*, which, as we said, is the turning-point for his whole analysis of *historicity*. Repetition, for him, means more than a mere reversal of the basic orientation of Care towards the future. It means the retrieval of our ownmost potentialities inherited from our own past in the form of personal fate and collective destiny. The question, then, is whether we may go so far as to say that the function of narratives – or at least of some of them – could be to establish human action at the level of genuine historicity, i.e., of repetition. If such were the case, the temporal structure of narrative would display the same hierarchy as the one established by the phenomenology of time experience.

c / In order to acknowledge this new temporal structure of some narratives, we have to question some of the initial presuppositions of the previous analysis, and above all, of those which rule the selection of the paradigmatic case of narrative in modern literary criticism. Vladimir Propp, in his *Morphology of Tales*, opened the way, by focusing on a category of tales – Russian tales – which may be characterized as complying with the model of the heroic quest. In those tales, a hero meets a challenge – either mischief or some lack – which he is sent to overcome. Throughout the quest he is confronted with a series of trials which require that he choose to fight rather than to yield or to flee, and which finally end in victory. The paradigmatic story ignores the non-chosen alternatives – yielding and losing. It knows only the chain of episodes which leads the hero from challenge to victory. It is not by chance if, after Propp, this schema offered so little resistance to the attempts by structural analysis to dechronologize Propp's paradigmatic chain. Only the linear succession of episodes had been taken into account. Furthermore, the segmentation of the chain had led to the isolation of temporal segments held as discrete entities that were externally connected. Finally, these segments were treated as contingent variations of a limited number of some abstract narrative components, the famous thirty-one 'functions' of Propp's model. The *chronological* dimension was not abolished, but immediately deprived of its temporal constitution as plot. The segmentation and the concatenation of 'functions' had paved the way for a reduction of the chronological to the logical.

In the new phase of structural analysis, with Greimas and Barthes, the atemporal formula, which generates a chronological display of functions, transforms the structure of the tale into a machinery whose task it is to compensate for the initial mischief or lack by a final restoration of the disturbed order. Compared to this logical matrix, the quest itself appears as a mere diachronical residue, as a retardation or suspension in the epiphany of order.

The question is whether it is not, rather, the initial need to reduce the chronological to the logical – a need arising from the method itself – which rules the strategy of structural analysis in Propp's successive phase: first, the selection of the quest as the paradigmatic case, then the projection of its episodes on a linear time, the segmentation and the external connection of this 'function,' and finally the dissolution of the chronological into the logical.

There is an alternative to dechronologization. It is repetition. Dechronologization implies the logical abolition of time; repetition, its existential deepening. But, to support this view, we have to question the implications and even the choice of the paradigmatic cases of narratives in current literary criticism.

Without putting aside the model of the quest, we may emphasize some of its temporal aspects, aspects which have been ruled out by the method itself. Before projecting the hero forward for the sake of the quest, many tales send the hero or heroine into some dark forest where he or she goes astray or meets some devouring beast (*Little Red Riding Hood*), or where the younger brother or sister has been kidnapped by some threatening birds (*The Swan-Geese Tale*). These initial episodes do more than merely introduce the mischief which is to be suppressed. They bring the hero or heroine *back* into a primordial space and time which is more akin to the realm of dream than to the sphere of action. Thanks to this preliminary disorientation, the linear chain of time is broken and the tale assumes an oneiric dimension which is more or less preserved alongside the heroic dimension of the quest. Two qualities of time are thus intertwined: the circularity of the imaginary travel and the linearity of the quest, as such. I agree that the kind of repetition involved in this travel towards the origin is rather primitive, if not even regressive, in the psychoanalytic sense of the word. It has the character of an immersion and confinement in the midst of dark powers. This is why this repetition of the origin has to be superseded by an act of rupture, depicted, for example, in the episode of the woodcutters breaking open the belly of the wolf with an axe. Nevertheless, the imaginary travel suggests the idea of a metatemporal mode which is not the atemporal mode of narrative codes in structural analysis. This timeless – but not atemporal – dimension duplicates, so to speak, the episodic dimension of the quest and contributes the 'fairy' atmosphere of the quest itself.

This first mode of repetition must, in turn, be superseded, to the extent that it constitutes only the reverse side of the time of quest and conquest, brought forward by the call for victory. Finally, the time of quest prevails over that of the imaginary travel through the break, thanks to which the world of action emerges from the land of dreams – as though the function of the tale was to elicit the progressive time of the quest out of the regressive time of imaginary travel.

Repetition tends to become the main issue of the narrative in the kind of narratives in which the quest itself duplicates a *travel* in space which assumes the shape of a return to the origin. Odysseus's travels are the paradigm of the narrative as travel and return. As Mircea Eliade writes in *The Trial of the Labyrinth* (p. 109),

> Ulysses is for me the prototype of man, not only modern man, but the man of the future as well, because he represents the type of the 'trapped' voyager. His voyage was a voyage towards the center, towards Ithica, which is to say, towards himself. He was a fine navigator, but destiny – spoken here in terms of trials of initiation which he had to overcome – forced him to postpone indefinitely his return to hearth and home. I think that the myth of Ulysses is very important for us. We will all be a little like Ulysses, for in searching, in hoping to arrive, and finally, without a doubt, in finding once again the homeland, the hearth, we rediscover ourselves. But, as in the Labyrinth, in every questionable turn, one risks 'losing oneself' (*se perdre*). If one succeeds in getting out of the Labyrinth, in finding again one's home, then one becomes a new being.[4]

The retardation of which Eliade speaks here is no longer the mere 'suspension' in the epiphany of order. Retardation now means growth.

The Odyssey, accordingly, could be seen as the form of transition from one level of repetition to another, from a mere fantasy repetition which is still the reverse side of the quest, to a kind of repetition which would generate the quest itself. With the *Odyssey*, the character of repetition is still imprinted in time by the circular shape of the travel in space. The temporal return of Odysseus to himself is supported by the geographical return to Odysseus's birthplace, Ithica.

We come closer to the kind of repetition suggested by Heidegger's analysis of historicity with stories in which the return to the origin is not merely a preparatory phase of the tale and is no longer mediated by the shape of the travel back to Ithica. In these stories, repetition is constitutive of the temporal form itself. The paradigmatic case of such stories is Augustine's *Confessions*. Here the form of the travel is interiorized to such a degree that there is no longer any privileged place in space to return to. It's a travel 'from the exterior to the interior, and from the interior to the superior.' (*Ab exterioribus ad interiora, ab interioribus ad superiora.*) The model created by Augustine is so powerful and enduring that it has generated a whole set of narrative forms down to Rousseau's *Confessions* and to Proust's *Le Temps retrouvé*. If Augustine's *Confessions* tell 'how I became a Christian,' Proust's *Le Temps* tells 'how Marcel became an artist.' The quest has been absorbed into the movement by which the hero – if we may still call him by that name – becomes *who he is*. Memory, then, is no longer the narrative of external adventures, stretching along episodic time. It is itself the spiral movement which, through anecdotes and episodes, brings us back to the almost motionless constellation of potentialities which the narrative retrieves. The end of the story is what equates the present with the past, the actual with the potential. The hero *is* who he *was*. This highest form of narrative repetition is the equivalent of what Heidegger called Fate – individual Fate – or destiny – communal destiny – i.e., the complete retrieval in resoluteness of the inherited potentialities in which *Dasein* is thrown by birth.

At this point the objection could be made that only fictional narrative, and not history, reaches this deep level of repetition. I do not think this is the case. It is not possible to ascribe only to *inquiry* – as opposed to traditional narrative – all the achievements of history in the overcoming of legendary accounts, i.e., the release from mere apologetic tasks related to the heroic figures of the past, the attempt to proceed from mere narrative to truly explanatory history, and finally the grasp of whole periods under a leading Idea. We may wonder whether the shift described by Maurice Mandelbaum in the *Anatomy of Historical Knowledge* from sequential history to *explanatory* history does not find its complete meaning in the further shift from explanatory to what he calls *interpretive* history. 'While an interpretive account is not usually confined to a single cross-section of time but spans a period ... the emphasis in such words is on the manner in which aspects of society or of the culture of the period, or both, fit together in a pattern, defining a form of life different from that which one finds at other times or in other places' (pp. 39f.).

Am I stretching the notion of *interpretation* too far if I put it in the Heideggerian terms of repetition? Professor Mandelbaum may dislike this unexpected proximity to Heideggerian ideas. I find, nevertheless, some confirmation and some encouragement to take this daring step in the profound analysis of action that Hannah Arendt gives in her brilliant work *The Human Condition*. As is well known, Arendt distinguishes between labour, work, and action. Labour, she says, aims merely at survival in the fight between man and nature. Work aims at leaving a mark on the course of things. Action deserves its name when, beyond the concern for submitting nature to man or for leaving behind some monuments bearing witness to our activity, it aims only at being recollected in stories whose function it is to provide an identity to the Doer, an identity which is merely a *narrative identity*. Thus history *repeats action* in the figure of the memorable.

Such is the way in which history itself – and not only fiction – provides an approximation of what a phenomenology of time experience may call repetition.

My conclusion will be less a summary of the previous analysis than a set of suggestions for further inquiry.

First, to what extent can we say that narrative activity solves the ambiguities and paradoxes of our experience of time? It can achieve no speculative resolution, but perhaps may achieve a *poetic* one. By that I mean that by telling stories and writing history we provide 'shape' to what remains chaotic, obscure, and mute. But the complete account of this function of narrative as *shaping* time would imply a development and a reformulation of all our previous analysis in terms of *productive imagination*, to use Kant's terminology. We should have to show that historical narrative and fictional narrative *jointly* provide not only 'models of' but 'models for' articulating in a symbolic way our ordinary experience of time. This has not been done in this paper.

And this could not have been done, because we have not overcome the abstraction thanks to which we were able to isolate the *plot* as the structure of *sense* common to history and to fiction. In order to show the way in which history and fiction *jointly* shape our experience of time, we should have to proceed from *sense* to *reference*, i.e., to show how the obvious differences between history as 'true' story and *fictional* story work together, so to speak, beyond the asymmetry in truth-claims. This task cannot be achieved within the boundaries of a mere epistemology of narrative forms. It requires a hermeneutical approach able to encompass both forms under a broader concept of truth than the epistemological one which is assumed when we oppose 'true' story to 'fictional story.' I don't deny that this task can be partially achieved within a framework which can still be called epistemological. On the one hand, it can be shown, with such writers as Hayden White, that history-writing is more fictional than positivist writers would allow us to say. On the other hand, it can be shown, with a whole school of literary criticism arising from Aristotle's *Poetics*, that fiction is more *mimetic* than the same positivistic trend of thought would acknowledge. Between a fictional history and a mimetic poetry some striking convergences could therefore be discerned, and an intersection between the direct referential claim of 'true' story and the indirect referential claim of fictional story could appear as a plausible horizon for inquiry into narratives at large. But I have no difficulty in acknowledging that this *intersection* remains a plausible horizon for research only as long as we keep talking in epistemological terms. The gap between historical and fictional narrative could only be bridged if we could show that both are grounded in the same basic temporality which provides to repetition itself an existential foundation. Then, it could be shown that the reasons for which we write history and the reasons for which we tell stories are rooted in the same temporal structure that connects our 'élan' towards the future, our attention to the present, and our capacity to emphasize and to recollect the past. Then 'repetition' would no longer appear as a dubious procedure divided between fictional repetition and historical repetition. It would be able to encompass history and fiction to the extent that both are rooted in the primordial unity between future, past, and present.

But this ontological part of the inquiry is, unfortunately, beyond the scope of this study.

Notes

1 William Dray, *Laws and Explanations in History* (London: Oxford University Press, 1957)
2 W.H. Walsh, '"Meaning" in History,' in *Theories of History*, ed. by Patrick Gardiner (New York: The Free Press, 1959), pp. 295–307
3 Dray, *Laws and explanation in History*
4 Ricoeur's translation

The Function of Fiction
in Shaping Reality

The theme of this paper may seem intriguing. Yet, no taste for paradox animates it. It must be understood in the sense of Nelson Goodman's first chapter in *Languages of Art*, entitled 'Reality Remade.' My own approach is in agreement with this book's general thesis that symbolic systems 'make' and 'remake' the world, and that our aesthetical grasping of the world is a militant understanding that 'reorganizes the world in terms of works and works in terms of world' (p. 241). My title could as well correspond with certain works in epistemology such as that of Mary Hesse in *Models and Analogies in Science*, where scientific models are interpreted as sustained metaphors aiming at a *redescription* of reality. I shall not extend my inquiry to this theory of models, but I want to draw attention to this potential expansion of the present topic, which is not necessarily bound to aesthetics. It is not even bound to cognition, to the extent that fictions also 'remake' human action or praxis as the practical fictions which are called ideologies and utopias. I shall not consider here that category of fictions, but limit myself to the region of cognitive symbols with an emphasis on aesthetics.

I shall proceed in the following way. I shall first discuss the concept of *fiction* and designate its place in a general theory of imagination, by contrasting it with the notion of image as a portrait or a replica. This analysis will pursue the distinctive ways in which portraits and fictions *refer to* reality. I shall thus elaborate the crucial concept of *productive* reference as equivalent to *reality shaping*.

Then I shall test this working hypothesis by putting it in two different frameworks, that of *verbal* symbols and that of *pictorial* symbols.

1. Fictions and Copies

It is a fact that no articulate theory of imagination is available which does justice to the basic distinction between image as fiction and image as copy. Stubborn prejudices tend to identify the notion of image with that of a replica of a given reality.

These prejudices may be traced back to common sense. Ordinary language tends to impose as the paradigmatic case either the physical replica (a photograph, a copy in the ordinary sense of the word) of some absent thing which could be shown and perceived elsewhere, or the mental equivalent of such a physical replica as the mental image, in the usual sense of the word. Philosophies of ordinary language, following ordinary use, tend to take for granted the definition of the image as the intuitive representation of some existing *in absentia*. To have an image of something is to 'see' it in our mind's eye, without the presence of the actual thing. If we put the problem in the terms of a general theory of denotation or reference (which is, to my mind, the most appropriate approach for the philosophy of mind or for a philosophical psychology), we have to say that the image as copy raises no specific question of reference, since it is the same thing, by hypothesis, that is to be perceived in *praesentia* or imagined *in absentia*. Image and perception differ only as regards their *modes of givenness*. I don't mean to say that this difference is not important. Rather it raises a tremendous range of questions. I shall mention only three of them: first, does the mental image imply some kind of *analogon* of the thing represented, similar to the material analogon of the physical portrait? This is Sartre's question in *L'Imaginaire*. Second, when we say that we have an image of something, is there something intuitively 'seen' in our mind's eye, as we usually say, meaning by that a kind of mental presentation of the thing absent, or do we merely 'pretend' to see, as Ryle claims? Third, as concerns the mode of belief linked to the specific mode of givenness of the image, how is it possible that we believe enough in the quasi presence of the represented things or persons to the point of preserving and cherishing their portraits, but not to the point of mistaking the image for the thing? What is the meaning of this partial illusion or partial magic displayed by faithful copies? Paradoxy which plagues the theory of image as copy (paradox of the non-physical analogon; paradox of intuitive absence; paradox of quasi belief) explains partially why philosophers have so easily endorsed the bias of common sense and of ordinary language that an image is a physical or mental replica of an absent thing.

But philosophers have reinforced this prejudice by adding arguments of their own. Two arguments keep recurring in the literature on the subject. First, images *derive* in one way or the other from perceptions. This argument may already be found in Aristotle's *De Anima*. Whatever may be the specificity of the *phantasia* for Aristotle, it is by comparison to perception that *phantasia* is described. And it *resembles* it, because it proceeds from it. It is a movement deriving from the previous exercise of a sensible faculty. The mode of dependence then rules the difference as well as the similarity. Spinoza and Hume do not proceed in such very different ways. For Spinoza, there is first the real action, of real physical bodies on a real human body, then, thanks to the repeated action of those stimuli, the formation of a trace which, when reactivated, reinstates the belief in the existence of the thing. Thus, the image and the original perception have the same cause. As concerns Hume, everyone knows, his insistence on treating the image as a weak impression; between a simple image and a simple impression there is only a difference of force and vivacity.

The second argument is that fictions, in turn, proceed from simple images by the means of new combinations. Fictions are merely complex ideas whose components are derived from previous experience.

The classical example of the centaur of the chimera shows with what mistrust the classical philosophy of imagination approaches the question of fiction. Reminiscences from the past must be found at all cost in all new ideas and images. The components are old; only the combination is new. But the enigma remains unexplained, since all experience is, in a sense, based on a selection and a combination of elements. The problem is precisely the newness occurring in the order of appearances. But the truth is that thought does not like what is new and does its best to reduce the new to the old.

This reductive stand explains the whole strategy of the philosophy of imagination: the choice of the portrait as the paradigmatic case, the derivation of the mental image from the physical portrait by interiorization of the analogon up to the point that the image becomes a mere nothing, then the derivation of the fiction from the simple image in terms of complex images.

But what is wholly overlooked in the transition from the image as replica to the image as fiction is the shift in the referential status. This shift constitutes to my mind the critical point in the theory of imagination and the criterion of the difference between fiction and portrait.

Let us elaborate this point with utmost accuracy.

The portrait image and the corresponding perception, we said, have the same referent, which is the existing thing. They differ only as two different modes of givenness of one and the same thing. In the argument of Sartre, my friend Peter, over there in Berlin, is the same that I could see if I were there and whose photograph I contemplate here in my room. This defines the status of absence. Absence and presence are modes of givenness of the same reality.

In the case of fiction, on the contrary, there is no given model, in the sense of an original already there, to which it could be referred. Of course, if you treat fiction as a complex image you may refer your elementary images one by one to corresponding entities in the world. But you have only displaced the difficulty. It's the new combination which has no reference in a previous original to which the image would be the copy. And this defines the status of unreality. Unfortunately, absence and unreality are very often confused. The original of a photograph is absent but may be real or may have been real. That does not mean that there is not something negative in a photograph. It is *not* its model. Furthermore, it is not even, as image, the sum of the material lines and colours making up what we see, touch, and move. But this nothingness proper to the representation of an absent thing belongs to the mode of givenness of the image, not to its referent. The referent of the portrait is a real thing aimed at *in absentia*. In that sense, the non-existence of the object of the fiction is the true form of unreality. There is no symmetry between absence as a mode of givenness of the real, and non-existence as the contrary of the real. The centaur, to return to the classical examples, exists nowhere. Its unreality is not opposed to the absence of Peter, in the example of Sartre, but to Peter's reality. The phenomenology of fiction has its starting-point in this lack of symmetry between the nothingness of unreality and the nothingness of absence. The nothingness of absence concerns the mode of givenness of a real thing *in absentia*, the nothingness of unreality characterizes the referent itself of the fiction.

But, if the phenomenology of fiction has its starting-point in the character of the nothingness of its referent, as opposed to the nothingness of a mere mode of givenness, the recognition of this difference is not the last word in this connection. The denial of the primacy of the original opens rather new ways of *referring to* reality for the image. Because fictions do not refer in a 'reproductive' way to reality as already given, they may refer in a 'productive' way to reality as intimated by the fiction. This lecture will be an attempt to make some sense of the concept of *productive reference*, which I take to be the ultimate criterion of the difference between fiction and picture.

That fiction changes reality, in the sense that it both 'invents' and 'discovers' it, could not be acknowledged as long as the concept of image was merely identified with that of picture. Images could not increase reality since they had no referents other than those of their originals. The only originality of the image had thus to be found in the spontaneity characteristic of the production of the image. For Sartre, this spontaneity sends us back to our freedom, not to new ways of looking at reality. This spontaneity appears to a reflective consciousness as concerns only its non-thetic activity. For Ryle, a mock-performance seems to exhaust its meaning in the abstention from the straight performance and the likeness of the mock-performance. Both abstention and likeness seem to belong to a second order of discourse which corresponds to Sartre's reflective consciousness.

It is at this point, precisely in opposition to the limited concept of image found in these two thinkers, that we discover the paradox of fiction. Because it has no previous referent, it may refer in a productive way to reality, and even *increase* reality, as we will say later. However, this 'productive' reference of fiction requires several important changes in the framework within which the problem is construed in order to arrive at a solution to the problem. This paper will specifically address two of these changes.

The first change concerns the shift from the framework of perception to that of language. What prevents recognition of the 'productive' reference of fiction is the classical assumption that images are derived from perception. This trait is common to Aristotle and to Hume, although the derivation in question is in terms of 'motion' for Aristotle and in terms of 'copies of impressions' for Hume. A theory of fiction must first break with this way of putting the problem and cease asking to what extent an image differs from a perception. Our first positive step, therefore, will be to shift the problem of images from the sphere of perception to the sphere of language. After this shift in the problematic itself, we expect to find that the 'productive' aspects of imagination will appear to be linked to some 'productive' aspects of language. The theory of metaphor will provide us with this new starting-point. This, therefore, will be our first task: to show how the emergence of new meanings in the sphere of language generates an emergence of new images.

The second change made at the level of the problematic will be an attempt to link fiction tightly to work. With both Ryle and Sartre, images are taken in isolation; they are taken in isolation because they are not 'wrought.' When I see Helvellyn in my mind's eye and when I produce the image of my friend Peter, no further labour is required than to 'see' and to 'imagine.' The image remains within the poverty of its own appearance. One of the reasons why the *mental* picture is able to be understood in an other than 'productive' context, and why the accounts of Sartre and Ryle seem convincing, is that *physical* pictures may be handled in such an isolated way. We may, for instance, withdraw a photograph from a collection and contemplate it, as it were, out of context. Thus, the kinship between physical and mental pictures suggests that one is able to transfer his capacity from the former to the latter.

Yet, this does not seem to be the main reason why the aspect of work has been divorced from the notion of image. Actually, the power to deal with images in isolation is more deeply rooted in the 'reproductive' character of pictures. Pictures may be taken out of context because their originals enjoy innumerable relations with the rest of the world. And these relations are already constituted. This explains why isolated images present the kind of poverty which Sartre rightly ascribes to them. It is not by chance that at a further stage of the same analysis, Sartre speaks of the magical aspect of the imagination. This magical attribute consists of the self-deceptive attempt to 'possess' the object of desire in spite of its absence. This fascination with the object 'in image' is a kind of reaction to the poverty of the image as such. Now, the magic of quasi possession is exactly the opposite of what we here call a context of work. Even if magic is only one among several possible reactions to the image as picture, it shows in a kind of caricatural way to what extent reproductive imagination may become parasitic on the picture's original.

This contrast between fascination and work suggests that imagination is 'productive' when thought is at work. Writing a poem; telling a story; construing a hypothesis, a plan, or a strategy: these are the kinds of contexts of work which provide a perspective to imagination and allow it to be 'productive.' In the last part of this paper we will draw from *painting* one example of this 'productive' state of imagination in the context of work, that of 'iconic augmentation.' It will appear that, in such a context, imagination is 'productive' not only of unreal objects, but also of an expanded vision of reality. Imagination at work – in a work – produces itself as a world.

II. Metaphor and Image

As we said above, the theory of metaphor offers us the occasion to shift the problem of the image from the sphere of perception to that of language. The theory of metaphor does this in the aspect of *semantic innovation* characteristic of the metaphorical usage of language. Semantic innovation creates the display of images, or rather, that which ordinary language and literary criticism identify as 'images,' but which actually comprise the metaphors of an author.

The change involved in this approach to the problem is significant in two ways. On the one hand, modern semantics since Frege and Husserl has tended to exclude image from the sphere of meaning. For these two philosophers, the break between *Sinn* (sense) and *Vorstellung* (representation) is total. 'Sense' is a logical dimension, 'image' a psychological one. Likewise, image is relegated to the status of a weak impression, of a representative, of a sign substituted for an empirical presence. But the semantic operation of the metaphor appears to open the way to a joint reinterpretation of sense and representation. In the measure to which image gives a body, a contour, a shape to meaning, it is not confined to a role of accompaniment, of illustration, but participates in the *invention* of meaning.

On the other hand, image appears to be able to play this appropriately semantic role only if it leaves the unstableness of the sensible impression in order to pass into that of language. It is therefore necessary to renounce the prejudice according to which image would be an appendage or shadow of perception. To say that our images are spoken before being seen is to disclaim a first false evidence, according to which, image would be at first and in essence a 'scene' displayed upon some mental 'theatre' before the gaze of an internal 'spectator.' But it is at the same time to disclaim a second false evidence, according to which, this mental entity would be the material out of which we shape our abstract ideas or concepts, as if image were the basic ingredient of some supposed mental alchemy. Therefore, the characteristic of the approach proposed here is to go from language to image. But if we do not derive image from perception, how are we to derive it from language?

An examination of the poetic image taken as a paradigmatic case will provide a beginning of the response. The poetic image is something that the poem, as a certain work of discourse, displays in certain circumstances and according to a certain procedure. This procedure is that of 'reverberation,' to use an expression borrowed by Gaston Bachelard from Eugene Minkowski.[1] But to understand this procedure, one must first admit that the reverberation proceeds not from things *seen*, but from things *said*. The question to which we must now return is therefore that which concerns the circumstances of discourse in which use engenders imagination.

Elsewhere I have studied the operation of metaphor, which has such great consequences for the theory of the imagination. I have shown that this operation remains totally misunderstood as long as one sees in metaphor only a deviating use of nouns, a mistake in denomination. Instead, metaphor is a deviating use of predicates within the framework of the entire phrase. It is necessary to speak of a metaphorical statement rather than of nouns used metaphorically. The question, then, is that of the strategy which rules the use of bizarre *predicates*. With certain French- and English-language authors, I place the accent on predicative impertinence as a way to describe the production of a clash between semantic fields. In order to respond to the challenge issued by the semantic clash, we produce a new predicative pertinence, which is the metaphor. In its turn, this new appropriateness, produced at the level of the entire sentence, creates, at the level of the isolated word, the extension of meaning by which classical rhetoric identified the metaphor.

If this approach has any value, it is in shifting one's attention towards the problem of the restructuring of semantic fields at the level of predicative usage.

It is precisely at this point that the theory of metaphor is of interest to philosophy of the imagination. This bond between the two theories has always been suspected, as witnessed by the expression *figurative* language and *figure* of style. It is as if metaphor gives a body, a contour, a face to discourse ... But how? It seems to me, it is in the moment of the emergence of a new meaning from the ruins of literal predication that imagination offers its specific mediation. In order to understand this, let us begin with Aristotle's famous remark that 'to make good metaphors ... is to see similarity.' But one is mistaken about the role of resemblance if one interprets it in terms of the association of ideas, as association by resemblance (as opposed to association by contiguity which would rule metonymy and synecdoche). This resemblance is itself a function of the use of bizarre predicates. It consists of the *rapprochement* which suddenly abolishes the logical distance between previously remote semantic fields in order to engender the semantic clash which, in turn, creates the spark of meaning of metaphor. Imagination is the apperception, the sudden insight, of a new predicative pertinence, specifically a pertinence within impertinence. One could speak here of *predicative assimilation*, in order to underline by the word 'assimilation,' on the one hand, that it is not a question of a passively recorded similitude, but of an active operation, coextensive with the *rapprochement* performed by the metaphorical statement, and, on the other hand, by the word 'predicative' that the entire weight of the operation rests on the copula of the metaphorical statement: X is like Y.

This predicative assimilation enables the imagination to work as 'to see' ... 'to see similarity.'

But why to see and not to think? Or rather, why is thinking posited as seeing?

This is the case for a fundamental reason which pertains precisely to the logical nature of the predicative assimilation in the case of the metaphor. Several others have stressed the paradoxical character of this predicative assimilation which approximates Gilbert Ryle's category–mistake, which consists of presenting the facts of one category in the idioms appropriate to another. Every metaphor, in bringing together two previously distant semantic fields, strikes against a prior categorization, which it shatters. Yet, the idea of semantic impertinence preserves this: an order, logically antecedent, resists, and is not completely abolished by, the new pertinence. In effect, in order that there be a metaphor, it is necessary that I continue to perceive the previous incompatibility through the new compatibility. Therefore, predicative assimilation contains a new sort of tension, one no longer solely between subject and predicate, but between incompatibility and the new compatibility. Remoteness persists in closeness. This is why to see similarity is to see the likeness in spite of the difference. To speak of one thing in terms of another which resembles it is to pronounce them alike and unlike. Imagination – in its semantic sense – is nothing but this 'competence' which consists of producing the genre through the difference, again not beyond the difference, as in the concept, but in spite of the difference.

Imagination is that stage in the production of genre, where the generic relationship has not acceded to the quietness of the concept, but lives in the conflict of 'proximity' and 'distance.' We have arrived here at what Gadamer calls metaphoricity in general, which is a better name for this stage of apperception of the generic relationship. Metaphor is the figure of style which enables the preparatory stage to interrupt conceptual formation because, in the metaphorical process, the movement towards genre is arrested by the resistance of the difference and, in some way, intercepted by the figure of rhetoric.

Imagination thus identified is doubtless the productive, schematizing imagination. The benefit of a semantic theory of imagination lies precisely in approaching the image through its verbal nucleus, then proceeding from the verbal to the non-verbal, from the semantic to the sensible, and not vice versa. Treated as schema, the image is, in the words of Bachelard, a being of language. Before being a tarnished percept, it is a nascent signification. Here, one could adopt the term 'icon' to designate this aspect of the image which is homogeneous with language. Icon is to language what schema is to concept. In the same way that the schema is the matrix of the category, the icon is the matrix of the new semantic pertinence which is born of the collapse of the semantic kinds under the clash of contradiction. In short, I would say that the icon is the schematization of metaphorical attribution.

One will object that schema is not image. That is true. But one could understand how schema is displayed in images, in the same way that the metaphorical attribution is articulated in the schema. The path we follow is that which Kant has opened in the theory of schematism when he defined the schema as 'a universal procedure of imagination in providing an image for a concept.[2] In the schema, the liaison between logical component and sensible component, or, if one prefers, between the verbal and the non-verbal movement of the image, is effectuated. The theory of metaphor furnishes the exemplary occasion for recognizing the insertion of the psychological into the semantic. It is necessary to acknowledge that this transition is delicate. The tradition of the image as picture is so strong that one is tempted to see in the image an intrinsic factor with regard to discourse. Image remains a mental representation 'associated' from without with the linguistic message, unless it adds whatever it is to the information already conveyed by the message. But if one starts with the schema–image, one could understand that it is in producing some images that the predicative assimilation is schematized. It is in giving a body to images that discourse produces the alterations of distance, the semantic *rapprochement* of which the unusual attribution consists.

The deployment of schema in image has been implicitly recognized by all the theoreticians who have recognized in metaphor not only a tension between semantic fields, but also a tension between the levels of effectuation of the ideas brought together. 'The tropes through resemblance,' writes Fontanier, 'consist in presenting one idea under the sign of another more striking or better known idea, which, moreover, is bound to the first by no other bond than that of a certain conformity or analogy.'[3] I.A. Richards, in *The Philosophy of Rhetoric*, expresses this difference between the levels of abstraction as a harmony between *tenor* and *vehicle*. The metaphor is neither tenor nor vehicle, but their indissoluble unity. Moreover, the same correspondence could be expressed in some other metaphors of the metaphor: lens, grid, screen, and stereoscopic vision. Consequently, to form an image is not to have an image, in the sense of having a mental representation; instead, it is to read, through the icon of a relation, the relation itself. Image is less 'associated' than evoked and displayed by the schematization. Language remains the bearer of the predicative relation, but in schematizing and illustrating itself in a pictorial manner, the predicative relation can be read through the image in which it is invested. The seeing created by language is therefore not a seeing of this or that; it is a 'seeing-as.' This 'seeing-as' has little to do with the Humean image, image as a simple residue of an impression. To see-as is to apprehend the meaning alluded to in a display of regulated images.

Image thus evoked or excited is not exactly the kind of 'free' image with which associationistic psychology deals. The experience of *reading* suggests, instead, that images which exercise the iconic function with regard to nascent significations are 'bound' images, i.e., images engendered by poetic diction itself. This is because the poet is an artisan of language, who, by the sole means of language, produces and shapes images. 'Free' images, presenting the character of occurring images described by classical psychology – images as pictures – are instead interruptions and diversions to reading. It is when we stop ourselves from reading and *dream* that we see in our mind's eye scenes, pictures which escape the control of the meaning that they interrupt or divert. At the lower limit we rejoin the fascinating image described by Sartre as the self-deceptive attempt to possess magically the object of desire. But this last step represents a sort of relaxing of all the semantic tensions which constitute the metaphorical process.

The intermediate level of depiction is therefore the most interesting, *between* what we have called the schematization of the metaphorical attribution and the 'free' (or even 'wild') image. This intermediate level is what Bachelard had in mind when he spoke of 'reverberation.' It is also what Marcus B. Hester describes in *The Meaning of Poetic Metaphor*. To read a poem, he says, is not only to bind 'sense' and 'sensa,' as most poeticians have put it, but 'sense' and 'images' as well. In order to account for the role of these images bound by meaning, he transposes Wittgenstein's analysis of 'seeing-as' from the plane of the perception and the interpretation of perceived figures to the plane of reading and the interpretation of the read poem. To read meaning into the images is to see the meaning as that which the image describes.

Thus understood, the role of the imagination is not merely an accessorial one and the role of reverberation not a secondary phenomenon. If, on the one hand, the free image seems to weaken and disperse meaning into floating reverie, then, on the other hand, the bound image introduces into the whole process an effect of neutralization, in a word, a negative moment, thanks to which the entire phenomenon of reading is placed in a dimension of unreality, the neutralized atmosphere of fiction. The ultimate role of the image is not only to diffuse meaning across diverse sensorial fields, to *hallucinate* thought in some way, but, on the contrary, to effect a sort of *epoché* of the real, to suspend our attention to the real, to place us in a state of non-engagement with regard to perception or action, in short, to suspend meaning in the neutralized atmosphere to which one could give the name of the dimension of fiction. In this state of non-engagement we try new ideas, new values, new ways of being-in-the-world. Imagination is this free play of possibilities. In this state, fiction can, as we said above, create a *redescription* of reality. But this positive function of fiction, of which the *epoché* is the negative condition, is understood only when the fecundity of the imagination is clearly linked to that of language, as exemplified by the metaphorical process. In that case, we grasp this truth: we *see* some images only to the extent that we first *hear* them.

III. Painting and Image

We can now approach the central paradox of the theory of fiction, namely, that only the image which does not already have its referent in reality is able to display a world. This paradox is the paradox of productive reference. But, as we suggested in the introduction to this paper, fiction reveals its ability to transform or transfigure reality only when it is inserted into something as a labour, in short, when it is a work. Thus we are referred to the primary meaning of the word fiction: *fictio* comes from *facere*. When the image is made, it is also able to remake a world. It is at this stage that the break with philosophic tradition is most difficult to perform and preserve. The constant tendency of classical philosophy to reduce fiction to illusion closes the way to any ontology of fiction. Kant himself has rendered this step most difficult both in insisting on the subjectivity of the judgment of taste and in placing fiction within the aesthetics of genius. It is finally to the reflecting judgment that fiction is relegated for him. As for the Sartrean conception of the imagination, we have seen to what extent it overemphasizes the function of absence and negativity in order to underscore the capacity of freedom to make itself absent from the world.

In this third section, we will take *painting* as the principal paradigm of this power of fiction to transform. The choice is doubly motivated. To begin with, it allows us to extend to non-linguistic symbols the theory of fiction which had first been broached in the previous analysis of the poetic image. But above all, the example of painting clearly shows in what sense fiction must be a labour and must be embodied in a work in order that reality in its turn be worked by it.

In thus taking a point of departure outside of the sphere of language, we make it possible to include two partial analyses, those of the poetic image and the pictorial fiction, under a larger category. This larger category could be called the iconic function, or, to be more precise, the iconographic function, in order to underline the profound relationship between this function of the image and the graphic nature of writing, as François Dagognet has brilliantly demonstrated in his work *Ecriture et iconographie* (1973).

In thus linking the vicissitudes of the icon to those of writing, we are taking seriously Plato's argument in the *Phaedrus* (274c–277a).[4]

The attack is inserted within a myth concerning the origin of the major inventions of culture: numbers, geometry, astronomy, games of chance, and *grammata* (written characters). One god, Theuth, is credited with having given these to man. Thamus, king of Thebes, inquires of him as to the powers and benefits of his inventions. Concerning letters, Theuth answers that written signs would make the Egyptians wiser and give them better memories. But, the king replies, souls would actually become more forgetful for having placed their confidence in 'external marks' instead of cultivating, in themselves and by themselves, true recollection. As for their 'instructional' value, written signs supply not reality but only its semblance, not wisdom, but only apparent knowledge. Then Socrates adds: 'I cannot help feeling, Phaedrus, that writing is unfortunately like painting: for the creations of the painter have the attitude of life, and yet if you ask them a question they preserve a solemn silence.' The spoken word also, when one questions it, 'always gives one unvarying answer.' Furthermore, written words can circulate anywhere, little caring with whom they come in contact; and when a quarrel is raised or they are unjustly scorned, they find 'they have no parent to protect them; and they cannot protect or defend themselves.' An intelligent word, on the other hand, is accompanied by wisdom and, being 'graven in the soul of the learner, can defend itself, and knows when to speak and when to be silent.' 'You mean,' Phaedrus asks, 'the living word of knowledge which has a soul, and of which the written word is properly no more than an image?' 'Yes,' replies Socrates, 'of course that is what I mean.'

Thus, for Plato, images are less than reality, composed of simple shadows. As for paintings, they are shadows of shadows, supposing it true that sensible things are already themselves shadows of the real.

The thesis which I want to elaborate here, and incorporate within the problematic of fiction, is that images created by the talent of the artist are not less real but more real because they *augment* reality. It is here that Dagognet introduces the concept of *iconic augmentation* in order to characterize the power of the image to condense, spell out, and develop reality. He opposes this iconic augmentation to the simple function of reduplication in shadow-images. Resorting to the vocabulary of thermodynamics, he states that if shadows express the entropic tendency towards the equalization and effacement of enegetic differences in the world, iconic activity merits the name 'negentropic' in so far as it stems the inclination to entropy and fights against the tendency to annul contrasts and differences in the universe. This remarkable way of putting in new terms the ancient problem of the productive imagination only has meaning if one is able to defeat the Platonic argument. This one can do if one is able to juxtapose writing and painting for purposes of mutual clarification, and if one apprehends the dialectic of externality that they have in common. Painting, in effect, keeps the analysis from turning its back on the classic problematic of the mental image conceived as an entity internal to the mind and of familiar character. Painting presents to thought a kind of image which is, at first glance, public because it is essentially external. It is exactly on this point that writing and painting pose a similar problem (as Plato had perfectly perceived, but in order to condemn them together). Their error, he said, was in entrusting thought to 'external marks.' Yet, the history of the adventures of man as painter suggests, instead, that it is precisely the exteriorization of thought in external marks which has encouraged the creation of images which not only are shadows or similarities, but also offer new models for perceiving the world. If some promotion of reality results from this adventure, it is primarily because projects, human designs, have been externalized in a material medium.

To this notion of a material medium corresponding to what Plato called 'external marks' we now need to link the concept of work. The second idea implied by the concept of iconic augmentation is that the surplus which fiction engenders is tied not only to the choice of a material medium but also to the construction of an instrument essentially destined to abridge and condense the relevant traits of reality. It is sufficient to consider that a picture is enclosed in a frame which delimits a minute segment of space in order that, as if through a window, the immensity of the world may appear. However, this condensation, which makes a miniature of all painting, is a question not only of scale and size, but of parsimony in the usage of what we have just called relevant traits as well.

It is now writing which can facilitate our understanding of painting. In effect, what occurs in painting is entirely comparable to the invention of the phonetic alphabet through a succession of stages, from pictograms and hieroglyphics to ideograms and the phonetization of the alphabet. The history of this invention clearly shows that the capacity to express thought in writing was constantly enhanced by the progressive reduction of the number of elementary signs. This process of abbreviation appears to be a decisive condition of all iconic augmentation, for it is in abridging his alphabet that man simultaneously increases the generative power contained in the combinative resources of the completed ensemble of discrete units. In the same manner, the progress and change which one can observe in the history of painting are linked to some inventions comparable to that of the alphabet and offering the same character of conciseness, distinctiveness, and combinative power. Painting also appears to be an attempt to capture the universe in a web of abridged signs. I certainly do not mean to obliterate the considerable difference between verbal and non-verbal messages. However, if Plato has not erred completely in comparing painting and writing, we are not entirely mistaken when we attempt to vindicate one by the other. Their manifest difference can be subsumed under a general function of iconicity, and it is the structure of this general function which is in question here. The problem, in this sense, is similar to that addressed by Nelson Goodman in *Languages of Art*. For him the symbols of art and of language also have in common the same pretension to 'remake reality' ('Reality Remade' is the title of his first chapter). The differences between what he calls the discrete symbols of language and the dense symbols of the plastic arts can be placed within the unique framework of what he calls the symbolic function and what we have here called the iconic function.

What would be the concrete procedures of painting which one could compare to the abbreviation of the alphabet? A complete response to this question would entail a detailed discussion of highly technical problems. I will, therefore, confine myself to two or three particularly instructive examples suggested by the reading of Dagognet. Let us first consider what is implied by the invention of oil paint by Flemish painters in the fifteenth century. In mixing coloured pigments with oil and, consequently, in selecting a new range of materials, they were able to meet the challenge presented by the erosion of colour oppositions in ordinary vision and to fight against the tendency of visual qualities to be neutralized, of their boundaries to be blunted, and of their contrasts to be blurred. Among all their strategies, the way in which they intertwined depth refraction and surface reflection reveals that, with labour, the luminosity of the universe can be re-created. Painting, with them, remains mimetic in the sense that aspects of the reality are restored, but painting reaches its goal only under the condition of inventing the medium of that mimesis. Ever since, imitation is no longer a reduplication of reality but a creative rendering of it.

One could make a similar analysis of the art of impressionism. At the time of the invention of photography – which, by the way, is never a simple replica of reality, even in its less imaginative forms – the problem was to capture something other than the alleged objective dimensions of proportion, form, and colour and to hold the transitory and the fleeting by means of a magic of correspondences. Once again, reality was remade, but this time with an accent on atmospheric values and luminous appearances.

These two examples, even very modestly commented on, suffice to lead us to the threshold of what I have called the paradox of iconic augmentation. The more imagination deviates from that which is called reality in ordinary language and vision, the more it approaches the heart of the reality which is no longer the world of manipulable objects, but the world into which we have been thrown by birth and within which we try to orient ourselves by projecting our innermost possibilities upon it, in order that we *dwell* there, in the strongest sense of that word. But this paradox is only sustainable if we happen to concede that we have to amend not only our ideas as to what an image is, but also our prejudices as to what reality is. Under the shock of fiction, reality becomes problematic. We attempt to elude this painful situation by putting beyond criticism a concept of reality according to which the 'real' is what our everyday interests project upon the horizon of the world. This prejudice is not displaced but reinforced by our scientific culture in that for science, reality is what science declares it to be; only scientific discourse denotes reality. Consequently, poetry and painting do not denote, but are content to display some subjective connotations totally lacking in truth-claims.

It is this double prejudice of ordinary language and of the popular conception of science which the concept of iconic augmentation shatters. Because we have seen paintings we can now perceive the universe as landscape. Painting enables us to see the world in another way; it augments our vision of the world. Employing another language suggested by the theory of models and by the work of Mary Hesse in *Models and Analogies in Science*, we may say that fiction redescribes reality. One sort of language describes reality; then, as an outcome of the crisis in the vision of things supported by this first language, a second sort of language arises to redescribe the world.

If we now join the two halves of the present analysis, we can, without hesitation, apply to poetry what we have just said of painting. Poetry, even more than painting, appears at first sight to be a retreat of language into itself, a pure and simple abolition of reality. But, what is denied by poetry is the ordinary vision of reality as it is described in ordinary language. This suspension is the condition for the emergence of new dimensions of experience and reality, exactly those which are redescribed by fiction. In this manner, what we have called iconic augmentation is the rule for poetic language as well as painting. It is in this way that we retrieve one of Aristotle's affirmations in the *Poetics*. Tragedy – which for him is poetry *par excellence* – is a *mimesis* of reality, but under the condition that the poet creates a new mythos of this reality. Thus mimesis is not simply reduplication but creative reconstruction by means of the mediation of fiction.

Conclusion

In conclusion, I would like to say a word about the further steps which I believe should be taken in order to liberate the theory of fiction from the yoke of imagination as picture. We have just considered the first two steps. One concerned the shift from the framework of perception to that of language; the second, the link between fiction and work. Our contention was that only imagination at work – in a work – could produce a world out of itself. But the liberation of the theory of fiction would not be complete without taking two other steps. Although this will not be done in any complete way here, I would at least like to hint at what they involve.

The third step would be the most decisive. It would be to overthrow the prejudice that it is only in poetry, in the plastic arts, and, in general, in the kinds of works with which aesthetics is concerned that imagination is productive. This prejudice is very often perpetuated by aestheticians themselves who renounce all truth-claims for the arts. They agree too easily with the description which assigns denotation to science and reserves connotation for the arts, meaning by this last expression that the arts merely evoke feelings, emotions, and passions devoid of any ontological weight. Nothing is more harmful for a sound recognition of the productive reference of the imagination than this dichotomy between the sciences and the arts. Therefore, the denial of the dichotomy between poetic imagination and epistemologic imagination would be the active principle of this further inquiry. Our task, consequently, would be to extend the concept of fiction beyond language and the plastic arts, and to acknowledge the work of the analogies, models, and paradigms in the conceptual field of scientific knowledge. The ground for this extension has already been prepared by the interpretation of metaphor in terms of semantic innovation. If metaphor is not merely decorative device, then it has already escaped any emotionalist theory. It could even provide a clue for what happens in the scientific sphere with the 'displacement of concepts' (in the words of Donald Schon) or the explanatory function of models (this time using an expression of Mary Hesse). But this extension of the theory of metaphor to that of models is only one side of the coin. Models, in turn, provide us with the most accurate account of what we have attempted to describe as productive reference. To the extent that models are not models of ... i.e., still pictures of a previously given reality, but models for ... i.e., heuristic fictions for redescribing reality, the work of the model becomes, in turn, a model for construing in a meaningful way the concept of the productive reference of all fictions, including the so-called poetic fictions. Thus, if the metaphorical process is the key to the *transfer* of meaning proper to all displacement of concepts, the work of the model shows the way in which poetic fictions themselves effect the metamorphosis of reality. The creative *mimesis* of reality proceeding from the poetic *mythos* would be, in the terms of this analysis, a case of redescription by models.

One further extension of this problematic should be tried. This fourth step in a theory of fiction freed from picture would deal with another dichotomy, that of *theory* and *praxis*, and would attempt to overcome it within a general theory of fiction. Ideology and utopia would provide a concrete context for this inquiry. (Elsewhere,[5] I have explored the possible application of the dialectics between fiction and picture to the sphere of cultural phenomena.)

These, then, are four steps to be taken to liberate fiction from its bondage to picture. It must not be forgotten, however, that moving in this way entails, as its negative moment, the struggle against the profound prejudices of ordinary language and of philosophy, both ancient and modern. Yet, there is something positive to be gained by this liberation of fiction. It is that new realities become open to us and old worlds are made new.

Notes

1 See Gaston Bachelard's *Poetics of Space* (Boston: Beacon Press, 1969), p. xxi; 'retentissement' in French
2 *Critique of Pure Reason*, trans. by Norman Kemp Smith (New York: St Martin's Press, 1929, p. 182
3 Pierre Fontanier, *Les Figures du discours* (1830; Paris: Flammarion, 1968)
4 The text used here is B. Jowett's translation of *The Dialogues of Plato*, Vol. I (New York: Random House, 1970)
5 See my contribution to the Symposium on 'Humanness' held at Ohio University in 1974. My paper 'Ideology and Utopia as Social Imagination' is published in *Being Human in a Technological Age*, ed. by O.M. Borchert and D. Stewart (Athens: Ohio University Press, 1979), pp. 107–25

Mimesis and
Representation

For contemporary philosophy, representation is a great culprit. Some philosophers even speak of a representative illusion, just as Kant spoke of a transcendental illusion. This representative illusion allegedly stems from the impossible claim of uniting the interiority of a mental image in the mind and the exteriority of something real that would govern from outside the play of the mental scene within a single entity or 'representation.' The illusory nature of this claim is said to be even clearer if one says that the interior presence and the exterior presence can be made present to each other through some process of adequation which would define the truth of the representation. Representation, accordingly, it is said, should be denounced as the reduplication of presence, as the re-presenting of presence.

My project will be to try to extricate representation from the impasse to which it has been relegated, to return it to its field of play, without, however, in any way weakening the critique I have just mentioned. I shall attempt to do this by tying its fate to that of the term *mimesis*, which seems to me less shut-in, less locked-up, and richer in polysemy, hence more mobile and more mobilizing for a sortie out of the representative illusion.

I do not think I am being arbitrary in giving myself the right to appeal to a mimetic opening to the closure of representation. After all, Erich Auerbach gave his important post-war book, *Mimesis*, the subtitle: 'The Representation of Reality in Western Literature.' And just recently, several intrepid French translators of Aristotle's *Poetics* have not hesitated in translating his term *mimesis* by the term 'representation.'

What polysemic resources does *mimesis* have that may assist us in emigrating from the closure of representation? The rupture initiated by the Aristotelian use of the term in relation to the Platonic one is already instructive. As is well known, Plato made an almost unlimited use of this word and particularly one that is easily interpreted in terms of a redoubled presence, works of art and of language being taken for weakened copies of things, whereas the things themselves borrow whatever tenor of meaning they have from their intelligible models, the Ideas. In Aristotle, there is a twofold rupture with this usage. On the one hand, for Aristotle *mimesis* takes place only within the area of human action, or production, or *poiesis*. It is an operation, as is indicated by the *-sis* ending that it shares with *poiesis* and with some other terms that we shall consider below. Accordingly, for Aristotle, there is *mimesis* only where there is *poiesis*. On the other hand, far from producing a weakened image of pre-existing things, *mimesis* brings about an augmentation of meaning in the field of action, which is its privileged field. It does not equate itself with something already given. Rather it produces what it imitates, if we continue to translate *mimesis* by 'imitation.' This idea of a creative imitation will be the central concern of my whole discussion that follows.

At the same time, this double break in the use of *mimesis* between Plato and Aristotle offers a particularly noteworthy example of an early fissuring of the specular model of representation. This mutation in the meaning of the term *mimesis* is linked to its being applied just to works of art and to its privileged application to such verbal arts as Greek epic, tragedy, and comedy; that is, to those modes of discourse which today we discuss in terms of the theory of narrative. Within this one micro-universe of discourse, *mimesis* is the *mimesis* of an action, and what makes such imitating a *poiesis*, i.e., a productive activity, is the activity of arranging incidents into a plot: the activity of emplotment that Aristotle calls *mythos*. Here, too, Aristotle displaced the meaning of another Greek word, a pre-Platonic one this time. He uses the term *mythos* strictly – at least in the *Poetics* – to designate the working of *mimesis*, that is, the act of composing, bringing together, and arranging the incidents into a unique and complete action. Thus, chapter six of the *Poetics* defines *mythos* as *sýnthesis tôn pragmáton*, the arrangement of the incidents.

Our problem has now become more precise: how is it possible that the activity of emplotment constitutes at the same time the imitation of an action? In other words, how may we bring together *mythos* and *mimesis*, where *mythos* is the synthesis of incidents into one story and *mimesis* is the imitation of action? At least one negative response may already be set aside. It cannot be a question of imitation as a copy, reflection, replica, or however one might wish to state it. The poet imitates or represents to the extent that he or she is a maker, a composer of plots. The three terms *poiesis*, *sustasis* (which can be substituted for *mythos*), and *mimesis* thus form a chain that has to do with *praxis*, where each term must be understood in terms of its relations to the others.

Once removed from the enchanted precincts of re-presented presence, *mimesis* may deploy for us, on the level of the modern theory of narrative, a range of meaning liberated from the representative illusion by its being qualified in terms of *praxis*. I would like to suggest that we attempt to articulate this polysemy of *mimesis* in terms of three moments, which I shall playfully, yet seriously, call $mimesis_1$, $mimesis_2$, and $mimesis_3$. The pivot term is obviously $mimesis_2$ – I mean the stage issuing from the split *mimesis* brings about within the empire of *poiesis*, a term that, as we have seen, covers all artificial fabrication and production. Word artisans, I shall say, do not produce things but just quasi things. They invent the 'as if.' In this median sense, the term *mimesis* is the emblem of that split [*décrochage*] that opens up the world of fiction, or, to use current vocabulary, that institutes the literariness of the literary work. Aristotle ratifies this pivotal sense when he says, 'the plot *is* the imitation of the action.'

I in no way propose to eliminate this interpretation of *mimesis* as a kind of simulacre, something 'quasi,' or 'as if.' For here is the birth of the world of fiction, in the sense precisely that fiction is *fingere*, to feign and figure, or better configure, if we keep in mind the operation of composing – of the *sustasis* of – poetic discourse. My proposal is rather to frame this leap into fiction with the two operations I am calling $mimesis_1$ and $mimesis_2$, which constitute, so to speak, the upstream and the downstream sides [*l'amont et l'aval*] of *mimesis* as fiction. By so doing, I propose to show that $mimesis_2$ gets its intelligibility from its mediating function, which is to lead the text from one side to the other, to transfigure the one side into the other by its configurating power.

In this, my enterprise differs from what many theoreticians of the text call textural semiotics. In my opinion, these theoreticians build upon an abstraction, that of $mimesis_2$, by considering only the internal laws of the literary work. It is the task of hermeneutics, on the contrary, to reconstruct the set of operations by means of which a work arises from the opaque depths of living, acting, and suffering, to be given by an author to readers who receive it and thereby change their own actions. For a semiotic theory that abstracts from this whole span of meaning, the work is constituted as an interior that alone is relevant, while the two sides are the irrelevant exterior. The antecedent side of fiction is referred to as merely the psychobiography of the author, while the second side is taken as merely the psycho-sociology of the reception of literary works. For this kind of textual semiotics, in other words, the only remaining operative concept is that of the literary text. For hermeneutics, on the contrary, which seeks to reconstruct the whole arc of operations by which practical experience is turned into works, authors, and readers, there is neither an inside nor an outside to the work – the distinction of inside and outside being a methodological artefact – instead, there is a concrete process in which the textual configuration conjoins the practical prefiguration and the practical transfiguration.

As a corollary to this, at the end of our analysis the reader will appear as that operator *par excellence* who takes up the unity of the whole traversal from *mimesis*$_1$ to *mimesis*$_3$ by way of *mimesis*$_2$ through his or her doing something: reading.

Mimesis$_1$

Let us therefore begin by considering *mimesis*$_1$. Why should we claim that understanding *mimesis*$_2$ requires a side of the text that is already a form of *mimesis*? To see why, let us return to Aristotle's key expression which says that the poem is the imitation of action. He makes this more specific by adding that it is not so much a question of an imitation of human beings acting, as it is of their action, as such, in so far as it leads to good or bad fortune. It is this acting that implies the 'characters' of this or that quality and the 'thoughts' which are given an appropriate language. Now the simple mentioning of an action brings into play the pre-understanding common to the poet and his or her public of what action, or rather acting, signifies. It is this familiarity, this prior acquaintance with the order of action that, by way of the mediation of fiction, will be intensified, magnified, and, in the strong sense of the word, transfigured.

It should not be objected that there is nothing to be said about this pre-understanding because it lacks form, structure, and meaning. Instead, allow me to call our attention to three major traits of what I have just called the order of action, traits which we have always already understood when we enter a fiction.

The first trait is that the intelligibility engendered by emplotment finds its first anchorage in our competence for using in intelligible ways such terms as project and intention, motive and reason for action, circumstance, obstacle and occasion, agent and capacity to do something, interaction, adversary and helper, conflict and co-operation, amelioration and deterioration, success and failure, happiness and misfortune. All these terms mutually signify one another. To use any one of them in an appropriate way implies having mastered the whole network of practical categories by means of which the semantics of action is distinguished from that of physical movement and even from psychophysiological behaviour. This knowing how to do something constitutes a 'repertory' common to the writer and his or her reader, and it inaugurates between them a community of meaning preliminary to any entering into fiction. This repertory attests to the fact that the condition of action and suffering, far from being ineffable, is always already understood.

A second trait allows us to understand what it is about such doing something, such being able to do something, and such knowing how to do something that makes possible, and even perhaps calls for, the transposition into fiction. If human action can be recounted and poeticized, in other words, it is due to the fact that it is always articulated by signs, rules, and norms. To use a phrase from Clifford Geertz, human action is always symbolically mediated. An intentional activity of poetic representation can be grafted to these symbolic mediations because they already confer a basic readability on action. To understand a rite, for example, is to be capable of tying together the structured set of conventions thanks to which a gesture of the hand, say, counts as a salutation, a benediction, or a supplication. In this sense, symbols sometimes function as rules for interpreting action. So, before being themselves submitted to interpretation, symbols are sometimes interpretants – to use C.S. Peirce's term – internal to human action. Properly representative symbols are added to such constitutive symbols to augment their readability.

The third trait brings us up to the confines of fiction. The pre-understanding of the order of action has temporal characteristics upon which the narrative time proper to fiction grafts its own configurations. Stephen Crites has even spoken in this regard of a 'narrative quality of experience.' And, in the last chapter of Heidegger's *Being and Time*, we find a phenomenological description of the first threshold that such temporality – even though still inauthentic temporarily – crosses in going beyond the simple succession of 'nows' that characterizes the vulgar representation of linear time. Without reaching the depths of the abyss of mortal time, this time, which is the time of works and days, is the time with which we count and measure, and we can measure only because we can first reckon with it. It is the time for doing this or that, the time that can be won or lost. In a word, it is the time 'in' which we live and act.

I have said that this temporal trait illumines the transition from *mimesis*$_1$ to *mimesis*$_2$. It might be objected that it already expresses the structuring action of narrative time on lived experience. Nevertheless, I shall maintain, without fearing the apparently vicious circle involved, the thesis of a narrative or pre-narrative quality of experience as such. As evidence of this, I would like to refer to some important forms of experience whose point is preserved in our ordinary language. For example, we speak of a life story, as though life were a story in search of a narrator. In the same way, Hannah Arendt, in her magnificent work *The Human Condition*, distinguished action, properly speaking, from labour and from work by means of the fact that action is what calls for narration, as though any action worthy of the title expects no other confirmation than fame and glory. Similarly, we speak of stories we are caught up in or entangled in, and which we find it difficult to relate. Here I am thinking of the fine title of a book by Wilhelm Schapp: *In Geschichten verstrickt*. From such 'being implicated' in stories that happen to us emerge from the depths of our lives the stories we tell. Whatever may be the status of these stories which somehow are prior to the narration we may give them, our mere use of the word 'story' (taken in this pre-narrative sense) testifies to our pre-understanding that action is human to the extent it characterizes a life story that deserves to be told.

Mimesis$_1$ is this pre-understanding of what human action is, of its semantics, its symbolism, its temporality. From this pre-understanding which is common to poets and their readers arises fiction, and with fiction comes the second form of *mimesis* which is textual and literary. It is true that under the rule of fiction the pre-understanding of the world of action withdraws to the rank of being a 'repertory,' to speak as W. Iser does in his *The Act of Reading*, or to the rank of 'mention' as opposed to 'use,' to use another terminology more familiar to analytic philosophy. But it remains true that despite the break [*coupure*] it introduces, fiction would never be understandable if it did not configurate what is already figured in human action.

Mimesis₂

With *mimesis₂* we enter the field where modern poetics and semiotics apply. In part, but only in part, these prolong Aristotle's poetic theory. For him poets and poems imitate action only on the condition that they configure it according to specific rules of emplotment. Only in invented plots do such-and-such actions count as a beginning, a middle, or an end. Only in such plots does contingency count as *peripeteia*, or a reversal of fortune. Only in such plots does some new surprise count as recognition, or does this or that frightening or pitiable incident count as a complication of the plot, while still others count as its dénouement. *Mimesis*, at this stage, signifies the production of a quasi world of action through the activity of emplotment. Far from being an effigy or a replica of action, this emplotment is its intelligible schema [*épure*]. It imitates in that it is intelligible.

But what intelligibility is involved at this level of fiction? The possibility or impossibility of traversing our three stages of *mimesis* in a single movement depends on our answer to this question.

Modern semiotics offers one type of answer which rests solely on isolating the text. It does so for good reasons. Thanks to writing, and also thanks to emplotment, the narrative text acquires a semantic autonomy that cuts it off in three ways: first, from the presumed intention of its author; second, from the capacity of its first audience to receive it; third, from the socio-cultural conditions of its genesis. *Mimesis₂* is the emblem of this triple autonomy. In turn, this semantic autonomy engenders a profound alteration in the process of communication, as has been described by Roman Jakobson – an alteration that provides the step to what Jakobson calls the 'poetic function' at the expense of the 'referential' one, where the poetic function in the broad sense of this term means accentuating the message 'for its own sake.' Whereas ordinary language and scientific language depend on the extralinguistic reality that they describe, the poetic function suspends this concern for an external reference and turns language back on itself in order to celebrate itself, to use one of Roland Barthes's apt expressions. To accentuate this cutting function of *mimesis*₂ following modern semiotics, we might say that the semantic autonomy of the text and the poetic nature of language turned in upon itself engender a new type of relation between texts, an intertextuality which serves to cut fiction off from the world of actual action, in such a way that texts, in completing, correcting, quoting, and crossing out one another, form a closed chain, a library [*bibliothèque*] in the precise sense of this term. It follows, then, that the fiction of action, far from evaporating like a fleeting dream, takes on the consistency of a distinct universe, the literary universe.

Then, too, the distinction between outside and inside returns in force. Yet semioticians believe they have given up the representative illusion by having constituted the text as an inside without an outside, or rather as an inside whose outside (be it author, audience, or sociocultural circumstances) has become irrelevant. The referent of the text has become a function of the text. Within the narrative field, it is the narrated story as narrated and nothing more. Just as we can speak of an implied author or an implied audience, we must speak of a referential field implied by the text, which is sometimes called the 'world' of the text.

Having said this, we may again take up our question stemming from Aristotle's *Poetics:* If the plot is an intelligible schema of action, what intellegibility is involved?

Here, it seems to me, contemporary semiotics or poetics does not give the appropriate answer. The rationality of its models – I have in mind Greimas's narrative semiotics – to my mind provides only a simulation of the basic intelligibility preliminary to the activity of emplotment. This intelligibility is closer to the practical reasoning that Aristotle called *phronèsis* than to the logical reasoning that may be ascribed to theoretical thinking. It is the shift from the practical understanding to which emplotment pertains to the theoretical rationality which the 'logic of possible narratives' advocates that requires the shift from the surface of the text towards its deep syntax. This deep syntax is what governs the narrative codes that may be constructed on the basis of logical requirements that are as independent as possible of the surface narrative chronology. The transformative algorithms for moving from an initial state of affairs to a terminal one that preside over such a narrative logic are well known. Greimas, for example, holds that all the discursive operations of narrativity, that is, the transformative algorithms that lead from an initial state of affairs to a terminal one, can be engendered beginning from the relations of contrariety, contradiction, and supposition inscribed upon his famous 'semiotic square.' Every transformation, every interlinking of action segments, every conflict between narrative programs, and every transference of a valuable object are contained ideally in the one great topography that follows the semiotic square's lines of force, to the point of bringing them back to their starting-point and closing the square.

Hermeneutics, which I referred to earlier, is in no way opposed to this enterprise with its laws, its restrictions, its rigour, and its fecundity for research. It adds nothing to it. And it has nothing to teach it. What it does do is to interrogate the conditions of intelligibility of the rational process that presides over the whole process. It shows that semiotic rationality actually produces a new text, one constituted by the narrative codes inscribed in a new form of writing where the concrete narratives are taken to be only a manifestation of this new text. This new text does have its readers, but they are readers of codes rather than of messages; readers for whom the message is significant only as a 'display' of its immanent code. For these code readers, *mimesis* is not just the emblem of the text's semantic autonomy and its corollary intertextuality, but also the emblem of the reversal that submits the level of manifestation to that of immanence.

My thesis here is that this rationalizing operation stands in a parasitic relation to that first-order intelligibility which alone is capable of mediating between the two sides of the text. It is this form of intelligibility, this comprehending of narrative configurations, that I should like to describe now in terms of the mediation between the prefiguration of the world of action and its transfiguration – in other words, in terms of the mediation between $mimesis_1$ and $mimesis_3$.

To convey some idea of this ordering comprehension upon which the semiotician's codifying rationality is constructed as a metalanguage, I shall return to some of the traits of the plot, or rather of emplotment, in an Aristotelian perspective. These are those traits that give the initial intelligibility to the surface of the text which the semiotician then tries to reconstruct in terms of the requirements of another logical order.

The first one is that emplotment is an operation about which we may say equivalently either that it draws an intelligible story *from* the various events or incidents (what Aristotle calls the *pragmata*) or that it makes these events or incidents *into* a story. The reciprocal prepositions 'from' and 'into' characterize the plot as mediating between the events and the told story. An event, accordingly, must be more than a singular occurrence. It is qualified as an event by its contribution to the progression of the plot. A story, on the other hand, must be more than an enumeration of events in a series. It has to organize them into an intelligible whole.

Second, emplotment brings together such heterogeneous factors as circumstances, agents, interactions, ends, means, and unintended results. From this composition we get a synthetic comprehension in the act of 'following a story,' or better, in the act of retelling a story, to the extent that, in this second situation, we are less prey to the unexpected and more attentive to the way, as Marx would have put it, human beings make their history in circumstances they themselves have not made, and – I would add – with results they had not intended.

Third, emplotment mediates, from another point of view, the temporality proper to poetic composition. This temporality interweaves two temporal components: on the one hand, the pure, discrete, and interminable succession of what we may call the story's incidents; on the other hand, the aspect of integration, culmination, and closure brought about by what Louis O. Mink calls the act of narrative configuration. This act consists in 'grasping together' the details, or what we have called the incidents, of the story. From these diverse events it draws the unity of one temporal whole. We cannot overemphasize the kinship between this 'grasping together' proper to the configurating act and Kant's presentation of the operation of judging, where the transcendental meaning of a judgment consists not so much in joining a subject and a predicate as in placing some intuitive manifold under one concept.

This configurating act entails two other new traits which definitively mark the gap between the ordering comprehension at work in narrative composition and the codifying rationality proper to narrative semiotics. Still in a Kantian vein, we should not even hesitate in ascribing the configurating act to the productive imagination. This should be understood as a transcendental, not a psychological function. This productive imagination is not without its own rules and it lends itself to the type of typology of emplotment used by Northrop Frye in his *Anatomy of Criticism*. This typology of emplotment cannot be derived from a logic of narrative possibilities which has to be ascribed to a second-degree form of rationalization. The typology of emplotment arises rather from a schematism of the narrative function from which derives the categorical order semioticians use in their constructions, with the help of a logic that is unaware of the transcendental genesis of this schematism of emplotment.

In its turn, this schematism – and this will be the last trait with which I shall characterize narrative comprehension – does not share the atemporality of the logical and syntactical laws which the semioticians appeal to. Instead, this schematism is constituted within a history, a history that has all the characteristics of a *tradition*. By this, I do not mean the inert transmission of some dead deposit but the living transmission of an innovation that is always capable of being reactivated through a return to the most creative moments of poetic making.

This phenomenon of traditionality illumines the functioning of the narrative paradigms. Through the interplay of innovation and sedimentation, the production of individual works is revealed to be a much more complex phenomenon than the simple manifestation of a deep grammar indifferent to history. The paradigms that constitute a typology of emplotment – or, as we put it, of its schematism – have issued from a sedimented history whose genesis has been obliterated. This is why individual works can enter into a variable relation to these paradigms. The range of solutions is deployed between the two poles of servile repetition and calculated deviance, passing through all the degrees of systematic deformation. Folktales, myths, and traditional narratives in general stand close to the pole of repetition. This is why they constitute the privileged kingdom of structuralism. In the metalanguage of semiotics they can be reduced without excessive violence to the simple manifestation of the deep grammar constructed by the semiotician. But as soon as we move beyond such traditional narrative, deviance and a gap or separation become the rule. Thus the contemporary novel, for example, may in large part be defined as an anti-novel to the extent that disputing the paradigms prevails over simply varying their application.

This play with the constraints of the paradigms is what provides emplotment with its historicity. As a background to such play, the combining of sedimentation and invention defines traditionality, as such, on the basis of which we obey the models or experiment with them.

Such is the realm of *mimesis*$_2$ between the antecedence and the descendance of the text. At this level *mimesis* may be defined as the

configuration of action. This configuration is governed by a schematization that is historically structured in a tradition or traditions,
and it is expressed in individual works which stand in varying relations to the constraints generated by this schematism.

Mimesis₃

Now I should like to show how *mimesis₂*, when led back to its first-
order intelligibility, requires as its complement a third stage which
also is worthy of being called *mimesis*.

This stage corresponds to what Hans-Georg Gadamer, in his
philosophical hermeneutics, calls 'application.' And Aristotle himself suggests this third sense of *mimesis tēs práxeōs* at various places
in his *Poetics*, although he is less concerned with the audience there
than in his *Rhetoric*, where the theory of persuasion is entirely governed by the capacity of being received by the audience. Still, when
he says that poetry 'teaches' the universal, that tragedy 'arouses pity
and fear, effecting the proper purgation of these emotions, 'or even
when he refers to the pleasure we take in seeing frightening or
pitiable incidents which lead to that reversal of fortune that makes a
tragedy, he indicates that it is in the audience or the reader that the
process [*parcours*] of mimesis ends.

Generalizing beyond Aristotle, I shall say that *mimesis₃* marks the
intersection of the world of the text and the world of the hearer or
reader. Therefore it is the intersection of the world unfolded by
fiction and the world wherein actual action unfolds.

Some may be tempted to refuse the problem, to hold the question
of literature's impact on life as irrelevant. But then, paradoxically, on
the one hand, we ratify the positivism we ordinarily struggle against –
that is, the prejudgment that the real is the given, such as it can be
empirically observed and scientifically described – and, on the other
hand, we lock literature up in a world in itself and when it breaks out
as subversion, it turns against the moral and social order. We forget
that fiction is precisely what makes language that supreme 'danger,'
about which Walter Benjamin spoke with such awe and admiration,
following Hölderin.

Now the intersection between the configured world of the plot and
the transfigured world of the reader constitutes in itself a very
complex problematic. This is due first of all to the diversity of its
modalities. A whole range of cases is open, running from ideological

confirmation of the established order, as in official art, to social criticism, and even to derision for everything 'real.' Even the case of extreme alienation from the 'real' is another such intersection.

Next, the shock of the possible, which is not a lesser shock than is the shock of the 'real,' is required by the internal interplay within works between the received paradigms and the production of gaps by the deviance of individual works. In this sense, narrative literature models practical efficacity by its gaps as well as by its paradigms.

So we may take up again each of the three traits by means of which I characterized the pre-understanding of action: the network of intersignifications among practical categories, its immanent symbolic system, and above all its properly practical temporality. I shall say that each of these traits is intensified, that it is 'iconically augmented.'

I shall not dwell upon the first two traits. The intersignification among projects, circumstances, and chance is precisely what is put in order by the plot in so far as we have described it as a synthesis of what is heterogenous. As for the symbolization internal to action, we may say that it is exactly this that is resymbolized or desymbolized (or resymbolized through desymbolization) thanks to the schematism which is, in turn, traditionalized and subverted by the historicity of the paradigms. Most of all, however, it is the time of action that is transfigured through emplotment. In this regard, we ought to confront Augustine's analysis of experienced time – the *distentio animi*, the inner stretching out of the present – with the order inherent in emplotment. We would then see this order by turns denying then intensifying the *distentio animi*, without ever letting it come to rest. But even today when Joyce or Robbe-Grillet or Marguerite Duras mixes together all the ways of time, it is still always a more refined, a more unmade and remade, modelling that produces the narrative. And in this regard the paradox is that art skirts its own death whenever its systematic subversion of paradigms leads the work of art, by way of a resolute use of rule-governed deformations, to the repetition of the alleged fragmentation of our modern sense of time. Frank Kermode refers to this limit, which is doubtless never fully attained, in his *The Sense of an Ending*. It would be the case where the dissolution of every paradigm would lead to a situation that is no longer one of rule-governed deviance but rather of systematic schism, one where no schematization any longer appears to be at work. But at least we can say that the work iconically augments the *distentio animi* itself by making it over-signifying [*sur-significant*]. This again is a limit case of temporal modelling, but perhaps it is then, as I shall suggest in a moment, that the reader is invited to do the work that the artist delights in undoing.

If, therefore, we accept, as I think we must, the problematic of the reception of a work as an integral part of the constitution of its meaning, the question arises how we are to understand this final stage of *mimesis* and how we are to link it to the second one. This is where the pitfalls of representation are the most redoubtable and where the science of semiotics is least helpful to us. On the one side, we may be tempted to look at the 'teaching of the universal' as a description of what human action already essentially is. We then come back to the 'imitation copy' at a higher degree of subtlety. It is no longer what is accidental to action that is re-presented or made present anew but what is essential. I would like to show that my reinterpretation of *mimesis*$_2$ as a structuring operation or as a configurating act allows us both to escape this impasse of re-presentation and to think of the passage from *mimesis*$_1$ to *mimesis*$_3$ by way of *mimesis*$_2$ as one continuous operation.

To do this, we must cling to the language of *praxis* from one end to the other in order to escape the representative illusion. *Mimesis* is an action about action. What it prefigures in the first stage and configures in the second, it transfigures in the third. To transfigure is still to do something. To use the language of Nelson Goodman's *Languages of Art*, works of literature ceaselessly make and remake our world of action – the first chapter of this book is entitled 'Reality Remade.' Goodman also offers this maxim: think of works in terms of worlds, worlds in terms of works.

Using another language, I shall say that the transformation of action proceeds from what François Dagognet, in speaking of painting and writing, calls 'iconic augmentation,' by means of which the world signifies something more and does so in another manner. This transfiguration is the return on the prefiguration we spoke of in discussing *mimesis*$_1$. What is thereby iconically augmented is the preliminary readability that action owes to the interpretants that are already at work in it. Human action can be oversignified because it is already pre-signified by all the modalities of its symbolic articulation.

In an earlier work I said that poetry redescribes the world through its plot or *mythos*. Today, in order to distance myself from the representative illusion, I shall say that poetic making resignifies the world to the extent that recounting or narrating remakes action following the poem's invitation.

But how are we to overcome the constantly reborn and apparently invincible exteriority between the inside of fiction and the outside of life? There is just one way – dissolve the opposition between inside and outside, which itself arises from the representative illusion. We must stop seeing the text as its own interior and life as exterior to it. Instead we must accompany that structuring operation that begins in life, is invested in the text, then returns to life.

To do this, we must balance the autarchy of a theory of writing through a theory of reading and understand that the operating [*opérativité*] of writing is fulfilled in the operating of reading. Indeed, it is the reader – or rather the act of reading – that, in the final analysis, is the unique operator of the unceasing passage from *mimesis₁* to *mimesis₃* through *mimesis₂*. That is, from a prefigured world to a transfigured world through the mediation of a configured world.

This fulfilment of writing in reading is understandable only if we articulate the act of reading on the basis of the structuring activity of emplotment and not on the metalanguage of codifying rationality. The subordination we have proposed of semiotic rationality which thinks in terms of codes to narrative intelligibility centred on emplotment, schematization, and traditionality may contribute to our better hearing this connection of reading and writing.

The act of reading is what accompanies the configuration of the narrative and what actualizes its capacity for being followed. To follow a story is to actualize it by reading it.

And if emplotment can be described as an act of judgment and as an act of the productive imagination, as I have suggested, this occurs inasmuch as this act is the conjoint work of the text and its reader, just as Aristotle said that sensation is the common work of sensing and what is sensed.

It is also the act of reading that accompanies the interplay of innovation and sedimentation of the paradigms that schematize emplotment. In the act of reading, the recipient plays with the narrative constraints, brings about deviations, takes part in the fight between the novel and the anti-novel, and feels that pleasure Roland Barthes called the pleasure of the text.

Finally, it is the reader who completes the work in so far as, following Roman Ingarden and Wolfgang Iser, we say the written work is a sketch for the reader. Indeed, the written text may involve holes, lacunae, and indeterminate zones which, as in Joyce's *Ulysses*, defy the reader's capacity to configure the work which the author seemingly finds a mischievous pleasure in defiguring. In this extreme case, it is the reader, whom the work almost abandons, who bears the burden of emplotment.

So I maintain that the act of reading is that operation that conjoins *mimesis*$_3$ to *mimesis*$_1$ through *mimesis*$_2$. It is the final vector of the transfiguration of the world of action in terms of fiction.

To end this brief traversal of *mimesis*, I would like to raise the following questions and suggestions for further discussion.

1 / Can we keep the classical concept of reference – which I have forbidden myself using until now – for speaking about the transfiguring action of *mimesis*? Not if we take it in the sense of descriptive reference. But yes if we admit that *mimesis*$_3$ splits open descriptive reference and suggests that we forge the notion of a non-descriptive referential dimension. In that case, we must dare to form the paradoxical idea of a productive form of reference. The advantage of this paradox – which also has its drawbacks – is that it allows us to give the notion of reference its full amplitude. It also allows us to affirm as vehemently as possible that, in the final analysis, all discourse is about ... In other words, language never exists just for itself. Even when it seems to withdraw into itself, it still celebrates what it lifts above its confines.

2 / This shaking or breaking open of reference's claim to univocity has another effect as its corollary. It also affects our concept of the real. Earlier I also avoided as much as I could expressions such as the real or irreal world. I preferred to use, instead, the notion of efficacity, of effective action, keeping in mind one sense of the German term *Wirklich*, which is related to the verb *wirken*. However must we say that, at the stage of *mimesis*$_3$, the poem still imitates real action? Not if real means already there and available. But yes if real means that human action is 'effectively' refigured through the fact of being configured. Then the word real denotes the effectiveness of 'dangerous' speech, as when Solzhenitsyn's telling the story of the Gulag shatters our conventional view of death and life, of hatred and love; as when we say that the Word dwelt among us, was with us, and we did not receive him.

This point once again makes us feel the force of attraction

exercised on all our thinking by representation understood as re-presented presence. But it is also at this point that the interpretation of *mimesis* in terms of *praxis* resists most. According to this interpre-tation, the real is everything already prefigured that is also transfig-ured. The thought effort required here is considerable. We might even go so far as to say that for thinking there is a vanishing-point where invention and discovery can no longer be separated. And it is vain therefore to ask whether the universal that poetry 'teaches,' according to Aristotle, already existed before it was invented. It is as much found as invented. And once invented, it is recognized as that which, in one way or another, had to be brought to language. It is this kind of requirement in what must be said that torments and some-times even tortures the artist.

3 / My last question – or at least one more question – is whether we can still speak of truth at the level of *mimesis₃*. This question is even more redoubtable than those regarding reference and the real. Nelson Goodman, for example, holds that reference occurs wherever a symbolic system contributes to the making of a world. But he rejects the term truth as part of his theoretical language, admitting only 'rightness' and 'fitness.' He thereby thinks he can account for the artist's conviction that one way of 'rendering' the world is better than another. But why should we not say that the univocity of truth is also exploded by *mimesis* – to the point that it indicates this fitness, this appropriateness? Is it not the model of truth as adequation, the accomplice of the representative illusion, that blocks our way? I do admit, however, that we lack a sufficiently multivocal concept of truth, one that would fuse, at its margins, with the concept of right-ness. It is not even certain that Heidegger's substitution of truth as manifestation for truth as adequation responds to what *mimesis* demands of our thinking about truth. For is it still a matter of manifestation, there where there is a fitting production?

Mimesis, in this sense, is ahead of our concepts of reference, the real, and truth. It thus engenders a need as yet unfilled to think more. This is why I shall limit myself to a more modest conclusion, one that I shall express in terms of a wish. It is the wish that my deploying the meaning of *mimesis* be credited to representation's account; the wish that the concept of representation, upon which converge philosophy's most serious attempts to question itself, rediscovers, in turn, the polysemy and mobility that will make it available for new adventures of thinking.

Bibliography

Arendt, Hannah. *The Human Condition*. Chicago: University of Chicago Press, 1958

Aristotle. *La Poetique*. Ed. by R. Dupont-Roc and J. Lallot. Paris: Seuil, 1980

– *The Rhetoric and the Poetics*. New York: Random House, 1954

Auerbach, Erich. *Mimesis: The Representation of Reality in Western Literature*. Trans. by Willard R. Trask. Princeton: Princeton University Press, 1953

Augustine. *Confessions and Enchiridion*. Trans. by Albert C. Outler. Philadelphia: The Westminster Press, 1955

Barthes, Roland. *The Pleasure of the Text*. Trans. by Richard Miller. New York: Hill & Wang, 1975

Benjamin, Walter. *Illuminations*. New York: Schocken Books, 1969

Crites, Stephen. 'The Narrative Quality of Experience.' *Journal of the American Academy of Religion* 39 (1971): 291–311

Dagognet, François. *Ecriture et iconographie*. Paris: J. Vrin, 1973

Frye, Northrop. *Anatomy of Criticism*. Princeton: Princeton University Press, 1957

Gadamer, Hans-Georg. *Truth and Method*. Trans. and ed. by Garret Barden and John Cumming. New York: Seabury, 1975

Geertz, Clifford. *The Interpretation of Cultures: Selected Essays*. New York: Basic Books, 1973

Goodman, Nelson. *Languages of Art*. Indianapolis: Hackett, 1976

– *Ways of Worldmaking*. Indianapolis: Hackett, 1978

Greimas, A.-J. *Sémantique structurale: Recherche de méthode*. Paris: Larousse, 1966

– *Du Sens: Essais sémiotiques*. Paris: Seuil, 1970

Heidegger, Martin. *Being and Time*. Trans. by John Macquarrie and Edward Robinson. New York: Harper & Brothers, 1962

Ingarden, Roman. *The Literary Work of Art*. Trans. by George G. Grabowicz. Evanston: Northwestern University Press, 1973

Iser, Wolfgang. *The Act of Reading: A Theory of Aesthetic Response*. Baltimore: Johns Hopkins University Press, 1979

Jakobson, Roman. 'Closing Statements: Linguistics and Poetics.' In T.A. Sebeok, ed., *Style in Language*, pp. 350–77. Cambridge: MIT Press, 1960

Kant, Immanuel. *Critique of Pure Reason*. Trans. by Norman Kemp Smith. New York: St Martin's Press, 1965

– *Critique of Judgment*. Trans. by J.H. Bernard. New York: Hafner, 1966

Kermode, Frank. *The Sense of an Ending: Studies in the Theory of Fiction*. London: Oxford University Press, 1966

Mink, Louis O. 'Interpretation and Narrative Understanding.' *The Journal of Philosophy* 69 (1972): 735–7

– 'The Autonomy of Historical Understanding.' *History and Theory* 5 (1966): 24–57

Peirce, Charles Sanders. *Collected Papers,* Vol. 2: *Elements of Logic.* Cambridge: Harvard University Press, 1932

Ricoeur, Paul. 'The Human Experience of Time and Narrative.' *Research in Phenomenology* 9 (1979): 17–34

– 'The Narrative Function.' In *Hermeneutics and the Human Sciences.* Trans. by John B. Thompson, pp. 274–96. Cambridge: Cambridge University Press, 1981

– 'Narrative Time.' *Critical Inquiry* 7 (1980): 169–90

– 'Review of Nelson Goodman, *Ways of Worldmaking.' Philosophy and Literature* 4 (1980): 107–20

Schapp, Wilhelm. *In Geschichten verstrickt: Zum Sein von Mensch und Ding.* Hamburg: Meiner, 1953

II

The Dialectic of
Engagement

Habermas

In this paper I shall discuss Habermas's theory of ideology, which is presented in terms of a critique, a critique of ideology. I shall focus mainly on the parallelism claimed between psychoanalysis and the critique of ideology, since Habermas bases his theory of ideology on the transfer of some psychoanalytic insights into the field of the critical social sciences.

Before turning to this discussion, however, we need to situate the character of psychoanalysis and ideology-critique as critical social sciences. In establishing the distinctiveness of critical social sciences, Habermas moves from a twofold division between instrumental and practical sciences to a threefold division between instrumental, historical-hermeneutic, and critical social sciences. This change in Habermas's framework is set out in the appendix to *Knowledge and Human Interests*. The appendix does not belong to the German edition of *Knowledge and Human Interests*; it was added to the English translation.[1] This essay is the inaugural address Habermas delivered upon assuming his chair at Frankfurt in 1965, a chair he left only a few years later after receiving condemnation for his support of German student protests in the late 1960s. The appendix is addressed not to Marx but rather to the tradition of phenomenology in Husserl and its offshoot, the hermeneutics of Gadamer. While never named, Gadamer is clearly the major person the address is directed against. Habermas's threefold division of both knowledge-constitutive interests and their corresponding sciences is central to his response to Gadamer, who maintains a twofold division. A second reason for Habermas's formulation may be that this division comes from his friend and colleague Karl-Otto Apel. Apel is a much more systematic thinker, even an architectonic thinker.

Apel is interested more in epistemology, whereas Habermas's focus is the sociology of knowledge. When Habermas shifts from a sociology of knowledge to an epistemology, the discrepancy in framework may therefore be the change from his own portrayal of the former's duality between the instrumental and the practical to acceptance of Apel's tripartite characterization of the latter.

I shall not examine in any detail the first four sections of the appendix, because the critique of Husserl presented there is not very good. The sections are directed against the theoretical claims of philosophy, but it is a weak argument to oppose praxis to theory and to say that everything is theory which is not post-Marxist thought. Husserl is accused of committing the Platonic sin, because he remains under the spell of theory. Positivism is also treated as an heir of this theoretical illusion, and as a result the fight between Husserl and positivism becomes meaningless. I question even more whether this opposition between praxis and theory does not weaken Habermas's own position, because how can there be a critical position that does not participate in the theoretical trend of philosophy? The critical moment within praxis is surely a theoretical moment; the capacity for distanciation is always a part of theory.

The interesting part of the appendix is the fifth section, and I shall restrict myself to that because it gives us a good summary of Habermas's project here as a whole. There are two main ideas. The first is that an interest, which is an anthropological concept, is at the same time a transcendental concept in the Kantian sense of the word. A transcendental concept is the condition of possibility of a certain type of experience. Each interest then rules a certain domain of experience and provides this domain with its major categories. We have already discussed this in considering labour as a synthesis; in acting as a synthesis, labour is both an anthropological and an epistemological concept. The concept offers a principle of classification, and it also provides the major rules of a given science. A type of science corresponds to an interest because an interest supplies the expectations for what can be accepted, identified, and recognized in a given field.

Habermas's second idea delimits this relationship by suggesting that there are three interests which rule three types of sciences. The first interest is one we have already discussed, the instrumental. An equivalence is drawn between the technical-instrumental, which rules the domain of the empirical sciences, and what can be put under control by empirical knowledge. 'This is the cognitive interest in technical control over objectified processes' (p. 309). Habermas owes more than he claims to Husserl's critique in *The Crisis of European Sciences*, since Husserl there tried to show that we have natural sciences because we have objectified and expressed in mathematical law the domain of nature within which we live. What is post-Marxist is Habermas's identification of objectification with the notion of control and manipulation. As we have briefly noted before, for Habermas the modern ideology may be defined as the reduction of all other interests to this interest. This is the Marcusean component of Habermas, an argument that the hierarchies of interests and sciences have been flattened to one dimension only. When a cognitive interest supersedes and rules a communicative interest, there arises the situation of modern ideology in which science and technology function ideologically, because they justify the reduction of human being to this one-dimensional figure.

The second interest is called a historical-hermeneutic interest, and it too has methodological implications. What is striking here is that this interest is defined in Gadamerian terms: 'Access to the facts is provided by the understanding of meaning, not observation. The verification of lawlike hypotheses in the empirical-analytic sciences has its counterpart here in the interpretation of texts. Thus the rules of hermeneutics determine the possible meaning of the validity of statements of the cultural sciences' (p. 309). Each interest is transcendental, that is, a space for a particular kind of validation. We do not validate all statements in the same way; the kind of validation we resort to depends on the nature of our interest. We do not want to verify or falsify historical propositions; instead, we validate them by their capacity to enlarge our communication. As Habermas puts it in some more recent essays, historical-hermeneutic validation centres on the possibility of building a narrative of our own life. One way Habermas attempts to interpret psychoanalysis is in terms of its ability to construct a consistent narrative. The notion of a text is then decisive, and the rule of hermeneutics concerns this text.

The third kind of interest, that found in the critical social sciences, is not hermeneutic. Pursuit of Habermas's argument about the distinctiveness of the critical social sciences will orient our examination of his portrayal of psychoanalysis, which Habermas finds the prototypical example of this science. The appendix lays the ground-work for and provides the transition to this discussion. Habermas distinguishes between systematic and critical social sciences; not all social sciences are critical. 'The systematic sciences of social action, that is economics, sociology, and political science, have the goal, as do the empirical-analytic sciences, of producing nomological knowl-edge' (p. 310). Nomological knowledge means that individual cases are put under more general regulative laws; explanation takes the form, as Hempel expresses it, of a covering law. (It seems that any social science that is not critical belongs to the first, instrumental kind of interest, and this is one reason why Habermas's division is not so satisfying.) A critical social science, on the other hand, is not content with producing nomological knowledge. 'It is concerned with going beyond this goal to determine when theoretical statements grasp invariant regularities of social action as such and when they express ideologically frozen relations of dependence that can in principle be transformed' (p. 310). The task of the critical social sciences is therefore to draw a line between cases where theoretical statements grasp the real human situation and cases where the laws developed describe in actuality the situation of reification. As we may remem-ber, this is an argument Marx used at the beginning of the *Manuscripts* against the British political economists, claiming that they correctly described the character of capitalism but did not see that its underly-ing principle was alienation. What they took as a regularity was, in fact, the disguise of a situation of alienation. According to Habermas, then, the more standard social sciences are unable to differentiate between what is really human in what they describe and what is already reified and so has the appearance of a fact. The factuality of the social sciences is ambiguous because it includes two elements which are not distinguished: that which belongs to the fundamental possibilities of communication, symbolization, institutionalization, and so on, and that which is already reified and appears as a thing. The critique of ideology takes on a central role, because its function is to distinguish between these two kinds of social facts.

The final point about the third kind of interest, says Habermas, is that to the extent that it makes a distinction between the two kinds of facts, 'the critique of ideology, as well, moreover, as psychoanalysis, take into account that information about lawlike connections sets off a process of reflection in the consciousness of those whom the laws are about' (p. 310). The critique is a process of understanding that advances by means of a detour through a process of scientific explanation. This detour encompasses explanation not only of what has been repressed but of the system of repression, explanation not only of distorted content but of the system of distortion. It is because of this emphasis on systemic analysis, Habermas claims, that critical social science cannot be regarded as an extension of hermeneutics. According to Habermas, hermeneutics tries to extend the spontaneous capacity of communication without having to dismantle a system of distortion. Its concern is only local mistakes, misunderstanding, not the distortion of understanding. The model for hermeneutics is biography and philology. In biography we understand the continuity of a life on the basis of both its self-understanding and the direct understanding of others and not by digging under appearances. In philology we rely on the universal capacity of understanding based on the similarity between minds. The critical social sciences are distinctive because they allow us to make the detour required to explain the principle of distortion, a detour necessary so that we may recapture for understanding and self-understanding what in fact has been distorted.

I do not want to press too far, however, this opposition between hermeneutics and critique. I take this position for two reasons. First, I cannot conceive of a hermeneutics without a critical stage itself. This critical stage is exemplified in the development out of philology of modern structuralism and other objective approaches. Second, the critical sciences are themselves hermeneutical, in the sense that besides tending to enlarge communication they presuppose that the distortions of which they speak are not natural events but processes of desymbolization. The distortions belong to the sphere of communicative action. I try to minimize the discrepancy between a twofold and threefold division of the sciences, then, by saying that a division *within* the practical introduces the distinction between hermeneutic and critical social sciences. As the argument developed in the last lecture maintains,[2] the element of critique is itself the key to the process of re-establishing communication; excommunication and the re-establishment of communication therefore belong to the practical. I do not agree with the threefold division, which tends to identify the practical with the third kind of science and isolates the second as a distinct sphere. I am therefore more and more inclined to take the conflict between Habermas and Gadamer as a secondary one. There is, of course, the difference of their generations and also of their political stands. For Habermas, Gadamer is an old gentleman who must vote on the right, and so hermeneutics represents the conservation of the past in a kind of museum. Gadamer, on the other hand, sees Habermas as the radical who made concessions to the students and was punished for it. I no longer find interesting this opposition between the two figures, because I do not see how we can have a critique without also having an experience of communication. And this experience is provided by the understanding of texts. We learn to communicate by understanding texts. Hermeneutics without a project of liberation is blind, but a project of emancipation without historical experience is empty.

In order to recover a conceptual framework of two stages and not three, I turn back from the appendix of *Knowledge and Human Interests* to the main part of the text. Recognition of Habermas's tripartite analysis helps us to understand why he depicts psychoanalysis and the critique of ideology as critical social sciences, but the two-part conceptual framework allows us to comprehend more adequately the topic to which we now turn, the transfer of concepts from psychoanalysis to the critique of ideology. This topic is Habermas's most interesting contribution. For this part of our discussion, I rely mainly on chapters ten through twelve of Habermas's text, and I shall raise two questions. The first asks what is paradigmatic for the critique of ideology in psychoanalysis. At issue is the nature of psychoanalysis as a model. The second question concerns the adequacy of this model; we must consider whether there are any significant differences between the psychoanalytic situation and the position of critique in the social sciences. In concluding this paper, I shall link this second issue to one of the main questions that generates my reading of Habermas: is it not on the basis of a utopia that we can do critique?

To anticipate this conclusion, I might note that there is little in Habermas concerning the question of the differences between psychoanalysis and critique, because he is more interested in finding a certain support in psychoanalysis that in identifying divergences. It may be that the principal difference has precisely to do with the absence in critique of something comparable to the experience of communication in the transference situation. The absence of transference in social critique makes more obvious the utopian status of its claim to cure the diseases of communication. The psychoanalyst does not need to be utopian, because he or she has the experience, even if a limited one, of the successful re-establishment of communication. The sociologist, on the other hand, does not have this experience, since he or she remains at the level of the class struggle, and so without this miniature of recognition that is the situation of the psychoanalyst.

The fundamental thesis of chapters ten through twelve is that psychoanalysis is distinctive because it incorporates a phase of explanation in a process that is fundamentally self-reflective. Psychoanalysis is self-reflection mediated by an explanatory phase. Explanation is not an alternative to understanding but a segment of the process as a whole. In exploring the nature of the psychoanalytic model, Habermas proceeds in three steps. The first examines the paradoxical structure of psychoanalysis, paradoxical because it encompasses both understanding and explanation. This paradoxical structure explains why there are so many misunderstandings of psychoanalysis, misunderstandings which are not entirely unfounded. Freud and his followers did not themselves maintain the relation between understanding and explanation but instead attempted to reduce the process to an explanatory, even merely casual, framework of thought. In the eleventh chapter Habermas calls this an 'energy distribution model' (p. 247). Habermas, though, insists that the paradoxical structure of psychoanalysis must be upheld, because psychoanalysis deals with both linguistic analysis and casual connection. Freud's genius is that he preserved the balance between these two factors, even though he did not maintain this balance in his metapsychology. The paradoxical structure of psychoanalysis is a consequence of the psychoanalytic situation itself, since it involves not only a distorted text but a systematically distorted text. We must insist that the distortions are systematic. Philology, in comparison, is an instance of mere linguistic analysis. It examines distortions – mutilated texts, errors in copying a text, and so on – and requires us to establish the text through the critique, but it does not encompass systematic distortions. We must not only interpret what is distorted; we must explain the distortions themselves. Thus we have the conjunction of 'linguistic analysis with the psychological investigation of causal connections' (p. 217). This conjunction is also the fundamental reason for the epistemological ambiguity of psychoanalysis.

Psychoanalytic interpretation is concerned with those connections of symbols in which a subject deceives itself about itself. The *depth herme-neutics* that Freud contraposes to Dilthey's philological hermeneutics deals with texts indicating *self-deceptions of the author.* Beside the man-ifest content ... such texts document the latent content of a portion of the author's orientations that has become inaccessible to him and alien-ated from him and yet belongs to him nevertheless. Freud coins the phrase 'internal foreign territory' to capture the character of the alien-ation of something that is still the subject's very own. (p. 218; emphasis in original; quoting *New Introductory Lectures on Psychoanalysis*)

Because the latent content is inaccessible to the author, a detour through an explanatory method is required. Note also in this passage that Habermas calls Freud's method 'depth hermeneutics.' Again this reinforces that a dividing line between hermeneutics and critical science cannot be maintained.

A good example of the duality of language in psychoanalysis may be found in analysis of the dream. On the one hand, a certain linguistic analysis is required. The dream needs hermeneutic decod-ing; it is a text to decipher. Here the language of the method is philological. On the other hand, however, the need to explain the distortion of the dream calls for a theory of dream work and a technique addressed to the resistances opposed to interpretation. Here the language is quasi-physical. All the terms in the sixth chap-ter of Freud's *The Interpretation of Dreams* involve mechanisms of distortion: condensation, displacement, representability, and sec-ondary revision. This vocabulary of censorship and repression be-longs to an energetics and not to a hermeneutics. Yet this does not prevent us from saying that the distorted meaning is still a question of communication. The dreamer is excommunicated from the lin-guistic community, but excommunication is a distortion of commu-nication. Habermas has several phrases that circle this paradox. To excommunicate is to 'exclude from public communication.' Relations are 'delinguisticized'; language is 'privatized.' We have 'the degram-maticized language of the dream' (p. 224). Present is the Wittgen-steinian notion of language games; the excommunication of the dream is a disease in the language games that make up communica-tion. 'The object domain of depth hermeneutics comprises all the places where, owing to internal disturbances, the text[s] of our every-day language games are interrupted by incomprehensible symbols. These symbols cannot be understood because they do not obey the

grammatical rules of ordinary language, norms of action, and cultur-
ally learned patterns of expression ... Because the symbols that
interpret suppressed needs are excluded from public communication,
the speaking and acting subject's communication with himself is
interrupted' (pp. 226–7). The first point about the psychoanalytic
model, then, is that it treats symptoms, dreams, and all pathological
or quasi-pathological phenomena as cases of excommunication based
on systematic distortion, and these systematic distortions all require
explanation in order to be dissolved.

Habermas's second point is that in psychoanalysis the analytic
situation is paradigmatic. This theme will be central to our discussion
of the relationship between psychoanalysis and the critique of ideology. For Habermas, the most interesting philosophic contribution of
Freud is his papers on analytic technique, that is, his papers on the
situation of transference. Here an artificial circumstance of communication is created in which the basic situation of excommunication is
transposed and dealt with. Habermas's claim is that we must construe a metapsychology upon the paradigm supplied by these papers
on technique and not the reverse. In his metapsychology Freud
elaborated two different models, first the topological model for the
mental apparatus – the unconscious, preconscious, and conscious –
and second the model of superego, ego, and id. Habermas argues
that these models are diagrammatic representations of something
which happens in the situation of transference. Therefore, the analytic
technique must rule the metapsychological model and not the contrary. Unfortunately, says Habermas, the stance that evolved in both
Freud and the Freudian school was to start from the model and to
interpret what happens in the analytical situation according to this
model; Freud and his followers forgot that the model was in fact
derived from the analytical experience.

Habermas's assessment of Freud here has an interesting parallelism with his approach to Marx. As we have seen, Habermas argues
that what Marx's inquiry actually does is more important than what
Marx says that it does. Marx's inquiry maintains the distinction
between relations of production and forces of production, even
while this dialectic is abolished in a unidimensional model involving
only the structures of production. In order to rescue Marx we have to
rescue Freud, for Freud's insights into the situation of transference
help to revitalize understanding of the import of the relations of
production. In a sense, our task is the same in both Marx and Freud:

we must appeal to their real, concrete contribution to technical inquiry and must plead on the basis of these inquiries' real indications against Marx's and Freud's explanatory models. Their actual inquiries must rule their models and not the reverse.

Before saying something about the transcription of Freud's inquiry into the psychoanalytic model, we should say something about the analytic experience itself. This common experience between patient and analyst is the experience of a genesis of self-consciousness (p. 228). This, for Habermas, is a central perception of psychoanalysis and a key to the critique of ideology. The aim of class struggle is recognition, but we know what recognition means on the basis of the psychoanalytical situation. Freud's important formula summarizes the analytic insight: 'Wo Es war, soll Ich werden'; where the id was, the ego must become. The first reason why the analytic situation is paradigmatic for psychoanalysis, then, is because self-recognition rules its whole process.

The second reason why the analytic situation is paradigmatic is because self-recognition is an aim achieved by dissolving resistances. The concept of resistance in psychoanalysis will become the model for ideology. An ideology is a system of resistance; it resists recognition of where we are, who we are, and so on. The crucial insight of psychoanalysis here is that intellectual understanding of the system of resistance is not sufficient. Even if a patient understands his or her situation intellectually, this information is useless as long as it has not led to a restructuration of the libidinal economy. For a parallel in the social world, we might look to the role of the mass media. To whatever extent that media inform us about the real nature of power in society, this knowledge is useless in itself because it has no impact on the distribution of power. The liberal system of information is neutralized by the real system of power. This is my own example and not in the text. In fact, Habermas himself does not offer explicit comparisons between Freud and Marx on this question of the proper model for the critical sciences. We are the ones who have to make this effort. Habermas draws a connection between Freud and Marx only later, when speaking in the twelfth chapter of Marx's theory of culture. At the present stage, Habermas's focus is on Freud alone. The analytic situation is an exemplary model for the critical social sciences because it is based on a theory of resistance. The task of analysis is to dissolve resistances by a kind of work, what Freud called *Durcharbeitung*, a working-through. 'Working-through designates the dynamic component of a cognitive activity that leads to recognition only against resistances' (p. 231). This is a good definition, because it integrates three concepts: a cognitive activity that leads to recognition through dealing with resistances.

I shall only allude to the fact that Habermas incorporates into this process the reconstruction of a life history (p. 233). For those of us interested in the constitution of narratives – as story, as history – there is much available in Habermas's discussion of the narrative structure of the analytic experience. Because it involves a life history, its criteria are not those of verification. Its concern is not with facts but with the capacity to make a significant whole of our life story. The reconstruction of one's life history reverses the process of splitting-off that typifies excommunication.

If cognitive activity, the overcoming of resistance, and recognition are the implications of the psychoanalytic situation, this kernel experience is transformed by Freud into a structural model (p. 237). This transformation is Habermas's third general point about psychoanalysis. Habermas thinks of this development as applicable particularly to *The Ego and the Id*, written in 1923, but the transformation is apparent in all Freud's successive models, as in the writings of 1895 and in the model of the seventh chapter of *The Interpretation of Dreams*, written in 1900. Habermas argues that the structural model is legitimate because we have to introduce causal connections within a process that is more generally interpretive. The process is interpretive but includes causal episodes. As long as we remain aware of the derivation of the structural model from the analytic situation, there is no danger of its abuse. When this model is isolated from the situation that it describes, however, then it becomes an ideology. ('Ideology' at this point is not Habermas's term but my own.) When separated from the analytic experience, the structural model becomes an objectification by which psychoanalysis denies its affiliation with depth hermeneutics and claims to imitate the natural sciences.

Indeed, many texts in Freud do maintain that psychoanalysis is a natural science. There are several reasons, I think, why Freud takes this step. First, Freud had to fight so hard for recognition that he had to claim to be a scientist. The only way for him to be recognized was as a scientist. Second, his own training in physiology led him to think that psychoanalysis was only a provisory stage and that one day it would be replaced by pharmacology. Psychoanalysis is necessary only because we ignore or do not understand some of the workings of the brain. This point is odd, because his emphasis throughout on self-understanding is incompatible with a science like pharmacology.

In any event, we may reappropriate the structural model if we keep in mind its derivation from the experience of analysis. Within this framework a term like the id makes sense because we may take it as literally the neutral. Because some parts of ourselves are no longer recognized, are excommunicated not only from others but from ourselves, they then must appear as a thing. The id describes well the existence of a part of our experience that we no longer understand, something to which we no longer have access and so is like a thing. The id is the name of what has been excommunicated.

The concept of excommunication rules the structural model. Because excommunication itself belongs to the system of the concepts of communicative action, a species of communicative action provides the key for a model that is quasi-naturalistic.

> It seems to me more plausible to conceive the act of repression as a banishment of need interpretations themselves. The degrammaticized and imagistically compressed language of the dream provides some clues to an excommunication model of this sort. This process would be the intrapsychic imitation of a specific category of punishment, whose efficacy was striking especially in archaic times: the expulsion, ostracism, and isolation of the criminal from the social group whose language he shares. The splitting-off of individual symbols from public communication would mean at the same time the privatization of their semantic content. (pp. 241–2)

I like very much this part of Habermas's analysis. Only by a process of internal banishment is there something like an id. The id is not a given but a product of expulsion. I think that this is an orthodox interpretation of Freud; repression is produced not by natural forces but by forces under certain cultural circumstances. Repression is not a mechanical phenomenon, it is the expression in causal language of what happens when we do not recognize ourselves, when we banish ourselves from our own company.

In concluding our discussion of Habermas's characterization of psychoanalysis, we may say that his general argument is: 'The language of [psychoanalytic] theory is narrower than the language in which the technique was described' (p. 245). For Habermas this comment is just as important as when he said that an interpretation of Marx in mechanistic terms cannot give an account of Marx's critique, since the critique is not a part of the mechanistic system. Similarly, in Freud, if we deal with a mechanistic model of psychoanalysis, we cannot give an account of the process of self-reflection that the analytic experience requires. 'Strangely enough, the structural model denies the origins of its own categories in a process of enlightenment' (p. 245). This statement provides us with the transition to the last topic in our analysis of Habermas. We must discuss how the process of enlightenment – *Aufklärung*, the name of the eighteenth-century philosophy – orients Habermas's critique, a critique whose interest is in emancipation. To what extent is enlightenment, understood as emancipation, a utopian element at the centre of the critique of ideology?

Two problems merit our attention here. First, we must consider to what extent the psychoanalytic model helps us to construe the concept of a critique of ideology. We must ascertain the principle of this parallelism and the range of its extension. We must consider, second, to what extent there is a utopian component in the concept of self-reflection and in the concept of critique in general. I shall link these two questions, because I think that the difference finally between psychoanalysis and ideology-critique is that the element of utopia in the latter is irreducible. This conclusion is more a personal interpretation than a strict reading of Habermas's text.

As I have mentioned previously, in *Knowledge and Human Interests* Habermas strangely says only very little about the possibility of transferring to the critique of ideology some of his conclusions about psychoanalysis. The reader is the one who generally has to extract these consequences. On the basis of our reading, I shall try to draw these comparisons between psychoanalysis and ideology-critique, and I shall proceed in a certain order, from what is the most similar to what is the least similar. We shall end by raising the question of these two enterprises' fundamental difference.

There are four main points where the psychoanalytic model is transferable to the critique of ideology. The detour through psychoanalysis illustrates first that self-reflection is the principal motive of the critical social sciences as a whole. Psychoanalysis is exemplary because it is a process of self-recovery, of self-understanding. A second transferable aspect is that in both psychoanalysis and ideology-critique, distortions belong to the same level of experience as emancipation. Distortions occur within the process of communication.

Thus, we are compelled to speak even of class struggle in terms of communication. Class struggle involves not only conflicting forces but a disruption of a process of communication between human beings. People become strangers; in different classes people do not speak the same language. Excommunication extends even to the level of style, grammar, the amplitude of the lexicon, and so on. The difference is not only between groups' linguistic tools, though, but between the symbolic systems through which they look at one another. 'Just as in the clinical situation, so in society, pathological compulsion itself is accompanied by the interest in its abolition. Both the pathology of social institutions and that of individual consciousness reside in the medium of language and of communicative action and assume the form of a structural deformation of communication' (p. 288). Freud helps us to reread Marx in terms of processes of communication not just when Marx speaks of forces but throughout.

The third point of commonality between psychoanalysis and the critique of ideology is that because their distortions are systematic, we cannot expect dissolution of these distortions by mere extension of our ordinary capacity to communicate. The ordinary means of interpretation which constitute conversation are useless, because we are faced not with misunderstanding but with systematic distortion. This requires us to apply an intermediary technique, the detour of causal explanation. In both psychoanalysis and ideology-critique, then, the movement from excommunication to the re-establishment of communication has an explanatory phase which implies that we construe a theoretical model for dealing with this segment of concealed and reified processes.

This leads us to the fourth and final parallelism: the structural model in which we deal with the casual connections must always be derived from the situation of communication, but the model can become abstracted from this situation and so reified. For Habermas there is a complete parallelism here between what happened in Marxism and in psychoanalysis; the model of each was abstracted from the original situation for which it was conceived and became a reified structural model. The energy distribution model in Freud has the same ambiguous status as superstructure and infrastructure in the orthodox Marxist model.

Turning to a second group of statements, we can see where the comparison between psychoanalysis and ideology-critique begins to fail. Discrepancy starts to arise when we attempt to identify what

Marx and Freud each emphasize in the human fabric of culture. 'What interests [Marx] as the natural basis of history is the physical organization specific to the human species under the category of possible labor: the tool-making animal. Freud's focus, in contrast, was not the system of social labor but the family' (p. 282). A human being is described by Marx as a tool user and by Freud as someone who remains a child even after having moved beyond the age of childhood. With Freud the fundamental problem is not labour but the instinctual renunciations by which a cultural system may function. In Freud's three great texts on culture – *The Future of an Illusion*, *Civilization and Its Discontents*, and *Moses and Monotheism* – everything is measured in terms of libidinal loss, the libidinal pleasures that must be sacrificed in order that one may be a member of society. Freud's view of culture is a pessimistic one, because he thinks society functions only on the basis of the compensations, prohibitions, and sublimations that protect the social system. Freud 'concentrates on the origins of the motivational foundation of communicative action' (p. 283).

This divergence between Marx and Freud begins to appear in chapter twelve of the text, the only place where there is a direct comparison between both figures. Habermas writes of 'the psychoanalytic key to a social theory that converges in a surprising manner with Marx's reconstruction of the history of the species while in another regard advancing specifically new perspectives' (p. 276). The parallelism does not extend all that far because Freud's concern is limited to the fact that a human being is more than an animal only because of the renunciation of instinct. Habermas quotes a striking and in many ways terrifying assertion from Freud's *The Future of an Illusion*: 'every individual is virtually an enemy of civilization' (p. 277). Society must take measures against this destructive dimension, a dimension linked by Freud to sadism and to the death instinct. The latter in particular seems to have no parallel in Marx. For Freud guilt is the guardian of the city against disruption by the individual. Habermas comments:

> The last assertion, that *everyone* is virtually an enemy of civilization, already points up the difference between Freud and Marx. Marx conceives the institutional framework as an ordering of interests that are immediate functions of the system of social labor according to the relation of social rewards and imposed obligations. Institutions derive

their force from perpetuating a distribution of rewards and obligations that is rooted in force and distorted according to class structure. Freud, on the contrary, conceives the institutional framework in connection with the repression of instinctual impulses. (p. 277; emphasis in original)

Repression is fundamental for Freud, whereas in Marx it is a supplement, a distortion introduced by the division of labour and by the class structure. For some time Freud had a certain sympathy for the Bolshevik enterprise, but he also viewed it with caution, because he perceived that a political experiment which did not fundamentally change the balance of instincts was not a real revolution.

In spite of these differences between Freud and Marx, however, Freud may still be helpful at this second level of comparison. At this second stage, there is a balance of difference and similarities between psychoanalysis and ideology-critique, whereas in the first part there were only similarities. What remains paradigmatic in Freud is the kind of hope that he proposes. This may be more difficult to find in Marx, because as long as the class structure has not been overcome, then the rationality of human existence cannot be established. In contrast, we may observe in the process of psychoanalysis something of the emergence of self-understanding and self-reflection.

To discuss this dimension of psychoanalysis, which affects not only the second stage of its comparison with the critique of ideology but the third, where the lack of parallelism comes to the fore, I shall concentrate on pages 284–90 of the text. As far as I know, these are the only pages outside the appendix where the word 'utopia' occurs. Habermas views Freud as a man of the eighteenth century, a man of the Enlightenment, and this is surely correct. Habermas understands the aim of the Enlightenment to be advocacy of the rationality of utopia, promotion of rational hope. 'The ideas of the Enlightenment stem from the store of historically transmitted illusions. Hence we must comprehend the actions of the Enlightenment as the attempt to test the limit of the realizability of the utopian content of cultural tradition under given conditions' (p. 284). This statement is linked to an idea developed in the late writings of Freud, when Freud differentiates between illusion and delusion. A delusion is an irrational belief, whereas an illusion represents the possibilities of rational human being. Habermas quotes Freud's *New Introductory Lectures*: ' "My illusions are not, like religious ones, incapable of correction. They have not the character of a delusion. If experience should show ... that we have been mistaken, we will give up our expectations"' (p. 284). Freud advances the notion of a tempered utopian mind, a mind tempered by the spirit of the Enlightenment, by the spirit of rationality. Why is this notion present in Freud? 'Freud encounters this unity of reason and interest in the situation in which the physician's Socratic questioning can aid a sick person's self-reflection only under pathological compulsion and the corresponding interest in abolishing this compulsion' (p. 287). There is an identity of interest and reason which gives to hope a rational content. This quality may be what is lacking in any suggested parallelism between ideology-critique and psychoanalysis.

We now reach the point where emphasis should be placed on the lack of parallelism between psychoanalysis and the critique of ideology. To my mind, the fundamental difference is that there is nothing in the critique of ideology comparable to the psychoanalytic relation between patient and physician. It is not by chance that Habermas never speaks of the parallelism between ideology-critique and psychoanalysis when developing the notion that the patient-physician relation is paradigmatic in psychoanalysis and that the structural model is derived from this situation. We must inquire ourselves whether there is anything similar in the critique of ideology. The important text here is the one just cited for the stage of transition. Let me begin several lines earlier than before: 'The analytic situation makes real the unity of intuition and emancipation, of insight and liberation from dogmatic dependence, and of reason and the interested employment of reason developed by Fichte in the concept of self-reflection ... Freud encounters this unity of reason and interest in the situation in which the physician's Socratic questioning can aid a sick person's self-reflection' (p. 287). The analytic situation makes real (*wirklich*) the unity of intuition and emancipation, and the physician's Socratic questioning supplies the aid for this to occur. This relationship between patient and physician is unique to the psychoanalytic situation. It is sometimes presented, at least in this country, even as a contractual relationship. Someone calls himself or herself the patient, and someone else is trained as a physician and recognized as the physician by the patient. There is recognition of the situation that I am ill, I call for help, and you are the one who can help me. The situation is, in Habermas's definition of the term, dialogic, not in the sense of shared experience – the analyst is abstinent and shares nothing – but in the sense that the analyst is present to the patient and offers aid.

This initial situation of the doctor–patient relationship has no parallel in ideology-critique. In ideology-critique no one identifies himself or herself as the ill, as the patient, and no one is entitled to be the physician. Some might argue that to a certain extent the sociologist or the writer is able to take on the role of physician, but this raises the problem of whether there can really be a value-free thinker. In a way the psychoanalyst in the analytic situation may be a value-free thinker, because he or she is the object of transference. I do not see, however, what would be a similar position in ideology-critique, because even the thinker is part of the polemical situation. The thinker does not transcend the polemical situation, and so the notion of ideology remains a polemical concept for the thinker also. The psychoanalyst, on the other hand, does not use the concept of neurosis as a polemical tool against the patient. The lack of parallelism here between psychoanalysis and ideology-critique has dreadful consequences for the status of the latter, since it becomes a member of its own referent. The status of ideology-critique itself belongs to the polemical situation of ideology. This is the first point where the parallelism between psychoanalysis and the critique of ideology fails.

The second point where the parallelism fails is that there is nothing in ideology-critique comparable to the psychoanalytic situation of transference. Transference is the decisive procedure where what happened on the neurotic scene is transposed onto the miniature and artificial scene of the patient–physician relation. It constitutes an intermediary scene between the neurotic scene and the original infantile scene. The art of creating this intermediary and artificial situation gives the psychoanalytic experience its efficiency. Once again I wonder whether, for example, an ideology-critique's examination of class affiliation can play the same role as this transference situation.

The third and final point where parallelism fails is in the lack of recognition intrinsic to ideology-critique. The relation between physician and patient is not only a situation of contract and not only a procedure of transference; it is also an occasion where mutual recognition is finally implied. We cannot say, however, that recognition is at work in *Ideologiekritik*. In *Lenin and Philosophy*, for example, Althusser radically denies the possibility of recognition. We must draw the party line, he says, between the Marxist intellectual and the bourgeois intellectual. At least for the orthodox Marxists the situation is one of war, and we must take this perspective as exemplary rather than that of those other Marxists who are more tamed and humanized. In the orthodox claim, the notion of recognition is a projection only about the classless society. In the classless society there will be recognition, but we cannot say that recognition gives its thrust to the current enterprise.

My criticism is not so much an argument against Habermas as an analysis for the sake of the problem itself, that psychoanalysis and ideology-critique have different criteria of success. We may agree that there are certain therapeutic moments in ideology-critique. Even if we are not Marxists, when we read Marx it is a personal event, and one that transforms our outlook on society. We are less deceived by the appearances of democracy and so on. So this change has both direct and indirect political implications. Dissident voices are fundamental to the democratic process itself. We must preserve this margin of dissidence for the sake of inner critique. We may also say that ideology-critique can lead to conscientization, a theme developed by Latin American thinkers such as Paulo Freire. This, too, is a form of political therapy. In general, though, ideology-critique lacks an immediate, experiential component. It functions much more at the level of analysis of the wheels of the social machinery. Though ideology-critique may have some therapeutic results, its purpose is still critique. Psychoanalysis, on the other hand, includes both critique and cure. The function of therapy is to cure, but virtually no one is cured by the process of ideology-critique. Many are wounded but very few are cured.

Ideology-critique is part of a process of struggle and not one of recognition. The idea of free communication remains an unfulfilled ideal, a regulative idea, an 'illusion' in the sense that Freud distinguishes the term from delusion. Perhaps here a utopian element fills the gap that the experience of recognition satisfies in the psychoanalytic situation. The utopian element is linked to the absent counterpart of the psychoanalytic situation. What suggests this relationship is Habermas's appeal to the utopian thematic at this point in his discussion of Freud. 'That is why for the social system, too, the interest inherent in the pressure of suffering is also immediately an interest in enlightenment; and reflection is the only possible dynamic through which it realizes itself. The interest of reason inclines toward the progressive, critical-revolutionary, but tentative realization of the major illusions of humanity, in which repressed motives have been elaborated into *fantasies* of hope' (p. 288; emphasis added). Habermas adds, several lines later: 'The "good" is neither a convention nor an essence, but rather the result of fantasy. But it must be fantasied so exactly that it corresponds to and articulates a fundamental interest: the interest in that measure of emancipation that historically is objectively possible under given and manipulable conditions.' The German for fantasy is *Phantasie*, and it means not fancy but imagination. So Habermas's discussion, I was pleased to see, is about the social imagination.

In more recent work, Habermas tries to respond to criticisms about the lack of parallelism between psychoanalysis and ideology-critique by advancing the notion of communicative competence. Communicative competence is a utopian construction, an ideal speech situation, the possibility of undistorted communication. Recourse to this concept, however, raises questions about the nature of the utopian element that are similar to those arising from our reading of *Knowledge and Human Interests*. The word 'competence' is used ambiguously. On the one hand, a competence is something at our disposal, a potentiality that we can either use or not use. It is the correlate of performance in Chomsky. Because I am competent to speak French, I can perform a sentence in French. Communicative competence, however, is not something at our disposal but rather something that must appear as a Kantian Idea, a regulative idea. My question is whether we can have this idea without a certain anthropology or an ontology in which it makes sense for dialogue to succeed. This is the permanent argument of Gadamer in his discussion with Habermas. If we do not understand the poet Hölderlin when he speaks of *das Gesprach das wir sind*, the dialogue that we are, then we cannot make sense of the dialogue that we ought to be. If we have no ontology in which dialogue is constitutive of who we are, then can we have this communicative ideal? Perhaps it is merely a matter of emphasis, though, and Habermas's question is how can we understand the dialogue that we are if not through the utopia of a communication without boundary and constraint.

As for myself, I assume completely the inextricable role of this utopian element, because I think that it is ultimately constitutive of any theory of ideology. It is always from the depth of a utopia that we may speak of an ideology. This was the case with the young Marx when he spoke of the whole human being, the famous person who went fishing in the morning, hunting in the afternoon, and in the evening did critique. This reconstruction of a totality lying beyond the division of labour, this vision of an integral human being, is the utopia which allows us to say that the British economists did not dig beneath the surface of the economic relations between wage, capital, and work.

I want to conclude by saying a few words about the structure of utopia. For my part, I see utopia as itself a complex network of elements with different origins. It is not something simple but a cluster of forces working together. Utopia is supported first by the notion of self-reflection. This is the main notion of utopia, and it is the teleological component of all critique, of all analysis, of all restoration of communication. I call it the transcendental component. This factor preserves the unity between ideology-critique and Germanic idealism and also finally the unity between ideology-critique and the whole tradition of philosophy in spite of Habermas's claim that we have broken with theory for the sake of praxis. What remains common to theory and praxis is this element of self-reflection, something which is not historical but transcendental, in the sense that it has no date, no point of historical origin, but is instead the fundamental possibility of being human. When the young Marx speaks of the difference between animal and human being, he draws a line; the difference is an element of transcendence available only to human being. I prefer to say this factor is transcendental, because it is the condition of possibility for doing something else.

The second component of the utopian structure is cultural. This attribute is modern and comes from the tradition of the Enlightenment; it adds to the element of fantasy the possibility of correction, of testing the limits of realizability. To repeat a quotation already cited: 'The ideas of the Enlightenment stem from the store of historically transmitted illusions. Hence we must comprehend the actions of the Enlightenment as the attempt to test the limit of the realizability of the utopian content of cultural tradition under given conditions' (p. 284). The ideas are transmitted historically. The utopia is then not merely a transcendental element without history, for it is part of our history. This allows me to say that perhaps the great difference between Gadamer and Habermas is that they do not have the same traditions. Gadamer relies more on the tradition of German idealism plus Romanticism, whereas for Habermas it is more the Enlightenment plus German idealism. That Habermas and Gadamer are both situated historically is inevitable; no one is outside all tradition. Even emphasis on self-reflection has a certain tradition. Self-reflection has both an ahistorical factor, what I have called its transcendental component, and a cultural component, a history. When Habermas speaks of the unity of interests and reason (pp. 287, 289), this is typically a theme of the Enlightenment.

The third element of the utopian structure is fantasy. Fantasy is Habermas's term for what Freud calls illusion. Illusion is differentiated, we remember, from delusion, where delusion is both the unverifiable and the unrealizable. Illusion or fantasy is the element of hope, a rational hope. Habermas develops this theme not only in his discussion of Freud but also in his systematic theses in the appendix. In the latter, Habermas says that humanity is rooted in fundamental structures like work, language, and power. He adds, though, that there is also something in us which transcends this conditionality, and this is the utopian. Habermas specifically uses the word 'utopian' in this context' 'Society is not only a system of self-preservation. An enticing natural force, present in the individual as libido, has detached itself from the behavioral system of self-preservation and urges toward utopian fulfillment' (p. 312). Fantasy is that which 'urges toward utopian fulfillment.' Habermas's opposition between utopia and self-preservation is a good insight into the relation between ideology and utopia in their best senses. As we shall see with Geertz [in the next essay], the fundamental function of an ideology is to establish identity, whether the identity of a group or of an individual. Utopia, on the other hand, breaks with the 'system of self-preservation and urges toward utopian fulfillment.' For Habermas, realization of this utopian element's role leads to the thesis that 'knowledge equally serves as an instrument and transcends mere self-preservation' (p. 313). Utopia is precisely what preserves the three knowledge-constitutive interests – the instrumental, the practical, and the critical – from being reduced to one. The utopian opens the spectrum of interests and prevents it from being closed or collapsed to the instrumental.

It may be, then, that utopia, in the positive sense of the term, extends to the boundary line between the possible and the impossible which perhaps cannot be rationalized finally even in the form of rational hope. May we not say therefore that this utopian factor is irreducible, that ideology-critique cannot rely on an experience similar to that of transference in psychoanalysis, where the process of liberation may lead to self-recognition under the guidance of an actual, mutual recognition? It may even be that full mutual recognition is a utopian element in all therapy itself. The utopian fantasy is that of an ideal speech act, an ideal communicative situation, the notion of communication without boundary and without constraint. It may be that this ideal constitutes our very notion of humankind. We speak of humanity not only as a species but as, in fact, a task, since humanity is given nowhere. The utopian element may be the notion of humanity that we are directed towards and that we unceasingly attempt to bring to life.

[...] We shall close our analysis of ideology with the following paper on Clifford Geertz. Habermas has been a figure of transition. He establishes the possibility of a social critique that avoids Mannheim's paradox, the division between ideology and science, he builds on Weber and shows that only at the end of the process of critique can we recover as our own work what are the claims of authority, and he alerts us that this recovery moves from excommunication and desymbolization to recognition and communication. On the last point he anticipates Geertz, who demonstrates that ideology must be understood on the basis of the symbolic structure of action, a conclusion that moves us beyond distortion and legitimization to the third and final level of ideology, a non-pejorative concept of ideology as integration.

Notes

1 Jurgen Habermas, *Knowledge and Human Interests*, trans. by J. Shapiro (Boston: Beacon Press, 1971)
2 Ricoeur refers here to the first lecture on Habermas given in the series published by George H. Taylor, *Lectures on Ideology and Utopia* (New York: Columbia University Press, 1986), pp. 216–31.

Geertz

We end our regressive analysis of ideology[1] by discussion of Clifford Geertz. Discussion of Geertz is the last step in an analysis that covers three main stages. We started from the surface concept of ideology as distortion. When we read *The German Ideology*, we asked how can we make sense of Marx's assertion that a ruling class is expressed by ruling ideas, ideas which become the ruling ideas of an epoch. We recognized that at this stage the concept of ideology was systematic distortion, and we saw that in order to approach this first concept, we had to take into account a concept of interest – class interest – apply an attitude of suspicion, and proceed to a causal dismantlement of these distortions. Here the paradigmatic model was the relation between superstructure and infrastructure.

We then raised the question, how does it make sense to have a distorting thought caused by such structures as class structures? We were led to ask what is implied in the notions of ruling class and ruling idea. Our answer was the problem of authority. This uncovered the second concept of ideology, ideology as legitimation. Here we introduced discussion of Max Weber, since the paradigmatic case was no longer a class interest but the claim to legitimacy made by all forms of authority. Our focus was the gap within a group between the leader's claim to authority and the members' belief in this authority. The attitude of analysis at this second stage was not suspicion but the value-free attitude of the sociologist. Further, the conceptual framework was not causality but motivation, and we spoke of this framework not in terms of structures and forces but in terms of the ideal types of the authority's claims. In this second stage the ideal types of claims played the same role as the superstructure in the first stage.

It is to build a third concept of ideology as integration or identity that we finally resort to Geertz. At this stage, we reach the level of symbolization, something that can be distorted and something within which lies the process of legitimation. Here the main attitude is not at all suspicion, nor even the value-free attitude, but conversation. Geertz himself comes to this attitude as an anthropologist. In *The Interpretation of Cultures*, Geertz says of his ethnographic research: 'We are seeking, in the widened sense of the term in which it encompasses very much more than talk, to converse with [people of another culture], a matter a great deal more difficult, and not only with strangers, than is commonly recognized' (p. 13). 'Looked at in this way,' Geertz continues, 'the aim of anthropology is the enlargement of the universe of human discourse ... It is an aim to which a semiotic concept of culture is peculiarly well adapted. As interworked systems of construable signs (what, ignoring provincial usages, I would call symbols), culture is not a power, something to which social events, behaviors, institutions, or processes can be causally attributed; it is a context, something within which they can be intelligibly – that is, thickly – described' (p. 14).

In conversation we have an interpretive attitude. If we speak of ideology in negative terms as distortion, then we use the tool or weapon of suspicion. If, however, we want to recognize a group's values on the basis of its self-understanding of these values, then we must welcome these values in a positive way, and this is to converse.

This attitude is linked to a conceptual framework which is not causal or structural or even motivational but rather semiotic. What particularly interests me in Geertz is that he tries to deal with the concept of ideology by the instruments of modern semiotics. Geertz declares early in the text, 'The concept of culture I espouse ... is essentially a semiotic one.' What he means by this is that analysis of culture is 'not an experimental science in search of law but an interpretive one in search of meaning.' Geertz is thus not far from Max Weber, since he follows Weber in believing that 'man is an animal suspended in webs of significance he himself has spun' (p. 5). At this level we address ourselves to motives not as motivational but as expressed in signs. The signitive systems of the motives constitute the level of reference.

Because culture is understood as a semiotic process, the concept of symbolic action is central for Geertz. This theme is most present in his article 'Ideology as a Cultural System,' which is included in *The Interpretation of Cultures*. This article will be our focus for the rest of the discussion in this paper. Geertz borrows the concept or at least the term 'symbolic action' from Kenneth Burke (p. 208). It seems that what Geertz borrows is more the term than the actual concept, because in the book of Burke's that Geertz cites for this notion, *The Philosophy of Literary Form: Studies in Symbolic Action*, symbolic action appears to have a different meaning than it does for Geertz. Burke says that language, in fact, is symbolic action. Geertz's point, though, is that action is symbolic just like language. The notion of symbolic action may therefore be deceiving in the context that Geertz intends. I prefer to speak of action as symbolically mediated. This seems less ambiguous than the term 'symbolic action,' because symbolic action is not an action which we undertake but one which we replace by signs. This is Burke's concept, that in literature we have symbolic action. Literature is symbolic action, whereas here we want to say that action itself is symbolic in the sense that it is construed on the basis of fundamental symbols.

Geertz also utilizes the doubtful concept of an extrinsic symbol, in the sense of an extrinsic theory of symbolic systems (pp. 214ff.). If I am correct in my understanding of Geertz on this point, I think that the expression is unfortunate. Geertz wants to show that action is ruled from within by symbols, and he calls these symbols extrinsic, in contrast to another set of symbols provided by genetics, where the codes are incorporated in the living organism. This differentiation between extrinsic and intrinsic models is an attempt to draw the line between models that we find in biology and those developed in cultural life. In the later, all the symbols are imported instead of being homogeneous to life. There is a heterogeneity between the cultural model and the biological potentiality of life. Geertz's point is that the biological plasticity or flexibility of human life does not give us guidance for dealing with various cultural situations – scarcity, labour, and so on. Therefore, we need a secondary system of symbols and models which are no longer natural but cultural models. The salient consideration, then, is not so much the fact that these symbols and models are extrinsic to the organism as that they function exactly in the same way as the intrinsic models.

The defining proposition of the extrinsic theory is that symbol systems are matched with other systems. 'Thought consists of the construction and manipulation of symbol systems, which are employed as models of other systems, physical, organic, social, psychological, and so forth, in such a way that the structure of these other

systems ... is, as we say, "understood."' We think and understand by
matching 'the states and processes of symbolic models against the
states and processes of the wider world' (p. 214). If we enter into a
ceremony but do not know the rules of the ritual, then all the
movements are senseless. To understand is to pair what we see with
the rules of the ritual. 'An object (or an event, an act, an emotion) is
identified by placing it against the background of an appropriate
symbol' (p. 215). We *see* the movement *as* performing a mass, *as*
performing a sacrifice, and so on. The notion of pairing or matching
is the central theme. Cultural patterns are therefore programs. They
provide, says Geertz, 'a template or blueprint for the organization of
social and psychological processes, much as genetic systems provide
such a template for the organization of organic processes' (p. 216).
The semiotic process provides a plan.

There is a further implication of Geertz's analysis which is I think
the most significant part of his article, and that is the possibility of
comparing an ideology with the rhetorical devices of discourse. This
may be the point where Geertz goes the farthest. In the earlier part
of his article, Geertz criticizes the more usual theories of ideology –
ideology as the representation of certain interests, ideology as the
product of certain socio-psychological strains – for always assuming
something that they do not understand: how the release of a strain
becomes a symbol or how an interest is expressed in an idea. He
claims that most sociologists take for granted what it means to say
that an interest is 'expressed by' something else. How do interests
become expressed, though? Geertz argues that we can provide an
answer only be analysing 'how symbols symbolize, how they function
to mediate meaning' (p. 208). 'With no notion of how metaphor,
analogy, irony, ambiguity, pun, paradox, hyperbole, rhythm, and all
the other elements of what we lamely call 'style' operate ... in casting
personal attitudes into public form,' we cannot construe 'the import
of ideological assertions' (p. 209). Geertz takes as an example an
attack by organized labour on the Taft-Hartley Act, where labour
assailed the act as being a '"slave labor law"' (p. 209). This metaphor
should not be reduced to its literal meaning, Geertz says, because it
derives its informative value from being a metaphor. Its language is
not merely distortion, because it says what it wants to say by the
comparison to and the metaphor of slave labour. The phrase is not a
literal label but a metaphoric trope (p. 210).

What is especially intriguing here is Geertz's attempt to connect analysis not only to semiology in the broad sense of the word but to the part of semiology that deals with figures of speech, with tropology, with rhetorical devices that are not necessarily intended to deceive either oneself or others. The possibility that rhetoric can be integrative and not necessarily distortive leads us to a non-pejorative concept of ideology. If we follow this path, we may then say that there is something irreducible in the concept of ideology. Even if we separate off the other two layers of ideology – ideology as distortion and as the legitimation of a system of order or power – the integrative function of ideology, the function of preserving an identity, remains. It may be that our regressive analysis can go no farther, because no group and no individual are possible without this integrative function.

Here I find a provocative similarity between Geertz and Erik Erikson. Let me draw the connection briefly. In Erikson's *Identity: Youth and Crisis*, there are several statements about ideology that are very close to Geertz. These statements are completely independent of Geertz's influence, we may note, since they were written many years before Geertz's article. (Geertz himself makes no reference to Erikson.) Erikson calls ideology the guardian of identity. 'For the social institution which is the guardian of identity is what we have called ideology' (p. 133). A number of pages later, he writes: 'More generally... an ideological system is a coherent body of shared image, ideas, and ideals which ... provides for the participants a coherent, if systematically simplified, over-all orientation in space and time, in means and ends' (pp. 189–90). Because Erikson raises the problem of the condition of identity, he says that we must go beyond the propagandist concept of ideology, where ideaology is 'a systematic form of collective pseudologia' (p. 190).

On the basis of this analysis of ideology as integrative, I would like to emphasize three points. First, by transforming how the concept of ideology is construed, we stress the symbolic mediation of action, the fact that there is no social action which is not already symbolically mediated. Therefore, we can no longer say that ideology is merely a kind of superstructure. The distinction between superstructure and infrastructure completely disappears, because symbolic systems belong already to the infrastructure, to the basis constitution of human beings. The only aspect of the notion of superstructure that we can say possibly remains is the fact that the symbolic is 'extrinsic,' in the sense that it does not belong to organic life. This is perhaps more a problem in the term 'extrinsic,' however, for what is called extrinsic is still constitutive of human beings.

A second point is the correlation established between ideology and rhetoric. In some ways Habermas prepared us for this connection, since he discussed the problem of ideology in terms of communication or excommunication. Now the correlation is more positive, though, because ideology is not the distortion of communication but the rhetoric of basic communication. There is a rhetoric of basic communication because we cannot exclude rhetorical devices from language; they are an intrinsic part of ordinary language. In its function as integration, ideology is similarly basic and ineluctable.

My third point questions whether we are allowed to speak of ideologies outside the situation of distortion and so with reference only to the basic function of integration. Can we speak of the ideologies of non-modern cultures, cultures which have not entered into the process that Karl Mannheim describes as the collapse of universal agreement, if that ever existed? Is there ideology where there is no conflict of ideologies? If we look only at the integrative function of a culture, and if this function is not challenged by an alternative form for providing integration, may we have ideology? My doubt is whether we can project ideology on cultures outside the post-Enlightenment situation in which all modern cultures are now involved in a process not only of secularization but of fundamental confrontation about basic ideals. I think that integration without confrontation is pre-ideological. Nevertheless, it is still most important to find among the conditions for the possibility of having a distorted function a legitimating function and under this legitimating function an integrative function.

We may also note that the process of deriving the three forms of ideology can proceed in the reverse direction. As Geertz observes quite accurately, ideology is finally always about power. 'It is through the construction of ideologies, schematic images of social order, that man makes himself for better or worse a political animal.' 'The function of ideology,' he continues, 'is to make an autonomous politics possible by providing the authoritative concepts that render it meaningful, the suasive images by means of which it can be sensibly grasped' (p. 218). The notion of the authoritative is a kernel concept, because when the problem of integration leads to the problem of a system of authority, the third concept of ideology sends us back to the second. It is not by chance that a specific place for ideology exists in politics, because politics is the location where the basic images of a group finally provide rules for using power. Questions of integration lead to questions of legitimation, and these in turn lead to questions of distortion. We are therefore forced to proceed backwards and upwards in this hierarchy of concepts.

A question might be raised asking why I take Geertz's notion that ideology provides the 'authoritative concepts' that 'make an autonomous politics possible' as necessarily a statement that ideology is finally about political power. Could not the 'authoritative concepts' be provided by religion, for example? In response, I would say that, consistent with themes running throughout the lectures, I understand the concept of the authoritative as the transition from the integrative function to the legitimation of hierarchy. Geertz comes to my aid here, observing in a footnote to the text just cited: 'Of course, there are moral, economic, and even aesthetic ideologies, as well as specifically political ones, but as very few ideologies of any social prominence lack political implications, it is perhaps permissible to view the problem here in this somewhat narrowed focus. In any case, the arguments developed for political ideologies apply with equal force to nonpolitical ones' (p. 281 n). I am tempted to say that ideology has a broader function than politics to the extent that it is integrative. When integration comes to the problem of the authoritative function of models, however, then politics becomes the focus and the question of identity becomes the frame. What is at stake finally in the process of integration – as we have learned from Weber – is how we can make the transition from the general notion of a social relationship to the notion of rulers and ruled.

The problem of religion is yet a significant one. We may compare Geertz's analysis of ideology with his analysis of religion in 'Religion as a Cultural System,' an article also included in *The Interpretation of Cultures*. It is not the case that ideology replaces religion in modern life; Geertz does not relegate religion simply to past societies. I see three basic points on which Geertz establishes the continuing role of religion. First, religion is the attempt to articulate an ethos and a world-view. He never says that about ideology. Geertz makes a long analysis about the problem of suffering and death and says that the function of a religious system with regard to this issue is not to elude suffering but to teach us how to endure suffering. It is difficult to say that this is a function only of past societies, because at the point when we learn how to suffer, the difference between the ethical and the cosmic collapses; we are taught both a way of looking at life and a way of behaving. Religion is beyond the opposition between the traditional and the modern in a second sense, because its dispositional function allows it to establish a mood. Religion provides a fundamental stability at the level of our most basic feelings. It is a theory of feelings, and as such it again deals with both the ethical and the cosmic. The third point about religion is that it stages these feelings through rituals, and we have some residues and perhaps even some permanent traditions representing that in modern society. Ideology arises not on the collapse of the ritual dimension but from the open conflictual situation of modernity. Systems – even religious ones – are confronted with other systems which raise similar claims of authenticity and legitimacy. We are caught in a situation of ideologies, in the plural.

We may say that Geertz's purpose is not so much to eliminate current theories about ideology – ideology as interests or strains – as to found them at a deeper level. Finally, though, Geertz is more on the side of a strain theory of ideology. The concept of integration precisely has to do with the threat of the lack of identity, what is discussed by Erikson in psychological terms as crisis and confusion. What a group fears most is no longer being able to identify itself because of crises and confusions creating strain; the task is to cope with this strain. Once again the comparison with religion is relevant, because suffering and death play exactly the same role in personal life as a crisis and confusion in the social sphere. The two analyses tend to overlap.

I would add that another positive element about ideology as integration is that it supports the integration of a group not simply in space but in time. Ideology functions not only in the synchronic dimension but also in the diachronic dimension. In the latter case, the memory of the group's founding events is extremely significant; re-enactment of the founding events is a fundamental ideological act. There is an element of a repetition of the origin. With this repetition begin all the ideological processes in the pathological sense, because a second celebration already has the character of reification. The celebration becomes a device for the system of power to preserve its power, so it is a defensive and protective act on the part of the rulers. Can we imagine, though, a community without the celebration of its own birth in more or less mythical terms? France celebrates the fall of the Bastille, and the United States celebrates the Fourth of July. In Moscow a whole political system is based on a tomb, Lenin's tomb, perhaps one of the only cases in history after the Egyptians where a tomb is the source of a political system. This permanent memory of the group's founders and founding events, then, is an ideological structure that can function positively as an integrative structure.

It may be that Geertz's point of view as an anthropologist is the decisive reason for his emphasis on integration and thus on strain theory. As an anthropologist, Geertz has a different perspective from someone like Habermas, who is a sociologist of modern industrial society. In the kind of societies with which Geertz deals – the main sources of his field-work are Indonesia and Morocco – the problematic is not that of industrial or post-industrial society but that of societies which are developing, in every sense of that word. For these societies the critique of ideology is premature; their focus is more the constitutive nature of ideology. When intellectuals or other dissidents in these societies use the tools of ideology-critique, whether in the sense of Habermas or, more typically, in the sense of Althusser, they are usually sent to prison if not killed. Dissidents become marginal when they apply the critical tools of an advanced society to the birth of a new society. The methodological point, then, is to consider to what extent Geertz's viewpoint as an anthropologist commits him to an analysis which cannot be that of a Habermas.

It may be too simple, though, to say that developing countries have only to deal with the constitutive character of ideology, because their arduous task is to find their own identity in a world already marked by the crisis of industrial societies. Not only have the advanced industrial societies accumulated and confiscated most of the means and the tools for development; they have engendered a crisis of advanced society which is now a public and world phenomenon. Societies are entering into the process of industrialization at the same time as nations at the top of this development are raising questions about the process. Countries have to incorporate technology at the same time that the critique and trial of technology has begun. For intellectuals in these countries, the task is an especially difficult one, because they live in two ages at the same time. They live at the beginning of the industrial period, let us say the eighteenth century, but they are also part of the twentieth century, because they are raised in a culture which has already entered into the crisis of the relation between its goals and the critique of technology. The concept of ideology has now become universal, therefore, because the crisis of the industrial societies is a universal crisis; it is part of the education of any intellectual at any place in the world. I remember travelling a number of years ago in Syria, Lebanon, and other parts of the Middle East, and in their libraries one finds the works of Simone de Beauvoir, Sartre, and so on. Everyone is now the contemporary of everyone else. People in developing countries are educated at the same time with the intellectual tools of their own culture and the tools of the crisis of the developed countries.

If ideology is now a universal issue, the Marxist claim is that the concept of ideology came into being with the development of social classes. The argument is that ideology did not exist prior to the rise of class structures. Althusser goes so far as to say that before the bourgeoisie there was no ideology. There are creeds and beliefs, but only the class structure created the situation that an important part of the population did not share the values of the whole. As we have seen, the Marxist perspective emphasizes the distortive aspects of ideology rather than its integrative function. In response to this emphasis, I would claim that the primitive concept of ideology as integration cannot be used in political practice except for the purpose of preserving, even in the situation of struggle, the problematic of recognition. If I understand that the distorting function could not appear if there were not a symbolic structure of action, then at least I know that it is because an integrative process is under way that there may be some class conflicts. Class conflicts are therefore never exactly situations of total war. Realization of the integrative character of ideology helps to preserve the appropriate level of class struggle, which is not to destroy the adversary but to achieve recognition. To put it in Hegelian terms, the struggle is for recognition and not for power. The underlying integrative function of ideology prevents us from pushing the polemical element to its destructive point – the point of civil war. What prevents us from making a plea for civil war is that we have to preserve the life of our adversary; an element of belonging together persists. Even the class enemy is not a radical enemy. In some sense he or she is still a neighbour. The concept of ideology as integrative puts a limit on social war and prevents it from becoming a civil war. Some of the European communist parties – particularly in Italy and now in France and Spain – have formulated the idea that the problem is to develop a society better integrated than in the class structure. The point, then, is really to integrate and not to suppress or destroy one's enemy.

The grounds for this transformation may already exist in class society. Even in class society integrative processes are at work: the sense of a common language, a common culture, and a common nation. People share at least the linguistic tools and all the communicative means that are linked to language, so we have to locate the role of language in a class structure. Resolution of this question was an important battle among Marxists earlier this century. At least for a time Stalin was on the correct side against those Marxists who said that even grammar has a class structure. Stalin argued instead that the language belongs to the nation as a whole. The status of the nation in Marxist theory is difficult to elaborate because it cuts across class lines. We may say that Geertz's concept of ideology is more appropriate for an issue like this, since the status of the nation is not radically affected by the class structure. In attempting to define the nature of the nation, the question is as problematic as the definition of sex roles: it is difficult to say what is really fundamental and what is merely cultural. Only by changing traits or roles do we discover what cannot be changed. It is by questioning class affiliations that we may be able to identify what is constitutive of a community beyond or above its class structure. Many Marxists now say in fact that Marxism must be realized according to the different cultural situations in which it finds itself. These situations are then defined precisely by what Geertz calls an ideological system. We have to deal with the norms and the images that project a group's identity in the same way as some psychologists speak of the body image. There is a social group image, and this image of identity is particular to each group.

We may take the ideology of the United States as an example. The first point about this ideology is that it cannot be defined in isolation from its relations with other countries and their own ideological patterns. The United States is hardly in the position of isolation that would shield it from confrontation with other national ideologies. As Lenin was quite conscious, the stage is now the world. We should note that this situation is of rather recent origin. Before the First World War, the inner conflicts of Europe ruled the world situation. Now that Europe has collapsed by its inner wars, though, the conflict is more global. The relation, for example, between the Third World and the industrial world is currently a fundamental battle. Thus, the ideology of the United States is defined in part by its external relations.

As for judging the internal determinants of this ideology, we have more difficulty responding if we no longer rely solely on the Marxist concept of class, where one group is the dominant class and sets forth the ruling ideas – the ideology – of the nation. Someone like Mannheim is both quite clever and quite cautious on this issue, because he always speaks of a social stratum. He leaves us the task of identifying which groups are at work in society and in what way. In fact, the task is precisely to consider all the various social groupings and not to preclude other determinants than the notion of class. Perhaps class is only one structure among many. Consider, for instance, the question of racial and ethnic minorities, a most prominent issue in this country. In what category do we put minorities? They are not a class nor a nation. We must be flexible with the concept of social stratum; perhaps the connection between a stratum and an ideology or utopia is what gives unity to both. It may be, as some argue, that the United States is shifting from a melting-pot to a mosaic. This means that many groups and consequently many ideologies make up whatever is the whole. Ethnic consciousness is now a collective component of a broader national ideological mixture.

It is still true, though, that the United States does have a common ideology. As a foreigner, I am quite conscious of the unity of the ideology in this country, and I take the term 'ideology' here in a neutral sense. Consider the question of unemployment. For me, this is a typical difference between Europe and the United States. In Europe, to be unemployed is an injustice; one has a right to work. Here unemployment is seen as an individual failure. It is not an accusation directed against the system but a personal problem. The unemployed must rely on welfare and food stamps, which makes them still more dependent on the system. The failure of being unemployed is accentuated by this dependence. Although the concept of free enterprise may be an object of criticism, it is finally taken for granted. Everyone is competing against everyone else. Even the way students work in this country – individual against individual – is quite different from Europe. This pervasive individualism has some healthy implications but also implies that while everything run by private enterprise is in good condition, public enterprises like the railroad suffer. There is no sense of the common property. The United States does have something like a collective ideology, then, though I know that those who live within it are more aware of its subideologies or subcultures.

To conclude this last paper on ideology, let me say that the concept of integration is a presupposition of the two other main concepts of ideology – legitimation and distortion – but actually functions ideologically by means of these two other factors. Further, the nexus between these three functions may be situated by relating the role of ideology to the larger role of the imagination in social life. My presupposition at this more general level, which I shall develop further in the lectures on utopia, is that imagination works in two different ways. On the one hand, imagination may function to preserve an order. In this case the function of the imagination is to stage a process of identification that mirrors the order. Imagination has the appearance here of a picture. On the other hand, though, imagination may have a disruptive function; it may work as a breakthrough. Its image in this case is productive, an imagining of something else, the elsewhere. In each of its three roles, ideology represents the first kind of imagination; it has a function of preservation, of conservation. Utopia, in contrast, represents the second kind of imagination; it is always the glance from nowhere. As Habermas has suggested, perhaps it is a dimension of the libido itself to project itself *aus* – outside, nowhere – in this movement of transcendence, whereas ideology is always on the brink of becoming pathological because it has a conservative function in both the good and the bad senses of that word. Ideology preserves identity, but it also wants to conserve what exists and is therefore already a resistance. Something becomes ideological – in the more negative meaning of the term – when the integrative function becomes frozen, when it becomes rhetorical in the bad sense, when schematization and rationalization prevail. Ideology operates at the turning-point between the integrative function and resistance.

Note

1   Here and throughout this essay, Ricoeur makes reference to the other lectures in the series 'On Ideology and Utopia' that he delivered at the University of Chicago in autumn 1975. The entire series was edited by George H. Taylor and published as *Paul Ricoeur: Lectures on Ideology and Utopia* (New York: Columbia University Press 1986).

In the final lecture on Fourier, Ricoeur clarifies his use of the term 'regressive' to refer to a method that 'attempts to dig under the surface of the apparent meaning to the more fundamental meaning. [Ed.]

Construing and Constructing:
A Review of *The Aims of Interpretation*
by E.D. Hirsch, Jr

In 1967, E.D. Hirsch published *Validity in Interpretation*. Now, nearly ten years later, in *The Aims of Interpretation*, he proposes 'to amplify important subjects that were dealt with only briefly in the earlier book.' In speaking of amplification, the author denies having introduced any 'substantive revisions of the earlier argument.' I would say, for my part, that *The Aims of Interpretation* actually takes a middle course between amplification and revision.

On two points the earlier work left the reader in some confusion. The first concerned the relationship between the internal meaning of a work of art, what Professor Hirsch called the 'verbal meaning,' and the intention of the author, or 'authorial meaning.' He defended with equal vigour the idea that meaning must be determinate, i.e., self-identical, in order to be sharable and the object of a valid interpretation, and the idea that the ultimate norm of validation of all interpretation was 'authorial meaning.' His purpose was to reinforce the autonomy of the meaning in order to prevent its usurpation by the reader, but he thereby risked falling into what W.K. Wimsatt called 'intentional fallacy.'

The second ambiguity in *Validity in Interpretation* was this: if in principle Professor Hirsch distinguished between the meaning of the work and its significance for the reader and critic, he did not succeed in elucidating this distinction, for this problem was finally overshadowed by the problem of validating our 'guesses' about the possible ways of constructing the meaning of a text. The great originality of *The Aims of Interpretation* is to have made the distinction between 'meaning' and 'significance' the main line of his argument. The second ambiguity is thus resolved, but perhaps at the cost of an untenable separation. As for the first ambiguity, we shall see later on to what extent the reorientation of all hermeneutics as a function of the couplet meaning/significance removes that.

Criticism must therefore be concerned with the major distinction between meaning and significance. In my opinion Professor Hirsch is better when he argues and polemicizes in order to introduce his distinction than when he gets down to resolving the difficulties which result from it. Broadly speaking, the distinction is one between 'content' and 'context': the term 'meaning' refers to the verbal meaning within the text; the word 'significance' designates the relevance of the text beyond itself, as a function of the interests, values, and norms which preside over its evaluation. This demarcation extends beyond the confines of literature; it alone ensures in a general way the identity of the same objects of experience in time. Within the framework of literature, the autonomy of meaning in relation to significance achieves its full prominence once one recognizes that the private processes of verbal understanding follow the same rules as the public processes of validation.

Consequently, there are not two things: to understand and to validate. To understand is already to construe for oneself a scheme, a genre, a type, which together yield expectations and are in their turn susceptible or not of being confirmed. In thus conceiving understanding to be a 'validating, self-correcting process,' Professor Hirsch transfers on to his theory of meaning all the weight of his earlier theory of validation. His purpose in so doing is to provide himself with weapons against all forms of relativism, thus giving his work a deliberately polemical tone. Among the relativists he naturally puts those literary critics who deny that meaning can be separated from significance, but he also includes all those who, following Heidegger, insist on the circular character of understanding: to these he adds, for good measure, French theorists like Barthes, Foucault, and Derrida, who become, in his terms, 'theologians of dogmatic relativism' and 'cognitive atheists.' I must confess that to me this process of amalgamation seems very debatable. In this work no more than in the earlier one has Professor Hirsch perceived the difference between a hermeneutic philosophy and a relativistic literary criticism which would impose the perspective of the reader as the criterion of meaning. To this mistake he now adds a second by enrolling under the same relativist banner the new wave of French theorists and the hermeneutists stemming from Heidegger.

If one forgets temporarily the universalizing pretensions of this work, its critique of some of the relativist arguments seems very persuasive. This is the case first of all with the 'paradoxes of perspectivism': the author establishes in a very convincing fashion that the visual metaphor of perspective suggests exactly the opposite of what relativism sees in it; I can understand that the same object is seen by another spectator from a different angle than mine because I can depart from my own perspective, co-ordinate it with others, and recognize the identical object which relates my perspective to other people's. Professor Hirsch quite rightly concludes that all acts of interpretation necessarily include two perspectives, that of the author and that of the interpreter. (However, he refuses to see that H.-G. Gadamer's notion of the 'fusion of horizons' proceeds from a precisely similar reflection on double perspective.)

The same clear-sightedness shines out in the chapter 'Stylistics and Synonymity.' The author at first picks his way between two extreme positions. If two different sentences are taken as synonyms, this is not to say that they are substitutable in every context, which would be to reduce them to an empty tautology; but neither is it to say that they do not have any meaning in common, which would be to ignore the independence of the stylistic level with respect to that of the structural analysis of content. Professor Hirsch reckons to escape these two pitfalls by distinguishing the proposition which is the kernel identical to both synonyms from the synonymous phrases themselves. One might think that the indeterminacy of the form with respect to the content furnishes an argument rather in favour of relativism. No, answers Professor Hirsch, for in freeing meaning from the tutelage of form, meaning recovers its identity at the level of the proposition. Thus, synonymity becomes an argument in favour of the fundamentally determinable character of meaning. But Professor Hirsch does not tell us how one could transpose to the interpretation of a text the distinction between the identical proposition, underlying several synonymous sentences, and the sentences themselves.

Be that as it may, these two more technical studies are remarkably good. But Professor Hirsch's thesis finally stands or falls on whether it is possible clearly to separate meaning from significance, i.e., the descriptive from the normative aspects of interpretation. In a certain sense, the thesis becomes more radical the more it is clarified. Thus, the author now confesses that he gave too narrow a definition of the meaning of a text when he identified it with the 'author's original meaning'; that is the second ambiguity of which I spoke earlier. How far is it resolved in the present book? The logic of the separation of meaning from significance would require that the author's intention be a case of 'meaning-for-another,' and therefore belong on the side of significance. However, Professor Hirsch does not wish to draw this conclusion: he concedes that the intention of the author is not the only *possible* norm of interpretation, but maintains that it is, in the strong sense of the word, the only *practical* norm. All verbal significance must be constructed; but there is no construction without choice, and no choice without a norm. It is at this point that the original authorial meaning asserts its claim: the most fundamental moral imperative of discourse is to respect the intention of the author.

I understand this answer. But it raises an even more fundamental problem which calls into question the distinction between meaning and significance. I have just said that meaning must be constructed – it is not given in the written signs; further, it is the minimal presupposition of a theory of validation that the meaning be first guessed before being validated. We must therefore admit that the identity of meaning with itself is not given in any intuition of essence, but yielded only by the test of validation. Now, it is precisely in the work of construction that choices occur, and with choice, aims, values, and norms. In other words, questions of choice are an integral part of the construction of meaning. We no longer have to deal with only the two aspects of interpretation – meaning and significance – but with the 'three dimensions of hermeneutics' (which is the title of the fifth essay in this book). The third dimension is the ethical choice itself which, on the one hand, intervenes in the field of description, since there must be a norm in order to realize the meaning of a text, but on the other, already belongs to the problematics of evaluation (which is why the fifth essay is meant to be a chapter of transition between the two parts of the book).

Part Two, which is devoted to evaluation, confirms the reader's suspicions that the demarcation between meaning and significance cannot be maintained without equivocation. Professor Hirsch is not prepared to say that Northrop Frye, rather than René Wellek, is right in their quarrel over the possibility of separating value and meaning. On the one hand, the 'separatists' are partially correct, in so far as description and evaluation constitute two distinct poles of interpretation. The argument of Professor Hirsch's work is solidly entrenched on this thesis, which is less clear-cut than that of demarcation. It is perfectly legitimate to ask of criticism that it situate its disagreements about the value of a work in relation to the meaning on which it tries to agree.

It is entirely legitimate even to give free rein to conflicts of evaluation as long as one strives elsewhere for a common description of the text. But in the concrete work of interpretation the two tasks never cease to become confused, and this means that the 'anti-separatists' too are partially correct. This impossibility was foreseeable inasmuch as our knowledge of the meaning is in no way authorized by any intuitive insight into it. Because meaning has to be constructed, value and meaning are necessarily joined. In fact, Professor Hirsch's recourse to the 'Analytics of the Beautiful' in Kant's third *Critique* can only reinforce the thesis of the indissoluble liaison between fact and value, because it is a subjective judgment of values which, in the Kantian theory of 'common sense,' is taken as communicable, sharable, and in this sense universal. One can understand why Professor Hirsch should insist in his final essay that, once conceded, this 'interference' must not weaken the basic distinction between meaning and significance. That is the thesis which has to remain as the chief thrust of the book if the enemy to be overcome is relativism and if the latest form of this relativism is found among the French theorists, who are accused of reducing all textual commentary to a mere fiction. It is Professor Hirsch's combative spirit which leads him to subordinate the unstable realm of value to the stable realm of meaning. But has he not himself undermined the stability of this realm by showing that all textual meaning has to be constructed, that all construction requires choice, and that all choice involves ethical values?

Review of Nelson Goodman's
Ways of Worldmaking

The seven chapters which compose Goodman's new book will be no
surprise for readers of *Fact, Fiction, and Forecast* and *Languages of
Art*. But these readers will be confronted by the most radical and the
most condensed exposition of the author's philosophy (plus some
internal excursions, if I dare say so, which add the pleasure of
discovery to that of recognition).

I

The thesis is simple, rigorous, and uncompromising. For the sake of
didactic clarity, I analyse it in three partial theses:

1 / *We 'make' the world by construing symbolic systems* (in a sense of
the word symbol akin to Ernst Cassirer's use of the term)[1] *which are
numerous and equally legitimate: descriptive theories, perceptions,
novels, paintings, musical scores, etc. (Thesis I)*
    In order to help the reader to exercise the thesis, the author starts
with a familiar example which implies only statements, but whose
truth-claims are at odds with each other: 'The sun always moves,'
'The sun never moves.' We are ready to rewrite the two statements in
such a way that the emphasis is shifted from what is described to
systems of description: 'Under frame of reference A, the sun always
moves, and under frame of reference B, the sun never moves.' A
more difficult step is taken when we juxtapose and conjoin two
pictures, say, a Van Gogh and a Canaletto, or a picture and a statement. All of them are equally versions or visions (I shall return in my
critical part to this duplication of terms) of the world.
    This first phase of the theory recalls Cassirer, but more strikingly

radicalizes him. In the *Philosophy of Symbolic Forms*, linguistic forms, mythical and aesthetical forms, and scientific forms were indeed held as distinct and irreducible (in a cultural rather than transcendental sense of the term 'form'), but Cassirer's pluralism was still a mixed one to the extent that symbolic forms taken together constitute a teleological development ruled by the mind's thrust towards objectivity, i.e., scientific knowledge. In that sense the system of symbolic forms remains a hierarchical system. Unlike Cassirer, Goodman sees no such hierarchy obtaining between versions and visions. 'Just this, I think: that many different world-versions are of independent interest and importance, without any requirement or presumption of reducibility to a single base' (p. 4). In that sense, his pluralism is a radical pluralism.

2 / Each of these ways of world making is a world-version rather than a version of the world, in the sense that there is no world in itself before or beneath these versions. (Thesis II)

This thesis is supported by the lack of any test that could allow us to compare a version to a world which would be neither described, nor perceived, nor depicted. Here, too, Goodman radicalizes a thesis that Cassirer had developed in *Function and Substance*, before writing his *Philosophy of Symbolic Forms*: by dissolving substance into function, Cassirer had completed the demolition of the thing in itself, insofar as the priority of the category of substance over that of causality among the triadic set of Kant's categories of relation could still offer a basis for reinstating the thing in itself. The same negative argument may be put in the following terms: there is no way of showing that two versions are of the *same* world, because the question 'same or not the same?' must be complemented by the addition of 'same what?' Then the use of the term *same* is always relative to a homogeneous kind. We may only say that versions differ in that not everything belonging to one belongs to the other, or that there is no more a unique world of worlds than there is a unique world (p. 17).

Therefore we must drop the idea that versions are versions of one and the same neutral and underlying world. As a corollary to this second stage of the thesis, we have to say that no version is the basic one and the others derivative, as physicalism does say of the physical world, phenomenalism of the perceptual world, and the man in the street of interpretations based on custom and prejudice. And if somebody asks out of what worlds are made, we have to answer:

from other worlds, from worlds already on hand. The making is a remaking. In that way, the radical pluralism of the author is at the same time a radical relativism.

3 /*World versions other than the scientific one are neither true nor false. And yet some may be said to be right and others wrong. There must be therefore criteria to assign or to deny rightness to non-descriptive world versions. (Thesis III)*

This thesis first imposes a twofold limit to the concept of truth. First the question of truth makes sense only if a version is verbal and consists in statements. For non-verbal versions and verbal versions without statements, truth is irrelevant. Second, within these limits, truth cannot be defined or tested by agreements with the world, since one cannot compare a description to a non-described world. We can only say that 'a version is taken to be true when it offends no unyielding beliefs and none of its own precepts' (p. 17). '"The truth, the whole truth, and nothing but the truth" would thus be a perverse and paralyzing policy for any worldmaker' (p. 19). Now, what is *rightness* has still to be shown. But it is impossible to proceed farther without incorporating within the thesis some fundamental *rules of categorization* concerning the functioning of symbolic systems which are mainly imported from *Languages of Art.*

II

This reference to the scheme of organization governing symbolic systems proposed in *Languages of Art* requires from the reader of *Ways of Worldmaking* a rare mental effort. 'The pluralists' acceptance of versions other than physics implies no relaxation of rigor but a recognition that standards different from yet no less exacting than those applied in science are appropriate for appraising what is conveyed in perceptual or pictorial or literary versions' (p. 5). The difficulty is duplicated by the fact that this last book proceeds mainly by allusions and footnotes sending back to the appropriate chapters of *Languages of Art.* This is why it may be helpful to give at least a rough draft of this scheme.

The reader must take as a guideline the statement which closes the first chapter of *Ways of Worldmaking* that arts are *cognitive*: 'All the processes of world making I have discussed enter into knowing' (p. 22). Then he must learn to master the technical tools which allow us to ascribe reference and rightness to symbols which are neither verbal nor descriptive. The key distinctions occur within the framework of the *referential* function of all symbols, which implies nothing else and nothing more than that all symbolic systems are capable of making and remaking the world, of 'reorganizing the world in terms of works and works in terms of the world' (*Languages of Art*, p. 241). The key distinctions concern the appropriate use of such terms as denotation, description, depiction, exemplification, and expression, which together constitute the conceptual network of both books. Denotation defines the kind of referential function obtaining in the subclass of symbols which may be said to be *applied* to items. Exemplification, as we shall see, does something other than denoting, in spite of the fact that it refers in its own way. The two main kinds of denotation symbols are verbal descriptions and non-verbal depictions. Verbal descriptions apply 'labels' to occurrences. These 'labels' may be applied literally or metaphorically. Metaphors are merely unusual applications of 'labels,' i.e., applications of familiar labels (whose usage consequently has a past) to new objects: 'metaphor is an affair between a predicate with a past and an object that yields while protesting' (*Languages of Art*, p. 73). In that sense, we may speak of metaphorical truth, to the extent that we already speak of literal truth. Now the grouping of description and depiction under the same heading of denotation has as its aim to assimilate the relation between a picture and what it depicts to that between a predicate and that to which it is applied. At the same time, it says that representing (or depicting) is not imitating in the sense of resembling or copying. In that way, pictures are one of the ways through which nature becomes a product of discourse and of art. (By extension we may call 'labels' all symbols which denote: nouns, predicates, gestures, pictures.) We leave the subclass of denotative symbols when we introduce 'samples' and 'exemplifications.' Here, we no longer apply a given label to a something. We have the sample and we look for the property, the feature which is thus exemplified and which the sample 'possesses.' 'Samples' in that way refer too, but reference, here, runs in the opposite direction from denotation (i.e., description and depiction). 'Exemplification and expression, though running in the opposite direction from denotation – that is from the symbol to a literal or metaphorical feature of it instead of to something the symbol applies to – are no less symbolic referential functions and instruments of worldmaking' (*Ways of Worldmaking*, p. 12). What is most interesting for our discussion of *Ways of Worldmaking* is 1 / that such non-linguistic symbols as forms, feelings, affinities, contrasts may be exemplified; 2 / that exemplification, as well as application, may be literal or metaphorical, i.e., unusually extended or expanded. It is in that guise that we say that a painting 'expresses' sadness. Sadness is exemplified literally by human faces or gestures and expressed metaphorically by paintings, musical pieces, etc. Exemplification and expression are thus referential without being denotational. One may give a graphic sketch of this schema of categorization by saying that it proceeds by the way of a succession of extensions of the sphere of referentiality: 1 / starting from description (verbal symbol), 2 / adding metaphorical to literal description, 3 / then conjoining depiction (non-verbal symbol) to description, 4 / then adding metaphorical to literal depiction to complete the field of denotation, 5 / then complementing denotation by exemplification and expression. 'Worlds are made not only by what is said literally but also by what is said metaphorically, and not only by what is said either literally or metaphorically but also by what is exemplified and expressed – by what is shown as well as by what is said' (*Ways*, p. 18). 'A non-representational picture such as a Mondrian denotes nothing, pictures nothing, and is neither true nor false, but shows much. Nevertheless, showing or exemplifying, like denoting, is a referential function; and much the same considerations count for pictures as for the concepts or the predicates of a theory' (p. 19). This last extension is the most significant for our topic. It implies that abstract paintings and other works that have no subject nevertheless inform our worlds, through the feelings, rhythms, structures, and forms that they exemplify or express.

One may wonder whether this categorization of the system of symbols may be itself true or false. The answer is that it may be right or wrong, not true or false. We shall return to that sensible topic at the end of the present section.

This rough sketch allows me to give a brief account of the four studies that Goodman has, so to speak, interpolated between his first and two last broader studies. The author acknowledges in his foreword that 'this book does not run a straight course from beginning to end. It hunts ... And it counts not the kill but what is learned of the territory explored' (p. ix). This writer does not therefore need to be 'plus royaliste que le roi,' as we say in French. Nevertheless it is his task to find the unity underneath. This unity, we shall see, is provided by the conceptual network which we just described.

'The Status of Style' (chap. 2) has at its aim the delineation of the stylistic features of a work. If such distinctions as how and what, style and subject, style and feeling, extrinsic and intrinsic features are misleading oppositions, there remain two distinctive features. First, style functions like signature to identify an individual or a group as the 'place' of the work (in that way, Goodman denies that questions of authorship have nothing to do with the understanding of a work [p. 38]). Furthermore, style designates the symbolic function as such of the work, i.e., the kind of referential function that it assumes (description, depiction, exemplification, or expression). It is in that indirect way that the identification of the style of a work contributes to the understanding of its way of world-making. And this is not a secondary task, since nothing is more hidden than the actual stylistic traits of a work. 'Styles are normally accessible only to the knowing eye or ear, the tuned sensibility, the informed and inquisitive mind' (p. 39). The author may conclude his chapter by saying that 'the discernment of style is an integral aspect of the understanding of works of art and the worlds they present' (p. 40).

'Some Questions Concerning Quotation' (chap. 3) is, perhaps, a better sample of hunt than of kill. The main question is whether we may speak of quotation in non-verbal symbolic systems. If I am right, the question is relevant for the purpose of the present work to the extent that it gives an opportunity for testing the analogy between description and depiction. Furthermore, 'as ways of combining and constructing symbols, [pictorial and musical quotations] are among the instruments for world-making' (p. 56).

'When Is Art?" (chap. 4) is also linked to the main topic through indirect and tortuous links. Starting from the more classical question What is art? the author meets the purist (or formalist) thesis according to which any representational or expressive feature of a work is irrelevant to art criticism because it is external to the work. A dilemma confronts us here. Either 'we seem to be advocating lobotomy on many great works,' or 'we seem to be condoning impurity in art, emphasizing the extraneous' (p. 60). The solution to this dilemma is that the purist is both right and wrong – right in excluding everything which is extrinsic to the work, wrong in overlooking the kind of referential function inherent to the work. It is at that stage that our previous analysis of exemplification and expression becomes helpful: as any 'sample,' a work free of representation may still exemplify certain patterns of shape, colour, texture, that it shows forth and that contribute to world-making. 'Art without representation or expression or exemplification – yes; art without all three – no' (p. 66). But the confirmation of the referential thesis is not the only outcome of the analysis. The very initial question What is art? appears to be a wrong question. The functions of exemplifying symbols impose another more appropriate question: When is art? There is art *when* the 'symptoms' of what counts as art are there. Altogether they provide to a work of art a specific non-transparency which derives mainly from the integration and interaction of its multiple and complex references.[2]

The indirect contribution of this study to the overall undertaking of the book has now become quite clear. The way in which an object or event functions in certain circumstances as a work of art through certain modes of reference is a part of the way in which it contributes 'to a vision of – and to the making of – a world' (p. 70).

'A Puzzle about Perception' (chap. 5) seems to be more remote from the mainstream of the book. But it reminds us that perception, too, makes a world. We had learned that from Gombrich's analysis of perspective in *Art and Illusion.* Goodman adds here an argument borrowed from experimental psychology concerning the perception of apparent movement (apparent in the sense that it is 'not there' for the observer). Goodman does not only review some of the puzzles yielded by the experiments, but adds his own puzzle. Psychologists have only considered apparent changes in position, form, and size of moving objects and noticed that apparent transition in those cases is smooth. Goodman observes something new when we add colour to movement; for example, when a black square moves at moderate speed from left to right against a white background, at each moment, the left edge of the black flicks to white merging with the background (the same from black to white for the other edge), without passing through intermediate greys. This contrast between the smooth shape change and the colour-jumps *is* the puzzle. The puzzle evaporates, Goodman claims, when we consider that those jumps preserve the identity of the object in motion-perception. Object-identity, then, appears to be a construct, not a given.

The example of motion-perception is not therefore marginal. It is rather a striking example 'of how perception makes its facts' (p. 89), in other words, of how the perceptual version of the world is *made.*

'The Fabrication of Facts' (chap. 6) is a kind of summary of the intermediary chapters and brings the reader back to the main thesis of chapter 1: 'worlds are made by making such versions with words, numerals, pictures, sounds, or other symbols of any kind in any medium; and the comparative study of these versions and visions and of their making is what I call a critique of worldmaking' (p. 94).

The main thing to say about this critique is that the *radical relativism* implied by the thesis allows no laxity. On the contrary, as in Kant and Cassirer, the task is to analyse with the utmost accuracy the *ways* of world-making proper to each kind of version. The technical examples selected above by Goodman show how demanding the task is. The most demanding cases are those belonging to versions that are not literal, not denotational, not verbal. Metaphors, exemplifications and expressions, pictures or sounds or gestures or other non-linguistic symbolic systems are the most difficult topics of the critique of world-making.

But the ultimate test of this critique is without any doubt the status of *rightness* of non-verbal versions. We gave above (at the end of the first part of this discussion) a first draft of the thesis that truth is relevant only for statements, but that there are criteria of rightness for non-verbal versions which are as cogent as those of truth for statements. Goodman returns to this thesis in the last chapter of his book, 'On Rightness of Rendering' (chap. 7), and supports it with the acquisitions made in the preceding parts of his book. Goodman resumes here the notion of *fitness* introduced in *Languages of Art* but brings it a bit farther. Two claims are made. First, truth is not even the only consideration in descriptive versions of the world. That choice among statements or versions requires some tests in *judging* truths already requires criteria of rightness, such as utility or coherence, or better validity in deductive or inductive arguments, or still better *rightness of categorization*: 'Such rightness is one step farther removed from truth; for while deductive and inductive rightness still have to do with statements, which have truth-value, rightness of categorization attaches to categories or predicates – or systems thereof – which have no truth-value' (p. 127).

This thesis about rightness of categorization is all the more important since the whole critique of world-making falls under it, to the extent that this critique itself relies on the categorization of the symbolic systems. Therefore, Goodman has to apply to his own work what he says about categorial systems: 'For a categorial system, what needs to be shown is not that it is true but what it can do. Put crassly, what is called for in such cases is less arguing than selling' (p. 129).

Thus, it is the rightness of the whole proposed scheme of categorization which supports the very analysis of rightness of non-verbal versions. This can be shown in great detail. The test is fitness in exemplification. To the question: 'When is a sample right?' the only answer is nearly tautological: when it may be 'rightly projected to the pattern or mixture or other relevant feature of the whole or of further samples' (p. 135). Right projectability is fairness in exemplification. Yet, projectability is no mere equivalent of fairness, to the extent that to establish projectability is a quite demanding task; it depends upon conformity to good practice in interpreting samples, therefore, in the last resort, 'upon habit in continual revision under frustration and invention' (p. 137). Discovering what is exemplified requires taste, as Kant would say: 'what counts as success in achieving accord depends upon what our habits, progressively modified in the face of new encounters and new proposals, adopt as projectible kinds' (p. 137). In this arduous task we are no longer helped by arguments of universal and atemporal acceptability. To return to Kant, his criterion of the universality of the judgment of taste crumbles, since there is no universal and eternal acceptability. Test results are transient and what is once maximally acceptable may later be unacceptable. Nevertheless, we have to keep ultimate acceptability as what we mean by rightness, if rightness must remain parallel to truth. We are not that far from what Kant called 'aesthetic Ideas' in the third *Critique*, with the following pragmatic qualification: 'ultimate acceptability, though as inaccessible as absolute rightness would be, is thus nevertheless explicable in terms of the tests and their results' (p. 139).

Because of the circularity of the definition of rightness within a conceptual framework which cannot claim to be true but right, Goodman is *right* to conclude by these words: 'My readers could weaken that latter conviction [that any approach to universal accord on anything significant in artistic and even scientific judgment is exceptional] by agreeing unanimously with the foregoing somewhat tortuous and in a double sense trying course of thought' (p. 140). The last sentence of the book is more than a joke intended to capture the benevolence of the reader. Bordering the argument of the 'Liar,' it underscores the difficult epistemological status of a categorial system which unavoidably defines its own validity in the terms of the major category that the organizational scheme yields. We are therefore sent back to the aphorism: 'For a categorial system, what needs to be shown is not that it is true but what it can do' (p. 129).

III

My personal assessment of Goodman's work is a mixture of agreement and disagreement – but at different levels.

I have no hesitation in acknowledging that I heartily approve the daring attempt to go farther than Cassirer in the recognition of the plurality and irreducibility of world-versions. This thesis is not only liberal but liberating. To go farther than Cassirer, Goodman had to give up the still hierarchical conception of symbolic forms whose outcome was to put the scientific version at the top of the ascending scale of forms.

With an equal conviction I hold as plausible the organizational scheme of symbolic forms that Goodman transfers from *Languages of Art* to *Ways of Worldmaking*. I hold it not only as plausible, but as *right*, in the sense that the author ascribes to *rightness*. I adhere accordingly to the idea that a categorial system may be neither true nor false – in the sense of the term true that I shall discuss later – but right or wrong. Here, to be right means to *fit* with our current experience with symbols. And it fits to the extent that it provides guidelines for using such terms as 'description,' 'depiction,' 'denotation,' 'exemplification,' 'expression,' and so on, appropriately to the way we *already make sense* with statements or paintings, whether representational or not. In that sense, Goodman offers a modern version of what Kant called transcendental deduction, i.e., the justification (in the juridical sense) of the claim that the categorial network shows the condition of the possibility of meaningfulness in our use of symbolic structures. This transcendental deduction presupposes therefore that we have already recognized in a non-reflective way the variety of the referential modes of our world-versions. This previous recognition entails what we could call a spontaneous, i.e., non-reflective, phenomenology of the meaningfulness of statements and paintings. It is this spontaneous phenomenology of the universal and varied referentiality of all our symbols that justifies or warrants the construction of any organizational system of symbolic forms.

I should like now to inquire into this spontaneous phenomenology. It seems to me that it may entail some suggestions, even some requirements other than those displayed by Goodman's *Ways of Worldmaking.*

Let us return to the three major theses which we commented on in our presentation of Goodman's book. It is within these theses that I find motives for both agreement and disagreement.

My praise of Goodman's pluralism seemed to endorse *Thesis 1* without qualifications. Nevertheless my disagreement starts there. And it starts with the very expression world-*making.* On the one hand, Goodman makes a vibrant plea for the *cognitive* significance of works of art. His fights against the emotionalist and ornamental theory of metaphor – his defense of the referential capacity of non-representational painting – are the most striking examples of his declared intellectualism. Furthermore, he assumes M. Polanyi's use of the concept of understanding (p. 22). On the other hand, he transfers into the realm of knowledge categories which have their first use in the field of production. This transfer is not indeed wrong in all regards. Aristotle, speaking of the composition of a literary work such as epic and tragedy, applies to it the concept of *poiesis,* i.e., fabrication of something exterior to the maker, and the very expression 'work of art' witnesses to this right use of the term *making.* But, if the composition of a work (of discourse, of art, or whatever you have in the field of symbolic works) pertains to the order of making, is the referential aiming of the work itself fully characterized as making? What supports the partial identification between knowing and making is the description by Goodman of such *ways* of world-making as composition and decomposition, weighing, ordering, deletion and supplementation, deformation.[3] But these modes of construction do not exhaust the intentionality constitutive of the referentiality of symbols. The factor of otherness proper to this intentionality is overshadowed by the factor of fabrication proper to the ways of world-making described above.

My argument here is merely phenomenological. It intends to give an account of our dealing with symbols to which the symbolic system is supposed to be attuned. Does a painter like Cézanne make a version of the world in the same way as one makes a car? The deep thrust that moves him to paint, and which is the origin of that which Merleau-Ponty describes as 'Cézanne's Doubt' in a famous essay, seems to arise from a stubborn attempt to 'render' what he keeps calling Nature (with a capital N). Let us put aside for the moment the word *Nature,* and let us focus on the term '*render.*' Goodman too uses it. His last chapter is entitled 'On Rightness of Rendering.' My contention is that making and rendering are not substitutable terms but form together a dynamical and dialectical pair at the phenomenological level. Tell a creator, say Van Gogh or Cézanne, that he is fabricating a world-version. He will not recognize himself in this account of what he is doing. And if by chance he accepted it, he would stop painting, because he would lose faith in the kind of constraint which makes his predicament. The painter – at least this kind of painter – understands himself as the servant – if not the slave – of that which has to be said, depicted, exemplified, expressed. Because a gap keeps recurring between *making* and *rendering*, he is never relieved from the duty of painting. Cézanne, facing 'la montagne sainte Victoire' or simply 'un compotier de pommes,' feels himself the bearer of an infinite debt as regards that which Merleau-Ponty calls the visibility of the visible. By the way, the English verb 'to render' displays a full array of potential meanings ranging from 'making' to 'giving in return or requital,' even to 'giving up' and 'surrendering.' The experience of the artist, it seems to me, encompasses the whole range of meanings from making to surrendering, through representing and interpreting.

At that point *Thesis II* (see above) awaits us. I hear Nelson Goodman telling me: In sum, you take my complete pluralism, but you claim to drop my radical relativism. This is impossible. You cannot get the one without paying the price of the other. I think, nevertheless, that there is something to say on behalf of a concept of world that would not fall under the blows of Goodman's critique. We could, in effect, wonder why Goodman does not get rid of the term *world* as the term common to all versions. Of course, he does not contradict when he substitutes world-versions for versions of the world. But is this substitution more than an artifice of writing? This way of speaking has not at all the same intent as in the case of such fictions as chimeras, for which it is perfectly right to say that the fiction *of* a chimera is a chimera-fiction, i.e., the member of a class of fictions. Here we speak within the framework of a theory of denotation, and the chimera is a case of null-denotation. But Goodman himself teaches us that denotation does not cover the whole field of referential symbols and that works of art with null-denotation – as is the case with non-representational paintings – keep referring in a non-denotational way, for example by exemplifying and expressing. What, then, compels Goodman to preserve reference at all costs, if not a dimension of experience entailed in the term *world* that he has not considered? The irreducible difference, it seems to me, between world-versions and versions of the world arises from the conviction that no version exhausts that which requires to be, literally or metaphorically, described, depicted, exemplified, or expressed. Otherwise why, throughout cultural changes, would men have wanted or needed to make new kinds of versions and new versions of the known kinds *again and again*? What are they after, what are they seeking for, by making new world-versions?

Here, Nelson Goodman would reply: either the world is apart from all versions and then you fall back to the absurd thesis of the *Ding an sich*, or you favour one version, most likely the phenomenist one, and then you make an arbitrary and imperialist claim.

I think that it is possible to escape this alternative choice. Contrary to the first alternative, the world may be more than each version without being apart from it. It is the very experience of making that yields that of discovering. And discovering is to confront the opacity of the world. The world is included – excluded as the horizon of each intentional aiming. It is not something to which versions refer, but that out of which, or against the background of which, versions refer. Contrary to the second alternative, the world is not either a phenomenon in the perceptual sense, although a phenomenology of perception, as well as that of the creative experience of painting alluded to above, is particularly suited to teach the difference between phenomenon and horizon. This capability of perception arises from the fact that our own body – as lived body – is implied in a unique way in perception. Now our body, as our own, is the basic medium of our being in the world as the place where we dwell. Dwelling, construing, and thinking, these are – according to the wonderful title of one of Heidegger's essays – human acts of an inexhaustible significance. To dwell is to be received as a guest. And construing is making, but in such a way that we do not make the world less worthy of dwelling in. Some kind of humility, accordingly, is entailed in the act of dwelling. This kind of humility in turn says something of the openness proper to perception. In that sense the significance of the world as horizon excludes any hypostasis of the phenomenist version.

The phenomenist version, as version, is exemplified by the perception of apparent movement so beautifully expounded by Goodman. It is only a version, in the sense that it is isolated by the artificial but necessary constraints of the experiment itself from the whole concrete context which makes observation inexhaustible, i.e., the interplay between all the perceptual fields, the movement of attention which expands or focuses alternately and the indefinite flight of the perceptual horizon. Whether we call this trait of perceptual experience inactuality or potentiality (Husserl), it makes the difference between world-version and version *of* the world. Deprived from the contextual feature, the perceived world becomes a phenomenon, in the Kantian sense of a 'representation' which abides in the mind. This reduction engenders the false problematics of the *Ding an sich*, to compensate, as it were, the phenomenist impoverishment of experience. Ultimately the old dichotomy, subject–object, has to be questioned, to the extent that the dichotomy phenomenon – *Ding an sich* – belongs to the same mistaken problematics of *Vorstellung*. For the same reason, the so-called realism of the *Ding an sich* is only and always the counterpart and the penalization of the idealism of *Vorstellung*. I find myself suddenly quite in agreement with this statement by Goodman: 'The realist will resist the conclusion that there is no world; the idealist will resist the conclusion that all conflicting versions describe different worlds. As for me, I find these views equally delightful and equally deplorable – for after all, the difference between them is purely conventional' (p. 119). *Bravo!*

A further reason not to hypostasize the perceptual version is that its own inexhaustibility, displayed by the experience of observing, makes possible the shift to other versions – among them, to the pictorial version. When Van Gogh depicts the furniture of his room and when he exemplifies by his painting some features, rhythms, moods, pertaining to his surroundings, does he not make visible certain textures and even certain non-Euclidean spatial structures that our usual perception, overloaded by traditions and prejudices (including the prejudice that the perceptual space is Euclidean), prevents us from seeing? In that sense the perceptual inexhaustibility of the world and its opacity are hints of, and clues to, the function of the world as horizon, as that which makes possible, suggests, and sometimes requires the transition from one version of the world to another. The possibility and the fact of such transitions are one more implication of the significance of the term 'world' without any regression to the logical concept of *sameness* that Goodman correctly excludes.

In conclusion, I should like to sketch a critical reflection on *Thesis*

III. This thesis about the difference between rightness and truth is itself right as long as one decides to limit the meaning of the term *true* to the domain of denotations and among them to that of descriptions and finally of statements. Nevertheless, the duality rightness–truth seems to me to be a residue of the philosophy that the author condemns, i.e., the reduction of reference to denotation and to statements. By the same token, does he not remain captive of a verificationist (or falsificationist) prejudice that his whole philosophy of symbolic forms denies? If one gives back to the world its character of horizon, of inexhaustibility, and of opacity, has one not to question anew the concept of truth and to acknowledge that its amplitude is equal to that of world? Someone may say that the change is only of a semantic kind, to the extent that it entails merely the convention of including rightness in truth. I do not think that our contention bears merely on terminology. By calling rightness truth, we respond, I think, to a phenomenological requirement, namely to the same requirement which compelled us to distinguish between making and rendering.

I find in Nelson Goodman himself some symptoms of this requirement. First, his full respect for the cognitive function of the arts,[4] then his quasi-instinctive doubling of the term version by vision ('versions and visions,' pp. 2–5), then his right use of the term *rendering* when combined with rightness (would he say: rightness of making, with the same ... rightness?), and finally and above all, his fight on behalf of the reference of symbols in the absence of denotation. Why should this plea be so stubborn, if the search for truth were not, under the garment of rightness, the concern for doing justice to that which Hölderlin called *das Offene* – The Open – and which requires that we, literally or metaphorically, keep describing, depicting, exemplifying, and expressing *again and again*?

For my part, I have great difficulty in conceiving a philosophy of generalized reference which would not be stirred by the passionate concern for an equally generalized sense of truth.

Notes

1 The first chapter, 'Words, Works, Worlds,' was read at the University of Hamburg on the 101st anniversary of the birth of Ernst Cassirer.
2 To the four 'symptoms' dealt with in *Languages of Art* – syntactic density, semantic density, relative repleteness, exemplification – *Ways of Worldmaking*

adds a fifth 'symptom,' that of 'multiple and complex reference, where a symbol performs several integrated and interacting referential functions' (p. 68).

3 One may notice that the expression 'ways of worldmaking,' taken in this more technical sense, becomes a subtitle within a chapter which bears the same title (pp. 7–17). See also pp. 101–2 in chapter 6, 'The Fabrication of Facts.'

4 A major thesis of this book is that the arts must be taken no less seriously than the sciences as modes of discovery, creation, and enlargement of knowledge in the broad sense of advancement of understanding, and thus that the philosophy of art should be conceived as an integral part of metaphysics and epistemology' (p. 102).

The Conflict of Interpretations:
Debate with Hans-Georg Gadamer

Gadamer

My introductory remarks to our joint discussion will be brief. But I hope they will provide an initial theme. After my short conversation with Professor Ricoeur about what he would be saying, I feel quite sure our two contributions will complement each other.

My proposal for our topic, the conflict of interpretations, was by way of honouring Ricoeur, who, in his book on this question, formulated a problem I have been working on for a long time. I am not offering a solution to this conflict of interpretations. My aim is rather a better understanding of the methodological and philosophical involvements of the different directions of interpretation which stand in such striking conflict.

The first point I have to make is this. Interpretation is a word that has been, as it were, charged with an electricity, at least since the days of the later Nietzsche, as expressed, for example, in the typically provocative fashion in the famous statement: I do not know moral phenomena: I know only moral interpretations of phenomena. Indeed, in Nietzsche the philologist, the philological skill reattained the position of predominance that had been taken for granted in the higher education of former days. For example, everybody knows that Bacon called his own enterprise the *interpretation* of nature, because in his time philology was *not* the secondary thing in the eyes of common opinion that it has become today. But our problem, of course, is to show how this new shift-in-meaning of interpretation fits in the context of today's philosophy.

It was not the professors of philosophy that achieved this change. They were preoccupied with epistemology, i.e., the justification of the positive sciences. It was mainly Nietzsche that brought about this new style of interpretation; though it was embodied as well in the works of the great novelists of the nineteenth century. Then, of course, both the critique of ideology and psychoanalysis call for the same new sense of interpretation. For it is clear that interpretation in Nietzsche's usage constitutes a new approach to the whole problem: It means unmasking *pretended* meaning and signification. It does not mean simply philological skill in clarifying or articulating the meaning of a text. And the whole question of course is: Is it possible for philosophy and critical reflection to accept two different and quite irreconcilable attitudes towards any given meaningful whole?

For the sake of simplicity, I shall speak of a meaningful total or whole as a *text*. I am choosing that way of putting the matter, of course, as an old philologist. But philosophical hermeneutics is not restricted to exercising philological skill in interpreting texts. As Galileo or perhaps Nicholas of Cusa first expressed it, I believe, the book of nature is a book written with the finger of God. And since Hegel a similar claim has been made, namely, that the book of history was written by the world spirit. Consequently, by text-interpretation is implied the totality of our orientation of ourselves in the world, together with the assumption that deciphering and understanding a text is very much like encountering reality.

This is why the Idealist theory of interpretation can no longer suffice. That was Heidegger's point, as well as crucial for what I learned from Heidegger. To be sure, hermeneutics is an old method in some of the fields of the humanities, especially in theology, where since the Reformation there has been a special commitment to the authentic access to the '*text*' as *kerygma*, in opposition to the dogmatic tradition of the Roman Church. Another and obviously permanent field of hermeneutics is law. In the case of legal interpretation, the ordering of civic life by codified or uncodified laws includes an immense distance between the prescriptions of the law and the ideal of justice in any particular case.

So these two fields of hermeneutical labour are well-known in the modern epoch. But the evolution of hermeneutics reached a climax in the Romantic era. At that time, the task of rediscovery and re-entry seemed to apply not just to the Bible in relation to the special dogmatic tradition of the Roman Church; and not just to the law in any given jurisdiction; but especially in modern states where, after the adoption of Roman law, the conflict between the scientifically elaborated Roman law and the traditional, uncodified legal customs of the people reached a high-water mark. The Romantic era came to realize that in the wake of the French Revolution, *the whole tradition* of Western civilization was at stake. From this moment onward the question was how to bridge the abyss between our post-revolutionary epoch and the almost indisputable self-evidence of the Christian humanistic tradition of previous centuries.

That is the background for modern-day hermeneutics. Schleiermacher was the first to introduce hermeneutics as a common human concern for mutual understanding and for gaining access to the very *ground* of what is at stake – especially, in Schleiermacher's case, the truth claim of Holy Scripture.

Well, given the radical questioning of Nietzsche, Idealist hermeneutics can no longer suffice. Nietzsche was less the inventor of some other particular philosophical doctrine than the symbolic expression of the crisis of modern life. We have here, I think, a unique case in world history, namely, that somebody said of himself: I am dynamite – *and he was*. Normally, people who say, I am dynamite, are insane!

The problem, therefore, is this: What is the meaning of hermeneutics if 'interpretation' can no longer be understood and defined as the explicit *fulfilment* of the intentionality of discourse actually created in a tradition – in other words, of the text, of what someone means and everyone accepts as discourse; so that the gap between the interpreter and the interpreted text could ultimately disappear? It seems to me no longer unproblematic to interpret the Christian humanistic heritage of our history in almost monolithic solidarity. This was the illusion of the Romantic era formulated in the Hegelian concept of the absolute spirit. Certainly, Hegel's saying that the absolute transparence of the other occurs in the experience of art and in the experience of religion has something convincing to it. I mean that in both these fields, nobody feels this unbridgeable gap between oneself and another, between oneself and the truth. The basic assumption in such experiences is that I and thou are no longer in our differences. The work of art and the message of religion collect and bring together a new community, since even historical distances disappear in the contemporaneity of art or the kerygma.

But how can we make this truth-claim of our tradition compatible with the new concept of interpretation introduced by Nietzsche and elaborated by the others mentioned? How can we hope to reconcile this radicalism of interpretation as unmasking with an attitude of participation in a cultural heritage which forms and transforms itself in a process of mediation? I think Heidegger opened up the way to do this by raising a question even more radical than the radicalism of Nietzsche.

Here let me recall briefly the now familiar entry of Heidegger into the philosophic scene of our century by way of his destructive criticism of modern subjectivism, including that of his own teacher and admired master, Husserl. This criticism concerned the notion of consciousness. It did not of course claim that the labour of research done by phenomenological philosophy and especially by Husserl had not been valid at all. Heidegger did not deny the radicality and intensity of Husserl the thinker. But he saw an unsolvable problem behind his foundation of phenomenology as rigorous science; and he became aware at the same time of the challenge issuing from the heritage of Hegel.

In his first books he suggests that Hegel was the one who integrated historicity into the content of the investigation of truth in the most radical way. In Heidegger's eyes this integration was, of course, further mediated by Dilthey, in particular. It was in connection with Dilthey's work that the word *hermeneutics* came up in Heidegger: indeed, in a very provocative expression that implies a revision of the hermeneutical foundation of Dilthey's historicism – 'hermeneutics of facticity.' 'Of facticity' – I want to emphasize the radicalism of this formulation, especially after listening yesterday to some of the discussion. I would stress that Heidegger was penetrating enough to realize that it is impossible, not to say ridiculous, for a philosopher today to write an ethics. How can any philosopher *invent* something that does not exist? We should recognize that Heidegger was consistent enough to ask: What real basis for solidarity is left for posing philosophical questions after the rise of the nihilism predicted by Nietzsche? *Facticity* – this emphatic word means something that is not capable of being chosen. So our 'existence' is not a matter of our free choice, but simply *is* a fact. We are given any moment of our lifetime. Facticity in this emphatic sense means something that is absolutely opaque in relation to any form of interpretation. Hence, the claim of doing a hermeneutics of facticity was a real battle-cry.

We have to realize that, with this paradoxical demand, Heidegger pointed to what may, in our spiritual, cultural, and philosophical situation with its belief in science, be asked by anyone and to which science can never adequately respond: the problem of death. This ultimate point of solidarity is common to all human beings. While the answers to this question offered by religions may differ and be accepted or rejected, science cannot really give a proper answer at all, despite all the advances of modern medicine.

On this basis, Heidegger developed his hermeneutics of facticity. He interpreted the temporal structure of *Dasein* as the movement of interpretation such that interpretation doesn't *occur* as an activity in the course of life, but *is* the *form* of human life. Thus, we are interpreting by the very energy of our life, which means 'projecting' in and through our desires, wishes, hopes, expectations, as well as in all our life-experience; and this process culminates in its expression of an orientation by means of speech. The interpretation of another speaker and his speech, of a writer and his text, is just a special aspect of the process of human life as a whole.

Heidegger had a good reason for eventually dropping the word *hermeneutics*. I have learned myself that it is dangerous to use this word, because it always invites the expectation that here is a new wonder-weapon: that one can learn how to interpret more reliably, more surely, and with a deeper meaning than was ever done before. Hermeneutics is a new skill of mastering something – that is not what we learned and have to learn from Heidegger. I think Heidegger demonstrated that, behind the whole activity of human life, seeking its points of orientation as *In-der-Welt-Sein*, is this mysterious openness to being which is inseparably connected with our finitude; an openness to questioning, an openness which lays the constant charge upon our human living to break through the illusions of our self-sufficiency.

My aim here is not to interpret Heidegger and his raising of the question of being. It is simply to place the question of hermeneutics, of interpretation, in the centre of philosophy, and to go behind the conflict of interpretations that may preoccupy our scientific and methodological interests. From the viewpoint of 'interpretation,' we should not just focus on the idea of the finite structure of human life, or on the idea that there is death. To be sure, that represents a radical break with the Idealist claim of absolute knowledge and self-realization of the spirit. Our facticity is not only represented by the anticipation of the end. It is the same with the beginning. That we are thrown into the world and not invited is just the symbol for the constitutive fact that we are always on the way; and that is true for interpretation, too. Perhaps the key insight in my own work is that we are never at the zero-point, we are never starting out new, we are always already en route, *wir haben immer schon angefangen.* A good way to put this point across is the familiar story about a child's first spoken word. It is made up of the illusion on the part of the parents. For it cannot be what it seems, since a first word cannot exist as such. It is not language. It is not a word, if there is just this one word. Consequently, the story illustrates why interpretation is the element in which we live, and not something into which we have to make entry.

The question, therefore, becomes: how can we expect that in interpreting (which means elaborating our experience in life as a legitimate way to develop self-understanding) we can escape the illusions of objective self-consciousness and the foundations of knowledge upon self-conscious method? In posing this question we are confronted by the two extremes mentioned above. On the one hand, there is interpretation in the Nietzschean sense that refers to any form of interpretation as was practised by Marx or by Freud. On the other hand, there is the experience of life in communicative processes, the actual working-out of daily life, where communication as the exchange of words in use structures the whole of social reality and encompasses the cultural features of this reality; sciences, the humanities, etc. What then is the place in social interaction for unmasking interpretation, this interpretation that goes behind the apparent meanings? An example from the social pathology of every-day life spoken about by Freud may serve to illustrate the question: I make a blunder in speaking. The other person stops to listen to what I say to him and starts to think: 'Oh, there is something behind it all. One should no longer take this man's explanations at face value. He is concealing something, or at least something within him is conceal-ing itself subconsciously.' I think you see the conflict immediately. Is there a continuous process of understanding each other going on for the most part; or is the direct opposite what is usually taking place? Does the analyst – in this case, everyone – who sets out to reveal the sub- or unconscious background of the interlocutor attest to commun-ication? Certainly not. This is not to deny the tremendous task and astonishing results being achieved by the investigation of the uncon-scious; or to question the therapeutic effort to heal obtrusive con-flicts between the conscious and unconscious in order to reintroduce the patient into communication. But going behind, unmasking, showing forth hidden desires that are longing for their fulfilment as revealed by the inner tension in our souls – that is something besides communication. We have to assume as the basis of our social life that the other means what he is saying, and we have to accept his utterances without straight-away interpreting him against his own intentions – at least until there is sufficient evidence to suspect that the opposite obtains. Where a gap becomes actual, communication is broken down; then we begin to consider his utterances as a mask of the unconscious. At any rate, there is no easy solution to these problems from a theoretical point of view. There is, however, a similar set of problems in the field of politics. The intrinsic analogy between psychoanalysis and the critique of ideologies has often been stressed.

Be that as it may, it might be helpful to think about these issues in the context of Heidegger's insight that interpretation is not a sovereign attitude over against a pre-established context of meaning, so that I can decipher it and possess it exhaustively and definitively. Interpretation is an ongoing process of life in which there is always something behind and something expressly intended. Both an opening of a horizon and a concealing of something take place in all our experiences of interpretation.

That is true. Nor did Heidegger neglect to insist that thinking we can penetrate this deepest darkness of one's own mind was an illusion of Idealism. We can objectify ourselves; we can decipher the text of our own life, seeing it as a full series of symptoms of an illusion. And yet how can we make our way through this in a way that does justice to concrete life as an interpretive process? For me the pre-eminent model has been the *dialogue*. Plato was right in saying that thinking is at best a dialogue with oneself. But in a *real* dialogue, like the dialogues he wrote, the key point to be grasped is that there is no subject who states and fixes the objective content of an utterance, and then argues this fixed idea as the whole point. Instead there is an interplay between two persons, so that both expose themselves to one another with the expectation that each tries in his own way to find a common point between himself and the interlocutor. Whereas if we find no common point, *wir reden an einander vorbei.*

I could of course take up two hours speaking about this problem, but I think it is neither in your interest nor my duty as a human being! My point is that the dialogue is a good model for the process of overcoming the structure of two opposing postures. Finding a common language is not contributing to a new handbook of science or thought; it is sharing in a social act. This is a rather useful conclusion

– to discover that the process of dialogue and all that is involved in its unfolding actually consists in an ongoing effort to bridge any form of alienation and to bring persons together so that nobody stays rigidly where he started, but rather integrates and appropriates what is other. Both partners to a genuine dialogue change and move and eventually find some small ground of solidarity.

In this sense I think even the conflict of interpretations could have a resolution. For the critique of ideologies, psychoanalysis, and every radical form of critique should be and needs to be reintegrated into this basic process of social life – a way which I call (in a manner I find satisfactory) *hermeneutical*.

Ricoeur

I want to address my remarks to the last part of the paper by Professor Gadamer, to his proposal regarding the reintegration of conflictual situations in hermeneutics within the encompassing framework of a dialogical relationship. I am quite aware that to start immediately with the most radical and most dramatic condition of conflict between a hermeneutic of suspicion and a hermeneutic of re-enactment is to put oneself in the situation of the unhappy consciousness. But I don't think that it's the task of the philosopher merely to brood over this situation of conflict, but rather to try to bridge it. It is, I think, always the task of philosophical rationality to try to mediate, to work out a mediation, and to do so with passion. To that purpose, I think that the paradigmatic case which has to be taken up here is not one of the most extreme conflict, but on the contrary, one in which the conflict is more manageable. The way I shall proceed is to start with conflict *within* interpretation in order then to move step by step towards conflict of a more radical kind. My studies in these last years have followed this kind of progression through the following fields of inquiry: the theory of texts, the theory of action, the theory of history, and lastly, psychoanalysis. Among these different fields a certain homology of problematics may be discerned and at the same time a certain progression, if I may say so, in the conflictual structure of the problematic. This similarity and this progression suggests, therefore, the treatment case by case and step by step of the conflictual situation of hermeneutics.

My proposal here, then, is first, to reflect on the global situation of conflict and then to take a more analytical approach. My purpose is not to fill the gap between the two extreme modes of interpretation, namely, that of a recapitulation in a Hegelian sense and that of the archaeology of a deconstruction in a Nietzschean sense. I have no answer myself for this situation but at least as a philosopher, I shall try to approach it by this procedure of the progressive construction of mediation. Accordingly, as we shall see, psychoanalysis may not allow a direct approach, but may stand as an extreme case, as a kind of borderline case, a marginal case, for this procedure, for this progressive procedure. Because, as we shall see, between the three first steps, there is not only an homology, an analogy of structure, but also a progressive complexity in the structure of the problematic itself, an increasing complexity.

I

The central problematic which appears to be common to the three fields just mentioned is the conflict between comprehension and explanation. And this central problematic is not only homologous among the three fields but suggests the idea of an order of increasing complexity from one field to the other, in such a way that the further case of psychoanalysis may appear less appreciated and, therefore, less manageable. I shall devote less time here to an exposition of the theory of texts, for I discuss it in detail elsewhere. As a first point, I want to insist only on the strategic position of this theory in relation to the whole pattern of inquiry. By holding the question of texts as the paradigmatic case for the conflict of interpretation, I give to the concept of hermeneutics an orientation and a scope somewhat different from the one which was implied by an earlier emphasis on the conflict between suspicion and re-enactment. In that previous orientation, the problem of symbol existence was predominant, and the emphasis on symbols implied that there are several ways of reading symbols and therefore that the discrepancy between these ways of reading was intolerable. But if we put the emphasis on the concept of texts, and if we give to hermeneutics the same rights as that of texts extended in the sense which I shall propose, the problem of the double meaning of symbols seems to be the crucial issue. We might emphasize here that a hermeneutical question arises wherever there is a move from misunderstanding to better understanding.

My next point now is the epistemological conflict – and a typical one for this field – between comprehension and explanation. This is not an intractable conflict, but one that can be mediated within the hermeneutical field itself. It is not a conflict *of* interpretation but a conflict *within* interpretation. This, I think, is the predominant contribution of the theory of the texts to hermeneutical theory in general, which to my mind has not been confined within the borders of linguistics, as we shall see later. Let us, therefore, consider for a while what is specific in the dialectic of explanation and comprehension.

First, dialectic is unavoidable because it belongs to the nature of the text to display a verbal autonomy with respect to the author's intention, the capacity of the understanding of its original audience, and the circumstances which constitute its transmission in written form. This autonomy of the verbal meaning of the text generates an objectification of a specific kind which, broadly speaking, is contemporaneous with the emergence of recent literature. Of course, it should be said against any type of thesis on writing, that the most primitive condition of any kind of inscription may be found in the very constitution of discourse, even oral, to the extent that that which is said in my discourse is already distant from the act of saying it and *endures*, as Hegel said in the first chapter of the *Phenomenology of the Spirit*. But literature exploits this interval, this gap, in innumerable ways, and generates situations of communication quite different from those of dialogual intercourse. And one of the most remarkable aspects of this objectification of discourse into text is the reliance on specific codes which are to broad works of discourse what grammar is to the generation of meaningful sentences in natural languages. Such is the starting-point for insisting that the objectification of discourse in texts is not the deplorable case of alienation that Plato suggested in the myth of the *Phaidos*, where writing is held to be lost remembrance against the pure interiority of knowledge and of wisdom. The inscription in external marks and the encoding of discourse according to the rules of specific literary genres constitute rather the necessary distanciation thanks to which linguistic communication is raised to the level of the written traditions on which our cultural existence relies. Hence a second consideration: if the objectification of discourse in text is a natural step in the development of our linguistic competence, explanatory devices applied to texts are not then as such doomed to pervert and eventually to destroy its objective comprehension. It is the very process of exteriorization which calls for the detour through explanatory devices; and among these devices, I should consider the structural treatment of such classes of texts as narrative, and maybe some others, as the most appropriate approach to those exteriorized forms of discourse. It is, therefore, perfectly legitimate to consider the texts as the manifestation at the level of surface structures of the deep structures which rule the encoding of, for example, the mythology of a given cultural space. The decoding, therefore, has to be homogenous to the encoding.

However, as this is the first dimension of the problem and the most polemical point, any non-mediated dichotomy between a structural and an existential approach to texts would bring us back to the dead-end of hermeneutics of the Dilthey type. It is not because explanatory procedures are no longer borrowed from natural sciences but rely on semiotic models that the gap between *Erklären* and *Verstehen* would be more easy to breach. A return to a dichotomy situation is always possible. On the one hand, some structuralists would claim that the surface structures of a text are only the epiphenomenon of their deep structure, that messages are only instantiations of codes, that texts are semiotic machines in regards to which all questions about their meaning and their reference is irrelevant. On the other hand, some romantic and existential hermeneuts would claim that any structural analysis is already an alienation which does violence to the message of the text, and that the aim of study is to establish a soul to soul relationship between author and reader. My contention is that understanding without explanation is blind as much as explanation without understanding is empty.

I already said in what sense the necessity of the detour through explanation is grounded in the exteriorization of discourse in written signs. We must now say that reciprocally the finality of explanation is understanding. Why? Because the codes themselves, say, narrative codes, like grammatical codes, have no other function than to generate the concrete texts at the level of which human communication is exerted. Considered in analysis simply as code, a narrative is, as it were, made simply virtual, I mean deprived of its actuality as an event of discourse. Only the reverse move from code to message, from system to event, makes possible this ultimate stage of the hermeneutical process which Professor Gadamer calls *Anwendung* or *Eneignung*, application, appropriation. The analytic stage would then supply mere segments on the interpretative arc which proceeds from naïve understanding to mature understanding through learned explanation. Such is the kind of conflict which I consider as paradigmatic. Once more it's not so much a conflict *between* interpretations as a movement of *many* interpretations, a movement between phases of understanding and phases of explanation, between phases of objectification and phases of appropriation.

In accord with its paradigmatic status for our analysis here, I wish to emphasize that the theory of texts is both the topic of a specific discipline linked to the actualization of discourse in literary genres and the first term of a series of analogous cases which can be put under the title of quasi texts; and in the second part of my paper now, I shall try to show how the present status of the theory of action and the theory of history may be considered as analogous to the present status of the theory of texts.

II

Concerning the theory of action, we could find in the Anglo-American discussion a situation quite comparable to that of hermeneutics as discussed in Germany fifty years ago. The claim that the language-game of nature, events, and causation and the language game of action, intention, and motive have nothing in common and that the task of philosophy is merely to disentangle their confusion, that, I think, is a situation quite comparable to the situation in which Dilthey left the problem of the *Geisteswissenschaften*, namely, where understanding has to be disentangled from a confusion with explanation. But precisely I think that this mere disconnection between understanding of motives and explanation of causes is as untenable in the sphere of action as it is in the sphere of the texts. And here we should have to consider what is, in fact, a motive. If a motive is not merely a redescription of an intention, it must have some explanatory force, and here all the arguments of Donald Davidson against G.E.M. Anscombe and others are very strong. For my part it seems that in order for a motive to have explanatory force, it must be given in the form of a kind of small autobiography. By that I mean that I must put my motive under the rules of story-telling; and it is quite possible that this process of story-telling might accompany the generation of intentions themselves, as if retrospection were always suffocating the prospective mood of action. There is therefore always a subtle discrepancy between the intentional movement of decision and this retrospection through which I tell the story of my motive. It is in this process of story-telling that explanatory procedures may be introduced comparable in the theory of action to the explanatory procedures that we found in the theory of the text. The intersection between the theory of texts and the theory of action becomes more obvious when the point of view of the onlooker is added to that of the agent, because the onlooker will consider action not only in terms of its motive, but also in terms of its consequences, perhaps of its unintended consequences. A different way of making sense with actions occurs then, and also a different way of reading it as a quasi text. Detached from its agent, a course of action acquires an autonomy similar to the semantic autonomy of a text. It leaves its mark on the course of events and eventually it becomes sedimented into social institutions. Human action has become archive and document. Thus it acquires potential meaning beyond its relevance to its initial situation.

This way of reading action has been pursued theoretically by Clifford Geertz. According to his interpretation of culture, we see that it is the writing of symbolic systems in ethnography which transforms the quasi text of action into the text of ethnography. It is not surprising that the theory of action gives rise to the same dialectic of comprehension and explanation as the theory of the text. To construe the motivational basis of the string of action is an attempt similar to the construing of the meaning of the text. And this construing encompasses explanatory phases to the extent that motives must be causes in order to have an explanatory force. These explanatory phases may lead to inquiries of different kinds according to the principle of description which governs them. It is in that sense that the theory of action tends to increase the gap between explanation and understanding. But as wide as this gap is, no explanation can remain an explanation of human action which does not return to the initial connection between a motive and an intention. Even if the motive is not the real description of the intention, it is related to action in a way which is irreducible to the logical exteriority between the cause and effect. Understanding is the milieu within which all explanation extends up to the breaking-point in the motivational link.

This reciprocal relation between the theory of texts and theory of action receives not only support but amplification in the third field where the same dialectic of explanation and understanding may be described, the theory of history. And by that I mean, of course, historical inquiry. History generates the same problems and debates as the theory of texts (the theory, namely, of narrative texts) and as the theory of action. This does not happen by chance. On the one hand, historiography is a kind of narrative, and therefore, a kind of text. On the other hand, since history is about human action, it's not extraordinary that we find the same structure of interpretation and explanation. This twofold allegiance justifies our putting the theory of action in this third place. But also, the fact that the dialectic here is more distended, right to the point of breaking, justifies that we take it as an introduction to the problem of psychoanalysis. Here too we could find in the history of the problem the two opposite sides, the same non-dialectical confrontation between the school of understanding comprising French (i.e., Jacques Le Goff, Henri I. Marrou, and Ferdinand Braudel) and German (i.e., Wilhelm Dilthey and J.-G. Droysen) historians (and Collingwood) and the school of explanation that adopts Carl G. Hempel's model of historical explanation.

I don't intend to go very deeply into this aspect here, but I do want to emphasize that here, too, the mere dichotomous approach to the problem cannot get us very far. Starting from the claim that explanation as historical has to be substituted for mere understanding, my point would be that the model proposed here by Hempel and his school cannot be applied since, in fact, the practice of history is the permanent denial of what is claimed by the model. Hempel himself has to recognize that at best we find in history explanatory sketches, not full-fledged explanations. But, more than that, the kind of accounts that the historian gives have no predictive value. They speak of important conditions and not causes, and conditions that are important according to certain kinds of interest. History has to speak in ordinary language, and counter-examples abound that do not function in historical inquiry the same way as in the physical sciences. It is only to narrow down their scope to try to specify precise places, times, and circumstances where the adduced explanation is to apply. Anomalies like these suggest that the model has to be recast into the form of a dialectic of understanding and explanation. And together with some authors like W.B. Gallie my suggestion is that historical understanding at its first stage has to be grafted onto a more primitive competence, namely, that of following a story. To follow a story is to understand something as a succession of actions, faults, and feelings that present coherent direction as well as surprises. The conclusion of a story is accordingly not something deducible, or predictable, but it does have to be both consistent and acceptable. Without this basis there is no story and no history. The interest of the hearer, of the reader, is not in the underlying laws but in following the plot as unfolded in a story.

This starting-point is, I think, more appropriate than the romanticist's starting-point, for example, the idea of a transfer over to an alien other person; because here we have a specific structure, a narrative structure, which makes possible a transition from mere understanding to developed explanation. It is interesting perhaps to see how the procedures of explanation are called for and required as much as the functioning of understanding itself, exactly as in the theory of the text where the surface structure calls for explanation in terms of the deep structure. Consider a situation viewed as at the level of simply following a story. In historical inquiry, the problem is not that of following, because we know what happens, but that of writing down what has been followed. The problem of the organization of the pattern of the story is more important than the surprise in the outcome of the story. A silent conflict therefore is generated here between the pattern which we try to recognize and the sequence of the story, the sequence which is intrinsic to all narrative. The trend of historical explanation is to subordinate the sequential to the pattern, to subordinate the aspect of sequence to the structural planes of a pattern. The process of explanation tends then to be more and more separated from that of understanding. The next step here would be to say that history is not a description of what past agents did in terms of their own motivation, but a prescription in terms of some consequences unknown to them. Then, too, through the narrative, sentences about past events in history enter the description of consequences which only the historian knows. Configurations of events emerge therefore which are ruled by connections quite different from those that link motives and intentions for the agents themselves. This does not mean that the historian knows better, but that he knows otherwise, in another way. And it is here that all the explanatory procedures described by Hempel and others must be introduced because now the historians will bring in categories, principles, and rules which are unknown to the agents themselves. For example, if we speak of class struggle in the Roman Empire, we are using categories which were unknown to the Romans. For them there were no classes as, let us say, for a medieval painter there were no rules of perspective. As to how far we can go towards explanations *without* understanding, my view is that the substitution, the complete substitution, of explanation for understanding would simply destroy history. What we want here is reflection upon the *function* of explanation and not just a study of its structure. It is quite possible that Hempel describes the structure of explanation quite well when he analyses it as not very different from that of physical explanation; but, in the end, its function is to follow the story better. Consequently what has to be done is not posit a substitute for the story but rather inquire into its sequential order.

III

It is only after these preliminary considerations that we now can return to the case of psychoanalysis. The point of the exercise of the mediations practised so far is that it is the task of the philosopher to learn how to master mediation before being confronted with *un*mediated conflict. To do that in the case of psychoanalysis, however, may well imply some important changes in the way the problem is approached, and may even require the de-emphasis of the theory. For my part, I see now that I paid too much attention to the theory as such, whereas it is quite possible that the theory is only the metalanguage of the experience, of the psychoanalytic experience, and that we should therefore start with what constitutes this experience. This experience taken in itself *is* a hermeneutical experience, since the patient has to live with his own feelings and impulses in terms of what can be said of them, and said of them to somebody else – within the framework of a kind of narrative of his own experience. An explanation in psychoanalysis, eccentric as it can be in regard to all the kinds of explanation of which we spoke in the theory of the texts, of action, and of history, nevertheless preserves a link with these other explanations by virtue of being inquiry as sequential understanding. What is new with the psychoanalytic experience cannot be denied, namely, the fact that we have to do with distorted symbolic actions and symbolic systems, that it is the principle of distortion which makes for the problem and not simply the content as such of symptoms and dreams. It is the fact that to give an account of this distortion we must introduce new theoretical terms which do not belong to the experience itself, terms such as libido, repression, cathexis, and so on. It is perfectly legitimate, therefore, that the explanation be not written in the terms native to the experience itself. But it seems to me that this explanation becomes a myth if it cannot be reappropriated within the experience itself in the following way. First, we have to understand that, as distorted as symbolic systems may be, they remain symbolic systems. As far as we have to go in the direction of quasi-material processes, compensation, displacement, investment, and so on, repressed symbols remain symbols and thus retain the meaningfulness of symbolic systems. Therefore, we have to forge the concept of the processes of desymbolization, that is, of what happens when symbolic structures are not only objectified (objectification being, as I said, always a natural and wholesome process) but reified, petrified. Some German interpreters, Freud, Lorenson, and others, speak of delinguisticized logic in privatized language. Here we may have a situation comparable to that of banishment or political ostracism; in other words, what occurs here is a state, let us say, of excommunication. We therefore have to preserve the concept of excommunication in order to make sense within hermeneutical theory of the process of resymbolization which is the whole process of psychoanalysis. It is quite possible, then, that reified symbols *imitate* natural processes. It is quite possible that man functions like a thing; but psychoanalysis is a procedure of investigation, and the method of treatment proves that this symbolization can only be understood as the negative side of the process of resymbolization.

To conclude, my position is that the whole process of the objectification of language, of human action, and of symbolic systems makes procedures of explanation possible, but that the problem of self-alienation has always to be grafted onto the process of objectification in order to be understood. Self-alienation, left unconnected with the process of objectification, appears absolutely cryptic and impenetrable, and the conflict with hermeneutics then seems intractable. It is in this way that I think dialogical rationality may, from a position on the border between elements in opposition, mediate unmediated conflicts, which perhaps are the core of our cultural situation.

Thank you.

Discussion

Q: Professor Gadamer, you were talking about the discovery of the necessary opacity involved in a hermeneutic of facticity. I think before, as with Hegel and people like Dilthey, the idea of interpretation was to overcome opacity. Now, for you is it the task of hermeneutics to make things as transparent as possible regarding this necessary opacity as a negative thing, or is your idea that this opacity isn't necessarily a bad thing, and that hermeneutics should *not* overcome it but take a positive attitude towards it?

Gadamer: I spoke about opacity in opposition to the idealistic optimism concerning the possibility of overcoming every trace of the opaque. In that way I take it certainly as a restriction upon the possibility of insight or spirituality; but I would say that exactly this limitation upon our understanding has, how shall I say, a moment of reality. So that the limitations in our understanding of something are a part of our own real being. To show what I mean, take this illustration. One of my standard examples (I hope nobody is acquainted with it) is Mommsen's *History of Rome*. Opening one page of this work I know immediately that it can only be written by a historian who was a democrat in the so-called *Vormärz*. That means a democratic historian who had a special preference for the Republic and therefore never wrote the fourth volume about the era of Augustus, because that was not his job. But in seeing that he was in a way narrow and limited in his own interests, in his own insights, I gain a profile of his own spiritual character. This example is, of course, taken from a very intellectual academic field, but I think you can shift it to any form of life experience.

Q: I would like to ask Professor Gadamer what is perhaps a naïve question concerning the ongoing dialogue between unmasking and re-enacting interpretation. Would Professor Gadamer agree or would he deny that the idea of unmasking the text implies that there is some real meaning or some true interpretation which does lie behind it, even if we in our constant efforts fail to reach it? If our efforts to interpret a text might be compared, say, to the continuous removal of the skin of an onion, so that ultimately we arrive at nothing, does that not mean that the whole conception of hermeneutic or interpretation is simply meaningless to us?

Gadamer: I am not of course the infinite spirit that knows the kernel of the onion. But I find it very important to say that this assumption, this anticipation of meaning or of significance, is a pre-condition for our effort to understand. In this I would agree with you that as an *intentional* factor, this assumption that there is meaning *in* breeds our whole effort. But I think that is exactly so as a universal condition of our finite structure. I would claim it as belonging to our hermeneutical approach to the world, that we can never reach the position which would allow us to demonstrate what the kernel of the onion is.

Q: I find that response reassuring, but would Professor Gadamer not have something more to say for Plato, and perhaps even Hegel, regarding this claim that while the dialogue is a continuous ongoing process, in our finite condition we never reach the kernel. Despite this, what we are aiming at, what we do intend – if you can put it that way – is the idea that there is an ultimate truth, as the Hegelians put it.

Gadamer: But you know that Hegel at least is on my side. He says it is dialectic. God may *know* but human beings *seek* truth. No God philosophizes. He does not need this ongoing approach of articulation; but this is a subject with so many sides, and there is not time enough here now to take it up. As to Plato, his insight was not the conception of the totality of what we could call, in a philosophical experiment, the entire system of possible relations, like the central monad of Leibniz, encompassing the whole relationship of all the monads, so that the full coincidence of the entire system of monads is a universe. That is not Plato. Plato saw, I think, that to re-enact a relation, to see something under an aspect, 'shadows' by necessity other aspects. About Hegel, I have my reservations, but in my contribution here I tried to find a way of overcoming the Hegelian end-point, and of assuming, so far as I can, the whole content of his dialectical description, in so far as I can re-enact it in this way. This movement of dialectically furthering our insight, that of course is common in Plato and Hegel; but when you give me the choice, I am for Plato.

Q: I would like to ask both Professor Ricoeur and Professor Gadamer about this shift from opacity to the idea of the *continuation* of opacity. This was touched upon in the final comments of both papers, first, in Professor Gadamer's notion of the reintegration of critique as a definition or at least another account of what hermeneutics may be, and then in Professor Ricoeur's notion of unmediated conflict. This notion of mediation seems to me to be central to the discussion here, and what I would like to ask is whether hermeneutics is to include a form of mediation, whether there is something which passes between two poles, and thus is mediated – so that there is interpretation of texts or of history, or of the other forms which Professor Ricoeur discussed – or whether the vision or mode of understanding involved in interpreting these forms is *un*mediated. Perhaps each of you might take up that question.

Ricoeur: My contribution was not fundamentally different from that of Professor Gadamer, because what he called dialogue is, in fact, a position of mediation. In dialogue I have to encounter the other as he is, I have to presume that he *means* something, that he *intends* something, and I have to bring myself into that which is meant and intended. And so the exchange of positions, what Professor Gadamer called the fusion of horizons, is a fundamental presupposition of the philosophical overcoming of unmediated conflicts. What I tried to do was to focus on certain epistemological situations in which we may proceed accurately in this task of mediation, instead of starting from, let us say, the cultural situation of our time, this desperate situation in which there is no bridge to build between the ongoing process of what Nietzsche called the devaluation of the highest values, and our desperate attempt to make sense of our whole heritage. We are surely the children of these two processes; we belong to both. There is a part of our self which participates in this ongoing process of suspicion, using not only the sciences but also this specific kind of hermeneutics which was invented by Nietzsche. (We can find it as well, retrospectively, already in Marx, in his deconstruction of what he called the world of representation in relation to the world of praxis.) We belong to this current. But we have a *double* allegiance as modern man: on the one hand, to continue this task of suspicion and, yet, an opposite obligation, to recover the past because there would be no sense in doing archaeology, or being interested in foreign cultures or in the deep past. It makes no sense for *suspicion*, but it surely does for *recollection*. So, I tried to say that if we stay in this state of affairs, then there is a kind of repetition of the situation of the unhappy consciousness; and in that situation there is nothing for philosophy to do except to hope that somewhere, someday, some mediation will appear between these opposites. My hope is that if we could narrow down somewhat the scope and then proceed analytically, then a certain aspect of the philosophical task could be fulfilled, which is to solve the problems one by one. We find Plato in all this. He says somewhere that there are those who reach the one too quickly, and others who remain in the many; but the philosopher proceeds through progressive mediations. That is what I tried to do by giving an ordered place to a number of problems which occur in the region between the explanatory sciences and hermeneutical disciplines; and it was this area of intersection which interested me as the place where we can do some positive work of mediation. I do not claim that this solves the huge and global problem of the contradiction of modern culture; but if we do this modest philological work in the interval between the one and the many, maybe thereafter we may be able to say something less incoherent about the one itself.

Gadamer: Following Professor Ricoeur's response I should like to add a question of my own, on a point which has never been quite clear to me. I agree with him completely in the observation that this gap or conflict of interpretations is, in a way, abstraction, with the result that we have a serious problem about mediating links. How can we describe them convincingly? Again, how much might there remain of the extreme positions one is attempting to mediate? It is possible that they cannot be brought together on a new level and in a new form of approach. What I mean may be helped by an example. When we take a historical problem, say, the beginning of a war which changes the world, and our analytical research convinces us the man who was responsible for the beginning of this war was a special kind of man. My example is not fictitious. Something like this was said about Frederick II. Well I think it is obvious that there are two absolutely different topics: one to explain the individual behaviour and psychology of a political man in this situation, and another to have a historical interest in the beginning of the Silesian wars. I cannot see what you mean in this case by a connection, or a mediation, in so far as it is not mediation to say: Well, of course, there is a layer of individual, personal biographies, but history is certainly not the *sum* of that.

Here we reach my last point in alluding to another of your fine papers from recent years, from which I learned a lot, because you know we Germans were much more isolated than you in the last decades and so we had much to pick up. Well, you described the hermeneutic and the structuralist approaches, and then applied a hermeneutic also to that contrast. I could not see that it had the same level. I have no doubt that one can elaborate and use many forms of explanation. There is not just structuralism; there are many other ways to interpret a text. I certainly need a great deal of knowledge about language and historical conditions and cultural habits and so on, that is one thing. But to *concretize* all that in this unique statement or text that must recollect all these externalized and objectifiable aspects, to live through the meaning in concrete fullness, that is quite another thing. It seems to me, as well as I can describe it following your explanation, that we have here the attempt at a reintegration of a disintegrating system of special approaches. I have real difficulty here about how you will get things to combine. It is to aim for combining to say hermeneutic has the right and the goal to reconcretize any form of general description. And it remains the ultimate goal of any understanding. I would be satisfied if you could say yes to this, but I think you cannot; and I would like to know your reasons.

Ricoeur: Let us take a concrete example of a structural analysis to show how it redirects us towards understanding. Let me take the most extreme case, that of the structural analysis of the Oedipus myth by Lévi-Strauss in *Structural Anthropology*. His claim is that we have to forget the chronology of the story, take all the sentences and distribute them into classes, and then look for patterns of relationships. But, at bottom, what results do we obtain? We finally reach the recognition of what Jaspers has called the boundary situations of birth, death, love, hatred, and so on. What we get from a structural analysis, as I put it, is a kind of depth semantics of the narrative, of what is at issue in the narrative, of what makes the narrative structure a place of conflict, and of what mediates its conflict. It would be a dead end if we were to say that these structures merely comprise codes, or perform a merely logical mediation, if they do not help us to read the narrative, not at the anecdotal level, but at the level of its plotting, as Northrop Frye would say. It shows us, therefore, the way in which the narrative moves from crisis to dénouement. I may thereafter reincorporate the structural analysis into an understanding which will be no longer a kind of naïve reading, but a learned reading. This is what I think we all do when we read a poem, first at the surface of the work, and then in a final reading, when we understand the underlying structure. In this final reading we forget all the analytical approaches; it is a kind of second life taken up in the reading itself. Isn't this what we do when we study, for example, the sonata structure of the first movement of a symphony of Beethoven? It's not lost time to see how the first phrase and the second theme work out in the composition, and finally in the coda – that does not spoil our pleasure. On the contrary, the understanding of the underlying structure comes also to underlie our pleasure. I think that we can give good examples of this reintegration of an explanation within an understanding. If, on the other hand, it were impossible, then I should ask the reverse question: what can we do with a philosophy of dialogue if it is not able to be reconnected with the discipline of the human sciences, if it is merely a face-to-face relationship, and if it cannot provide us with, if it cannot structure, an epistemology? The risk would otherwise be that we would oppose truth to method, instead of rethinking the method itself according to the requirements of truth.

Gadamer: Well, I thank you for your full agreement! That was exactly what I had in mind, that structural analysis as an analysis of the structure of some elements schematized in a generalizing approach must be reintegrated in the second, learned reading. But, now, how do you reintegrate the Freudian interpretation of individuals? You did it – you *felt* that you did it – in your book, you insist that these two should be brought together. You gave an excellent description of what, for my own orientation, King Oedipus *means*, of why we *are* lost and terrified. But this works *not* by what we learned in our quite special interest in incest and shock and the Oedipus complex and so on. We are to link those things together in such a way that we see this tragedy of self-cognition which occurs in the story as at the same time the re-enactment of archaeology of our own soul, of our own childhood! I cannot bring it together like that. And I cannot say that that is the bankruptcy of philosophy. I think it is the opposite. It demonstrates, for example, in a concrete form, that psychoanalytic interest involves a special social commitment to avoid the edges.

Ricoeur: I shall never defend the psychoanalytic explanation of a literary text because a psychoanalytic explanation has its function only in the psychoanalytic situation with the patient. Sophocles is not on the couch. Psychoanalytic explanation is analytical only because something happens in a myth which has some analogy in dreams. That is what is interesting. But a second remark is needed here: I should not say that the tragedy of *Oedipus Rex* is a psychoanalytic tragedy. On the contrary, it is overcome, because it is a tragedy of truth about sex. But nevertheless what we learn from that is that *good* symbols, symbols which have a cultural impact, have two dimensions. On the one hand, they are deeply rooted in conflicts, in archeconflicts. On the other hand they are the process of overcoming these conflicts. Consequently, what is needed is the recognition of the dialectic of symbols which embraces both, so that these symbols emerge from all regressive trends and the regression is overcome. We recognize the multidimensionality of *good* symbols to re-enact some primitive conflicts by overcoming them. So it is the movement of overcoming the regression of conflicts that I discover in the tragedy of Sophocles, in this story of marrying one's mother and killing one's father. Just to say that is what the story is about is trivial; it is to enact the tragedy of truth, because the problem is to recognize the resistance to recognition which is the tragedy of Sophocles. But if we have not identified the depths of the conflictual situation, perhaps we fail somewhat to overcome the situation. We therefore enrich our understanding of the tragedy by understanding how the tragedy of truth is overcome when it supersedes the tragedy of sex (which is not a tragedy, but comedy!).

Q: Professor Ricoeur, do you distinguish between modes of comprehension which *can* take an explanatory character into themselves, and modes of comprehension which are such that they won't admit this reintegration of explanation into their structure?

Ricoeur: It is quite evident that, when we raise different questions, we get the answers which we deserve on the basis of our question. If you are raising a question about Frederick II concerning his libidinal structure, what do we expect here? A better understanding of what he did, or a better understanding of psychoanalysis and its types? It depends on the question that we are raising. But my claim is that it is always possible to return to the fundamental question: How do we enlarge the sphere of communication? This, finally, is the hermeneutical question. The aim here is, if possible, to integrate the most erratic human behaviour into the broader field of communication with our contemporaries and our predecessors. Finally, it is the structure of historicity which is thereby enriched. However, it is quite possible to raise questions which do not allow of being thus reincorporated. Such may be scientific inquiries which have their own aim apart from all this. On the other hand, there are scientific questions that return to the enlargement of self-understanding by the detour of the understanding of what made man, mankind, what it is. I think as the horizon of all questions we find the expansion of communication. The dialogue model is therefore all-encompassing. It is a paradigmatic structure not only for the I–thou relationship but also for the totality of our relationships.

Gadamer: That means that one cannot say for any single point of view that the reintegration of an explanation and a comprehension is altogether impossible. That is not a question concerning principles. It is an empirical question. And I would say that the last point is a question even of social responsibility, because I think that this disintegration of a society is in the end suicidal.

Q: I think there is an aspect to the comprehension of the conflict of interpretations that tends to come out as a result of some of the answers that Professor Ricoeur is offering. His reference to Beethoven does more to explain how the reintegration of explanation into an interpretative procedure is possible. Now I think everyone knows that, say, Georg Solti and Von Karajan or any of a dozen other conductors all know how to analyse the first movement of Beethoven's *Eroica*. And yet every one of them conducts it in a different way, which means that we have a dozen interpretations, a dozen integrations. What is the connection of the theoretical component in this interpretation? And what, on the other hand, is the significance of the interpretative aspects? The conflict of interpretations comes not between the explanatory and the interpretative in this case, but between one interpretation and another. For instance, there is a conflict between a Marxist interpretation of a historical event and a Hegelian interpretation of a historical event. And despite the fact that Hegel has now been dead since 1831, one can still entertain the possibility of that kind of conflict. Despite the fact that Professor Gadamer no longer finds Hegelian optimism possible, one can still understand the possibility of a Hegelian interpretation. So there's a conflict between Marxist and liberal historical interpretations of the Second World War or the First World War. Should one even try to do something about those conflicts, or rather should one attempt, instead of mediating them, to multiply them, and do something about holding all the multiplicities together?

Gadamer: Thank you very much for your question. You described these two fields as showing a conflict of interpretation. I would prefer to speak about a *competition* of interpretations; so that, in the end, there is a possible discrimination in terms of adequacy and inadequacy. In the ten reproductions of Beethoven, we have a doubled doubling of the whole problem of ambiguity because we have the text, the notes, and the different possibilities of performance in a situation that is a little more complicated than in the other examples. Nevertheless, different facets occur in these different interpretations. An *interpreter* of these interpretations would claim: Well, I see some points which are covered better in this, better in that interpretation. And so, in the end, my inner ear feels superior to any given performance. I think you would agree to the way I have put it here. Thank you.

Q: Professor Ricoeur, by discussing the conflict of interpretation as dialectical, do you do so on the Hegelian ground of recognizing these all as object, as product of the spirit, or what? On the other hand, Professor Gadamer's pessimism about the reconciliation of conflicting interpretations, and his distinction between surface meaning and deeper text seem to me to imply a kind of return to a Kantian *Ding an sich*, with all the paradoxes that go with that for Hegel. Would you be so kind as to comment on *that*, Professor Gadamer?

Ricoeur: I am entirely on the side of Professor Gadamer when he said that we have to do without a philosophy of absolute knowledge. This is, in fact, the lament of modern philosophy, that we have to raise Hegelian problems without the Hegelian solution. Each time we speak of negation, of dialectics, we are in fact the heirs of the system in ruins. In a sense, I perceive phenomenology, existential philosophy, and hermeneutics as an attempt to do the promised rational job in this situation of the impossibility of the system, and with the limiting idea not of there being something *an sich*, but simply *agreement*. But this was also the rhythm of the Socratic discourse, discussion, *homologia*; but with *homologia* as a horizon, we have only the history of interpretations. I think that we must live with that, but having as well the dialogual recognition that the other makes sense. Perhaps I cannot incorporate the other's interpretation into my own view, but I can, by a kind of imaginary sympathy, make room for it. I think that it is a part of intellectual integrity to be able to do that, to recognize the limit of my own comprehension and the plausibility of the comprehension of the other. It is in that way that I preserve *homologia* as the limiting idea of us all. But just as one recognizes there is no absolute performance of a symphony, so there is this recognition, at least of difference, the capacity to situate differences with respect to or within my own interpretation. I would say the same with all-encompassing theories of history. I have a great deal of reluctance to do that because, in keeping with what I have said about narratives, I don't think the narration of history allows all-encompassing theories like those of Marx and others. I may however understand these as a kind of working hypothesis, as the proposing of global images. Maybe we cannot have passionate history without a certain expectation of what *could be* the global meaning of history, but that must remain at the level, I think, of hypothesis; that must remain a kind of working hypothesis.

Northrop Frye's *Anatomy of Criticism,* or the Order of Paradigms

This essay on interpreting Northrop Frye's *Anatomy of Criticism* is governed by an underlying hypothesis which I want to set forth before testing it out in the reading that follows. It is my belief that, despite its systematic aspect, this work does not belong to the same system of thought that governs the narrative theory of the French school of structuralism. I see in the latter an attempt to reconstruct, to simulate at a higher level of rationality, what is already understood on a lower level of narrative understanding, the level brought to light for the first time by Aristotle in his *Poetics*. This attempted reconstruction has the same ambitions and arises out of the same second-order rationality that we see at work in the domain of historiography; its best illustration is provided by nomological models of historical explanation. It has the same ambition and the same legitimacy, that of bringing into play in the human sciences a logic of explanation akin to the one governing the exact sciences. In this sense, the vast body of work already produced in the field of narrative studies cannot be questioned. What is philosophically disputable is the claim to substitute this form of rationality for the narrative understanding that precedes it, not just as a fact in the history of culture, but also as a rule in the epistemological order of derivation. Such a substitution depends upon forgetting how rooted semiotic rationality is in narrative understanding, for which it attempts to provide an equivalent or a simulacrum on its own level.

Yet the precedence of narrative understanding in the epistemological order can neither be claimed nor maintained unless we restore to it those features of intelligibility that serve as the original model which semiotic rationality undertakes to simulate.

It is to just this intelligibility that Aristotle attributes poetry's power to 'teach,' to present 'universals' to thought – poetry, in the context of his *Poetics*, referring to the composing of tragic, comic, or epic works. But these universals are not those of theoretical reason. Rather they are akin to the universals operative in *phronesis*, 'prudence,' in the practical, ethical, and political order. Indeed, the configurational act (to use a term Louis Mink has introduced into the philosophy of history), by means of which the tragic, comic, or epic *mythos* imitates an action, is intelligible by virtue of this single fact: that the arrangement of incidents in a plot calls upon our capacity for 'grasping together' scattered events, circumstances, ends, means, interactions, contingencies, and unintended and unexpected results. It is this synthesis of the heterogenous in the configurational act that we understand as meaningful.

The multiple typologies we find in Northrop Frye's *Anatomy of Criticism* are grafted to this first order of intelligibility, without any recourse to the structuralists' narratological rationality, which begins by setting aside on principle every chronological, and therefore every narrative, feature in its models of the deep grammar of narration.

How then does one establish a typology that stays close to narrative intelligibility? This will be the guiding question of the remainder of my inquiry.

Two conditions for the possibility of such a typology are to be found in narrative understanding itself. First, that the creation of new plots arises from the eminently synthetic operation which Kant designated in terms of the productive imagination. Unlike the simply reproductive imagination, which is limited to representing already-existing objects *in absentia*, the productive imagination brings about new syntheses without any prior models. Yet, for Kant, the productive imagination does not work in a random fashion. It is the model for all rule-governed behaviour, in the sense that it is the creative matrix for the categories that critical philosophy proceeds to constitute in following its own *Leitfaden* (or guideline) stemming from transcendental logic. Even this constructive process, however, is subterraneously guided by the order of the schematism. The schematism has such power because the productive imagination itself performs a basically synthetic function. It connects the level of understanding (in the Kantian sense of *Verstand*) with that of intuition by generating new syntheses that are both intellectual and intuitive. In the same way, emplotment, that is, the formation (or *poiesis*) of plots, generates a mixed intelligibility between what can be called the thought – the 'theme,' the topic of a story – and the intuitive presentation of situations, characters, episodes, changes of fortune, and so on. We may thus speak of a schematism of the narrative function to characterize the work of intelligibility proper to the configurational act of emplotment.

And we may say that it is thanks to such potential intelligibility that individual plots lend themselves to typologies of the kind Northrop Frye construes in his *Anatomy of Criticism*. Such typologies, I believe, reflect a sustained familiarity with the individual works of our narrative tradition or traditions, and they constitute the schematism of the narrative function, whereas individual plots express the productive imagination at work on the level of poetic composition.

In this way, we can transpose into more contemporary terms – with Kant's help! – Aristotle's thesis that poetry teaches us universals. These universals, as I said, are not those of theoretical reason. Let us now add that they are the universals of the schematism of the narrative function.

The second condition for the possibility of a typology that is not reducible to a 'logic' of narrative is close to the first one. Its universals are taught through reflection upon the structuring acts of our narrative traditions in the course of our history. In other words, the narrative schematism is constituted in and through a history that has all the features of a tradition. By this I do not mean some inert transmission of dead materials but rather the living transmission of a chain of interactions which can always be reactivated by a return to the most creative moments of poetic composition. This phenomenon of 'traditionality' is the key to the functioning of the narrative paradigms. The constituting of any tradition relies on the interplay between innovation and sedimentation; and it is to sedimentation – that is, the preservation of innovations through a cumulating time – that we can ascribe those paradigms that constitute the typology of emplotment. They – or rather their schematisms – stem from a sedimented history whose genesis has largely been obliterated.

However, sedimentation does not occur without its contrary process, innovation, just as innovation does not occur apart from sedimentation. It is easy to see why. Paradigms that are generated by some previous innovation in turn provide guidelines for further experimentation in the narrative field. These paradigms change under the pressure of new innovations, but they change slowly and even resist change by virtue of the process of sedimentation. This dialectic of sedimentation and change gives rise to a whole range of combinations, deployed between the two poles of servile application and calculated deviance, and passing through every degree of rule-governed deformation. Most folk-tales, myths, and traditional narratives in general stand close to the pole of servile application. But to the extent that we move beyond such traditional forms of narrative, deviance prevails. For example, many contemporary novels may be defined as anti-novels. A range of variations is thus delineated beyond which we should no longer speak of deviance but rather of 'schism,' to use Frank Kermode's term. But rule-governed deformation remains the axis along which the various modalities of paradigm change get distributed. These variations confer a historicity of its own upon the productive imagination, one that keeps the narrative tradition alive.

It is to this schematism of narrative understanding, considered in terms of the unity of its style of traditionality, that I attach the typologies that abound in the first essay of Frye's work 'Historical Criticism: Theory of Modes,' and even more in the third essay, 'Archetypal Criticism: Theory of Myths.' These typologies do not justify themselves by some abstract form of coherence or by their deductive virtues, but just by their capacity for rendering an account, by an openly inductive process, of the greatest possible number of works included in our cultural heritage.

Anatomy of Criticism, in its very construction, poses a delicate problem of interpretation in that it seems to develop fully a theory of 'modes' (wherein tragedy, epic, and modern forms of narrative find their place) before it develops the theory of symbols that, in the final analysis, contains the profound motivation justifying the cyclic distribution of the modes. The author no doubt wanted us to be able to read his theory of modes independently of his theory of symbols. But to anyone who has read the remainder of this book, it seems as though the theory of modes is established only on the basis of the theory of symbols that follows it.

Taken alone, the theory of modes is a vast taxonomy on the level of what I have called a narrative schematism. Let us concentrate our attention on the fictional modes, here leaving aside the thematic ones. In opposition to the thematic modes, which group together all the traits that link a poem to its speaker, the fictional modes refer only to internal structural relations. Their distribution is governed by a single basic criterion, their hero's power of action, which may be, as we read in Aristotle's *Poetics*, greater than our own, less than our own, or more or less similar to our own. Frye applies this criterion along two parallel planes, that of tragedy and that of comedy, which in fact are not modes but classes of modes. In tragic modes, the hero is isolated from society (to which isolation corresponds the spectator's aesthetic distance, as we see in the 'purifying' emotions of terror and pity). In comic modes, the hero is reincorporated into his society. Frye applies his criterion of the power of action along these two lines of tragedy and comedy. And he distinguishes on each line five modes divided into five columns. In the first column, that of myth, the hero is superior in kind. In the second, that of romance, he is no longer superior in kind but in degree, in relation to other people and their environment. In the third column, that of high mimetic, the hero is superior to others but not to their environment, as we see in epic and in tragedy. In the fourth column, that of low mimetic, the hero is the equal of his fellows and their surroundings. Finally, in the fifth column, that of irony, the hero is inferior to us in strength and intelligence; we look down at him from above.

If we limited ourselves to this taxonomy, there would be hardly any place for more than the little parlour game of endlessly adding new subdivisions or of proving the author wrong by 'inventing' a category that would be unclassifiable according to this taxonomy. However, the real interest lies elsewhere than in the question of completeness. Beyond the fact that Frye adds differential features to his model equal in importance to those of the fictional modes, under the title 'thematic modes,' he also adds two rules for reading which profoundly transform the simply taxonomic character of the classification. On the one side, it is said that fiction, in the West, ceaselessly displaces its centre of gravity from above to below, that is, from the divine hero towards the hero of tragedy and of ironic comedy, including the parody of ironic tragedy. This law of descent is in no way a law of decadence, as may be seen by its counterpart. To the extent that the sacred in the first column and the marvellous in the second column decrease, we see the mimetic tendency increase, first in the form of high mimetic, then of low mimetic. We also see the values of plausibility, then of resemblance increase. What is more, by means of the diminution of the hero's power, the values of irony are liberated and allowed to develop. And in one sense, irony is already potentially present as soon as we have a *mythos* or plot in the broad sense. Every *mythos* implies an 'ironic withdrawal from reality' (p. 82). This explains the apparent ambiguity of the term 'myth': in the sense of sacred myth, the term designates the stories of heroes superior to us in every way; in the Aristotelian sense of *mythos*, it covers the entire region of fiction. The two senses are connected by irony. Irony is implicitly present in all *mythos*, but it only becomes a separate mode with the decline of sacred myth. Only thus does irony become a terminal mode, in accordance with the law of descent mentioned above. The irony inherent in plot, as such, appears to be connected in this way to the whole set of fictional modes. As we shall see, this first appended thesis introduces an orientation into the taxonomy.

The second thesis is still more unsettling. It states that, in one way or another, irony moves back towards myth (see pp. 42, 48–9), for Northrop Frye is anxious to catch hold of an indication of a return towards myth underlying what he calls 'ironic myth.' This indication is the basis of the scale that runs from ironic comedy through the irony of the *pharmakos* or scapegoat, to the irony of the inevitable and the incongruous.

Now these two rules for reading – the law of descent, which orients the taxonomy, and the law of return, which gives a circular shape to the linear succession of modes – define what I would call the style of European or Western traditionality for Northrop Frye. But these two rules are incomprehensible and appear entirely arbitrary unless the theory of modes finds its hermeneutical key in the theory of symbols that informs the three other essays of *Anatomy of Criticism*.

For the purposes of our discussion, let us consider two important points of that theory: the definition of what counts as a symbol for literary criticism, and the distinguishing of phases, which is the real object of *Anatomy of Criticism*.

For Northrop Frye, literary symbolism does not imply a category of symbols in the broad sense that Cassirer gave this term. Instead, the definition of literary symbolism is quite specific. It follows from a prior definition of what a poem is, namely a 'hypothetical verbal structure' (p. 71). Correlatively, a symbol is 'any unit of any literary structure that can be isolated for critical attention' (ibid.). The three words used in defining a poem – and, by implication, a symbol – are equally important. It is a question of language phenomena that present a delimited, closed texture, and whose relation to external things is neutralized. This last point is most important because schematically a symbol can be considered as moving in two different directions, one towards the outside, the other towards the inside. If we follow the first direction, the symbol stands for or points towards external things. It 'represents' them (p. 73). This class of symbols is that of 'signs.' If we follow the other direction, the symbol unifies a verbal structure. It 'connects' it and hence we can speak of a 'motif.' These two kinds of symbols appear in every form of reading, but in descriptive reading the ultimate direction is towards the outside. Conversely, 'in all literary verbal structures the final direction of meaning is inward' (p. 74). This is why literary meaning is 'hypothetical.' A 'hypothetical' or assumed relation to the external world is part of what is usually meant by the word 'imaginative' (ibid.), a term that Northrop Frye clearly distinguishes from 'imaginary,' which designates a failed assertion. Literature is made of such hypothetical verbal structures, and symbols are the units that critical interest isolates.

If Northrop Frye chooses to use the term *symbol*, in spite of all the risks of confusion in this overloaded concept, it is because it allows him to take up in a new way the problem of multiple meanings arising from the medieval exegetical theory of the four senses of Scripture. The polysemy of a symbol is nothing other than the possibility of placing it in a succession of contexts or networks of relations which define its 'phases.'

As in the hermeneutic of the four senses of Scripture, the first phase is the literal one. It is defined exactly by our taking the hypothetical character of poetic structure seriously. To understand a poem literally is to understand everything that constitutes it as it stands. It is to interest ourselves in the unity of its structure, to read it as a poem. A poem is then taken by the reader to represent a certain 'mood,' which is nothing other than the unifying emotion that informs it and that arises from the references from one poetic image to another. In this sense, the mood is just as hypothetical as is the *mythos* or plot. We can even say that they share the same ironic relation with regard to reality, the same 'ironic withdrawal from reality.'

With the second phase, which Frye calls the formal one to distinguish it from the literal one, the symbol begins its hermeneutic course paralleling the four senses of the medieval tradition. With this stage, the author introduces the mimetic function of the poem, whether it be a mimesis of action in narrative plots or *mimesis logou* with the *dianoia* poetically transposed. To the reader's surprise, this second phase introduces the symbol into the cycle of nature. 'The poem is not natural in form, but it relates itself naturally to nature' (p. 82). Is the critic about to deny his allegiance to the hypothetical? No. Just as the non-literal senses of the medieval tradition presuppose the literal one, Frye's formal phase presupposes it too. But since the literal for Frye means something hypothetical, the mimetic relation to nature which constitutes the second phase must be constructed on the basis of the hypothetical one. Mimesis therefore cannot be a copy unless we abolish the difference between poetry and description. And if we wish to conserve the metaphor of a mirror, we must understand it precisely in the sense of a poem holding up a mirror to nature, 'the poem is not itself a mirror' (p. 84). We can therefore explore this stage of the symbol as an image if we keep in mind that the image is not the replica of some natural object but rather a relation to nature based upon the hypothetical status of the poem and its symbols. Given this condition, an autonomous type of criticism is possible, one that would be the examination of the imagery recurring in this or that poem. We can then risk calling this phase an 'allegorical' one, recalling the older terminology, as long as we do not mean by 'allegory' an illustration in images of abstract ideas arising from anything but the poem itself. On the contrary, allegory is the very movement from the literal sense of the poem to another kind of sense. And in this sense, the initial irony of the literal sense puts us on guard against taking a poem's ideas too seriously in the wrong way – I mean, in a way contrary to its hypothetical status.

For myself, I understand this turn in Northrop Frye's theory of symbols as follows. Even within that state of suspension wherein fiction holds the poem, there subsists an oblique reference to the real world, either as a form of borrowing or as a subsequent resymbolization of it. Therefore I see Frye's second phase as the nexus or turning-point between suspended reference and re-created reference, what I would call, in a vocabulary close to Hans-Georg Gadamer's, reference to the world of the text. To the extent that the poem unfolds in some hypothetical dimension, it also projects a world that we might inhabit.

There is evidence for such an interpretation, I submit, in the following statements from *Anatomy of Criticism*. Literature, Frye says, must be seen ' as a body of hypothetical creations which is not necessarily involved in the worlds of truth and fact, nor necessarily withdrawn from them, but which may enter into any kind of relationship to them, ranging from the most to the least explicit ... The conception of art as having a relation to reality which is neither direct nor negative, but potential, finally resolves the dichotomy between delight and instruction, the style and the message' (pp. 92–3).

The third stage, that of the symbol as archetype, marks the place for a third type of criticism, archetypal criticism. We should not rush to denounce the latent 'Jungianism' of this type of criticism. On the contrary, it is a question of following the rigorous movement inaugurated by the literal phase, that is, by the hypothetical status of the poem, and continued across the second stage, that of the symbol as an image. Within this perspective, we see that the term *archetype* designates the genesis of a conventional and generic bond, stemming from a poem's external relations with every other poem. This bond derives from the eminently communicable character of poetic art, that is, its social or sociable character. No poem is without precedent. The new always appears within an already existing order of words. 'Poetry can only be made out of other poems; novels out of other novels. Literature shapes itself' (p. 97). Thus to talk about an archetype is to presuppose that the order of words is not pure chaos, that it has its own recurrences. And a symbol considered as an archetype designates some communicable form of unity. 'I mean by an archetype a symbol which connects one poem with another and thereby helps to unify and integrate our literary experience' (p. 99). In this sense, I recognize in the concept of an archetype an equivalent of what I have called the schematism issuing from the sedimentation of tradition.

It is true that Northrop Frye gives his notion of an archetype a more pregnant and, at first glance, a more opaque meaning. But this meaning becomes more accessible if we consider its filiation not just from the first phase, but also from the second, the mimetic dimension added to the hypothetical one. If an archetype designates a stable conventional order, this order can be established in terms of its correspondence to the order of nature and its recurrences – day and night, the seasons, the years, life and death. To see the order of nature as imitated by a corresponding order of words is a perfectly legitimate enterprise, if we know how to construct it on the basis of the mimetic conception that is itself built upon the hypothetical conception of the symbol. These two approaches to the archetype are then conjoined in archetypal criticism in which the individuality of any poem is entirely absorbed into the order of words born both from social conventionality and from imitation of the natural order. Jungian or not, this way of understanding symbols from the point of view of an order that goes beyond individual creations does not betray its premises; rather, it enriches them without destroying them. Archetypal criticism in this sense is not fundamentally different from the type of criticism practised by Gaston Bachelard in his theory of a 'material' imagination governed by the 'elements' of nature – water, air, earth, fire – but operating within the realm of language. It is also akin to the way in which Mircea Eliade orders hierophanies in terms of such cosmic dimensions as the sky, water, life, and so on – dimensions that go beyond all spoken or written rituals. This is why the archetypes most laden with cosmic meaning in *Anatomy of Criticism* are still 'learned cultural archetypes' (p. 102). It is their belonging to the sphere of language that makes them suitable for comparative and morphological study, which, by right, extends from folk-tales and legends to all the rest of literature.

Finally, the last symbolic phase is one where the symbol is a 'monad.' This phase corresponds to the anagogical sense of medieval biblical exegesis. By a monad, Frye means imaginative experience's capacity to attain totality in terms of some centre. As he states, 'difficult' writers lead one to think that 'the learned and the subtle, like the primitive and the popular, tend toward a center of imaginative experience – there *is* a center of the order of words' (pp. 117–18, his emphasis). On these terms, then, we can again speak of a world of the text. In the last analysis, we must choose between an endless labyrinth or a total form.

We cannot doubt that the whole of Northrop Frye's enterprise hangs on the thesis that the narrative order finally refers to this 'still center of the order of words.' This centre is 'what our whole literary experience has been about' (p. 117). In any case, we would misconceive the whole point of archetypal criticism, and even more that of anagogical criticism, if we saw it as some kind of interest in mastery or domination, in the fashion of rational reconstructions of a phenomenon or a process. On the contrary, the schematisms arise from these two phases more than from some order whose cyclic composition we cannot master. We can hardly speak of the blossoming division of literary creations in terms of the myths of spring, summer, fall, and winter as taxonomy. Why? Because the imagery whose secret order we seek to discern is dominated from above by apocalyptic imagery that, through forms difficult to number, turns on reconciliation in a unity – the unity of a one yet triune God, the unity of humanity, the unity of the animal world in terms of the symbol of the lamb, of the vegetable world in terms of the symbol of the tree of life, and of the mineral world in terms of the heavenly city.

It is true that this symbolism has its demonic side, as expressed in such figures as Satan, the tyrant, the monster, the barren fig tree, and the 'primitive sea,' the symbol of 'chaos.' But this polar structure is itself unified by the strength of the desire that configures both the infinitely desirable and its contrary, the infinitely detestable, at the same time. From an archetypal and an anagogical perspective, then, all imagery is inadequate in relation to the apocalyptic imagery of fulfilment and yet at the same time in search of it. Consequently literature is to be characterized overall as a quest, whether we consider the romantic, the high-mimetic, or the low-mimetic modes, or the ironic one represented by satire. All of literature derives its movement and its amplitude from this structure. So while we should not really speak of process in apocalyptic/demonic imagery, all imagery, in that it does not measure up to this ideal, is nothing but process: the alternation of life and death, of labour and rest, of sorrow and joy. Within the cyclical character of these changes appears the reigning mark of the apocalyptic/demonic order. This is why we have to put the cycle of seasons, which plays such a large part in the fourth phase, under the sign of the Apocalypse. This reference to the Apocalypse divests this theory of seasonal myths of every naturalistic characteristic, not just, as I have said, because it is taken up into the hypothetical register of the poem or because of the non-reduplicating character of poetic mimesis, but still more because of the attraction that the apocalyptic/demonic imagery exercises on the verbal order. On the archetypal level, nature still contains man. On the anagogical level, man contains nature. Even his cities and his gardens are figures of a human universe configured by the infinitely desirable. In this sense, the Apocalypse is what draws the potent symbolism of nature, arising from the archetypal level, into the orbit of the mythical order of language.

For Northrop Frye, our whole literary experience stands in relation to this 'still center of the order of words.' It is 'what our whole literary experience has been about.' However, if we run through the four phases of the symbol in reverse, it seems as though it is this reasonable belief in the power of a centre to order and contain everything that, retroactively, confers its plausibility on the search for an archetypal order. It is this which, if we return to the earlier phase, allows us to expect to find those 'images' that are capable of being put into patterns. If we return to our starting-point, it is this belief that allows us to say of each poem that it constitutes a hypothetical verbal structure. What is more, we must not fail to include the progressive movement from the literal sense to the anagogical one in this retrogressive move. The symbol can assume the mimetic, then the archetypal and the anagogical functions because it had from the beginning established the difference between the hypothetical and the actual. *The hypothetical is retained in the anagogical.* This explains the fine definition of literature in the anagogic phase as 'existing in its own universe, no longer a commentary on life or reality, but containing life and reality in a system of verbal relationships' (p. 122).

We would completely misconceive the meaning of this assertion if we concluded that, for Northrop Frye, in the end literature and religion become identical. For Frye, religion remains on the realistic and, therefore, descriptive side of language, even if its language traverses phases comparable to those we have described. We must say, instead, that, within its hypothetical order, literature is driven by the same desire as is religion. And in this sense, nothing is closer to Blake's dream than Mallarmé's statement that 'tout au monde existe pour aboutir à un livre' (cited, ibid.).

This analogy between literature and religion, an analogy which the hypothetical character of poetry prevents us from ever reducing to an identity, finds its highest expression in the symbol of the Apocalypse. In literature this symbol marks the internal limit, not the external boundary, of a desire that aims at wholeness by means of the imagination. Precisely because the bond with the natural cycle has been broken, it can only be imitated and becomes an immense reservoir of images. The Apocalypse reconstructs the cycle that, on the level of nature, has been lost on the successive levels of the hypothetical, the imaginative, the archetypal, and finally on the level of a universal gravitation of symbols around a centre. 'The conception of a total Word is the postulate that there is such a thing as an order of words' (p. 126). Once again this formula sounds like a religious one, but religion for Northrop Frye is too devoted to what *is* and literature too devoted to what *may be* for them to be identified with each other. Culture 'interposes, between the ordinary and the religious life, a total vision of possibilities, and insists on its totality – for whatever is excluded from culture by religion or state will get its revenge somehow' (p. 127). Culture thus establishes its autonomy precisely by developing itself fully in its imaginative mode. 'Between religion's "this is" and poetry's "but suppose *this* is," there must always be some kind of tension, until the possible and the actual meet at infinity' (pp. 127–8).

This aiming at totality through language in the mode of the imaginative and the hypothetical which is characteristic of literature cannot be fully appreciated, in my opinion, without reference to the dialectic of innovation and sedimentation by means of which above I tried to characterize the traditionality of the narrative schematism.

Two problems, the one the contrary of the other, then arise. On the one hand, we can ask to what extent the literary tradition, by virtue of its principle of sedimentation, allows us to discern a style of development, an order of paradigms. Such an order of paradigms, if it can be identified without doing violence to individual works, would make our tradition into a coherent heritage, in spite of the contingent appearance of individual works. However, we can also ask what amount of variation is authorized by the space of variation which tradition opens, before we have to talk of a 'schism,' that is, of a death of paradigms. Walter Benjamin, for example, in his essay 'The Storyteller,' seems to consider the extinction of the narrative function as a *fait accompli:* 'Familiar though his name may be to us, the storyteller, in his living immediacy, is by no means a present force. He has already become something remote from us and something that is getting more distant ... The act of storytelling is coming to an end ... It is as if something that seemed inalienable to us, the securest among our possessions, were taken from us: the ability to exchange experience' (*Illuminations*, p. 83).

Benjamin thus seems to pose a problem diametrically opposed to that of Northrop Frye, as does Frank Kermode when he refers to the passage from deviance to 'schism' in contemporary literature, and as do, too, the deconstructionists when they ferociously attack the very idea of a 'still center of the order of words.' For me, the most valuable question that Northrop Frye raises for us is this: whether the question of deviance or even of schism, of the death of paradigms, can receive an intelligible answer apart from the prior question of the order of paradigms. In relation to what, in effect, could there be deviance or schism or death, if not in relation to a style of development capable of being identified? What would there be to deconstruct if literature did not itself posit the postulate 'that there is such a thing as an order of words'?

Anatomy of Criticism attempts to answer this first, primary question. Its enterprise is plausible to the extent that the level where it occurs is not that of semiotic rationality but rather that of narrative understanding, and it does so in the first place by means of Northrop Frye's great familiarity with the works of which we are the inheritors, then in virtue of the twofold phenomenon of the schematism of traditionality which I described above. The order of paradigms that *Anatomy of Criticism* establishes is not atemporal inasmuch as it proceeds from the sedimentation that gives this schematism the unity of a style. Nor is it historical in the sense that it follows the chronology of the history of literature. Neither ahistorical nor historical, it is rather trans-historical, in the sense that it traverses history in a cumulative and not simply an additive mode. Even if this order includes breaks, these do not ignore what precedes them or that from which they separate themselves. They too are part of the phenomenon of tradition and its cumulative style.

The decisive test of Northrop Frye's conception of literary criticism would be to demonstrate that the phenomena of deviance, schism, and the death of paradigms constitute the inverse side of the problem posed by *Anatomy of Criticism* of an order of paradigms constituting the schematism of narrative understanding.

Greimas's Narrative Grammar

What is interesting about Greimas's narrative grammar is the way it constructs, degree by degree, the necessary conditions for narrativity, starting from a logical model which is the least complex possible and which, initially, includes no chronological import at all. The question is whether, in the attempt to arrive at the structure of those stories which are, in fact, produced by oral and written traditions, the author, in the successive additions with which he enriches his initial model, does indeed build upon the specifically narrative characteristics of the initial model or whether his development includes extrinsic presuppositions. Greimas believes that, despite these additions to the initial model, an equivalence is maintained, from beginning to end, between that initial model and the final matrix. The validity of this belief must be tested theoretically and practically. Here this will be done at the theoretical level, that is, by following the author step by step as he constructs his final model, without including examples which might verify *a posteriori* the fruitfulness of the method.

The question concerning the equivalence between the initial model and the final matrix can be broken down into several stages, following the order the author himself sets out in 'Eléments d'une grammaire narrative.'

In the model we can identify four stages of narrativization.

The first is at the level which the author calls fundamental grammar, where he introduces for the first time the notion of 'narrativization,'[1] this being something contained within the fundamental grammar.

The second is found as we move from the fundamental grammar to the 'surface narrative grammar.' Here the author introduces the

notion of 'doing,' then those of 'wanting to do' and 'being able to do.'
On these he bases the notion of 'narrative utterance.'

We find the third in the course of the development of the surface
grammar, where a *polemical* factor is introduced which shapes the
notion of 'performance,' taken to be an exemplary 'narrative unit.'

The fourth is found in the further development of the surface
grammar, where the exchange structure provides the author with a
'topological' way of representing narrative phenomena. Here we
have a reformulation of all the generative operations of narrativity in
terms of *transfer* from one place to another: the 'performance series'
thus obtained provide the semiotic foundation of the narrative structure itself.

At each stage the question is whether equivalence to the initial
model is maintained – that is, whether or not the successive degrees
of narrativization are limited to a development of the logical forces
of the initial model alone, making them explicit in such a way as to be
their manifestation, making the deep structure *apparent*.

This simple presentation of the skeletal outline of the author's
argument gives an idea of the rigorous and fine distinctions used to
bridge gradually the distance between what the author calls 'fundamental *ab quo* instances' and 'final *ad quem* instances.'[2] The intellectual process we are going to describe here is, strictly speaking, a
process of *mediation* whose progressive stages must be understood
before its value is judged. We must therefore be very attentive to
such highly refined distinctions as: 1 / 'narrativization' (of the taxonomic model); 2 / 'narrative utterance'; 3 / 'narrative unit' or 'performance'; 4 / 'performance series.' These will now become the titles of
our four levels of description and discussion of this body of theory.

I. At the Fundamental Grammar Level:
The First Stage of 'Narrativization'

We have to remember the requirements made of the initial model: it
must first be constructed at the so-called immanent level, that is, a
stage that precedes its 'manifestation' by some linguistic substance,
or even by a non-linguistic substance (painting, cinema, and so on);
then it must show a *discursive* character, that is, it must be constructed of
units that are much larger than utterance (which is manifested as
sentence). These two requirements dictate the *semiotic* level of anal-

ysis. We must say right away that the second requirement introduces the minimal condition of narrativity – namely, that it, of its essence, includes a characteristic of 'composition' (to use Aristotle's term) of sentences used in discourse, a characteristic that is not deducible from the phrastic structure (that is, from the predicative relationship, as indeed is the case in the theory of metaphor).[3]

Thus the initial model must from the outset present an articulated character, if indeed it is going to be able to be narrativized. The stroke of genius – and this is not too strong – is to have sought this already-articulated nature in a logical structure that is as simple as possible, that is, in the 'elementary structure of signification.' This structure has to do with the conditions of grasping of meaning, any meaning. If something – anything at all – *signifies*, it is not because one might have some intuition as to what it signifies, but because one can lay out in the following way an absolutely elementary system of relations: a relation of contradiction – white/non-white; a relation between contraries – white/black; and one of implication or presupposition – non-white/black. Here we have the famous *semiotic square*, whose logical force is supposed to bring about all subsequent enrichment of the model. To understand primary narrativization, that is, narrativization which occurs at this so-called deep level, we must understand the manner in which semantics and syntax are linked at this very level. The constitutive model is semantic in that what it structures is a signification. More precisely, 'this elementary structure of signification gives us a semiotic model which allows us to explain the articulation of meaning within a semantic micro-universe' (p. 161). By semantic micro-universe let us agree that we refer to the capacity of a simple element of signification – the 'seme' – to be part of the triple relation that we have just mentioned.[4] This elementary structure, the author tells us, 'is capable of enabling meaning to signify' (p. 162). In other words, it makes a micro-universe of the unit of meaning, that is, a relational microsystem. What constitutes it is also what organizes it. It is also what, subsequently, will allow for the 'manipulation' of meaning. It is what shapes all of the transformations we are now going to present.[5]

How does this constitutive model enter into narrativization?

Semantically speaking – or, to say the same thing differently, from the point of view of morphology – the model is rigorously achronic. It is a taxonomy, that is, a system of unoriented relations. The mutual defining of its four poles presents an absolutely static network of relations. But one can represent the model dynamically. One just has to move from the morphological point of view to the syntactic one, that is, treat the constituent *relations* of the taxonomic model as being *operations*. Indeed, syntax is no more than a regulating of these operations. Treating relations as operations amounts to viewing signification 'as a grasping or a production of meaning by the subject' (p. 164).

This must be emphasized: semantics is taxonomic; syntax has to do with operations. The operations taking place are *transformations*. By so saying, we prepare the way for the introduction of the key notion which will underlie all subsequent developments of the model, that is, the notion of a 'syntactic doing.' But, as we shall see, there is more in 'doing' than there is in 'operation.' Nevertheless the idea of a subject who is a producer of meaning already underlines the 'dynamization' of the constitutive model which shapes that meaning. Reformulated in terms of operations, our three relations of contradictions, contraries, and presuppositions can appear as *transformations* by which a given content is *negated* and others *affirmed*. We will call the transformation by negation 'disjunction,' and the transformation by affirmation '*conjunction*.' If we view these transformations as *oriented* operations we end up with the primary condition of narrativity. This is nothing more than the setting into motion of the taxonomic model.[6]

Discussion

Before moving from the deep grammar to the surface narrative grammar, let us pause to make a critical comment. Three questions are raised. The first has to do with the principle itself by which a distinction is made between a deep grammar and a surface narrative grammar. The second has to do with the logical rigour of the constitutive model. The third deals with the 'narrativization' of that model.

1 / As for the general relation between fundamental (or deep) grammar and surface grammar, one might ask if, in fact, this is a relation of the 'immanent' (that is, as premanifestation) to the 'manifest.' The complete answer to this question cannot be given at this stage of the discussion inasmuch as it amounts to asking whether or not the surface grammar is richer than the deep grammar in terms of relations and operations. But given the extent to which the distinction between immanent structure and manifestation brings into play

the general relations between the *semiotic* and the *linguistic*, one might wonder whether the hierarchy of these two levels does not *a priori* bring into play relations of another order, already noted by de Saussure: that is, that the linguistic order is at the same time one semiotic system among other semiotic systems and the paradigm within which one can discover the general characteristics of semiotics in general. Proof for this is found in the analysis of Greimas's constitutive model which shows itself to be, of its essence, 'semic' (the binary schema s_1/non-s_1). I do not contest the rightness of reaching the semiotic *through* the linguistic. I do contest the correctness of a procedure that articulates the semiotic *before* it articulates the linguistic. This way the semiotic and the linguistic reciprocally precede each other: the first by virtue of its general nature, the second by virtue of its exemplary status.

This objection is not inconsequential as far as narrativity is concerned. If, in fact, the semiotic and the linguistic precede each other according to different points of view, it is possible that sometimes a semiotic analysis, operating in the context of a preliminary narrative intelligibility, might legitimately construct *a priori* the semiotic square (or squares) which structure that text. In this case, semiotic analysis has a real heuristic value and really can show how the text should be read. But it can happen that a semiotic analysis might also be feigned. What I mean is that the analysis, shaped by a narrative force which establishes its own criteria, might be not so much constructed *a priori*, but reconstructed, instead, after the fact, in order to meet the demands of the semiotic approach. Finally – and this is, in my opinion, the most frequent case, if indeed not the norm – the constitutive model for the semiotic level and the specific criteria for narrativity which the following discussion will identify can come together in a *mixed* or complex conceptual understanding of narrativity which is an accurate reflection of the complex relationship according to which the semiotic and the linguistic mutually precede each other from different points of view.

2 / As for the logical rigour of the constitutive model, the *constraints* that it imposes upon semiotic analysis, and even more understandably upon subsequent linguistic analysis, are perhaps those that one would expect from a model that is too rigid for what must subsequently be codified by it, and, as often happens when one interprets in a given area according to models constructed *a priori*,

certain of the model's requirements might have to be attenuated in order to function well in subsequent applications.

We note immediately that all is based upon semic analysis,[7] and that while, indeed, this analysis identifies certain discursive characteristics, in the sense of articulations, which lend themselves to being narrativized, they are not established at the transphrastic level as had been promised. The analysis does not begin at a point beyond utterance, but within it, at the level of a fundamental semantics. In this sense, the model is not discursive in the sense of discourse being a wider unit than utterance. We have therefore to presuppose the existence of a homological arrangement of the infra- and supraphrastic structures which is not thematically developed here.[8]

It will also be noted that the semic analysis has to be completed first, or at least to have reached the stage at which it allows for a 'limited inventory of the semic categories' (p. 161), as in the example of white versus black. This requirement is rarely met.

But above all, it will be noted that the taxonomic model has a strictly logical significance only if it remains a very powerful model. Let us be clear: the three relations of contradictions, contraries, and presuppositions are what they are only if contradiction signifies no more than the relation between s_1 and non-s_1; if the relation of contraries between s_1 and s_2 truly constitutes a binary semic category of the white-versus-black type, that is, within the precise framework of a polar opposition between semes of the same category; and finally if the presupposition of non-s_1 by s_2 is truly preceded by two relations of contradictions and contraries which obey the rigorous conditions just mentioned. Now, one can justifiably doubt that all three conditions will be met rigorously in the area of narrativity. If they were, all subsequent operations would have to be 'predictable and calculable' (p. 166). But then nothing would happen. There would be no events. There would be no surprise. There would be nothing to tell. One can suppose that the surface grammar will more often be dealing in quasi contradictions, quasi contraries, quasi presuppositions. As we shall see, many of the author's 'schemata' (so he calls the twosome constructed from the relation of contradiction) are analogous only to contradictions. Many of the 'correlations' between two such 'schemata' are weak contraries (that is, they could not sustain a true semic analysis and cannot be authenticated by pointing to their resting on a binary semic category of the white-versus-black type). Finally – and above all – the crucial point for the proper functioning of the constitutive model has to do with the kind of constraints – introduced by the relation of presupposition, which links non-s_1 to s_2 – which regulate the *deixes*. These constraints are entirely dependent upon the force of the other two relations between contradictions and contraries. Therefore, only in a case where these three requirements have not been weakened can we speak of the 'unity of meaning' of the four-term model and of the isotopy of the semantic micro-universe articulated by the constitutive model. In a case in which the relations are too attenuated, too much just a fact of analogy, if not simply counterfeiting, the relation of presupposition no longer holds. The unity of meaning is broken up and the isotopy vacillates. It is perhaps at this point that some *novelty* is included in the operations made upon, and the manipulations of, the constitutive model.

3 / What of the 'narrativization' of the taxonomic model? It is supposed to be guaranteed by the fact of one's moving from the idea of relation to that of operation. This is assuredly the key point and is within the deep grammar itself.

At first sight – and if one reads the 'Eléments d'une grammaire narrative' in the light of 'Les Jeux des contraintes sémiotiques' – primacy is given to morphology in a reading which is avowedly paradigmatic. The emphasis is thus not on the difference between relations and transformations, but on the fact that the constitutive model is, of its essence, of a discursive nature – or at least an articulated one. Since each case of signification constitutes a relational micro-universe, reformulation in terms of operations appears to be no more than a corollary of this signification network arrangement. The equivalence between relations and operations remains unthreatened, but one cannot understand how an achronic model can contain the conditions for narrativity. Is it enough to take relations as *operations*? Is it enough for these operations to be *oriented*[9] and form *series*? Do these things allow us to speak of narrativization? Even more, the whole enterprise can be suspected of having, from the outset, misunderstood the narrative dimension of discourse.

For reading that takes more closely into account the shift in emphasis seen between the 'Contraintes' and the 'Eléments' (to which the author himself attests),[10] moving from the idea of relation to that of operation implies the need for wholesale additions to the taxonomic model which really change its nature and also give it an authentic chronological nature. These additions are evident in the

'Eléments' in the notion of 'production of meaning by the subject' (p. 164). What subject? If it is not yet the actant of surface grammar, it is already the subject of a doing, of a syntactic doing which will precisely bring about the transition to a general doing, a central point for all of the anthropomorphic meanings of the story. We thus have here much more than reformulation. Instead, it is the introduction, on an equal footing, of a syntagmatic factor alongside the paradigmatic factor. This is in fact a process involving 'already established terms' (p. 164), or 'terms with already invested values' (p. 164). In a case where you have a relation of contradiction, you effectuate the negation of one of the terms. You change it into its contradictory, which you then affirm. It is this transformation of invested content into other content that constitutes narrativization. There is thus a syntactic initiative applied to the simple taxonomic model. But if that is so then the notion of equivalence loses its meaning in terms of reciprocal relations, when we move from morphology to syntax.[11] It even loses its strict meaning in terms of isotopic, although not isomorphic, relations: In what way are a stable relation and its transformation equivalent, if orientation is what is important?[12] To go even farther, one might ask whether the construction of the taxonomic model was not guided by the idea of the transformations to be made to its terms. This question, as we shall see, can and will be asked at all levels: the final point of an operation should be the next operation, ending with the narrative's completed project. And if the taxonomic model was constructed in view of the syntactic operations to be grafted onto it, is it not true that these operations in turn become conditions for narrativity only retrospectively? This follows from their use in the narrative surface grammar – where they are linked with characteristics which appear and occur only in terms of phenomena unique to the surface grammar.

For my part, I am inclined to think that the enterprise, from beginning to end, obeys a twofold postulate: on the one hand, in an unfolding process, it applies, to all levels of narrativization, the logical force of the initial taxonomic model in such a way as to elevate semiotics to the rank of a deductive science; on the other hand, the enterprise, in a reverse process, seeks to construct the stages of the conditions for narrativity in the light of the end-point of a given narrative. To satisfy the first requirement, all additions to the model must appear to be equivalent transformations between isotopic metalanguages (p. 167). To meet the second demand, new specifications must be introduced at each stage in order to enhance the initial model, given its ultimate application in terms of the end-point of the narrative. Movement from one level to the other thus loses all its deductive nature. The complex interplay of these two requirements gives the whole enterprise the ambiguous appearance of reducing narrative to logic or of seeing narrative as a surpassing of logic. This ambiguous nature is obvious even at the initial stage, where narrativization appears to be the object of a reluctant recognition, half denied, scarcely avowed.

II. From the Fundamental Grammar to the Surface Narrative Grammar: The Narrative Utterance

The decisive grammatical shift is that which takes us from the 'deep' or fundamental level to the level which Greimas calls 'surface,' even though it is still, in his view, an intermediate plane between the strictly conceptual one we have been looking at, and the strictly 'figurative' one, the one at which actors accomplish tasks, undergo tests, reach goals. Although the differences between deep and surface structures may be easy to characterize, the difference between the superficial and figurative levels is difficult to describe. The level that we are now going to concentrate upon is, like the preceding one, a metalanguage level *vis-à-vis* the figurative language. The discussion of 'figurative' will come later.

The distinctive feature of this level is the *anthropomorphic* representation of the operations described earlier. If one says 'anthropomorphic' one means interpreting the notion of operation in terms of 'doing.' In other words, 'doing is an operation that is made specific by the addition of a human classeme' (p. 167). The syntactic operations of affirming and negating by conjunction and disjunction are thus rewritten as a syntactic doing. To this doing, which is syntactic because the reformulated operations were themselves syntactic, Greimas adds all the doing of human activity, to the extent that, in semiotics, all doing, whether performing an action ('Peter goes out') or recounting a doing ('Peter tells'), comes into play only when transcoded into a message. That is, it becomes an object of communication circulating between a sender and receiver. So it is that the notion of a syntactic doing, equivalent to that of an operation (itself being equivalent to a relation), provides the mediation required to generate the kind of utterance needed in order for the author legitimately to characterize a surface grammar as being a narrative grammar. This utterance is the *narrative utterance*. It expresses a process which articulates a function, in Propp's sense, and an actant. This can be represented as NU = F(A). 'One can thus say that any operation upon the deep grammar can be converted into a narrative utterance whose minimal canonic form is F(A)' (p. 168).

As can be seen, the equivalences upon which the entire enterprise rests are the homogeneity between syntactic operation and syntactic doing, on the one hand, and, on the other, between syntactic doing and any utterance expressing the doing of an actant.

Once this 'isotopy without isomorphism' has been allowed (p. 167), the theory of the narrative utterance develops in a remarkable way. In a thoroughly felicitous way the author has the narrative utterances spawn utterances which describe an effective doing and others which describe a wanting-to-do. If you consider that the complete utterance of the wanting-to-do is of the following form: X wants Y to do, then you can see that this wanting-to-do, formulated within the left-hand side of the complete utterance, modalizes the narrative utterance which, in turn, becomes the object of the wanting. It modalizes it in the sense that it makes it possible, thus causing it to go through the succession of the possible, the real, and the necessary modalities. Thus we will call modal utterances – so that we can distinguish them from simple narrative utterances, which we will from now on refer to as descriptive utterances – those utterances of the wanting-to-do form and those showing the same form which will be presented later. The introduction of *wanting*, in fact, constitutes the first in a series of 'predetermined semantic restrictions' (p. 168) which identify actants as subjects, that is, as potential operators of doing. The narrative utterance is itself specified as being a program which a subject wishes to carry out. In a general way, we call the complete modal utterance of the following type a program: 1 / 'X wants Y to do ...' Greimas next constructs a series of model utterances of the same form. First: 2 / 'X wants X to do ...' In this case, the same actor both wants and does. Then: 3 / 'X wants to have ...'; 4 / 'X wants to be ...' In these cases the object of the wanting is an attribution of objects or values. We will speak of attributive utterances (which will play a key role in the last phase in the construction of the completed model) when dealing with utterances of types 3 and 4. We still have left those modal utterances of the form: 5 / 'X wants to know (how to do ...)'; 6 / 'X wants to be able (to do ...).' Here, the model utterance is doubled to become a wanting-to-know-how and a wanting-to-be-able. At the end of this remarkable reconstruction of the typology of descriptive and modal utterances, the author believes that he has kept the equivalence between the elementary units of the surface grammar and those of the deep grammar (p. 172).

Discussion

Discussion of the second segment of the semiotic reconstruction of narrativity will follow the same order as the discussion of the first segment.

1 / The general question concerning the relation between deep and surface grammar can now be taken up in more detail. Does the logical level purely and simply precede the anthropomorphic level? This is certainly true in terms of the order of the exposition, since it is necessary to introduce determining factors which 'specify,' which 'transcribe in a more complex way' the operations of the deep grammar. But can the same be said concerning the order of discovery on the part of a reader? It is the anthropomorphic level which, in my opinion, carries all of the significations of doing. All these cases of signification are born of what I would call the *semantics of action*. We already know, concerning a knowing that is immanent to doing itself, that doing is the object of utterances whose structure differs in essence from that of predicative utterances of the type 's is p,' as it does also from the relational utterances of the type 'X is between Y and Z.' This structure of the descriptive utterance of action has been the object of precise study in analytic philosophy and I give an account of this in 'La Sémantique de l'action' (in which I refer particularly to Anthony Kenny).[13] One remarkable characteristic of these utterances is that their structure allows for everything from 'Socrates speaks ...' to 'Brutus killed Caesar on the Ides of March in the Roman Senate with a dagger ...'

It is this semantics of action which in fact is presupposed in the narrative utterance. Here, doing is substitutable for all verbs of action (as with the English *to do*) and is equated with them in the canonic form $NU = F(A)$.

I therefore now make the above suggestion more precise. It will be remembered that it dealt with the relation between semiotics and linguistics and saw them in terms of a mutual precedence. The semiotic square gives us its network of interdefined terms and its system of contradictions, contraries, and presuppositions. Semantics of action offer us the principal significations of doing and the specific structure for utterances which refer to action. In this sense, surface grammar is a mixed grammar: semiotic-praxic.

Nowhere is the specificity of the semantics of action more evident than in the movement from utterances on doing to utterances on being able to do. What makes it certain that wanting to do brings about doing? Nothing in the semiotic square allows us to believe this. Furthermore, the typology of wanting to do, of wanting to be, of wanting to have, of wanting to know, and of being able to want, is excellent. But, from the point of view of linguistics, it is implicated in a very specific grammar which analytic philosophy has developed with great sophistication under the name of intensional logic. But if a special grammar is required to put into logical form the relations between modal utterances of the 'wanting that ...' type and descriptive utterances of doing, it is the phenomenology implicit in the semantics of action which gives meaning to Greimas's declaration that 'modal utterances which have wanting as their function set the subject up as a virtuality of doing, whereas the other two modal utterances, characterized by the knowing-how-to and being-able-to modalities, determine this potential doing in two different ways: as a doing resulting from knowing how to or as one founded exclusively on being able to' (p. 175). This implicit phenomenology is brought to light when 'one can interpret the modal utterances as "the desire to realize" a program which is present in the form of a descriptive utterance and is at the same time part of, as an object, the modal utterance' (p. 169). One might say, in terms of 'desire,' that we have already moved from the anthropomorphic level to the figurative one (hence the quotation marks around 'desire to realize'). But can these two levels be distinguished from each other within modal utterances?[14] Can an utterance with two actants which links a virtual subject with an object which is itself a doing in fact utter anything else but desire? The author contradicts himself when he again takes up the term *desire* (without quotation marks this time) in order to account for the structure of modal utterances: 'the axis of desire which links [the two actants: the subject and the object] legitimizes, in turn, a semantic interpretation of them as a virtual *performing subject* and an *object set up as a value*' (p. 171). Likewise, if the figurative level is 'that at which human or personified actors accomplish tasks, submit to tests, reach goals' (p. 166), one might wonder if the anthropomorphic level, given that it includes utterances on wanting to do. being able to do, knowing how to do, hence 'the desire to realize' a program, can be defined without tasks, tests, and goals. Here again, the meanings proferred by the semantics of action precede the semiotic square even if that square, by its logical simplicity, precedes the complexity of the categories of the surface grammar.

2 / We can move on to the next point and inquire into the equivalence of the two metalanguages – that of the conceptual order and that of the anthropomorphic order. This equivalence, as we have seen above, has as guarantor the notion of syntactic doing, a doing which is homogeneous simultaneously to syntactic operations and to ordinary doing transcoded into message. I fear that, in this reasoning, we have a certain paralogism.[15] Syntactic doing can designate only the operations of conjunction and disjunction which give rise to affirmations and negations on the semiotic square. You cannot, without ambiguity, call ordinary doing transcoded into message a syntactic doing. The transcoding operation which transforms doing into an object message within a relation of communication does not prevent the descriptive utterance from precisely describing a doing which is not the equivalent of a syntactic operation, but is rather the formal term that is substituted for all terms of action. This is why the utterance of a doing cannot be equivalent to syntactic doing, which reformulates, in an anthropomorphic language, syntactic operations. On the contrary, it is because utterances of doing are specific that one is saying something new when one reformulates logical operations as a syntactic doing. Even in the expression 'syntactic doing,' the author is borrowing from the semantics of action.[16]

What can conceal the paralogism is the fact that doing, transcoded into message, develops its own syntax (a predicate with two arguments, specific grammar for the verbal tenses, open structure of the utterance, and so on). But the syntax of doing, which praxiology discusses, and that of wanting, of being able to, and of knowing how to do, which intensional logic studies, do not derive from syntactic doing in the strict sense defined above.

It is therefore very difficult to find an equivalence between the structures used by the semantics of action and the operations implied by the semiotic square. It is true that the simple narrative utterance is still an abstraction within the surface grammar, to the extent that the polemical relation between contradictory programs has not yet been introduced. Only this relation can give rise to series admitting of comparison with the syntactic series of operations following the taxonomic model. This is why we must postpone the complete discussion concerning the isotopy of the two metalanguages to the third stage in the construction of the complete model. However, to the extent that the author himself hints at this isotopy at the level of syntactic doing, we must oppose this hint, by making reference to the discontinuity, which is introduced by doing and its syntax, between the logical and the anthropomorphic levels.

3 / The preceding remark concerning the abstract character of the narrative utterance in relation to the unfolding narrative, of which more later, leads us to a third observation. This concerns the narrative qualifying of the descriptive utterance (X does A) and of the modal utterance (X wants to do A). If we examine doing, and even more, wanting to do and other modalities, this brings us, decisively, to the order of story. However, I will not call the utterances of these two types narrative. What they lack, in order to be narrative, is the fact of being articulated in a series of utterances of the same kind which together construct a plot, with a beginning, a middle, and an end. I will call such simple utterances action utterances rather than narrative utterances. This is based on Arthur Danto's definition of 'narrative phrases.'[17] Greimas would probably allow me this reservation, since from the outset he established, as the criteria for the autonomous level of narrative structures, the requirement that the latter contain units of meaning that are longer than a simple utterance.

Having reached the end of these two stages, we see the following results: 1 / we have set up two conditions for narrativity, but not narrativity itself; 2 / these two conditions are irreducible, one to the other: one is of a logical order, and the other of a praxic order; 3 / the praxic condition sets a semantics of action into play, and this latter sets up a syntax whose intelligibility is itself not unalloyed: phenomenological and linguistic.

III. From the Narrative Utterance to the Narrative Unit: 'Performance'

By introducing relations of confrontation and resistance, therefore by giving a polemical representation of the whole schema, we give to the relations of the semiotic square their truly anthropomorphic equivalent. But, more precisely – and this will have consequences for our discussion – it is of contradiction that a confrontation between a subject s_1 and an anti-subject s_2 gives an anthropomorphic representation *par excellence*. None the less, it is the succession of transformations of content, along the axes of contrariety and presupposition, which then gives rise to a chain of narrative utterances which, taken together, constitute the narrative units. According to this new reformulation, negation presents itself as *domination* and affirmation as *attribution* (attribution of a value-object according to whether the utterance is wanting to be or wanting to have).

We thus obtain a syntagmatic succession of the type: confrontation (NU_1), domination (NU_2), attribution (NU_3). This succession constitutes a unit of a syntactic nature which, it is decided, will be called *performance*. Since narrative utterances can be of two kinds, according to whether they involve doing or wanting to do (or the other modalities of doing), we will have performance not only of doing, but of wanting to do, knowing how to do (manifested as ruse and trickery), and of being able to do (manifested as real or magical power).

For the discussion of the equivalence between the two metalanguages, it is absolutely necessary to emphasize the complex and articulated character of the phenomenon which, in relation to the performance series (see below), appears as a 'narrative unit.' Again we emphasize that what is here called 'narrative unit' is not the same thing as the simple narrative utterance. It is, in fact, a syntactic unit in the sense that it is a unified syntagmatic succession. It is this unit which appropriately can be superimposed upon the interplay of taxonomic relations and upon the interplay of disjunction and conjunction operations.[18]

This is why it is from the complex makeup of performance, much more than from the simple narrative utterance, that we should be able to read an *equivalence* between deep and surface grammar. Greimas sees this equivalence at play between the orientation of the relations of the taxonomic schema and the relation of implication by which NU_3 (attribution) implies NU_2 (domination) which implies NU_1 (confrontation): 'with, nonetheless, this difference, if the orientation follows the order of the utterances $NU_1 \rightarrow NU_2 \rightarrow NU_3$, implication is oriented in the reverse direction' (p. 174). Thanks to the equivalence between orientation and implication, we can say that the final narrative utterance of a performance – attribution – is 'the equivalent, at the surface level, of the logical affirmation of the deep grammar' (p. 175).

Discussion

1 / This discussion will not dwell on the general relationship between the deep and the surface grammars: since performance derives from the narrative utterance, all of the semantics of action, whether at the level of doing or at the level of wanting to do, knowing how to do, and being able to do, is found here. None the less, a complementary argument appears with the *polemical* representation of logical relations. This representation brings with it several new characteristics which, before taking on a logical significance (which is, however, dubious, as we shall see) of the contradiction/contrariety type, possess an autonomous praxic significance. Confrontation and resistance are figures for the orientation of action towards others, that is, of a significant phenomenon which Max Weber places at the head of the constitutive categories of his comprehensive sociology.[19] Context or resistance (*Kampf*) is a specifying of the orientation towards others which comes into play later when the semantics of social action are constructed.[20]

To the extent that performance, for Greimas, complements the idea of program with that of polemic, we have to say that performance, in which the author sees 'the most characteristic unit of narrative syntax' (p. 173), is also the most characteristic unit of the mixed character – logical and praxic – of the whole of the narrative order. A more important problem is to evaluate the degree of equivalence that can subsist in this alloy of logic and praxis which we see between the two metalanguages, the logical and the anthropomorphic.[21]

2 / Let us consider the reasoning upon which Greimas bases this equivalence.

Three remarks: (a) We are surprised to read that confrontation is the anthropomorphic representation of contradiction (therefore at the level of each of the schemata s_1 versus non-s_1 and s_2 versus non-s_2) and also that two subjects, s_1 and s_2 (subject and anti-subject), correspond to two contradictory doings (p. 172). Has the author confused contrariety and contradiction? It is unlikely. Thus several hypotheses suggest themselves: for example, if confrontation does not correspond to contradiction, contrariety cannot have anthropomorphic representation. To fill this lack do we have to posit confrontation/contrariety alongside confrontation/contradiction? This seems to be the case, to the extent that it is the correlation between two schemata, therefore contrariety, which allows for completion of the trajectory through four poles, s_1, non-s_1, s_2, non-s_2, of the semiotic square. But this attenuating of the logical model allows only for establishing the equivalence of confrontation with both contrariety and contradiction. And, indeed, this still requires that very weak forms of contrariety be postulated which are far removed from the white/black type. Indeed this is so and we are given a 'limited inventory of semic categories' (p. 161). We can thus expect that the equivalence will be proportionately attenuated.

(b) This attenuation is particularly necessary when the author tries to establish a correspondence between the function of attribution (NU$_3$) and instances of affirmation. Let us come back to the semiotic square: the final affirmation is the one which posits s_2 through presupposition from non-s_1. But have we not already said that presupposition cannot take place unless the accompanying contrariety is a strong contrariety? And have we not just seen that contrariety here remained without a determinate polemic?

(c) What is even more serious is that the chain of the narrative utterances NU$_1$, NU$_2$, NU$_3$, which are constitutive of performance, does not constitute a chain of implication unless, as the author himself admits, you reverse the order of the utterances and thereby move from attribution to domination and confrontation. Now, orientation was necessary for the narrativization of the taxonomic model. Does this not amount to an admission that the correspondence between the relations that are internal to performance and those that are internal to the taxonomic model does not apply to the very condition for narrativity as engendered by the model? Here, the equivalence is no longer just weak. It is forced.

Indeed, the notion of polemic, so felicitously introduced by Greimas at the root of narrativity, brings into play a type of negativity which Kant was the first to show, in his *Versuch, den Begriff der Negativen Grössen in die Weltweisheit einzuführen*, to be irreducible to contradiction. Opposing a subject to an anti-subject does not set up an opposition between two contradictory doings. It is legitimate to fear that it is not at all like contrariety either.

If I now bring together the last series of remarks concerning 1 / the mixed logical and praxic model and 2 / the weakness of the equivalence between the two metalanguages, we can expect two kinds of results from the correspondence between the logical properties of the semiotic square and the praxic categories which are the most determined by the polemical nature of action. To the extent that the logical model, even when weakened, retains a certain priority in the reading of a narrative text, the semiotic square exercises a heuristic function which I happily admit. However, to the extent that the praxic relations of a strictly polemical nature escape logical contradiction representation – even logical contrariety representation – the semiotic square runs the risk of being reduced to a presentational artifice by which the semiotician conforms his readings, after the fact, to his models.

3 / As to the strictly narrative tenor of the syntagmatic succession which articulates performance, I would say that it is superior to that of the simple narrative utterance, by virtue of the introduction of the polemic factor. However, performance still does not go beyond the stage of the conditions for narrativity. The author admits this: it is only with the performance series, which we will speak of shortly, that he is able to constitute the complete set of conditions for story.

This is why he, quite properly, designates performance by the term *narrative unit.* Will we nevertheless say that the syntagmatic succession of confrontation, domination, attribution constitutes of itself a microstory? We can without doubt say so, but only if we emphasize that this oriented succession presents relations which are inverse to the relation of implication which alone can legitimize the statement that NU_3 'is the equivalent, at the surface level, of logical affirmation at the deep-grammar level' (p. 175). Now it is precisely in this inverse relation of implication that *something new* happens, of which a story can be born.

IV. The Last Stage: The Performance Series

Greimas's final stroke of inspiration is to complete the constitution of his narrative model by adding the polemical category, the anthropomorphic doublet of the relation of contradiction, the category of *transfer* borrowed from the communication schema or more generally from the structure of *exchange.* Here is how this new structure is applied to the previous system. We pointed out that the last of the three narrative utterances which constituted performance could be expressed as an attributive utterance, according to which a subject acquires an object or a value. To reformulate attribution in terms of exchange, one could say that a subject acquires what another subject is deprived of. Attribution can thus be broken down into two operations: deprivation, which is equivalent to disjunction, and an attribution proper, which is equivalent to a conjunction.

This reformulation – the last one proposed by the author – leads to the notion of the performance series, an abbreviated form for the 'syntagmatic series of performances.' Such a series can be seen as the formal framework of every narrative. It is only at this stage that the narrative grammar is complete (or, as we shall see, almost complete).

The general advantage of this reformulation is that it permits one to represent all the previous operations as changes of 'place' – the initial and final places of transfers. In other words, it corresponds to a topological syntax of translative utterances. In turn, the richness of this topological syntax can be observed as the topological analysis is carried out at the two levels of doing and wanting to do.

If one first of all considers only value-objects, acquired or transferred by doing, then the topological syntax enables us to represent the ordered series of operations on the semiotic square along the lines of contradiction, contrariety, and presupposition as a *circular transmission of values*. One can say without hesitation that this topological syntax of transfers is the true motivation of narration as the creative process of values (p. 178).

If one now considers no longer only the *operations*, but the *operators*.[22] that is to say, in the exchange schema, the senders/receivers of the transfer, then the topological syntax regulates the transfer of the capacity to do, and therefore operates the transfers of the values considered above. In other words, it regulates the *institution* proper of the syntactic operators by creating subjects endowed with the virtuality of doing.

Separating the topological syntax therefore corresponds to separating doing and wanting (being able to do, knowing to do) – corresponds, that is, to dividing narrative utterances into descriptive and modal utterances, or dividing them into two series of performances: acquisition then corresponds to transfer, bearing either on object-values or on modal values (acquiring the being able, the knowing, the wanting to do).

The second series of performances is the most important one from the point of view of the activation of the syntactic trajectory. The operators must be instituted as being able, knowing, and wanting, in order in turn for transfers of value-objects to take place. If one wishes to know where the first actant comes from, it is necessary to evoke the contract which institutes the subject of desire by attributing to him the modality of wanting. The specific narrative unity in which the wanting of the 'knowing' or 'able' subject is posited constitutes the first performance of the narrative.

The 'completed narrative' (p. 180) combines the series of transfers of value-objects with the series of transfers instituting the 'knowing' or 'able' subject.

Discussion

1 / The last stage of the completed constituent model enables us to raise for the last time the general question of the mixed nature – logical and praxic – of this model. The new addition to be considered is the transfer by which a subject is deprived of what is attributed to another. Now anyone can see that to deprive and to give signify more than to disjoin and to conjoin. Lack and deprivation are categories the anthropomorphic nature of which becomes manifest only if one considers, as was so well shown by Claude Bremond in *Logique du récit*, the relationship between *being subjected to* and *acting*: 'We define as playing the role of patient every person which the narrative presents as being affected in one way or another by the course of the events narrated.'[23] The notion of a patient affected by a certain state logically precedes that of any modification (or conservation) of state. The deprivation of a value-object, suffered by a subject, and the attribution of this same object to another subject are modifications affecting a patient. What the last stage of the constitution of the model therefore adds is a phenomenology of suffering-acting, in which notions such as deprivation and donation take on meaning. As far as I am concerned, it is this implicit phenomenology which permits Greimas to write: 'actants are conceived no longer as operators, but as places where value-objects can be situated, places where they can be brought or from where they can be taken' (p. 176). The topological language of this last phase is thus a mixture of logical conjunction/disjunction and modifications which happen not only in the practical field, but also in the *pathetic* one. The operative value cannot therefore come exclusively from the logical aspects of attribution, but also, in turn, from the topological syntax and the seman-

tics of acting and suffering according to whether the topological syntax plays an effectively heuristic role in the reading of the text, or whether it is an artifice of exposition in relationship to interplay of the pathico-praxic categories.[24]

2 / This composite nature of the topological syntax results in a new weakening of the equivalence between logical metalanguage and anthropomorphic metalanguage. In fact, just as the author attempted to link the polemical values of narrativity solely to the relation of contradiction of the taxonomic model, now the circular transmission of values, in the topological syntax of the transfers, rests on the correlation[25] between the two schemata (d_1 versus non-d_1, d_2 versus non-d_2):

This opposition is what creates spatial heterotopy. Consequently, it is the relation of presupposition (non-$d_2 \rightarrow d_1$ and non-$d_1 \rightarrow d_2$) which bears the entire logical weight of the topological apparatus. Two schemata, two programs, can in fact be *correlated* in various ways. The logical projection of this correlation can be called contrariety only if the terms are in the same relation as black and white, which is rarely borne out in the praxic and pathetic order. All sorts of modifications can affect a state, without the correlation of roles being reduced to their contrariety. Now if the correlation is reduced to a weak contrariety, indeed analogical, then presupposition in turn loses its characteristic of logical constraint. That is not to say that correlation and presupposition become relations empty of all meaning. Greimas characterizes, and justly so, the places occupied or attained by the correlated programs as '*heterotopic spaces* whose deixes are *disjoined*, because they do not belong to the same schemata, but *conformed*, since they are linked by the relation of presupposition' (p. 177). When correlation moves away from strong contrariety, conformity moves away from strong presupposition (or implication). Must one not now say that the hypotactic axes (non-$d_2 \rightarrow d_1$ and non-$d_1 \rightarrow d_2$), the functioning of which from the beginning seems to have constituted the critical point of this entire logical system, have only a narrative content, insofar as, lacking categorical unity (as in the case of the polar terms black/white), it is the unity of plot which ensures the 'conformity of the heterotopic spaces'? To what do they conform? They conform to what Aristotle calls the *dianoia*, correlative to the *mythos* of narrative. In this vein, Northrop Frye remarks that the typology of *mythos* is systematically coupled with a typology of *dianoia*. It is the history of culture which engenders the schematization of this *dianoia* and these *mythoi*, which are the matrix of the weak logical operations and relations.

This conclusion should not be surprising if it is true that the topological syntax of the transfers, which functions in conjunction with the trajectory of the logical operations of the semiotic square, 'organizes narration as a process creating values' (p. 178). How can this reduplication account for the passage from the syntactic operations, which in the taxonomic framework were 'predictable and calculable' (p. 166), to 'process creating values'? Of necessity, logicity must somehow be inadequate in relationship to creativity, which characterizes narrative. This gap becomes obvious at the level of transfer, in so far as correlation and presupposition move away from the strong logical model and express the dissymmetry of deprivation and attribution and the *newness* proper to attribution. The nature of newness linked to attribution is more evident when being able to, knowing how to, and wanting to do – that is to say, the actual virtuality of the doing – is granted the subject. The word 'institution' – in the expression 'institution of the syntactic operators' – is not too strong to express the newness in 'the contract instituting the subject of desire through the attribution of the modality of wanting' (p. 179).

This gap between the initial schema, where all the relations compensate for one another, and the final schema, where new values are produced, is masked by the particular case of Propp's Russian folktales, where the circulation of values ends up restoring the initial state. The king's daughter, carried off by the villain who transfers her elsewhere to hide her, is found by the hero and brought back to her parents! In *Structural Semantics*, Greimas himself admits that the most general function of narrative is to re-establish an order of threatened values. Now we know, thanks to the schematization of plots produced by the cultures we have inherited, that this restoration characterizes only one category of narratives, and even probably of folk-tales. Diverse are the ways in which plot articulates 'crises' and 'conclusion'! And diverse are the ways in which the hero (or anti-hero) is modified in the course of the intrigue! Is it even certain that every narrative can be projected onto this teleological matrix, having two programs, a polemical relation and a transfer of values? Although this methodological *a priori* can help the reader respect the text and discover its hidden articulations, it also risks becoming the Procrustean bed on which the text is racked.

3 / There remains the question of confidence: are the conditions of narrativity *complete*, once the syntactic operators are instituted and the topological syntax of the modal values added to those of the objective values? That the terminal model constitutes the most rigoros approximation of the narrative structure permitted by the method is undeniable. But how far is this approximation from what constitutes narrative proper, that is to say, from plot?

With exemplary lucidity, the author himself suggests at the end of his essay that he has sketched out the main point of 'only part' of the superficial narrative syntax, that is to say, the part 'dealing with the body proper of narrative.' 'What is missing in this sketch,' he says, 'is the examination and the establishment of the syntactic units which frame narrative, and which correspond to the initial and final sequences of the manifest narrative' (p. 181). Now, are these sequences not as essential to plot as opening and closing? It is true that the superficial grammar has the potential to describe its own inadequacies. We already alluded to the contract by which the first actant is instituted into a subject of desire. We can add that 'the opening of narrative would be represented as the establishment of a *conjunctive* contractual relation between a sender and a receiver subject, followed by a spatial *disjunction* between the two actants. The closing of narrative would be marked, on the contrary, by a spatial conjunction and a last transfer of values, instituting a new contract by means of a new distribution of values, which can be either objective or modal' (pp. 181–2). Why then have these characteristics not been incorporated into the surface grammar and why are they attributed to a lack in the sketch? The author circumscribes the difficulty when he observes that these framing sequences correspond to 'what are, at the level of the deep grammar, the hypotactic relations of the taxonomic model, that is to say, to the relations which can be established in the model between the terms s_1 and non-s_2, on the one hand, and between the terms s_2 and non-s_1 on the other' (p. 181). Now, what are these hypotactic relations, if not relations of presupposition whose weak logicality was demonstrated every time the relation of contrariety completing the relation of contradiction in the semiotic square was weakened? Does the critical point revealed by the incompleteness of the sketch not correspond to the critical point in the logical structure of the sketch itself?

This technical discussion shows how difficult it is, on the basis of the 'predictable and calculable' (p. 166) syntactic operations, to derive the topological operations of transfer which 'organize narration as a process creating values' (p. 178). The fundamental question raised by Greimas's attempt is related to the nature of the generation, from one deep level of the semiotic model to another. Does the stratification into levels of depth function as the extension into each new stage of the initial virtues of the taxonomic model? Or, on the contrary, does the introduction, at each level, of new semantico-syntactic components (anthropomorphic representation, addition of figurativity) confer richness on the apparatus? In an 'Interview' published by Frédéric Nef, Greimas admits that 'a theoretical apparatus, no matter how satisfactory it seems at first, could easily remain hypothetical as long as the problem of *equivalences* between various levels of depth has not been clearly posited, as long as the procedures of *conversion* from one level to another have not been elaborated' (p. 24). To raise the question in somewhat different terms, one must ask how the paradigmatic and the syntagmatic are equated in Greimas's model. The author's intention is never in doubt: to find for each new syntagmatic addition a paradigmatic equivalent, that is to say, to extend the 'squaring' of every process. In this same interview Greimas declares: 'If one now considers narrative from its syntagmatic perspective where each narrative program appears as a process made up of the acquisition and loss of values, of the enrichment and the impoverishment of subjects, then one notices that each step forward on the syntagmatic axis corresponds to (and is defined by) a topological displacement on the paradigmatic axis' (p. 25). But if, as we attempted to demonstrate, it is true that a syntagmatic newness appeared at each level, under the pressure first of all of a semantics of action, then of praxico-pathetic categories of polemics and exchange, then the innovative power is situated in these praxico-pathetic investments and not in the initial taxonomic model. The author almost admits as much in the very same interview. 'However it is only a question there of a manipulatory syntax, through use of disjunctions and conjunctions, of utterances of *state* which only give a static representation of a series of narrative states of the narrative. Just as the taxonomic square must not be considered simply as a place where logical operations happen, the series of utterances of state are organized and manipulated by utterances of doing and by the transforming subjects which are inscribed there' (p. 26).

Greimas's topological preoccupations can be seen as an ultimate attempt to extend the paradigmatic as far as possible into the heart of the syntagmatic. Nowhere else does the author feel that he is closer to realizing the dream of making linguistics an algebra of language: 'The figurative circulation can thus be considered as the result of the conversion of communications, taking place according to a predictable order, value objects passing from one subject to another, communications that can be represented as disjunctions and conjunctions' (p. 25). Thus the topological trajectory simply explicates the principle of the polemical structure of narrative discourse. Greimas can then declare that 'each step forward on the syntagmatic axis corresponds to (and is defined by) a displacement on the paradigmatic axis' (p. 25). But, once again, should the priorities not be switched about? In the same way that the syntactic transformations are linked to the morphological relations and the polemical structures are linked to the syntactic transformations, should it not be admitted that the topological displacements in turn are linked to the simple representation of the states at the extremities of the paradigmatic axes?

In conclusion, Greimas's model seems to be bound by a dual constraint, on the one hand logical, and on the other praxico-pathetic. But it can satisfy the former, that of the inscription of the components of narrativity introduced at each new level and pushed on to the following one, only if together the understanding we have of the narrative and of the plot establishes the necessary additions of a decidedly syntagmatic order without which the taxonomic model would remain inert and sterile.

To recognize the mixed nature of Greimas's model is not at all to refute it: on the contrary, it is to clarify the conditions of its application and to explain to readers of works stemming from this school why the semiotic square sometimes seems to have a true heuristic value, and sometimes to be simple transcription, which can be more or less elucidating but sometimes corresponds to a more or less forced understanding of narrative which proceeds not according to the logical component, but according to the praxico-pathetic component of the mixed model.

Notes

1 Algirdas Julien Greimas, 'Eléments d'une grammaire narrative,' in *Du sens: Essais sémiotiques* (Paris, 1970), p. 164; hereafter cited in text. Here and elsewhere, unless otherwise noted, translations are by Frank Collins and Paul Perron.

2 'To do this, one must think of semiotic theory in such a way that between the fundamental instances *ab quo*, where semantic substance takes on its first articulations and constitutes its signifying form, and the last instances *ad quem*, where signification is manifested through its multiple languages, a vast area must be set up in which a *mediating instance* is established where semiotic structures having an autonomous status would be situated – the narrative structure would be part of these – a place where the complementary articulations of content and a sort of grammar, at the same time general and fundamental, commanding the institution of articulated discourses would be worked out' (pp. 159–60). A year earlier, Greimas wrote: 'Perhaps out of a desire for intelligibility, we can imagine that the human mind, in order to achieve the construction of cultural objects (literary, mythical, pictorial, etc.) starts with simple elements and follows a complex course, encountering on its way constraints to which it must submit, as well as choices which it can make.' See Algirdas Julien Greimas, 'Les Jeux des contraintes sémiotiques,' in *Du sens*, p. 135.

3 'In other words: the generation of signification does not pass through, first of all, the production of utterances and their combination into discourse; it is relayed, in its trajectory, by the narrative structures and it is these that produce meaningful discourse articulated by means of utterances' (p. 161).

4 'The constitutive model is, henceforth, only the elementary structure of signification utilized, as form, to articulate the semantic substance of a micro-universe' (p. 161).

5 For the reader of the 'Eléments d'une grammaire narrative,' the representation of the semiotic square in its purely morphological form, thus independent of the operations which introduce the first concept of narrativization, seems transparent. This is not the case when one attempts to reconstitute the stages of the constitution of the model by Greimas since *Structural Semantics* (1966), by taking into account 'Les Jeux des contraintes sémiotiques' (1968). The difficulties overcome, the traces of which are more or less erased in the axiomatic presentations of 1968 and 1969, can only be reconstructed if one compares the Greimassian square with its logical and linguistic ancestors and if one measures the distance separating it from its antecedents. It is, first of all, clear that the semiotic square has nothing in common with Aristotle's, or rather Apuleus's, square: first, the latter is concerned with propositions (labelled A, E, I, O), whereas the level at which Greimas operates is that of the

analysis of signification into semes – that is to say, into units which are to lexemes what distinctive features are to phonemes (this is the main feature linking 'Les Jeux des contraintes sémiotiques' and 'Eléments d'une grammaire narrative' with *Structural Semantics*). Next, the oppositions in Apuleus's square rest on the choice of two pertinent features of the propositions: the quality (affirmation–negation), and the quantity (universal–particular). Hence the meaning given to contradiction as the complete opposition between the universal affirmative (I) and the universal negative (E), and to contrariety as the partial opposition between the universal affirmative (1) and the particular negative (0). For Greimas, contradiction and contrariety are not distinguished on this basis, since s_1, non-s_1, s_2, non-s_2 as semes are *simple* terms. For the same reasons, the semiotic square is not derived from Blanché's hexagon. Of course, the latter is concerned not with propositions, but with predicates belonging to the same category of thought; but these predicates are lexicalized terms, whereas for Greimas the basis of the construction is the semantic axis linking the semes. As for the Piaget group, the psychological application of Klein's group, the distinction between contradiction and contrariety, as in Apuleus's square, is founded on the dual nature of the opposed terms (black square, white square, black circle, white circle). Contradiction is therefore a total inversion (black square vs. white circle, black circle vs. white square) and inversion (black square vs. white circle, black circle vs. white square) and contrariety is a partial opposition (black square vs. white square, etc.). From two things one can thus derive the relation: AB, $\bar{A}B$, $A\bar{B}$, $\bar{A}\bar{B}$. In spite of the fact that Piaget's group operates with lexically perceived objects, its double terms do correspond to Greimas's semic opposition. (For a further development of this, see *Structures élémentaires de la signification*, ed. by Frédéric Nef et al. [Brussels, 1976], esp. pp. 9–17, 20–1, 28–33, 49–55). The true filiation of the semiotic square must be sought elsewhere. One must begin with de Saussure's thesis that a sign is defined by its difference with other signs in the same system; but one must abandon the Saussurean level of sign for that of seme. Here one encounters the linguist Brøndal's epistemology, the role of opposition in Lévi-Strauss's theory of myth, and especially – this is the decisive stage – binary oppositions applied on the phonological level by Jakobson to distinctive features, thus to units of the subphonematic level. But it is also in restoring this filiation that the difficulties adumbrated by Greimas's didactic expositions appear. In particular, it is very difficult to make contrariety and contradiction according to Greimas correspond to one or other of Jakobson's binary oppositions, in particular those referred to by Greimas in 'La Mythologie comparée,' in *Du sens*, p. 129: that is to say, a vs. non-a (marked vs. nonmarked), and a vs. –a, where –a is the negation of a. The equivalences, or rather the comparisons, proposed by Nef between Greimas and Jakobson are, in turn, far from convincing; see Frédéric Nef, 'Preésentation,' in *Structures élémentaires*, p. 15. On this point the interview with Greimas throws no new light; see Frédéric Nef, 'Entretien avec A.J. Greimas,' in *Structures élémentaires*, p. 21, hereafter cited in text. In fact what does contrariety between s_1 and s_2 mean? It opposes two equally positive semes, in which one is the contrary of the other only if one can oppose them as poles, as the extremes of a graded series, consequently as polar qualities of the same category (of the type high vs. low, white vs. black). Will the rigorous conditions of this polar opposition between semes always be respected in the course of the successive investments of the constitutive model?

6 In 'Les Jeux des contraintes sémiotiques,' the distinction between relations and operations, thus between morphology and syntax, is not worked out: thus the name of operations is often given to relations, and the relations of contrariety and contradiction are immediately labelled disjunction and conjunction (p. 137). This is no longer the case in 'Eléments d'une grammaire narrative.' Rigour now demands that morphology be the domain of *relations* of contrariety, contradiction, and homology, as well as the notion of contrary, contradictory, and homologous *terms*. It is only on the syntactical level that one can speak about the *operations* of negation/ assertion (manifesting the contrary terms of the axis), of negation/assertion (manifesting the contradictory terms of the *schemata*), of implication/presupposition (manifesting the homologous terms on the *deixis*). For further discussion see Georges Combet, 'Complexification et carré performatoire,' in *Structures élémentaires*, pp. 68–9.

7 I will not raise again the issue that semiotics and linguistics are in a relationship of reciprocity. Greimas is correct to say that his semiotics is based on a 'fundamental semantics which is different from the semantics of manifestation in linguistics' (p. 160). It none the less remains true that it is within the latter that it is effectively constructed. And Greimas characterizes as 'universals of language' (p. 162) the categories necessary to formalize the elementary structure of signification. Here linguistics is the paradigm of semiotics.

8 The postulation of this homology is characteristic of structuralism, as Roland Barthes clearly says in his 'Introduction à l'analyse structurale des récits,' *Communications*, 8 (1966), 3–4, reproduced in Roland Barthes et al., *Poétique du récit* (Paris, 1977), pp. 10–13.

9 One should remark Greimas's hesitation concerning the relation of implication: 'If the existence of this type of relation seems undeniable, the problem of its orientation ($s_1 \rightarrow$non-s_2 or non-$s_2 \rightarrow s_1$) is not yet settled. We will not raise the issue here since its solution is not necessary for the rest of the demonstration'; see 'Les Jeux des contraintes,' p. 37, n. 1. Cf. on this point 'Présentation,' in Nef, p. 15; and Combet, 'Complexification,' pp. 68–9.

10 In the 'Entretien avec A.J. Greimas,' it seems that in the eyes of the author himself the operations must be stressed rather than the relations, or the relations in terms of the operations: 'In relationship to "Contraintes," which only raises the problem of the narrative states, "Eléments" attempts to make explicit the *operations* giving rise to narrativizations' (p. 22). Consequently, in the syntactic interpretation the dominant question remains that of 'representing how signification is *produced* by a series of operations creating differentiated positions' (p. 22). Hence the phenomenon of narrativization can be conceived as 'a series of logically oriented operations taking place within the framework anticipated by the semiotic square' (p. 22).

11 Again, the critical point remains (cf. above, n. 9) that of the relation of

presupposition: 'the operation of contradiction which, in negating, for example, the term s_1, posits at the same time the term non-s_1, must be followed by a new operation of presupposition giving rise and conjoining to the term non-s_1 the new term s_2' (p. 165). Can the operation be at the same time 'predictable,' thus 'calculable,' (p. 166) and 'new'?

12 The commentators in Frédéric Nef's work suggest that by thus putting the main accent on the operations of transformation, Greimas in a way increases the initial gap between logical opposition and semiotic square. Thus, Alain de Libéra, 'La Sémiotique d'Aristote,' in *Structures élémentaires*, p. 41, begins by stating that Apuleus's square was already more than a simple pedagogical device in so far as it engendered a series of permitted operations (concerning the contradiction couples: who refutes E proves I, etc.; the contraries: who proves A, destroys E, but who destroys A does not prove E, etc.); but he does so only in order to deny that the Apulean square is in any way productive (p. 41). Going further, the commentator denies that thought founded on disjunction can have the virtue of a founding *a priori*: 'Disjunction,' he says, 'is the stabilizing operator of forms necessary for any ontology and for any idealist thought' (p. 47); 'logical disjunction borne by the verb to be is the inaugural exterior which represses all dialectic' (p. 48). Turning one's back on Aristotle must one now turn to Hegel to give meaning to a productive opposition? This is suggested by de Libéra when he compares Jakobson and Greimas. It is said that one must radically distinguish the logical square from the semiotic square: 'There is not (in fact) contradiction in inscribing at the same time s_1 and $-s_1$. They are not on the same level. S_1 is a term (seme), $-s_1$ is an operation on the term (s_1), or again: the illocutionary negation of this term' (p. 53). A little farther on: 'In fact with Greimas (as with Lévi-Strauss) contradiction must be understood in the *Hegelian* sense' (p. 53). Following Utaker, Alain de Libéra, in 'Note sur "On binary opposition" de Arild Utaker,' in *Structures élémentaires*, p. 55, interprets the semiotic square as the dual interaction of the qualitative opposition and the privative opposition: 'One can thus consider the logical square as a logical apparatus which produces privative oppositions starting with qualitative oppositions. The productivity of the square makes it an open model, a generative structure: all complex or neutral terms of any square can be taken at another level as the simple term generating a new semiotic square. Here is where its applicability resides: myths, tales, etc., and in a general way, every domain where an opposition is "negated" by the production of a new opposition which at the same time seems to reproduce and not to reproduce the original' (p. 55). In the same vein, Nef's work contains various attempts to engender one semiotic square from another one and thus to complexify the model by a chain of 'squarifications' (see Combet, in Nef, pp. 67–72). In the 'Entretien,' Greimas shows interest in this attempt which accentuates the logical and deductive aspects of semiology; see Nef, · 'Entretien,' pp. 22–4. But is this logic Aristotelian, Hegelian, or ... other?

13 Anthony Kenny, *Action, Emotion and Will* (London, 1963). On the analytical philosophy of action, see Paul Ricoeur, *Sémantique de l'action* (Paris, 1977), pp. 3–137.

14 Greimas proposes the following example of a wanting which would be anthropomorphic without being figurative: 'this rule requires that ...' (p. 168). The example, it seems to me, is not valid, since the rule cannot precisely function as the virtual subject of a possible action. The obligation by the rule is of another status than wanting is.

15 The paralogism is the following: 'narrative utterances are syntactic utterances, that is to say independent of content which can be invested by such-and-such a doing' (p. 168). To substitute doing for all action verbs is not to transform them into a syntactic doing.

16 This could have been foreseen: already at the deep level, virtual narrativization consisted in the fact that the dynamic representation of the semiotic square was considered as 'a bringing together or as the production of meaning by the subject' (p. 164).

17 See Arthur Danto, *Analytical Philosophy of Action* (Cambridge, 1973).

18 The result is 'the construction of a particular narrative unit, performance: due to the fact that it constitutes the operative schema of the transformation of contents, it is probably the most characteristic unit of narrative syntax' (p. 173).

19 See Max Weber, *Wirtschaft und Gesellschaft*, 5th ed. (Tübingen, 1972).

20 See Weber, 'Begriff des Kampfes,' in *Wirtschaft und Gesellschaft*, pp. 20–1.

21 In the 'Entretien,' Greimas insists that the polemic structure of narrative is what permits the unravelling of the initial *paradigmatic* articulation of the taxonomic model into the entire *syntagmatic* unfolding of the narrative (p. 25). By opposing an anti-subject to a subject, an anti-program to a program, by even multiplying actantial squares by dividing every actant into actant, negactant, anatactant, negantactant. The polemic structure ensures the infiltration of the paradigmatic order into all syntagmatic order: 'It is not surprising then that the analysis of even slightly complex texts necessitates the multiplication of the actantial positions and so reveals, besides its syntagmatic unravelling, the paradigmatic articulation of narrativity' (p. 24). But one can also say the inverse: It is because something happens of a conflictual nature between two subjects that one can project it onto the square. And this projection is in turn possible because the square itself has been treated 'as the place where the logical operations are carried out' (p. 26), in short it has been narrativized beforehand. The entire progress of 'squarification' from level to level can appear in turn as the progression of the paradigm to the heart of the syntagmatic, or as the addition of new syntagmatic dimensions (quest, struggle, etc.) secretly finalized by the dual paradigmatic and syntagmatic structure of the finished narrative.

22 'That is, a *syntax of operators* must be constructed independently from a *syntax of operations*: a metasemiotic level must be worked out in order to justify the transfer of values' (p. 78).

23 Claude Brémond, *Logique du récit* (Paris, 1973).

24 Is it for this reason that the author writes that 'a metasemiotic level must be worked out in order to justify the transfer of values'? (see n. 23 above).

25 The reader can here formulate a doubt which is the opposite of the one raised by the interpretation of the polemic category. The latter was explicitly superimposed on the relation of contradiction, but also seemed to permit an anthropomorphic interpretation of contrariety. On the other hand, topological syntax, after having been explicitly related to the correlation between schemata, and thus to contrariety (p. 176), is then superimposed onto contradiction, which opposes the two subjects s_1 and s_2 foreseen by the construction of the performance: 'Consequently, it is the axis of exchange between these two subjects which constitutes the place of transfer of the modal values; the attribution of any modal value to s_1 presupposes that s_2 is at the same time deprived of that value' (p. 180).

On Narrativity:
Debate with A.J. Greimas

Ricoeur: It is a pleasure to share once again a discussion session with Professor Greimas. Our paths have often crossed over the years and our friendship has increased along with these exchanges. Let me first say how my own agenda not only led me to cross Greimas's path but also led me along the same road with him. Coming from the disciplines of phenomenology and hermeneutics, I was first interested in the way semiotics responds to the aporias of hermeneutics, which is fundamentally based on the notion of pre-understanding that is necessary before scientific discourse on literature, and more specifically on narrative, can be elaborated.

My initial conviction was, and to a large extent still is, that we have a first mode of understanding narrative configuration before having the slightest notion about semiotics. When linguists speak of phonemes, they are dealing with objects that have no social or institutional existence. Narratives, by contrast, already have their social functions, and they are understood in a certain way in social intercourse among writers, narrators, readers, and speakers, for example. Therefore, this first-order intelligibility, if I may so call it, has in a sense its own rules, which are, if not thought out, at least understood. The best document concerning this type of understanding prior to any semiotics is provided by Aristotle's *Poetics*, which has a very articulate system of categories that ignores the difference between deep structures and surface structures. Aristotle speaks of the 'mythos' as the configuration of incidence in the story and uses the term 'sustasis' to refer to a sort of system of events. But the kind of intelligibility linked to our acquaintance with the way stories are plotted is closer to what Aristotle in the rest of his work called 'forensis,' that is to say, practical intelligence, which is closer to the way we use our intelligence in ethical and political matters than it is to the kind of episteme that functions in physical and social sciences at their systematic level.

My first approach to semiotics was therefore to consider the kind of rationality it introduced in this field as being a second-order rationality that has as its object not narratives themselves but the pre-understanding we have of them. Hence, I would say that the rationality at work in semiotics derives from this first-order intelligibility, without being subordinated to it, for it has its own function precisely because it introduces a new kind of rationality into this first-order intelligence and understanding. This can be compared to what happens in the field of history, where there is a sense of belonging, a tradition of having expectations of the future. Thus, there is a kind of inner intelligence, an intelligibility of the historicality that characterizes us. But when historians bring their rules of explanation to bear on a topic, an inquiry and a dialectic is introduced between first-order intelligibilty, the intelligibility of being historical, and historiography, the writing of history.

My main theme would therefore be that to explain more is to understand better, and it is in the exchange between understanding better and explaining more that semiotics makes sense for me. It increases the readability of texts which we have already understood to a certain extent without the help of semiotics. Hence the following three problems that we shall discuss since Professor Greimas kindly accepted the format of my own questions, for which I am most grateful.

The first problem I would like to raise is the relationship in Greimas's semiotic system between deep structures, with their paradigmatic principles, and superficial or surface structures.[1] I would like to go even farther and raise the problem of the relationship between these deeper structures and the text understood at the locus of figuration, the figurative level of the story. My hunch here would be that if the rules of transformation that belong to a logic of narrative have a narrative character, it is to the extent that they go from the peripeteia of the surface to the dynamics, without which the system would not exist. My claim here is that surface is more than a kind of reflection of deep structure, it is more than the instantiation of narrative rules that can be construed at the deeper level. Something happens at the level of figuration that makes the dynamism of the processes described possible. In other words, to use vocabulary familiar to semioticians, in the shift from paradigmatic structures to their syntagmatization, the historicization of the story occurs at the surface and then it is by reflection of the surface at the deep level that the deep level itself may be said to transform, to provide transformations from a first state of effect to a last state of effect.

To illustrate this point I will take two examples, the second from Greimas's work itself. The first example is the study by one of Greimas's former students, Louis Marin, on narrative in the Gospels, in which he examined the role of the traitor who may be defined as an opponent.[2] In the actantial system it is easy to recognize the place of the traitor in the system, but the fact that this traitor is Judas, and that he has individual characteristics, is not secondary. For we can see that, in the development of the character, say, from Mark to John, there is an increasing enrichment that at the same time enriches the story itself, the plot itself. In Mark, Judas is simply one of the twelve apostles who shares the same meal with Jesus. He fulfils the prophecy that the Son of Man will be delivered to His enemies, but there is something contingent at every moment, since 'Judas' is a proper name that connects the function of delivering the Son of Man to the traitor who makes treason happen. Making something happen therefore seems to introduce a contingency, the equivalent of what Aristotle called the peripeteia, which belongs, I think, to the surface of the text. It would therefore seem to me that we cannot apply to the relation between deep structures and surface structures something which would be too close, for example, to the unfortunate distinction between infrastructure and superstructure in Marx, where the superstructure would be a mere reflection of the infrastructure. We have here instead a dialectic of a kind that needs to be recognized.

I will take my second example from Greimas's wonderful book, *Maupassant: The Semiotics of Text: Practical Exercises*, a 250-page analysis of a 6-page short story, 'Two Friends.'[3] The surface of the text narrates the story of a failed fishing expedition that will end with a reversal of roles because the enemy who has captured the unfortunate fishermen does not succeed in making them confess they are spies and that the fishing expedition is a cover story. The two friends refuse to accept the role of spies, and they are executed by a firing squad. The important event is that they are cast into the water and given back to the fish. At the end of the tale the Prussian officer catches the fish and has them fried up for himself. According to Greimas's analyses, in fact, it is the unfortunate fishermen who offer the fish to the officer. Greimas comes to this conclusion by constructing all the proper semiotic squares. He sets in the right place the oppositions between life and non-life, death and non-death and therefore all the exchanges among the four poles of the square. But it seems to me there is something decisive that does not belong to the model as a logical model, namely, the way in which the homologation of the individual characters is made in relation to the roles. This homologation of the sun with cold life, the empty sky with cold non-life, Mount Valerian with cold death, and the water with cold non-death is brought about through the initiative of the enunciator. It is very important for this homologation to be decisive since it gives the clue to the whole story and makes the immersion of the unfortunate fishermen into a quasi resurrection. The enunciator's initiation of this very homologation makes the story unique. This is the story in which the miraculous fishing expedition in the end becomes the loser's victory. Therefore one could ask if it is not the surface of the text that provides the element of contingency and the series of unpredictable decisions which keep the story moving. Pushing this to the limit, I would say finally that the deep structure reflects the surface and not the contrary.

Greimas: In order to understand the questions raised by Professor Ricoeur and the objections that could be made to semiotic theory, it is necessary for me to make the following general points. I feel that not only in semiotics but also in linguistics more generally, and, again, in the whole of the social sciences, the first major methodological step necessary is the identification of pertinent levels. It is only when a scientific project posits the objects it wishes to describe or construct at a specific level, and not at ten different levels, that it can hold a coherent discourse on these objects. This constitutes, I believe, the superiority of linguistics over the other human sciences. Yet, this is also the general rule to be followed if one wishes to carry out rigorous semiotic practice. Thus, the distinction between the deep and surface levels is an important methodological choice. When developing models of description of narrative structures, it is necessary once again to identify two levels: an abstract deep level and a more concrete surface level. The difference between the two is that the surface level is an anthropomorphic level, because all syntax of natural languages is anthropomorphic. There exist subjects, objects, beneficiaries; qualifications are attributed to subjects, for example. Linguists generally try to hide this fact, but it cannot be hidden when one investigates discourse from a semantic perspective. This narrative level of an anthropomorphic nature posits relations between subject and object, the sender and receiver, which are fundamental. The deeper level we try to establish is the level of abstract operations, that is to say, operations in which the operating subject is no longer a human subject but, just as science demands, a substitutable subject. This is what guarantees the transmissibility of scientific knowledge. Often people do not understand the necessity I felt to posit the existence of this deep abstract level.

As to the semiotic square, it could be a square or a cube or a circle. The shape is of no importance whatsoever. It was necessary to formulate a minimum number of relational tools, and in this case, a fundamental structure of discourse that was as simple as possible. The other problem raised is related to the passage from one level to another. When passing from the surface level, what always raised problems for Chomsky's generative grammar is that he wanted to keep the equivalence of forms between the unfolding at one level and the syntactic unravelling at the other, whereas in semiotics, when passing from one level to another level towards the surface, we posit a progressive increase in signification. Hence, there is an increase in meaning as we go from deep structures toward the surface, and this increase in meaning must be distinguished from the increase in horizontal meaning which Paul Ricoeur spoke about. Within a story, meaning increases syntagmatically. We notice – simply, for example, by consulting a reader such as the one published by Dell Hymes, *Language in Culture and Society* – that three thousand human communities fabricate proverbs, riddles, stories, and so on in the same way, and that they narrate these by using forms which are, *mutatis mutandis,* identical.[4] Consequently, when we speak about semio-narrative structures we are in fact dealing with kinds of universals of language, or rather with narrative universals. If we were not afraid of metaphysics we could say that these are properties of the human mind. The collective actant possesses these narrative universals and so does humanity. However, the semio-narrative level must be distinguished from what I call the discursive level since individuals are the ones who fabricate discourse. They do so by using narrative structures that already exist, that actually coexist with individuals. I thus imagine the subject of enunciation as a kind of funnel into which the narrative structures are poured drop by drop, and from which discourse emerges. This discourse, that is the product of the instance of enunciation, can also be divided into levels of depth, a thematic level and a figurative level. This I feel is the beginning of an answer to your question.

The set of constraints that is presupposed, that exists prior to all discourse, language, and thought, is so great that many semioticians do not know how to come to grips with it. For example, in his inaugural discourse at the Collège de France, my friend Roland Barthes said that language was fascist. I believe that he attributed too great an honour to fascism. We live by our organs, by our desires, in a circumscribed world, and our possibilities are limited. There are a great many restrictive things in human activity, and there is nothing fascist or communist about this. It is simply a question of the common human condition. However, if we raise the question of the instance of enunciation, then all of the lovers of liberty can take heart. The subject of enunciation partakes of all possible liberties. Once again a semiotic deviation appears where each one makes use of all the possible specificities and liberties of discourse. We should take things much more seriously. The characteristics of discursive semiotics and what happens with the setting into discourse, or with discursivization, is essentially a phenomenon of spatialization, temporalization, and actorialization. Actants also are transformed into actors. But to say that discourse is dependent upon space and time is already to inscribe discourse, as well as the subject pronouncing it, within exteriority. In fact, it corresponds to projecting discourse outside the I, the subject of enunciation, and starting to relate stories about the world.

This level of discourse is extremely important and is probably the least studied of all in semiotics. It is also the least organized since we have only a very few ideas and projects to create models to account for it. In any case, a hypothetical provisional distinction can be made between the thematic and figurative levels. For example, when Chateaubriand says that 'my life was as sad as the autumn leaves carried off by the wind,' you can see that 'my life was as sad' is thematic, let us say, more abstract than 'the autumn leaves carried off by the wind.' But one part of the sentence says the same thing as the other. They can thus be superimposed, and we obtain a metaphor that will be the figurative level. The figurative is a way of speaking in either temporal or spatial figures, and if we examine our own discourse we note that everything belongs to one or the other of these. The concept of figures is of major theoretical importance for us not only, as some claim, because in painting we distinguish abstract art from figurative art, but also because this term, which is taken from Hjelmslev's linguistic theory, corresponds to the non-sign, or the semantic part of the sign. On the other hand, 'figure' also permits us to exploit the concept of 'gestalt,' the psychology of forms. The problem is to know how discourse is composed – not with these photographic representations of objects, but with schemata, so to speak, of objects – and how it is used in the most diverse situations. Chains of figures essentially constitute so-called narrative discourse; and what narrative, from this perspective, happens to correspond to is the exploitation of narrative structures from the deep level. We use parts of the narrative structures that we need, and we set them in our own discourse and clothe our own discourse in a figurative manner. Yet there do exist more or less abstract discourses.

Ricoeur: Figures are much more than a garment. What I mean to say is that at this level there is more than an investment, in the sense of an instantiation; in fact, there is something productive. Precisely what is productive is that you cannot have spatialization, temporalization, and actorialization without plot. The different kinds of plot produced in the history of narrative show us that what we are dealing with is not merely an application and projection at the surface, but that there is something really productive which follows rules, and that these rules for plot construction belong to the figurative level. Hence, there is productivity of the figurative level. I would like to return to this problem later. The point I want to make here is that the figurative level provides the dynamics for the rules of transformation and that they are projected backwards from the surface to the deep structures.

Greimas: You are right to take me to task for having said that the figurative clothed narrative structures. This is a bad metaphor and certainly not the way to express the problem. One should first of all take into account that the mode of existence of narrative structures is a virtual mode of existence. Narrative structures do not exist per se but are a mere moment in the generation of signification. When the subject of enunciation says something, he utters a durative discourse and proceeds by means of figures that are linked up. It is the figures that bear the traces of narrative universals.

Ricoeur: I want to approach the problem from a different angle. Are there not ways of dealing with narrative which, in a sense, bypass this distinction between deep structure and surface structure? Because

of all the difficulties in connecting the levels, the freedom of enunciation, and also the constraints of the last level, I insist that on this last,
or third level, this level of figurativization has its own rules. Let us
start with a comment made a few decades ago by Kate Hamburger in
her book *The Logic of Literature,*[5] when she writes that the great feat
of narratives – 'epic,' in her own terms – is to explore minds in the
third-person narrative, to take all the narrative procedures through
which we make judgments on the thoughts, feelings, actions of third
persons, and to transfer them into first-person narrative, thereby
creating a pseudo-autobiography. If we then say that the function of
narrative is to provide a kind of mimesis of other minds, we need new
categories, and we need to know whether these categories belong to
the development of your own semiotics, or whether they are foreign
to it. This is not a critique but, rather, a question.

Let us therefore look at what is required if we begin this way, the
way Dorritt Cohn did in her work *Transparent Minds,*[6] where she
showed that narratives always have this function of exploring other
minds. If we do so, we get constraints of another kind which are more
of a typological than a structural nature. This is the route first
followed by Franz Stanzel in his attempt to work out a typology of
narrative situations and, more powerfully, by Lubomir Dolezel in his
attempt to set up a dialectic between the discourse of the narrator
and the discourse of the character. The next step is to introduce the
category of narrator, a kind of figure that is the part of the text where
someone says something about other minds. You therefore have the
narrator's discourse, the character's discourse, and then it is necessary to develop a typology to show what the constraints are. But my
claim would be that these constraints bypass the distinction between
deep structure and surface structure in your semiotics. They belong
to other systems of categorization, and I would like to know how
these systems intersect with yours. Here, notions such as point of
view and narrative voice would have to be introduced. (When I
speak about point of view, I am thinking about the work done by the
Tartu School. Uspensky, for example, who tried to show that the
interplay between points of view is a principle of composition.) If,
like Dorritt Cohn following Kate Hamburger, we speak of procedures
between narrator and character, we are in fact attempting to structure
enunciation itself. This is, I think, a third dimension which should be
added to the Proppian categories of functions and actants that you
have expanded. We would then be dealing with enunciation, with the

enunciator inscribed in the text as narrator, but also with characters. If I raise the point it is because I think that ultimately the figurative has its own dimension, its own structuration, which is more a part of a sort of typology than of a logic of transformation.

I would also add that I question your own theory when you say that there is an increase in meaningfulness when we proceed from deep structures to surface structures. My question is, where does this increase in meaningfulness come from? I do not think that it is implied only in the transformative capacities of the deep structures, which are constraints.[7] But it is a new kind of constraint that belongs to the level of figurativization and all the resources provided by notions such as narrator, characters, point of view, narrative voice, and so on. These are constraints of a different kind which are immediately figurative but not by derivation. I am aware that your school of thought is not a closed system but is proceeding step by step, from the most abstract to the more concrete. I feel you have reached the point precisely where you have to come to grips with contributions that do not come from your own semiotics. The development of the third stage of your semiotics requires that either you reject these categories or you reconstruct them within your own system of reference.

Greimas: I have always claimed that semiotics is not a science but rather a scientific project, still incomplete or unfinished; and I leave the task of completing and transforming it, starting from a few theoretical principles that I have attempted to establish, to future generations of semioticians. To begin with the deep structures and go toward the surface structures is perhaps a question of strategy. Personally, and on an anecdotal level, I was troubled by the way Jerrold S. Katz and J.A. Fodor presented semantics as an appendix to Chomskian theory. They simply took sentences, aligned them next to one another, and established connections by drawing lines. They thought that discourse could be structured in this way. I found the same thing in Germany, where a type of text linguistics was developed that also treated only surface phenomena.

The second point you raised is related to the increase in signification that results from passing from one level to another. First of all, the way I present things is not by means of a combination of elements; that is to say, I do not usually start with simple units and then combine them to arrive at a more complex level. The problem as I see it is related to the passage from meaning to signification. As a linguist I see this in the procedure of articulation, a sort of continuous explosion. The production of meaning is the production of difference, the production of oppositions, and when discourse happens it takes place by a sort of series of successive explosions that produce the totality, the richness of discourse. On the other hand, we can very well imagine that an analyst dealing with a realized discourse would begin with the surface before going on to the deep structures. That would be another way of proceeding.

The third point I would like to bring up is related to point of view. What I will say about this does not come directly from my own personal research but from work done by one of my students, Jacques Fontanille, who wrote a thesis on the problem of point of view in discourse.[8] He studied cinema, painting, Marcel Proust, advertising, and also quantum theory. He made use of common knowledge, especially when dealing with the concept of the narrator that you yourself mentioned. From a linguistic perspective, we notice that, in addition to modalities, there exists the fundamental element of the modulation of sentences constituted by aspectualities. These aspectualities can be imagined and described only if one posits an observer who is watching the process being actualized, whether it happens to be inchoative, durative, or terminative. Thus, natural language already utilizes the simulacrum of the observer to account for linguistic phenomena, even at the level of the sentence. If one examines narrative discourse one sees that these observers can be situated anywhere. When analysing a text by Proust one notices that the observer changes point of view at almost every sentence. What Fontanille did was to posit that all discourse has a cognitive level and that it is at this cognitive level that a diad – two actants – is located: the observer–actant and the informer–actant. Between the two a sort of exchange of information takes place that can be integrated into the total or partial knowledge of either actant according to the wish of the subject of enunciation, who can be a narrator. This would then be a case of syncretism between the actor–subject of the enunciation and the observer. However, this is not a generalizable actantial structure. I would therefore insist on the need to distinguish in the narrative flow between different levels – especially the cognitive and the pragmatic levels, for example.

As for the last question related to figurativity, I must say that I attach a great deal of importance to research being done in this area. During a year-long seminar given over to the study of these problems some progress was made, but it still is not satisfying, since this level of analysis is extremely complex. My first observation is that we can encounter figurative expression at different levels of depth. To take a very simple case, for example indirect discourse, when I say that it is warm, this can mean 'open the window.' Therefore, 'it is warm' is a figure for saying something else. Another type is parabolic discourse, which is found for example in the Gospels. If you take the parable of the Prodigal Son you can see that the four or five partial parables, which do not start at exactly the same point, narrate the story figuratively. Each parable is displaced a little in relation to the other, but one can establish, by partial parables, so to speak, the common thematic level that can account for the figurativization of the whole. This is another way of grasping figurativity, the type of discourse which we have studied most.

Finally, figurativity is found at the deep level of discourse, as was illustrated, for example, by Denis Bertrand in his thesis on Zola's *Germinal*.[9] In Zola's story about miners living underground, spatial configurations and spatial figures are transformed and become, so to speak, an autonomous language. When we read the novel we think that the lives of the miners are being narrated but, in fact, what is narrated is the great mystery of the mediation within this underground universe. Spatiality becomes an almost abstract sort of language to speak about something other than surface figurativity. These few examples are meant simply to point out that what I call the discursive level of semiotics is a level in which there is an articulation, a level at which other levels of depth can be found. The problematics of levels is a strategy because the number of levels can be increased or diminished in order to facilitate the analysis and the construction of the model.

Ricoeur: I find this answer satisfactory, satisfactory because I acknowledge and welcome this capacity of semiotics to expand. But I wonder whether the initial model is not undermined by this expansion, and whether the price to pay for such an expansion is not a complete reformulation of the basic terms of depth and surface. It is not by chance you ended up speaking about the depth of the surface, which, if I may say so, now has a meaning quite different from your original usage. We are no longer dealing with the idea that there are logical, semantic rules having a logic of transformation which are subsequently invested with anthropomorphic roles, and that then those anthropomorphic roles are once more invested in figures.

Here figure itself has depth, and a quite different use is being made of the term *figure* from that of the term *figura*, to which Auerbach devoted one of his most extraordinary essays. Here we are dealing with the polysemantic capacity of discourse, and it is no longer possible to know if we are at the level of the depth of the surface. The same story may be read in different ways because it is multilayered, and this multilayered nature of any story calls for the role of a reader, which we have not discussed at all. I think that by necessity we have to reintroduce the dialectic between the text and the reader because of this polysemanticism. I will give one example of bringing out the complexity of the figure, to which we bring meaningfulness but also introduce something that Kermode called secrecy. He took the example of parables and the strong interpretation given them by Mark. Parables are narrated in order not to be understood, that is to say, there is an increase of secrecy. The actual title of his work is *The Genesis of Secrecy*.[10] We therefore have to take into account the possibility of another kind of deep meaning, and in so doing we join up with the whole tradition of symbolism concerning the four meanings of the Scriptures, for example. This is a tradition which, I think, has a scope quite different from that of deep structure as it is defined by semiotics. Finally, the best stories, those of Kafka, for example, are not intended to increase intelligibility but to increase perplexity and to call into question the reader's understanding. Here productivity of the surface level is all the more striking as it increases both meaningfulness and puzzlement.

Greimas: I agree in part with what you say. None the less, I would like to make a brief observation. What scientific status can be given to this type of task? Both of us have been speaking about intelligibility, but intelligibility can be situated at different levels. We can understand the main line, the essential; we can also attempt to understand the greater and greater complexity of discourse. I once investigated automatic translation. At that time it was said that to translate the syntax of simple sentences the computer had to carry out two thousand binary operations. Now, if we were to take a short story as complex as Maupassant's 'Deux amis,' we could ask how many binary operations would be necessary to analyse such a text. At each level I feel we would reach the sum of several million at least. Discourse is a complex object and so is the world. Hence, there are no objections in principle if we deepen our knowledge of this phenomenon.

Now, regarding accessibility to the secret that language is, I agree with you, except that the hidden will perhaps remain hidden because we wish to hide things, or because we cannot speak about them. No matter, I would simply say that we linguists or semioticians have extremely poor tools to speak about the secret of language. To speak about meaning or signification, one of the rare means we have at our disposal is transcoding, that is, to take a discourse, a sentence, and to translate it into another discourse, with other words, in a different way. This is how we understand what the first sentence or the first discourse signified. Operations of transcoding are the only means we have to grasp signification and, consequently, when I take a parable such as the Prodigal Son, I am obliged to try and translate it. In doing so perhaps I have not exhausted the totality of meaning, which is regrettable, but unfortunately it is impossible to do otherwise.

Notes

1 See also Paul Ricoeur, 'Greimas's *Narrative Grammar,*' this volume, pp. 256–86.

2 Louis Marin, *Sémiotique de la passion: Topiques et figures* (Paris: Aubier-Montaigne, 1971)

3 Algirdas Julien Greimas, *Maupassant: The Semiotics of Text: Practical Exercises*, trans. by Paul Perron (Amsterdam: J. Benjamin, 1988)

4 See *Language in Culture and Society: A Reader in Linguistics and Anthropology*, ed. by Dell Hymes (New York: Harper and Row, 1964).

5 Kate Hamburger, *The Logic of Literature*, trans. by Marilyn G. Rose (Bloomington: Indiana University Press, 1973)

6 Dorritt Cohn, *Transparent Minds: Narrative Modes for Presenting Consciousness in Fiction* (Princeton: Princeton University Press, 1978)

7 For a detailed discussion of this point, see Jean Petitot-Cocorda, *Morphogenèse du sens* (Paris: Presses Universitaires de France, 1985), esp. pp. 260–8. See also Paul Perron, 'Introduction,' *On Meaning: Selected Writings in Semiotic Theory*, by Algirdas Julien Greimas, trans. by Paul Perron and Frank Collins (Minneapolis: Minnesota University Press, 1987), pp. xxiv–xlv

8 Jacques Fontanille, *Le Savoir partagé: Sémiotique et théorie de la connaissance chez Marcel Proust* (Paris: Hadès-Benjamins, 1987)

9 Denis Bertrand, *L'espace et le sens: 'Germinal' d'Emile Zola* (Paris: Hadès-Benjamins, 1985)

10 Frank Kermode, *The Genesis of Secrecy: On the Interpretation of Narrative* (Cambridge: Harvard University Press, 1979)

III

Aspects of a
Post-Structuralist
Hermeneutics

Metaphor and the
Main Problem of Hermeneutics

I begin this paper with the assumption that the main problem of hermeneutics is that of interpretation. Not interpretation in any undetermined sense of the word, but interpretation with two qualifications: one concerning its scope or field of application, the other its epistemological specificity. As concerns the first point, I should say that there are problems of interpretation because there are *texts, written* texts, the autonomy of which (as regards either the intention of the author, or the situation of the work, or the destination to privileged readers) creates specific problems; these problems are usually solved in spoken language by the kind of exchange or intercourse which we call dialogue or conversation. With written texts, the discourse must speak by itself. Let us say, therefore, that there are problems of interpretation because the relation writing–reading is not a particular case of the relation speaking–hearing in the dialogical situation. Such is the most general feature of interpretation as concerns its scope or application field.

Second, the concept of interpretation occurs, at the epistemological level, as an alternative concept opposed to that of explanation (or explication); taken together, they both form a significant contrasting pair, which has given rise to many philosophical disputes in Germany since the time of Schleiermacher and Dilthey; according to that tradition, interpretation has specific subjective implications, such as the involvement of the reader in the process of understanding and the reciprocity between *text*-interpretation and *self*-interpretation. This reciprocity is usually known as the 'hermeneutical circle' and has been opposed, mainly by logical positivists, but also for opposite reasons by Romantic thinkers, to the kind of objectivity and to the lack of self-involvement which is supposed to characterize a scientific explanation of things. I shall say later to what extent we may be led to amend and even to rebuild on a new basis the opposition between interpretation and explanation.

Whatever the outcome of the subsequent discussion may be, this schematic description of the concept of interpretation is enough to delineate the two main problems of hermeneutics: that of the status of written texts versus spoken language, and that of the status of interpretation versus explanation.

Now for the metaphor! The aim of this paper is to connect together the problems raised in hermeneutics by *text-interpretation* and the problems raised in rhetoric, semantics, stylistics – or whatever may be the discipline concerned – by metaphor.

I. Text and Metaphor as Discourse

Our first task will be to find a common ground for the theory of text and for that of metaphor. This common ground has already a name – discourse; it has still to receive a status.

One first thing is striking: the two kinds of entities which we are now considering are of different length and may be compared from the standpoint of length of the basic unity of discourse, the sentence. Of course a text may be reduced to only one sentence, as in proverbs or aphorisms; but texts have a maximal length which may go from paragraphs to chapters, to books, to 'selected works,' to 'complete works' (*Gesammelte Werke!*), and even to full libraries. I shall call a *work* the closed sequence of discourse which may be considered as a text. Whereas texts may be identified on the basis of their maximal length, metaphors may be identified on the basis of their minimal length, that of the words. Even if the remainder of the analysis tends to show that there are no metaphors, in the sense of metaphorical *words*, without certain contexts, even therefore if we shall have to speak of metaphorical *statements* requiring at least the length of a sentence, or of a phrase, nevertheless the 'metaphorical twist' (to speak like Monroe Beardsley) is something which happens to words; the shift of meaning which requires the whole contribution of the context affects the word; it is the word that has a 'metaphorical use,' or of a non-literal meaning, or a novel, 'emergent meaning' in specific contexts. In that sense the definition of metaphor by Aristotle – as a transposition of an alien *name* (or word) – is not cancelled by a theory which lays the stress on the contextual action which creates the shift of meaning in the word. The word remains the 'focus,' even if this focus requires the 'frame' of the sentence, to use the vocabulary of Max Black.

This first remark – merely formal – concerning the difference of length between text and metaphor, that is, between *work* and *word*, will help us to elaborate our initial problem in a more accurate way: to what extent may we treat metaphor as a work in miniature? The answer to this first question will help us afterwards to raise the second question: to what extent may the hermeneutical problem of text-interpretation be considered as a large-scale expansion of the problems condensed in the explication of a local metaphor in a given text?

Is a metaphor a work in miniature? May a work – say, a poem – be considered as an expanded metaphor? The answer to the first question relies on the general properties belonging to *discourse*, since both text and metaphor, work and word, fall under one and the same category, that of discourse.

I shall not elaborate the concept of discourse at length, but limit my analysis to those features which are necessary for the comparison between text and metaphor. For the sake of this analysis, I shall consider only the following characteristics. All of them present the form of a paradox, that is, of an apparent contradiction.

First, all discourse occurs as an *event*; it is the opposite of language as 'langue,' code, or system; as an event, it has an instantaneous existence, it appears and disappears. But, at the same time – here lies the paradox – it can be identified and reidentified as the same; this sameness is what we call, in the broad sense, its *meaning*. All discourse, let us say, is effectuated as an event, but all discourse is understood as meaning. We shall see in what sense metaphor concentrates on the character of event and of meaning.

Second, metaphor as a pair of contrasting traits: the meaning is carried by a specific structure, that of the proposition, which involves an inner opposition between a pole of singular identification (this man, the table, Mr Jones, London) and a pole of general predication (mankind as a class, lightness as a property, equality with such-and-such as a relation, running as an action). Metaphor, as we shall see, relies on this 'attribution' of characters to the 'principal subject' of a sentence.

Third, discourse, as an act, may be considered from the point of view of the 'content' of the propositional act (it predicates such-and-such characters of such-and-such things) or from the point of view of what J.L. Austin called the 'force' of the complete act of discourse (the 'speech act' in his terms): what is *said* of the subject is one thing; what I 'do' *in* saying that is another thing: I may make a mere description, or give an order, or formulate a wish, or give a warning, etc. Hence the polarity between the locutionary act (the act *of* saying) and the illocutionary act (that which I do *in* saying); this polarity may seem to be less useful than the preceding ones, at least at the level of the structure of the metaphorical statement; it will play a significant role when we shall have to replace the metaphor in the concrete setting, say, of a poem, of an essay, of a fictional work.

Fourth, metaphor as a pair of opposite features: discourse, mainly as sentence, implies the polarity of *sense* and *reference*, that is, the possibility to distinguish between *what* is said, by the sentence as a whole and by the words as parts of the sentence, and *about what* something is said. To speak is to say something about something. This polarity will play the central role in the second and the third parts of this paper, since I shall try to connect the problems of explanation to the dimension of 'sense,' that is, to the immanent design of the discourse – and the problems of interpretation to the dimension of 'reference' understood as the power of discourse to apply to an extralinguistic reality *about* which it says what it says.

But, before developing this dichotomy of sense and reference as the ground for the opposition between explanation and interpretation, let us introduce a last polarity which will play a decisive role in the hermeneutical theory. Discourse has not only one kind of reference, but two kinds of reference: it refers to an extralinguistic reality, say, the world or a world, but it refers equally to its own speaker by the means of specific devices which function only in a sentence, therefore in discourse, such as personal pronouns, verbal tenses, demonstratives, etc. In that way, language has both a *reality*-reference and a *self*-reference. And it is the same entity – the sentence – which has this twofold reference, intentional and reflective, thing-bound and self-bound. As we shall see, this connection between the two directions of reference will be the key of our theory of interpretation and the basis of our reappraisal of the hermeneutical circle.

I enumerate the basic polarities of discourse in the following condensed way: event and meaning, singular identification and general predication, propositional act and illocutionary acts, sense and reference, reference to reality and self-reference.

Now, in what sense may we say that text and metaphor rely on this same kind of entity which we called discourse?

It is easy to show that all texts are discourse, since they proceed from the smallest unity of discourse, the sentence. A text is at least a set of sentences. We shall see that it has to be something more in order to be a work. But it is at least a set of sentences, therefore a discourse.

The connection between metaphor and discourse requires a specific justification, precisely because the definition of metaphor as a transposition occurring to *names*, or to words, seems to put it in a category of entities smaller than the sentence. But the semantics of the word demonstrates very clearly that words have *actual* meanings only in a sentence and that lexical entities – words in the dictionary – have only potential meanings and for the sake of their potential uses in sentences. As concerns the metaphor itself, semantics demonstrates with the same strength that the metaphorical meaning of a word is nothing which may be found in a dictionary (in that sense we may continue to oppose the metaphorical sense to the literal sense, if we call literal sense *whatever* sense may occur among the partial meanings enumerated in the dictionary, and not a so-called original, or fundamental, or primitive, or proper meaning). If the metaphorical sense is more than the actualization of one of the potential meanings of a polysemic word (and all our words in common discourse are polysemic), it is necessary that this metaphorical use is only *contextual*; by that I mean a sense which emerges as the result of a certain contextual action. We are led in that way to oppose *contextual* changes of meaning to *lexical* changes, which concern the diachronistic aspect of language as code, system, or *langue*. Metaphor is such a *contextual* change of meaning.

By saying that, I agree partially[1] with the modern theory of metaphor, from I.A. Richards to Max Black and Monroe Beardsley; more specifically, I agree with these authors on the fundamental issue: a word receives a metaphorical meaning in specific contexts within which they are opposed to other words taken literally; this shift in meaning results mainly from a clash between literal meanings, which excludes a literal use of the word in question and gives clues for the finding of a new meaning which is able to fit in the context of the sentence and to make sense in this context.

This contextual action creates a word meaning which is an event, since it exists only in this context; but it can be identified as the same when it is repeated; in that way the innovation of an 'emergent meaning' (Beardsley) may be recognized as a linguistic creation; if it is adopted by an influential part of the speech community, it may even become a standard meaning and be added to the polysemy of the literal entities, contributing in that way to the *history* of language as *langue*, code, or *system*. But, at that ultimate stage, metaphor is a dead metaphor. Only genuine metaphors are at the same time 'event' *and* 'meaning.'

The contextual action requires in the same way our second polarity, that between singular identification and general predication; a metaphor is said of a 'principal subject'; as a 'modifer' of this subject, it works as a kind of 'attribution.' The three theories to which I refer here rely on this predicative structure, either when they oppose the 'vehicle' to the 'tenor,' or the 'frame' to the 'focus,' or the 'modifier' to the 'principal subject.'

That metaphor requires the polarity between sense and reference will demand a complete section of this paper; the same must be said of the polarity between reference to reality and self-reference. You will understand later why I am unable to say more about sense and reference, and about reality-reference and self-reference at the level of metaphoric statements. Here the mediation of the theory of text will be required.

We have so far delineated the framework of our comparison. We are now prepared for the second part of our task, in which we shall answer our second question: to what extent may *text* explanation and interpretation, on the one hand, and the explication of metaphor, on the other hand, be said to be similar processes, only applied at two different levels of discourse, the level of the *work* and the level of the *word*?

II. Explanation and Metaphor

I want to explore the following working hypothesis. From one standpoint the process of understanding a metaphor is the key for that of understanding larger texts, say, literary works; this point of view is that of explanation and develops only this aspect of the meaning which we called the *sense* – the immanent design of discourse. But, from one other standpoint, it is the understanding of a work as a whole which gives the key to metaphor; this other point of view is that of interpretation properly, which develops the second aspect of the meaning which we called the reference, that is, the intentional direction towards a world and the reflective direction towards a self. Therefore, if we apply explanation to sense as the immanent design of the work, we may reserve interpretation to the kind of inquiry devoted to the power of a work to project a world of its own and to initiate the hermeneutical circle between the apprehension of those projected worlds and the expansion of self-understanding in front of these novel worlds.

Our working hypothesis invites us therefore to proceed from metaphor to text at the level of the 'sense' and of the 'explanation' of the sense – then from text to metaphor at the level of the reference of the work to a world and to a self, that is, at the level of interpretation, properly said.

What aspects of metaphor explication may serve as paradigms for text explication or explanation?

These aspects are features of the *work* of explanation which do not appear when we start from trivial cases, such as: man is a wolf, or a fox, or a lion. (You could look at most of the good authors on metaphor and notice interesting variations within the bestiary which furnishes them with examples!) With those examples we elude the major difficulty, that of *identifying a meaning which is a word meaning*. The only way of doing it is to *construct* it so that the whole sentence makes sense.

On what do we rely in the case of trivial metaphors? Max Black and Beardsley argue that the meaning of a word does not only depend on the semantical and syntactical rules which govern its use as *literal* use, but by other rules – which are nevertheless rules – to which the members of a speech community are committed, and which determines what Black calls the 'system of associated commonplaces' and Monroe Beardsley the 'potential range of connotations.' In the statement 'man is a wolf,' the principal subject is qualified by one of the traits of the animal which belong to the 'wolf-system of related commonplaces' (p. 41);[2] this implication system works as a filter or as a screen; it does not only select, but brings forward aspects of the principal subject.

What may we think of this explication in the light of our description of metaphor as a word meaning occurring in a new context?

I agree entirely with the 'interaction view' implied by this explication; the metaphor is more than a mere substitution for another literal word which an exhausting paraphrase could restitute at the same place. The algebraic sum of these two operations of substitution by the speaker and of restitution by the hearer or the reader equals zero. No new meaning emerges and we learn nothing. As Max

Black says: 'Interaction-metaphors are not expandable ... this use of a subsidiary subject to foster insight into a principal subject is a distinctive intellectual operation'; this is why you cannot translate an interaction metaphor in plain language without 'a loss in cognitive content' (p. 46).

But are we doing better justice to the power of metaphor 'to inform and enlighten,' by merely adding to the semantic polysemy of the word in the dictionary and to the semantic rules which govern the literal use of the lexical terms, the 'system of associated commonplaces' and the cultural rules – I coin the term – which govern their use? Is not this system something dead, or at least something already established?

Of course, this system of commonplaces has to be assumed in order that the contextual action follow the guidelines of some directions for the construction of the new meaning. And Max Black's theory reserves the possibility that metaphors are 'supported by specially constructed systems of implication as well as by accepted commonplaces' (p. 43). The problem is precisely that of these 'specially constructed systems of implication.' We have therefore to inquire into the process of interaction itself in order to explain the cases of novel metaphors in novel contexts.

Beardsley's theory of metaphor leads us a step farther in that direction when he emphasizes the role of logical absurdity – or of clash between literal meanings within the same context. 'And in poetry,' he says, 'the chief tactic for obtaining this result is that of *logical absurdity*' (p. 138).[3] How? Logical absurdity creates a situation in which we have the choice between either preserving the literal sense of both the subject and the modifier and concluding to the meaninglessness of the whole sentence – or attributing a new meaning to the modifier such as the whole sentence makes sense. Then we have not only a self-contradictory attribution, but a significant self-contradictory attribution. When I say 'man is a fox' (the fox has chased the wolf), I must shift from a literal to a metaphorical attribution *if* I want to save the sentence. But, where do we have this new meaning from?

As long as we raise this kind of question – *from where* – we are sent back to the same kind of solution; the potential range of connotations does not say more than the system of associated commonplaces; indeed we enlarge the notion of meaning by including the 'secondary meanings' as connotations within the scope of the full meaning; but we keep linking the creative process of metaphor-forming to a non-creative aspect of language.

Is it sufficient to add to this 'potential range of connotations,' as Beardsley does in the 'revised theory of controversion' (*the metaphorical twist*), the range of *properties* which do not yet belong to the range of connotations of my language? At first sight this addition improves the theory; as Beardsley says very strongly, 'the metaphor transforms a property actual or attributed into a sense.' The shift in the theory is important, since we have now to say that 'the metaphors would not only actualize a potential connotation, but establish it as a staple one'; and further: 'some of the relevant properties are given a new status as elements of verbal meaning.'

But to speak of properties *of things* (or *of objects*) which were not yet meant is to concede that the novel meaning is not *drawn from* anywhere, in language at least (property is a thing-implication, not a word-implication). And to say that a novel metaphor is *not drawn at all* is to recognize it for what it is, that is, a momentaneous creation of language, a semantic innovation which has no status in language, as already established, neither as designation nor as connotation.

At that point it could be asked how one can speak of a semantic innovation, of a semantical *event* as of a *meaning* which can be identified and reidentified (such was the first criterion of discourse in our first part).

Only one answer remains possible: to take the standpoint of the hearer or of the reader and to treat the novelty of an emergent meaning as the counterpart, from the side of the author, of the *construction* from the part of the reader. Then the process of explanation is the only access to the process of creation.

If we don't take this way, we do not get rid of the theory of *substitution*; instead of substituting for the metaphorical expression some literal meaning restituted by the paraphrase, we substitute the system of connotations and commonplaces. This task must remain a preparatory task which relates literary criticism to psychology and sociology. The decisive moment of explication is that of the construction of the network of interaction, which makes of this context an actual and unique context. In doing that, we point to the semantic event as to the point of intersection between several semantic lines; this construction is the means by which all the words taken together make sense. Then – and only then – the 'metaphorical twist' is both an event *and* a meaning, a meaningful event and an emerging meaning in language.

Such is the fundamental feature of the explication of metaphor which makes of it a paradigm for the explanation of a literary work. We construct the meaning of a text in a way which is similar to the way in which we make sense of all of the terms of metaphorical statement.

Why have we to 'construct' the meaning of a text? First because it is a *written* thing: in the asymmetric relation of the text and the reader, only one of the partners speaks for two. Bringing a text to speech is always something else than hearing somebody and listening to his words.

A second reason concerns more specifically the fact that a text is not only a *written* thing, but a work, that is, a closed chain of meaning. Now a work has to be constructed because a text – especially if it is a literary work – is more than a linear succession of sentences. It is a cumulative, holistic process.

From these two reasons what we may give for the necessity of construing the meaning of a *text* or more precisely of a *work*, of a literary work, we may draw more suggestions concerning the 'how' of this construction. It is at that stage that the pole of text understanding is homologous to the understanding of a metaphorical statement.

On the one hand, this construction necessarily takes the form of a guess. As Hirsch says in his book *Validity in Interpretation*, there are no rules. As concerns the place of *guessing* in the construction, it follows from what we said about the absence of the author's intention as a guideline and the character of a work as a system of whole and parts. We may summarize in this way the corresponding features which are the grounds for the analogy between the explication of a metaphoric statement and a literary work as a whole.

In both cases the construction relies on the 'clues' contained in the text itself: a clue is a kind of index for a specific construction, both a set of permissions and a set of prohibitions; it excludes some unfitting constructions and allows some others which make more sense of the same words.

Second, in both cases a construction may be said more probable than another, but not true. The most probable is that which 1 / accounts for the greatest number of facts provided by the text, including potential connotations, and 2 / offers a better qualitative convergence between the traits which it takes into account. A poor explication may be said to be narrow or farfetched.

I agree here with Beardsley that a good explication satisfies two principles: that of congruence and that of plenitude. I have spoken so far of convergence. The principle of plenitude will provide us with a transition to our third part. This principle reads: 'all the connotations that can fit are to be attached; the poem means all it can mean.' This principle leads us farther than mere concern for the 'sense.' It already says something of the reference. Since it takes as a measure of plenitude the requirements raised by an expression which wants to be said and to be equated by the semantic density of the text. The principle of plenitude is the corollary at the level of the *sense* of a principle of integral expression which draws our inquiry in a quite different direction.

A quotation from Wilhelm von Humboldt will help us approach this new field of inquiry: 'A language,' he said, 'language as discourse (*die Rede*) stands on the boundary line between the expressed and the unexpressed. Its aim and its goal is to always repel this boundary a bit farther.'

Interpretation conforms to this aim.

III. From Hermeneutics to Metaphor

1 / At the level of interpretation, text-understanding gives the key for metaphor-understanding.

Why? Because some features of discourse begin to play an explicit role only when discourse takes the form of a literary *work*. These features are those which we put under the two headings of reference and self-reference. I oppose reference to sense by identifying 'sense' with 'what' and 'reference' with 'about what' of discourse. Of course, these two traits may be recognized in the smallest unity of language as discourse, in sentences. The sentence is about a situation which it expresses and refers back to its own speaker by the means of specific devices. But reference and self-reference do not give rise to perplexing problems until discourse has become a text and has taken the form of a work.

Which problems? Let us start once more from the difference between written and spoken language. In spoken language, what a dialogue ultimately refers to is the situation common to the interlocutors, that is, aspects of reality which can be shown or pointed at;

we say then that reference is 'ostensive.' In written language, reference is no longer ostensive: poems, essays, and fictional works speak of things, events, states of affairs, characters which are evoked, but which are not there. Nevertheless, literary texts are about something. About what? About a world, which is the world of this work.

Far from saying that the text is there without a world, I will now say without paradox that only man has a world, and not just a situation, a *Welt* and not just an *Umwelt*. In the same manner that the text frees its meaning from the tutelage of the mental intention, it frees its reference from the limits of ostensive reference. For us, the world is the ensemble of references opened up by texts. Thus we speak about the 'world' of Greece, not to designate any more what were the situations for those who lived then, but to designate the nonsituational references which outlive the effacement of the first and which henceforth are offered as possible modes of being, of symbolic dimensions of our being-in-the-world.

This nature of reference in the case of literary works has an important consequence for the concept of interpretation. It implies that 'the meaning of a text is not behind the text, but in front of it. It is not something hidden, but something disclosed.' What has to be understood is what points towards a possible world thanks to the non-ostensive references of the text. Texts speak of possible worlds and of possible ways of orientating oneself in those worlds. In that way disclosure becomes the equivalent for written texts of ostensive reference for spoken language. And interpretation becomes the grasping of the world-propositions opened up by the non-ostensive references of the text.

This concept of interpretation expresses a decisive shift of emphasis within the Romanticist tradition of hermeneutics; here the emphasis was put on the ability of the hearer or of the reader to transfer himself in the spiritual life of another speaker or writer. The emphasis now is less on the *other*, as a spiritual entity, than on the world that the work displays. *Verstehen* – understanding – is to follow the dynamics of the work, its movement from what it says to that about which it speaks. 'Beyond my situation as reader, beyond the author's situation, I offer myself to the possible ways of being-in-the-world which the text opens up and discovers for me.' This is what Gadamer calls 'fusion of horizons' (*Horizontverschmelzung*) in historical knowledge.

The shift of emphasis from understanding the other to understanding the world of his work implies a corresponding shift in the conception of the 'hermeneutical circle.' By 'hermeneutical circle' Romanticist thinkers meant that the understanding of a text cannot be an objective procedure in the sense of scientific objectivity, but necessarily involves a precomprehension which expresses the way in which the reader has already understood himself and his world. Therefore, a kind of circularity occurs between understanding a text and understanding oneself. Such is in condensed terms the principle of the 'hermeneutical circle.' It is easy to understand that thinkers taught in the tradition of logical empiricism could only reject as sheer scandal the mere idea of a hermeneutical circle and consider it as an outrageous violation of all the canons of verifiability.

For my part, I do not want to deny that the hermeneutical circle remains an unavoidable structure of interpretation. No genuine interpretation which does not end in some kind of appropriation – of *Aneignung*, if by that term we mean the process of making one's own (*eigen*) what was other, foreign (*fremd*). But my claim is that the hermeneutical circle is not correctly understood when it is presented 1 / as a circle between two subjectivities, that of the reader and that of the author, and 2 / as the projection of the subjectivity of the reader in the reading itself. Let us correct the first assumption in order to correct the second one.

That which we make our own, we appropriate for ourselves, is not a foreign experience or a distant intention, it is the horizon of a world towards which this refers: the appropriation of the reference no longer finds any model in the fusion of consciousness, in 'empathy' or in sympathy. The coming to language of the sense and the reference of a text is the coming to language of a world and not the recognition of another person.

The second correction of the Romanticist concept of interpretation follows from the first one. If appropriation is the counterpart of disclosure, then the role of subjectivity is not correctly described as projection. I should rather say that the reader understands himself before the text, before the world of the work. To understand oneself before, in front of, a world is the contrary of projecting oneself and one's beliefs and prejudices; it is to let the work and its world enlarge the horizon of my own self-understanding.

Hermeneutics, therefore, does not submit interpretation to the finite capacities of understanding of a given reader; it does not put the meaning of the text under the power of the subject who interprets. Far from saying that a subject already masters his own way of being in the world and projects it as the *a priori* of his reading ... I say that interpretation is the process by which the disclosure of *new modes of being* – or, if you prefer Wittgenstein to Heidegger, of new *forms of life* – gives to the subject a new capacity of knowing himself. If there is somewhere a project and a projection, it is the reference of the work which is the project of a world; the reader is consequently enlarged in his capacity of self-projection by receiving a new mode of being from the text itself.

In that way the hermeneutical circle is not denied, but it is displaced from a subjectivistic to an ontological level; the circle is between my way (or my mode) of being – beyond the knowledge which I may have of it – and the mode (or the way) of being disclosed by the text as the work's world.

2 / Such is the model of interpretation which I want now to transfer from texts as long sequences of discourse to metaphor as 'a poem in miniature' (Beardsley). Indeed the metaphor is too short a discourse to display this dialectic between disclosing a world and understanding one's self in front of this world. Nevertheless this dialectic points towards some features of metaphor which the modern theories I quoted above do not seem to consider, but which were not absent from Greek theory of metaphor.

Let us return to the theory of metaphor in the *Poetics* of Aristotle. Metaphor is only one of the 'parts' *(merê)* of that which Aristotle calls 'diction' (*lexis*); as such it belongs to a family of language procedures – use of foreign words, coining of new words, shortening or lengthening of words – all of which depart from common (*kyrion*) use of words. Now, what makes the unity of *lexis*? Only its *function* in poetry. *Lexis*, in its turn, is one of the 'parts' *(merê)* of tragedy, taken as the paradigm of the poetic work. Tragedy, in the context of the *Poetics*, represents the level of the literary work as a whole. Tragedy, as a poem, has sense and reference. In the language of Aristotle, the 'sense' of tragedy is secured by what he calls the 'fable,' or the 'plot' (*mythos*). We may understand the *mythos* of tragedy as its sense, since Aristotle keeps putting the emphasis on its structural characters; the *mythos* must have unity and coherence and make of the actions represented something 'entire and complete.' As such, the *mythos* is the principal 'part' of the tragedy, its 'essence'; all the other 'parts' of the tragedy – the 'characters,' the 'thoughts,' the 'diction,' the 'spectacle' – are connected to the *mythos* as the means or the conditions or the performance of the tragedy as *mythos*.

We must draw the inference that it is only in connection with the *mythos* of tragedy that its *lexis* makes sense, and, with *lexis*, *metaphora*. There is no local meaning of metaphor beside the regional meaning provided by the *mythos* of tragedy.

But, if metaphor is related to the 'sense' of tragedy by the means of its *mythos*, it is related to the 'reference' of tragedy thanks to its general aim which Aristotle calls *mimesis*.

Why do poets write tragedies, elaborate fables and plots, and use such 'strange' words as metaphors? Because tragedy itself is related to a more fundamental project – that of *imitating* human action in a *poetic* fashion. With these master words – *mimesis* and *poiesis* – we reach the level of what I called the referential world of the work. Indeed, the Aristotelian concept of *mimesis* involves already all the paradoxes of reference. On the one hand, it expresses a world of human action which is already there; tragedy is bound to express human reality, the tragedy of life. But, on the other hand, *mimesis* does not mean duplication of reality; *mimesis* is *poiesis*, that is, fabrication, construction, creation. Aristotle gives at least two hints of this creative dimension of *mimesis*: the fable itself as a coherent construction of its own, and above all the definition of tragedy as the imitation of human actions as better, nobler, higher than they actually are. Could we not say, then, that *mimesis* is the Greek name for what we called the unostensive reference of the literary work, or in other words, the Greek name for world disclosure?

If we are right, we may now say something about the *power* of metaphor. I say here the 'power,' and no longer the 'structure,' no longer even the 'process of metaphor.' The power of metaphor proceeds from its connection, within a poetic and work: *first*, with the other procedures of 'diction' (*lexis*); *second*, with the 'fable,' which is the essence of the work, its immanent 'sense'; *third*, with the intentionality of the work as a whole, that is, its intention to represent human actions as *higher* than they actually are: and this is *mimesis*. In that sense the power of metaphor proceeds from that of the poem as a whole.

Let us apply these remarks borrowed from Aristotle's *Poetics* to our own description of metaphor. Could we not say that the feature of metaphor that we put above all other features – its nascent or emerging character – is related to the function of poetry as a creative imitation of reality? Why should we invent novel meanings, meanings which exist only in the instance of discourse, if it were not for the sake of the *poiesis* in the *mimesis*? If it is true that the poem creates a world, it requires a language which preserves and expresses its creative power in specific contexts.

Link together the *poiesis* of the *poem* and metaphor as an emergent meaning, then you will make sense of both at the same time: poetry and metaphor.

Such is the way in which the theory of interpretation paves the way for an ultimate approach to the power of metaphor. This priority given to text interpretation in this last stage of the analysis of metaphor does not imply that the relation between both is not reciprocal. The explication of metaphor as a local event in the text contributes to the interpretation itself of the work as a whole. We could even say that, if the interpretation of local metaphors is enlightened by the interpretation of the text as a whole and by the disentanglement of the kind of world it projects, the interpretation of the poem as a whole is controlled, reciprocally, by the explication of metaphor as a local phenomenon. I should venture, as an example of this reciprocal relation between regional and local aspects of the text, the possible connection, in Aristotle's *Poetics*, between the function of *imitation*, as making human actions *higher* than they actually are, and the structure of metaphor, as *transposing* the meaning of ordinary language into *strange* uses. Is there not a mutual affinity between the project of making human actions look *better* than they actually are and the special procedure of metaphor as an emerging meaning?

Let us express that relation in more general terms. Why should we draw new meanings from our language, if we had nothing *new* to say, no new worlds to project? Linguistic creations would be meaningless if they did not serve the general project of letting new worlds emerge from poetry.

Allow me to conclude in a way which would be consistent with a theory of interpretation which lays the stress on 'opening up a world.' Our conclusion should also 'open up' some new vistas. On what? Maybe on the old problem of imagination, which I cautiously put aside. We are prepared to inquire into the power of imagination, no longer as the faculty of deriving 'images' from sensory experiences, but as the capacity to let new worlds build our self-understanding. This power would not be conveyed by emerging images but by emerging meanings in our language. Imagination, then, should be treated as a dimension of language. In that way, a new link would appear between imagination and metaphor.

Notes

1 My main disagreement concerns their use of 'field of associated commonplaces' or of the 'potential range of connotations' which concerns more trivial metaphors than genuine metaphors. In that case, which is alone paradigmatic, the contextual effect goes farther than mere actualization of the potential range of commonplaces or connotations. I shall return to this point in the second part. The theory of metaphor must address itself directly to the novel metaphor and not proceed through an expansion from flat metaphors to novel metaphors.

2 Max Black, *Models and Metaphors: Studies in Language and Philosophy* (Ithaca: Cornell University Press, 1962), page references cited in the text.

3 Monroe C. Beardsley, *Aesthetics: Problems in the Philosophy of Criticism* (New York: Harcourt, Brace and World, 1958), page references cited in the text.

Writing as a Problem for Literary Criticism and Philosophical Hermeneutics

To the extent that hermeneutics is a text-oriented interpretation, and that texts are, among other things, instances of written language, no interpretation theory is possible that does not come to grips with the problem of writing. Therefore the purpose of this essay is twofold. I want first to show that the transition from speaking to writing has its conditions of possibility in the structures of discourse itself, then to connect the kind of intentional exteriorization which writing exhibits to a central problem of hermeneutics, that of distanciation. This same concept of exteriority, which in the first part of this paper will be more used than criticized, will become problematic in the second part. Plato's critique of writing as a kind of alienation will provide the turning-point from the descriptive to the critical treatment of the exteriorization of discourse proper to writing.

I. From Speaking to Writing

What happens in writing is the full manifestation of something which is in a virtual state, something nascent and inchoate in living speech, namely the detachment of the 'said' from the 'saying.'

This seclusion of the said from the saying is implied by the dialectical structure of discourse which may be described as the dialectic of event (the 'saying') and meaning (the 'said').

The event-character of discourse may be emphasized by a simple comparison between the stable structure of the codes which constitute the rules of the game for any given language and the vanishing existence of the message. This vanishing status is the counterpart of the fact that the message alone is actual, the code being merely virtual. Only the discrete and, each time, unique acts of discourse actualize the code.

But this first criterion alone would be more misleading than illuminating if the 'instance of discourse,' as Benveniste calls it, was merely this vanishing event. Then science would be justified in discarding it and the ontological priority of discourse would remain vain and without consequence. An act of discourse is not merely transitory and vanishing, however. It can be identified and reidentified as the same, so that we may say it again or in other words. We may even say it in another language or translate it from one language into another. Through all these transformations it preserves an identity of its own which can be called the propositional content, the 'said as such.'

We have therefore to reformulate our first criterion – discourse as event – in a more dialectical way in order to take into account the relation which constitutes discourse as such, the relation between event and meaning.

This is not the place to elucidate in detail the inner constitution of the 'said as such,' the role of the predicate as the kernel and the criterion on the minimal unit of discourse – the sentence – the combination between singular identification and universal predication within one and the same propositional act, etc. We must limit ourselves to saying that this inner constitution testified that discourse is not merely a vanishing event, it has a structure of its own based on its predicative form.

Discourse therefore is the dialectical unity of event and meaning in the sentence. The event character has to be stressed over against all attempts to reduce the message to the code. Every apology for speech as an event is significant if it makes visible the necessary actualization of our linguistic competence in performance. But the same apology becomes abusive when this event character of discourse is extended from the problematic of actualization, where it is valid, to another problematic, that of understanding. *If all discourse is effectuated as an event, it is understood as meaning*, that is, as the propositional content which can be described as the synthesis of two functions, the identification and the predication.

It is this dialectic of event and meaning which makes possible the detachment of meaning from the event in writing. But this detachment is not such as to cancel the fundamental structure of discourse. The semantic autonomy of the text which now appears is still governed by the dialectic of event and meaning. Moreover, we may say that this dialectic is made obvious and explicit in writing. Writing is the full manifestation of discourse. To hold, as Jacques Derrida does, that writing has a root distinct from speech and that this foundation has been misunderstood due to our having paid excessive attention to speech, its voice, and its *logos*, is to overlook the grounding of both modes of the actualization of discourse in the dialectical constitution of discourse.

I propose that we begin from the schema of communication described by Roman Jakobson in his article 'Linguistics and Poetics.' To the six main 'factors' of communicative discourse – the speaker, hearer, medium or channel, code, situation, and message – Jakobson relates six 'functions,' each function correlating with one of the factors: these functions are called the emotive, conative, phatic, metalinguistic, referential, and poetic functions. Using this terminology, our questions about writing can be raised as an inquiry into what alterations, transformations, or deformations affect the interplay of factors and functions when discourse is inscribed in writing.

A. Message and Medium: Fixation

The most obvious change from speaking to writing concerns the relation between the message and its medium or channel. At first glance, it concerns only this relation, but upon closer examination, this first alteration irradiates in every direction, affecting in a decisive manner all the factors and functions. Our task therefore will be to proceed from this central change towards its various peripheral effects.

As a simple change in the nature of the medium, the problem of writing is identical to that of the fixation of discourse in some exterior bearer, whether it be stone, papyrus, or paper, which is other than the human voice. This inscription, substituted for the immediate vocal, physiognomic, or gestural expression, is in itself a tremendous cultural achievement. The human face disappears. Now material 'marks' convey the message. This cultural achievement concerns the event character of discourse first and subsequently the meaning as well. It is because discourse only exists in a temporal and present instance of discourse that it may flee as speech or be fixed as writing. Because the event appears and disappears, there is a problem of fixation, of inscription. What we want to fix is discourse, not language as *langue*. It is only by extension that we fix by inscription the alphabet, lexicon, and grammar, all of which serve that which alone is to be fixed, discourse. The atemporal system neither appears nor disappears, it simply does not happen. Only discourse is to be fixed, because discourse as event disappears.

But this non-dialectical description of the phenomenon of fixation does not reach the core of the process of inscription. Writing may rescue the instance of discourse because what writing does actually fix is not the event of speaking, but the 'said' of speaking, i.e., the intentional exteriorization constitutive of the couple event–meaning. What we write, what we inscribe, is the noema of the speaking act, the meaning of the speech event, not the event as event. This inscription, in spite of the perils that we shall later evoke following Plato in the second part of this essay, is discourse's destination. Only when the *sagen* – the 'saying' – has become *Aussage*, enunciation, only then, is discourse accomplished as discourse in the full expression of its nuclear dialectic.

Now, does the problematics of fixation and inscription exhaust the problem of writing?

In other words, is writing only a question of a change of medium, where the human voice, face, and gesture are replaced by material marks other than the speaker's own body?

When we consider the range of social and political changes which can be related to the invention of writing, we may surmise that writing is much more than mere material fixation. We need only to remind ourselves of some of these tremendous achievements. To the possibility of transferring orders over long distances without serious distortions may be connected the birth of political rule exercised by a distant state. This political implication of writing is just one of its consequences. With the fixation of rules for reckoning may be correlated the birth of market relationships, therefore the birth of economics. To the constitution of archives, that of history. To the fixation of law as a standard for decisions, independent of the opinion of the concrete judge, the birth of justice and of juridical codes, etc. Such an immense range of effects suggests that human discourse is not merely preserved from destruction by being fixed in writing, but that it is deeply affected in its communicative function.

We are encouraged to pursue this new thought by a second consideration. Writing raises a specific problem as soon as it is not merely the fixation of a previous oral discourse, the inscription of spoken language, but is human thought directly brought to writing without the intermediary stage of spoken language. Then writing takes the place of speaking. A kind of short-cut occurs between the meaning of discourse and the material medium. Then we have to do with literature in the original sense of the word. The fate of discourse is delivered over to *littera*, not to *vox*.

The best way to measure the extent of this substitution is to look at the range of changes which occur among the other components of the communication process.

B. Message and Speaker

The first connection to be altered is that of the message to the speaker. This change indeed is itself one of two symmetrical changes which affect the interlocutionary situation as a whole. The relation between message and speaker at one end of the communication chain and the relation between message and hearer at the other are together deeply transformed when the face-to-face relation is replaced by the more complex relation of reading to writing, resulting from the direct inscription of discourse in *littera*. The dialogical situation has been exploded. The relation writing–reading is no longer a particular case of the relation speaking–hearing.

If we consider these changes in more detail we see that the reference of the discourse back to its speaker is affected in the following way. In discourse the sentence designates its speaker by diverse indicators of subjectivity and personality: personal pronouns centred around the 'I,' adverbs of space and time centred around the 'here' and 'now,' tenses of the verbs centred around the 'present indicative,' etc. But in spoken discourse this ability of discourse to refer back to the speaking subject presents a character of immediacy because the speaker belongs to the situation of interlocution. He is there, in the genuine sense of being-there, of *Dasein*. Consequently the subjective intention of the speaker and the discourse's meaning overlap each other in such a way that it is the same thing to understand what the speaker means and what his discourse means.

The ambiguity of the German *meinen* and the English 'to mean' attests to this overlapping in the dialogical situation. With written discourse, however, the author's intention and the meaning of the text cease to coincide. This dissociation of the verbal meaning of the text and the mental intention of the author gives to the concept of inscription its decisive significance, beyond the mere fixation of previous oral discourse. Inscription becomes synonymous with the semantic autonomy of the text which results from the disconnection of the mental intention of the author from the verbal meaning of the text, of what the author meant and what the text means. The text's career escapes the finite horizon lived by its author. What the text means now matters more than what the author meant when he wrote it.

This concept of semantic autonomy is of tremendous importance for hermeneutics. Exegesis begins with it, i.e., it unfolds its procedures within the circumscription of a set of meanings that have broken their moorings to the psychology of the author. But this depsychologizing of interpretation does not imply that the notion of authorial meaning has lost all significance. Here again a non-dialectical conception of the relation between event and meaning would tend to oppose one alternative to the other. On the one hand, we would have what W.K. Wimsatt calls the intentional fallacy which holds the author's intention as the criterion for any valid interpretation of the text, and, on the other hand, what I would call in a symmetrical way the fallacy of the absolute text, the fallacy of hypostasizing the text as an authorless entity. If the intentional fallacy overlooks the semantic autonomy of the text, the opposite fallacy forgets that a text remains a discourse told by somebody, said by someone to someone about something. It is impossible to cancel out this main characteristic of discourse without reducing texts to natural objects, i.e., to things which are not man-made, but which are like pebbles found in the sand.

The semantic autonomy of the text makes the relation of event and meaning more complex and in this sense reveals it as a dialectical relation. The authorial meaning becomes properly a dimension of the text to the extent that the author is not available for questioning. When the text no longer answers, then it has an author and no longer a speaker. The authorial meaning is the dialectical counterpart of the verbal meaning and they have to be construed in terms of each other. The concepts of author and authorial meaning raise a hermeneutical problem contemporaneous with that of semantic autonomy.

C. Message and Hearer

At the opposite end of the communication chain the relation of the textual message to the reader is no less complex than is the relation to the author. Whereas spoken discourse is addressed to someone who is determined in advance by the dialogical situation – it is addressed to you, the second person – a written text is addressed to an unknown reader and potentially to whoever knows how to read. This universalization of the audience is one of the more striking effects of writing and may be expressed in terms of a paradox. Because discourse is now linked to a material support, it becomes more spiritual in the sense that it is liberated from the narrowness of the face-to-face situation.

Of course this universality is only potential. In fact, a book is addressed to only a section of the public and reaches its appropriate readers through media which are themselves submitted to social rules of exclusion and admission. In other words, reading is a social phenomenon which obeys certain patterns and therefore suffers from specific limitations. Nevertheless, the proposition which says that a text is potentially addressed to whoever knows how to read must be retained as a limit on any sociology of reading. A work also creates its public. In this way it enlarges the circle of communication and properly initiates new modes of communication. To that extent, recognition of the work by the audience created by the work is an unpredictable event.

Once again the dialectic of meaning and event is exhibited in its fullness by writing. Discourse is revealed as discourse by the dialectic of the address which is both universal and contingent. On the one hand, it is the semantic autonomy of the text which opens up the range of potential readers and, so to speak, creates the audience of the text. On the other hand, it is the response of the audience which makes the text important and therefore significant. This is why authors who do not worry about their readers and despise their present public keep speaking to their readers as a secret community, sometimes projected into a cloudy future. It is part of the meaning of a text to be open to an indefinite number of readers and therefore of interpretations. This opportunity for multiple readings is the dialectical counterpart of the semantic autonomy of the text.

It follows that the problem of the appropriation of the meaning of the text becomes as paradoxical as that of the authorship. The right of the reader and the right of the text converge in an important struggle which generates the whole dynamic of interpretation. Hermeneutics begins where dialogue ends.

D. Message and Code

The relation between message and code is so fundamental to the production of language as discourse that it may be said that it defines discourse as such, either oral or written. The code, or rather the codes (phonological, lexical, and syntactical), provide the speaker with the set of discrete units and the combinatory rules with which he produces the most elementary unit of discourse, the sentence. Writing changes nothing with regard to this fundamental polarity message-code. If it alters it, it does so only in a somewhat indirect way. What I have in mind here concerns the function of literary genres in the production of discourse as such and such a mode of discourse, whether poem, narrative, or essay. This function undoubtedly concerns the relation between message and code since genres are generative devices to produce discourse as ... Before being classificatory devices used by literary critics to orient themselves in the profusion of literary works, therefore before being artefacts of criticism, they are to discourse what generative grammar is to the grammaticality of individual sentences. In this sense these discursive codes may be joined to those phonological, lexical, and syntactical codes which rule the units of discourse, sentences. Now the question is to what extent literary genres are genuinely codes of writing? Only in an indirect, but nevertheless decisive way.

Literary genres display some conditions which theoretically could be described without considering writing. The function of these generative devices is to produce new entities of language longer than the sentence, organic wholes irreducible to a mere addition of sentences. A poem, narrative, or essay relies on laws of composition which, in principle, are indifferent to the opposition between speaking and writing. They proceed from the application of dynamic forms to sets of sentences for which the difference between oral and written language is unessential. Instead, the specificity of these dynamic forms seems to proceed from another dichotomy than that of speaking and hearing: for the application to discourse of categories borrowed from another field, that of practice and work. Language is submitted to the rules of a kind of craftsmanship which allow us to speak of production and of works of art, and, by extension, of words of discourse. The generative devices which we call literary genres are the technical rules presiding over their production. And the style of a work is nothing else than the individual configuration of a singular product or work. The author here is not only the speaker, but also the maker of this work which is his work.

But, if the dichotomy between theory and practice is irreducible to the pair speaking–writing, writing plays a decisive role precisely in the application of the categories of practice, technique, and work to discourse. There is production when a form is applied to some matter in order to shape it. When discourse is transferred to the field of production it is also treated as a stuff to be shaped. It is here that writing interferes. Inscription as a material support, the semantic autonomy of the text as regards both the speaker and the hearer, and all the related traits of exteriority characteristic of writing help to make language the matter of a specific craftsmanship. Thanks to writing, the works of language become as self-contained as sculptures. It is not by chance that literature designates the status of language both as written (*littera*) and as embodied in works according to literary genres. With literature the problem of inscription and that of production tend to overlap. The same may be said for the concept of text, which combines the condition of inscription with the texture proper to the works generated by the productive rules of literary composition. Text means discourse both as inscribed and as wrought.

Such is the specific affinity that reigns between writing and specific codes which generate the works of discourse. This affinity is so close that we might be tempted to say that even oral expressions of poetic or narrative composition rely on processes equivalent to writing. The memorization of epic poems, lyrical songs, parables, and proverbs, and their ritual recitation tend to fix and even to freeze the form of the work in such a way that memory appears as the support of an inscription similiar to that provided by external marks. In this extended sense of inscription, writing and the production of works of discourse according to the rules of literary composition tend to coincide without being identical processes.

E. Message and Reference

We have postponed considering the most complex changes which occur in the functioning of discourse which may be ascribed to writing until the end of this inquiry. They concern the referential function of discourse in the schema of communication proposed by Roman Jakobson, which are the most complex effects of all for two reasons. On the one hand, the distinction between sense and reference introduces in discourse a more complex dialectic than that of event and meaning which provides us with the model of exteriorization which makes writing possible. It is, so to speak, a dialectic of the second order where the meaning itself, as immanent 'sense,' is externalized as transcendent reference, in the sense that thought is directed through the sense towards different kinds of extralinguistic entities such as objects, states of affairs, things, facts, etc. On the other hand, most of the alterations of reference which will be considered are not to be ascribed to writing as such but to writing as the ordinary mediation of the modes of discourse which constitute literature. Some of these alterations are even directly produced by the strategy proper to specific literary genres such as poetry. Inscription, then, is only indirectly responsible for the new fate of reference.

Yet despite these reservations, the following may be said. In spoken discourse the ultimate criterion for the referential scope of what we say is the possibility of showing the thing referred to as a member of the situation common to both speaker and hearer. This situation surrounds the dialogue, and its landmarks can all be shown by a gesture or by pointing a finger. Or it can be designated in an ostensive manner by the discourse itself through the oblique reference of those indicators which include the demonstratives, the adverbs of time and place, and the tenses of the verb. Or finally they can be described in such a definite way that one and only one thing may be identified within the common framework of reference. Indeed, the ostensive indicators and, still more, the definite descriptions work in the same way in both oral and written discourse. They provide singular identifications, and singular identifications need not rely on showing in the sense of a gestural indication of the thing referred to. Nevertheless singular identifications ultimately refer to the here and now determined by the interlocutionary situation. There is no identification which does not relate that about which we speak to a unique position in the spatio-temporal network, and there is no network of places in time and space without a final reference to the situational here and now. In this ultimate sense, all references of oral language rely on monstrations which depend on the situation perceived as common by the members of the dialogue. All the references in the dialogical situation are consequently situational.

It is this grounding of reference in the dialogical situation which is shattered by writing. Ostensive indicators and definite descriptions continue to identify singular entities, but a gap appears between identification and monstration. The absence of a common situation generated by the spatial and the temporal distance between writer and reader, the cancellation of the absolute here and now by the substitution of material external marks for the voice, face, and body of the speaker as the absolute origin of all the places in space and time, and the semantic autonomy of the text which severs it from the present of the writer and opens it to an indefinite range of potential readers in an indeterminate time, all these alterations of the temporal constitution of discourse are reflected in parallel alterations of the ostensive character of the reference.

Some texts merely restructure for their readers the conditions of ostensive reference. Letters, travel reports, geographical descriptions, diaries, historical monographs, and in general all descriptive accounts of reality may provide the reader with an equivalent of ostensive reference in the mode of 'as if ...' ('as if you were there'), thanks to the ordinary procedures of singular identification. The heres and theres of the text may be tacitly referred to the absolute here and there of the reader thanks to the unique spatio-temporal network to which both writer and reader ultimately belong and which they both acknowledge.

This first extension of the scope of reference beyond the narrow boundaries of the dialogical situation is of tremendous consequence. Thanks to writing, man and only man has a world and not just a situation. This extension is one more example of the spiritual implications of the substitution of material marks for the bodily support of oral discourse. In the same manner that the text frees its meaning from the tutelage of the mental intention, it frees its reference from the limits of situational reference. For us, the world is the ensemble of references opened up by the texts, or, at least, for the moment, by descriptive texts. It is in this way that we may speak of the Greek 'world,' which is not to imagine anymore what were the situations for those who lived there, but to designate the non-situational references displayed by the descriptive accounts of reality.

A second extension of the scope of reference is much more difficult to interpret. It proceeds less from writing as such than from the open (or sometimes covert) strategy of certain modes of discourse. Therefore it concerns literature more than writing, or writing as the channel of literature. In the construction of his scheme of communication, Roman Jakobson relates the poetic function – which is to be understood in a broader sense than just poetry – to the emphasis of the message for its own sake at the expense of the reference. We have already anticipated this eclipsing of the reference by comparing poetic discourse to a self-contained sculptural work. The gap between situational and non-situational reference, implied in the 'as if' reference of descriptive accounts, is now unbridgeable. This can be seen in fictional narratives, i.e., in narratives that are not descriptive reports. A narrative time, expressed by specific tenses of the verbs, is displayed by and within the narrative without any connection to the unique space-time network common to ostensive and non-ostensive description.

Does this mean that this eclipse of reference, in either the ostensive or descriptive sense, amounts to a sheer abolition of all reference? No. My contention is that discourse cannot fail to be about something. In saying this, I am denying the ideology of absolute texts. Only a few sophisticated texts, along the line of Mallarmé's poetry, satisfy this ideal of a text without reference. But this modern kind of literature stands as a limiting case and an exception. It cannot give the key to all other texts, even poetic texts, in Jakobson's sense, which includes all fictional literature whether lyric or narrative. In one manner or another poetic texts speak about the world. But not in a descriptive way. As Jakobson himself suggests, the reference here is not abolished, but doubled. ('La suprématie de la fonction poétique sur la fonction referentielle n'oblitère pas la référence [la dénotation], mais la rend ambigüe. A un message à double sens correspondent un destinateur dédoublé, un destinataire dédoublé et, de plus, une référence dédoublé.') The effacement of the ostensive and descriptive reference liberates a power of reference to aspects of our being in the world which cannot be said in a direct descriptive way, but only alluded to, thanks to the referential values of metaphoric and, in general, symbolic expression.

We ought, therefore, to enlarge our concept of the world not only to allow for non-ostensive but still descriptive references, but also non-ostensive and non-descriptive references, those of poetic diction. The term *world* then has the meaning that we all understand when we say of a new-born child that he has come into the world. For me, the world is the ensemble of references opened up by every kind of text, descriptive or poetic, that we have read, understood, and loved. And to understand a text is to interpolate among the predicates of our situation all the significations which make a *Welt* out of our *Unwelt*. It is this enlarging of our horizon of existence which permits us to speak of the reference opened up by the text or of the world opened up by the referential claims of most texts.

In this sense, Heidegger rightly says, in his analysis of *Verstehen* in

Being and Time, that what we understand first in a discourse is not another person, but a 'project,' that is, the outline of a new way of being in the world. Only writing – given the two reservations made at the beginning of this section – in freeing itself, not only from its author and from its originary audience, but from the narrowness of the dialogical situation, reveals this destination of discourse as projecting a world.

II. A Plea for Writing

The preceding analysis has reached its goal. It has shown the full manifestation of the nuclear dialectic of event and meaning and of the intentional externalization already at work in oral discourse, although in an inchoative way. But, by pushing it to the forefront, it has made problematic what could be taken for granted as long as it remained implicit. Is not this intentional externalization delivered over to material marks a kind of alienation?

This question is so radical that it requires that we assume in the most positive way the condition of exteriority, not only as a cultural accident, as a contingent condition for discourse and thought, but as a necessary condition of the hermeneutical process. Only a hermeneutic using distanciation in a productive way may solve the paradox of the intentional externalization of discourse.

A. Against Writing

The attack against writing comes from afar. It is linked to a certain model of knowledge, science, and wisdom used by Plato to condemn exteriority as being contrary to genuine reminiscence. (Phaedrus 274e–277a). He presents it in the form of a myth because philosophy here has to do with the coming to being of an institution, a skill, and a power, lost in the dark past of culture and connected with Egypt, the cradle of religious wisdom. The king of Thebes receives in his city the god Theuth, who has invented numbers, geometry, astronomy, games of chance, and *grammata* or written characters. Questioned about the powers and possible benefits of his invention, Theuth claims that the knowledge of written characters would make Egyptians wiser and more capable of preserving the memory of things. No, replies the king, souls will become more forgetful once they have put their confidence in external marks instead of relying on themselves from within. This 'remedy' (*pharmakon*) is not reminiscence, but sheer rememoration. As to instruction, what this invention brings is not the reality, but the resemblance of it; not wisdom but its appearance.

Socrates's commentary is no less interesting. Writing is like painting, which generates non-living being, which in turn keeps silent when asked to answer. Writings, too, if one questions them in order to learn from them, 'signify a unique thing always the same.' Besides this sterile sameness, writings are indifferent to their addressees. Wandering here and there, they are heedless of whom they reach. And if a dispute arises, or if they are injustly despised, they still need the help of their father. By themselves they are unable to rescue themselves.

According to this harsh critique, as the apology for true reminiscence, the principle and soul of right and genuine discourse, discourse accompanied by wisdom (or science), is written in the soul of the one who knows his subject, how to define and divide it, and how to address it to the soul whom he is addressing.

This Platonic attack against writing is not an isolated example in the history of our culture. Rousseau and Bergson, for different reasons, link the main evils which plague civilization to writing. For Rousseau, as long as language relied only on the voice, it preserved the presence of oneself to oneself and others. Language was still the expression of passion. It was eloquence, not yet exegesis. With writing began separation, tyranny, and inequality. Writing ignores its addressee just as it conceals its author. It separates men just as property separates owners. The tyranny of the lexicon and grammar is equal to that of the laws of exchange, crystallized in money. Instead of the word of God, we have the rule of the learned and the domination of the priesthood. The break-up of the speaking community, the partition of the soil, the analycity of thought, and the reign of dogmatism were all born with writing. An echo of Platonic reminiscence may therefore still be heard in this apology for the voice as the bearer of one's presence to oneself and as the inner link of a community without distance.

Bergson directly questions the principle of exteriority, which witnesses to the infiltration of space into the temporality of sound and its continuity. The genuine word emerges from the 'intellectual effort' to fulfil a previous intention of saying, in the search for the appropriate expression. The written word, as the deposit of this search, has severed its ties with the feeling, effort, and dynamism of thought. The breath, song, and rhythm are over and the figure takes their place. It captures and fascinates. It scatters and isolates. This is why authentic creators such as Socrates and Jesus have left no writings, and why the genuine mystics renounce statements and articulated thought.

Once more the interiority of the phonic effort is opposed to the exteriority of dead imprints which are unable to 'rescue' themselves.

B. Writing and Iconicity

The rejoinder to such critiques must be as radical as the challenge. It is no longer possible to rely on just a description of the movement from speaking to writing. The critique summons us to legitimate what has been hitherto simply taken for granted.

A remark made in passing in the *Phaedrus* provides us with an important clue. Writing is compared to painting, the images of which are said to be weaker and less real than living beings. The question here is whether the theory of the *eikon*, which is held to be a mere shadow of reality, is not the presupposition of every critique addressed to any mediation through exterior marks.

If it could be shown that painting is not this shadowy reduplication of reality, then it would be possible to return to the problem of writing as a chapter in a general theory of iconicity such as Dagognet elaborates in his recent book, *Ecriture et Iconicité*.

Far from yielding less than the original, pictorial activity may be characterized in terms of an 'iconic argumentation,' where the strategy of painting, for example, is to reconstruct reality on the basis of a limited optic alphabet. This strategy of contraction and miniaturization yields more, so to speak, by handling less. In this way, the main effect of painting is to resist the entropic tendency of ordinary vision – the shadow image of Plato – and to increase the meaning of the universe by capturing it in the network of its abbreviated signs. This effect of saturation and culmination, within the tiny space of the frame and on the surface of a two-dimensional canvas, in opposition to the optical erosion proper to ordinary vision, is what is meant by iconic argumentation. Whereas in ordinary perception qualities tend to neutralize one another, to blur their edges, to shade off their contrast, painting – at least since the invention of oil-painting by Dutch artists – enhances the contrasts, gives colours back their resonance, and lets appear the luminosity within which things shine. The history of the techniques of painting teaches us that these meaningful effects followed the material invention of pigments made active by being mixed with oil. This selection of what we just called the optic alphabet of the painter allowed him to preserve the colours from diluting and tarnishing and to incorporate the deep refraction of light beneath the mere reflective effect of surface luminosity into his pictures.

Because the painter could master a new alphabetic material – because he was a chemist, distillator, varnisher, and glazer – he was able to write a new text of reality. Painting for the Dutch masters was neither the reproduction nor the production of the universe, but its metamorphosis.

In this respect, the techniques of engraving and etching are equally instructive. Whereas photography – at least unskilled photography – grasps everything, but holds nothing, the magic of engraving, celebrated by Baudelaire, may exhibit the essential because, as with painting, although with other means, it relies on the invention of an alphabet, i.e., a set of minimal signs, made up of syncope points, strokes, and white patches, which enhance the trait and surround it with absence. Impressionism, and abstract art as well, proceed more and more boldly to the abolition of natural forms for the sake of a merely constructed range of elementary signs whose combinatory forms will rival ordinary vision. With abstract art, painting is close to science in that it challenges perceptual forms by relating them to non-perceptual structures. The graphic capture of the universe, here too, is served by a radical denial of the immediate. Painting seems to only 'produce,' no longer to 'reproduce.' But it catches up with reality at the level of its elements, as does the god of the *Timeaus*. Constructivism is only the boundary case of a process of augmentation where the apparent denial of reality is the condition for the glorification of the non-figurative essence of things. Iconicity, then, means the revelation of a real more real than ordinary reality.

This theory of iconicity as esthetic augmentation of reality gives us the key to a decisive answer to Plato's critique of writing. Iconicity is the rewriting of reality. Writing, in the limited sense of the word, is a particular case of iconicity. The inscription of discourse is the transcription of the world, and transcription is not reduplication, but metamorphosis.

This positive value of the material mediation by written signs may be ascribed in writing as in painting to the invention of notational systems presenting analytical properties: discreteness, finite number, combinatory power. The triumph of the phonetic alphabet in Western cultures and the apparent subordination of writing to speaking stemming from the dependence of letters on sounds, however, must not let us forget the other possibilities of inscription expressed by pictograms, hieroglyphs, and, above all, by ideograms, which represent a direct inscription of thought meanings and which can be read differently in different idioms. These other kinds of inscription exhibit a universal character of writing, equally present in phonetic writing, but which the dependence on sounds there tends to dissimulate: the space-structure not only of the bearer of the marks, but of the marks themselves, of their forms, position, mutual distance, order, and linear disposition. The transfer from hearing to reading is fundamentally linked to this transfer from the temporal properties of the voice to the spatial properties of the inscribed marks. This general spatialization of language is complete with the appearance of printing. The visualization of culture begins with the dispossession of the power of the voice in the proximity of mutual presence. Printed texts reach man in solitude, far from the ceremonies which gather the community. Abstract relations, telecommunications in the proper sense of the word, connect the scattered members of an invisible public.

Such are the material instruments of the iconicity of writing and the transcription of reality through the external inscription of discourse.

III. Inscription and Productive Distanciation

We are now prepared for a final step. It will lead us to find in the process of interpretation itself the ultimate justification of the externalization of discourse.

The problem of writing becomes a hermeneutical problem when it is referred to its complementary pole which is reading. A new dialectic then emerges, that of distanciation and appropriation. By appropriation I mean the counterpart of the semantic autonomy which detached the text from its writer. To appropriate is to make 'one's own' what was 'alien.' Because there is a general need for making our own what was foreign to us, there is a general problem of distanciation. Distance, then, is not simply a fact, a given, just the actual spatial and temporal gap between us and the appearance of such-and-such work of art or of discourse. It is a dialectical trait, the principle of a struggle between the otherness which transforms all spatial and temporal distance into cultural estrangement and the ownness by which all understanding aims at the extension of self-understanding. Distanciation is not a quantitative phenomenon; it is the dynamic counterpart of our need, our interest, and our effort to overcome cultural estrangement. Writing and reading take place in this culture struggle. Reading is the *pharmakon*, the 'remedy,' by which the meaning of the text is 'rescued' from the estrangement of distanciation and put in a new proximity, a proximity which suppresses and preserves the cultural distance and includes the otherness within the ownness.

This general problematic is deeply rooted both in the history of thought and in our ontological situation.

Historically speaking, the problem which we are elaborating is the reformulation of a problem to which the eighteenth-century Enlightenment gave its first modern formulation for the sake of classical philology: how to make once more present the culture of antiquity in spite of the intervening cultural distance. German Romanticism gave a dramatic turn to this problem by asking how we can become contemporaneous with past geniuses. More generally, how to use the expressions of life fixed by writing in order to transfer oneself into a foreign psychic life. The problem returns again after the collapse of the Hegelian claim to overcome historicism in the logic of the Absolute Spirit. If there is no recapitulation of past cultural heritages in an all-encompassing whole delivered from the one-sidedness of its partial components, then the historicity of the transmission and reception of these heritages cannot be overcome. Then the dialectic of distanciation and appropriation is the last word in the absence of absolute knowledge.

This dialectic may also be expressed as that of the tradition as such, understood as the reception of historically transmitted cultural heritages. A tradition raises no philosophical problem as long as we live and dwell within it in the naïveté of the first certainty. Tradition only becomes problematic when this first naïveté is lost. Then we have to retrieve its meaning through and beyond estrangement. Henceforth the appropriation of the past proceeds along an endless struggle with distanciation. Interpretation, philosophically understood, is nothing else than an attempt to make estrangement and distanciation productive.

Placed against the background of the dialectic of distanciation and appropriation, the relation between writing and reading accedes to its most fundamental meaning. At the same time, the partial dialectical processes, separately described in the opening section of this essay, following Jakobson's model of communication, make sense as a whole.

Narrated Time

What I have in mind here is a schematic presentation of the interpretation of human time that I formulate at the end of *Time and Narrative III*. That interpretation comes at the end of a long journey which took me through the most noteworthy forms of narrative activity, divided between the history of the historians and narrative fiction, from the epic to the novel. The question to which I am trying to respond is the following: in what way is the ordinary experience of time, borne by daily acting and suffering, refashioned by its passage through the grid of narrative?

The response I offer is prepared at length by an analysis of the operations of configuration that one can assign to narrative activity in the two fields considered. I say nothing here of the rather serious problems met in the parallel exploration – unhappily separated by the requirements of publication – of historical narrative and fictional narrative from the strict point of view of the narrative formation of discourse. There I discuss the question of knowing whether the Aristotelian notion of *muthos*, which I translate as 'emplotment,' can establish the point of comparison appropriate to this dual investigation of configuring activity. Here I wish to concentrate on the set of problems which gravitate, no longer around the *configuration* of time on the formal level of narrative composition, but around the *refiguration* of the time of acting and suffering by narrative considered within the total scope of its discursive expressions. The problem which I pose here is parallel to that which I treat in *The Rule of Metaphor* under the title of metaphorical reference. If, in *Time and Narrative*, I abandon the Fregean vocabulary of sense and reference for that of *configuration* and *refiguration*, it is first of all to avoid the equivocations inevitably raised by the extension to a foreign domain of a vocabulary specifically tied to the descriptive usage of language and to the propositional logic appropriate to that usage; it is, in addition, to place myself from the beginning in the frankly hermeneutic perspective of the *ars applicandi* which, according to Gadamer, follows the *ars comprehendi* and the *ars explicandi*, which I treated in the first parts of that work; finally, the term *refiguration* seems to me to be more appropriate than that of reference because, by reason of its derivation from the term *figure*, it recalls the belongingness of the whole problematic of configuration and refiguration to the preconceptual order of the schematism of the productive imagination. By refiguration I mean, therefore, the power of revelation and transformation achieved by narrative configurations when they are 'applied' to actual acting and suffering. Doubtless one will have recognized, under this particular word, the old problem of *mimesis*, a word which I refrain from rendering by 'imitation,' and whose meaning, and therefore translation, I suspend, to the degree that what is at stake is precisely the meaning which is suitable to attribute to the famous notion of *mimesis praxeos*, which Aristotle joins to that of *muthos*. Hence my question can be formulated thus: what happens to *mimesis praxeos*, to the mimetic activity applied to human action (and suffering), when we make the question of time the touchstone of the meaning of this *mimesis*?

I try to respond to this question with a conversation between three partners – phenomenology, historiography, and literary criticism. The last two have already been called upon to answer the question of knowing if and how the elaborate forms of historical explanation and explanation by the logic of literary narrative allow derivation from the matrix of emplotment, such as our familiarity with particular narratives carried by our culture gives us an initial understanding of it. If historiography and literary criticism are called upon a second time, it is to ask them in what different and complementary manner they refigure what we call reality in a non-critical way. And if a third questioner, in the person of phenomenology, must be introduced here, it is because the reformulation of the problem of reality as revealed and transformed by narrative cannot emerge from a direct confrontation between historiography and narratology. At a first approximation, their dissymmetry might appear to be total, particularly when the problem is stated in terms of reference and referent. We are aware that the ambition of the historian is that his constructions be also more or less approximate reconstructions of events which have actually happened in the past; whereas the novelist, even if, as I have shown in a previous analysis, he projects something like a world of the text, leaves indeterminate the relation between his imaginary worlds and the actual world where the activity of the reader is situated. Put differently, it is with the passage from configuration to refiguration that the difference between history and fiction deepens, without thought being able yet to give a determinate sense to the difference in the relation to the real which is supposed to explain the dissymmetry between history and fiction. It is here that the third partner, the phenomenologist, enters the scene. Not at all, as I had anticipated at the beginning of my investigation, because phenomenology would speak the truth about experience of time in relation to which history and fiction would have to locate themselves in a univocal fashion, but quite the contrary, because phenomenology raises the problem of time to an extreme degree of *aporia*. If my work has any originality, it is to the degree that it succeeds in pointing out, within what one calls the referential aim of history and fiction respectively, two different but complementary replies to the aporias which the phenomenology of time brings to light. This reply is that of a *poetics* to the extent that history and fiction *produce* the resolution that speculation is powerless to contribute to the aporias of time. Hence the strategy of the last part of my work with the title *Narrated Time*. It consists, first of all, in raising the aporia of time to its highest degree by means of phenomenology, then of linking to this aporetic of time the presumed dissymmetry between the respective referential aims of history and fiction so as to exhibit the poetic – or better *poïétique* – quality.

I. The Aporetic of Time

I begin the first volume of *Time and Narrative* with a sketch of the aporetic of time based solely on the Augustinian meditation of Book XI of the *Confessions*. I centre that aporetic on three points: the paradox of the triple present (present of the past, present of the future, present of the present), the paradox of the *distentio animi* and of the *intentio* – a paradox that allows us to characterize time according to Augustine as concordant-discordance, the paradox of the originality of the present, confronted with its indigence in comparison with the fullness of the eternal present.

I deepen that aporetic in two ways in the last part of my work.

First, by pursuing the examination of phenomenology beyond Augustine, specifically in Husserl and Heidegger: then, by showing two series of aporias: those that phenomenology reveals in the experience of time and those which it engenders as phenomenology by virtue of the initial decision to prescind from aspects of time alien to all phenomenology.

I will say little here of things adduced in the phenomenology of time by Husserl and Heidegger. I will dwell more on the aporias that they deepen at the very heart of the experience of time. Concerning the first point, I limit myself to recalling from Husserl: the analysis of retention and protention which prolongs, *mutatis mutandis*, the Augustinian paradox of triple present; the distinction between primary memory and secondary memory of remembrance, which corresponds in its fashion to the paradox of concordant-discordance; the constitution of the unitary form of time by recovery among all the imaginary quasi presents and the living present, a constitution which takes the place of the Augustinian contrast between the human present and the divine present. For brevity also I limit myself to recalling the great achievements of the hermeneutic phenomenology of *Sein und Zeit*: here within the structure of care that principle of temporalization is sought out; direct consequence: beginning with the pole of the future the three *extases* of time – to come/having-been/make-present – are engendered. But the most decisive advance brought about by *Sein und Zeit* appears to me to be the hierarchization of the process of temporalization which Heidegger takes to three successive levels of temporality properly so called – a unification by resoluteness in the face of death; a datable and public historicality recapitulated only in repetition; a within-time–ness splintered and consumed by the preoccupation which gives to the things dispersed under our care a step towards the unified structure of care in its originary and authentic intimacy.

I cannot conceal my admiration for these analyses of a phenomenology ever more refined and aware of the conditions of its own discourse. All the more baffling (and, for a long time, discouraging) was the discovery which I resisted for a long time, namely, that by its very advance phenomenology creates aporias, as if the part of time which it left out of its field increased, to the extent that it internalized itself. A failure to cover the whole problematic of time is already present in Augustine. His ambition to derive the extension of physical time from the simple distention of the soul hit up against the

Aristotelian reef: referring time to movement and to the root of movement, the accomplishment of the unaccomplished of *phusis*. All of which falls outside a psychology of time. It is this initial failure that in my opinion undermines Husserlian phenomenology and perhaps even more so the hermeneutic phenomenology of *Sein und Zeit*. The ambition of Husserl to make time itself a pure experience [*vécu pur*], by the setting aside of objective time, strikes another reef, the Kantian one: it is from Kant that we learned that time as such is invisible, that it could not appear in any living experience, that it is always presupposed as the condition of experience, and from this fact could only appear indirectly on objects apprehended in space and according to the schemata and the categories of objectivity. This constraint explains why the phenomenology of internal time-consciousness must, to be articulated and to be said, borrow its structure from this objective time that the reduction holds in suspense. Paradoxically, it is the heremeneutic phenomenology of *Sein und Zeit* that reveals most completely the inability of phenomenology to engender the very thing it excludes. I say paradoxically: for never has there been such an effort to multiply the levels of temporalization. But this very effort comes up against *the other* of phenomenological time: the 'popular' concept of time, made up of an infinite series of indifferent nows. Even the most decentred level of temporality – within-time-ness – where the 'in' of being in time is highlighted, never rejoins this 'ordinary' time which is simply removed from the phenomenological field by the allegation of an enigmatic levelling of the 'in' of 'within-time–ness.' It seems to me it is in vain that Heidegger puts the whole history of the philosophy of time from Aristotle to Hegel under the pseudoconcept of 'ordinary' time, pretending to be unaware that this is also the time of all the sciences having to do with time and that the sciences have diversified it as geology, biology, thermodynamics, quantum physics, and physical cosmology define the functions of temporal parameters in their respective fields.

Understand me well: this failure of phenomenology is for me the underside of its very success; it is the increasing price you have to pay for an endless radical interiorizing of the internal consciousness of time; time of movement with Aristotle, objective time with Kant, 'ordinary' time with Heidegger – all sciences point, at three different levels of knowledge, to the recognition of *that other* of lived time which the most acute phenomenology never catches up with. Should I add that wisdom from time immemorial has always known this failure? It has always known the disproportion between time that, on the one hand, we deploy in living, and that, on the other, envelops us everywhere. It has always told of the brevity of human life in comparison with the immensity of time. There is the real paradox: on a cosmic scale our life span is insignificant, yet this brief period of time when we appear in the world is the moment during which all meaningful questions arise.

II. Historical Time and the Aporetic of Phenomenological Time

This acknowledgment leads me to the threshold of my main hypothesis – that historical time effects, by specific means, a mediation between the two poles of which the aporetic of time will have shown their non-congruence. To introduce this decisive step, I will adopt the distinction proposed by J.T. Fraser, in his recent work *The Genesis and Evolution of Time* (1982), between two notions of time: a time without a present, resulting from an oriented succession of indifferent instants, and a time with a present, which allows us to determine the before as past and the after as future. The *disproportion* with which we ended the first step of our investigation, and which in a Pascalian mood is intuitively sensed as human misery, finds its conceptual expression in this heterogeneity of the pin-pointed instant and of the living present pregnant with the nearest past and the next future. We have here our announced hypothesis – that historical time is constituted at the juncture of our shattered concept of time. It is this hypothesis that I now wish to put to the test. That historical time is like a bridge thrown over the chasm which separates cosmic time from lived time is attested to by several procedures characteristic of the work of refiguration of time by history. These procedures are familiar to historical practice but remain conceptually unreflected. They draw their meaning from their role of mediation and from the connection they establish between mortal time and the immensity of cosmic time. I shall limit myself here to the examination of three connectors which make of historical time the *tertium quid*, the mixed remembrance. The first of these connectors is calendar time. The institution of the calendar has the remarkable effect of joining determinations of astronomical time with determinations of temporality which Heidegger puts on the level of the historical – which has the extensive, public, and datable character of the temporality of being-there. On the one hand, the calendar is an offshoot of astronomy. On the other, it is an institution in the political sense of the word. Under this double heading, it harmonizes work with days and festivals with the seasons and the years. It integrates the community and its customs into the cosmic order. Benveniste and Dumézil join hands here: the latter underscores the function of order exercised by what he calls the great time which both encompasses and articulates the rhythms of life in society; the former accents the orientation function of what he calls the temporal axis, the year zero, which joins the presentness [*présent présentifié*] of a founding event commemorated by the community with some instant of succession. Here we touch on a fundamental phenomenon, that of *dating*: in assigning to each significant event a place in the ultimate scheme of all possible dates (a reference to and a distance from the temporal axis) calendar time reinscribes lived time as private or common destiny upon cosmic time. This reinscription is the first response of historical practice to the major aporia brought to light by the phenomenology of time. We see later on that it is also the key to the dissymmetric relation between historical time and the time of fiction.

I propose as the second connector the notion of the sequence of generations. Biblical curses and blessings are transmitted from generation to generation. This mediation results from the fact that biological time underlies lived time. At the foundation we find a biological fact, the incessant replacing of the dead by the living at a rhythm of approximately thirty years, marked by the average age of reproduction. Onto this biological phenomenon are grafted two remarkable cultural phenomena which interest both Dilthey and Mannheim – belonging to the same generation and the coexistence of several generations at the same time. This remarkable coincidence of contemporaneity with the non-contemporaneous supports the chain of individual and collective memories. I remember the times in my childhood when my grandfather shared with me memories of his own childhood. In the same way we order the triple reign of contemporaries, predecessors, and successors (to allude to a remarkable study of Alfred Schutz, his *Phenomenology of Social Being*). What I have called the grounding of lived time on biological time is thus added to the *inscription* of lived time upon astronomical time.

I would like to end this second stage through historical time with the examination of the third connector implied by history's recourse to documents and monuments. This connector is nothing but the trace, in the sense in which F. Simiand defines history as knowledge by traces. In this sense I place the trace among the connectors between lived time and physical time by reason of its double, its mixed, nature. What, actually, is a trace? It is, in a primitive sense, a vestige left by the passage of a human being or of an animal. A trace is *left*, a trace *remains*. We speak thus of *remnants* of the past as of remnants from a dinner, or of the relics of a saint or the ruins of an ancient monument. The important point here about the trace is its double status which refers it to two heterogeneous temporal levels. On the first level, the physical, the trace as a substitute must be a *mark* left by something. As such, it is handed over to the contingencies of preservation or of destruction: this is why documents must not only be collected but conserved in archives. As a physical entity, the trace is something of the present. Traces of the past exist now: they are remnants to the extent that they are *still* there, while the past context of the trace – people, institution, actions, passions – no longer exists. It is there that the other face of the phenomenon enters the picture. On a second level, the noetic, there is a trace only for one who can deal with the mark as a present sign of an absent thing, or better, as the present vestige of a passage that exists no longer. A trace, then, is a present thing which stands for [*vaut*] an absent past. The whole enigma of the trace is here. What creates the enigma is the interconnection of a relation of causality with a relation of meaning. To follow a trace, to trace back a trace, is to effect practically the fusion of two sides of the trace, to constitute it as effect-sign. The temporal implication is considerable: to follow a trace is to effect the mediation between the *no-longer* of the passage and the *still* of the mark. At this price we now no longer have to say that the past is something over and done with in any negative sense but can say that it is something that has been and, because of this, is now preserved in the present. The historian as such does not ask himself about the ontological status of the trace; he limits himself to the epistemological problem of *inference*, that is, to the argumentative procedures such as S. Toulmin, for example, discusses in *The Uses of Argument*. This epistemological debate, however, should not eclipse the ontological debate raised by the status of the trace as a present mark standing for an absent past.

This ontological status has been clearly recognized by Heidegger in *Sein und Zeit*, but I do not think that his solution there holds. The past, he says correctly, is not written on the face of a remnant [*vestige*]. The past-character, the 'pastness' [*passéité*] belongs to a world which no longer exists. But a world is always world for *Dasein*. Only because of *having-been-there*, does *Dasein* have a meaning. It is by the levelling of the traits of within-time–ness that we break the connection between the past of things and the *having-been* of *Dasein*. So be it. The difficulty returns precisely whenever one asserts the levelling which separates the pastness of subsisting and manipulable things from the having-been-there of *Dasein* and from the world which belongs to its structure. For how does *Dasein* interpret its having-been-there if not by relying on the autonomy of marks left by the passage of former humans? Heidegger's failure to understand the phenomenon of the trace reflects the failure of *Sein und Zeit* to give an account of the time of the world, which has no care for our care. Therefore the double allegiance of the trace to heterogeneous temporal orders is an original phenomenon. In this, the phenomenon of the trace is affirmed to be kin to the *inscription* of lived time upon astronomical time, from which calendar-time comes, and also kin to the founding of lived time on biological time, from which the sequence of generations comes.

At the conclusion of our second stage, I will say this: the aporetic of time has not been in vain, since it opened the way to the justification of the concept of historical time. Historical time is justified in the sense that it brings about the conjunction of lived time as mortal time and cosmic time, whose immensity escapes us. In this way we have begun – but only begun – to give a poetic response, the response of a *poiesis*, to the aporetic of time. We have, actually, only made a space where it is possible to locate (to oppose first of all, and then to make intersect) the dissymmetrical and heterogeneous truth – claims of the historical and the fictional narrative. Let us begin with the truth-claim of the historical narrative.

III. The Reality of the Historical Past

What do we mean when we say that something has really happened? If the answer is difficult, the question is unavoidable. The intentionality of knowledge cannot deceive us. You need only let yourself be guided by the strong conviction of the historian: whatever one says – and whatever one ought to say – of the relative character of the collecting, of the conserving and consulting of documents (indeed, of the ideological implication of all of these – de Certeau) – the recourse to documents signals a dividing line between history and fiction.

Unlike the novel, the constructions of the historian want to be reconstructions of the past. With the document and by way of documentary proof, the historian is subject to what once happened. He has a *debt* to the past, a debt of recognition of the dead, which makes of him an insolvent debtor. Because of this, he is delegated to remember for all of us. It is indeed this conviction that is expressed in the notion of the trace. In so far as it remains and is *interpreted*, as mentioned above, it represents the past: but not in the same sense that the past would appear in the mind [*Vorstellung*], but in the sense that the trace is a stand-in [*tient lieu*] for the past [*Vertretung*], of the absent past of historical discourse. I risk speaking of place-taking [*lieu-tenance*] to distinguish this relation of *Vertretung* from the relation of *Vorstellung*. It characterizes the *indirect* reference proper to a knowledge by trace, and distinguishes this from all other references to the past.

Let us try to clarify the structure of this relation of representing for which the idea of a reinscription of mortal time upon cosmic time constitutes only a formal framework. That we apprehend the 'pastness' of the past in the two ways of *ne plus* (no longer) and of *encore* (still) suggests that this relation of representing can be approached only in an oblique and dialectical fashion. At the beginning of this dialectic, we have for a guide only the sense of a debt and the vague, unanalyzed idea of a *vis-à-vis*, of a *Gegenüber*, as Karl Heussi says in *Die Krisis des Historismus*. To conceptualize this sense of debt and its correlate, *Gegenüber*, I shall risk using some general categories somewhat like those Plato uses in the *Sophist*. I have thus tried to locate the idea of the '*past-ness*' *of the past* successively within the general categories of the Same, the Other, and the Analogue. By doing this, I give an account of the spontaneous structure of historical intentionality by using the resources of transcendental analysis.

Under the sign of the *Same*, to be brief, I would place the attempt by Collingwood to define the task of the historian by *re-enactment* – the re-effectuation of the past in the present – under the sign of the *Same*. This notion of *re-enactment* in no way takes the place of epistemology. It has no pretension to understanding through empathy. On the level of method, it is perfectly compatible with the exercise of historical imagination. The *re-enactment* defines the historical aim as such, the task of *rethinking* and not of reliving what has once been thought, by calling thought the *inside* [*l'intérieur*] of the event and by including in it the entire field of the motives for action. In this sense, the re-effectuation is indeed the first dialectical moment: that is past which can be rethought, the identity of the first and of the second instance of the same thought. What escapes is the temporal distance dissimulated in the *re-* of the *re-enactment*.

From this comes the dialectical reversal, thinkable precisely as the reversal from the Same to the Other. Under the sign of the Other, I am placing the variants of a negative ontology of the past. The thought of the difference goes back to Dilthey who takes as his model of the past the alien consciousness and as model for understanding of the past the transfer into such a foreign consciousness. This is also the way taken by Aron and Marrou. With the latter an ethics of friendship corrects the agnosticism of the former whose 'shocking' expression is still remembered – the dissolution of the object.

Otherness is deepened when curiosity about the radically different replaces friendship, as we see in Paul Veyne's *L'inventaires de différences*. Otherness is radicalized to a degree when difference is no longer seen as the variable of an invariant (as in Paul Veyne) but as escaping from any kind of subjection to models, as with de Certeau. But if the Other is thought non-dialectically in relation to the Same – I would say in relation to the intent of a *re-enactment* – how would it not remain the unknowable about which one can say nothing and with regard to which we would be freed from all acknowledgment of debt? How could temporal distance be played out as distance *traversed*, to speak like Proust, as distance which transmits – *Überlieferung*? In brief, how could an absence, a difference, a gap, take on the function of substitution [*lieu-tenance*], how could it take the place of what, absent and dead today, once existed and was living?

Hence my third suggestion: to place the pastness of the past under the sign of the Analogue and to try, with Hayden White in *Metahistory* and *Tropics of Discourse*, a tropological approach to the problem. In this way the formula of Leopold Ranke could be reinterpreted: to describe the past *Wie es eigentlich gewesen*. Some have scoffed at the claim to complete integral restitution. They have not perceived the metaphoric import of the *wie: as* this was, in fact. To say *what* things were *as*, is to *see* them *as* ... in a metaphoric relation of assimilation, which brings together identity and difference. Tropology offers in addition the panoply of its tropes – synecdoche, metonymy, irony, to use the ancient classifications that preceded contemporary binarism

– which tropes, by modulating the metaphor, enrich the intent of correspondence without repetition.

Thus the wish of the historian that his constructions be reconstructions is dialectically clarified – and also the sense that he is shouldering for us an unpaid debt: 'render' the painter says, and 'render' says the historian, to give its due to what is no longer but once was. I do not say at all that the pastness of the past thus becomes transparent to us: I am only saying something reasonable about it as I successively think of it under the sign of re-effectuation, as difference or gap, as an analogizing grasp or hold. And what we have called reasonable here must always be restored to the formal schema where lived time is reinscribed upon cosmic time. This latter must always be the formal framework within which we dialectically think pastness as such, what we call in ordinary language the reality of the past, or better yet, the real in the past, the *having been.*

IV. The Conjunction of Fiction and History in the Refiguration of Time

To gauge the risk of this last stage, we must return to the initial dissymmetry between the referential aims of history and fiction.

Let us say first what this dissymmetry is not: it does not imply that only history aims at the 'real.' If that were the case, there would be no problem with the *intersection* of history and fiction in the refiguration of time. We have tried to give a meaning to the idea of the *reality* of the past by our analyses of the reinscription of the trace, then by the dialectic of re-effectuation of the gap and the analogical assimilation. A similar task is indicated on the side of fiction which would give a plausible meaning to the idea of crossed-reference between history and fiction.

First, in a preliminary analysis, starting again with literary criticism, and parallel to what I have done in my first volume *à propos* of historical intentionality, I developed the notion of the *world* of the text. A text, actually, is not a self-enclosed entity. It has not only a formal structure, it points beyond itself to a possible world, a world I could inhabit, where I could actualize my own possibilities in so far as I am in the world. Certainly, this world of the text is still something textual: but it is already an indirect aiming at the real, a mimetic relation by which the text is externalized. The world of the text is a transcendence in the immanence of the text, an outside intended by an inside. Among narrative fictions – my special interest – some have the remarkable property of projecting an experience in which time as such is thematized; these are the 'stories about time,' like the novels of Virginia Woolf, *Mrs. Dalloway, To the Lighthouse, The Waves,* or the *Zauberberg* of Thomas Mann, and of course, *A la recherche du temps perdu* of Proust, to say nothing of the novels of Conrad and Joyce. These works are veritable laboratories for a fictive experience of time. Thus it is in *reading* that the world of the text and the fictive experience of time that emerges from it intersect with the actual world of the reader, the world of my actual acting and suffering. The meaning of the work in the full sense of the word, its significance, if you will, is complete only in that more or less conflictual encounter between the world of the text and the world of the reader. It is at this intersection of a fictive world, already externalized [*exorbité*] with respect to the literary work, and an actual world of action itself mediated by all sorts of symbolic structures, that we find what Gadamer has called the fusion of horizons. This mediation through reading, which I understand as Wolfgang Iser and Robert Jauss (in his *Esthétique de la réception*) do, lets me reconsider the notion of metaphorical redescription that I elaborated in the *Rule of Metaphor*. There I too readily attributed to the poem itself the power of the reader. The literary work, I would now say, redescribes, or better *refigures*, the world only on the condition that there is a critical or naïve appropriation of the world of the text by a reader. Without some go-between who receives the text there is no refiguring of the real world of action. Having said this, I would readily say of narrative fictions what I said regarding lyrical fictions: both teach us to see the world, and more precisely to act and suffer *as* we imagine things in our fictions. Seeing *as* ... is the Spirit [*âme*] common to metaphor and narrative. Narrative fictions can be called *metaphorical* as long as we mean nothing more by this term than the work of seeing as ... which is what narrative fiction achieves in the world [*milieu*] of acting and suffering.

It would be the task of an empirics of receptivity to sketch the typology of the modalities by which narrative is applied to life. That is not our task here. Let me simply say that this *application* – to use the hermeneutical terminology used by Gadamer – must be thought of as revelatory and transforming at the same time. Revelatory, in the sense that it brings out into the open the traits dissimulated but already sketched out at the heart of our practical and empathetic experience; transforming, in the sense that a life thus examined is a life changed, a different life. We reach here a place where the notion of reference no longer functions, and doubtless even less so that of redescription. A place where in order to signify something like a productive reference, the problematic of refiguration must be freed definitively from that of reference.

These are the analyses I made before confronting the specific problem of the *intersection* of the two refigurations of *time* by fiction and history, respectively. Still lacking is a common medium between these two processes of refiguration, the initial dissymmetry which the preceding analyses only sanctioned and reinforced.

It is here that the examination of the original relation of fiction to the aporias of time brought out into the open by phenomenology can reveal the missing link in our investigation. Can we not just say that history and fiction bring two different but complementary responses to the discordance between mortal and cosmic time? The response of history was the reinscription of the former upon the latter by means of specific connectors such as the calendar, the sequence of generations, documents as traces. Would not the response of fiction be to invent imaginative variations with respect to the cosmic reinscription effected by history, imaginative variations on the theme of the fault which separates the two perspectives on time? The detailed study which I have made of *Mrs. Dalloway,* of the *Zauberberg,* and of the *Recherche du temps perdu* has convinced me at least of the plausible character of my hypothesis. It is a matter each time, and in various ways in each work, according to the vision of such or such character, of relating oneself to this fault, of overcoming it otherwise than in the historical mode, or of failing to overcome it, like Septimus in *Mrs. Dalloway* since his failure leads to suicide. If these imaginative variations can be multiplied endlessly, it is because in the kingdom of fiction the specific constraints of historical knowledge have been suspended beforehand – this knowledge that is dependent upon the stringencies of calendar time, of the implacable replacement of the dead by the living, as a counterpart of this lifting of the restraint of reinscription, a greater freedom to explore the unexpressed modalities of discordant-concordance or of the hierarchization of the levels of temporalization. The imaginary here *empowers* the common temporal experience, lightens the burden of the debt towards people of the past, and thus liberates in human acting and suffering the possibilities that were blocked or aborted. The exploration of the possible can thus give free rein to imaginative variations which have the experiental value of eternity, and this in multiple and reduced senses, as one sees in the stories about time of Virginia Woolf, Thomas Mann, and Marcel Proust. A characteristic of the Augustinian experience of time is thus restored, even though differently articulated – the 'eternity experience.' In all these ways, the discovering and transforming power of fiction is in proportion to its derealizing power with respect to the constraints of calendar time and knowledge by traces. This does not mean that other constraints that are more subtle do not bind the imagination – other forms of debt with regard to the vision of the world to which the creator is each time committed.

In a sense this is a new dissymmetry that shows up between history and fiction. But now it is found together with the common problematic that the phenomenology of time has articulated. Phenomenology thus comes as a referee between the documentary reinscriptions characteristic of history and the imaginative variations of fiction. It brings some norm for measuring their successes and their aporias. The successes are like a common cloth on which are embroidered history and fiction, each in its own way. The aporias, as much if not more than the successes, make a place for the ground rules of quite different games, games governing the responses given to these aporias by history, and fiction, respectively. Although dissymetrical, history and fiction are commensurable because of the common bond they have with the phenomenology of time and its battery of aporias.

To conclude I want to test my hypothesis concerning the mediation by phenomenological time and its aporias between the constraint of documentary redescription proper to history and the imaginative variations of fiction in the phenomena of intersection between the respective intentional aims of history and fiction. With an inadequate vocabulary, I introduced in *Time and Narrative I* the notion of crossed-reference. This refers to the exchanges in which history and fiction mediate each other, each accomplishing its aim only by borrowing from the other. It is easy to show that history makes use of fiction and fiction of history as each refigures time. Mediation by fiction was implicit all along our investigation of the intentional aim of history: the role of the imaginary is clearly evident in the non-observable character of the past. The connectors that reinscribe mortal time upon cosmic time are all institutions, inventions that witness to the ingenuity of the productive imagination. The relation in representing or place-taking is no less the work of imagination, as witnessed by the bond between historical imagination and *re-enactment* in Collingwood. There are also imaginary testings in the divergences. Finally and above all, the metaphorical relation of present consciousness to the 'having-been.' But I would like to give a new illustration of this mediation of knowledge of the past through fiction. When the expression of our debt to the dead takes on the colour of indignation, of lamentation, or compassion, the reconstruction of the past needs the help of imagination that can place it 'right before our eyes,' according to a very striking expression of Aristotle in speaking of metaphor. I would like to mention here those *horrible* events which we must not forget. It is true that there is something like an individuation in the horrible as well as in the admirable. Help with this comes nowhere more than from the quasi intuitivity of the imaginary. Fiction gives eyes to the horrified narrator. Eyes to bear witness as much as to weep. The present state of Holocaust literature verifies this. We get either an unreliable body count or the tales of the victims. In thus joining history, fiction leads this latter back to their common matrix, the epic. More precisely, what the epic does for the admirable, the stories of the victims do for the horrible. But the carefully guarded illusion is but a detour (compelled by modesty) of the memory of suffering – the highest form of the debt.

Does fiction have traits that favour its *historization* similar to the traits of history (due to the characteristics I have just mentioned) that call for a kind of *fictionalization* on behalf of its intention to represent the past? I think so. I even believe that these traits reinforce the convergence of fiction and history in the refiguration of time. There is a sense in which fiction imitates the historical narrative. To tell any story whatsoever is, in effect, to tell it as if it were past. A strong indication that this *as if*, essential to the efficacy of fictional narrative, is of the grammatical order. It is a fact that narratives are told about past times.

The 'once upon a time' in the story marks the door to narrative. We can certainly turn the words around and say with Harold Weinrich in *Tempus* that the use of past tenses signals to the reader only the entrance into narrative. There is still the fact that these tenses are also those of memory and history. The relation here cannot be purely contingent. Does it not account for the fact that fictive things, in their telling, are considered as quasi past? But for whom? I suggest this: they are such for the *narrative voice* which we can take here as identical with the implied author, that is, a fictional disguise for the real author. A voice speaks which tells what *for it* has taken place. To enter into fiction is to include within the pact with the reader the belief that the events related by the narrative voice belong to the past of that voice.

The interpretation which I propose here of the quasi-historical character of fiction cross-checks with what I propose concerning the quasi-fictional character of the historical past. It is because of its quasi-historical character that fiction can exercise its liberating function with respect to possible hidden elements in the actual past. What 'could have taken place' – the object of poetry as opposed to history according to Aristotle – fuses the potentialities of the 'real' past and the 'irreal' possibilities of pure fiction.

This profound kinship between the quasi past of fiction and the 'unrealized' potentialities of the historical past explains, perhaps, why, as we suggested above, the liberation of fiction from the constraints of history is not the last word concerning the freedom of fiction. It is only the Cartesian moment: the free choice in the kingdom of the imaginary. But is not fiction's rapport with the quasi past the source of more subtle constraints which indicate the Spinozist moment of freedom – interior necessity? Free *from* the exterior constraint of documentary proof, must not the creator still make himself free *for* – on behalf of the quasi past? If this were not the case, how would we explain the anguish and the sufferings of artistic creation? Does not the quasi past of the narrative voice bring an interior constraint to novelistic creation – all the more telling if it is not confused with the exterior constraint of documentary fact? And the harsh law of creation – to 'render' in the most perfect way the vision of the world that inspires the narrative voice – does it not simulate almost perfectly the debt that history owes to men of the past, to the dead? Debt for debt, which is more unpayable – that of the historian or that of the novelist?

Whatever we make of these questions, it is in the intersection of history and fiction in the refiguration of time that we discover or invent – its all the same – what we might suitably call *human time*. Human time, that fragile mix where the representing of the past of history and the imaginative variations of fiction are joined against a background of the aporias of the phenomenology of time.

Time Traversed:
Remembrance of Things Past

Are we justified in looking for a 'tale about time' in *Remembrance of Things Past*?[1]

This has been contested, paradoxically, in a number of different ways. I shall not linger over the confusion, which contemporary criticism has dispelled, between what might be considered a dissimulated autobiography of Marcel Proust, the author, and the fictional autobiography of the character who says 'I.' We now know that if the experience of time can be what is at stake in a novel, this is not due to what the novel borrows from the experience of its real author but rather to literary fiction's power to create a narrator-hero who pursues a certain quest of him/herself, in which what is at stake is, precisely, the dimension of time. It remains to be determined in just what sense this is so. Regardless of the partial homonymy between 'Marcel,' the narrator-hero of *Remembrance*, and Marcel Proust, the author of the novel, the novel does not owe its fictional status to the events of Proust's life, which may have been transposed to the novel and have left their scar there, but to the narrative composition alone, which projects a world in which the narrator-hero tries to recapture the meaning of an earlier life, itself wholly fictive. Time lost and time regained are thus to be understood together as the features of a fictive experience unfolded within a fictive world.

My first reading hypothesis will therefore be to consider, uncompromisingly, the narrator-hero as a fictive entity supporting the tale about time that constitutes *Remembrance*.

A more forceful way of challenging the exemplary value of *Remembrance* as a tale about time is to say, with Gilles Deleuze in *Proust and Signs*, that what is principally at stake in *Remembrance* is not time but truth.[2] This challenge grows out of the very strong argument that 'Proust's work is based not on the exposition of memory, but on the apprenticeship to signs' (p. 4) – signs of the social world, signs of love, sensuous signs, signs of art. If, nevertheless, 'it is called a search for lost time, it is only to the degree that truth has an essential relation to time' (p. 15). To this I would reply that this mediation by means of the apprenticeship to signs and the search for truth is in no way damaging to the characterization of *Remembrance* as a tale about time. Deleuze's argument undercuts only those inter- pretations that have understood *Remembrance* solely in terms of the experiences of involuntary memory and that, for this reason, have overlooked the long apprenticeship to disillusionment that gives *Remembrance* the scope that is lacking in the brief and fortuitous experiences of involuntary memory. If the apprenticeship to signs imposes the long, circuitous path that *Remembrance* substitutes for the shortcut of involuntary memory, this interpretation does not, in its turn, exhaust the meaning of *Remembrance*. The discovery of the extratemporal dimension of the work of art constitutes an eccentric experience in relation to the entire apprenticeship to signs. As a result, if *Remembrance* is a tale about time, it is so to the extent that it is identified neither with involuntary memory nor with the appren- ticeship to signs – which, indeed, does take time – but poses the problem of the *relation* between these two levels of experience and the incomparable experience that the narrator puts off and finally reveals only after almost three thousand pages.

The singular character of *Remembrance* is due to the fact that the apprenticeship to signs, as well as the irruption of involuntary memo- ries, represents the form of an interminable wandering, interrupted rather than consummated, by the sudden illumination that retro- spectively transforms the entire narrative into the invisible history of a vocation. Time becomes something that is at stake again as soon as it is a question of making the inordinately long apprenticeship to signs correspond to the suddenness of a belatedly recounted visita- tion, which retrospectively characterizes the entire quest as lost time.[3]

From this follows my second reading hypothesis. In order to avoid granting an exclusive privilege either to the apprenticeship to signs, which would deprive the final revelation of its role as a hermeneuti- cal key for the entire work, or to the final revelation, which would divest the thousands of pages preceding the revelation of any signifi- cation and eliminate the very problem of the relation between the quest and the discovery, the cycle of *Remembrance* must be represented in the form of an ellipse, one focus being the search and the second the visitation. *The tale about time is then the tale that creates the relation between these two foci of the novel.* The originality of *Remembrance* lies in its having concealed both the problem and its solution up to the end of the hero's course, thus keeping for a second reading the intelligibility of the work as a whole.

A third, even more forceful way of undercutting the claim that *Remembrance* constitutes a tale about time is to attack as Anne Henry does in *Proust romancier: Le Tombeau égyptien*, the primacy of the narrative itself in *Remembrance* and to see in the novel form the projection, on the plane of anecdote, of a philosophical knowledge forged elsewhere and therefore external to the narrative.[4] According to the author of this brilliant study, the 'dogmatic corpus that was to support the anecdote at every point' (p. 6) is to be sought nowhere but in German Romanticism, in particular the philosophy of art first proposed by Schelling in *The System of Transcendental Idealism*,[5] then continued by Schopenhauer in *The World as Will and Representation*,[6] and finally, reworked in psychological terms in France by Proust's philosophy teachers, Séailles, Darlu, and, especially, Tarde. Considered on its narrative level, the work therefore rests on a 'theoretical and cultural base' (Henry, p. 19) that precedes it. The important thing to us here is that what is at stake for this philosophy that governs the narrative process from outside is not time but what Schelling called 'Identity,' that is, the suppression of the division between the mind and the material world, their reconciliation in art, and the necessity of establishing the metaphysical evidence of this in order to provide it with a lasting and concrete form in the work of art. *Remembrance*, is, as a result, not only a fictive autobiography – everyone agrees on this today – but a feigned novel, the 'novel of *Genius*' (pp. 23ff., her emphasis). This is not all. Among the theoretical prescriptions governing the work is the psychological transposition undergone by the dialectic in order to become a novel – a transposition that also belongs to the epistemological base preceding the construction of the novel. What is more, in the opinion of Anne Henry, this transfer of the dialectic to the psychological plane indicates less a new conquest than a deterioration of the Romantic heritage. So if the passage from Schelling to Tarde by way of Schopenhauer explains that lost unity, according to Romanticism, could have become lost time, and that the double redemption of the world and the subject could have been transmuted into the rehabilitation of an individual past. In short, if, in a general manner, memory could have become the privileged mediator for the birth of genius, the fact must not be concealed that this translation of the combat to within one consciousness expresses the collapse as much as the continuation of the great philosophy of art received from German Romanticism.

My recourse to Proust to illustrate the notion of the fictive experience of time is thus doubly contested. Not only does the theoretical core, with regard to which the novel is held to be a demonstration, subordinate the question of time to a higher question, that of identity lost and recovered, but the passage from lost identity to lost time presents the scars of a shattered belief. By tying the promotion of the psychological, of the self, of memory, to the deterioration of great metaphysics, Anne Henry tends to disparage all that has to do with the novel as such. The fact that the hero of the quest is a bourgeois leading a life of leisure, dragging his boredom from one unhappy love to another, and from one silly salon to another, expresses an impoverishment corresponding to the 'translation of the combat within a consciousness' (p. 46). 'A life that is flat, bourgeois, never shaken by cataclysms ... offers the ideal mediocrity for an experimental type of narrative' (p. 56).[7] A remarkably vigorous reading of *Remembrance* results from this suspicion that saps from within the prestige of the narrative genre as such. Once the major stake has been shifted from lost unity to lost time, all the prestige attaching to the novel of genius loses its lustre.

Let us admit, provisionally, this thesis that *Remembrance* is generated out of the 'transposition of the system into a novel.' The problem of narrative *creation* thereby becomes, in my opinion, all the more enigmatic and its solution all the more difficult. Paradoxically, we return here to an explanation in terms of sources. We have, of course, done away with a naïve theory of elements borrowed from Proust's life, but only to end up with a more subtle theory of elements borrowed from Proust's thought. The birth of *Remembrance* as a novel requires instead that we look in the narrative composition itself for the principle of the narrative's acquisition of 'allogenic speculations,' coming from Séailles and Tarde as well as from Schelling and Schopenhauer. The question is then no longer how the philosophy of lost unity could have degenerated into a quest for lost time but how the search for lost time, taken as the founding matrix of the work, accomplishes, through strictly narrative means, the recovery of the Romantic problematic of lost unity.[8]

What are these means? The only way to reintegrate the 'allogenic speculations' of the author into the narrative work is to attribute to the narrator-hero not only a fictive experience but 'thoughts' that form its sharpest reflexive moment.[9] Have we not recognized, since Aristotle's *Poetics*, that dianoia is a major component of poetic muthos? Moreover, narrative theory offers us irreplaceable assistance here, and this will become my third reading hypothesis, namely, the resource of distinguishing several narrative voices in the fiction of the narrator.

Remembrance makes us hear at least two narrative voices, that of the hero and that of the narrator.

The hero tells his worldly, amorous, sensuous, aesthetic adventures as they occur. Here, utterance takes the form of a march directed towards the future, even when the hero is reminiscing; hence the form of the 'future in the past' that launches *Remembrance* towards its dénouement. And it is the hero again who receives the revelation of the sense of his past life as the invisible history of a vocation. In this respect, it is of the greatest importance to distinguish between the hero's voice and that of the narrator, not only to place the hero's memories themselves back into the stream of a search that advances, but in order to preserve the event-like character of the visitation.

However, we must also be able to hear the voice of the narrator, who is ahead of the hero's progress because he surveys it from above. It is the narrator who, more than a hundred times, says, 'as we shall see later.' But, above all, the narrator gives the meaning to the experience recounted by the hero – time regained, time lost. Before the final revelation, his voice is so low that it can barely be distinguished from the hero's voice (which authorizes us to speak of the narrator-hero).[10] This is no longer the case in the course of and following the narrative of the great visitation. The narrator's voice takes over to such an extent that it ends up covering over that of the hero. The homonymy of the author and the narrator is then given free reign, at the risk of making the narrator the spokesman for the author in his great dissertation on art. But even then, it is the narrator's exposition of the author's conceptions as his own that is at issue for our reading. His conceptions are then incorporated into the narrator's thoughts. These thoughts of the narrator, in their turn, accompany the hero's lived experience and shed light on it. In this way, they participate in the event-like character of the birth of the writer's vocation as it is lived by the hero.

In order to put these reading hypotheses to the test, let us ask a series of three questions: 1 / What would be the signs of time lost and time regained for the reader who is unaware of the conclusion to *Remembrance*, which we know was written during the same period as *Swann's Way*, in *Time Regained*? 2 / By what precise narrative means are the speculations on art in *Time Regained* incorporated into the invisible history of a vocation? 3 / What relation does the project of the work of art, stemming from the discovery of the writer's vocation, establish between time regained and time lost?

The first two questions place us in turn in each of the two foci of *Remembrance*, and the third allows us to bridge the gap separating them. It is on the basis of the third question that the interpretation I am proposing for *Remembrance of Things Past* will be decided.

Time Lost

The reader of *Swann's Way* – lacking the retrospective illumination projected by the end of the novel onto its beginning – has as yet no way to compare the bedroom in Combray, where, between waking and sleeping, a consciousness experiences the loss of its identity, its time, and its place, to the library in the Guermantes home, where an excessively vigilant consciousness receives a decisive illumination. On the other hand, this reader could not help but notice certain singular features of this opening section. From the very first sentence, the narrator's voice, speaking out of nowhere, evokes an earlier time that has no date, no place, a time that lacks an indication of distance in relation to the present of the utterance, an earlier time that is endlessly multiplied. (The uniting of the compound past with the adverb *longtemps* has been commented upon time and time again: 'For a long time I used to go to bed early [*Longtemps, je me suis couché de bonne heure*]. Sometimes ...' [I: 3].) In this way the beginning for the narrator refers back to an earlier time that has no boundaries (the only conceivable chronological beginning, the birth of the hero, cannot appear in this duo of voices). It is in this earlier time, in the zone between waking and sleeping, where childhood memories are set away, that the narrative moves two steps away from the absolute present of the narrator.[11]

These memories express themselves in reference to a unique episode, the experience of the madeleine, an episode which itself is characterized by a before and an after. Before it are only archipelagos of unrelated memories; the only thing that emerges is the memory of a certain goodnight kiss, itself placed against the backdrop of a daily ritual:[12] mother's kiss refused at the arrival of M. Swann; kiss awaited in anguish; kiss begged for still as the evening comes to an end; kiss obtained at last but immediately divested of the expected happiness.[13] For the first time, the narrator's voice is heard distinctly. Evoking the memory of his father, the narrator observes, 'Many years have passed since that night. The wall of the staircase up which I had watched the light of his candle gradually climb was long ago demolished ... It is a long time, too, since my father has been able to say to Mamma: "Go along with the child." Never again will such moments be possible for me' (I: 39–40). The narrator thus speaks of time lost in the sense of time gone, abolished. But he also speaks of time regained. 'But of late I have been increasingly able to catch, if I listen attentively, the sound of the sobs which I had the strength to control in my father's presence, and which broke out only when I found myself alone with Mamma. In reality their echo has never ceased; and it is only because life is now growing more and more quiet round about me that I hear them anew, like those convent bells which are so effectively drowned during the day by the noises of the street that one would suppose them to have stopped, until they ring out again through the silent evening air' (I: 40). Without the recovery of the same thoughts at the end of *Time Regained*, would we recognize the dialectic of time lost and time regained in the barely audible voice of the narrator?

Then comes the episode of the overture – told in the preterite – the experience of the madeleine (I: 48). The transition with its aftermath is made by means of a remark by the narrator on the incapacities of voluntary memory and on leaving to chance the task of rediscovering the lost object. For someone who is unaware of the final scene in the Guermantes library, which expressly connects the recovery of lost time to the creation of a work of art, the experience of the madeleine may misdirect readers and put them on the wrong track, if they do not set aside, within their own expectations, all of the reticences that go along with the evocation of this happy moment. 'An exquisite pleasure had invaded my senses, something isolated, detached, with no suggestion of its origin' (ibid.). From this arises the question, 'Whence could it have come to me, this all-powerful joy? I sensed that it was connected with the taste of the tea and the cake, but that it infinitely transcended those savours, could not, indeed, be of the same nature. Whence did it come? What did it mean? How could I seize and apprehend it?' (ibid.). Posed in this way, however, the question holds within it the trap of an overly brief reply, which would simply be that of involuntary memory.[14] If the answer given by this 'unknown state were fully accounted for by the sudden rush of memory of the first little madeleine offered long ago by Aunt Leonie, then *Remembrance* would already have reached its goal when it had only just got underway. It would be limited to the quest for similar reawakenings, of which the least we could say is that they do not require the labour of art. That this is not the case is conveyed by a single clue that speaks to the reader with a keen ear. It is a parenthesis and it says '(although I did not yet know and must long postpone the discovery of why this memory made me so happy)' (I: 51). It is only on a second reading, instructed by *Time Regained*, that these remarks, bracketed by the narrator, will take on meaning and force.[15] Nevertheless they are already perceptible on a first reading, even if they offer only a weak resistance to the hasty interpretation according to which the fictive experience of time in Proust would consist in equating time regained with involuntary memory, held to superimpose spontaneously two distinct but similar impressions owing to chance alone.[16]

If the ecstasy of the madeleine is no more than a premonitory sign of the final revelation, it at least already possesses certain of its qualities, opening up the door to memory and allowing the first sketch of *Time Regained*: the Combray narrative (I: 52–204). For a reading not acquainted with *Time Regained* the transition to the Combray narrative seems to partake of the most naïve of narrative conventions, even if it does not seem artificial and rhetorical. For a second, more educated reading, the ecstasy of the madeleine opens up the recaptured time of childhood just as the meditation in the library will open up that of the time when the vocation, recognized at last, is put to the test. The symmetry between the beginning and the end is thus revealed to be the guiding principle of the entire composition. If Combray springs out of a cup of tea (I: 51), just as the narrative of the madeleine emerges out of the state between waking and sleeping experienced in a bedroom, it does so in the way that the meditation in the library will govern the chain of subsequent experiences. This series of insets that govern the narrative composition does not prevent consciousness from advancing. To the confused consciousness of the first pages – 'I was more destitute than the cave-dweller' (I: 5) – replies the state of a consciousness that is awake, when the day dawns (I: 204).

I do not want to leave the section on 'Combray' without having attempted to say what it is in the childhood memories that carries us away from speculation about involuntary memory and already directs our interpretation in the direction of an apprenticeship to signs, without for all that making this apprenticeship to disconnected aspects fit too easily within the history of a vocation.

Combray is first and foremost its church, 'epitomising the town' (I: 52). On the one hand, it imposes on everything that surrounds it, owing to its enduring stability,[17] the dimension of a time that has not vanished but that has been traversed. On the other hand, through its stained glass and tapestry figures, through its gravestones, it imparts to all living beings that the hero meets the general character of images to be deciphered. Along with this, the fact that the young hero is constantly absorbed in books tends to make the image the privileged access to reality (I: 91).

Combray is also the encounter with the writer Bergotte (the first of the three artists to be introduced in the narrative, in accordance with a carefully planned progression, long before Elstir, the painter, and Vinteuil, the musician). The encounter contributes to transforming surrounding objects into beings to be read.

In particular, however, the time of childhood continues to be made up of scattered islands, just as incommunicable among themselves as the two 'ways,' that of the Méséglise, which turns out to be that of Swann and Gilberte, and that of the Guermantes, that of the fabulous names of an out-of-reach aristocracy, especially that of Madame de Guermantes, the first object of an inaccessible love. Georges Poulet is correct to draw a sharp parallel here between the incommunicability of the islands of temporality and that of the sites, places, beings.[18] Distances that cannot be measured separate the instants evoked as much as the places traversed.

Combray is also, in contrast to the happy moments, the reminder of some events that foreshadow disillusionment, the meaning of which is postponed until a later inquiry.[19] Thus the Montjouvain scene, between Mlle de Vinteuil and her friend, where the hero, who is shown to be a voyeur, is introduced for the first time into the world of Gomorrah. It is not without importance for the subsequent understanding of the notion of lost time that this scene contains some abominable features: Mlle de Vinteuil spitting on her father's portrait, set on a small table in front of the sofa. A secret tie is thus established between this profanation and lost time, but it is too deeply hidden to be perceived. The reader's attention is directed instead to the reading of signs by the voyeur and his interpretation of the intimations of desire. More precisely, as a result of this strange episode, the art of deciphering is guided towards what Deleuze calls the second circle of signs, that of love.[20] The evocation of *The Guermantes Way* also acts as a springboard for a reflection on signs and their interpretation. Guermantes represents, first of all, fabulous names attaching to the tapestry and stained-glass figures. With an almost imperceptible touch, the narrator connects up this oneirism of names with the premonitory signs of the vocation that *Remembrance* is said to recount. Yet these dream thoughts, like his reading of Bergotte, create a sort of barrier, as if the artificial creations of dreams revealed the emptiness of his own talent.[21]

And if the impressions collected during walks also create an obstacle to the artist's vocation, this is so to the extent that material exteriority seems to govern them, maintaining 'the illusion of a sort of fecundity' (I: 195) which spares one the effort of seeking what 'lay hidden beneath them' (ibid.). The episode of the Martinville steeples, which corresponds to the experience of the madeleine, draws its meaning precisely from this contrast with the excessive richness of ordinary impressions, just as is the case with recurrent dreams. The promise of something hidden, something to be looked for and found, is closely associated with the 'special pleasure' (I: 195) of the impression. These walks themselves guide the search. 'I did not know the reason for the pleasure I had felt on seeing them upon the horizon, and the business of trying to discover that reason seemed to me irksome; I wanted to store away in my mind those shifting, sunlit planes and, for the time being, to think of them no more' (I: 197). This is, however, the first time that the search for meaning goes first by way of words and then by way of writing.[22]

Regardless of the remarks, still quite infrequent and entirely negative, relating to the history of a vocation, and, in particular, regardless of the hidden relation between this vocation and the two happy episodes connected to Combray, what seems to dominate the still inchoate experience of time in the section on Combray is the impossibility of co-ordinating the bundles of undated events,[23] which are compared to 'the deepest layer of my mental soil' (I: 201). An indistinct mass of memories, which only something resembling 'real fissures, real geological faults' (I: 201) can make distinct. In sum, the lost time of Combray is the lost paradise in which 'the faith which creates' (I: 201) cannot yet be distinguished from the illusion of the bare and silent reality of external things.

It is doubtless in order to stress the character of autobiographical fiction of *Remembrance* as a whole that the author decided to intercalate 'Swann in Love' – that is, third-person narrative – between 'Combray' and 'Place-Names,' which are both first-person narratives. At the same time, the illusion of immediacy that may have been produced by the childhood narratives, due to their classical charm, is broken by this emigration of the narrative into another character. In addition, 'Swann in Love' constructs the diabolical mechanism of a love gnawed away by illusion, suspicion, disappointment; a love condemned to pass through the anguish of expectation, the bite of jealousy, the sorrow accompanying its decline, and the indifference that meets its death. This construction will serve as a model for the narration of other loves, in particular the hero's love for Albertine. It is due to this role of paradigm that 'Swann in Love' says something about time.

There is no point in insisting on the fact that the narrative is not dated. It is loosely connected to the reveries, which are themselves relegated to an indeterminate past by the sleepy narrator who speaks in the opening pages of the book.[24] In this way, the narrative of 'Swann in Love' is set within the hazy memories of childhood, as what occured before birth. The artifice suffices to break the chronological line once and for all and to open the narrative up to other qualities of past time, indifferent to dates. More important is the distension of the tie between this narrative and the history of a vocation, held to govern *Remembrance* as a whole. This tie occurs on the level of the 'association of memories,' referred to at the end of the 'Combray' section. The little phrase of Vinteuil's sonata appears to serve as a relay station between the experience of the madeleine (and the Martinville steeples) and the revelation of the final scene, due to its repeated appearances in the hero's story, reappearances that are reinforced in *The Captive* by the memory of Vinteuil's septet, the forceful homology to this little phrase.[25] This function of the musical phrase in the unity of the narrative may remain unperceived due to the close tie between the phrase and Swann's love for Odette. It is as someone who has fallen in love with the musical phrase (I: 231) that Swann clings to his memory. And this memory, henceforth, is too closely tied up with his love for Odette to provoke the interrogation contained in its promise of happiness. The entire field is occupied by a more pressing interrogation, pushed to the point of frenzy, one which is constantly generated by jealousy. The apprenticeship in the Verdurin salon to the signs of love, interwoven with that of the signs of society, is alone capable of making the search for lost time coincide with the search for truth, and lost time itself coincide with the defection that ravages love. Nothing, therefore, allows us to interpret lost time in terms of some time regained, the evocation of the phrase itself still being rooted in the soil of love. As for the 'passion for truth' (I: 298) which is mobilized by jealousy, nothing allows it to be crowned with the prestige of time recaptured. Time is quite simply lost in the twofold sense of being over and done with and of having been scattered, dispersed.[26] At the very most, all that might suggest the idea of time regained would be either the weight accorded to a few rare moments when memory 'joined the fragments together, abolished the intervals between them' (I: 342), characterizing a time in tatters, or the quietude of a secret vainly pursued at the time of jealousy and finally pinned down at the time when love has died (I: 346). The apprenticeship to signs would then come to an end in this context once a certain detachment is attained.

It is worthwhile to look at the way in which the third part of *Swann's Way*, entitled 'Place Names: The Name' (I: 416–62), links up with what precedes it concerning the interconnection of time spans.[27] For, indeed, the same 'long nights of sleeplessness' (I: 416) that were recalled in order to serve as a setting for the childhood narratives associated with Combray are also used here in order to connect, in the dreamlike memory, the rooms at the Grand Hotel of Balbec beach with the rooms at Combray. It is therefore not surprising that a dream of Balbec precedes the real Balbec, at a period in the hero's adolescence when names foreshadow things and state reality before all perception. Thus are the names of Balbec, Venice, Florence, generators of images and, through images, of desire. At this stage of the narrative, what can readers make of this 'imaginary time' in which several voyages are gathered together under a single name? (I: 425–6). They can only keep it in the back of their minds, once the Champs-Elysées, quite real enough, and the games with Gilberte hide the dreams from sight: 'in this public garden there was nothing that attached itself to my dreams' (I: 427). Is this hiatus between the 'similacrum' of an imaginary realm (ibid.) and reality another figure of lost time? Undoubtedly. The difficulty in joining this figure and all the others that follow to the general story-line is made even greater by the absence of any apparent identity between the earlier characters of Swann and, especially, of Odette – who could be thought to have 'disappeared' at the end of the intermediary third-person narrative – and the Swann and Odette who turn out to be Gilberte's parents, at the period when the hero plays in the park near the Champs-Elysées.[28]

For the reader who breaks off the reading of *Remembrance* at the last page of *Swann's Way*, lost time would be summed up in 'how paradoxical it is to seek in reality for pictures that are stored in one's memory, which must inevitably lose the charm that comes to them from memory itself and from their not being apprehended by the senses' (I: 462). *Remembrance* itself would seem to be limited to a hopeless struggle to combat the ever-increasing gap that generates forgetfulness. Even the happy moments at Combray, where the distance between the present impression and the past impression is magically transformed into a miraculous contemporaneousness, could appear to have been swallowed up in the same devastating oblivion. These moments of grace will never be brought up again – except in one instance – after the pages on 'Combray.' Only the savour of the phrase of Vinteuil's sonata – a savour we know only through a narrative within a narrative – carries with it another promise. But a promise of what? This enigma, just as the enigma of the happy moments at Combray, can be solved only by the reader of *Time Regained*.

In the long deciphering of the signs of the world, of love, and of sensory impressions, extending from *Within a Budding Grove* to *The Captive*, only the way of disillusionment remains open before this turn-about.

Time Regained

Let us now move in one fell swoop to *Time Regained*, the second focal point of the great ellipse of *Remembrance of Things Past*, saving for the third stage of our investigation the interval, enormously amplified, that separates these two foci.

What does the narrator mean by time regained? To attempt to reply to this question, we shall take advantage of the symmetry between the beginning and the end of the great narrative. Just as the experience of the madeleine in *Swann's Way* marks a before and an after, the before of the state between waking and sleeping and the after of the time regained with respect to Combray, the great scene in the Guermantes library demarcates, in its turn, a before to which the narrator has given significant amplitude and an after in which the ultimate signification of *Time Regained* is discovered.

It is not actually *ex abrupto* that the narrator relates the event marking the birth of a writer. He prepares for the illumination by passing through the two initiatory stages. The first, which takes up by far the greatest number of pages, is made up of a mist of events that are poorly co-ordinated among themselves, at least in the state in which the unfinished manuscript of *Time Regained* was left to us, but which all bear the double sign of disillusionment and detachment.

It is significant that *Time Regained* begins with the narrative of a stay in Tansonville, not far from the Combray of childhood, the effect of which is not to rekindle memory but to extinguish desire.[29] In the moment, the hero is moved by this loss of curiosity, to such an extent it seems to confirm the feeling once experienced in the same place 'that I would never be able to write' (III: 709). One must give up an attempt to relive the past if lost time is ever, in some as yet unknown way, to be found again. This death of the desire to see things again is accompanied by the death of the desire to possess the women he has loved. It is noteworthy that the narrator considers this 'incuriosity' to be 'brought by Time,' the personified entity that will never be assigned wholly either to lost time or to eternity, and which to the end will be symbolized, as in the adages of ancient wisdom, by its power of destruction. I shall return to this at the end of our discussion.

All of the events recounted, all the encounters reported in what follows, are placed under the same sign of decline, of death. Gilberte's narrative of the poverty of her relations with Saint-Loup, now her husband; the visit to the church in Combray, where the power of what endures accentuates the precariousness of mortal beings; and, especially, the sudden mention of the 'long years' that the hero has spent in a sanatorium, contributing a realistic aspect to the feeling of separateness and of distanciation required by the final vision.[30] The description of Paris at war adds to the impression of erosion that affects everything.[31] The frivolity of Parisian drawing-rooms has an air of decadence about it (III: 746–7). The campaigns for and against Dreyfus have been forgotten. Saint-Loup's visit, home from the front lines, is that of a ghost; we learn of Cottard's death, then of the death of M. Verdurin. The chance encounter with M. de Charlus in a Paris street during the war places on this sinister initiation the seal of a deadly abjection. From the degradation of his body, of his loves, rises a strange poetry (III: 789) which the narrator ascribes to a complete detachment, something the hero is not yet able to attain. (III: 799). The scene in Jupien's bordello, where the baron has himself whipped with a chain by soldiers on leave, reduces the painting of a society at war to its quintessence of abjection. The interconnection in the narrative between Saint-Loup's last visit, rapidly followed by the news of his death – evoking another death, that of Albertine[32] – and the narrative of Charlus's ultimate turpitudes, leading to his arrest, gives these pages the tone of a funereal maelstrom, which will again prevail, although with an entirely different signification, in the symmetrical scene that follows the great revelation, the scene of the dinner surrounded by death's-heads, the first test of the hero converted to eternity.

To stress once again the sort of nothingness that surrounds the revelation, the narrator introduces a sharp break in his story. 'The new sanatorium to which I withdrew was no more successful in curing me than the first one, and many years passed before I came away' (III: 885). One last time, during a return trip to Paris, the hero takes stock of his pitiful state: 'the falsehood of literature,' 'the non-existence of the ideal in which I had believed,' 'an unattainable inspiration,' 'absence of emotion' (III: 886–7).

This first stage of initiation by the shadows of reminiscence is followed by a much briefer second stage, marked by premonitory signs.[33] The tone of the narrative is indeed reversed the moment the hero allows himself to be seduced, as in the early days of Combray, by the name Guermantes, printed on the invitation to the afternoon party given by the prince. This time, however, the journey by car is experienced as an airplane flight. 'And like an airman who hitherto has progressed laboriously along the ground, abruptly 'taking off' I soared slowly towards the silent heights of memory' (III: 890). The encounter with misfortune, in the personage of M. de Charlus, convalescent after an attack of apoplexy – 'upon the old fallen prince this latest illness had conferred the Shakespearean majesty of a King Lear' (III: 891) – is not enough to foil this take-off. Instead, the hero sees in his wasted figure 'a sort of gentleness, an almost physical gentleness, and of detachment from the realities of life, phenomena so strikingly apparent in those whom death has already drawn within its shadow' (III: 892). It is then that the hero receives as a salvific 'warning' a series of experiences that resemble entirely, through the happiness they give him, the experiences of Combray, 'of which the last works of Vinteuil had seemed to me to combine the quintessential character' (III: 899): tripping against the uneven paving stones, the noise of a spoon knocking against a plate, the stiffness of a starched and folded napkin. But, whereas formerly the narrator had to postpone until later clarifying the reasons for this happiness, this time he has made up his mind to solve the enigma. It is not that, as early as the period of Combray, the narrator failed to perceive that the intense joy felt resulted from the fortuitous conjunction between two similar impressions despite their distance in time. This time, too, the hero is not long in recognizing Venice and the two uneven paving stones in the baptistry of Saint Mark's under the impression of the uneven stones in Paris. The enigma to be solved therefore is not that temporal distance can be abolished in this way 'by chance,' 'as if by magic,' in the identity of a single instant – it is that the joy experienced is 'like a certainty and which sufficed, without any other proof, to make death a matter of indifference to me' (III: 900). In other words, the enigma to be solved is that of the *relation* between the happy moments, offered by chance and involuntary memory, and the invisible history of a vocation.

Between the considerable mass of narratives that extend over thousands of pages and the critical scene in the library, the narrator has thus worked in a narrative transition that shifts the sense of the

Bildungsroman from the apprenticeship to signs to the visitation. Taken together, the two wings of this narrative transition serve at once to separate and to suture the two foci of *Remembrance*. Separation, through the signs of death, confirming the failure of an apprenticeship to signs that lacks the principle of their decipherment. Suture, through the premonitory signs of the great revelation.

We now find ourselves at the heart of the great visitation scene that determines the primary – but not the final – meaning to be ascribed to the very notion of time regained. The narrative status of what may be read as a grand dissertation on art – even as Marcel Proust's *ars poetica*, forcibly inserted into his narrative – is maintained by the subtle diegetic tie that the narrator establishes between this major scene and the earlier narrative of the events that function as transitional points in the hero's initiation. This tie involves two levels at once. First, on the anecdotal level, the narrator has been careful to situate his narrative of the final signs of warning in the same place as the narrative of the great revelation: 'the little sitting-room used as a library' (III: 900). Next, on the thematic level, the narrator grafts his meditation on time onto the moments of happiness and the premonitory signs. The speculation on time thereby arises out of the thoughts of the narrator, reflecting on what had heretofore been provided by chance.[34] Finally, on a deeper level of reflection, the speculation on time is anchored in the narrative as a founding event in the vocation of the writer. The role of origin, assigned in this way to speculation in the history of a vocation, assures the irreducibly narrative character of this very speculation.

What may seem to place this speculation at a distance from the narrative is the fact that the time it brings to light is not, at first, time regained, in the sense of time lost that is found again, but the very suspension of time, *eternity*, or to speak as the narrator does, 'extratemporal' being (III: 904).[35] And this will continue to be the case as long as speculation has not been taken in hand by the decision to write, which restores to thought the intention of a work to be done. Several remarks by the narrator confirm to us that the extratemporal is only the first threshold of time regained. First, there is the fugitive character of contemplation itself; then, there is the necessity to support the hero's discovery of an extratemporal being that constitutes him through the heavenly nourishment of the essences of things; finally, we find the immanent, and non-transcendent, character of an eternity that mysteriously circulates between the present and the past, out of which it creates a unity. Extratemporal being, therefore, does not exhaust the entire meaning of *Time Regained*. It is, of course, *sub specie aeternitatis* that involuntary memory performs its miracle in time[36] and that the intelligence can encompass in the same look the distance of the heterogeneous and the simultaneity of the analogous. And it is indeed extratemporal being, when it makes use of the analogies offered by chance and by involuntary memory, as well as the work of the apprenticeship to signs, that brings the perishable course of things back to their essence 'outside time' (III: 904). Nevertheless, this extratemporal being still lacks the power 'to make me rediscover days that were long past' (ibid.). At this turning-point the meaning of the narrative process constituting the tale about time is revealed. What remains to be done is to join together the two valences assigned side-by-side to 'time regained.'[37] Sometimes this expression designates the extratemporal, sometimes it designates the act of rediscovering lost time. Only the decision to write will put an end to the duality of meaning of time regained. Before this decision is made, this duality seems insurmountable. The extratemporal is, in fact, related to a meditation on the very origin of aesthetic creation, in a contemplative moment unconnected to its inscription in an actual work, and without any consideration of the labour of writing. In the extratemporal order, the work of art, considered with respect to its origin, is not the product of the artisan of words – its existence precedes us; it has only to be discovered. At this level, creating is translating.

Time regained, in the second sense of the term, in the sense of lost time revived, comes out of the fixing of this fugitive, contemplative moment in a lasting work. The question is then, as Plato said of Daedalus's statues that were always on the point of fleeing, to tie down this contemplation by inscribing it within duration. 'To this contemplation of the essence of things I had decided therefore that in the future I must attach myself, so as somehow to immobilise it. But how, by what means, was I to do this?' (III: 909). It is here that artistic creation, taking over from aesthetic meditation, offers its mediation. 'And this method, which seems to be the sole method, what was it but the creation of a work of art?' (III: 912). Swann's mistake, in this respect, was to have assimilated the happiness afforded by the phrase of the sonata to the pleasures of love: 'he was unable to find it in artistic creation' (III: 911). It is here, too, that the deciphering of signs comes to the assistance of fugitive contemplation, not to substitute itself for the latter, and even less to precede it, but, under its guidance, to clarify it.

So the decision to write has the capacity to transpose the extratemporal character of the original vision into the temporality of the resurrection of time lost. In this sense we may say, in all truth, that Proust's work *narrates the transition from one meaning of time regained to the other*; and it is for this reason that it is a tale about time.

It remains to say in what way the narrative character of the birth of a vocation is assured by the act of testing that follows the revelation of the truth of art as well as by the hero's involvement in the work to be accomplished. This testing takes through the challenge of death. It is not an overstatement to say that it is the relation to death that makes the difference between the two meanings of time regained: the extratemporal, which transcends 'my anxiety on the subject of my death' and makes me 'unalarmed by the vicissitudes of the future' (III: 904), and the resurrection in the work of lost time. If the fate of the latter is finally handed over to the labour of writing, the threat of death is no less in time regained than in time lost.[38]

This is what the narrator meant to indicate by having the narrative of the conversion to writing followed by the astonishing spectacle offered by the guests at the Prince de Guermantes's dinner party. This dinner, where all the guests appeared to have 'put on a disguise [*s'être 'fait une tête'*]' (III: 920) – actually, a death's-head – is expressly interpreted by the narrator as a 'spectacular and dramatic effect' (III: 959), which, he says, 'threatened to raise against my enterprise the gravest of all objections' (III: 959–60). What is this, if not the reminder of death, which, without any hold on the extratemporal, threatens its temporal expression, the work of art itself.

Who are the characters in this dance of death?

A puppet-show, yes, but one in which, in order to identify the puppets with the people whom one had known in the past, it was necessary to read what was written on several planes at once, planes that lay behind the visible aspect of the puppets and gave them depth and forced one, as one looked at these aged marionettes, to make a strenuous intellectual effort; one was obliged to study them at the same time with one's eyes and with one's memory. These were puppets bathed in the immaterial colours of the years, puppets which exteriorized Time, Time which by

> Habit is made invisible and to become visible seeks bodies, which wherever it finds it seizes, to display its magic lantern upon them. (III: 964)[39]

And what do all these moribund figures announce, if not the hero's own approaching death? (III: 967). Here lies the danger. 'I had made the discovery of this destructive action of Time at the very moment when I had conceived the ambition to make visible, to intellectualize in a work of art, realities that were outside Time' (III: 971). This admission is of considerable importance. Might not the old myth of destructive time be stronger than the vision of time regained through the work of art? Yes, if the second meaning of time regained is separated from the first one. And this is indeed the temptation that haunts the hero up to the end of the narrative. It is a powerful temptation, inasmuch as the labour of writing takes place in the same time as lost time. Worse, the narrative that has preceded has, in a certain way, precisely as a narrative, stressed the fugitive nature of the event, related to the discovery of its abolition in the supra-temporal. But this is not the final word. For the artist who is capable of preserving the relation between revived time and the extra-temporal, time reveals its other mythical side: the profound identity that beings preserve despite their altered appearance attests to 'the power to renew in fresh forms that is possessed by Time, which can thus, while respecting the unity of the individual and the laws of life, effect a change of scene and introduce bold contrasts into two successive aspects of a single person' (III: 977–8). When we shall later discuss recognition, as the key concept of the unity between the two foci of the ellipse of *Remembrance*, we should recall that what makes beings recognizable is still 'Time, the artist' (III: 978). 'He was an artist, moreover, who works very slowly' (ibid.).

A sign that this pact between the two figures of *Time Regained* can be made and preserved is seen by the narrator in the unexpected encounter, totally unforeseen in all that has gone before: the appearance of the daughter of Gilberte Swann and Robert de Saint-Loup, who symbolizes the reconciliation of the two 'ways' – Swann's way through her mother, the Guermantes way through her father. 'I thought her very beautiful: still rich in hopes, full of laughter, formed from those very years which I myself had lost, she was like my own youth' (III: 1088). Is this appearance, which concretizes a reconciliation, one announced or anticipated several times in the work, intended to suggest that artistic creation has a pact with youth – with 'natality' as Hannah Arendt would say – which makes art, unlike love, stronger than death?[40]

Unlike the preceding ones, this sign is neither an announcement of something to come nor a premonition. Rather, it is a 'spur.' 'The idea of Time was of value to me for yet another reason: it was a spur, it told me that it was time to begin if I wished to attain to what I had sometimes perceived in the course of my life, in brief lightening-flashes, on the Guermantes way and in my drives in the carriage of Mme de Villeparisis, at those moments of perception which had me think that life was worth living. How much more worth living did it appear to me now, now that I seemed to see that this life that we live in half-darkness can be illumined, this life that at every moment we distort can be restored to its true pristine shape, that a life, in short, can be realised within the confines of a book!' (III: 1088).

From Time Regained to Time Lost

At the time of this inquiry into *Remembrance of Things Past*, considered as a tale about time, we have still to describe the relation that the narrative establishes between the two foci of the ellipse: the apprenticeship to signs, with its lost time, and the revelation of art, with its exaltation of the extratemporal. It is this relation that characterizes time as time regained, more precisely as time *lost-regained*. In order to understand this adjective, we must interpret the verb – what is it, then, to regain lost time?

To answer this question, we are interested, once again, only in the thoughts of the narrator, meditating on a work not yet written (in the fiction, this work is not the one we have just read). The result is that the meaning to be given to the act of regaining time is best designated by the difficulties expected of a work yet to be realized.

We find these difficulties condensed in the declaration by which the narrator attempts to characterize the meaning of his past life in relation to the work to be realized. 'And thus my whole life up to the present day might and yet might not have been summed up under the title: A Vocation' (III: 936).

The ambiguity, carefully nourished, between the yes and the no deserves our attention. No, 'literature had played no part in my life' (ibid.); yes, this whole life 'formed a reserve,' an almost vegetative domain in which the germinating organism was to be nourished. 'In the same way my life *was linked to* [*en rapport avec*] what, eventually, would bring about its maturation' (ibid., my emphasis).

What difficulties, then, must the act of regaining lost time overcome? And why does their resolution bear the mark of an ambiguity?

An initial hypothesis presents itself. Could the relation upon which the act of regaining time on the scale of *Remembrance* as a whole is built, be extrapolated from that discovered by reflection on the canonical examples of reminiscence that are elucidated and clarified? In turn, might not these infinitesimal experiences constitute the laboratory in miniature where the relation is forged that they will confer unity upon the whole of *Remembrance*?

An extrapolation such as this may be read in the following statement: 'what we call reality is a certain connexion between these immediate sensations and the memories which envelop us simultaneously with them – a connexion that is suppressed in a simple cinematographic vision, which just because it professes to confine itself to the truth in fact departs widely from it – a unique connexion which the writer has to rediscover in order to link for ever in his phrase the two sets of phenomena which reality joins together' (III: 924). Every element carries weight here: 'unique connexion,' as in the happy moments and in all the similar expressions of reminiscence, once these are clarified – a connection (or relation) to be 'rediscovered' – a connection in which two different terms are 'linked forever in his phrase.'

The first trail is now open, and it leads us to look for others, those of the stylistic figures whose function is precisely to posit the relation between two different objects. This figure is *metaphor*. The narrator confirms this in one statement in which, along with Roger Shattuck, I am prepared to see one of the hermeneutical keys to *Remembrance*.[41] This metaphorical relation, brought to light by the elucidation of happy moments, becomes the matrix for all the relations in which two distinct objects are, despite their differences, raised to their essence and liberated from the contingencies of time. The entire apprenticeship to signs, which contributes to the considerable length of *Remembrance*, thus falls under the law that is apprehended in the privileged examples of a few premonitory signs, already bearing the twofold sense that the intelligence has only to clarify. Metaphor reigns where cinematographic vision, which is purely serial, fails to relate sensations and memories. The narrator has perceived the general application that can be made of this metaphorical relation when he holds it to be 'analogous in the world of art to the unique connexion which in the world of science is provided by the law of causality' (III: 924). It is thus not an overstatement to say that sensations and memories, on the scale of *Remembrance* in its entirety, are enclosed within 'the necessary links of a well-wrought style' (III: 925). Style, here, does not designate anything ornamental but the singular entity resulting from the union, in a unique work of art, of the questions from which it proceeds and the solutions it gives. Time regained, in this first sense, is time lost eternalized by metaphor.

This first trail is not the only one. The stylistic solution, placed under the aegeis of metaphor, calls for, as its complement, a solution that could be termed 'optical.'[42] The narrator himself invites us to follow this second trail, without pausing to identify the point where they cross, by declaring that 'style for the writer, no less than colour for the painter, is a question not of technique but of vision' (III: 931).

By vision we are to understand something other than a revivification of what is immediate: a reading of signs, which, as we know, calls for an apprenticeship. If the narrator calls the experience of regained time 'vision,' it is so in so far as this vision is crowned with a 'recognition' that is the very mark of the extratemporal on lost time.[43] Once again, happy moments illustrate in miniature this stereoscopic vision set up as a form of recognition. But the idea of an 'optical view' applies to the entire apprenticeship to signs. This apprenticeship, in fact, is shot through with optical errors, which retrospectively take on the sense of a misunderstanding. In this respect, the sort of dance of death – the death's-heads at the Guermantes dinner party – which follows the great meditation, is not marked simply by the sign of death but also by that of non-recognition (III: 971, 990, etc.). The hero even fails to recognize Gilberte. This is a crucial scene, for it places the entire foregoing quest retrospectively at once under the sign of a comedy of errors (optical errors) and on the path of a project of integral recognition. This overall interpretation of *Remembrance* in terms of recognition authorizes us to consider the meeting between the hero and Gilberte's daughter as an ultimate recognition scene, to the extent that, as I said above, the young girl incarnates the reconciliation between the two ways, that of Swann and that of the Guermantes.

The two trails we have just followed intersect at some point.

Metaphor and recognition share the common role of elevating two impressions to the level of essence, without abolishing their difference. 'For to 'recognize' someone, and, *a fortiori*, to learn someone's identity after having failed to 'recognize' him, is to predicate two contradictory things of a single subject' (III: 982). This crucial text establishes the equivalence between metaphor and recognition, making the first the logical equivalent of the second ('to predicate two contradictory things of a single subject'), and the second the temporal equivalent of the first ('it is to admit that what was here, the person whom one remembers, no longer exists, and also that what is now here is a person whom one did not know to exist' [ibid.]). Thus metaphor we may say is in the order of style what resemblance is in the order of stereoscopic vision.

The difficulty, however, reappears at this very point. Just what is the relation between style and vision? By this question we touch on the problem that predominates throughout *Remembrance*, that of the relation between writing and impressions, that is to say, in an ultimate sense, between literature and life.

A third sense of the notion of time regained will be discovered along this new trail. Time regained, I will now say, is *the impression regained*. But what is the impression regained? Once again, we must start from the exegesis of happy moments, and extend this to the entire apprenticeship to signs pursued throughout *Remembrance*. In order to be regained, the impression must first have been lost as an immediate pleasure, prisoner to its external object. The initial stage of the rediscovery is that of the complete internalization of the impression.[44] A second stage is the transposition of the impression into a law, into an idea.[45] A third stage is the inscription of this spiritual equivalent in a work of art. There is supposed to be a fourth stage, which is alluded to only once in *Remembrance*, when the narrator mentions his future readers. 'For it seemed to me that they would not be "my" readers but the readers of their own selves, my book being merely a sort of magnifying glass like those which the optician at Combray used to offer his customers – it would be my book, but with its help I would furnish them with the means of reading what lay inside themselves' (III: 1089).[46]

This alchemy of the impression regained perfectly presents the difficulty that the narrator perceives as he crosses the threshold of the work: How to prevent substituting literature for life, or again, under the patronage of laws and ideas, how to keep from dissolving the impression in a psychology or an abstract sociology, divested of all narrative character. The narrator replies to this danger by his concern for preserving an unsteady balance between impressions, of which he says, 'their essential character was that I was not free to choose them, that such as they were they were given to me' (III: 913), and, on the other side, the deciphering of signs, guided by the conversion of the impression into a work of art. Literary creation therefore seems to go in two opposite directions at once.

On the one hand, the impression must act as 'the very proof of the trueness of the whole picture' (ibid.).[47] Along this same line, the narrator comes to speak of life as an 'inner book of unknown symbols' (ibid.). This book, we have not written, and yet 'the book whose hieroglyphs are patterns not traced by us is the only book that really belongs to us' (III: 914).[48] Better, it is 'our true life ... reality as we have felt it to be, which differs so greatly from what we think it is that when a chance happening brings us an authentic memory of it we are filled with an immense happiness' (III: 915). Writing the work to be realized is thus based on 'the faculty of submitting to the reality within' (III: 917).[49]

On the other hand, reading the book of life is 'an act of creation in which no one can do our work for us or even collaborate with us' (III: 913). Everything now seems to swing to the side of literature. The following text is well known. 'Real life, life at last laid bare and illuminated – the only life in consequence which can be said to be really lived – is literature, and life thus defined is in a sense all the time immanent in ordinary man no less than in the artist. But most men do not see it because they do not seek to shed light upon it' (III: 931). This statement should not mislead us. It in no way leads to an apology for 'The Book' as Mallarmé conceived it. Rather it posits an equation which, at the end of the work, should be completely reversible between life and literature, which is to say, finally, between the impression preserved in its trace and the work of art that states the meaning of the impression. This reversibility, however, is nowhere simply given. It must be the fruit of the labour of writing. In this sense *Remembrance* could be entitled the search for the lost impression, literature being nothing other than the impression regained – 'the joy of rediscovering what is real' (III: 913).

A third version of time regained thus offers itself to our meditation. It is not so much added to the two preceding versions as it includes them both. In the impression regained, the two paths we have followed cross and reconcile what might be called the two 'ways' of *Remembrance*: on the level of style, the way of metaphor; on the level of vision, the way of recognition.[50] In return, metaphor and recognition make explicit the *relation* upon which the impression regained is itself constructed, the relation between life and literature. And in every instance this relation includes forgetfulness and death.

Such is the wealth of meaning of time regained, or rather of the operation of rediscovering lost time. This meaning embraces the three versions that we have just explored. Time regained, we might say, is the metaphor that encloses differences 'in the necessary links of a well-wrought style.' It is also the recognition, which crowns stereoscopic vision. Finally, it is the impression regained, which reconciles life and literature. Indeed, inasmuch as life is the figure of the way of time lost, and literature the way of the extratemporal, we have the right to say that time regained expresses the recovery of lost time in the extratemporal, just as the impression regained expresses the recovery of life in the work of art.

The two foci of the ellipse formed by *Remembrance of Things Past* do not merge into one another – a distance remains between the lost time of the apprenticeship to signs and the contemplation of the extratemporal. But this will be a distance that is traversed.

And it is with this final expression, 'traversal,' that I shall conclude, for it marks the transition from the extratemporal, glimpsed in contemplation, to what the narrator calls 'Time embodied' (III: 1105).[51] The extratemporal is only a point of passage; its virtue is to transform into a continuous duration the 'retorts of discontinuous periods.' *Remembrance*, then, is far from a Bergsonian vision of a duration free of all extension; instead, it confirms the *dimensional* character of time. The itinerary of *Remembrance* moves from the idea of a distance that separates to that of a distance that joins together. This is confirmed by the final figure of time proposed in *Remembrance*, that of an accumulated duration that is, in a sense, beneath us. Thus the narrator-hero sees people 'perched upon living stilts which never cease to grow until sometimes they become taller than church steeples, making it in the end both difficult and perilous for them to walk and raising them to an eminence from which suddenly they fall' (III: 1107). As for himself, having incorporated into his present 'all this length of Time,' he sees himself 'perched on its giddy summit' (III: 1106). This final figure of time regained says two things: that time lost is contained in time regained but also that it is finally Time that carries us within it. *Remembrance*, in fact, closes not with a cry of triumph but with 'a sensation of weariness and almost of terror' (ibid.). For time regained is also death regained. *Remembrance* has generated, in the phrase of Hans Robert Jauss, only an interim time, that of a work yet to be accomplished, one that may be destroyed by death.

The fact, in the final analysis, that time envelops us, as we are told in the old myths, we have known from the start – the beginning of the narrative possessed the strange feature of referring us back to an indefinite earlier period. The narrative closure is not different. The narrative stops when the writer sets to work. All the tenses then pass from the future to the conditional. 'But my task was longer… my words had to reach more than a single person. My task was long. By day, the most I could hope for was to try to sleep. If I worked, it would only be at night. But I should need many nights, a hundred perhaps, or even a thousand. And I should live in the anxiety of not knowing whether the master of my destiny might not prove less indulgent than the Sultan Shahriyar, whether in the morning, when I broke off my story, he would consent to a further reprieve and permit me to resume my narrative the following evening' (III: 1101).[52]

Is it for this reason that the final words place the self and all other people back *in* Time? This is certainly 'a very considerable place compared with the restricted one which is allotted to them in space' (ibid.) but none the less a place 'in the dimension of Time' (III: 1107).

Notes

1 Marcel Proust, *Remembrance of Things Past*, trans. by C.K. Scott Moncrieff, Terence Kilmartin, and Andreas Mayor (New York: Random House, 1981), 3 vols. I shall refer to this work throughout this chapter by volume and page number.
2 Gilles Deleuze, *Proust and Signs*, trans. by Richard Howard (New York: George Braziller, 1972)
3 The quasi-synchronic table of signs in Deleuze's work and the hierarchy of · temporal configurations that correspond to this grand paradigm of signs must not make us forget either the historicity of this apprenticeship or, especially, the singular historicity that marks the event of the Visitation itself, which

changes after-the-fact the meaning of the earlier apprenticeship, and first and foremost its temporal signification. It is the eccentric character of the signs of art in relation to all the others that engenders this singular historicity.

4 Anne Henry, *Proust romancier: Le Tombeau égyptien* (Paris: Flammarion, 1983)

5 Henry (ibid., pp. 33 and 40) gives two significant extracts from Part VI of *The System of Transcendental Idealism*. Cf. F.W.J. Shelling, *The System of Transcendental Idealism* (1800), trans. by Peter Heath (Charlottesville: University of Virginia Press, 1978).

6 Schopenhauer, *The World as Will and Representation*, trans. by E.F.J. Payne (New York: Dover Books, 1966), 2 vols

7 'The realization of Identify did foresee its place of accomplishment as the artist's consciousness, but it was a metaphysical essence, not a psychological subject – a feature that the novel will inevitably end up concretizing' (Henry, p. 44). And further along: 'Proust thought only about placing himself in the intermediary zone between the system and concrete reality which the genre, novel, permits' (ibid., p. 55).

8 Anne Henry is not unaware of the problem. 'Nothing will have been accomplished so long as one has not yet shed light on this ever so peculiar presentation that Proust gives of Identity, its realization at the heart of reminiscence' (ibid., p. 43). But the answer she gives leaves the difficulty intact, when the key to the psychologizing process to which the aesthetics of genius is subjected is still sought outside the novel in a mutation of intellectual culture at the end of the nineteenth century. This reversal of the relationship between the theoretical foundation and the narrative process leads to the question of what revolution *Remembrance* provoked in the tradition of the *Bildungsroman*, which Thomas Mann's *Der Zauberberg* reoriented in the way I have tried to indicate above. The decentring brought about by *Remembrance* of the redemptive event in relation to the long apprenticeship to signs leads us rather to understand that, by placing his work within the tradition of the *Bildungsroman*, Marcel Proust subverts the law of the novel of apprenticeship in a different way than Mann does. Proust breaks with the optimistic vision of a continuous, ascending development of the hero in quest of himself. Compared in this way to the tradition of the *Bildungsroman*, Proust's novelistic creation resides in the invention of a plot that joins together, by strictly narrative means, the apprenticeship to signs and the maturation of a vocation. Anne Henry herself mentions this kinship with the *Bildungsroman* but, for her, the choice of this novel formula participates in the overall degradation that affects the philosophy of lost identity when it becomes a psychology of lost time.

9 The problem posed is not without analogy to that posed by Genette's structural analysis. He also saw, in the 'art of Poetry' inserted into the hero's meditation on the eternity of the work of art, an intrusion of the author into the work. My retort was to introduce the notion of a world of the work and of an experience that the hero of the work has within the horizon of this world. This accorded the work the power to project itself beyond itself in an imagi-

nary transcendence. The same reply holds with respect to Anne Henry's explanation. It is to the extent that the work projects a narrator-hero who *thinks* about his experience that it can include, within its transcendent immanence, the scattered debris of philosophical speculation.

10 Nevertheless, this voice can be easily recognized in the aphorisms and maxims that allow us to see the exemplary character of the experience recounted. It is also readily apparent in the latent irony that prevails throughout the narrative of the hero's discoveries in the world of society. Norpois, Brichot, Madame Verdurin, and, one after the other, bourgeois and aristocrats fall victim to the cruelty of a cutting remark, perceptible to an ear with a moderate amount of experience. On the other hand, it is only on the second reading that the reader who knows the outcome of the work perceives what, in deciphering the signs of love, would be the equivalent of irony in deciphering worldly signs: a tone of disillusionment, which forces the day of disappointment and thus ascribes meaning without expressly stating it – the meaning of time lost that comes out of every amorous experience. In other words, it is the narrative voice that is responsible for the overall pejorative tone that predominates in deciphering the signs of love. The narrative voice is more restrained in deciphering sensory signs, and yet their voice insinuates a questioning tone, an interrogation, a request for meaning at the heart of impressions, to the point of breaking this charm and dissolving their spell. The narrator thus constantly makes the hero a consciousness who is awakening to underlying reality.

11 These moments between waking and sleeping serve as an initial pivot for the inset memories, one within the other: 'my memory had been set in motion' (I: 9). A second pivot is provided by the association of one bedroom with another: Combray, Balbec, Paris, Doncières, Venice (ibid.). The narrator does not fail to recall, at the appropriate moment, this inset structure. 'And so it was that, for a long time afterwards, when I lay awake at night and revived old memories of Combray, I saw no more of it than this sort of luminous panel, sharply defined against a vague and shadowy background' (I: 46). This will be the case until the conclusion of this sort of 'prelude' (as Hans Robert Jauss calls it in his *Zeit und Erinnerung in Marcel Proust 'A la Recherche du Temps Perdu'* [Heidelberg: Carl Winter, 1955]) in which all the narratives of childhood, as well as the story of Swann's love, are included.

12 As we would expect, this ritual is recounted in the *imparfait*: 'that frail and precious kiss which Mamma used normally to bestow on me when I was in bed and just going to sleep had to be transported from the dining-room to my bedroom where I must keep it inviolate all the time that it took me to undress' (I: 24).

13 'I ought to have been happy; I was not' (I: 41).

14 The trap lies in the transitional question, 'Will it ultimately reach the clear surface of my consciousness, this memory, this old, dead moment, which the magnetism of an identical moment has travelled so far as to importune, to disturb, to raise up out of the very depths of my being? I cannot tell' (I: 50).

15 The entire section *Time Regained* is announced in this statement by the

narrator, reflecting on the hero's effort to make the ecstasy return: 'And then for the second time I clear an empty space in front of it; I place in position before my mind's eye the still recent taste of that first mouthful, and I feel something start within me, something that leaves its resting-place and attempts to rise, something that has been embedded like an anchor at great depth; I do not know yet what it is but I can feel it mounting slowly; I can measure the resistance, I can hear the echo of great spaces traversed' (I: 49). The expression 'great spaces traversed' will be, as we shall see, our final word.

16 Hans Robert Jauss interprets the experience of the madeleine as the first coincidence between the narrating self and the narrated self. In addition, he sees in this the primary *nunc*, always already preceded by an abyssal before, yet still able to open the door to the hero's forward progress. A double paradox, therefore: from the start of the narrative the self that narrates is a self remembering what preceded it. By narrating backwards, however, the narrative offers the hero the possibility of beginning his journey forward. And by virtue of this, to the end of the novel, the style of 'the future in the past' is preserved. The problem of the relations between the orientation towards the future and the nostalgic desire for the past is at the centre of the chapters devoted to Proust in Georges Poulet's *Etude sur le temps humain* (Paris: Plon, Ed. du Rocher, 1952–68), Vol. 1: 400–38; Vol. 4: 299–355.

17 An edifice occupying, so to speak, a four-dimensional space – the name of the fourth being Time – extending through the centuries its ancient nave, which, bay after bay, chapel after chapel, seemed to stretch across and conquer not merely a few yards of soil, but each successive epoch from which it emerged triumphant' (I: 66). It is not by chance that, closing the circle, *Time Regained* ends with a final evocation of the Combray church. The steeple of Saint Hilaire is already one of the symbols of time; in Jauss's expression, one of its symbolic figures.

18 Georges Poulet, *Proustian Space*, trans. by Elliot Coleman (Baltimore: Johns Hopkins University Press, 1977), pp. 57–69

19 The different epochs are never dated: 'That year' (I: 158); 'that autumn' (I: 167, 169); 'at that moment, too' (I: 170).

20 'It is perhaps from another impression which I received at Montjouvain, some years later, an impression which at the time remained obscure to me, that there arose, long afterwards, the notion I was to form of sadism. We shall see, in due course, that for quite other reasons the memory of this impression was to play an important part in my life' (I: 173). This 'we shall see, in due course' followed by 'was to' helps to rebalance in a forward direction the overall backward orientation of the work. The scene is at once recollected and projected towards its own future, and so placed at a distance. On the relation between temporality and desire in Proust, cf. Ghislaine Florival, *Le Désir chez Proust* (Louvain/Paris: Nauwelaerts, 1971), pp. 107–73.

21 'And these dreams reminded me that, since I wished some day to become a writer, it was high time to decide what sort of books I was going to write. But as soon as I asked myself the question, and tried to discover some subject to which I could impart a philosophical significance of infinite value, my mind

would stop like a clock, my consciousness would be faced with a blank, I would feel either that I was wholly devoid of talent or that perhaps some malady of the brain was hindering its development' (I: 188–89). And a bit farther on: 'And so, utterly despondent, I renounced literature for ever, despite the encouragement Bloch had given me' (I: 189–90).

22 'Without admitting to myself that what lay hidden behind the steeples of Martinville must be something analogous to a pretty phrase, since it was in the form of words which gave me pleasure, that it had appeared to me, I borrowed a pencil and some paper from the doctor, and in spite of the jolting of the carriage, to appease my conscience and to satisfy my enthusiasm, composed the following little fragment, which I have since discovered and now reproduce with only a slight revision here and there' (I: 197).

23 'But by the same token, and by their persistence in those of my present-day impressions to which they can still be linked, they give those impressions a foundation, a depth, a dimension lacking from the rest' (I: 197).

24 'Thus would I often lie until morning, dreaming of the old days at Combray ... and, by an association of memories, of a story which, many years after I had left the little place, had been told me of a love affair in which Swann had been involved before I was born' (I: 203).

25 For the reader, a passage such as the following speaks clearly and distinctly: 'Swann found in himself, in the memory of the phrase that he had heard, in certain other sonatas which he had made people play to him to see whether he might not perhaps discover his phrase therein, the presence of one of those invisible realities in which he had ceased to believe and to which, as though the music had had upon the moral barrenness from which he was suffering a sort of recreative influence, he was conscious once again of the desire and almost the strength to consecrate his life' (I: 230). And again: 'In its airy grace there was the sense of something over and done with, like the mood of philosophic detachment which follows an outburst of vain regret' (I: 238).

26 It is not without importance that Swann is a failure as a writer. He will never write his study on Vermeer. As is already suggested, in his relation to the phrase of the Vinteuil sonata, he will die without ever having known the revelation of art. *Time Regained* states this clearly (III: 902).

27 In order to anchor his narrative of 'Swann in Love' in the main narrative, the narrator common to the third- and first-person narratives is careful to have Odette appear for the last time (at least the first Odette, who the reader is unable to guess will later be Gilberte's mother in the hero's fictive autobiography) 'in the twilight of a dream' (I: 411), and then in his thoughts as he awakes. In this way, 'Swann in Love' ends in the same semi-dreamlike region as the 'Combray' narrative.

28 The author – and no longer the narrator – is in no way bothered by having the young Marcel and Gilberte encountered on the little footpath in Combray meet on the Champs-Elysées (her indelicate gesture in those early days [I: 154] will remain an enigma until *Time Regained* [III: 711–12]). Novelistic coincidences do not disturb Proust. For it is the narrator who, transforming them first into the peripeteia of his story, then ascribing an almost supernatural

sense to chance encounters, succeeds in transforming all coincidences into destiny. *Remembrance* is full of these unlikely encounters that the narrative makes productive. The final, and most meaningful, will be, as we shall see below, the joining together of *Swann's Way* and *The Guermantes Way* in the appearance of the daughter of Gilberte and Saint-Loup in the final pages of the book.

29 'When I found how incurious I was about Combray' (III: 709). 'But, separated as I was by a whole lifetime from places I now happened to be passing through again, there was lacking between them and me that contiguity from which is born, even before we have perceived it, the immediate, delicious and total deflagration of memory' (III: 710).

30 Even the famous pastiche of the Goncourts (III: 728–36), which serves as a pretext for the narrator to thrash out at a memorialist type of literature, based on the immediate capacity for 'looking and listening' (III: 737) helps to reinforce the general tone of the narrative in which it is interpolated, through the disgust that the reading of the pages, fictitiously attributed to the Goncourts, inspires in the hero with respect to literature and by the obstacles it sets up to the advancement of his vocation (III: 728, 737–8).

31 It is true that the transfiguration of the Parisian sky by the light of the searchlights and the way the airmen are taken for Wagnerian Valkyries (III: 781, 785–6) adds to the spectacle of Paris at war a touch of aestheticism, with respect to which it is hard to say whether it contributes to the spectral character of all the surrounding scene, or whether it already partakes of the literary transposition consubstantial with time regained. In any case, frivolity continues alongside the danger of death. 'Social amusements fill what may prove, if the Germans continue to advance, to be the last days of our Pompeii. And if the city is indeed doomed, that in itself will save it from frivolity' (III: 834).

32 'And then it had turned out that their two lives had each of them a parallel secret, which I had not suspected' (III: 879). The rapprochement between these two disappearances gives the narrator the opportunity to engage in a meditation on death, which will later be incorporated into the perspective of time regained. 'Yet death appears to be obedient to certain laws' (III: 881); more precisely, accidental death, which, in its own way, combines chance and destiny, if not predestination (ibid.).

33 'But it is sometimes just at the moment when we think that everything is lost that the intimation arrives which may save us; one has knocked at all the doors which lead nowhere, and then one stumbles without knowing it on the only door through which one can enter – which one might have sought in vain for a hundred years – and it opens of its own accord' (III: 898).

34 Note that this narrativized speculation is related too in the *imparfait*, the background tense according to Harald Weinrich, in contrast to the preterite, the tense of occurrence, from the point of view of what in the narrative is put into relief. The meditation on time indeed constitutes the background against which the decision to write stands out. A new preterite of anecdotal occurrence is required in order to interrupt this meditation. 'At this moment the butler came in to tell me that the first piece of music was finished, so that I

could leave the library and go into the rooms where the party was taking place. And thereupon I remembered where I was' (III: 957).

35 'A minute freed from the order of time has re-created in us, to feel it, the man freed from the order of time' (III: 906).

36 Speaking of this extratemporal being that the hero had been without knowing it in the episode of the madeleine, the narrator specifies, 'And only this being had the power to perform that task which had always defeated the efforts of my memory and my intellect' (III: 904).

37 The narrator anticipates this role of mediator between the two valences of time regained, when he admits, 'And I observed in passing that for the work of art which I now, though I had not yet reached a conscious resolution, felt myself ready to undertake, this distinctness of different events would entail very considerable difficulties' (III: 903). It should be noted, as Georges Poulet points out, that the fusion in time is also a fusion in space: 'Always, when these resurrections took place, the distant scene engendered around the common sensation had for a moment grappled, like a wrestler, with the present scene' (III: 908).

38 The 'universal language' (III: 941) into which impressions must be translated is also not unrelated to death. Like history for Thucydides, the work of art, for the narrator of *Remembrance*, may 'make out of those who are no more, in their truest essence, a lasting acquisition for the minds of all mankind' (III: 941). Lasting? Under this ambition is hidden the relation to death: 'Sorrows are servants, obscure and detested, against whom one struggles, beneath whose dominion one more and more completely falls, dire and dreadful servants whom it is impossible to replace and who by subterranean paths lead us toward truth and death. Happy are those who have first come face to face with truth, those for whom near though the one may be to the other, the hour of truth has struck before the hour of death!' (III: 948).

39 I shall return in my conclusion to this visibility of 'externalized' time, which illuminates mortals by the light of its magic lantern. Later on, in the same sense, we also read, 'now it was not merely what had become of the young men of my own youth but would one day become of those of today that impressed upon me with such force the sensation of Time' (III: 987). It is still a question of 'the sensation of time having slipped away' (III: 1000) and of the alteration of beings as 'an effect operative not so much upon a whole social stratum as within individuals – of Time' (III: 1010). This figuration of time, in the dance of death, is to be included in the gallery of symbolic figures' (Jauss, pp. 152–66) which, throughout *Remembrance*, constitute the many figurations of invisible time: Habit, Sorrow, Jealously, Forgetfulness, and now Age. This system of emblems, I would say, makes visible to 'the artist, Time.'

40 'Time, colourless and inapprehensible Time, so that I was almost able to see it and touch it, had materialised itself in this girl, moulding her into a master-piece, while correspondingly, on me alas! it had merely done its work' (III: 1088).

41 This statement follows the one just cited and is worth quoting in its entirety. 'He can describe a scene by describing one after another the innumerable objects which at a given moment were present at a particular place, but truth

will be attained by him only when he takes two different objects, states the connexion [*rapport*] between them – a connexion analogous in the world of art to the unique connexion which in the world of science is provided by the law of causality – and encloses them in the necessary links of a well-wrought style; truth – and life too – can be attained by us only when, by comparing a quality common to two sensations, we succeed in extracting their common essence and in reuniting them to each other, liberated from the contingencies of time, within a metaphor' (III: 924–5). Cf. Roger Shattuck, *Proust's Binoculars: A Study of Memory, Time, and Recognition in 'A la Recherche du Temps Perdu'* (New York: Random House, 1963). Shattuck begins his study, the merits of which I shall acknowledge below, with this famous passage.

42 For the remarks that follow I am indebted to Shattuck's book cited in the previous note. He does not just confine himself to noting the optical images scattered throughout *Remembrance* (magic lantern, kaleidoscope, telescope, microscope, magnifying glass, etc.) but also attempts to discover the rules governing a Proustian dioptics based on binocular contrast. Proustian optics is not a direct but a split optics which allows Shattuck to describe *Remembrance* as a whole as a 'stereo-optics of Time.' The canonical passage in this regard reads as follows. 'For all these reasons a party like this at which I found myself ... was like an old-fashioned peepshow, but a peepshow of the years, the vision not of a moment but of a person situated in the distorting perspective of time' (III: 965).

43 Shattuck points this out very nicely. The high point of Proust's work is not a happy moment but one of recognition (*Proust's Binoculars*, p. 37): 'After the supreme rite of recognition at the end, the provisional nature of life disappears in the discovery of the straight path of art' (ibid., p. 38).

44 'Since every impression is double and the one half which is sheathed in the object is prolonged in ourselves by another half which we alone can know, we speedily find means to neglect this second half, which is the one on which we ought to concentrate' (III: 927).

45 'In fact, both in one case and in the other, whether I was concerned with impressions like the one which I had received from the sight of the steeples of Martinville or with the reminiscences like that of the unevenness of the two steps or the taste of the madeleine, the task was to interpret the given sensations as signs of so many laws and ideas, by trying to think – that is to say, to draw forth from the shadow – what I had merely felt, by trying to convert it into its spiritual equivalent' (III: 912).

46 We shall return to this final phase of the alchemy of writing in the course of Part IV in Volume 3, within the framework of my reflections on the way the work finds its completion in the act of reading.

47 'I had not gone in search of the two uneven paving-stones of the courtyard upon which I had stumbled. But it was precisely the fortuitous and inevitable fashion in which this and the other sensations had been encountered that proved the trueness of the past which they brought back to life, of the images which they released, since we feel, with these sensations, the effort that they make to climb back towards the light, feel in ourselves the joy of rediscovering what is real' (III: 913).

48 The entire problematic of the trace, to be taken up again in Volume 3, is contained here. 'This book, more laborious to decipher than any other, is also the only one which has been dictated to us by reality, the only one of which the 'impression' has been printed in us by reality itself. When an idea – an idea of any kind – is left in us by life, its material pattern, the outline of the impression that it made upon us, remains behind as the token of its necessary truth' (III: 914).

49 In this respect, artists no less than historians owe a debt to something that precedes them. This is another topic I shall take up in Volume 3. But here is another passage indicative of it: 'the essential, the only true book, though, in the ordinary sense of the word it does not have to be 'invented' by a great writer – for it exists already in each of us – has to be translated by him. The function and the task of a writer are those of a translator' (III: 926).

50 Meditating on the outcome in the person of Mademoiselle de Saint-Loup of the two 'ways' along which the hero had taken so many walks and engaged in so many reveries, the narrator tells himself that his entire work will be made of all the 'cross-sections' reuniting impressions, epochs, and sites; as many ways as cross-sections, as distances traversed.

51 The figuration corresponding to this embodied time is the repetition, at the beginning and the end of *Remembrance*, of the same memory of the church in Combray, Saint Hilaire: 'it occurred to me suddenly that, if I still had the strength to accomplish my work, this afternoon – like certain days long ago at Combray which had influenced me – which in its brief compass had given me both the idea of my work and the fear of being unable to bring it to fruition, would certainly impress upon it that form of which as a child I had had a presentiment in the church at Combray but which ordinarily, throughout our lives, is invisible to us: the form of Time' (III: 1103). (To relate this final illumination, the narrator uses the preterite joined to the adverb 'suddenly.') One last time the church at Combray restores proximity in the distance that, from the beginning of *Remembrance*, has marked the evocation of Combray. *Time Regained* is, then, a repetition. 'This notion of Time embodied, of years past but not separated from us, it was now my intention to emphasize as strongly as possible in my work. And at this very moment, in the house of the Prince de Guermantes, as though to strengthen me in my resolve, the noise of my parents' footsteps as they accompanied M. Swann to the door and the peal – resilient, ferruginous, interminable, fresh and shrill – of the bell on the garden gate which informed me that at last he had gone and that Mamma would presently come upstairs, these sounds rang again in my ears, yes, unmistakably I heard these very sounds, situated though they were in a remote past' (III: 1105).

52 On the question of writing, that is, of the impossibility of writing, cf. Gérard Genette, 'La Question de l'écriture,' and Léo Bersani, 'Déguisement du moi et art fragmentaire,' in Roland Barthes et al., *Recherches de Proust* (Paris: Seuil, 1980), pp. 7–12 and 13–33.

Between the Text and
Its Readers

To what discipline does a theory of reading belong? To poetics? Yes, in so far as the composition of the work governs its reading; no, in so far as other factors enter into play, factors that concern the sort of communication that finds its starting-point in the author, crosses through the work, and finds its end-point in the reader. For it is, indeed, from the author that the strategy of persuasion that has the reader as its target starts out. And it is to this strategy of persuasion that the reader replies by accompanying the configuration and in appropriating the world proposed by the text.

Three moments need to be considered then, to which correspond three neighbouring, yet distinct, disciplines: 1 / the strategy as concocted by the author and directed towards the reader; 2 / the inscription of this strategy within a literary configuration; and 3 / the response of the reader considered either as a reading subject or as the receiving public.

This schema allows us to take a brief look at several theories of reading that I have expressly arranged starting from the pole of the author and moving towards that of the reader, who is the ultimate mediator between configuration and refiguration.

From Poetics to Rhetoric

At the first stage of our itinerary, we are considering a strategy from the point of view of the author who carries it through. The theory of reading then falls within the field of rhetoric, inasmuch as rhetoric governs the art by means of which orators aim at persuading their listeners. More precisely, for us, and this has been recognized since Aristotle, it falls within the field of a rhetoric of fiction, in the sense that Wayne Booth has given to this phrase in his well-known work *The Rhetoric of Fiction.*[1] An objection, however, immediately comes to mind: in bringing the author back into the field of literary theory, are we not denying the thesis of the semantic autonomy of the text, and are we not slipping back into an outmoded psychological analysis of the written text? By no means. First, the thesis of the semantic autonomy of the text holds only for a structural analysis that brackets the strategy of persuasion running through the operations belonging to a poetics as such; removing these brackets necessarily involves taking into account the one who concocts the strategy of persuasion, namely, the author. Next, rhetoric can escape the objection of falling back into the 'intentional fallacy' and, more generally, of being no more than a psychology of the author inasmuch as what it emphasizes is not the alleged creation process of the work but the techniques by means of which a work is made communicable. These techniques can be discerned in the work itself. The result is that the only type of author whose authority is in question here is not the real author, the object of biography, but the implied author. It is this implied author who takes the initiative in the show of strength underlying the relation between writing and reading.

Before entering this arena, I should like to recall the terminological convention I adopted in introducing the notions of point of view and narrative voice in Volume 2 of *Time and Narrative*, at the end of the analyses devoted to 'Games with Time.' There I considered these notions only to the extent that they contributed to the understanding of the narrative composition as such, apart from their effect on the communication of the work. But the notion of implied author belongs to this problematic of communication inasmuch as it is closely bound up with a rhetoric of persuasion. Conscious of the abstract character of this distinction, I stressed at that time the role of transition brought about by the notion of narrative voice. The narrative voice, I said, is what offers the text as something to be read. To whom does it make this offer if not to the virtual reader of the work? It was a deliberate choice on my part, therefore, not to consider the notion of implied author when we talked about point of view and narrative voice, but instead to emphasize at this time the ties between this implied author and the strategies of persuasion stemming from a rhetoric of fiction, without making any further allusions to the notions of narrative voice and point of view, from which this notion of implied author obviously cannot be dissociated.

Set back within the framework of communication to which it belongs, the category of implied author has the important advantage of side-stepping a number of futile disputes that conceal the primary meaning of a rhetoric of fiction. For example, we shall not attach an exaggerated originality to the efforts of modern novelists to make themselves invisible – unlike previous authors, inclined to intervene unscrupulously in their narratives – as if the novel were suddenly to have emerged authorless. Effacement of the author is one rhetorical technique among others; it belongs to the panoply of disguises and masks the real author uses to transform himself or herself into the implied author.[2] The same can be said of the author's right to describe minds from the inside, which in so-called real life is something that can only be inferred with great difficulty. This right is part of the pact of trust concluded with the reader, which we shall discuss below.[3] Also, whatever the angle of vision chosen by the author,[4] this is in every instance an artifice to be attributed to the exorbitant rights the reader grants the author. Nor does the author disappear simply because the novelist has attempted to 'show' rather than to 'inform and instruct.' We discussed this in Volume 2 of *Time and Narrative* in connection with the search for verisimilitude in the realistic novel, and even more so in the naturalist novel.[5] Far from being abolished, the artifice proper to the narrative operation is augmented by the task of simulating real presence through writing. However much this simulation may be opposed to omniscience of the narrator, it conveys no less a mastery of rhetorical techniques. The alleged faithfulness to life merely hides the subtlety of the manoeuvres by which the work governs, on the side of the author, the 'intensity of the illusion' desired by Henry James. The rhetoric of dissimulation, the summit of the rhetoric of fiction, must not fool the critic, even if it may fool the reader. The height of such dissimulation would be that the fiction appear never to have been written.[6] The rhetorical procedures by which the author sacrifices his presence dissimulate his artifice by means of the verisimilitude of a story that appears to narrate itself and to let life speak, whether this be called social reality, individual behaviour, or the stream of consciousness.[7]

This brief discussion of the misunderstandings that the category of implied author is able to dissipate underscores the rightful place of this category in a comprehensive theory of reading. The reader has an intimation of the role it plays inasmuch as this reader intuitively apprehends the work as a unified totality.

Spontaneously, the reader does not ascribe this unification the rules of composition alone but extends it to the choices and to the norms that make the text, precisely, the work of some speaker, hence a work produced by someone and not by nature.

I would readily compare this unifying role intuitively assigned by the reader to the implied author with the notion of style, proposed by G. Granger in his *Essai d'une philosophie du style*.[8] If a work is considered as the resolution of a problem, itself arising out of prior successes in the field of science as well as in the field of art, then style may be termed the adequation between the singularity of this solution, which the work constitutes by itself, and the singularity of the crisis situation as this was apprehended by the thinker or artist. This singularity of the solution, replying to the singularity of the problem, can take on a proper name, that of the author. Thus we speak of Boole's theorem just as we speak of a painting by Cézanne. Naming the work in terms of its author implies no conjecture about the psychology of invention or of discovery, therefore no assertion concerning the presumed intention of the inventor; it implies only the singularity of a solution to a problem. This comparison reinforces the right of the category of implied author to figure in a rhetoric of fiction.

The related notion of a reliable or unreliable narrator, to which we now turn, is far from constituting a marginal notion.[9] It introduces into the pact of reading a note of trust that counterbalances the violence concealed in the strategy of persuasion. The question of reliability is to the fictional narrative what documentary proof is to historiography. It is precisely because novelists have no material proof that they ask readers not only to grant them the right to know what they are recounting or showing but to allow them to suggest an assessment, an evaluation of the main characters. Was it not just such an evaluation that allowed Aristotle to classify tragedy and comedy in terms of characters who are 'better' or 'worse' than we are, and, in particular, to give the *hamartia* – the terrible flaw – of the hero its full emotional power, inasmuch as the tragic flaw must be that of a superior individual and not of an individual who is mediocre, evil, or perverse?

Why is this category not applied to the narrator rather than to the implied author? In the rich repertory of forms adopted by the author's voice, the narrator is distinguished from the implied author whenever the narrator is dramatized as narrator. In this way, it is the unknown wise man who says that Job is a 'just' man; it is the tragic chorus that utters the sublime words of horror and pity; it is the fool who says aloud what the author thinks deep down; it is a character as a witness, possibly a scoundrel, a knave, who makes known the point of view of the narrator on his own narrative. There is always an implied author. The story is told by someone. There is not always a distinct narrator. But when there is one, the narrator shares the privilege of the implied author, who, without always being omniscient, does always have the power to reach knowledge of others from the inside. This privilege is one of the rhetorical powers invested in the implied author by reason of the tacit pact between the author and the reader. The degree to which the narrator is reliable is one of the clauses of this reading pact. As for the reader's responsibility, it is another clause of the same pact. Indeed, inasmuch as the creation of a dramatized narrator, whether reliable or unreliable, permits variation in the distance between the implied author and his characters, a degree of complexity is induced, at the same time, in the reader, a complexity that is the source of the reader's freedom in the face of the authority that the fiction receives from its author.

The case of the unreliable narrator is particularly interesting from the point of view of an appeal to the reader's freedom and responsibility. The narrator's role here may perhaps be less perverse than Wayne Booth depicts it.[10] Unlike the reliable narrator, who assures readers that in the journey they are embarking upon they need not bother about false hopes or groundless fears concerning either the facts reported or the implicit or explicit evaluations of the characters, the unreliable narrator foils these expectations by leaving readers uncertain about where this is all meant to lead. In this way, the modern novel will fulfil all the better its function of criticizing conventional morality, and possibly even its function of provocation and insult, as the narrator will be increasingly suspect and the author ever more invisible, the two resources of the rhetoric of concealment mutually reinforcing each other. In this regard, I do not share Wayne Booth's severity concerning the equivocal narrator cultivated by contemporary literature. Does not an entirely reliable narrator, such as that of the eighteenth-century novelist, so quick to intervene and lead the reader by the hand, thereby exempt the reader from taking any emotional distance from the characters and their adventures? And is not a disoriented reader, such as the reader of *The Magic Mountain*, led astray by an ironic narrator, summoned, on the contrary, to greater reflection? May we not make a plea on behalf of what Henry James, in *The Art of the Novel*, called the 'troubled vision' of a character, 'reflected in the equally troubled vision of an observer'?[11] Cannot the argument that impersonal narration is more clever than another type of narration lead to the conclusion that such narration calls for the active deciphering of 'unreliability' itself?

There is no denying that modern literature is dangerous. The sole response worthy of the criticism it provokes, of which Wayne Booth is one of the most highly esteemed representatives, is that this poisonous literature requires a new type of reader: a reader who responds.[12]

It is at this point that a rhetoric of fiction centred on the author reveals its limits. It recognizes just a single initiative, that of an author eager to communicate his vision of things.[13] In this regard, the affirmation that the author creates his readers[14] appears to lack a dialectical counterpart. Yet it may be the function of the most corrosive literature to contribute to making a new kind of reader appear, a reader who is himself suspicious, because reading ceases to be a trusting voyage made in the company of a reliable narrator, becoming instead a struggle with the implied author, a struggle leading the reader back to himself.

The Rhetoric between the Text and Its Reader

The image of a combat between a reader and an unreliable narrator, with which we concluded the preceding discussion, might easily lead us to believe that reading is added onto the text as a complement it can do without. After all, libraries are full of unread books, whose configuration is, none the less, well laid out, and yet they refigure nothing at all. Our earlier analyses should suffice to dispel this illusion. Without the reader who accompanies it, there is no configuring act at work in the text; and without a reader to appropriate it, there is no world unfolded before the text. Yet the illusion is endlessly reborn that the text is a structure in itself and for itself, and that reading happens to the text as some extrinsic and contingent event. In order to defeat this tenacious suggestion, it may be a good stratagem to turn to a few exemplary texts that theorize about their being read. This is the path chosen by Michel Charles in his *Rhétorique de la lecture*.[15]

Charles's choice of this title is itself significant. It is no longer a question of a rhetoric of fiction, carried out by an implied author, but of a rhetoric of reading, oscillating between the text and its reader. This is still a rhetoric, inasmuch as its stratagems are inscribed within the text and inasmuch as even the reader is in a way constructed in and through the work.

It is not without import, however, that Charles's work begins with an interpretation of the first strophe of Lautréamont's *Les Chants de Maldoror*. The choices with which the reader is confronted by the author himself in this case – whether to turn back or to continue on through the book, whether or not to lose himself in reading, whether to be devoured by the text or to savour it – are themselves prescribed by the text. The reader is set free, but what reading choices there are have already been encoded.[16] The violence of Lautréamont, we are told, consists in reading in place of the reader. Better, a particular reading situation is established in which the abolition of the distinction between reading and being read amounts to prescribing the 'unreadable' (p. 13).

The second text selected, the Prologue to Rabelais's *Gargantua*, is in turn treated as a 'mechanism for producing meanings' (p. 33).[17] By this, Michel Charles means the sort of logic by which this text ' "constructs" the reader's freedom, but also limits it' (p. 33). The Prologue does possess the remarkable feature that the relation of the book to the reader is built upon the same metaphorical network as is the relation of the writer to his own work: 'the drug contained within,' 'the outside form of Silenus,' taken from the Socratic dialogues, 'the bone and the marrow,' which the book holds within itself and allows to be discovered and savoured. The same 'metaphorical rhapsody' (pp. 33f) in which we can discern a recovery of the medieval theory of the multiple senses of Scripture and a recapitulation of Platonic imagery, Erasmian parable, and patristic metaphor governs the text's reference to itself and the reader's relation to the text. In this way, the Rabelaisian text attempts to interpret its own references. Nevertheless, the hermeneutic woven in the Prologue is so rhapsodic that the author's designs become impenetrable and the reader's responsibility overwhelming.

We might say as regards the first two examples chosen by Michel Charles that the prescriptions for reading already inscribed in these texts are so ambiguous that, by disorienting the reader, they free him. Charles admits as much. The task of revealing the text's incompleteness falls to reading, through the interplay of transformations it involves.[18] The efficacy of the text is, as a consequence, no different from its fragility (p. 91). And there is no longer any incompatibility between a poetics that, in Jakobson's definition, places the accent on orienting the message back towards itself and a rhetoric of effective discourse, oriented towards a receiver, once 'the message which is itself its own end, continues its *questioning*' (p. 78; his emphasis). As with the image of a poetics of an open work, the rhetoric of reading renounces setting itself up as a normative system, in order to become a 'system of possible questions' (p. 118).[19]

The final texts chosen by Michel Charles open a new perspective. By seeing the 'reading in the text' (the title of part three of *Rhétorique de la lecture*), what we find is a style of writing that allows itself to be interpreted only in terms of the interpretations it opens up. At the same time, the 'reading-to-come' is the unknown that the writing puts into perspective.[20] Ultimately, the very structure of the text is but an effect of reading. After all, is not structural analysis itself the result of a work of reading? But then the initial formulation – 'reading is part of the text, it is inscribed in it' – takes on a new meaning: reading is no longer that which the text prescribes; it is that which brings the structure of the text to light through interpretation.[21]

Charles's analysis of Benjamin Constant's *Adolphe* is particularly well-suited for demonstrating this, in that the author feigns to be merely the reader of a manuscript that has been found and in that, moreover, the interpretations internal to the work constitute so many virtual readings. Narrative, interpretation, and reading thus tend to overlap. Here Charles's thesis reaches its full strength, at the very moment when it is turned upside down. The reading is in the text, but the writing of the text anticipates the readings to come. With this, the text that is supposed to prescribe its reading is struck by the same indeterminacy and the same uncertainty as the readings to come.

A similar paradox results from the study of one of Baudelaire's *Petits Poèmes en prose*: 'Le chien et le flacon.' On the one hand, the text restrains its indirect receiver, the reader, by way of its direct receiver, the dog. The reader is really in the text and, to this extent, 'this text has no response' (p. 251). But, just when the text seems to close itself up upon the reader in a terrorist act, by splitting its receivers in two it reopens a play space that rereading can turn into a space of freedom. This 'reflexivity of reading' – in which I perceive an echo of what I shall below call, following Hans Robert Jauss, reflective reading – is what allows the act of reading to free itself from the reading inscribed within the text and to provide a response to the text.[22]

The final text chosen by Michel Charles – Rabelais's *Quart Livre* – reinforces this paradox. Once again, we see an author take a stand in relation to his text and, in doing this, set in place the variability of interpretations. 'Everything happens as if the Rabelaisian text had *foreseen* the long parade of commentaries, glosses, and interpretations that have followed it' (p. 287; his emphasis). But, as a repercussion, this long parade makes the text a 'machine for defying interpretations' (ibid.).

Rhétorique de la lecture appears to me to culminate in this paradox. On the one hand, the thesis of the 'reading contained in the text' taken absolutely, as Charles asks us to do time and time again, gives the image not of manipulated readers, as the readers seduced and perverted by the unreliable narrator described by Wayne Booth appeared to be, but of readers terrorized by the decree of predestination striking their reading. On the other hand, the perspective of an infinite reading that, interminably, structures the very text prescribing it restores to reading a disturbing indeterminacy. So we can understand, after the fact, why Michel Charles, from the opening pages of his work, gives equal measure to constraint and to freedom.

In the field of theories of reading, this paradox places *Rhétorique de la lecture* in a median position, half-way between an analysis that emphasizes the place of origin of the strategy of persuasion – the implied author – and an analysis that sets up the act of reading as the supreme authority. The theory of reading, at this point, ceases to belong to rhetoric and slips over into a phenomenology or a hermeneutics.[23]

A Phenomenology and an Aesthetic of Reading

From a purely rhetorical perspective, the reader is, finally, the prey and the victim of the strategy worked out by the implied author, and is so to the very extent this strategy is more deeply concealed. Another theory of reading is required, one that places an emphasis on the reader's response – the reader's response to the stratagems of the implied author. A new element enriching poetics arises here out of an 'aesthetic' rather than a 'rhetoric,' if we restore to the term 'aesthetic' the full range of meaning of the Greek word *aisthésis,* and if we grant to it the task of exploring the multiple ways in which a work, in acting on a reader, *affects* that reader. This being-affected has the noteworthy quality of combining in an experience of a particular type passivity and activity, which allows us to consider as the 'reception' of a text the very 'action' of reading it.

As I announced in Part I,[24] this aesthetic, as it complements poetics, encompasses in turn two different forms, depending on whether the emphasis is placed on the effect produced on the individual reader and his response in the reading process, as in the work of Wolfgang Iser,[25] or on the response of the public on the level of its collective expectations, as in the work of Hans Robert Jauss. These two aesthetics may appear to be opposed to each other, inasmuch as the one tends towards a phenomenological psychology while the other aims at reshaping literary history, but in fact they mutually presuppose each other. On the one hand, it is through the individual process of reading that the text reveals its 'structure of appeal'; on the other hand, it is inasmuch as readers participate in the sedimented expectations of the general reading public that they are constituted as competent readers. The act of reading thus becomes one link in the chain of the history of the reception of a work by the public. Literary history, renovated by the aesthetic of reception, may thus claim to include the phenomenology of the act of reading.

It is, nevertheless, legitimate to begin with this phenomenology, for it is here that the rhetoric of persuasion encounters its first limit, by encountering its first reply. If the rhetoric of persuasion is supported by the coherence, not of the work to be sure, but of the strategy – evident or concealed – of the implied author, phenomenology has its starting-point in the incomplete aspect of the literary text, which Roman Ingarden was the first to develop, in two important works.[26]

For Ingarden, a text is incomplete, first, in the sense that it offers different 'schematic views' that readers are asked to 'concretize.' They strive to picture the characters and the events reported in the text. It is in relation to this image-building concretization that the work presents lacunae, 'places of indeterminacy.' However well-articulated the 'schematic views' proposed for our execution may be, the text resembles a musical score lending itself to different realizations.

A text is incomplete, second, in the sense that the world it proposes is defined as the intentional correlate of a sequence of sentences (*intentionale Satzkorrelate*), which remains to be made into a whole for such a world to be intended. Turning to advantage the Husserlian theory of time and applying it to the sequential chain of sentences in the text, Ingarden shows how each sentence points beyond itself, indicates something to be done, opens up a perspective. We recognize Husserlian protention in this anticipation of the sequence, as the sentences follow one another. This play of retentions and protentions functions in the text only if it is taken in hand by readers who welcome it into the play of their own expectations. Unlike the perceived object, however, the literary object does not intuitively 'fulfil' these expectations; it can only modify them. This shifting process of the modification of expectations constitutes the image-building concretization mentioned above. It consists in travelling the length of the text, in allowing all the modifications performed to 'sink' into memory, while compacting them, and in opening ourselves up to new expectations entailing new modifications. This process alone makes the text a work. So this work may be said to result from the interaction between the text and the reader.

Taken up again by Wolfgang Iser, these observations borrowed from Husserl by way of Ingarden undergo a remarkable development in the phenomenology of the act of reading.[27] The most original concept here is that of the 'wandering viewpoint' (*The Act of Reading*, p. 108). It expresses the twofold fact that the whole of the text can never be perceived at once and that, placing ourselves within the literary text, we travel with it as our reading progresses. 'This mode of grasping an object is unique to literature' (p. 109). This concept of a wandering viewpoint fits perfectly with the Husserlian description of the interplay of protentions and retentions. Throughout the reading process there is a continual interplay between modified expectations and transformed memories (p. 111). In addition, this concept incorporates into the phenomenology of reading the synthetic process by which a text constitutes itself sentence by sentence, through what might be called an interplay of sentential retentions and protentions. I am also retaining here the concept of the depragmatizing of objects, borrowed from the description of the empirical world. Literary text 'depragmatize [objects], for these objects are not to be denoted [*Bezeichnung*] but are to be transformed' (p. 109).

Leaving aside the other riches of this phenomenology of reading, I shall concentrate on those features that characterize the reader's response,[28] or even retort, to the rhetoric of persuasion. These features stress the dialectical character of the act of reading and lead us to speak of the work of reading in the same way we speak of the dream-work. Reading works on the text thanks to these dialectical features.

First, the act of reading tends to become, with the modern novel, a response to the strategy of deception so well illustrated by Joyce's *Ulysses*. This strategy consists in frustrating the expectation of an immediately intelligible configuration and in placing on the reader's shoulders the burden of configuring the work. The presupposition of this strategy, without which it would have no object, is that the reader expects a configuration, that reading is a search for coherence. In my terms, I would say that reading itself becomes a drama of discordant concordance, inasmuch as the 'places of indeterminacy' (*Unbestimmtheitstellen*) – to borrow Ingarden's expression – not only designate the lacunae of the text with respect to image-building concretization, but are themselves the result of the strategy of frustration incorporated in the text as such on its rhetorical level. What is at issue is therefore something quite different from providing ourself with a figure, an image, of the work; the work has also to be given a form. At quite the other extreme from readers on the edge of boredom from following a work that is too didactic, whose instructions leave no room for creative activity, modern readers risk buckling under the load of an impossible task when they are asked to make up for this lack of readability fabricated by the author. Reading then becomes a picnic where the author brings the words and the readers the meaning.

The first dialectic, by which reading comes close to being a battle, gives rise to a second one. What the work of reading reveals is not only a lack of determinacy but also an excess of meaning. Every text, even a systematically fragmentary one, is revealed to be inexhaustible in terms of reading, as though, through its unavoidably selective character, reading revealed an unwritten aspect in the text. It is the prerogative of reading to strive to provide a figure for this unwritten side of the text. The text thus appears, by turns, both lacking and excessive in relation to reading.

A third dialectic takes shape on the horizon of this search for coherence. If it is too successful, the unfamiliar becomes familiar, and readers, feeling themselves to be on an equal footing with the work, come to believe in it so completely they lose themselves in it. Concretizing then becomes an illusion in the sense of believing that one actually sees something.[29] If the search for coherence fails, however, what is foreign remains foreign, and the reader remains on the doorstep of the work. The 'right' reading is, therefore, the one that admits a certain degree of illusion – another name for the 'willing suspension of disbelief' called for by Coleridge – and at the same time accepts the negation resulting from the work's surplus of meaning, its polysemanticism, which negates all the reader's attempts to adhere to the text and to its instructions. This process of 'defamiliarizing' on the side of the reader corresponds to that of depragmatizing on the side of the text and its implied author. The 'right' distance from the work is the one from which the illusion is, by turns, irresistible and untenable. As for a balance between these two impulses, it is never achieved.

Taken together, these three dialectics make reading a truly vital experience [*expérience vive*].

It is here that the 'aesthetic' theory of reading authorizes a slightly different interpretation than that provided by the rhetoric of persuasion. The authors who most respect their readers are not the ones who gratify them in the cheapest way; they are the ones who leave a greater range to their readers to play out the contrast we have just discussed. They reach their readers only if they share with them a repertoire of what is familiar with respect to literary genre, theme, and social – even historical – context, and if, on the other hand, they practise a strategy of defamiliarizing in relation to all the norms that any reading can easily recognize and adopt. In this regard, the unreliable narrator becomes the object of a more lenient judgment than that made by Wayne Booth. The unreliable narrator is one element in the strategy of illusion-breaking that illusion-making requires as its antidote. This strategy is one of those more apt to stimulate an active reading, a reading that permits us to say that something is happening in this game in which what is won is of the same magnitude as what is lost.[30] The balance of this gain and loss is unknown to readers; this is why they need to talk about it in order to formulate it. The critic is the one who can help to clarify the poorly elucidated potentialities hidden in this situation of disorientation.

In fact, it is what comes after reading that determines whether or not the stasis of disorientation has generated a dynamics of reorientation.

The advantage of this theory of response-effect is clear. A balance is sought between the signals provided by the text and the synthetic activity of reading. This balance is the unstable effect of the dynamism by which, I would say, the configuration of the text in terms of structure becomes equal to the reader's refiguration in terms of experience. This vital experience, in turn, is a genuine dialectic by virtue of the negativity it implies: depragmatization and defamiliarization, inversion of the given in image-building consciousness, illusion-breaking.[31]

Is the phenomenology of reading thereby entitled to make the category of 'implied reader' the exact counterpart to that of the 'implied author' introduced by the rhetoric of fiction?

At first sight, a symmetry does appear to be established between the implied author and the implied reader, each represented by its corresponding marks in the text. By implied reader we must then understand the role assigned to the real reader by the instructions in the text. The implied author and the implied reader thus become literary categories compatible with the semantic autonomy of the text. Inasmuch as they are constructed in the text, they are both fictional correlates of real beings. The implied author is identified with the unique style of the work, the implied reader with the receiver to whom the sender of the work addresses himself. This symmetry, however, proves finally misleading. On the one hand, the implied author is a disguise of the real author, who disappears by making himself the narrator immanent in the work – the narrative voice. On the other hand, the real reader is a concretization of the implied reader, intended by the narrator's strategy of persuasion. In relation to the narrator, the implied reader remains virtual as long as this role has not been actualized.[32] Thus, whereas the real author effaces himself in the implied author, the implied reader takes on substance in the real reader. This real reader is the pole opposite the text in the process of interaction giving rise to the meaning of the work. It is in fact this real reader who is in question in a phenomenology of the act of reading. This is why I would be more inclined to praise Iser for getting rid of the aporias arising out of the distinctions made at various points between intended reader, ideal reader, competent reader, reader contemporary with the work, today's reader, and so on. Not that these distinctions are groundless, but various figures of the reader do not take us even a single step outside the structure of the text, of which the implied reader continues to be a variable. To give full scope to the theme of interaction, the phenomenology of the act of reading requires a flesh-and-blood reader, who, in actualizing the role of the reader prestructured in and through the text, transforms it.[33]

The aesthetic of reception, as we stated above, can be taken in two senses: either in the sense of a phenomenology of the individual act of reading in the 'theory of aesthetic response' of Wolfgang Iser, or in the sense of a hermeneutic of the public reception of a work as in Hans Robert Jauss's *Toward an Aesthetic of Reception*.[34] However, as we have already hinted, these two approaches intersect at some point – precisely, in *aisthēsis*.

Let us therefore follow the movement by which the aesthetic of reception leads back to this point of intersection.

In its initial formulation,[35] Jauss's aesthetic of reception was not intended to complete a phenomenological theory of the act of reading but rather to renew the history of literature, which is said at the start of this essay to have 'fallen into disrepute, and not at all without reason' (p. 3).[36] Several major theses make up the program for this aesthetic of reception.

The basic thesis from which all the others are derived holds that the meaning of a literary work rests upon the dialogical (*dialogisch*)[37] relation established between the work and its public in each age. This thesis, similar to Collingwood's notion that history is but a re-enactment of the past in the mind of the historian, amounts to including the effect produced (*Wirkung*) by a work – in other words, the meaning a public attributes to it – within the boundaries of the work itself. The challenge, as it is announced in the title of Jauss's essay, consists in equating actual meaning with reception. It is not simply the actual effect but the 'history of effects' – to use an expression from Gadamer's philosophical hermeneutics – that has to be taken into account, which requires restoring the horizon of expectation[38] of the literary work considered; that is, the system of references shaped by earlier traditions concerning the genre, the theme, and the degree of contrasts for the first receivers between the poetic language and everyday practical language (we shall return to this important opposition).[39] In this way, we understand the sense of parody in *Don Quixote* only if we are capable of reconstructing its initial public's feeling of familiarity with chivalrous romances and, consequently, if we are capable of understanding the shock produced by a work that, after feigning to satisfy the public's expectation, runs directly counter to it. The case of new works is in this respect the most favourable for discerning the change of horizon that constitutes the major effect that occurs here. Hence the critical factor for establishing a literary history is the identification of successive aesthetic distances between the pre-existing horizon of expectation and the new work, distances that mark out the work's reception. Theses distances constitute the moments of negativity in this reception. But what is it to reconstitute the horizon of expectation of a yet unknown experience, if not to discover the interplay of questions to which the work suggests an answer? To the ideas of effect, history of effects, and horizon of expectations must be added, following once again Collingwood and Gadamer, the logic of question and answer; a logic whereby we can understand a work only if we have understood that to which it responds.[40] This logic of question and answer, in turn, allows us to correct the idea that history would be no more than a history of gaps or deviations, hence a history of negativity. As a response, the reception of a work performs a certain mediation between the past and the present or, better, between the horizon of expectation coming from the past and the horizon of expectation belonging to the present. The thematic concern of literary history lies in this 'historical mediation.'

Having arrived at this point, we may ask whether the horizons stemming from this mediation can stabilize in any lasting way the meaning of a work, to the point of conferring a transhistorical authority on it. In opposition to Gadamer's thesis concerning 'the classical,'[41] Jauss refuses to see in the enduring character of great works anything other than a temporary stabilization of the dynamic of reception; any Platonic hypostasizing of a prototype offered to our recognition would, according to him, violate the rule of questions and answers. For what, to us, is classical was not first perceived as something outside of time but rather as opening up a new horizon. If we admit that the cognitive value of a work lies in its power to prefigure an experience to come, then there must be no question of freezing the dialogical relation into an atemporal truth. This open character of the history of effects leads us to say that every work is not only an answer provided to an earlier question but a source of new questions, in turn, Jauss refers to Hans Blumenberg, for whom 'each work of art poses and leaves behind, as a kind of including horizon, the 'solutions' which are possible after it.'[42] These new questions are opened not only in front of the work but behind it as well. For example, it is after the fact, by a recoil-effect of Mallarmé's lyrical hermeticism, that we are able to release virtual meanings in baroque poetry that had hitherto remained unnoticed. But it is not only before and behind, in diachrony, that the work opens up distances; this also occurs in the present, as a synchronic cross-section of a phase of literary evolution will show. We may hesitate here between a conception that underscores the total heterogeneity of culture at any given moment, to the point of proclaiming the pure 'coexistence of the simultaneous and the non-simultaneous,'[43] and a conception where the emphasis is placed on the effect of totalization resulting from the redistribution of horizons through the interplay of question and answer. We thus find on the synchronic plane a problem comparable to that posed by 'the classical' on the diachronic plane; the history of literature must break a path through the same paradoxes and the same extremes.[44] just as it is true that at any given moment, a particular work may have been perceived as out of step, not current, premature, or outmoded (Nietzsche would say 'untimely'), so too it must also be admitted that, owing to the history of reception itself, the multiplicity of works tends to form one great tableau that the public perceives as the production of *its* time. Literary history would not be possible without a few great works serving as reference points, relatively enduring in the diachronic process, and acting as powerful forces of integration in the synchronic dimension.[45]

We can see the fruitfulness of these theses with respect to the old problem of the social influence of the work of art. We must challenge with equal force the thesis of a narrow structuralism which forbids 'moving outside the text' and that of a dogmatic Marxism which merely shifts onto the social plane the worn-out topos of *imitatio naturae*. It is on the level of a public's horizon of expectations that a work exercises what Jauss terms the 'creative function of the work of art.'[46] The horizon of expectation peculiar to literature does not coincide with that of everyday life. If a new work is able to create an aesthetic distance, it is because a prior distance exists between the whole of literary life and everyday practice. It is a basic characteristic of the horizon of expectation, against the background of which new reception stands out, that it is itself the expression of an even more basic non-coincidence, namely, the opposition in a given culture 'between poetic language and practical language, imaginary world and social reality' (p. 24).[47] What we have just indicated as literature's function of social creation arises quite precisely at this point of

articulation between the expectations turned towards art and literature and the expectations constitutive of everyday experience.[48]

The moment when literature attains its highest degree of efficacy
is perhaps the moment when it places its readers in the position of
finding a solution for which they themselves must find the appropriate questions, those that constitute the aesthetic and moral problem
posed by a work.

If *Toward an Aesthetic of Reception*, whose basic theses we have just
summarized, could link up with and complete the phenomenology of
the act of reading, this was through an expansion of its initial undertaking, which was to renew literary history, and from its insertion
within a more ambitious project, that of constituting a literary hermeneutics.[49] This hermeneutics is assigned the task of equalling the
other two regional hermeneutics, theological and juridical, under the
auspices of a philosophical hermeneutics akin to that of Gadamer.
Literary hermeneutics, as Jauss admits, continues to be the poor
relation of hermeneutics. A literary hermeneutics worthy of the
name must assume the threefold task, referred to above, of understanding (*subtilitas intelligendi*), explanation *subtilitas interpretandi*),
and application (*subtilitas applicandi*). In contrast to a superficial view,
reading must not be confined to the field of application, even if this
field does reveal the end of the hermeneutical process; instead,
reading must pass through all three stages. A literary hermeneutics
will, therefore, reply to these three questions: In what sense is the
primary undertaking of understanding entitled to characterize the
object of literary hermeneutics as an aesthetic one? What does
reflective exegesis add to understanding? What equivalent to a ser-
mon in biblical exegesis and to a verdict in juridical exegesis does
literature offer on the level of application: In this triadic structure,
application orients the entire process teleologically, but primary
understanding guides the process from one stage to the next by
virtue of the horizon of expectation it already contains. Literary
hermeneutics is thus oriented both towards application and by understanding. And it is the logic of question and answer that ensures
the transition to explanation.

The primacy accorded to understanding explains why literary
hermeneutics, unlike Gadamer's philosophical hermeneutics, is not
directly produced by the logic of question and answer. Finding the
question to which a text offers a reply, reconstructing the expectations

of a text's first receivers in order to restore to the text its original otherness – these are already steps in rereading, standing second in relation to a primary understanding that allows the text to develop its own expectations.

This primacy ascribed to understanding is explained by the wholly original relation between knowledge and enjoyment (*Genuss*) that ensures the aesthetic quality of literary hermeneutics. This relation parallels that between the call and promise, committing a whole life, characterizing theological understanding. If the specific nature of literary understanding in terms of enjoyment has been neglected, this is due to the curious convergence between the interdiction uttered by structural poetics, forbidding us to step outside the text or to move beyond the reading instructions it contains,[50] and the disfavour cast on enjoyment by Adorno's negative aesthetic, which sees in it merely a 'bourgeois' compensation for the asceticism of labour.[51]

Contrary to the common idea that pleasure is ignorant and mute, Jauss asserts that it possesses the power to open a space of meaning in which the logic of question and answer will subsequently unfold. It gives rise to understanding – *il donne à comprendre*. Pleasure is a perceptive reception, attentive to the prescriptions of the musical score that the text is, one that opens up by virtue of the horizonal aspect that Husserl attributed to all perception. By all these features, aesthetic perception is distinguished from everyday perception and thus establishes a distance in relation to ordinary experience, as this was underscored above in Jauss's theses on the renewal of literary history. The text asks its readers, first of all, to entrust themselves to this perceptive understanding, to the suggestions of meaning that a second reading will thematize, suggestions of meaning that will provide a horizon for this reading.

The passage from the first reading, the innocent reading – if there is one – to the second reading, a reading at a distance, is governed, as we stated above, by the horizontal structure of immediate under-standing. This structure is not simply staked out by the expectations stemming from the dominant tendencies in taste of the epoch when a text is read or from the reader's familiarity with earlier works. This horizontal structure gives rise, in turn, to expectations of meaning that are not satisfied, which reading reinscribes within the logic of question and answer. So reading and rereading have their respective advantages and weaknesses. Reading includes both richness and opacity; rereading clarifies but in so doing makes choices. It is based on the questions that remained open after the first passage through the text but offers only one interpretation among others. So a dialectic of expectations and of questions governs the relation between reading and rereading. Expectations are open but more undetermined; questions are determined but more closed-in upon themselves. Literary criticism must take its stand on the basis of this hermeneutical pre-condition of partiality.

The elucidation of this partiality gives rise to a third reading. This emerges from the question: what historical horizon has conditioned the genesis and the effect of the work and limits, in turn, the interpretation of the present reader? Literary hermeneutics delimits in this way the legitimate space for the historico-philological methods that predominated in the pre-structuralist era and that were dethroned in the age of structuralism. Their proper place is defined by their function of verification which, in a certain sense, makes immediate reading, and even reflective reading, dependent on the reading based on historical reconstruction. By a recoil-effect the reading of verification helps to disentangle aesthetic pleasure from the mere satisfaction of contemporary prejudices and interests, by tying it to the perception of the difference between the past horizon of the work and the present horizon of reading. A strong feeling of distancing is thus inserted at the heart of present pleasure. The third reading brings about this effect by redoubling the logic of question and answer that governed the second reading. What, it asks, were the questions to which the work was the answer? Yet this third 'historical' reading continues to be guided by the expectations of the first reading and by the questions of the second reading. The merely historicizing question – what did the text say? – remains under the control of the properly hermeneutical question – what does the text say to me and what do I say to the text?[52]

What becomes of application in this schema? At first sight, the application proper to this hermeneutics does not appear to produce any effect comparable to preaching in theological hermeneutics or to a verdict in juridical hermeneutics. The recognition of the text's otherness in scholarly reading seems to be the final word of literary aesthetics. This hesitation is understandable. If it is true that *aisthēsis* and enjoyment are not restricted to the level of immediate understanding but carry through all the levels of hermeneutical 'subtility,' we may be tempted to consider the aesthetic dimension that accompanies pleasure in its traversal of the three hermeneutical stages as the final criterion for literary hermeneutics. If so, then application does not constitute a genuinely distinct stage. *Aisthēsis* itself already reveals and transforms. Aesthetic experience draws this power from the contrast it establishes from the outset in relation to everyday experience. But it is 'refractory' to anything other than itself, it asserts its ability to transfigure the everyday and to transgress accepted standards. Before any reflective distanciation, aesthetic understanding as such appears to be application. Attesting to this is the range of effects it deploys: from the seduction and illusion so dear to popular literature, to the appeasement of suffering and the aestheticizing of the experience of the past, to the subversion and utopia characteristic of so many contemporary works. Through this variety of effects, aesthetic experience as it is invested in reading directly corroborates Erasmus's aphorism: *lectio transit in mores*.

It is possible, however, to discern a more distinct contour for application if it is set at the end of another triad, which Jauss interweaves with that of the three subtleties without establishing a term-by-term correspondence between the two series – the triad here is *poiēsis, aisthēsis, catharsis*.[53] A complex set of effects is attached to catharsis. It designates, first of all, the effect of the work that is more moral than aesthetic: new evaluations, hitherto unheard-of norms, are proposed by the work, confronting or shaking current customs.[54] This first effect is closely bound up with readers' tendency to identify with the hero, and to allow themselves to be guided by the reliable or unreliable narrator. Catharsis, however, has this moral effect only because, first of all, it displays the power of clarifying, examining, and instructing exerted by the work in virtue of the distanciation that takes place in relation to our own affects.[55] It is an easy passage from this sense to the one most strongly emphasized by Jauss, namely, the work's communicative efficacy. A clarification is, indeed, essentially communicative; through it, the work 'teaches.'[56] What we find here is not simply a notation from Aristotle but a major feature of Kantian aesthetics – the contention that the universal nature of the beautiful consists in nothing else than in its *a priori* communicability. Catharsis thus constitutes a distinct moment from *aisthēsis*, conceived of as pure receptivity; namely, the moment of communicability of perceptive understanding. *Aisthēsis* frees the reader from everyday concerns; catharsis sets the reader free for new evaluations of reality that will take shape in rereading. An even more subtle effect results from catharsis. Thanks to the clarification it brings about, catharsis sets in motion a process of transposition, one that is not only affective but cognitive as well, something like *allégorèse*, whose history can be traced back to Christian and pagan exegesis. Allegorization occurs whenever we attempt 'to translate the meaning of a text in its first context into another context, which amounts to saying: to give it a new signification which goes beyond the horizon of meaning delimited by the intentionality of the text in its original context.'[57] It is ultimately this allegorizing power, related to catharsis, that makes literary application the response most similar to the analogizing apprehension of the past in the dialectic of the *Gegenüber* and of indebtedness.

This is the distinct problematic arising from application, which, however, never entirely escapes the horizon of the perceptive understanding and the attitude of enjoyment.

At the end of our perusal of several theories of reading, chosen in view of their contribution to our problem of refiguration, several major features stand out that underscore, each in its own way, the dialectical structure of the operation of refiguration.

The first dialectical tension arose from the comparison we could not help but make between the feeling of a debt, which appeared to us to accompany the relation of standing-for the past, and the freedom of the imaginative variations performed by fiction on the theme of the aporias of time, as we described them in 'The Aporetics of Temporality,' in *Time and Narrative*, Volume 3 (pp. 11–96). The analyses we have just made of the phenomenon of reading lead us to nuance this overly simple opposition. It must be stated, first of all, that the projection of a fictive would consists in a complex creative process, which may be no less marked by an awareness of a debt than is the historian's work of reconstruction. The question of creative freedom is not a simple one. The liberation of fiction as regards the constraints of history – constraints summed up in documentary proof – does not constitute the final word concerning the freedom of fiction. It constitutes only the Cartesian moment: free choice in the realm of the imaginary. But its service to the world-view that the implied author strives to communicate to the reader is for fiction the source of more subtle constraints, which express the Spinozist moment of freedom: namely, internal necessity. Free from the external constraint of documentary proof, fiction is bound internally by the very thing that it projects outside itself. Free from ..., artists must still make themselves free for ... If this were not the case, how could we explain the anguish and suffering of artistic creation as they are attested to by the correspondence and diaries of a van Gogh or a

Cézanne? Thus, the stringent law of creation, which is to render as perfectly as possible the vision of the world that inspires the artist, corresponds, feature by feature, to the debt of the historian and the reader of history with respect to the dead.[58] What the strategy of persuasion, wrought by the implied author, seeks to impose on the reader is, precisely, the force of conviction – the illocutionary force, we might say in the vocabulary of speech-act theory – that upholds the narrator's vision of the world. The paradox here is that the freedom of the imaginative variations is communicated only by being cloaked in the constraining power of a vision of the world. The dialectic between freedom and constraint, internal to the creative process, is thus transmitted throughout the hermeneutical process that Jauss characterizes by means of the triad *poiēsis, aisthēsis, catharsis.* The final term of this triad is the very one in which this paradox of a constrained freedom, of a freedom released by constraint, culminates. In the moment of clarification and of purification, readers are rendered free in spite of themselves. It is this paradox that makes the confrontation between the world of the text and the world of the reader a struggle to which the fusion of horizons of expectation of the text with those of the reader brings only a precarious peace.

A second dialectical tension arises from the structure of the operation of reading itself. Indeed, it appeared impossible to give a simple description of this phenomenon. We had to start from the pole of the implied author and his strategy of persuasion, then to cross over the ambiguous zone of a prescription for reading, which at once constrains readers and sets them free, in order, finally, to reach an aesthetic of reception, which places the work and the reader in a synergetic relation. This dialectic should be compared with the one that appeared to us to mark the relation of standing-for resulting from the enigma of the pastness of the past. To be sure, it is not a matter of seeking a term-by-term resemblance between the moments of the theory of standing-for and those of the theory of reading. None the less, the dialectical constitution of reading is not foreign to the dialectic of the Same, the Other, and the Analogous.[59] For example, the rhetoric of fiction brings on stage an implied author who, through the ploy of seduction, attempts to make the reader identical with himself. But, when readers, discovering the place prescribed for them in the text, no longer feel seduced but terrorized, their only recourse is to set themselves at a distance from the text and to become fully conscious of the distance between the expectations developed by the text and their own expectations, as individuals caught up in everyday concerns and as members of a cultured public formed by an entire tradition of readings. This oscillation between Same and Other is overcome only in the operation characterized by Gadamer and Jauss as the fusion of horizons and that may be held to be the ideal type of reading. Beyond the alternatives of confusion and alienation, the convergence of writing and reading tends to establish, between the expectations created by the text and those contributed by reading, an analogizing relation, not without resemblance to that in which the relation of standing-for the historical past culminates.

Another remarkable property of the phenomenon of reading, one which also generates a dialectic, has to do with the relation between communicability and referentiality (if it is still legitimate to employ this term, with the appropriate reservations) in the operation of refiguration. We can enter this problem from either end. We can say, as in our sketch of *mimesis₃* in Volume 1, *Time and Narrative*, that an aesthetics of reception cannot take up the problem of communication without taking up that of reference, inasmuch as what is communicated is, in the final analysis, beyond the sense of the work, the world the work projects, the world that constitutes the horizon of the work[60] But, from the opposite direction, we must say that the reception of the work and the welcome given what Gadamer likes to call the 'issue' of the text are extracted from the sheer subjectivity of the act of reading only on the condition of being inscribed within a chain of readings, which gives a historical dimension to this reception and to this welcome. The act of reading is thereby included within a reading community, which, under certain favourable conditions, develops the sort of normativity and canonical status that we acknowledge in great works, those that never cease decontextualizing and recontextualizing themselves in the most diverse cultural circumstances. From this angle we return to a central theme in Kantian aesthetics, namely, that communicability constitutes an intrinsic component of the judgment of taste. To be sure, it is not to reflective judgment that we ascribe this sort of universality which Kant held to be *a priori* but, quite the contrary, to the 'thing itself' that summons us in the text. However, between this 'appeal structure,' to speak as Iser does, and the communicability characteristic of a reading-in-common, a reciprocal relation is established, intrinsically constitutive of the power of refiguration belonging to works of fiction.

A final dialectic concerns the two, if not antithetical at least divergent, roles assumed by reading. Reading appears, by turns, as an interruption in the course of action and as a new impetus to action. These two perspectives on reading result directly from its functions of confrontation and connection between the imaginary world of the text and the actual world of readers. To the extent that readers subordinate their expectations to those developed by the text, they themselves become unreal to a degree comparable to the unreality of the fictive world towards which they emigrate. Reading then becomes a place, itself unreal, where reflection takes a pause. On the other hand, inasmuch as readers incorporate – little matter whether consciously or unconsciously – into their vision of the world the lessons of their readings, in order to increase the prior readability of this vision, then reading is for them something other than a place where they come to rest; it is a medium they cross through.

This twofold status of reading makes the confrontation between the world of the text and the world of the reader at once a stasis and an impetus.[61] The ideal type of reading, figured by the fusion but not confusion of the horizons of expectation of the text and those of the reader, unites these two moments of refiguration in the fragile unity of stasis and impetus. This fragile union can be expressed in the following paradox: the more readers become unreal in their reading, the more profound and far-reaching will be the work's influence on social reality. Is it not the least figurative style of painting that has the greatest chance of changing our vision of the world?

From this final dialectic comes the result that, if the problem of the refiguration of time by narrative comes together in the narrative, it does not find its outcome there.

Notes

1 Wayne Booth, *The Rhetoric of Fiction* (Chicago: University of Chicago Press, 1961; 2d ed., 1981). The second edition contains an important Afterword. This work's objective, we read in the Preface, is to pursue 'the author's means of controlling his reader.' And further: 'My subject is the technique of non-didactic fiction, viewed as the art of communicating with readers – the rhetorical resources available to the writer of epic, novel, or short story as he tries, consciously or unconsciously, to impose his fictional world upon the reader.' The psychological analysis of written text (psycho-graphics) is not, for all that, stripped of all rights; a genuine problem stemming from the psychology of creation remains – that of understanding why and how a real author adopts a particular disguise, this mask rather than that one; in short, why and how the author assumes the 'second self' that makes him an 'implied author.'

The problem of the complex relations between the real author and the various official versions he gives of himself fully remains (ibid., p. 71). Cf. also Booth's essay, contemporary with *The Rhetoric of Fiction*, 'Distance and Point of View' in *Essays in Criticism* 11 (1961): 60–79.

2 As Booth says, 'though the author can to some extent choose his disguises, he can never choose to disappear' (*The Rhetoric of Fiction*, p. 20).

3 The realism of subjectivity is only apparently opposed to naturalistic realism. As realism it stems from the same rhetoric as does its contrary, striving for the apparent effacement of the author.

4 See Jean Pouillon, *Temps et roman* (Paris: Gallimard, 1946).

5 In this respect Sartre's polemic against Mauriac seems quite pointless. (Jean-Paul Sartre, 'François Mauriac and Freedom,' in *Literary and Philosophical Essays*, trans. by Annette Michelson [New York: Collier Books, 1962], pp. 7–25.) In assuming the raw realism of subjectivity, the novelist takes himself to be God no less than does the omniscient narrator. Sartre grossly underestimates the tacit agreement that confers upon the novelist the right to know what he is attempting to write about. It may be one of the clauses of this contract that the novelist knows nothing at all or not be allowed the right to know the mind of a character except through someone else's eyes; but jumping from one viewpoint to another remains a considerable privilege, compared to our resources for knowing other people in so-called real life.

6 Whether 'an impersonal novelist hides behind a single narrator or observer, the multiple points of view of *Ulysses* or *As I Lay Dying*, or the objective surfaces of *The Awkward Age* or Compton-Burnett's *Parents and Children*, the author's voice is never really silenced. It is, in fact, one of the things we read fiction for' (*The Rhetoric of Fiction*, p. 60).

7 Once again, these considerations do not lead us back to a psychology of the author; what the reader discerns in the markings of the text is the implied author. 'We infer [the implied author] as an ideal, literary, created version of the real man; he is the sum of his own choices' (ibid., p. 75). This 'second self' is the creation of the work. The author creates an image of himself, just as he does of me, the reader.

8 G.G. Granger, *Essai d'une philosophie du style* (Paris: Armand Colin, 1968)

9 In the opening lines of *The Rhetoric of Fiction*, it is stated that 'one of the most obviously artificial devices of the storyteller is the trick of going beneath the surface of the action to obtain a reliable view of a character's mind and heart' (ibid., p. 3). Booth defines this category in the following way. 'I have called a narrator *reliable* when he speaks for or acts in accordance with the norms of the work' (ibid., p. 158; his emphasis).

10 According to Booth, a narrative in which the author's voice can no longer be discerned, in which the point of view continually shifts, and in which reliable narrators are impossible to identify creates a confused vision, and plunges its readers into confusion. After praising Proust for guiding his reader towards an unambiguous illumination in which author, narrator, and reader join one another on the intellectual level, Booth does not conceal his misgivings about Camus's strategy in *The Fall*. Here the narrator seems to him to draw the

reader into Clamence's spiritual collapse. Booth is certainly not mistaken to stress the higher and higher price that has to be paid for a narration that lacks the counsel of a reliable narrator. He may even be justified in fearing that a reader who is thrown into confusion, mystified, puzzled, to the point of being thrown off balance' will be secretly tempted to give up the task that Eric Auerback ascribed to narration: 'To give meaning and order to our lives' (ibid., p. 371, quoting *Mimesis: The Representation of Reality in Western Literature*, trans. Willard Trask [Princeton: Princeton University Press, 1953], pp. 485–6). The danger is indeed that persuasion will give way to the seduction of perversity. this is the problem posed by the 'seductive rogues' who narrate much modern fiction (ibid., p. 379). Above all, however, Booth is right to stress, in contrast to every allegedly neutral aesthetic, that the viewpoint of characters as it is communicated to and imposed upon the reader possesses not only psychological and aesthetic aspects but social and moral ones as well. His whole polemic centred on the unreliable narrator tends to show that the rhetoric of impartiality, of impassibility, conceals a secret commitment capable of seducing readers and making them share, for example, an ironic interest in the fate of a character apparently bent on self-destruction. Wayne Booth can thus fear that a great part of contemporary literature goes astray, caught up in a demoralizing operation that is all the more effective in that the rhetoric of persuasion resorts to a more deeply hidden strategy. We may nevertheless wonder who is the judge of what is finally pernicious. If it is true that the ridiculous and odious trial of *Madame Bovary* does not justify *a contrario* every sort of insult to the strict minimum of ethical consensus without which no community could survive, it is also true that even the most pernicious, the most perverse attempt at seduction – the attempt, for instance, to ascribe value to the degradation of women, to cruelty and torture, to racial discrimination, or to advocate disinvolvement, ridicule (in short, ethical divestment), to the exclusion of any broader or higher system of values – can, at the limit, on the level of the imaginary, possess an ethical function: serving as a means of distanciation.

11 Henry James, *The Art of the Novel*, ed. by R.P. Blackmur (New York: Charles Schribner's Sons, 1934), pp. 153–4

12 This is why Booth can only mistrust authors who generate confusion. All his admiration is reserved for those who create not only clarity but worthy universal values as well. His reply to his critics appears in the Afterword to the second edition of *The Rhetoric of Fiction*, 'The Rhetoric in Fiction and Fiction as Rhetoric: Twenty-One Years Later' (ibid., pp. 401–57). In another essay, 'The Way I Loved George Eliot: Friendship with Books as a Neglected Metaphor,' *Kenyon Review* 11:2 (1980): 4–27, he introduces into the diagological relation between the text and the reader the model of friendship he finds in Aristotelian ethics. He thereby links up with Henri Marrou, who spoke of the relation of the historian to the people of the past. Reading, too, according to Booth, can be enriched by the reappearance of a virtue that was so dear to the ancients.

13 'In short, the writer should worry less about whether his *narrators* are realistic than about whether the *image he creates of himself*, his implied author, is one that his most intelligent and perceptive readers can admire' (*The Rhetoric of Fiction*, p. 395; his emphasis). 'When human actions are formed to make an art work, the form that is made can never be divorced from the human meanings, including the moral judgments, that are implicit whenever human beings act' (ibid., p. 397).

14 'The author makes his readers ... But if he makes them well – that is, makes them see what they have never seen before, moves them into a new order of perception and experience altogether – he finds his reward in the peers he has created' (ibid., pp. 397–8).

15 Michel Charles, *Rhétorique de la lecture* (Paris: Seuil, 1977). 'It is a matter of examining how a text presents, even "theorizes" about, explicitly or not, the reading or readings that we actually do or could do; how it leaves us free (*makes* us free) or how it constrains us' (ibid., p. 9; his emphasis). I will not attempt to draw a full-fledged theory from Charles's work, for he has insisted on preserving the 'fragmentary' character of his analysis of reading, which he perceives to be a 'massive, enormous, omnipresent object' (ibid., p. 10). Texts that prescribe their own reading and even inscribe it within their own borders constitute an exception rather than a rule. These texts, however, do resemble the limit-case of the absolutely unreliable narrator proposed by Wayne Booth. These limit-cases give rise to a reflection that can itself be said to go to the limit, a reflection that draws an exemplary analysis from exceptional cases. This is the legitimate extrapolation made by Charles when he states as 'an essential fact [that] reading belongs to the text, it is inscribed in it' (ibid., p. 9).

16 Concerning the oscillations between reading and reader, cf. ibid., pp. 24–5. The theory of reading does not escape rhetoric 'inasmuch as it presupposes that any reading transforms its reader and inasmuch as it controls this transformation' (ibid., p. 25). In this context, the rhetoric in question is no longer that of the text but that of any and all critical activity.

17 The borderline between reading and reader is not clearly drawn: 'At the point where we are, the reader is responsible for this scholarly reading that has been described to us, so that the opposition is now between the frivolousness of the writer and the seriousness of reading' (ibid., p. 48). This statement is counterbalanced by the following one. 'The brotherhood of readers and authors is obviously an effect of the text. The book presupposes a complicity that it, in fact, constructs out of bits and pieces' (ibid., p. 53). But later we read, concerning the appeal of the text, that 'a process is thus set in motion at the end of which, inevitably, the reader (the perfect reader) will be the author of the book' (ibid., p. 57). And farther on: 'The Prologue describes us, we who read it; it describes us as we are occupied in reading it' (ibid., p. 58).

18 'The postulate of the completeness of the work or of its closure conceals the ordered process of transformation that constitutes the "text-to-be-read"; the closed work is a work that has been read, which by this token has lost all efficacy and all power' (ibid., p. 61).

19 In saying this, Charles does not allow himself to waver from his thesis that
   reading is inscribed in the text. 'And to assume that decision is free is (again)
   an effect of the text' (ibid., p. 118). So the notion of an 'effect' makes us go
   outside the text while still remaining within it. This is where I see the limit of
   Charles's undertaking. His theory of reading never manages to free itself from
   a theory of writing, when it does not simply turn into one, as is evident in the
   second part of the book, where Genette, Paulhan, Dumarsais and Fontanier,
   Bernard Lamy, Claude Fleury, and Cordomoy teach us an art of reading that is
   totally implicated in the art of writing, speaking, and arguing, on the condition,
   however, that the design of persuasion remain perceptible. 'It is a matter of
   acting as though the text, writing, are "assimilated" by rhetoric; it is a matter of
   showing that a rereading of rhetoric is possible on the basis of the experience
   of the text, of writing' (ibid., p. 211). To be sure, aiming at the receiver does
   define the rhetorical point of view and is enough to keep it from dissolving into
   the poetical point of view. But what the receiver does is not taken into
   consideration here, inasmuch as aiming at the receiver is inscribed within the
   text, is its intention. 'To analyse *the* structure of *Adolphe* is therefore to
   analyse the relation between a text and its interpretation, as neither of these
   two elements can be treated in isolation; structure does not designate ... a
   principle of order preexisting in the text, but the "response" of a text to
   reading' (ibid., p. 215; his emphasis). Here Michel Charles's *Rhétorique de la
   lecture* overlaps Jauss's *Toward an Aesthetic of Reception*, which we shall
   discuss below, to the extent that the history of the reception of a text is
   included in a new reception of it and, in this way, contributes to its current
   meaning.
20 It is true that Charles takes such pains in rereading classical rhetoric in order
   to indicate the limits of a normative rhetoric that claims to control its effects.
   'A rhetoric that did not impose this limit on itself would deliberately "turn
   back into" an "art of reading" in which discourse is conceived of as a function
   of possible interpretations, its perspective being based on an unknown
   element: readings yet to come' (ibid., p. 211).
21 Remarque IV returns to this formulation: 'The reading of a text is indicated
   within the text.' But a correction follows: 'The reading is in the text, but it is
   not written there; it is the future of the text' (ibid., p. 247).
22 Speaking of 'the *infinite* reading that makes Rabelais's work *a text*,' Charles
   states that 'a typology of discourses must be coupled with a typology of
   readings; a history of genres with a history of reading' (ibid., p. 287; his
   emphases). This is what we shall do in the pages that follow.
23 Michel Charles both invites us to take this step and forbids us to do so. 'In this
   text by Baudelaire, there are thus elements with a *variable* rhetorical status.
   This variability produced a *dynamics of reading*' (ibid., p. 254; his emphasis).
   Only it is not this dynamics that interests Charles here but instead the fact that
   the interplay of interpretations is finally what constructs the text: 'A reflexive
   text, it reconstructs itself out of the debris of reading' (ibid., p. 254). The
   reflexity of reading moves back into the text. This is why his interest in the

art of reading is finally always obliterated by his interest in the structure that results from reading. In this sense, the theory of reading remains a variant of a theory of writing for Charles.

24 See *Time and Narrative*, I: 77.

25 Wolfgang Iser, *The Implied Reader: Patterns of Communication in Prose Fiction from Bunyan to Beckett* (Baltimore: John Hopkins University Press, 1974), pp. 274–94: 'The Reading Process: A Phenomenological Approach'; *The Act of Reading: A Theory of Aesthetic Response* (Baltimore: John Hopkins University Press, 1978). See also idem, 'Indeterminacy as the Reader's Response in Prose Fiction,' in *Aspects of Narrative*, ed. by J. Hillis Miller (New York: Columbia University Press, 1971), pp. 1–45.

26 Roman Ingarden, *The Literary Work of Art: An Investigation on the Border-lines of Ontology, Logic, and the Theory of Literature*, trans. by George G. Grabowicz (Evanston: Northwestern University Press, 1973); *The Cognition of the Literary Work of Art*, trans. by Ruth Ann Crowley and Kenneth R. Olson (Evanston: Northwestern University Press, 1973)

27 See *The Act of Reading*, Part III, 'Phenomenology of Reading: The Processing of the Literary Text,' pp. 105–59. Iser devotes an entire chapter (pp. 135–59) of his systematic work to a reinterpretation of the Husserlian concept of 'passive synthesis' in terms of a theory of reading. These passive syntheses take place before the threshold of explicit judgment, on the level of the imaginary. They take as their material the repertoire of signals scattered throughout the text and the variations in 'textual perspective,' depending on whether the accent is placed on characters, plot, narrative, voice, or, finally, on the successive positions ascribed to the reader. To this interplay of perspectives is added the mobility of the wandering viewpoint. In this way, the work of passive synthesis in large part escapes the reading consciousness. These analyses agree perfectly with those of Sartre in his *Imagination*, trans. by Forrest Williams (Ann Arbor: University of Michigan Press, 1962), and of Mikel Dufrenne in his *The Phenomenology of Aesthetic Experience*, trans. by Edward S. Casey and others (Evanston: Northwestern University Press, 1973). An entire phenomenology of image-building consciousness is thus incorporated into the phenomenology of reading. The literary object is, in fact, an imaginary object. What the text offers are schemata for guiding the reader's imagination.

28 The German term is *Wirkung* in the double sense of effect and response. In order to distinguish his own enterprise from that of Jauss, Iser prefers to use the expression *Wirkungstheorie* rather than *Rezeptionstheorie* (*The Act of Reading*, p. x). But the asserted interaction between the text and the reader implies something more than the unilateral efficacity of the text, as the study of the dialectical aspects of this interaction confirms. Moreover, to the allegation that a theory of reception is more sociological than literary – 'A theory of response has its roots in the text; a theory of reception arises from a history of readers' judgments' (ibid.) – we might reply that a theory of literary effects runs the danger of being more psychological than ... literary.

29 As E.H. Gombrich puts it, 'Whenever consistent reading suggests itself ...

illusion takes over' (*Art and Illusion* [Princeton: Princeton University Press, 1961], p. 204; quoted by Iser, *The Act of Reading*, p. 124).

30 Iser quotes this sentence from George Bernard Shaw's *Major Barbara*: 'You have learnt something. That always feels at first as if you had lost something' (ibid., p. 291).

31 In this brief study of the activity of reading proposed by Iser, I do not discuss the criticism he levels against efforts to ascribe a referential function to literary works. According to him, this would be to submit a literary work to a ready-made and pre-established meaning; for example, to a catalogue of established norms. For a hermeneutic such as ours, which seeks nothing behind the work and which, on the contrary, is attentive to its power of detection and transformation, the assimilation of the referential function to that of the denotation at work in the descriptions of ordinary language and in scientific language prevents doing justice to the effectiveness of fiction on the very level where the effective action of reading unfolds.

32 Gérard Genette expresses similar reservations in his *Nouveau Discours du récit* (Paris: Seuil, 1983). 'Unlike the implied author, who is, in the reader's mind, the idea of a real author, the implied reader, in the head of the real author, is the idea of a possible reader ... So perhaps the implied reader should actually be rechristened the *virtual reader*' (ibid., p. 103; his emphasis).

33 On the relation between the implied reader and the actual reader, cf. *The Act of Reading*, pp. 27–38. The category of implied reader serves mainly to reply to the accusations of subjectivism, psychologism, mentalism, or of the 'affective fallacy,' levelled at a phenomenology of reading. In Iser himself, the implied reader is clearly distinguished from any real reader, to the extent that 'the implied reader as a concept has his roots firmly planted in the structure of the text' (ibid., p. 34). 'To sum up, then, the concept of implied reader is a transcendental model which makes it possible for the structural effects of literary texts to be described' (ibid., p. 38). In fact, faced with the proliferation of literary categories of 'reader,' conceived of as heuristic concepts that mutually correct one another, the phenomenology of the act of reading takes a step outside the circle of these heurisitc concepts, as can be seen in Part III of *The Act of Reading*, devoted to the dynamic interaction between the text and the real reader.

34 Hans Robert Jauss, *Toward an Aesthetic of Reception*, trans. by Timothy Bahti (Minneapolis: University of Minnesota Press, 1982)

35 'Literary History as a Challenge to Literary Theory' (ibid., pp. 3–45). This long essay stems from Jauss's inaugural lecture given in 1967 at the University of Constance.

36 Jauss wants to restore to literary history the dignity and the specificity it has lost, through a series of misfortunes, owing to the way it continually slips back into psycho biography; owing also to the reduction by Marxist dogmatism of the social effect of literature to a mere reflection of the socio-economic infrastructure; and owing, finally, to the hostility, in the age of structuralism, of literary theory itself to any consideration extrinsic to the text, set up as a self-

sufficient entity; to say nothing of the constant danger that a theory of reception will be reduced to a sociology of taste, paralleling a psychology of reading, which is the fate threatening a phenomenology of reading.

37 The German *dialogische* need not be translated here by 'dialectical.' The works of Bakhtin and those of Francis Jacques give an unquestionable legitimacy to the term 'dialogical.' Jauss is to be commended for having connected his dialogical conception of reception to Gaetan Picon's *Introduction à une esthétique de la littérature* (Paris: Gallimard, 1953) and to André Malraux's *The Voices of Silence*, trans. by Gilbert Stuart and Francis Price (Garden City, N.Y.: Doubleday, 1967).

38 This concept is borrowed from Husserl, *Ideas I*, §§27 and 82.

39 It is important, in order to distinguish Jauss's enterprise from Iser's, to stress the intersubjective character of the horizon of expectations that founds all individual understanding of a text and the effect that it produces (*Toward an Aesthetic of Reception*, p. 41). Jauss has no doubt that this horizon of expectation can be reconstituted objectively (ibid., pp. 42–3).

40 A comparison is to be made here with the notion of style in Granger's *Essai d'une philosophie du style*. The singular character of a work is the result of the unique solution provided for a set of circumstances, grasped as a singular problem to be solved.

41 'The classical, according to Hegel, "signifies itself [*Bedeutende*] and interprets itself [*Deutende*]" ... What we call "classical" does not first require the overcoming of historical distance – for in its own constant mediation it achieves this overcoming' (*Truth and Method*, p. 257).

42 *Poetik und Hermeneutik*, 3 (Munich: Fink, 1968), p. 692, cited by Jauss, *Toward an Aesthetic of Reception*, p. 34.

43 Siegfried Kracaur (discussed by Jauss, pp. 36–7) states that the temporal curves of different cultural phenomena constitute so many 'shaped times,' resisting all integration. If this is the case, how could one hold, as Jauss does, that 'this multiplicity of literary phenomena ... when seen from the point of view of an aesthetics of reception, coalesces again for the audience that perceives them and relates them to one another as works of *its* present, in the unity of a common horizon of literary expectations, memories, and anticipations that establishes their significance'? (ibid., p. 38; his emphasis). It is perhaps too much to ask of the historical effect of works of art that it lend itself to a totalization such as this, if it is true that no teleology governs it. Despite the vigorous criticism levelled at the concept of the 'classical' in Gadamer, in which he sees a Platonic or Hegelian residue, Jauss is himself searching for a canonical rule, without which any literary history would perhaps be directionless.

44 Jauss mentions in this respect the sense of parody in Cervantes's *Don Quixote* and in Diderot's *Jacques the Fatalist* (ibid., p. 24).

45 This antinomy parallels that which appeared above with regard to inquiry. Jauss, again here, breaks an arduous path between the extremes of heterogeneous multiplicity and systematic unification. According to him, 'it must also

be possible ... to arrange the heterogeneous multiplicity of contemporaneous works in equivalent, opposing, and hierarchical structures, and thereby to discover an overarching system of relationships in the literature of a historical moment' (ibid., p. 36). But if we refuse every Hegelian-type teleology, as well as every Platonic-style archetype, how can we prevent the historicity characteristic of the chain of innovations and receptions from dissolving into pure multiplicity? Is any integration possible other than that of the last reader (concerning whom Jauss himself says he is the vanishing-point but not the goal of the process of evolution (ibid., p. 34)? Speaking of 'the historical dimension of literature,' he states that what determines 'this historical articulation ... [is] the history of influence: that "which results from the event" and which from the perspective of the present constitutes the coherence of literature as the prehistory of its present manifestation' (ibid., p. 39). However, for lack of any conceptually thought-out interconnection, the principle of this organic continuity must perhaps be seen as unnameable.

46 My conception of mimesis, which at one and the same time discovers and transforms, is in perfect agreement with Jauss's critique of the aesthetics of representation, presupposed by both the adversaries and the proponents of the social function of literature.

47 This first distance explains why a work like *Madame Bovary* influenced customs more by its formal innovations (in particular by introducing a narrator who is the 'impartial' observer of his heroine) than did the openly moralizing interventions or denunciations so dear to socially commited writers. The absence of any answer to the moral dilemmas of an epoch is perhaps the most effective weapon available to literature to act on social customs and to change praxis. A direct line runs from Flaubert to Brecht. Literature acts only indirectly on social customs by creating what could be called second-order gaps in relations to the first-order gap between imaginary and everyday reality.

48 The final chapter of this section will show how the action of literature on the reading public's horizon of expectation is placed within the more comprehensive dialectic between a horizon of expectation and a space of experience, which we shall use, following Reinhart Koselleck, to characterize historical consciousness in general. The intersection of history and fiction will serve as the privileged instrument for the inclusion of the literary dialectic within an encompassing historical dialectic. And it is indeed through the function of social creation that literary history is integrated, as a particular history, within general history (cf. ibid., pp. 39–45).

49 See Hans Robert Jauss, 'Ueberlegungen zur Abgrenzung und Aufgabenstellung einer literarischen Hermeneutik,' in *Poetik und Hermeneutik*, 9 (Munich: Fink, 1980), pp. 459–81, translated into French as 'Limites et tâches d'une herméneutique littéraire,' *Diogène* no. 109 (January–March 1980): 92–119; *Aesthetic Experience and Literary Hermeneutics*, trans. by Michael Shaw (Minneapolis: University of Minnesota Press, 1982), pp. 3–188.

50 Michael Riffaterre was one of the first to show the limits of structural analysis and, in general, of mere description of the text in his debate with Jakobson and Lévi-Strauss. Jauss commends him as the one who 'introduced the turn from the structural description to the analysis of the reception of the poetic text' (*Toward an Aesthetic of Reception*, p. 141), even if, he adds, Riffaterre is 'more interested in the pregiven elements of reception and in the "rule of actualization" than in the aesthetic activity of the reader who takes up or receives the text' (ibid.). Cf. Michael Riffaterre, 'The reader's Perception of Narrative,' in *Interpretation of Narrative*, ed. Mario J. Valdés and Owen Miller (Toronto: University of Toronto Press, 1971), pp. 28–37.

51 On the rehabilitation of aesthetic pleasure, cf. Hans Robert Jauss, *Kleine Apologie der aesthetischen Erfahrung* (Constance: Verlaganstalt, 1972). Jauss thus aligns himself with the Platonic doctrine of pure pleasure found in the *Philebus* and with the Kantian doctrine of disinterested aesthetic pleasure and the idea of its universal communicability.

52 The reader is thereby asked to 'measure and to broaden the horizon of one's own experience *vis-à-vis* the experience of the other' (ibid., p. 147).

53 I will not discuss *poiēsis* here. It is none the less of importance to the theory of reading in that reading is also a creative act replying to the poetic act that founded the work. Following Hans Blumenberg, 'Nachahmung der Natur! Zur Vorgeschichte des schöpferischen Menschen, '*Studium Generale* 10 (1957): 266–83, and Jürgen Mittestrass, *Neuzeit und Aufklärung: Studium zur Entstehung der neuzeitlichen Wissenschaft und Philosophie* (Berlin and New York: W. de Gruyter, 1970), Jauss retraces the conquest of the creative power freed from every model, from biblical and Hellenic antiquity, by way of the Enlightenment, up to our day.

54 Remember that in Aristotle's *Poetics* characters are classified as 'better' than, 'worse' than, or 'like' ourselves; remember, too, that in the discussion of the rhetoric of fiction the strongest reservations expressed by Wayne Booth had to do with the moral effects of the strategy of persuasion in the modern novel.

55 On the translation of catharsis by 'clarification' and 'purification,' cf. my chapter on Aristotle's *Poetics* in Volume I of *Time and Narrative*, in particular p. 50.

56 Cf. ibid., p. 49

57 Hans Robert Jauss, 'Limites et tâches d'une herméneutique littéraire,' p. 124

58 In the following chapter [Volume 3, Chapter 8] we shall return to this similarity, strengthening it, drawing support from the notion of narrative voice introduced in Volume 2, *Time and Narrative*, pp. 95–9

59 I have described elsewhere a comparable dialectic between appropriation and distanciation; see 'The Task of Hermeneutics,' *Philosophy Today* 17 (1973): 112–24.

60 See *Time and Narrative*, I: 77. No one has better clarified the indissociable relation between communicability and referentiality taken in its broadest generality than has Francis Jacques; cf. *Dialogiques: Recherches logiques sur le*

dialogue (Paris: Presses Universitaires de France, 1979) and *Dialogiques II: l'Espace logique de l'interlocution* (Paris: Presses Universitaires de France, 1985).

61 This distinction between reading as stasis or pause and reading as impetus [*envoi*] explains Jauss's oscillations in his estimation of the role of application in literary hermeneutics. As stasis, application tends to be identified with aesthetic understanding; as impetus, it detaches itself from this in rereading and displays its cathartic effects; it then functions as a means of correcting other applications which continue to be subject to the pressure of situations and to the constraints imposed by decisions to be made concerning direct action ('Limites et tâches d'une herméneutique littéraire,' p. 133).

Life: A Story in Search of a Narrator

That life has to do with narration has always been known and said;
we speak of the story of a life to characterize the interval between
birth and death. And yet this assimilation of a life to a history should
not be automatic; it is a commonplace that should first be subjected
to critical doubt. Such doubt is the outcome of all the knowledge
acquired in the past few decades concerning the narrative and the
narrating activity – knowledge that seems to remove the story from
life as lived and locks it away in the realm of fiction.

First I will traverse this critical zone with an eye to rethinking in a
different way this all too rudimentary and overly direct relation
between a story and a life, rethink it such that fiction helps to make
life – in the biological sense of the word – human. to the relation
between story and life I would apply the Socratic maxim according to
which the unexamined life is not worth living. As a starting-point for
crossing the critical zone I will take a commentator's statement:
Stories are told and not lived; life is lived and not told. In order to
clarify this relation between living and recounting I suggest that we
first investigate the act of narrating itself.

The theory of narration I am going to sketch here is quite recent
since in its elaborated form it hails from the Russian and Czech
formalists of the 'twenties and 'thirties and from the French structuralists of the 'sixties and the 'seventies. But it is a very old theory, too,
to the measure that I find it prefigured in Aristotle's *Poetics*. It is true
that Aristotle knew but three literary genres: the epic, the tragedy,
and the comedy. But already his analysis was sufficiently general and
formal to allow room for modern transpositions. For my part, from
Aristotle's *Poetics* I retain his central concept of 'composition' [*mise
en intrigue*], *mythos* in Greek, which means both 'fable' (in the sense

of imaginary story) and 'plot' (in the sense of well-constructed history). This second aspect of Aristotle's *mythos* I will take as guide; and from this concept of 'plot' I will draw all the elements that are able to help us towards reformulation of the relation between life and narrative.

That which Aristotle denotes as plot is not a static structure but an operation, an integrative process which, as I hope to show presently, does not come to fruition other than in the living receiver of the story being told. By 'integrative process' I mean the work of composition which confers on the narrated story an identity one can call dynamic; what is being told is precisely this or that story, singular and complete. It is this structuring process of the plot that I would put to the test in a first section.

I. The Act of Plotting

The operation of plotting may very broadly be defined as a synthesis of heterogeneous elements. Synthesis of what? First, it is a synthesis of multiple events or incidents with the complete and singular history; from this first point of view the plot has the power to make a single story out of the multiple incidents or, if you like, of transforming the manifold happenings into a story; in this connection an event is more than a mere occurrence, something that just happens: it is that which contributes to the progress of the story as much as it contributes to its beginning and its end. In correlation with this the narrated story, too, is always more than mere enumeration in a simple or serial or successive order of incidents or events. Narration organizes them into an intelligible whole.

From a second point of view as well, the plot is a synthesis: it unifies components as widely divergent as circumstances encountered while unsought, agents of actions and those who passively undergo them, accidental confrontations or expected ones, interactions which place the actors in relations ranging from conflict to co-operation, means that are well-attuned to ends or less so, and, finally, results that were not willed; gathering up all those factors into a single story turns the plot into a unity which one could call both concordant and discordant (which is why I like to speak of discordant concord or concordant discord). One gains understanding of such composition through the act of following this story; to follow a story is a very complex business, unceasingly guided by expectations concerning its course, expectations that we gradually adjust in line with the unfolding of the story right up until it reaches its conclusion. In passing I note that retelling a story reveals better this synthetic activity regarding the work on the composition, inasmuch as we are less captivated by the unexpected aspects of the story and more attentive to the manner in which it moves towards its close.

Finally, the plot is a synthesis of the heterogeneous in a profounder sense still, which will serve below in the characterization of the temporality proper to every narrative composition. One can say that two kinds of time are found in every story told: on the one hand, a discrete, open, and theoretically undefined succession of incidents (one can always ask: and then? and then?); on the other hand, the story told presents another temporal aspect characterized by the integration, the culmination, and the ending in virtue of which a story gains an outline. In this sense I would say: to compose a story is, from the temporal point of view, to derive a configuration from a succession. We already surmise the importance of this characterization of stories from the temporal viewpoint to the extent that, for us, time is that which is fleeting and passes away, as well as that which endures and remains. But we will come back to this below. Suffice for now the characterization of the narrated story as a temporal totality and the poetic act as the creation of a mediation between time as flux and time as duration. If one would speak of the temporal identity of a story, one must characterize it as something which endures and remains right across that which passes away.

From this analysis of a story as a synthesis of the dissimilar, then, we may retain three traits: the mediation between multiple incidents and the singular story accomplished in the plot; the primacy of concord over discord; finally, the struggle between succession and configuration..

I would like to present an epistemological corollary to this thesis regarding the plot viewed as synthesis of the incongruent. This consequence concerns the status of the intelligibility one should ascribe to the plotting activity. Aristotle did not hesitate to say that every well-told story teaches something; even more, he said that stories reveal universal aspects of the human condition and that, therefore, poetry is more philosophical than the history of historians, who are too dependent on anecdotic aspects of life. Whatever the relation of art and historiography may be, it is certain that the tragedy, the epic, and the comedy – to mention only the genres known through Aristotle – develop a kind of intelligence we could call narrative intelligence, and which is much closer to practical wisdom and moral judgment than it is to science and, more generally, to the theoretical use of reason. This can be shown quite easily. Ethics as conceived by Aristotle, and as it can still be understood, speaks abstractly of the relation between 'virtues' and the 'pursuit of happiness.' It is the function of poetry, in its narrative and dramatic forms, to set before imagination and meditation situations each of which make up thought-experiments by means of which we learn to join the ethical aspect of human behaviour to happiness and unhappiness, to fortune and misfortune. By means of poetry we learn how changes in fortune result from this or that behaviour, as put together in the plot of the story. On account of the acquaintance we have come to have with types of composition received from our culture, we learn to link the virtues or, rather, the excellences to happiness or unhappiness. These 'lessons' of poetry constitute the universals of which Aristotle spoke; but they are (in his view) universalia inferior to those of logic and of theoretical thought. Nevertheless, we must speak of 'intelligence,' though in the sense that Aristotle gave to *phronesis* (which the Latins translated with *prudentia*). In this sense I like to use 'pronetic intelligence' to distinguish it from theoretical intelligence. The story belongs to the first kind, not to the second.

This epistemological consequence of our analysis of the plot has, in turn, itself numerous implications for the efforts of contemporary narratology to elaborate a true *science* of the narrative; of all these undertakings, entirely legitimate in my view, I would say that they are justified only on account of the *simulation* of a narrative (or phronetic) intelligence always already there, simulation that puts into play depth-structures unknown to those who tell the stories or follow the telling of them, but which place narratology on a level of rationality equal to that of linguistics and the other sciences of language. I characterize the rationality of contemporary narratology in terms of its ability to simulate (in a second-level discourse) that which we understood to be a story already when we were children. This characterization is not meant to discredit modern efforts; it is meant only to situate them accurately within the levels of knowledge. I could just as well have looked for a model of thought more modern than Aristotle's, such as in the relation indicated by Kant in the *Critique of Pure Reason* between the schema and the categories.

Just as in Kant the schema points to the creative source of the categories and the categories designate the ordering principle of the mind, so also the plot constitutes the creative well-spring of the story and narratology forms the rational reconstruction of the rules hidden underneath the poetic activity. On account of this, it is a science with requirements of its own: it seeks to reconstruct all the logical and semiological constraints, together with the laws of transformation that direct the course of the story. My thesis, then, does not express any hostility towards narratology; it limits itself to saying that narratology is a second-level discourse [*discours de second degré*], always preceded by a narrative intelligence which issues from creative imagination. Throughout the remainder of this essay my analysis will stay at the level of first-level narrative intelligence.

Before moving on to the question regarding the relation between story and life, I would pause at a second corollary which puts me on the way of the reinterpretation of this very relation.

There is, I would say, a life of the narrative activity given with the traditionality characteristic of the narrative schema.

To say that the narrative schema has a history of its own, and that this history possesses all the characteristics of a tradition, is not at all to defend tradition understood as an inert transmission of dead sediment. On the contrary, it is to point to tradition, as a living passing-on of innovation which can always be re-activated by a return to the most creative moments of the poetic composition. That phenomenon of traditionality is the key to the functioning of narrative models and, consequently, to identifying them. The shaping of a tradition in effect rests on the interaction between the two factors of innovation and sedimentation. To sedimentation we ascribe the models that constitute in retrospect the typology of compositions which allows us to order the literary genres; but we must not lose sight of the fact that these models do not embody eternal essences: they derive from a sedimented tradition whose genesis is obliterated.

But while the sediment does enable us to identify a work as, for example, a tragedy, a moralizing novel, a social drama, such identification by way of embedded models is not exhaustive. the opposite phenomenon of innovation must be taken into account as well. Why should this be so? Because the models, themselves arising from a prior innovation, provide a guide to further experimentation in the narrative domain. The rules change under pressure of innovation, but they change slowly and even resist change in virtue of the sedimentation process. Thus, innovation remains the opposite pole of tradition. there is always room for innovation to the extent that whatever is produced in composing the poem is, ultimately, always a singular work, this particular work. The rules that together form a kind of grammar direct the composition of new works – new before becoming typical. Every work is an original production, a new being within the realm of discourse. The reverse, however, is no less true: innovation remains a strategy governed by rules; the work of the imagination does not come from nothing. In one way or another it is linked to models received through tradition. But it can enter into a variable relation to these models. The diversity in solutions is spread out between the two poles of servile repetition and calculated deviance, ranging through every degree of regulated deformation. Popular stories, myths, traditional narratives in general, stay closer to the pole of repetition. This is why they are the privileged realm of structuralism. But as soon as we move beyond the domain of these traditional stories deviance prevails over rule. Contemporary novels, for instance, can largely be defined as anti-novels to the measure that they themselves are the rules that become the object for new experimentation.

However that may be in the case of this or that work, the possibility of deviance is entailed in the relation between sedimentation and innovation which makes for tradition. The variations between these two poles confer on the productive imagination a historicity of its own and keep the narrative tradition alive.

II. From the Narrative to Life

We can now attack head-on our paradox: stories are told, life is lived. A chasm seems to open up between fiction and life. To bridge this gap, it seems to me, a serious revision of both terms of the paradox has to take place.

Let us stay for a moment on the side of the narrative, i.e., the side of fiction, and let us see how it leads back to life. My thesis here is that the process of composition, of configuration, does not realize itself in the text but in the reader, and under this condition configuration makes possible reconfiguration of a life by the way of the narrative. More precisely: the meaning or the significance of a story wells up from *the intersection of the world of text and the world of the reader.*

Thus the act of reading becomes the crucial moment of the entire analysis. On this act rests the ability of the story to transfigure the experience of the reader.

Allow me to stress the terms I just used: the world of the reader and the world of the text. To speak of the world of the text is to emphasize that trait of every literary work by which it opens up a horizon of possible experience, a world in which it would be possible to dwell. A text is not an entity closed in upon itself; it is the projection of a new universe, different from the one in which we live. Appropriating a work through reading it is to unfold the implicit horizon of the world which embraces the action, the personages, the events of the story told. The result is that the reader belongs to both the experiential horizon of the work imaginatively, and the horizon of his action concretely. The awaited horizon and the horizon meet and fuse without ceasing. In this sense Gadamer speaks of the 'fusions of horizons' (*Horizontverschmelzung*) essential to the act of understanding a text.

I know very well that literary criticism is much concerned to maintain the distinction between the inside of the text and its outside. Literary criticism prefers to look upon every exploration of the linguistic universe as foreign to its aims. Text analysis should therefore stop at the limit of the text and deny itself any departure from the text. I would say in this connection that the distinction between outside and inside is an invention of the method of textual analysis itself, and does not correspond to the experience of the reader. This opposition results from the extrapolation to literature of the characteristic properties of the kinds of units linguistics works with: phonemes, lexemes, words; to linguistics the real world is extra-linguistic. Reality is not contained within the dictionary or in grammar. It is precisely this extrapolation from linguistics to the poetic that seems to me open to criticism: the methodological decision, proper to structural analysis, to deal with literature in terms of linguistic categories which impose the distinction between inside and outside. From a hermeneutic point of view, that is, from the point of view of the interpretation of a literary experience, a text has an entirely different significance from that which a structural analysis, deriving from linguistics, accords to it; it is a mediation between man and the world, between man and man, between man and himself. Mediation between man and the world is called *reference*; mediation between man and man is *communication*; mediation between man and himself is *self-understanding*. A literary work brings together these three dimensions of reference, communication, and self-understanding. Thus, the work of hermeneutics begins where linguistics stops. Hermeneutics would uncover new traits of non-descriptive reference, of non-utilitarian communication, of non-narcissistic reflexivity – traits engendered by the literary work. In a word, hermeneutics takes hold of the hinge between the (internal) configuration of a work and the (external) refiguration of a life. As I see it, everything said above concerning the dynamics of composition proper to a literary creation is nothing but a lengthy preparation to understanding the real problem, i.e., that of the dynamics of transfiguration proper to the work. In this regard plotting is the work of the text and the reader jointly. One has to follow and accompany the composition, actualize its capacity of being followed, so that the whole work will have a configuration within its own proper limits. To follow a story is to reactualize the act of configuration which gave form to it. Furthermore, it is the act of the reader who accompanies the play between innovation and sedimentation, the play with narrative constraints, with the possibilities of deviating, even the battle between novel and anti-novel. Finally, it is the act of reading which completes the work, which transforms it into a reading *guide* with its zones of indetermination, its latent richness of interpretation, its ability to be reinterpreted in novel ways within historical context that are always new.

At this stage of the analysis we already anticipate how story and life can be reconciled to each other, since the reading itself already is a way of living in the fictitious universe of the work; in this sense we can already say that stories are told but also lived *in the imaginary mode.*

But now we must correct the second term of the alternative, that which we call 'life.' We must put in question the false evidence according to which life is lived and not told.

To this end I would insist on the pre-narrative capacity of that which we call a life. A life is no more than a biological phenomenon as long as it is not interpreted. And in the interpretation fiction plays a considerable, mediating role. To pave the way towards this new phase in the analysis we must attend to the mixture of doing and undergoing, of action and suffering which makes up the very texture of life. It is this mixture that the story seeks to imitate in a creative way. Indeed, in my reference to Aristotle I left out the definition itself which he gives to 'story'; it is, he says, the imitation of an action, *mimesis praxeos*. Hence we must first look for the points of support which the story can find in the living experience of acting and suffering; that which in this living experience requires insertion of the narrative and perhaps expresses a veritable need for it.

The first anchor-point we find for the narrative intelligibility in living experience lies within the structure of human acting and suffering itself. In this regard human life is profoundly different from animal life and *a fortiori* from mineral existence. We understand what action and passion are in virtue of our ability to utilize in a meaningful way the entire network of expressions and concepts which the natural languages supply us with in order to distinguish 'action' from simple physical 'movement' and from psycho-physiological 'behaviour.' Similarly, we understand the meaning of project, goal, means, circumstances, and so on. All such notions taken together make up the network of what could be called the *semantics of action*. Now, in this network, we rediscover all the components of the story which above appeared under the heading 'synthesis of the heterogeneous.' In this regard our familiarity with the conceptual network of human action is of the same order as the acquaintance we have with the plots of the stories we know; the same phronetic intelligence guides the concepts of action (and of passion) and that of the story.

The second anchor-point which the narrative proposition finds in practical understanding resides in the symbolic resources of the practical realm – a trait which will decide which aspects of making, of being able to make, and of knowing and being able to know [*du faire, du pouvoir-faire, et du savoir-pouvoir-faire*] come out of the poetic transposition.

If indeed action can be narrated it is because it is already articulated in signs, rules, and norms; action is always mediated symbolically. This characteristic of action has been emphasized vividly in cultural anthropology. I speak more precisely of 'symbolic mediation' in order to distinguish among symbols of a cultural kind those which underlie action to the point that they constitute its primary meaning before they are detached from the practical level as autonomous wholes connected with speaking and writing. Such autonomous symbols are met with in ideologies and utopias. Here I limit myself to what one could call *implicit, immanent* symbolism, in contradistinction to such explicit or autonomous symbolism.

That which actually characterizes the symbolism implicit in action is that it forms a *descriptive context* for the singular actions. In other words, it is in the context of this or that symbolic convention that we are able to interpret a given gesture as having this or that meaning; the same movement of the arm can, depending on the context, be understood as a way of greeting, of hailing a taxi, or of casting a vote. Before they are subjected to interpretation, symbols are the internal interpreters of an action. In this way symbolism confers on action a first readability. It makes of action a quasi text for which the symbols furnish the rules of significance, in the context of which such specific behaviour can be interpreted.

The third anchor-point of the story in life lies in what one could call the *pre-narrative quality of human experience*. Thanks to it we have the right to speak of life as of an incipient story, and thus of life as *an activity and a desire in search of a narrative*. Comprehension of an action is not limited to familiarity with its symbolic mediations. It extends even to recognition, in the action, of temporal structures that evoke narration. It is not by accident or by error that we are accustomed to speak of stories that happen to us or stories we are caught up in – or simply of the story of a life.

It may be objected here that my entire analysis rests on a vicious circle. If every human experience is already mediated by all sorts of symbolic systems, it is also already mediated by all kinds of stories we have heard. How then can one speak of a narrative quality of experience and of human life as an incipient story, since we have no access to the temporal drama of existence outside of the stories told to their subjects by others than ourselves?

To this objection I would oppose a number of situations which, I think, compel us to ascribe to experience as such already something like a virtual narrativity which does not proceed from – as is said – a projection of literature on life, but which makes for an authentic demand for a story. I introduced the phrase 'pre-narrative structure of experience' to characterize these situations.

Without moving away from daily experience, are we not inclined to see a certain chain of episodes of our live as *stories not yet told*, stories that seek to be told, stories that offer anchor-points for the narrative? I do not overlook how incongruous it seems to speak of a story not yet told. Once again, are not stories, by definition, *narratives*? As long as we are speaking of actual stories, this is undoubtedly the case. But is the notion of a potential story unacceptable?

I attend a moment to two less common situations in which the expression 'story not yet told' imposes itself on us with extraordinary force. The client who turns to a psychoanalist to present him with bits of lived histories, dreams, 'primitive scenes,' conflicting episodes; one can indeed say that the goal and effect of the analytic sessions is that the person analyzed draws out from these bits and pieces a story that is both more intelligible and more bearable. This narrative interpretation of psychoanalytic theory implies that the story of a life arises from untold and repressed stories, in the direction of effective stories which the subject can be responsible for and which he takes as constitutive of his personal identity. It is the search for this personal identity that guarantees the continuity of a potential or virtual story and the purposive story for which we assume responsibility.

There is another situation where the idea of a story not (yet) told seems appropriate. When a judge tries to understand a suspect by unravelling the knot of complications in which the suspect is caught, one can say that, before the story is told, the individual seems entangled in the stories that happen to him. This 'entanglement' thus appears as a pre-history of the story told in which the beginning is still chosen by the narrator. This pre-history of the story is what connects the latter to a larger whole and provides it with a background. This background is built up into a living, continuous overlap of all the lived stories. Thus, the stories told must emerge from this background. In this emergence the story guarantees man. The major consequence of this existential analysis of man as entangled in stories is that the telling is a secondary process grafted on our 'being entangled in stories.' Narrating, following, and understanding stories is nothing but the continuation of such untold stories.

From this double analysis we learn that fiction, particularly narrative fiction, is an irreducible dimension of *the understanding of the self*. If it is true that fiction cannot be completed other than in life, and that life can not be understood other than through stories we tell about it, then we are led to say that a life *examined*, in the sense borrowed from Socrates, is a life *narrated*.

What is a narrated life? It is a life in which we recover all the fundamental structures of the story enumerated in the first section. Mainly, it is the play of concord and discord which seemed to me to characterize a narrative. There is nothing paradoxical or outrageous about this conclusion. When we open St Augustine's *Confessions* at Book XI we discover a description of human time that answers completely to the structure of discordant concord that Aristotle, some centuries earlier, had discerned in poetic composition. In his famous treatise on time Augustine sees time as being born in the unceasing differentiation of the three aspects of the present: expectation, which he calls the presence of the future; memory, which he calls the presence of the past; awareness, which is the presence of the present. Hence the instability of time; nay, its ceaseless decomposition. Thus Augustine can define time as extendedness of the soul, *distentio animi*. It consists in the permanent contrast between the instability of the human 'now' and the stability of the divine 'now' which embraces past, present, and future in unity of creative vision and action.

One is led to juxtapose and confront Aristotle's notion of plot and St Augustine's definition of time. One could say that, in Augustine, discord is greater than concord; hence the misery of the human condition. To Aristotle concord outstrips discord; hence the incomparable value of the narrative to bring order to our temporal experience. But it would not do to push the opposition too far, since for Augustine himself there would be no discord if we did not tend towards a *unity of awareness*, as he shows in the simple example of reciting a poem: when I am about to recite a poem it is wholly present in my mind; next, as I am reciting it, its parts move one by one from being future to being past, crossing the present on the way, until finally, the future being exhausted, the whole of the poem has become past. Just so, a vision of totalizing intention guides the inquiry so that I feel the cruel talons of time that will not desist tearing my soul by bringing to hope, memory, and awareness discord without end. Nevertheless, if in this way discord outweighs concord in the living experience of time, even then the latter should be the permanent object of our desire.

In Aristotle's case we see the reverse. The narrative, I said, is a synthesis of the heterogeneous. But concord cannot be without discord. Tragedy is paradigmatic for this: no tragedy is without complications, with fickle fate, without terrible and sad events, without irreparable error committed in ignorance or by mistake rather than through evil-mindedness. If then concord wins out over discord, surely it is the battle between them that makes for the story.

Let us apply to ourselves this analysis of the discordant concord of the narrative and the concordant discord of time. It seems that our life, enveloped in one single glance, appears to us as the field of a constructive activity, deriving from the narrative intelligence through which we attempt to recover (rather than impose from without) *the narrative identity which constitutes us*. I emphasize the expression 'narrative identity,' because that which we call subjectivity is neither an incoherent succession of occurrences nor an immutable substance incapable of becoming. It is exactly the kind of identity which the narrative composition alone, by means of its dynamism, can create.

This definition of subjectivity in terms of the narrative identity has numerous implications. To begin with, it is possible to apply the play of sedimentation and innovation, which we recognized in the works in every tradition, to our understanding of ourselves. In the same manner we do not cease to re-interpret the narrative identity that constitutes us in the light of stories handed down to us by our culture. In this sense our self-understanding presents the same traits of traditionality as the understanding of a literary work does. In this way we learn to become the *narrator of our own story* without completely becoming the author of our life. It could be said that we appropriate in the application to ourselves the concert of narrative voices that make up the symphony of the great works, of the epics, the tragedies, dramas, and novels. The difference is that, in these works, the author has disguised himself as narrator and bears the masks of his many *personae* in whose midst he is the dominant narrative voice telling the story we read. We can become our own narrator, following these narrative voices, without becoming authors. That is the great difference between life and fiction. In this sense it is certainly true that life is lived and the story told. An unbridgeable distinction remains, but it is, in part, abolished through our capacity to appropriate in the application to ourselves the intrigues we received from our culture, and our capacity of thus experimenting with the various roles that the favourite *personae* assume in the stories we love best. And so we try to gain by means of *imaginative variation* of our *ego* a narrative understanding of ourselves, the only kind of understanding that escapes the pseudo-alternative of pure change and absolute identity.

Allow me to conclude by saying that the *subject* is never given at the beginning. Or, if it were so given, it would run the risk of reducing itself to a narcissistic ego, self-centred and avaricious – and it is just this from which literature can liberate us. Our loss on the side of narcissism is our gain on the side of the narrative identity. In the place of an ego enchanted by itself, a *self* is born, taught by cultural symbols, first among which are the stories received in the literary tradition. These stories give unity – not unity of substance but narrative wholeness.

IV

The Dialogical
Disclosure:
Interviews with
Paul Ricoeur

Phenomenology and
Theory of Literature

Erik Nakjavani (Q): Professor Ricoeur, I have followed with increasing interest your lectures on the application of the phenomenological method to the concept of action in sociology and political science. You have opened up new perspectives in these disciplines, and have brought to them an intense light of a certain specific quality. It is the particular nature of this light which seems to be of an enormous interdisciplinary significance.

By profession and by inclination, I find myself in another field, that of literature. For us, as René Wellek has so perceptively pointed out, the most urgent need appears to be a cohesive theory of literature, an organon of methods which could satisfactorily deal with such fundamental problems as the nature of the literary creative process, the mode of existence of a work of literature, and its classification, explanation, and evaluation.

The remarkable efforts of Freudian and Marxist literary theorists have provided us with some powerful extrinsic or egocentric approaches to the study of literature. Unfortunately, they remain approaches from without and seem to have failed to offer us an adequate theory of literature capable of grasping the complexities of a work of literature from within and as an independent, autonomous phenomenon.

It would be invaluable to us if you would care to discuss the possibility of an intrinsic or egocentric phenomenological approach to the theory of literature, and its potentials and limitations.

Paul Ricoeur: The first task of a phenomenological approach to the problem of literature would be to define the boundaries of the idea of text. What is a text? It is a question which includes several questions. First, what are the absolutely fundamental characteristics of discourse? By discourse, I don't mean at all language, which the linguist might mean, but the messages which we produce freely on the foundation and the structure of language. So, there is already a specific feature of discourse, in comparison to language, which constitutes the first boundary of the literary object. First, among the traits of discourse, I would put that discourse opens up a world. In short, it is a way of revealing a dimension of reality in relationship to dialogue with another person, the listener. Therefore, there is a triangular relationship among one who speaks, one who listens and answers, and, then, the world of things which one talks about. This triangular relationship is the very basis of the problem of literary criticism, because what is to be understood in a discourse is the quality of the world, the dimension of the world, isn't it?, which is opened up by communication. That would be the first level of an approach to the problem of the text.

The second level would be a reflection on what writing adds to this triangular relationship among one who speaks, one who listens, and the discovered reality which is made manifest by the dialogue. Primarily, through writing, the discourse slips away from the speaker, since writing has the power to preserve the discourse after the destruction and disappearance of the speaker. So, there is an autonomy of text in relationship to the occurrence of the discourse, which is at its origin and enables the text to have a destiny distinct from that of its author. The writer dies, but the text pursues its career, continues and produces its effects from time to time, which is vaster than the time of a human life. Therefore, if we go back to this triangular relationship, in regard to the author of the discourse, the text frees itself from the boundary of the history of its production and survives the occurrence of speech.

On the other hand, from the point of view of the listener, writing opens up a relationship which is much more comprehensive than the relationship of dialogue which remains locked up in the *I–thou* communication. A text opens up an audience, which is unlimited, while the relationship of dialogue is a closed relationship. The text is open to whoever knows how to read, and whose potential reader is everyone. There is, therefore, an opening in comparison to the closure of dialogue, which accounts, finally, for the literary work being an open work, an unlimited number of readings which are, for me, each a sort of new occurrence of speech taking possession of the text in order to give it a new actuality.

Third, the world which is opened up in this manner by writing is itself also a world which has an infinite horizon, while dialogue in spoken word is bound to the listener. Literature creates a world of fiction, of possibility, and, consequently, opens up a horizon of reality, too. Our sense of reality is multiplied by this world of fiction and possibility.

I think that that is the second approach to our problem of the nature of the text: What is a text?

I see, perhaps, a third problem which would be interesting: that would be to apply the category of work to utterance and discourse. In fact, we are constantly talking about a work of art. We talk about a piece of work. In English, the word work is very striking. Therefore, discourse may be the object of a work, and, as a result, one may apply the category of work to it.

If we define work as an activity through which we give form to matter, there is a literature because language is treated as matter which receives a form. The theory of forms is a part of literary criticism for this reason, because there are different genres of forms, whether they be the novel, poetry, or theatre. First of all, it is a paradox that one may think that work is contrary to speech; there is a literature because there is work done through speech and on speech, which is precisely to make a piece of work of it. That is particularly manifest in the case of poetry in which it is a veritable work done on language, because it is a work which consists in binding together, in an absolutely indissoluble manner, the sound and meaning, in such a way that the poem constitutes a sort of perfect object, closed on itself like a piece of sculpture.

If one adds these three categories: first, the category of discourse; second, the category of writing; third, the category of work, one discovers that the text is something to be interpreted, because it is open to an unlimited number of possible readings which will convert writing into living speech. Reading is a human act of considerable importance, which has rules distinct from listening to a dialogue. In short, it is something else to read a text than to listen to a spoken discourse. It is precisely because the text is mute and does not answer that it must be given life. There is a way of reanimating speech which is invested in the text. I would think that would be the function of hermeneutics to develop the theory of the act of reading which corresponds to this investment of discourse in writing and in literary work. The theory of hermeneutics, in my opinion, would consist of developing the parallel theory of genesis of text and of reading, and to show the flow of one to the other. This undertaking itself requires a very different operation, because the act of reading is, after all, a summing-up of numerous activities, going from the simple interpretation of sentences in their syntactic and semantic constitution to the comprehension of the work of an author in its living totality. Semantics does not go beyond the level of the isolated sentence, but hermeneutics begins with the work taken as a signifying totality, which is not simply a sum of sentences placed end-to-end but a relationship of all parts which has its own laws.

So, since the text has an autonomy in relation to the writer, and also in relation to the reader, one may certainly treat it primarily as a thing which is completely independent, both of the writer and the reader, and one may treat it as an absolute object. This is the tendency of French structuralism to treat a text as a structure which has its own laws and that one may study objectively, not in the least mixing it with the expectations, preferences, prejudices, or the hopes and affinities of the reader. This undertaking is perfectly legitimate, because it is justified by the very nature of the text as a kind of reality which has made itself autonomous in relation to the initial situation in which it was produced; therefore, it has become independent in relation to dialogue. Only, I would think that for me, this objective and absolutely disinterested study, in the right meaning of the word, therefore, without any relationship to our interest, is merely an abstract and preparatory phase for an appreciation of the text from which we make our own flesh and blood through a sort of appropriation which makes from what was strange something appropriate and familiar. I don't believe that these two attitudes, one much more objective, which triumphs in structuralism, the other much more subjective, which triumphs in what I have just called appropriation, contradict each other, because they mutually bring each other forth. A completely objective study kills the text, because one operates on a cadaver. But, inversely, reading which would be perfectly naive and would not have passed through all the mediations of an objective and structural approach would be only the projection of the subjectivity of the reader on the text. Consequently, it is necessary that subjectivity be held in some way at a distance and that the appropriation be in some way mediated by all the objectifying activities. I believe that phenomenology here is very enlightening, because it shows that all modes of relationship that one may have to another – and, after all, writing is a communicative relationship – pass through the mediation of the theory of objectifying acts, which Husserl develops in connection with an entirely different question, either the theory of perception or the theory of consciousness. This phase of objectification may be found everywhere in the lectures which I am giving at the moment on social and political theory, and plays a fundamental role. One sees that all social relationships pass through the intermediaries of institutions, of codes, of rules, which are very often anonymous and impenetrable. Well, literature is one of these mediations. But, contrary to the opaque mediations of politics, literature is a transparent mediation in which the institution becomes exactly a text. While the institutions are in great part indecipherable because the history which has produced them escapes us, the characteristic of literature is to create among us a transparent mediation, because it is entirely sustained by speech.

Q: You have talked about the phenomenology of the text. Now I would like to ask you what you think of the possibility of a phenomenology of the critic, because it seems to me that it would be useful to explore the relationship of the critic with the text.

Ricoeur: This is a very difficult question, for which I am not prepared, because I suspect that we lack here a wholly indispensable tool that comes from another discipline rather than from phenomenology. I am thinking about the critique of ideologies, in the fashion of the School of Frankfurt, which is a certain heritage of Marxism. But why introduce here the critique of ideologies, because the critic himself is always in a certain historical situation. He is tied to a certain culture and, consequently, he isn't this absolute, disinterested subject, a sort of non-involved ego. He is himself caught in the movement of the culture. So he doesn't have this kind of flight position or a view from above. He himself has a lateral vision of literary works. Consequently, he is exactly in the situation of a perceiving subject who always has only a side view; therefore, there is a sort of self-criticism of the critic, which is certainly an important part of the theory of literature.

You did very well to ask this question, because up to the present time we have chiefly had a theory of the literary object, and the activities on the literary object. But, what are the activities on the subject of the critic? There we have two extreme positions, which, it seems to me, would both be unacceptable. One would make of the critic a militant, who would be a person with a cause, and who, consequently, would like to show by means of literature that a certain morality, that a certain religion, that a certain politics is true. Then, at that moment, the criticism becomes apologetics. And then, at the other extreme, there would be the position which would claim that criticism has no set purpose, that criticism is neutral.

Between partisan criticism, which is an act of violence done to the text and, perhaps, to the reader, and this hypocritical claim that the critic belongs nowhere, there is this kind of self-criticism by the critic who knows that it is always from the basis of a prejudice that one understands something. in other words, it is necessary to understand that all comprehension implies a pre-comprehension; that is to say, a certain affinity with the object and, therefore, also a whole cultural equipment. It is from the depth of a certain culture that I approach a new object of the culture. As a result pre-comprehension and prejudice are necessarily a part of comprehension. There cannot be any self-criticism by a neutral critic. And, inversely, a critic cannot be partisan. So, there is an extremely delicate point of balance there between, on the one hand, the conviction that pre-comprehension and prejudgment are a vital part of comprehension of every object and, on the other hand and at the same time, the critique of the illusions of the subject which one may make with the aid of either Marxism or psychoanalysis.

But I myself don't believe that a single critique of ideologies suffices, because there is a truth in pre-comprehension. The question would then be posed again to the critic of ideologies: where does he stand himself and who will do the critique of the critic? Anyway, there is a pre-comprehension, because there is no comprehension without pre-comprehension. But pre-comprehension is at the same time prejudice. German is, however, very interesting from that point of view, because there is one word, *Vorurteil,* which means *préjugement* and *préjugé*, prejudgment and prejudice in English. Phenomenology of the critic is based upon the dialectic between prejudice and prejudgment.

Q: Mikel Dufrenne, in *Aesthetics and Philosophy*, talks about the triple function of the critic: to clarify, to explain, and to judge. I would like you to talk about his formulation, if you would, because I find it to be a sort of theorem of the critic's function.

Ricoeur: I believe that phenomenology only concerns, it seems to me, the first two, to clarify and to explain, because to clarify a work of literature, in the language which I was trying to develop in the beginning, is to understand the internal structure of it, to see how the different codes, the different subjacent structures, hold the message of the work; then, to explain is to put it in connection with its author, its public, its world in the triangular relationship which I have already explained, and which begins with discourse. I have an impression that judging comes from another discipline which would be aesthetics, properly speaking, and which would be passing judgment on what Kant has called the judgment of taste. I wouldn't like to make of phenomenology an almighty science. Not everything is phenomenological. I believe that phenomenology stops at the threshold of judgment. After that comes the function of aesthetics, which is a kind of decision, isn't it? It seems to me that in phenomenology there is an inclination to stop short of judgments – beautiful, ugly, successful, unsuccessful – in short, an appreciation which is after all a value judgment. Perhaps after that, there will be a phenomenology of this appreciative activity in terms of what I was trying to say about the phenomenology of the critic. But I think it is always the function of the critic to help the public to judge by proposing a judgment to them, it is an absolutely fundamental educative function, for the reason that, mainly, we have learned to discern great works from lesser works because, after all, the critics have already judged them. One could say that what we call tradition is a sort of continued critical judgment. The tradition has ratified somehow that Greek tragedy, for example, is a thing of grandeur. There is, briefly, a recognition of grandeur, which is not merely the work of the individual critic but a sort of continued criticism from one century to another. it is also true that there are works which are judged great in a certain period, then, later, fall into oblivion and disdain. There is also the history of this critical judgment, which is a completely specific history and which has its own rules.

Q: Thank you very much, Professor Ricoeur, for having talked to us.

Poetry and Possibility

Manhattan Review (Q): So, one of the things that we were just speaking about was that perhaps poetry in the United States is a little bit driven inward. I wanted to ask you about the mutual influence of poetry and philosophy. And I want to ask you a question with a lot of prepositions.

What do you think poetry and philosophy can do to, with, for, against each other?

Paul Ricoeur: The first thing I should like to emphasize is that poetry preserves the width, the breadth of language, because the first danger in our present culture is a kind of reduction of language to communication at the lowest level or to manipulate things and people. So it's full of language which becomes merely instrumental. This instrumentalization of language is the most dangerous trend of our culture. We have only one model of language – the language of science and technology.

Today, a part of philosophy considers only this form of language. So this would be, should be, one of the responsibilities of a philosophy of language: to preserve the varieties of the uses of language and the polarities between these different kinds of language, ranging from science through political and practical language and ordinary language, let us say, and poetry. And ordinary language, mediating between poetry, on the one hand, and scientific language, on the other hand.

Q: Ordinary language preserving a certain amount of the ... well, not as univocal, perhaps, as scientific and poetry being even richer.

Ricoeur: Yes, yes. Because all kinds of language rely ultimately on this very peculiar character of natural languages. I speak of natural languages in opposition to artificial languages constructed for the sake of computers and cybernetics, that is to say, languages which have a part in the culture and have been spoken by communities and so on.

But one basic feature of the language is this polysemy, the fact that for one word there is more than one meaning. So there is not a one-to-one relationship between word and meaning. And so it's a source of misunderstanding, but it's also the source of all richness in language, because you may play with this range of meanings which accompany one word.

We could say that in scientific language there is an attempt to reduce as much as possible this polysemy, this plurivocity to univocity: one word – one sense. But it is the task of poetry to make words mean as much as they can and not as little as they can. Therefore, not to elude or exclude this plurivocity, but to cultivate it, to make it meaningful, powerful, and therefore to bring back to language all its capacity of meaningfulness.

Q: Does this give poetry in this culture a subversive quality?

Ricoeur: Sure, in the sense that the reduction to utility and to mere functionalism requires a strong resistance, so, in that sense, poetry is – I think it's Nietzsche who said that it is dangerous. It is dangerous for this reductionism, which reigns over the use of language or unfortunately in ordinary speech, where there is a reduction to a very few words and the lack of the ... let us say the aura, the poetic aura of the words.

So, in fact, this reduction of language to one function, to one meaning starts with ordinary language but it is increased to the highest degree by scientific language. This is why, to answer your question, poetry is by necessity rebellious against this use of language which is at the same time a misuse of its capacities.

Q: Do you think that people are afraid of poetry because of this subversive quality, or resist it?

Ricoeur: Yes, they resist for good and bad reasons. For bad reasons, because they don't see the use of poetry. It seems to be language for the sake of language and therefore, I think ... but modern poetry has become very difficult precisely because it has to fight against this flattening of language. So it had to dig very deep under the surface of language to find the ... to rejuvenate language.

Therefore, modern poetry has to be difficult in a sense because it often has to re-create the syntax, sometimes the words, to bring the words back to their etymological meaning, or to a kind of fanciful etymology.

And this will help the philosopher because I should say that one part of philosophy, the one which is not only a discourse about scientific language but which is about the full capacity of language for expressing the relation between man and world, man and himself and man and the other ... therefore, the philosopher, too, is in need of words.

I like to quote a passage by Heidegger or by Husserl who said that here words are lacking. And then the poet is the one who saves the words and even expands the meaning of the words. In that sense, the philosopher relies on this capacity of poetry to enlarge, to increase, to augment the capacity of meaning of our language.

Q: But you implied that people are perhaps also right to resist.

Ricoeur: I understand why, because reading is a kind of pact between the writer and the reader. And when there is no possibility to make a new contract between the reader ... because, finally, the words, the syntax, the order of thought are so far from the reach of the reader, then the reader is left desperate on the shore.

It's a kind of big misunderstanding for which both are responsible.

Q: It's a desperate situation for both, as you paint it, because the poet, in order to fight this univocal language, has to dig deeper and deeper. And the reader, at the same time, is getting more and more desperate.

Ricoeur: Because he himself has lost his capacity to increase his own language. So since his language has shrunk, we may say, he cannot stretch his language to join the point where the poet himself stretches his own language. It's as though two people were stretching hands towards each other and cannot reach.

Q: Are we getting to the point where eventually these two figures, the writer and the reader, are just going to – especially with regard to poetry – are just going to diverge? What do you think could restore a different sort of movement, because you say that poetry is so necessary for enrichment of polysemy and the language as a whole?

Ricoeur: Maybe there is within poetry itself a kind of struggle, an attempt to give the proper expression, maybe at a high cost to what is human experience and which is covered by ordinary life and so on. But there is a kind of experience which is covered up and the task of the poet is to give a new chance to these experiences which are covered up by this practical language, this utilitarian language.

But there is the other trend of poetry to forget experience and to cultivate language for its own sake. So I see poetry caught between these two needs. On the one hand, to re-create expressions for deeply sunk experiences which are human experiences, which are common experiences at the root of human life concerning, I should say, life and death, guilt and love, and so on.

But, on the other hand, as poetry starts with a kind of break between language and things, language becomes its own object, and I see this fight either to recover lost experience or to cultivate possibilities of language which have nothing to do with any kind of experience but only for the sake of combinatory resources, for the connection between pattern and sound. And I see that especially in some kinds of poetry which cannot even be said, which have to be read, because the words are distributed on the page.

Q: Concrete poetry.

Ricoeur: Concrete poetry. And then the task for the reader is so great because he has to not only fight against his own narrowness but to fight also against his conviction that language is for the sake of bringing to language something which is lost and which should be common to both the poet and the reader.

Q: I think the ideas which you have written, as well as what you have just expressed, have an important bearing on this whole issue. I don't think that any particular movement of the two movements you've described is wrong or right but I think that at any particular time, maybe one might need to be stressed more than the other. And I have a feeling that in poetry –

Ricoeur: Far from saying that one is right and one is wrong, I should say that this polarity constitutes poetry. On the one hand, to give a voice to lost layers of experience and, on the other hand, to liberate language from its relation to things and to reality. And therefore, to increase the gap between, let us say, science and things.

So this is a two-edged situation for poetry.

Q: It would be a necessary dialectic.

Ricoeur: For example, we may say that in nineteenth-century romanticist poetry there was a priority given to the expression of feelings. Not ordinary feelings but precisely those delicate feelings which find expression only through the re-creation of language as poetry.

But then, at the end of the nineteenth century, mainly after Mallarmé, you have a kind of experiment in language, a complete disregard for experience. It's language for the sake of language. And surely it's a responsibility of the poet to free language from its bondage to things, to reality. But what keeps poetry wholesome, I think, is that the dialectic is preserved between the expressive function and the experimental function in language.

Q: Is this a particular area where philosophy could impinge, perhaps even in a harmful way, on poetry?

Structuralism is not in its full force at this point, but it's in the air. And I think it has affected writers' conception of themselves. It leads writers to stress one particular aspect of the dialectic you are talking about: the non-referential or self-referential qualities of literature at the expense of the referential qualities.

Ricoeur: Yes, yes, to catch up on this problem. When some critics – I speak of critics and no longer only of poets, but maybe also of poets, you will tell me where it is true for poets, too. When some critics say, but in poetry language is not referential, maybe it is because they have a very narrow idea of what could be and what should be referential. They mean if it is referential, it has to do with the things of my life and the things of scientific thought.

And therefore, we reinforce the prejudice that reality is only what is manipulatable. But if we have surmised that there is another layer of reality that only poetry may reach and express, then the suspension of referentiality is only one step and it is necessary that we must first lose contact with ordinary things in order maybe, thanks to this liberation of language, to redirect it once more towards some more deeply rooted forms of experience.

Q: This is what you say about the Majorcan story-tellers, that they make this little formula: the story I'm about to tell is true and is not true. That the particular way in which poetry and literature suspend reference to reality does not mean that there is no reference.

Ricoeur: Yes, you are right to introduce here the question of story-telling. I don't know whether you will agree with me, but I tend to take poetry not only in the sense of rhythmic and rhymed forms of language, in the broad sense of the word lyric fiction, but also narrative fiction is poetry in the sense that the plot of a narrative is a creation of productive imagination which projects a world of its own. And the stories are no less poetry than versified literature.

But I don't know whether you take, in your own review, the word poetry in the sense only of –

Q: Verse.

Ricoeur: Verse.

Q: Well, a number of contemporary poets are beginning to feel that the narrative element has unfortunately been lost in the last ten or twenty years. And I know that a lot of people are working to restore an element of narrative to contemporary poetry. There's a certain tiredness with the purely lyric.

But I am interested in a term you just introduced in speaking about story, the term *world*, which is very important in your writing. That a work of art projects a *world*: it's the way you have of escaping from a romantic conception of direct intersubjective communication. You say that a work of art, a poem, projects a world but that you don't mean it in a cosmological sense; you mean it ontologically.

Ricoeur: Yes, I mean in the sense ... I use the word *world* in both the very ordinary and very strong sense of the word when we say in French, for example, when we say that a child was born, we say that 'Il vient au monde.' He comes to the world.

And we speak of the Greek world, we speak of the Roman world, that is to say, a horizon of possibilities which constitute an environment for people ... where we could dwell. I like very much this notion of Heidegger when he links these three terms: dwelling – constructing the house, and dwelling, and thinking. So we are dwellers in a world. The relation of dwelling has its counterpart in the notion of a world. The world is where we dwell. The capacity to dwell and to exchange experiences.

And also there is in the notion of a world, the notion of horizon, that is to say, something which recedes when we approach it and, therefore, which has always an inexhaustible capacity. In each experience there is something there but also something which is only potential. And all potentialities of all our experiences constitute, so to say, a world.

Q: I see, so there's a tantalizing quality about the work of art in the sense that it projects a world whose horizons are never definite ... is that what you meant?

Ricoeur: Yes, I meant ... maybe it's the German philosopher who has said it best when he says that we don't try only to understand what is in the poem but to reach the kind of world to which this poem belongs or which it projects. And he speaks of the point of the merging of horizons.

Q: You are talking about Gadamer.

Ricoeur: Yes, of Gadamer, because it's at the limit of our experience that two horizons may merge.

Q: Now, this is the horizon of the author and the reader.

Ricoeur: Yes, we are the bearers of and the dwellers in a world, and so it's at the limits of this world that some covering is possible, how shall I say, some superimposition of the two borderlines of the two worlds.

Q: Isn't there a problem with this business of merging of the horizons? Lets's take an example of an SS man, who might have loved the poetry of Rilke. In a sense, he enters into this world, inhabits it, experiences it as a kind of play, and yet, at the threshold of the work of art, it ends.

It seems to me there's a problem. It presumes a good faith, but you don't mention this specifically.

Ricoeur: Good faith on the part of whom?

Q: The reader. In other words, where does this play ... maybe this play could end when you come out of the work of art, and then it doesn't affect you. It brings up the whole problem of how the world of the work of art really affects your world.

Ricoeur: It affects our capacity to see what we overlook in our ordinary life. It's Proust who says in *Time Recovered, Time Regained* that the reader is the reader of himself when he reads a book. So, in fact, I am taught by the work of art to read myself in terms of the work of art.

This is linked to a conviction of mine that I am not an ego, an ego which is finished. I am an unfinished ego, and therefore, what I call myself, the self of myself, is in fact the pupil of all the works of art, works of literature, works of culture which I read, which I loved, which I understood. And therefore, it's a kind of deposit, a treasure of all these experiences.

There is no ego ready-made before reading. The act of reading creates a new ego. I think that I said somewhere that when I read, I exchange the claims of an ego to know who he is –

Q: I think it was the essay on appropriation –

Ricoeur: Yes, and then I receive a self through the act of reading.

Q: It seems to me that your concepts of reading and of poetry are closely related to your religious concepts. You talk about the revelatory power of a text in opening out the possible. Isn't this closely linked to your notion of eschatology and the hope of what's to come?

Ricoeur: But to return to your first remark, that it's a kind of useful extension of religious language, I would say, in turn, that I see religious language as some kind of poetic language. This is why I don't think that I extrapolate beyond the field of religion, but from what is poetical in religion, that is to say, a capacity to create a new way of life and to open my eyes to new aspects of reality, new possibilities.

You may call that eschatology in the sense that it's the horizon of another world, the promise of a new life. But maybe it's already implied in the relationship that poetical language has with ordinary language. It reopens potentialities, where language has been reduced to its actuality, to its present functioning, therefore to its utility in the present.

Q: Do you think it would be useful or necessary to draw a distinction between poetry and kerygma? I know you admire Rilke –

Ricoeur: Yes, of course –

Q: A great deal. Would you even care to make a distinction between a great poet such as Rilke and kerygma as such? Because very often when you talk in Heideggerian terms of the word as bestowed, this has a strong religious dimension.

Ricoeur: Yes, but it's religion in a non-confessional sense. I should say that what makes the difference between poetry and religious kerygma is that poetry opens ways for my imagination to try, ways of thinking, ways of seeing the world, under the rule of play – that is to say, I am not committed. I have only to open my imagination.

Religious experience, whatever it may be, in whatever confessional sense it may be, adds at least three elements which are not the non-poetical side but which add to this capacity of opening an element of commitment. Second, the belonging to a certain community. And third, the attempt to connect that to a social, ethical, political stance.

So, whereas poetry is play, precisely because I do not have the burden of making a decision – what has been called in traditional Christianity conversion. It is not required from poetry, but there is a conversion from one impoverished world of language to an enriched one, but not in the sense of making a decision, taking a stand. So there is an element of promise and commitment in the religious attitude which is different from the pure play in imagination and through imagination that takes place in poetry.

That is why I should preserve both a strong kinship and a precise difference between the two, because I neither want to make everything poetical in religion nor to make everything religious in poetry – and to preserve this dialectic. This is one more example of the breadth of the uses of language. Religious language is and is not poetical language in the same sense as story-telling is and is not lyric poetry, and ordinary language is and is not poetical and so on. You have shades and slight shifts from one use of language and many overlappings. But, at the same time, some strong polarities.

This would be one of the functions of a philosophy which I should call a philosophy of interpretation: to be aware of these very subtle interplays with their tensions, polarities, but also their overlappings.

Q: I wanted to ask you, too, about your book *The Poetics of the Will,* the projected volume of the series on the will. Why do you call it a poetics? Does that have any relation to poetry, or just in a metaphorical sense?

Ricoeur: Neither one. I have in mind the use of the word poetics by Aristotle in his book and which is a way to return to the Greek sense of poesis, which is re-creation. And this is why I say poesis is broader than poetry in the sense of verse and why I also include fictional narratives to the extent that here we see our imagination, our productive imagination, at work. An imagination according to rules, a ruled imagination, but a creative imagination also, creating the rules and also breaking them.

So there is something common to all the forms of the poetics from the fictional narratives to lyric poetry.

Q: I know that in *Hermeneutics and the Human Sciences* you talk about history as text as well.

Ricoeur: Yes, I'm acquainted with some philosophers who tend to speak of history even in terms of a poetics, for example Hayden White, whose work I admire very much. Because the way in which the historian emplots the events of the past is as creative as the way the playwright emplots a fictional story. Both of them try to make sense with a manifold of events and try to take these together, and taking together, comprehending, is the very act of providing a configuration.

So this configurational act, either in fiction or in historiography, has the same quality of the productive imagination.

Q: So you really see all the human sciences under the sign of this productive imagination, and poetry would find itself –

Ricoeur: I don't want to say silly things about that, but I surmise that the opposition that was taken for granted at the beginning of this century, that there was a big gap between natural sciences, which had to obey facts and draw laws from facts, and the so-called human sciences, the *Geisteswissenschaften* as the Germans used to say, that there was a big gap because in sciences we should have facts and laws and in human sciences, we would have signs and interpretations ...

But now we have epistemologists who say, but this is a kind of fiction created by literary people who have a very poor idea of science and a false reverence for science. In science, too, there is a process of interpretation at work. For example, here my colleague Stephen Toulmin is working on that. He keeps saying, don't take as an opposite what scientists do because they, too, have a kind of poetical task. They have to organize fields and to elaborate configurations.

But then I don't want to go farther because this has to be verified.

Q: But this reminds me, too, of one of my favourite sections of *The Rule of Metaphor.* Section 7 is particularly interesting to me because of the very effective way in which you bring Aristotle into relation with Max Black's models and metaphors. There are, I'm sure, important differences between science and poetry, but at this stage of the game, it seems very useful to make the comparison.

We tend to think of science as a different enterprise, whereas the models that scientists construct are not so different, as a form of language. The poet, you say, is a kind of investigator.

What people think they're doing is very important in what they finally turn out. And if poets don't think of themselves as investigators, they might end up writing less important material, because they don't think of themselves as being part of a major enterprise.

Ricoeur: One point of intersection, let us say, between a logic of discovery, to use the vocabulary of Karl Popper, and the poetical enterprise is that logical discovery is an act of imagination to see new combinations and therefore to break a previous structure and to help a new structure to emerge.

But there are at least three criteria for scientific works which differ from those of a poetical work. First, there is a problem of falsification, and Popper is unbeatable on that, saying that a scientific proposition is meaningful to the extent that it includes the procedures which could falsify it.

And second, the scientist wants the recognition of his colleagues, so there is a problem of consensus, which makes no sense in poetry. The world-view of a poet, let us say, has not to be shared. So there is something like a scientific community which has no counterpart –

Q: There's no poetic community in the same sense, yes –

Ricoeur: This is part of the dramatic situation of the poet, who is always alone creating then re-creating the world.

And third, of course, each scientific discovery has to be in conformity with a body of acquired science to the point of rupture which Kuhn shows and then we have to change the paradigms. But there is nothing like a poetical system to which each poet would claim to contribute. So the idea of contributing to a body of truth is completely alien to my mind.

Even in fictional works, we could not say that a novel can be added to other novels and that constitutes a kind of a body of fictional work –

Q: But isn't that –

Ricoeur: Maybe I am wrong –

Q: I disagree, and this reminds me of a point that I meant to ask you about: the way you treat the world of the work. There's only one place in one essay, in *Hermeneutics and the Human Sciences*, where you talk about the worlds influencing each other. That would be a sense of a tradition. But almost always you talk about the unique world of each work, which goes along with what you just said.

Yet I meant to ask you about T.S. Eliot's concept of tradition as a sort of field. He was perhaps borrowing from the sciences. He did think that each individual work modifies all the relations very subtly of this field.

Ricoeur: Yes, but once more we must not be deceived by the too simplistic opposition between science and art and poetry ... in science, there is a body of truth to which each scientist contributes, whereas in poetry each one is a solitary inquirer. So maybe there is less coherence in science ... some now speak of science in rags. And, on the other hand, surely a poet does not start from scratch, even when he breaks the rules. There are rules to be broken, and he is in a certain relationship to these rules. And it's his way, the way of irony, so to say, to be linked to a tradition.

Maybe this notion of tradition is the most difficult concept because we have a strong distaste for the word. We tend to think in terms of a deposit, something which is dead. Whereas maybe a tradition deserves to be called a tradition if it keeps its dialectics, for there sedimentation and innovation always are at work.

I must say that I feel the tension, and maybe the contradiction, between the two claims that, on the one hand, each work of art is a solitary work, as I said a new world of its own ... On the other hand, all innovation has a kind of sedimentation as its background, consitituting a tradition, and tradition itself may be seen as a kind of tension between sedimentation and innovation.

Your were just speaking of T.S. Eliot, but I was thinking when you said that of Northrop Frye. It was in his *Anatomy of Criticism* that he tries to show that there is a network of works of art, because there are typologies of emplotment, of themes which make sense as a whole.

But then I wonder whether it does not belong to the self-consciousness of the poet or to the self-consciousness of the critic –

Q: Both –

Ricoeur: And then ... both?

Q: In some complex way, the poet writes –

Ricoeur: This is not part of his own project, to add to this body of literary works which is supposed to constitute a kind of structured universe of works of art, a kind of –

Q: But then the poet can be the reader, too, and when you talked about yourself before in terms of your appropriation of texts, you said 'treasure.' This, in a certain sense, constitutes a tradition in you as a reader. You are also a writer. This reminds me, too, of an aspect of the French tradition in poetry that I wanted to ask you about because of a comment you made in your book *Freud and Philosophy*. You say that the dream mainly conceals and the poem reveals. And in a passing remark you talk about the surrealists, implying their poetry isn't so good because it's too closely allied to the dream.

Ricoeur: No, I had in mind mainly the work of André Breton in *L'amour fou*. This was my main reference here, and surely it's a new pact, so to say, between dream and poetry. We are no longer allowed ... now when I read what I wrote at that time – the dream is merely archaic and poetry is prophetic – I have some reservations as to that. It's much more ... but I think that I say – I don't know the place in the same book – that in poetry there is a retrieval of the archaic. It's not my invention; it's Kris who said that regression for the sake of projection, something like that.

Q: Regression in the service of the ego?

Ricoeur: Yes ... so I transformed it and said, regression for the sake of progression or projection –

Q: You also say that the same symbol embodies both the teleological and the archaeological, but that you found it personally very difficult to think of the backward and the forward as the same. Do you still feel that difficulty?

Ricoeur: I was too, how to say, paralysed in this book, and what I wrote later was more articulate and also more aware of the subtle dialectics. There, I wanted to put some signposts. But, if I am right, in my treatment of Sophocles's *Oedipus Rex,* I tried to show that we have two tragedies, one a very archaic one, the repetition of an archaic dream, the Oedipus complex.

But grafted upon it, a tragedy of truth, since for Sophocles the problem is not that Oedipus killed his father and married his mother but that he denied that he was the man, so that it's a tragedy of truth, and a search for truthfulness. And the resistance in the Freudian sense is not resistance to the word of Teiresias, of the seer. And then it's the blindness, in fact his own blindness as opposed to the sight of the blind.

So you have here a very persuasive and very powerful link between the dream and the pure fancy in the philosophical tale which is told by Sophocles.

Q: Also, in regard to the statement that poetry reveals and the dream conceals, wouldn't certain schools of poetry, like symbolism, have as a conscious intention to conceal –

Ricoeur: Yes, I would like to catch up with this remark, because I wrote this book ten years ago, and since then I have learned a lot. I hope so. I am very fond of the work of Frank Kermode, and in his book *The Genesis of Secrecy,* he tries to say that its one of the functions of parables not to clarify but to obscure, to increase the opaqueness. It's a paradox, of course, but it's a way of breaking with this too easy opposition – the dream conceals and the poem reveals – because one way of revealing is also one way of making more obscure.

He builds heavily on this strange remark, this strange interpretation of the parables of Jesus by Mark, saying that they are not said to enlighten but to confuse those who claim to know; therefore, the increased opaqueness.

But it is not true also, I should say, with stories, story-telling, because at the first level, to tell a story is to clarify a situation? But the more we increase the complications of the story, the more it becomes opaque. And then the opaqueness of the creation retrieves the opaqueness of life.

So there is a kind of middle point where you have an acme, a summit of clarity, but for the sake of a new, not a second naïveté but a second opaqueness, so to say ... And we return here to the difficulty of poetry because this is what the reader has ... he was expecting a

kind of clarification of his own feelings, and he received more opacity.
Q: People don't want these other worlds, it's too much.
Ricoeur: Yes, it's too much.
Q: If you're having trouble with this world, why should you want to have trouble with another world, too? This reminds me of the graduate-school approach to a poet like Yeats who used all the ancient Irish names and symbols. In graduate school, you look it all up, but that's not why he did it. He wanted to give the depth, the feeling of a world.
Ricoeur: Wallace Stevens very often –
Q: Do you like Wallace Stevens?
Ricoeur: Yes, very, very much.
Q: Would you say that he is your favourite American poet?
Ricoeur: Yes, and Emily Dickinson, too. I have great admiration for both of them –
Q: Not Whitman?
Ricoeur: I don't know him enough to say that.
Q: What are the qualities of Wallace Stevens that you especially like?
Ricoeur: Of course, there is a kind of philosophy. This is the kind of philosophizing in poetry that exists only in German with Hölderlin and Stephan George, Paul Celan. Also, the two aspects of which we spoke at the beginning, expressing complex and very subtle feelings which don't find their own expression, that are lacking words. And then to bring to language some very deeply rooted experience, on the one hand, and, on the other hand, experiment with language, because it's also poetry about poetry. The two sides in Wallace Stevens.
Q: Yes, that's what perhaps makes him a very great poet.
Ricoeur: His capacity of dealing with language for the sake of language and because reality has been lost sight of you receive – as the Gospels say, look for the Kingdom of God and the rest will be given to you par-dessus le marché. So here reality is an unexpected gift from someone who seemed first to be in search of a quality of language, a way of saying. Then there is a re-creation of reality because there was no claim to say what is reality, what is experience.
Q: It reminds me of those lines of his from 'Esthetique du mal': 'Natives of poverty, children of malheur / The gaiety of language is our seigneur.'
Ricoeur: I like this double allegiance to the pure quality of language in terms of sonority and the horizon of this service of language for its

own sake, and the emergence of new shores –

Q: The world comes as a gift.

Ricoeur: Yes, because there was no attempt to express, but a kind of ascetic renouncement of expressing feelings like love and so on, death ... there is a creation of new feelings because there was a renouncement of the already known.

Q: Do you think that's the actual dynamic of it, that's the way it happens? The movement is towards language and the referential comes as a bonus?

Ricoeur: This would be my deep conviction. This is why I am not at odds with structuralists and all those who say, but poetic language is not referential or sui-referential. I say you are right and more right than you think, because it's precisely the blessing and the reward of this renunciation that may be a new link, a new bond with – should even say with nature or with creation.

At the beginning, you said but why do you speak of poetics. I gave only one-half of the answer, because Aristotle speaks of poetics for all kinds of making in terms of language, both in fiction and poetry. But also because through this recovery of the capacity of language to create and re-create, we discover reality itself in the process of being created. So we are connected with this dimension of reality which is itself unfinished, which is ... and then, once more I should like to use the vocabulary of Aristotle when he speaks of the *entelecheia,* the potentiality to see things in terms of potentialities and not in terms of actualities.

There is a place in my book on metaphor when I say that when language is itself in the process of becoming once more potential it is attuned to this dimension of reality which itself is unfinished and in the making.

Language in the making celebrates reality in the making.

Q: So the only reality we know is the reality that we reach in this way?

Ricoeur: And the rest of our language in ordinary speech and so on has to do with reality as it is already done, as it is finished, as it is there in the sense of the closedness of what is, with its meaning which is already asserted by the consensus of wise people.

The Creativity of Language

Richard Kearney (Q): How do your recent works on metaphor (*La Métaphore vive,* 1975) and narrativity (*Temps et récit,* 1983) fit into your overall program of philosophical hermeneutics?

Paul Ricoeur: In *La Métaphore vive,* (*The Rule of the Metaphor*) I tried to show how language could extend itself to its very limits forever discovering new resonances within itself. The term *vive* (living) in the title of this work is all important, for it was my purpose to demonstrate that there is not just an epistemological and political imagination, but also, and perhaps more fundamentally, a *linguistic* imagination which generates and regenerates meaning through the living power of metaphoricity. *La Métaphore vive* investigated the resources of rhetoric to show how language undergoes creative mutations and transformations. My work on narrativity, *Temps et récit,* develops this inquiry into the inventive power of language. Here, the analysis of narrative operations in a literary text, for instance, can teach us how we formulate a new structure of 'time' by creating new modes of plot and characterization. My chief concern in this analysis is to discover how the act of *raconter,* of telling a story, can transmute *natural* time into a specifically *human* time, irreducible to mathematical, chronological 'clock time.' How is narrativity, as the construction or deconstruction of paradigms of story-telling, a perpetual search for new ways of expressing human time, a production or creation of meaning? That is my question.

Q: How would you relate this hermeneutics of narrativity to your former phenomenology of existence?

Ricoeur: I would say, borrowing Wittgenstein's term, that the 'language-game' of narration ultimately reveals that the meaning of human existence is itself narrative. The implications of narration as a retelling of history are considerable. For history is not only the story (*histoire*) of triumphant kings and heroes, of the powerful; it is also the story of the powerless and dispossessed. The history of the vanquished dead crying out for justice demands to be told. As Hannah Arendt points out, the meaning of human existence is not just the power to change or master the world, but also the ability to be remembered and recollected in narrative discourse, to be *memorable*. These existential and historical implications of narrativity are very far-reaching, for they determine what is to be 'preserved' and rendered 'permanent' in a culture's sense of its own past, of its own 'identity.'

Q: Could you outline some such implications for a political rereading of the past? How, for example, would it relate to a Marxist interpretation?

Ricoeur: Just as novelists choose a certain plot (*intrigue*) to order the material of their fiction into a narrative sequence, so too historians order the events of the past according to certain choices of narrative structure or plot. While history has traditionally concerned itself with the plot of kings, battles, treaties, and the rise and fall of empires, one finds alternative readings emerging from the nineteenth century onwards whose narrative selection focuses on the story of the victims – the plot of suffering rather than that of power and glory. Michelet's romantic historiography of the 'people' was a case in point. And a more obvious and influential example is the Marxist rereading of history according to the model of the class struggle which champions the cause of the oppressed workers. In such ways, the normal narrative ordering of history is reversed and the hero is now the 'slave' rather than the 'master' as before; a new set of events and facts are deemed to be relevant and claim our attention; the relations of labour and production take precedence over the relations between kings and queens. But here again one must remain critical lest the new heroes of history become abstractions in their turn, thus reducing an alternative 'liberating' plot to another reified version of events which might only deepen the illusion that history somehow unfolds of its own accord independently of the creative powers of the labouring human subject. After such a manner, Marxism as an ideology of liberation, of the powerless, can easily become – as happened with the German Social Democrats or with Stalin – an ideology which imposes a new kind of oppressive power: the proletariat thus ceases to be a living human community of subjects and becomes instead an impersonal, abstracted concept in a new system of scientific determinism.

Q: Is narrative language primarily an intentionality of subjective consciousness, as phenomenology argued; or is it an objective and impersonal structure which predetermines the subjective operations of consciousness, as structuralism maintained?

Ricoeur: It is both at once. The invaluable contribution made by structuralism was to offer an exact scientific description of the codes and paradigms of language. But I do not believe that this excludes the creative expression of consciousness. The creation of meaning in language comes from the specifically *human* production of new ways of expressing the objective paradigms and codes made available by language. With the same grammar, for example, we can utter many novel and different sentences. Creativity is always governed by objective linguistic codes which it continually brings to their limit in order to invent something new. Whereas I drew from the objective codes of rhetoric in my analysis of the creative power of metaphor, in my study of narrativity I refer to the linguistic structures disclosed by the Russian formalists, the Prague school, and more recently the structuralism of Lévi-Strauss and Genette. My philosophical project is to show how human language is *inventive* despite the objective limits and codes which govern it, to reveal the diversity and potentiality of language which the erosion of the everyday, conditioned by technocratic and political interests, never ceases to obscure. To become aware of the metaphorical and narrative resources of language is to recognize that its flattened or diminished powers can always be rejuvenated for the benefit of all forms of language usage.

Q: Can your research on narrativity also be considered as a search for a shared meaning beyond the multiplicity of discourses? In other words, does the act of narrating history render it universal and common to all men?

Ricoeur: This problem of unity and diversity is central to narrativity and can be summarized in terms of the two following, conflicting interpretations. In the *Confessions* Augustine tells us that the 'human body is undone,' that human existence is in discord in so far as it is a temporal rupturing and exploding of the present in contrast to the eternal presence of God. To this Augustinian reading of human existence as *dispersion*, I would oppose Aristotle's theory of tragedy in *The Poetics* as a way of *unifying* existence by retelling it. Narrativity can be seen in terms of this opposition: the discordance of time (*temps*) and the concordance of the tale (*récit*). This is a problem which faces all historians, for example. Is history a narrative tale which orders and constructs the fragmentary, empirical facts offered by sociology? Can history divorce itself from the narrative structure of the tale, in its rapprochement to sociology, without ceasing to be history? It is interesting that even Fernand Braudel, who champions the sociological approach to history in his preface to *The Mediterranean in the Time of Philip II*, still retains the notion of history as temporal duration; he stops short of espousing atemporal paradigms, *à la* Lévi-Strauss, for that would spell the demise of history. Lévi-Strauss's social anthropology can afford to dispense with history since it is concerned only with 'cold societies': societies without historical or diachronic development, whose customs and norms – the incest taboo, for example – are largely unaffected by temporal change. History begins and ends with the reciting of a tale (*récit*); and its intelligibility and coherence rest upon this recital. My task is to show how the narrative structures of history and of the story (i.e., of the novel or fiction) operate in a parallel fashion to create new forms of human time, and therefore new forms of human community, for creativity is also a social and cultural act; it is not confined to the individual.

Q: What exactly do you mean by 'human' time?

Ricoeur: I mean the formulation of two opposing forms of time: public time and private time. Private time is mortal time, for, as Heidegger says, to exist is to be a being-towards-death (*Sein-zum-Tode*), a being whose future is closed off by death. As soon as we understand our existence as this mortal time, we are already involved in a form of private narrativity or history; as soon as the individual comes up against the finite limits of its own existence, it is obliged to recollect itself and to make time its *own*. On the other hand, there exists public time. Now I do not mean public in the sense of physical or natural time (clock time), but the time of language itself, which continues on after the individual's death. To live in human time is to live between the private time of our mortality and the public time of language. Even Chénu, who tends towards a quantitative assessment of history, acknowledges that the kernel of history is demography, that is, the regeneration of generations, the story (*histoire*) of the living and the dead. Precisely as this recollection of the living and the dead, history – as public narrativity – produces human time. To summarize, I would say that my analysis of narrativity is concerned with three interrelated problems: (i) narration as history; (ii) narration as fiction; and (iii) narration as human time.

Q: What can this analysis contribute to your study of the biblical patterns of narration in *La symbolique du mal*?

Ricoeur: The hermeneutics of narration is crucial to our understanding of the Bible. Why is it, for example, that Judaeo-Christianity is founded on narrative episodes or stories?; and how is it that these succeed in becoming *exemplary*, co-ordinated into laws, prophecies, and psalms, etc.? I think that the biblical co-ordination of narratives can perhaps be understood in terms of Kristeva's notion of *intertextuality*: the idea that every text functions in terms of another. Biblical narratives operate in terms of other prescriptive texts. The kernel of biblical hermeneutics is this conjunction of narrativity and prescription.

Q: What is the rapport between your earlier analysis of the 'creative imagination' as an 'eschatological hope' for the 'not yet' of history, and your more recent analysis of narrativity as the production of human time and history?

Ricoeur: Whereas the analysis of creative imagination dealt with creativity in its prospective or futural aspect, the analysis of narrativity deals with it in a retrospective fashion. Fiction has a strong relation to the past. Camus's *L'Etranger*, like most other novels, is written in the passive tense. The narrative voice of a novel generally retells something that has taken place in a fictional past. One could almost say that fictional narration tends to suspend the eschatological in order to inscribe us in a meaningful past. And I believe that we must have a sense of the meaningfulness of the past if our projections into the future are to be more than empty utopias. Heidegger argues in *Being and Time* that it is because we are turned towards the future that we can possess and repossess a past, both our personal past and our cultural heritage. The structure of narrativity demonstrates that it is by trying to put order on our past, by retelling and recounting what has been, that we acquire an identity. These two orientations – towards the future and towards the past – are not, however, incompatible. As Heidegger himself points out, the notion of 'repeating' (*Wiederholung*) the past is inseparable from the existential projection of ourselves towards our possibilities. To 'repeat' our story, to retell our history, is to re-collect our horizon of possibilities in a resolute and responsible manner. In this respect, one can see how the retrospective character of narration is closely linked to the prospective horizon of the future. To say that narration is a recital which orders the past is not to imply that it is a conservative closure to what is new. On the contrary, narration preserves the meaning that is behind us so that we can have meaning before us. There is always *more* order in what we narrate than in what we have actually already lived; and this narrative excess (*surcroît*) of order, coherence and unity, is a prime example of the creative power of narration.

Q: What about the modernist texts of Joyce and Beckett, etc., where the narrative seems to disperse and dislocate meaning?

Ricoeur: These texts break up the habitual paradigms of narrative order in order to leave the ordering task of creation to the reader himself. And ultimately it is true that the reader composes the text. All narrative, however, even Joyce's, is a certain call to order. Joyce does not invite us to embrace chaos but an infinitely more complex order. Narrative carries us beyond the oppressive order of our existence to a more liberating and refined order. The question of narrativity, no matter how modernist or avant-garde, cannot be separated from the problem of order.

Q: What compelled you to abandon the Husserlian phenomenology of consciousness, with its claim to a direct and immediate apprehension of meaning, and to adopt a hermeneutic phenomenology where the meaning of existence is approached indirectly through myth, metaphor, or narrativity, that is, through the detour of mediation?

Ricoeur: I think that it is always through the mediation of structuring operations that one apprehends the fundamental meaning of existence, what Merleau-Ponty called *l'être sauvage*. Merleau-Ponty sought this *l'être sauvage* throughout his philosophical career and consistently criticized its deformation and obfuscation in science. I for my part have always attempted to identify those mediations of language which are not reducible to the dissimulations of scientific objectivity, but which continue to bear witness to creative linguistic potentialities. Language possesses deep resources which are not immediately reducible to knowledge (particularly the intellectualist and behaviourist forms of knowledge which Merleau-Ponty rejected). And my interest in hermeneutics, and its interpretation of language which extends to the limits of logic and the mathematical sciences, has always been an attempt to detect and describe these resources. I am convinced that all figurative language is potentially conceptualizable and that the conceptual order can possess a form of creativity. This is why I insisted, at the end of *La Métaphore vive*, upon the essential connection or intersection between speculative and poetic discourse – evidenced, for example, in the whole question of analogy. It is simplistic to suggest that conceptualization is *per se* antagonistic to the meaning of life and experience; concepts can also be open, creative and living, though they can never constitute a knowledge which would be immediately accessible to some self-transparent *cogito*. Conceptualization cannot reach meaning directly or create meaning out of itself *ex nihilo*; it cannot dispense with the detour of mediation through figurative structures. This detour is intrinsic to the very working of concepts.

Q: In study 8 of *La Métaphore vive* you raised the complex philosophical problem of 'reference' in language. How does narrativity relate to this problem of reference?

Ricoeur: This question brings us to the intersection between history, which claims to deal with what actually happens, and the novel, which is of the order of fiction. Reference entails a conjunction of history and fiction. And I reckon that my chances of demonstrating the validity of reference are better in an analysis of narrativity than in one of metaphoricity. Whereas it is always difficult to identify the referent of poetic or metaphorical discourse, the referent of narrative discourse is obvious – the order of human action. Now, of course, human action itself is charged with fictional entities such as stories, symbols, and rites. As Marx pointed out in *The German Ideology*, when men produce their existence in the form of *praxis* they represent it to themselves in terms of fiction, even at the limit in terms of religion (which for Marx is the model of ideology). There can be no praxis which is not already symbolically structured in some way. Human action is always figured in signs, interpreted in terms of cultural traditions and norms. Our narrative fictions are then added to this primary interpretation of figuration of human action; so that narrative is a redefining of what is already defined, a reinterpretation of what is already interpreted. The referent of narration, namely human action, is never raw or immediate reality but an action which has been symbolized and resymbolized over and over again. Thus narration serves to displace anterior symbolizations on to a new plane, integrating or exploding them as the case may be. If this were not so, if literary narrative, for example, were closed off from the world of human action, it would be entirely harmless and inoffensive. But literature never ceases to challenge our way of reading human history and praxis. In this respect, literary narrative involves a creative use of language often ignored by science or by our everyday existence. Literary language has the capacity to put our quotidian existence into question; it is *dangerous* in the best sense of the word.

Q: But is not the hermeneutic search for mediated and symbolized meaning a way of escaping from the harsh, empirical reality of things, is it not always working at one remove from life?

Ricoeur: Proust said that if play was cloistered off in books, it would cease to be formidable. Play is formidable precisely because it is loose in the world, planting its mediations everywhere, shattering the illusion of the immediacy of the real. The problem for a hermeneutics of language is not to rediscover some pristine immediacy but to mediate again and again in a new and more creative fashion. The mediating role of imagination is forever at work in lived reality (le *vécu*). There is no lived reality, no human or social reality, which is not already *represented* in some sense. This imaginative and creative dimension of the social, this *imaginaire social*, has been brilliantly analysed by Castoriadis in his book, *L'Institution imaginaire de la société*. Literature supplements this primary representation of the social with its own narrative representation, a process which Dagonier calls 'iconographic augmentation.' But literature is not the only way in which fiction can iconographically mediate human reality. There is also the mediating role of models in science or of utopias in political ideologies. These three modes of fictional mediation – literary, scientific, and political – effectuate a metaphorization of the real, a creation of new meaning.

Q: Which returns us to your original question: what is the meaning of creativity in language and how does it relate to the codes, structures, or laws imposed by language?

Ricoeur: Linguistic creativity constantly strains and stretches the laws and codes of language that regulate it. Roland Barthes described these regulating laws as 'fascist' and urged the writer and critic to work at the limits of language, subverting its constraining laws, in order to make way for the free movement of *desire*, to make language festive. But if the narrative order of language is replete with codes, it is also capable of creatively violating them. Human creativity is always in some sense a response to a regulating order. The imagination is always working on the basis of already established laws and it is its task to make them function creatively, either by applying them in an original way or by subverting them; or indeed both – what Malraux calls 'regulated deformation.' There is no function of imagination, no *imaginaire*, that is not structuring or structured, that is not said or about-to-be-said in language. The task of hermeneutics is to charter the unexplored resources of the to-be-said on the basis of the already-said. Imagination never resides in the unsaid.

Q: How would you respond to Lévi-Strauss's conclusion, in *L'Homme nu*, that the structures and symbols of society originate in 'nothing' (*rien*)?

Ricoeur: I am not very interested in Lévi-Strauss's metaphysics of nothingness. The great contribution made by Lévi-Strauss was to identify the existence of enduring symbolic structures in what he called 'cold societies,' that is, societies (mainly South-American Indian) resistant to historical change. The Greek and Hebraic societies which combined to make up our Western culture are, by contrast, 'hot societies'; they are societies whose symbolic systems change and evolve over time, carrying within themselves different layers of interpretation and reinterpretation. In other words, in 'hot' societies the work of interpretation is not – as in 'cold' societies – something which is introduced from without, but an internal component of the symbolic system itself. It is precisely this diachronic process of reinterpretation that we call 'tradition.' In the Greek *Iliad*, for example, we discover a myth that is already reinterpreted, a piece of history that is already reworked into a narrative order. Neither Homer nor Aeschylus invented his stories; what they did invent were new narrative meanings, new forms of retelling the same story. The author of the *Iliad* has the entire story of the Trojan War at his disposal, but chooses to isolate the exemplary story of Achilles's wrath. He develops this exemplary narrative to the point where the wrath expires in the cathartic reconciliation – occasioned by Hector's death – with King Priam. The story produces and exemplifies a particular meaning: how the vain and meaningless wrath of one hero (Achilles) can be overcome when this hero becomes reconciled with his victim's father (Priam) at the funeral banquet. Here we have a powerful example of what it means to create meaning from a common mythic heritage, to receive a tradition and re-create it poetically to signify something new.

Q: And of course Chaucer and Shakespeare produced different 'exemplary' reinterpretations of the *Iliad* myth in their respective versions of Troilus and Cressida; as did Joyce once again in *Ulysses*. Such reinterpretation would seem to typify the cultural history of our

Hellenic heritage. Is this kind of historical reinterpretation also to be found in the biblical or Hebraic tradition?

Ricoeur: Yes, the biblical narratives of the Hebraic tradition also operate in this *exemplary* or exemplifying fashion. This is evident in the fact that the biblical stories or episodes are not simply added to each other, or juxtaposed with each other, but constitute a cumulative and organic development. For example, the promise made to Abraham that his people would have a salvific relation with God is an inexhaustible promise (unlike certain legal promises which can be immediately realized); as such it opens up a history in which this promise can be repeated and reinterpreted over and over again – with Moses, then with David, and so on. So that the biblical narrative of this 'not yet realized' promise creates a cumulative history of repetition. The Christian message of crucifixion and resurrection then inserts itself into this biblical history, as a double rapport of reinterpretation and rupture. Christianity plays both a subversive and preservative role *vis-à-vis* the Judaic tradition. Saint Paul talks about the overcoming of the Law; and yet we find the synoptic authors continually affirming that the Christian event is a response to the prophetic promise, 'according to the Scriptures.' The Judaic and Christian reinterpretations of biblical history are in 'loving combat,' to borrow Jaspers's phrase. The important point is that the biblical experience of faith is founded on stories and narratives – the story of the exodus, the crucifixion, and resurrection, etc. – *before* it expresses itself in abstract theologies which interpret these foundational narratives and provide religious tradition with its sense of enduring identity. The *future* projects of every religion are intimately related to the ways in which it remembers itself.

Q: Your work in hermeneutics always displays a particular sensitivity to this 'conflict of interpretations' – even to the point of providing one of the titles of your books. Your hermeneutics has consistently refused the idea of an 'absolute knowledge' which might reductively *totalize* the multiplicity of interpretations – phenomenological, theological, psycho-analytic, structuralist, scientific, literary, etc. Is there any sense in which this open-ended intellectual itinerary can be construed as a sort of odyssey which might ultimately return to a unifying centre where the conflicting interpretations of human discourse could be gathered together and reconciled?

Ricoeur: When Odysseus completes the circle and returns to his island of Ithaca there is slaughter and destruction. For me the philosophical task is not to close the circle, to centralize or totalize knowledge, but to keep open the irreducible plurality of discourse. It is essential to show how the different discourses may interrelate or intersect but one must resist the temptation to make them identical, the same. My departure from Husserlian phenomenology was largely due to my disagreement with its theory of a controlling transcendental *cogito*. I advanced the notion of a wounded or split *cogito*, in opposition to the idealist claims for an inviolate absolute subjectivity. It was in fact Karl Barth who first taught me that the subject is not a centralizing master but rather a disciple or auditor of a language larger that itself. At a broader cultural level, we must also be wary of attending exclusively to *Western* traditions of thought, of becoming *Europocentric*. In emphasizing the importance of the Greek or Judaeo-Christian traditions, we often overlook the radically heterogenious discourses of the Far East for example. One of my American colleagues recently suggested to me that Derrida's deconstruction of logocentricism bears striking resemblances to the Buddhist notion of nothingness. I think that there is a certain 'degree zero' or emptiness which we may have to traverse in order to abandon our pretension to be the centre, our tendency to reduce all other discourses to our own totalizing schemas of thought. If there is an ultimate unity, it resides elsewhere, in a sort of eschatological hope. But this is my 'secret,' if you wish, my personal wager, and not something that can be translated into a centralizing philosophical discourse.

Q: It appears that our modern secularized society has abandoned the symbolic representations or *imaginaire* of tradition. Can the creative process of reinterpretation operate if the narrative continuity with the past is broken?

Ricoeur: A society where narrative is dead is one where men are no longer capable of exchanging their experiences, of sharing a common experience. The contemporary search for some narrative continuity with the past is not just nostalgic escapism but a contestation of the legislative and planificatory discourse which tends to predominate in bureaucratic societies. To give people back a *memory* is also to give them back a *future*, to put them back in time and thus release them from the 'instantaneous mind' (*mens instans*), to borrow a term from Leibniz. The past is not *passé*, for our future is guaranteed precisely by our ability to possess a narrative identity, to recollect the past in historical or fictive form. This problem of narrative identity is particularly acute, for instance, in a country like France, where the

Revolution represented a rupture with the patrimony of legend and folklore, etc. (I have always been struck, for example, by the fact that most of the so-called traditional songs the French still possess are drinking songs.) Today the French are largely bereft of a shared *imaginaire*, a common symbolic heritage. Our task then is to reappropriate those resources of language which have resisted contamination and destruction. To rework language is to rediscover what we are. What is lost in experience is often salvaged in language, sedimented as a deposit of traces, as a thesaurus. There can be no pure or perfectly transparent model of language, as Wittgenstein reminds us in his *Philosophical Investigations*; and if there were it would be no more than a unversalized *vide*. To rediscover meaning we must return to the multilayered sedimentations of language, to the complex plurality of its instances, which can preserve what is said from the destruction of oblivion.

Q: In *History and Truth* you praise Emmanuel Mounier as someone who refused to separate the search for philosophical truth from a political pedagogy. What are the political implications, if any, of your own philosophical thinking?

Ricoeur: My work to date has been a hermeneutic reflection upon the mediation of meaning in language, and particularly in poetic or narrative language. What, you ask, can such hermeneutics contribute to our understanding of the rapport between the mediations of such symbolic discourses and the immediacy of political praxis? The fact that language is disclosed by hermeneutics (and also by the analytic philosophy of Wittgenstein) as a not-totalizable plurality of interpretations or 'language games' means that the rhetorical discourse of politics, which serves as a justification or critique of power, is but one among many other 'language-games' and so cannot pretend to the status of a universal science. Some recent exchanges I had with Czech philosophers and students in the Tomin seminar in Prague taught me that the problem of totalitarianism resides in the lie that there can be a universally true and scientific discourse of politics (in this instance, the communist discourse). Once one recognizes that political language is basically a rhetoric of persuasion and opinion, one can tolerate free discussion. An 'open society,' to use Popper's term, is one which acknowledges that political debate is infinitely open and is thus prepared to take the critical step back in order to continually interrogate and reconstitute the conditions of an authentic language.

Q: Can there be a positive rapport between language, as political ideology, and utopia?

Ricoeur: Every society, as I mentioned earlier, possesses, or is part of, a socio-political *imaginaire*, that is, an ensemble of symbolic discourses. This *imaginaire* can function as a rupture or a reaffirmation. As reaffirmation, the *imaginaire* operates as an '*ideology*' which can positively repeat and represent the founding discourse of a society, what I call its 'foundational symbols,' thus preserving its sense of identity. After all, cultures create themselves by telling stories of their own past. The danger is of course that this reaffirmation can be perverted, usually by monopolistic élites, into a mystificatory discourse which serves to uncritically vindicate or glorify the established political powers. In such instances, the symbols of a community become fixed and fetishized; they serve as lies. Over against this, there exists the *imaginaire* of rupture, a discourse of *utopia* which remains critical of the powers that be out of fidelity to an 'elsewhere,' to a society that is 'not yet.' But this utopian discourse is not always positive either. For besides the authentic utopia of critical rupture there can also exist a dangerously schizophrenic utopian discourse which projects a static future without ever producing the conditions of its realization. This can happen with the Marxist–Leninist notion of utopia if one projects the final 'withering away of the State' without undertaking genuine measures to ever achieve such a goal. Here utopia becomes a future cut off from the present and the past, a mere alibi for the consolidation of the repressive powers that be. The utopian discourse functions as a mystificatory ideology as soon as it justifies the oppression of today in the name of the liberation of tomorrow. In short, *ideology* as a symbolic confirmation of the past and *utopia* as a symbolic opening towards the future are complementary; if cut off from each other they can lead to a form of political pathology.

Q: Would you consider the Liberation Theology of Latin America to be an example of a positive utopian discourse insofar as it combines a Marxist utopianism with the political transformation of *present* reality?

Ricoeur: It also combines it with the *past*, with the memory of the archetypes of exodus and resurrection. This memorial dimension of Liberation Theology is essential, for it gives direction and continuity to the utopian projection of the future, thus functioning as a *garde-fou* against irresponsible or uncritical futurism. Here the political project of the future is inseparable from a continuous horizon of liberation, reaching back to the biblical notions of exile and promise. The promise remains unfulfilled until the utopia is historically realized; and it is precisely the not-yet-realized horizon of this promise which binds men together as a community, which prevents utopia detaching itself as an empty dream.

Q: How exactly does utopia relate to history?

Ricoeur: In his *History of the Concept of History*, Reinhart Kosselek argues that until the eighteenth century, the concept of history, in the West at any rate, was a plural one; one referred to 'histories' not History with a capital H. Our current notion of a single or unique history only emerged with the modern idea of progress. As soon as history is thus constituted as a single concept, the gap between our 'horizon of expectancy' and our 'field of experience' never ceases to widen. The unity of history is founded on the constitution of a common horizon of expectancy; but the projection of such a horizon into a distantly abstract future means that our present 'field of experience' can become pathologically deprived of meaning and articulation. The universal ceases to be concrete. This dissociation of *expectancy* from *experience* enters a crisis as soon as we lack the intermediaries to pass from the one to the other. Up to the sixteenth century, the utopian horizon of expectancy was the eschatological notion of the last Judgment, which had as mediating or intermediating factors the whole experience of the millennium of the Holy Roman and Germanic empires. There was always some sort of articulated path leading from what one had to what one expected to have. The liberal ideology of Kant and Locke produced a certain discourse of democracy which served as a path for the citizen towards a better humanity; and Marxism also promoted mediating stages leading from capitalism through socialism to communism. But we don't seem to believe in these intermediaries any more. The problem today is the apparent impossibility of unifying world politics, of mediating between the polycentricity of our everyday political practice and the utopian horizon of a universally liberated humanity. It is not that we are without utopia, but that we are without *paths* to utopia. And without a path towards it, without concrete and practical mediation in our field of experience, utopia becomes a sickness. Perhaps the deflation of utopian expectancies is not entirely a bad thing. Politics can so easily be injected with too much utopia; perhaps it should become more modest and realistic in its claims, more committed to our practical and immediate needs.

Q: Is there any place in contemporary politics for a genuine utopian discourse?

Ricoeur: Maybe not in politics itself but rather at the junction between politics and other cultural discourses. Our present disillusionment with the political stems from the fact that we invested it with the totality of our expectancies – until it became a bloated imposture of utopia. We have tended to forget that beside the public realm of politics, there also exists a more private cultural realm (which includes literature, philosophy and religion, etc.) where the utopian horizon can express itself. Modern society seems hostile to this domain of private experience, but the suppression of the private entails the destruction of the public. The vanquishing of the private by the public is a Pyrrhic victory.

Q: Are you advocating a return to the bourgeois romantic notion of private subjectivity removed from all political responsibility?

Ricoeur: Not at all. In my recent discussions with the Prague philosophers I spoke about the crisis of the subject in contemporary Continental philosophy, particularly structuralism. I pointed out that if one does away with the idea of a subject who is responsible for his or her words, we are no longer in a position to talk of the freedom or the rights of man. To dispense with the classical notion of the subject as a transparent *cogito* does not mean that we have to dispense with all forms of subjectivity. My hermeneutical philosophy has attempted to demonstrate the existence of an opaque subjectivity which expresses itself through the detour of countless mediations – signs, symbols, texts, and human praxis itself. This hermeneutical idea of subjectivity as a dialectic between the self and mediated social meanings has deep moral and political implications. It shows that there is an *ethic of the word*, that language is not just the abstract concern of logic or semiotics, but entails the fundamental moral duty that people be responsible for what they say. A society which no longer possesses subjects ethically responsible for their words is a society which no longer possesses citizens. For the dissident philosophers in Prague the primary philosophical question is the integrity and truthfulness of language. And this question becomes a moral and political act of resistance in a system based on lies and perversion. The Marxism of Eastern Europe has degenerated from dialectics to positivism. It has abandoned the Hegelian inspiration which preserved Marxism as a realization of the universal subject in history, and has become instead a positivistic technology of mass manipulation.

Q: So the hermeneutical interrogation of the creation of meaning in language can have a political content?

Ricoeur: Perhaps the most promising example of a political hermeneutics is to be found in the Frankfurt School synthesis between Marxist dialectics and Heideggerian hermeneutics – best expressed in Habermas's critique of ideologies. But here again one must be careful to resist the temptation to engage in an unmediated politics. It is necessary for hermeneutics to keep a certain distance so as to critically disclose the underlying mediating structures at work in political discourse. This hermeneutic distance is particularly important today with the post-1968 disillusionment, the demise of the Maoist ideology, and the exposure of Soviet totalitarianism by Solzhenitsyn and others.

Q: Is this disillusionment a world-wide phenomenon?

Ricoeur: It exists in varying degrees, but is most conspicuous in countries like France where the essential distinction between state and society has been largely occluded. The French Revolution apportioned political sovereignty to all levels of the community, from the government at the top to the individuals at the bottom. But in this process, the state became omnipresent, the citizen being reduced to a mere fragment of the state. What was so striking in the Solidarity movement in Poland was their use of the term 'society' in opposition to the term 'state.' Even in the Anglo-Saxon countries one finds certain national institutions – such as the media or universities – which are relatively independent of state politics. (It is difficult to find examples of this in France.) The weak ideologization of politics in America, for instance, means that it can at least serve as a sprawling laboratory where a multiplicity of discourses can be tried and tested. This phenomenon of the 'melting pot' is an example of what Montesquieu called the 'separation of powers.' It is interesting to remember that the state was originally conceived by the liberal thinkers as an agency of toleration, a way of protecting the plurality of beliefs and practices. The liberal state was to be a safeguard against religious and other forms of fanaticism. The fundamental perversion of the liberal state is that it came to function as a totalizing rather than a detotalizing agency. That is why it is urgent for us today to discover a political discourse which would not be governed by states, a new form of society guaranteeing universal rights yet dispensing with totalizing constraints. This is the enormous task of reconstituting a form of sociality not determined by the state.

Q: How does one go about discovering this new discourse of society?
Ricoeur: One of the first steps would be to analyse what exactly happened in the eighteenth century when the Judaeo-Christian horizon of eschatology was replaced by the Enlightenment horizon of humanism with its liberal notions of autonomy, freedom, and human rights. We must see how this Enlightenment humanism developed through the Kantian notion of the autonomous will, the Hegelian notion of the universal class (of civil servants), to the Marxist universal class of workers, etc. until we reached a secularized version of utopia which frequently degenerated into scientific positivism. We must ask: can there be any sort of continuity between the religious–eschatological projection of utopia and the modern humanist projection of a secularized utopia? The challenge today is to find alternative forms of social rationality beyond the positivistic extremes of both state socialism and utilitarian–liberal capitalism. Habermas's distinction between three forms of rationality is essential here: (i) *calculative rationality*, which operates as positivistic control and manipulation; (ii) *interpretative rationality*, which tries to represent the cultural codes and norms in a creative way; (iii) *critical rationality*, which opens up the utopian horizon of liberation. For a genuine social rationality to exist we must refuse to allow the critical and interpretive functions to be reduced to the calculative. Habermas is here developing Adorno's and Horkheimer's critique of *positivist rationality*, which exists in both state communism and in the argument of liberal capitalism that once the society of abundance has been achieved all can be distributed equally (the problem being, of course, that liberalism employs the means of a hierarchical and unequal society to achieve such an end of abundance – an end which never seems to be realized). So our task remains that of preserving a utopian horizon of liberty and equality – by means of interpretative and critical rationality – without resorting to a positivistic ideology of bad faith. I agree here with Raymond Aron's contention that we have not yet succeeded in developing a political model which could accommodate the simultaneous advancement of liberty and equality. Societies which have advocated liberty have generally suppressed equality and vice versa.
Q: Do you think that the critique of political power carried out by left-wing political philosophers in France, such as Castoriadis and Lefort, contributes to the hermeneutic search for a new discourse of sociality?
Ricoeur: Their contribution has been absolutely decisive. This cri-

tique has attempted to show that the error of Marxism resides not so much in its lack of a political horizon as in its reduction of the critique of power to the economic transfer of work to capital (that is, the critique of surplus value). Thus the Marxist critique tends to ignore that there can be more pernicious forms of power than capital – for example, the totalization of all the resources of a society (the resources of the workforce, of the means of discussion and information, education, research, etc.) by the central committee of the party or state. In this manner the handing over of the private ownership of the means of production to the state can often mean a replacement of the alienation of society by the alienation of the state. The power of the totalitarian party is perhaps more nefarious than the dehumanizing power of capital in so far as it controls not only the economic means of production but also the political means of communications. Maybe the economic analysis of class struggle is but one of the many plots that make up the complex of history. Hence the need for a hermeneutics of sociality that could unravel the plurality of power plots which enmesh to form our history.

Q: In 'Non-violent Man and His Presence in History' (*History and Truth*) you asked: 'Can the prophet or non-violent man have a historical task which would obviate both the extreme inefficacity of the Yogi and the extreme efficacity of the Commissar?' In other words, can one commit oneself to the efficacious transformation of political reality and still preserve the critical distance of transcendence?

Ricoeur: This idea of transcendence is essential for any sort of non-violent discourse. The pacifist ideal resists violence by attesting to values which transcend the area of political efficacity, without becoming irrelevant dreams. Non-violence is a form of genuine utopian vigil or hope, a way of refuting the system of violence and oppression in which we live.

Q: Is it possible to reconcile the exigency of an authentic social rationality with the eschatological hope of religion?

Ricoeur: This has never struck me as an insoluble problem for the basic cultural reason that our Western religiosity of Judaeo-Christianity has always functioned in the philosophical climate of Greek and Latin rationality. I have always objected to the simplistic opposition of Jerusalem and Athens, to those thinkers who declare that true spirituality can only be found in monotheism; or try to drive a wedge between Greek and Hebraic culture, defining the former as a thought of the cosmos and the latter as a thought of transcendence, etc. From the eleventh century onwards we find models for reconciling reason and religion – in Anselm, for example – and the Renaissance confirms this primary synthesis of rationality and spirituality. If it is true that the rationality of scientific positivism has divorced itself from spirituality, there are many signs today that we are searching for new forms of connection.

Myth as the Bearer of
Possible Worlds

Richard Kearney (Q): One of your first attempts at hermeneutic analysis concentrated on the way in which human consciousness was mediated by mythic and symbolic expressions from the earliest times. In *The Symbolism of Evil* (1960) you demonstrated how mythic symbols played an important ideological and political role in the ancient cultures of the Babylonians, Hebrews, and Greeks, etc. And in this same work you declared that 'myth relates to events that happened at the beginning of time which have the purpose of providing grounds for the ritual actions of men today' (p. 5). Are you suggesting that mythic symbols can play a relevant role in contemporary culture? And if so, could you elaborate on how it might do so?

Paul Ricoeur: I don't think that we can approach this question directly, that is, in terms of a direct relationship between myth and action. We must first return to an analysis of what constitutes the *imaginary nucleus* of any culture. It is my conviction that one cannot reduce any culture to its explicit functions – political, economic, legal, etc. No culture is wholly transparent in this way. There is invariably a hidden nucleus which determines and rules the *distribution* of these transparent functions and institutions. It is this matrix of distribution which assigns them different roles in relation to (1) each other, (2) other societies, (3) the individuals who participate in them, and (4) nature, which stands over against them.

Q: Does this ratio of distribution differ from one society to another?
Ricoeur: It certainly does. The particular relationship between political institutions, nature, and the individual is rarely if ever the same in any two cultures. The ratio of distribution between these different functions of a given society is determined by some *hidden*

nucleus, and it is here that we must situate the specific identity of culture. Beyond or beneath the self-understanding of a society there is an opaque kernel which cannot be reduced to empirical norms or laws. This kernel cannot be explained in terms of some transparent model because it is constitutive of a culture *before* it can be expressed and reflected in specific representations or ideas. It is only if we try to grasp this kernel that we may discover the *foundational mytho-poetic* nucleus of a society. By analysing itself in terms of such a foundational nucleus, a society comes to a truer understanding of itself; it begins to critically acknowledge its own symbolizing identity.

Q: How are we to recognize this mythical nucleus?

Ricoeur: The mythical nucleus of a society is only *indirectly* recognizable. But it is indirectly recognizable not only by what is said (discourse), but also by what and how one lives (praxis), and third, as I suggested, by the distribution between different functional levels of a society. We cannot, for example, say that in all countries the economic layer is determining. This is true for our Western society. But as Lévi-Strauss has shown in his analysis of many primitive societies, this is not universally true. In several cultures the significance of economic and historical considerations would seem to be minor. In our culture the economic factor is indeed determining; but that does not mean that the predominance of economics is itself explicable purely in terms of economic science. This predominance is perhaps more correctly understood as but one constituent of the overall evaluation of what is primary and what is secondary. And it is only by the analysis of the hierarchical structuring and evaluation of the different constituents of a society (i.e., the role of politics, nature, art, religion) that we may penetrate to its hidden *mytho-poetic nucleus*.

Q: You mentioned Lévi-Strauss. How would you situate your own hermeneutical analyses of symbol and myth in relation to his work in this area?

Ricoeur: I don't think that Lévi-Strauss makes any claim to speak of societies in general. He has focused on certain primitive and stable societies, leaving aside considerations of history. This is important to realize so as not to draw hasty conclusions from his analysis. Lévi-Strauss has deliberately chosen to speak of societies *without history*, whereas I think that there is something specifically historical about the societies to which we in the West belong, depending on the extent to which they are affected by Hebraic, Hellenic, Germanic, or

Celtic cultures. The development of a society is both synchronic and diachronic. This means that the distribution of power-functions in any given society contains a definite *historical* dimension. We have to think of societies in terms of both a set of simultaneous institutions (synchronism) and a process of historical transformation (diachronism). Thus we arrive at the panchronic approach to societies, i.e., both synchronic and diachronic, which characterizes the hermeneutical method. And we must also realize that the kinds of myth on which our societies are founded have themselves this twofold characteristic: on the one hand, they constitute a certain system of simultaneous symbols which can be approached through structuralist analysis; but, on the other hand, they have a history, because it is always through a process of interpretation and reinterpretation that they are kept alive. Myths have a historicity of their own. This difference of history typifies, for example, the development of the Semitic, pre-Hellenistic, and Celtic mythical nuclei. Therefore, just as societies are both structural and historical, so also are the mythical nuclei which ground them.

Q: In the conclusion to *The Symbolism of Evil* you state that 'a philosophy instructed by myths arises at a certain moment in reflection and wishes to answer to a certain situation in modern culture.' What precisely do you mean by this 'certain situation'? And how does myth answer to this problematic?

Ricoeur: I was thinking there of Jaspers's philosophy of 'boundary situations,' which influenced me so strongly just after the Second World War. There are certain boundary situations, such as war, suffering, guilt, death, in which the individual or community experiences a fundamental existential crisis. At such moments the whole community is put into question. For it is only when it is threatened with destruction from without or from within that a society is compelled to return to the very roots of its identity; to that mythical nucleus which ultimately grounds and determines it. The solution to the immediate crisis is no longer a purely political or technical matter but demands that we ask ourselves the ultimate questions concerning our origins and ends: Where do we come from? Where do we go? In this way, we become aware of our basic capacities and reasons for surviving, for being and continuing to be what we are.

Q: I am reminded here of Mircea Eliade's statement in *Myths, Dreams, Mysteries* that myth is something which always operates in a society regardless of whether this society reflectively acknowledges its existence. Eliade maintains that because modern man has lost his awareness of the important role that myth plays in his life, it often manifests itself in *deviant* ways. He gives as an example the emergence of fascist movements in Europe characterized by a mythic glorification of blood sacrifice and the hero-saviour together with the equally mythical revival of certain ancient rituals, symbols, and insignia. The suggestion is that if we do not explicitly recognize and reappropriate the mythic import of our existence it will emerge in distorted and pernicious ways. Do you think this is a valid point?

Ricoeur: You have hit here on a very important and difficult problem: the possibilities of a perversion of myth. This means that we can no longer approach myth *at the level of naivety.* We must rather always view it from a critical perspective. It is only by means of a selective reappropriation that we can become aware of myth. We are no longer primitive beings, living at the immediate level of myth. Myth for us is always mediated and opaque. This is not only because it expresses itself primarily through a particular apportioning of power-functions, as mentioned earlier, but also because several of its recurrent forms have become deviant and dangerous, e.g., the myth of absolute power (fascism) and the myth of the sacrificial scapegoat (anti-Semitism and racism). We are no longer justified in speaking of 'myth in general.' We must critically assess the content of each myth and the basic intentions which animate it. Modern man can neither get rid of myth nor take it at its face value. Myth will always be with us, but we must always approach it *critically.*

Q: It was with a similar scruple in mind that I tried to show in *Myth and Terror* (1978) that there are certain mythic structures operative in extreme Irish Republicanism – recurrence of blood sacrifice, apocalypse/renewal, etc. – which can become deviant manifestations of an original mythical nucleus. And I feel accordingly that any approach to myth should be as much a demythologization of deviant expressions as a resuscitation of genuine ones.

Ricoeur: Yes. And I think it is here that we could speak of the essential connection between 'critical instance' and the 'mythical foundation.' Only those myths are genuine which can be reinterpreted in terms of *liberation.* And I mean liberation as both a personal and collective phenomenon. We should perhaps sharpen this critical criterion to include only those myths which have as their horizon the liberation of mankind *as a whole*. Liberation cannot be exclusive. Here I think we come to recognize a fundamental convergence between the claims of myth and reason. In genuine reason as in genuine myth we find a concern for the *universal* liberation of men. To the extent that myth is seen as the foundation of a particular community to the absolute exclusion of all others, the possibilities of perversion – chauvinistic nationalism, racism, etc. – are already present.

Q: So in fact you suggest that the foundational power of myth should always be in some sense chaperoned by critical reason?

Ricoeur: In our Western culture the myth-making of man has often been linked with the critical instance of reason. And this is because it has had to be constantly interpreted and reinterpreted in different historical epochs. In other words, it is because the survival of myth calls for perpetual historical interpretation that it involves a critical component. Myths are not unchanging and unchanged antiques which are simply delivered out of the past in some naked, original state. Their specific identity depends on the way in which each generation receives or interprets them according to their needs, conventions, and ideological motivations. Hence the necessity of critical discrimination between liberating and destructive modes of reinterpretation.

Q: Could you give an example of such reinterpretation?

Ricoeur: Well, if we take the relation of *mythos* and *logos* in the Greek experience, we could say that myth had been absorbed by the *logos*, but never completely so; for the claim of the *logos* to rule over *mythos* is itself a mythical claim. Myth is thereby reinjected into the *logos* and gives a mythical dimension to reason itself. Thus the rational appropriation of myth becomes also a revival of myth. Another example would be the reinterpretative overlap between the mythical paradigms of the Hebraic exodus and the prophetic dimension in Hebrew literature. And then, at a second level, this Hebraic *mythos* came down to us through a Hellenization of its whole history. Even for us today, this Hellenization is an important mediation because it was through the conjunction of the Jewish *Torah* and Greek *logos* that the notion of law could be incorporated into our culture.

Q: You would not agree then with those modern theologians, such as Moltmann and Bultmann, who suggest that the Hellenization of the Judaeo-Christian culture is a perversion of its original richness?

Ricoeur: No. The tension between the Greek *logos* and the Semitic nucleus of exodus and revelation is fundamentally and positively constitutive of our culture.

Q: Several critics have described your hermeneutical approach to myth and symbol as an attempt, almost in the manner of psychoanalysis, to reduce myth to some hidden rational message. In *The Symbolism of Evil* you say that the aim of your philosophy is to disclose through reflection and speculation the *rationality* of symbols (p. 357). And again in *On Interpretation* you state that 'every *mythos* harbours a *logos* which requires to be exhibited.' (p. 17). But is it possible to extract the *logos* and yet leave the *mythos* intact? Or is myth something essentially enigmatic and therefore irreducible to rational content?

Ricoeur: This criticism must be understood in the following way. There are two uses of the concept of myth. One is myth as the *extension* of a symbolic structure. In this sense it is pointless to speak of a demythologization for that would be tantamount to desymbolization – and this I deny completely. But there is a second sense in which myth serves as an *alienation* of this symbolic structure; here it becomes reified and is misconstrued as an actual materialistic explanation of the world. If we interpret myth *literally*, we misinterpret it. For myth is essentially *symbolic*. It is only in instances of such misinterpretation that we may legitimately speak of demythologization; not concerning its symbolic content but concerning the hardening of its symbolic structures into dogmatic or reified ideologies.

Q: Do you think that Bultmann's use of the term demythologization had something to do with this confusion between two different types of myth (as creative symbol or reductive ideology)?

Ricoeur: Yes I do. Bultmann seems to ignore the complexity of myth. And so when he speaks, for example, of the necessity to demythologize the myth of the threefold division of the cosmos into Heaven, Earth, and Hell, he is treating this myth only in terms of its literal interpretation or rather misinterpretation. But Bultmann does not realize that there is a symbolic as well as a pseudo-symbolic or literal dimension in myth, and that demythologization is only valid in relation to this second dimension.

Q: Are myths *universal*, in terms of their original symbolic structures, or do they originate from *particular* national cultures?

Ricoeur: This is a very difficult problem. We are caught here between the claims of two equally valid dimensions of myth. And it is the delicate balance between them that is difficult to find. On the one hand, we must say that mythical structures are not simply universal any more than are languages. Just as man is fragmented between different languages, so also he is fragmented between mythical cycles, each of which is typical of a living culture. We must acknowledge, then, that one of the primary functions of any myth is to found the specific identity of a community. On the other hand, however, we must say that just as languages are in principle translatable one into the other, so too myths have a horizon of universality which allows them to be understood by other cultures. The history of Western culture is made up of a confluence of different myths which have been expatriated from their original community, i.e., Hebrew, Greek, Germanic, Celtic. The horizon of any genuine myth always exceeds the political and geographical boundaries of a specific national or tribal community. Even if we may say that mythical structures *founded* political institutions, they always go beyond the territorial limitations imposed by politics. Nothing travels more extensively and effectively than myth. Therefore we must conclude that while mythic symbols are rooted in a particular culture, they also have the capacity to emigrate and develop within new cultural frameworks.

Q: Is there not a sense in which perhaps the *source* and not only the historical *transmission* of symbols may be responsible for their universal dimension?

Ricoeur: It is quite possible that the supranational quality of myth or symbol may be ultimately traced back to a prehistorical layer from which all particular 'mythical nuclei' might be said to emerge. But it is difficult to determine the nature of this prehistory, for all myths as we know them come down to us through history. Each particular myth has its own history of reinterpretation and emigration. But another possible explanation of the universally common dimension of myth might be that because the myth-making powers of the human imagination are finite, they ensure the frequent recurrence of similar archetypes and motifs.

Q: Certainly the myth of the fall as you analyse it in *The Symbolism of Evil* would seem to be common to many different cultures.

Ricoeur: Yes. We could say that genuine myth goes beyond its claim to found a particular community and speaks to man as such. Several exegetes of Jewish literature, for example, have made a distinction between different layers of myth: those which are foundational for the Jewish culture – the 'chronicle dimension'; and those which make up a body of truths valid for all mankind – the 'wisdom dimension.' This seems to me an important distinction and one applicable to other cultures.

Q: In Irish literature over the last eighty years or so one finds a similar distinction between these dimensions. In the Fenian literature of the nineteenth century or the Celtic Twilight literature of Yeats, Lady Gregory, and others, myth seems to have been approached as a 'chronicle' of the spiritual origins of the race. For this reason it often strikes one as suffering from a certain hazy occultism and introversion. Joyce, on the other hand, used myth, particularly the myth of Finn, in its 'wisdom dimension'; that is, as an Irish archetype open to, and capable of assimilating, the rich resources of entirely different cultures. *Finnegans Wake* or *Ulysses* seem to represent an exemplary synthesis of the particular and universal clams of myth.

Ricoeur: The important point here is that the original potential of any genuine myth will always transcend the confines of a particular community or nation. The *mythos* of any community is the bearer of something which exceeds its own frontiers; it is the bearer of other *possible* worlds. And I think it is in this horizon of the 'possible' that we discover the *universal* dimensions of symbolic and poetic language.

Q: You have stated that what animates your philosophical research on symbolism and myth is not 'regret for some sunken atlantis' but 'hope for a re-creation of language' (*The Symbolism of Evil*). What precisely do you mean by this?

Ricoeur: Language has lost its original unity. Today it is fragmented not only geographically into different communities but functionally into different disciplines – mathematical, historical, scientific, legal, psychoanalytic, etc. It is the function of a philosophy of language to recognize the specific nature of these disciplines and thereby assign each 'language-game' its due (as Wittgenstein would have it), limiting and correcting their mutual claims. Thus one of the main purposes of hermeneutics is to refer the different uses of language to different regions of being – natural, scientific, fictional, etc. But this is not all. Hermeneutics is also concerned with the permanent spirit of language. By the spirit of language we intend not just some decorative excess or effusion of subjectivity, but *the capacity of language to open up new worlds*. Poetry and myth are not just nostalgia for some forgotten world. They constitute a disclosure of unprecedented worlds, an opening on to other *possible* worlds which transcend the established limits of our *actual* world.

Q: How then would you situate your philosophy of language in relation to Analytic Philosophy?

Ricoeur: I certainly share at least one common concern of Analytic Philosophy: the concern with ordinary language in contradistinction to the scientific language of documentation and verification. Scientific language has no real function of communication or interpersonal dialogue. It is important therefore that we preserve the rights of ordinary language where the communication of experience is of primary significance. But my criticism of ordinary language philosophy is that it does not take into account the fact that language itself is a place of prejudice and bias. Therefore, we need a third dimension of language, a critical and creative dimension, which is directed towards neither scientific verification nor ordinary communication but towards the disclosure of possible worlds. This third dimension of language I call the poetic. The adequate self-understanding of man is dependent on this third dimension of language as a *disclosure of possibility.*

Q: Is not this philosophy of language profoundly phenomenological in nature?

Ricoeur: Yes it is. Because phenomenology as it emerged in the philosophies of Husserl and Heidegger raised the central question of 'meaning.' And it is here that we find the main dividing line between the structuralist analysis and phenomenological hermeneutics. Whereas the former is concerned with the immanent arrangement of texts and textual codes, hermeneutics looks to the 'meaning' produced by these codes. It is my conviction that the decisive feature of hermeneutics is the capacity of world-disclosure yielded by texts. Hermeneutics is not confined to the *objective* structural analysis of texts or to the *subjective* existential analysis of the authors of texts; its primary concern is with the *worlds* which these authors and texts open up. It is by an understanding of the worlds, actual and possible, opened by language that we may arrive at a better understanding of ourselves.

World of the Text,
World of the Reader

Paul Ricoeur recently published *À l'école de la phénoménologie* (Vrin) and *Du texte à l'action* (Seuil), a short review of which can be read in the 'Philosophy' section of *Préfaces*. Although he returns to the question of reading in several articles collected in the latter volume, the essential part of his reflections on this problem is found in the third volume of *Temps et récit*, entitled *Le Temps raconté*, published in fall 1985 by Les Editions du Seuil. In the interview that he granted us, Paul Ricoeur explains how his interest in the question of reading was aroused in the course of his philosophical explorations.

(Joël Roman) Q: While reading is one of the major presuppositions of the philosophical practice, philosophers have rarely concerned themselves with it. In the 1960s, however, we saw a multiplication of readings, the most celebrated among them being Althusser's – in which the term reading strongly emphasizes that a relationship is constructed with the inherited text of tradition. How would you analyse this development?

Paul Ricoeur: I would say that there are three major reasons for this revaluation of reading. First of all, as the example of Althusser illustrates perfectly: the term reading has come to indicate one reading among others. We are talking about a selective principle in a context of several, possibly contradictory, readings. However – and this is the second reason – why do *multiple* readings exist? This attention given to the *multiplicity* of readings finds its origins in literary criticism, as a corrective to 'hard' structuralism, which had as its motto the text, and only the text. This predominance of the text was, for that matter, a necessary phase in the process of putting an end to the illusion of the author as sovereign creator. But the reader was put in brackets along with the author. Nevertheless, the practice of structuralist analysis has shown that it, too, is a reading. It leads to the question of the *dialectic* between text and reader, or, as I would prefer to say, between two worlds, the world of the text and the world of the reader: indeed, every text displays possibilities for inhabiting the world. The meeting between text and reader is a meeting between the whole of the text's claims, the horizon which it opens onto, the possibilities which it displays, and another horizon, the reader's horizon of expectation. The analyses of the Constance School, Hans Robert Jauss's reception aesthetics and Wolfgang Iser's phenomenology of reading, have drawn our attention to this aspect.[1]

Finally, the third reason for this revaluation of the theme of reading has to do with the structure of time: every projection into the future, whether it is a projection towards action or a utopian vision, has to be 'based on' something. In a way, reading is the recovery of a heritage that permits such a projection. But I would rather speak of traditionality than of tradition, in order to indicate the necessity with which all novelty must found itself on antecedents. Thus, reading stands in a relation to traditionality which would oppose submission to 'Tradition' seen as claiming that there is a non-temporal truth.

It is easy to see how these three reasons are interwoven, since it is because of the *dialectic* between the world of the text and the world of the reader that there are *multiple* readings, and that, consequently, a debate can develop on the relation to traditionality. But there is also an inflation of 'readings' when all reading is deemed to be interpretation, and all interpretation, reading.

Q: Yet, reading and interpretation are very closely related, if it is true that hermeneutics consists of revealing a meaning, of making an implicit meaning explicit, a meaning hidden in a text or even in a painting, an action, and so on. How would you locate the specificity of reading in relation to the whole of hermeneutics?

Ricoeur: You have used the word *reveal*, and it is certainly one of the two functions of the practice of reading to reveal a dimension, a structure, a potential, which are ignored, inhibited, or obscured. But I would not want to separate this activity, as indicated by the Heideggerian tern *revelation*, from the tranformative nature of reading. When a reader applies a text to himself, as is the case in literature, he recognizes himself in certain possibilities of existence – according to the model offered by a hero, or a character – but, at the same time, he is transformed; the becoming other in the act of reading is as important as is the recognition of self. Here we should undoubtedly use the concept of application, of *Verwendung*, as proposed by Gadamer when he distinguishes between the art of understanding, the art of explaining, and the art of application (*ars applicandi*).[2]

The moment of application, indispensable and overly neglected in the hermeneutic process, which is too often reduced to the first two activities, can be illustrated through the problems posed by the hermeneutics of *jurisdiction*. Betti, who examines the three origins of hermeneutics (biblical exegesis, classical philology, and *jurisprudence*), strongly emphasizes the value of the *jurisprudential* model. This model, moreover, is extremely important in the whole Anglo-Saxon common-law tradition. Application of the law is interpretation. The philosophical question touched upon here is analogous to Eric Weil's concern with our faculty of judgment, which he called the '*judicial sense.*' This moment of judgment may be one of the best examples of hermeneutic application.

Q: In the case of reading, however, it seems that we cannot evoke anything that decisive: there is nothing which would have 'the authority of having been decided.' In reading, is it not as if the judgment is always susceptible of being appealed?

Ricoeur: Absolutely. In reading, there is no instance which puts an end to the deliberation. None the less, they have something in common: that is, that all reading is a conflict of claims; that it can be understood as a court case. Of course, in the case of *jurisdiction*, the judge is decisiveness [itself]: it is the decisive act of favouring one interpretation considered to be more believable than others; in the situation with which we are concerned it can be an unending conflict, never resolved.

But let us take another example: the interpretations of great historic events. I am thinking of the readings of the French Revolution as François Furet studies them.[3] Probably because of the selective nature of reading, which attempts to construct a comprehensible 'arrangement' more compact than the explored field itself, there is a multiplicity of interpretations, every one of which claims to present the truth, and none of which fully exhausts historical reality, because there is always a residue of reading capable of being taken up in another reading.

Q: Application, then, has two sides [to it]. On the one hand, decision, judgment, the choice of one interpretation, and on the other, what you have referred to as imaginative variations of the ego,[4] which would preserve the open nature of reading...

Ricoeur: This is indeed the other side of reading: a non-decisive side which is, on the contrary, a kind of floating reading. Here we are in the domain of the imagination, no longer that of the judicial, where the imaginary has no place. Experimenting in our minds, we try different possible interpretations. Probably, the reading of literature is based on this: we are not forced to choose, we try to inhabit this or that character. I am thinking of what Henri Gouhier, or Gabriel Marcel, said about the theatre: there is a kind of equitable justice which can let everybody be right at the same time. A wonderful example of this is Hegel's reading of *Antigone*, in which he alternately agrees with Creon and Antigone. This is an important *moment in the reading process*, since several interpretations have the right to be admitted.

Q: There is another problem, corresponding to the changes that you acknowledge having made between *La Métaphore vive* and *Temps et récit*. You accuse *La Métaphore vive* of having made the text's reference to the world too direct, and of not having given enough consideration to the manner in which reading mediates between the world of the text and the world of the reader. It is this mediation which *Temps et récit* wants to promote. But is there not a risk of arbitrariness in interpretation, then, from which the 'referential realism' of *La Métaphore vive* could safeguard us?

Ricoeur: This is indeed the most important correction made to *La Métaphore vive* in *Temps et récit*. At the time I was irritated by these notions of *le texte pour le texte*, of the closed text. My response was that the text works directly on reality, that it 'denotes' reality. Since then I have re-evaluated this question of the mediating role of reading, through the work of Bakhtin, as well as through that of Jauss and Iser, and also through the American and Canadian influences of Northrop Frye and Wayne Booth. As for the risk which you refer to, it does exist. The American school of New Criticism, which had denounced the sophism of the intentional fallacy, then made me the target of the opposite criticism: you are giving in to the emotional fallacy. I would like to correct this impression by saying that reading is, first and foremost, a struggle with the text.

There is a type of reading which is fallacious recapitulation and identification, and of which we have two models in literature. Don Quixote and Emma Bovary, both of whom are victims of reading, trying to live their reading directly. In this regard, it is important to re-establish the importance of textual constraints: structuralism has had the merit of reminding us of these, and of limiting the arbitrary power of the reader. I am thinking of those exemplary structural analyses done by Greimas, in particular the one of Maupassant's short story 'Le Deux Amis.' The analysis of a text's formal constraints can lead to a better understanding of the place and role of the reader.

Finally, reading rarely consists only of the face-to-face presence of text and reader: that situation is an abstraction which erases all the *effects* of intertextuality. These demand that we take into account the dialectic relationships between the reader and the texts within a history of reading. From this point of view, the reader's expectations are decisive cultural *effects*.

Q: What distinction can be made between different kinds of texts, in particular between more explicit texts with theoretical claims, that propose an interpretation, and the others, the fictional texts, that appear to be more 'open'?

Ricoeur: This distinction should not be overestimated. For every text is open to interpretation, but also, each text limits interpretation to the extent that it resists. The act of interpretation would, here, be equivalent to a synthesis of the heterogeneous, a 'taking together' of a variety which, by the way, is not only temporal. But the theoretical text, the philosophical text for example, does not escape this interpretative destiny: just look at the multiplicity of interpretations of the *cogito*. None the less, the process of interpretation is undoubtedly more strictly regulated here than in literature.

Q: The difficulty lies in avoiding not only the temptation to believe that each text has its own correct interpretation, its own static, hidden meaning, to which we would have to gain access but which would be there, underneath, but also the inverse temptation of only reading what we ourselves project into the text. How do we establish norms for the practice of interpretation?

Ricoeur: This practice does not exclude a very great intellectual integrity: the right position has to be found, between the best of one's own 'expectations' and the most complete information, the recognition of the signs and signals of the text. Interpretation is a balance between these two. For a given interpreter, there is, indeed, a correct interpretation, an interpretation which is more plausible, given what he knows, what he is, what he expects. For another interpreter, who does not have the same information, the same expectations, the same cultural horizon, this balance will be found at a different point, but it will be no less compelling for him that for the first interpreter.

The struggle with the text is a struggle which has its own rules. I am thinking of someone whom I have admired infinitely: the historical philosopher Martial Guéroult. It cannot be said that he was always right in his debates with Gouhier or Alquié. But the power of his arguments is such that his reading becomes inevitably that of whoever retraces the same route. Here we could speak of an *ethics of reading*, to correct the impression of aesthetic preoccupations that may result from the freedom of interpretation.

An interpreter who has devoted many years to a text is subject to the same interior constraints as is an artist with high standards, like Cézanne, as if he were indebted to the mountain of Sainte-Victoire. Indebted in the aesthetic sense, but also in the sense of debt. This idea of debt is very important, to me. We may have to repay a debt owing to the authors we read. So we cannot say whatever we like, precisely because there is not just one interpretation. It is the status of the idea of truth, which is not of an unequivocal nature, that constitutes the horizon of these problems. Perhaps we should say that a text is a finite space of interpretations: there is not just one interpretation, but, on the other hand, there is not an infinite number of them. A text is a space of variations that has its own constraints; and in order to choose a different interpretation, we must always have better reasons.

Notes:

1　Hans Robert Jauss, *Toward an Aesthetic of Reception*, trans. by T. Bahti; intro. by P. de Man (Minneapolis: University of Minnesota Press, 1982) and Wolfgang Iser, *The Act of Reading* (Baltimore: Johns Hopkins University Press, 1978).

　　Paul Ricoeur integrates the analyses of these two authors into his own conception of reading 'Between the Reader and the Text' (this volume, pp. 390–424). Here he summarizes the interaction between the world of the text and the world of the reader as follows: 'to the extent that readers subordinate their expectations to those developed by the text, they themselves become unreal to a degree comparable to the unreality of the fictive world towards which they emigrate. Reading then becomes a place, itself unreal, where reflection takes a pause. On the other hand, inasmuch as readers incorporate – little matter whether consciously or unconsciously – into their vision of the world the lessons of their readings, in order to increase the prior readability of this vision, then reading is for them something other than a place where they come to rest; it is a medium they cross through.'

2 Hans-Georg Gadamer, *Truth and Method*, trans. by G. Barden and J. Cumming (New York: Seabury Press, 1975).

Ricoeur comments on the notion of application, which he also refers to as 'appropriation,' in 'Between the Reader and the Text' (see this volume, p. 401–2).

3 Cf. François Furet, *Penser la Révolution Français* (Paris: Gallimard, 1978).

4 'If fiction is a fundamental dimension of the text's *reference* it is no less a fundamental dimension of the reader's subjectivity. As a reader, I find myself only in losing myself. Reading introduces me into the imaginative variations of the *ego*. The metamorphosis of the world, according to the game, is also the playful metamorphosis of the *ego*': *Du text à l'action* (Paris: Seuil, 1986), p. 117.

Paul Ricoeur's Work in English

Seven of the twenty books by Ricoeur listed in this bibliography are collections of essays previously published in diverse journals and books; these essays have been gathered by the respective editors with a specific focus or under a general topic. This aspect of Ricoeur's work in English has given it far greater accessibility than would otherwise obtain, since many, if not most, of the original publications are not universally available.

I have listed the contents of these collections, but have not done so for the articles as they first appeared in English. The interested scholar will find a complete bibliography of and on Ricoeur in Frans D. Vansina, *A Primary and Secondary Systematic Bibliography of Paul Ricoeur 1935–1984* (Louvain-la-Neuve: Editions Peeters, 1985).

1965

Fallable Man. Trans., intro. C.A. Kelbley of *L'homme fallible*. Chicago: Henry Regnery. xxix + 224 pp.

History and Truth. Trans., intro. C.A. Kelbley of *Histoire et vérité*. Evanston: Northwestern University Press. xxxiv + 333 pp.
  Contents: 'Objectivity and Subjectivity in History'; 'The History of Philosophy and the Unity of Truth'; 'Note on the History of Philosophy and the Sociology of Knowledge'; 'The History of Philosophy and Historicity'; 'Christianity and the Meaning of History'; 'The *Socius* and the Neighbour'; 'The Image of God and the Epic of Man'; 'Emmanuel Mounier: A Personalist Philosopher'; 'Truth and Falsehood'; 'Note on the Wish and Endeavor for Unity'; 'Work and the Word'; 'Non-Violent Man and His Presence to History'; 'State and Violence'; 'The Political Paradox'; 'Universal Civilization and National Cultures'; 'True and False Anguish'; 'Negativity and Primary Affirmation'

1966

Freedom and Nature: The Voluntary and the Involuntary. Trans., intro E.V. Kohak of *Le volontaire et l'involontaire.* Evanston: Northwestern University Press. x + 498 pp.

1967

Husserl: An Analysis of His Phenomenology. Trans., intro. by E.G. Ballard and L.E. Embree. Evanston: Northwestern University Press. xxii + 238 pp.
  Contents: 'Introduction: Husserl (1859–1938)'; 'An Introduction to Husserl's *Ideas I*'; 'Husserl's *Ideas II* Analysis and Problems'; 'A Study of Husserl's Cartesian Meditations I–IV'; 'Husserl's Fifth Cartesian Meditation'; 'Husserl and the Sense of History'; 'Kant and Husserl'; 'Existential Phenomenology'; 'Methods and Tasks of a Phenomenology of the Will'

The Symbolism of Evil. Trans. E. Buchanan of *La Symbolique du mal.* New York: Harper and Row. xv + 357 pp; Boston: Beacon Press. 323 pp.

1970

Freud and Philosophy: An Essay on Interpretation. Trans. D. Savage of *De l'interprétatione: Essai sur Freud.* New Haven: Yale University Press. x + 573 pp.

1974

The Conflict of Interpretations: Essays in Hermeneutics Ed. D. Ihde, trans. of *Le Conflit des interprétations: Essais d'herméneutique.* Evanston: Northwestern University Press. xxv + 512 pp.
  Contents: 'Existence and Hermeneutics'; 'Structure and Hermeneutics'; 'The Problem of Double Meaning as Hermeneutic Problem and as Semantic Problem'; 'Structure, Word, Event'; 'Consciousness and the Unconscious'; 'Psychoanalysis and the Movement of Contemporary Culture'; 'A Philosophical Interpretation of Freud'; 'Technique and Non-technique in Interpretation'; 'Art and Freudian Systematics'; 'Nabert on Act and Sign'; 'Heidegger and the Question of the Subject'; 'The Question of the Subject: The Challenge of Semiology'; 'Original Sin: A Study of Meaning'; 'The Hermeneutics of Symbols and the Philosophical Reflection, I'; 'The Hermeneutics of

Symbols and the Philosophical Reflection, II'; 'The Demythization of Accusation'; 'Interpretation of the Myth of Punishment'; ' Preface to Bultmann'; 'Freedom in the Light of Hope'; 'Guilt, Ethics and Religion'; 'Religion, Atheism, and Faith'; 'Fatherhood: From Phantasm to Symbol'

Political and Social Essays. Ed. D. Stewart and J. Bien. Athens: Ohio University Press. ix + 293 pp.
Contents: 'Nature and Freedom'; 'A Critique of B.F. Skinner's *Beyond Freedom and Dignity*'; 'What Does Humanism Mean?'; 'Violence and Language'; 'Ye Are the Salt of the Earth'; 'Faith and Culture'; 'From Nation to Humanity: Task of Christians'; 'The Project of a Social Ethic'; 'Urbanization and Secularization'; 'Adventures of the State and the Task of Christians'; 'From Marxism to Contemporary Communism'; 'Socialism Today'; 'Ethics and Culture: Habermas and Gadamer in Dialogue'; 'The Task of the Political Educator'

1976

Interpretation Theory: Discourse and the Surplus of Meaning. Preface T. Klein. Fort Worth: Texas Christian University Press. xii + 107 pp.

1978

The Rule of Metaphor: Multi-Disciplinary Studies of the Creation of Meaning in Language. Trans. R. Czerny, K. McLaughlin, and J. Costello of *La métaphore vive.* Toronto: University of Toronto Press. vii + 384 pp.

The Philosophy of Paul Ricoeur: An Anthology of His Work. Ed. C. Reagan and D. Stewart. Boston: Beacon Press. vi + 262 pp.
Contents: 'The Unity of the Voluntary and the Involuntary as Limiting Idea'; 'The Antinomy of Human Reality and the Problem of Philosophical Anthropology'; 'The Hermeneutics of Symbols and Philosophical Reflection'; 'Philosophy of Will and Action'; 'Existential Phenomenology'; 'From Existentialism to the Philosophy of Language'; 'Existence and Hermeneutics'; 'Structure, Word, Event'; 'Creativity in Language: Word, Polysemy, Metaphor'; 'Metaphor and the Main Problem of Hermeneutics'; 'Explanation and Understanding: On Some Remarkable Connections among the Theory of Text, Theory of Action and Theory of History'; 'A Philosophical Interpretation of Freud'; 'The Question of God in Freud's Psychoanalytic Writings'; 'The

Critique of Religions'; 'The Language of Faith'; 'Listening to the Parables of Jesus'

1979

Main Trends in Philosophy. London: Holmes and Meier. xvii + 469 pp.

1980

The Contribution of French Historiography to the Theory of History. Oxford: Clarendon Press. 65 pp.

Essays on Biblical Interpretation. Ed. L.S. Mudge. Philadelphia: Fortress Press. ix + 182 pp.
  Contents: 'Reply to Lewis S. Mudge'; 'Preface to Bultman'; 'Toward a Hermeneutic of the Idea of Revelation'; 'The Hermeneutics of Testimony'; 'Freedom in the Light of Hope'

1981

Hermeneutics and the Human Sciences: Essays on Language, Action and Interpretation. Ed., trans., and intro. J.B. Thompson. Cambridge: Cambridge University Press. vii +314 pp.
  Contents: 'The Task Hermeneutics'; 'Hermeneutics and the Critique of Ideology'; 'Phenomenology and Hermeneutics'; 'The Hermeneutical Function of Distanciation'; 'What Is a Text? Explanation and Understanding'; 'Metaphor and the Central Problem of Hermeneutics'; 'Appropriation'; 'The Model of the Text: Meaningful Action considered as a Text'; 'Science and Ideology'; 'The Question of Proof in Freud's Psychoanalytic Writings'; 'The Narrative Function'

1984

The Reality of the Historical Past. Milwaukee: Marquette University Press. 51 pp.

Time and Narrative, Vol. I. Trans. K. McLaughlin and D. Pellauer of *Temps et récit I* Chicago: University of Chicago Press. xii + 274 pp.

1985

Time and Narrative, Vol. II. Trans. K. McLaughlin and D. Pellauer of *Temps et récit II*. Chicago: University of Chicago Press. 208 pp.

1986

Lectures on Ideology and Utopia. Ed. and intro. G.H. Taylor. New York: Columbia University Press. xxxvi + 353 pp.

1988

Time and Narrative, Vol. III. Trans. K. Blamey and D. Pellauer of *Temps et récit III*. Chicago: University of Chicago Press. 355 pp.

Index

THEORY/CULTURE SERIES